T0189300

Lecture Notes in Computer Science 12768

More information about this subseries at http://www.springer.com/series/7409

Margherita Antona · Constantine Stephanidis (Eds.)

Universal Access in Human-Computer Interaction

Design Methods and User Experience

15th International Conference, UAHCI 2021
Held as Part of the 23rd HCI International Conference, HCII 2021
Virtual Event, July 24–29, 2021
Proceedings, Part I

 Springer

Editors
Margherita Antona
Foundation for Research and Technology –
Hellas (FORTH)
Heraklion, Crete, Greece

Constantine Stephanidis
University of Crete and Foundation
for Research and Technology – Hellas
(FORTH)
Heraklion, Crete, Greece

ISSN 0302-9743 ISSN 1611-3349 (electronic)
Lecture Notes in Computer Science
ISBN 978-3-030-78091-3 ISBN 978-3-030-78092-0 (eBook)
https://doi.org/10.1007/978-3-030-78092-0

LNCS Sublibrary: SL3 – Information Systems and Applications, incl. Internet/Web, and HCI

This Springer imprint is published by the registered company Springer Nature Switzerland AG
The registered company address is: Gewerbestrasse 11, 6330 Cham, Switzerland

Foreword

Human-Computer Interaction (HCI) is acquiring an ever-increasing scientific and industrial importance, and having more impact on people's everyday life, as an ever-growing number of human activities are progressively moving from the physical to the digital world. This process, which has been ongoing for some time now, has been dramatically accelerated by the COVID-19 pandemic. The HCI International (HCII) conference series, held yearly, aims to respond to the compelling need to advance the exchange of knowledge and research and development efforts on the human aspects of design and use of computing systems.

The 23rd International Conference on Human-Computer Interaction, HCI International 2021 (HCII 2021), was planned to be held at the Washington Hilton Hotel, Washington DC, USA, during July 24–29, 2021. Due to the COVID-19 pandemic and with everyone's health and safety in mind, HCII 2021 was organized and run as a virtual conference. It incorporated the 21 thematic areas and affiliated conferences listed on the following page.

A total of 5222 individuals from academia, research institutes, industry, and governmental agencies from 81 countries submitted contributions, and 1276 papers and 241 posters were included in the proceedings to appear just before the start of the conference. The contributions thoroughly cover the entire field of HCI, addressing major advances in knowledge and effective use of computers in a variety of application areas. These papers provide academics, researchers, engineers, scientists, practitioners, and students with state-of-the-art information on the most recent advances in HCI. The volumes constituting the set of proceedings to appear before the start of the conference are listed in the following pages.

The HCI International (HCII) conference also offers the option of 'Late Breaking Work' which applies both for papers and posters, and the corresponding volume(s) of the proceedings will appear after the conference. Full papers will be included in the 'HCII 2021 - Late Breaking Papers' volumes of the proceedings to be published in the Springer LNCS series, while 'Poster Extended Abstracts' will be included as short research papers in the 'HCII 2021 - Late Breaking Posters' volumes to be published in the Springer CCIS series.

The present volume contains papers submitted and presented in the context of the 15th International Conference on Universal Access in Human-Computer Interaction (UAHCI 2021), an affiliated conference to HCII 2021. I would like to thank Margherita Antona for her invaluable contribution to its organization and the preparation of the proceedings, as well as the members of the Program Board for their contributions and support. This year, the UAHCI affiliated conference has focused on topics related to universal access methods, techniques and practices, studies on accessibility, Design for All, usability, UX and technology acceptance, emotion and behavior recognition for universal access, accessible media, and access to learning and education, as well universal access to virtual and intelligent assistive environments.

I would also like to thank the Program Board Chairs and the members of the Program Boards of all thematic areas and affiliated conferences for their contribution towards the highest scientific quality and overall success of the HCI International 2021 conference.

This conference would not have been possible without the continuous and unwavering support and advice of Gavriel Salvendy, founder, General Chair Emeritus, and Scientific Advisor. For his outstanding efforts, I would like to express my appreciation to Abbas Moallem, Communications Chair and Editor of HCI International News.

July 2021   Constantine Stephanidis

HCI International 2021 Thematic Areas and Affiliated Conferences

Thematic Areas

- HCI: Human-Computer Interaction
- HIMI: Human Interface and the Management of Information

Affiliated Conferences

- EPCE: 18th International Conference on Engineering Psychology and Cognitive Ergonomics
- UAHCI: 15th International Conference on Universal Access in Human-Computer Interaction
- VAMR: 13th International Conference on Virtual, Augmented and Mixed Reality
- CCD: 13th International Conference on Cross-Cultural Design
- SCSM: 13th International Conference on Social Computing and Social Media
- AC: 15th International Conference on Augmented Cognition
- DHM: 12th International Conference on Digital Human Modeling and Applications in Health, Safety, Ergonomics and Risk Management
- DUXU: 10th International Conference on Design, User Experience, and Usability
- DAPI: 9th International Conference on Distributed, Ambient and Pervasive Interactions
- HCIBGO: 8th International Conference on HCI in Business, Government and Organizations
- LCT: 8th International Conference on Learning and Collaboration Technologies
- ITAP: 7th International Conference on Human Aspects of IT for the Aged Population
- HCI-CPT: 3rd International Conference on HCI for Cybersecurity, Privacy and Trust
- HCI-Games: 3rd International Conference on HCI in Games
- MobiTAS: 3rd International Conference on HCI in Mobility, Transport and Automotive Systems
- AIS: 3rd International Conference on Adaptive Instructional Systems
- C&C: 9th International Conference on Culture and Computing
- MOBILE: 2nd International Conference on Design, Operation and Evaluation of Mobile Communications
- AI-HCI: 2nd International Conference on Artificial Intelligence in HCI

List of Conference Proceedings Volumes Appearing Before the Conference

1. LNCS 12762, Human-Computer Interaction: Theory, Methods and Tools (Part I), edited by Masaaki Kurosu
2. LNCS 12763, Human-Computer Interaction: Interaction Techniques and Novel Applications (Part II), edited by Masaaki Kurosu
3. LNCS 12764, Human-Computer Interaction: Design and User Experience Case Studies (Part III), edited by Masaaki Kurosu
4. LNCS 12765, Human Interface and the Management of Information: Information Presentation and Visualization (Part I), edited by Sakae Yamamoto and Hirohiko Mori
5. LNCS 12766, Human Interface and the Management of Information: Information-rich and Intelligent Environments (Part II), edited by Sakae Yamamoto and Hirohiko Mori
6. LNAI 12767, Engineering Psychology and Cognitive Ergonomics, edited by Don Harris and Wen-Chin Li
7. LNCS 12768, Universal Access in Human-Computer Interaction: Design Methods and User Experience (Part I), edited by Margherita Antona and Constantine Stephanidis
8. LNCS 12769, Universal Access in Human-Computer Interaction: Access to Media, Learning and Assistive Environments (Part II), edited by Margherita Antona and Constantine Stephanidis
9. LNCS 12770, Virtual, Augmented and Mixed Reality, edited by Jessie Y. C. Chen and Gino Fragomeni
10. LNCS 12771, Cross-Cultural Design: Experience and Product Design Across Cultures (Part I), edited by P. L. Patrick Rau
11. LNCS 12772, Cross-Cultural Design: Applications in Arts, Learning, Well-being, and Social Development (Part II), edited by P. L. Patrick Rau
12. LNCS 12773, Cross-Cultural Design: Applications in Cultural Heritage, Tourism, Autonomous Vehicles, and Intelligent Agents (Part III), edited by P. L. Patrick Rau
13. LNCS 12774, Social Computing and Social Media: Experience Design and Social Network Analysis (Part I), edited by Gabriele Meiselwitz
14. LNCS 12775, Social Computing and Social Media: Applications in Marketing, Learning, and Health (Part II), edited by Gabriele Meiselwitz
15. LNAI 12776, Augmented Cognition, edited by Dylan D. Schmorrow and Cali M. Fidopiastis
16. LNCS 12777, Digital Human Modeling and Applications in Health, Safety, Ergonomics and Risk Management: Human Body, Motion and Behavior (Part I), edited by Vincent G. Duffy
17. LNCS 12778, Digital Human Modeling and Applications in Health, Safety, Ergonomics and Risk Management: AI, Product and Service (Part II), edited by Vincent G. Duffy

38. CCIS 1420, HCI International 2021 Posters - Part II, edited by Constantine Stephanidis, Margherita Antona, and Stavroula Ntoa
39. CCIS 1421, HCI International 2021 Posters - Part III, edited by Constantine Stephanidis, Margherita Antona, and Stavroula Ntoa

http://2021.hci.international/proceedings

List of Conference Proceedings Volumes Appearing Hereinafter

38. CCIS 1420, HCI International 2021 Posters – Part II, edited by Constantine Stephanidis, Margherita Antona, and Stavroula Ntoa

39. CCIS 1421, HCI International 2021 Posters – Part III, edited by Constantine Stephanidis, Margherita Antona, and Stavroula Ntoa

http://2021.hci.international/proceedings

15th International Conference on Universal Access in Human-Computer Interaction (UAHCI 2021)

Program Board Chairs: **Margherita Antona,** *Foundation for Research and Technology – Hellas (FORTH), Greece,* **and Constantine Stephanidis,** *University of Crete and Foundation for Research and Technology – Hellas (FORTH), Greece*

- João Barroso, Portugal
- Rodrigo Bonacin, Brazil
- Laura Burzagli, Italy
- Pedro J. S. Cardoso, Portugal
- Silvia Ceccacci, Italy
- Carlos Duarte, Portugal
- Pier Luigi Emiliani, Italy
- Andrina Granic, Croatia
- Gian Maria Greco, Spain
- Simeon Keates, UK
- Georgios Kouroupetroglou, Greece
- Barbara Leporini, Italy
- I. Scott MacKenzie, Canada
- John Magee, USA
- Daniela Marghitu, USA
- Jorge Martín-Gutiérrez, Spain
- Troy McDaniel, USA
- Maura Mengoni, Italy
- Silvia Mirri, Italy
- Federica Pallavicini, Italy
- Ana Isabel Paraguay, Brazil
- Hugo Paredes, Portugal
- Enrico Pontelli, USA
- João M. F. Rodrigues, Portugal
- Frode Eika Sandnes, Norway
- J. Andrés Sandoval-Bringas, Mexico
- Volker Sorge, UK
- Hiroki Takada, Japan
- Kevin Tseng, Taiwan
- Gerhard Weber, Germany

The full list with the Program Board Chairs and the members of the Program Boards of all thematic areas and affiliated conferences is available online at:

http://www.hci.international/board-members-2021.php

HCI International 2022

The 24th International Conference on Human-Computer Interaction, HCI International 2022, will be held jointly with the affiliated conferences at the Gothia Towers Hotel and Swedish Exhibition & Congress Centre, Gothenburg, Sweden, June 26 – July 1, 2022. It will cover a broad spectrum of themes related to Human-Computer Interaction, including theoretical issues, methods, tools, processes, and case studies in HCI design, as well as novel interaction techniques, interfaces, and applications. The proceedings will be published by Springer. More information will be available on the conference website: http://2022.hci.international/:

General Chair
Prof. Constantine Stephanidis
University of Crete and ICS-FORTH
Heraklion, Crete, Greece
Email: general_chair@hcii2022.org

http://2022.hci.international/

Contents – Part I

Accessibility, Usability, User Experience and Technology Acceptance

Design for All Applications and Case Studies

Emotion and Behavior Recognition for Universal Access

Contents – Part II

Accessible Media

Universal Access in Virtual and Intelligent Assistive Environments

Universal Access Methods, Techniques and Practices

Implicit Measures as a Useful Tool for Evaluating User Experience

Rossana Actis-Grosso[1]([✉]), Roberta Capellini[1,2], Francesco Ghedin[2], and Francesca Tassistro[2]

[1] Department of Psychology, University of Milano-Bicocca, 20126 Milan, Italy
rossana.actis@unimib.it
[2] Avanade Italy, 20124 Milan, Italy

Abstract. With the increasing presence in our lives of interactive and technological items, the concept of "experience" becomes crucial in both the design and the evaluation phases. When aiming to measure such experience, researchers typically adopt self-report methodology. However, it has been established that also unconscious motives (i.e., emotions, implicit attitudes) - which people are not always aware of - need to be taken into account in understanding users' perception, by means of indirect measures. The present study investigates the possibility of measuring UX by both implicit and explicit attitudes measures. In an experimental study (N = 36), we asked participants to evaluate a conversational chatbot prototype, which had the fictional goal of pre-selecting candidates for a job, and to fix a date for the job interview. We manipulated between-participants the chatbot's gender (male vs. female) and the tone of voice (formal vs. informal). Explicit user experience's evaluation (i.e., UEQ) and implicit attitudes towards the chatbot (i.e., IAT) were the dependent variables, as well as self-reported measures of chatbot's efficacy and emotional experience. Our findings showed an implicit preference towards the informal version of the chatbot, as revealed by the IAT scores, whereas no differences emerged on explicit measures of the UEQ. Results are discussed in light of the effect of implicit attitudes on overall experience, and on the importance of comparing implicit and explicit measures, as well as objective usability measures, when evaluating the UX.

Keywords: User experience · Implicit measures · Chatbot · Tone of voice

1 Introduction

This study is based on the hypothesis that implicit attitudes should be measured when evaluating User Experience (UX), given that we are not necessarily aware of emotions, feelings and social constructs that shape our behavior together with more conscious (and therefore accessible for self-report explicit measures) beliefs. To measure implicit attitudes we used the Implicit Association Test (IAT; Greenwald et al. 1998) on a chatbot prototype, which had the fictional goal of pre-selecting candidates for a job in the "alfa group" of a private company, and to consequently fix the date for the job interview. The Research Questions guiding this study were (RQ1) whether it is possible to study UX

© Springer Nature Switzerland AG 2021
M. Antona and C. Stephanidis (Eds.): HCII 2021, LNCS 12768, pp. 3–20, 2021.
https://doi.org/10.1007/978-3-030-78092-0_1

by using IAT as a measure of implicit attitudes towards a chatbot and (RQ2) whether IAT could complement explicit measures of UX. We chose a chatbot to test our research questions because, having some human-like features, chatbots are likely to elicit implicit attitudes similar to social constructs applied to other humans and mindlessy applied to computer and new media as well (as demonstrated by the "Computers Are Social Actor" paradigm studies, Nass and Moon 2000). On the other hand chatbots are not *too* human-like, and thus they should not reasonably elicit the same implicit attitudes found in studies with humans, where interactions and experiences are far more complex. The first two paragraphs are dedicated to better illustrate this point, as well as studies conducted within the CASA paradigm. To test our hypothesis and research questions we develop different versions of a chatbot, with different (i) Tone of Voice (ToV, formal or informal) and (ii) gender (male or female). These versions were evaluated by participants with both explicit- (i.e. the UEQ+ and three explicit questions addressing different aspect of the interaction) and implicit-measures (i.e. a single category IAT, Karpinski and Steinman 2006) in a 2 × 2 factorial design experiment, where a preference for female and informal chatbot is expected. The third paragraph is dedicated to the experimental study.

2   Implicit Attitudes and Their Possible Influence on the Interaction Between Humans and Non-humans

Academic community and industry agree on the fact that product evaluation goes far beyond functionality and usability. With the increasing presence in our lives of inter-active and technological items, the concept of "experience", considered as the more or less engaging interaction with a device (and thus better shaped on user's feelings and emotions), becomes crucial in both the design and the evaluation phases.

In this perspective it is important to consider that our emotions are triggered not only by our cognitive (and therefore conscious) evaluations of a given situation, but also by implicit attitudes such as social rules, prejudices, stereotypes and expectations (e.g. Cuddy et al. 2008; Talaska et al. 2008; Alexander et al. 1999). Following Greenwald and Banaji's (1995) definition of implicit attitudes, an attitude is an association between a concept and an evaluation (e.g. negative or positive) and people have two type of attitudes: conscious, explicit attitudes that are experienced as their feelings and implicit attitudes that are not part of their conscious experience. This implies that implicit attitudes could be quite different from explicit attitudes. Studies on implicit attitudes have demonstrated that they tend to predict behaviors that are more spontaneous and difficult to control, because they are based on experience, while explicit attitudes reflect conscious values, beliefs, and desired responses and tend to predict behaviors that are deliberate and easy to control (Wilson et al. 2000). This has two important consequences: (i) implicit attitudes are strongly related with emotions and (ii) they shape not only our evaluation judgments but also (and more importantly) our consequent behavior.

Social desirability is one of the main reasons why implicit and explicit attitudes may diverge (e.g. Anderson 2019). For this reason studies on implicit attitudes are mainly focused on social interactions between humans. In this perspective it is important to consider that several studies on human social interaction demonstrate that, when interacting with another person, humans extract a number of information that could be entirely stimulus driven or influenced by top down processes. For example, when looking at a face, we automatically extract information about the person's age (e.g. Ciardo et al. 2014), gender, mean emotion (e.g. Haberman and Whitney 2007) attractiveness (e.g. Hung et al. 2016) and ethnicity (e.g. Yan et al. 2019), from its visual characteristics (these information are stimulus driven), but we also process information regarding what we know about that specific person (these information are semantic or top-down, and modulate the effect of stimulus driven information). Altogether this information contributes to person categorization, group membership and social valence and determines social interactions in everyday life. Implicit attitudes are more likely to be based on stimulus driven information, and some studies put in evidence that even semantic information could be at least partially based on visual information (e.g. Ciardo et al. 2021; Capellini et al. 2016). Thus not only implicit attitudes are not conscious, but also the information on which they are based are mainly automatically extracted from the physical appearance of the stimulus, and thus not under our deliberate control.

Given that implicit and explicit attitudes may diverge, studies aiming at understanding their influence on human behaviour are classically based on indirect measures, rather than self-report enquiries (e.g. face-to-face interviews, questionnaires, surveys, focus-group etc.). Indirect measures seek to circumvent the limitations of self-report methodological techniques (Dimofte 2010; Nevid 2010; Wittenbrink and Schwarz 2007), which could be grouped in (i) self-deception (e.g. false belief and a contradictory unconscious real belief), (ii) other deception (e.g. social desirability) and (iii) linguistic bias (e.g. how information is formulated). In the field of psychology and neuroscience, several ways of indirectly measuring human beliefs, emotions, preference and expectations have been conceived, such as eye-movements measures, skin conductance or neuroimaging. However, the methodology mostly used in psychological studies is based on reaction times, assuming that the time elapsed between sensory stimulus onsets and subsequent behavioral responses mirrors the mental processes involved between the onset and the response. This paradigm, generally known as mental chronometry, has been used to develop a number of measurement procedures specifically aimed at tapping implicit attitudes. Although differing in their procedural details, all these measurements could be considered slight variations of the Implicit Association Test (IAT; Greenwald et al. 1998), which provides a relative measure of implicit association strengths between target and attribute categories. The IAT indirectly measures the strengths of a person's automatic associations between two target concepts and evaluation attributes, by requiring participants to sort stimulus exemplars from two pairs of concepts using just two response options. The assumption behind the IAT is twofold: on the one hand it is supposed that it is easier to share the same response key when a target concept and an evaluation attribute are already associated in participant's mind, on the other hand the easier association is supposed to be faster. The IAT's association strength measure is labeled with the letter D and it is calculated on the basis of differences in reaction times between different blocks where target and attribute categories are differently associated.

Although implicit attitudes (and their influence on human behavior) are a well-established issue in the psychological literature, in the HCI field User Experience (UX) is still generally evaluated by means of self-report questionnaires (e.g. AttrakDiff, UEQ, and meCUE, to cite the most recognized questionnaires for UX evaluation). In such questionnaires several aspects are often intertwined, such as feelings, emotions, affective states and aesthetical experience (the so-called *look and feel*). By asking the user to report all these perceived aspects of the interaction, the expectation is not only that the user is perfectly aware of all his/her feelings and emotions, but also that s/he could distinguish between different aspects that trigger these emotions and feelings.

Exceptions are given by all those studies which explicitly acknowledge the crucial role of the social component in determining the success of the interaction (such as in the field of human-robot interaction, particularly with the so-called social robots) or studies where emotions are supposed to play a key-role in determining the behavior of the user/customer (such as in video games, virtual reality and in marketing-related studies).

We think that the reason why this issue has never been addressed in the HCI domain relies on the concept of "object", conceived as an artefact made by humans in order to help them accomplish specific tasks (and not having any human features). When (and if) an artefact shares some features with humans (such as verbal communication, as in chatbot, or human-like resemblance, as in social robots), then the implicit attitudes one might have towards it becomes an interesting object of study. On the other hand, when an artefact is not considered as human-like, the common assumption is that, whatever prejudice or stereotype we might have towards it, this is not affecting our interaction with it in a remarkable way. In our view this assumption is erroneously based on the idea that implicit attitudes determine our behavior only when humans are interacting with (i) other humans (ii) human-like devices (e.g. social robot) or, alternatively, the interaction (iii) has an high degree of social valence (e.g. a conversation with a chatbot) or (iv) has an high degree of emotional valence (as in video games or in the marketing domain, where many choices made by customers are not explainable without considering the emotional aspect related with them). On the contrary it is well established that in fact implicit attitudes, being largely based on stimulus driven information, are present in any sort of interaction where at least one human is present (thus they could influence the interaction with a social robot, a chatbot, a television and even a much simpler device). The strength of their influence in the interaction, and their relation with explicit attitudes and observable behavior is a matter of debate, and is strongly dependent on the context where the interaction takes place. We think that if we want to better understand UX, implicit attitudes should be measured, in order to tap the role of emotions, beliefs and feelings that the user is not able to verbalize (not only for social desirability but also because s/he is not aware of them). By using IAT in association with explicit measures, it would be possible to investigate the role of unconscious beliefs and stereotypes in shaping UX. We think that a good test bench for this possibility should be a conversational agent, as better detailed below.

2.1 Social Reactions to Technological Devices

Studies based on the Computers Are Social Actors (CASA) Theory shows that individuals consistently apply social cognitive constructs and stereotypes (typically associated with humans) to computers, television and new media, although users know that it is absurd to do so. For example we apply to computers gender-science stereotypes (Nass et al. 1997), politeness rules (e.g. Nass and Steuer 1993), Nass et al. (1999), and stereo-typical inferences (Nass and Moon 2000; Reeves and Nass 1996). Even though Nass and Moon (2000) proposed that social responses to various computer agents are often auto-matic, taking place spontaneously as a mindless process in which users focus on social cues instead of other agent characteristics, this assumption is still controversial. Several studies question whether the CASA theory applies only to "social agents" or could be extended to other categories of technological devices, providing that these devices share at least some characteristics with humans. When CASA paradigm was firstly proposed as a theoretical framework, it was limited to "new media", which indeed show a behavior which could be similar to a human agent as long as verbal competencies are concerned. Afterwards, several studies extended this paradigm to successfully investigate social responses to websites (Kim and Sundar 2012), computer agents used for interviews (Hasler et al. 2013; Pickard et al. 2016), Twitter bots (Edwards et al. 2014) and physical robots (Edwards et al. 2016). As it is apparent all these studies are concerned with new media, and with the increasing importance of the so-called human-robot interaction field, studies on how the visual appearance of a robot could influence the interaction with it are multiplying. In this perspective *anthropomorphism* (i.e. the tendency to attribute human traits, emotions and intentions to non-human entities) is somehow related to the fact that the object to be evaluated is in fact human-like. In other words, the more a technological device resembles a human person, the more it is generally accepted that humans would apply to it social cognitive constructs *as if* they are interacting with other humans. This point is particularly relevant when interacting with conversational agents (CA), which could be embodied or disembodied (e.g. Araujo 2018): Embodied CAs have a (virtual) body or face (usually human-like), disembodied CAs communicate with users primarily via a messaging-based interface, not allowing for a physical representation of the agent. While it is generally accepted that embodied CAs are treated as "social actors" (e.g., Etemad-Sajadi and Ghachem 2015; Verhagen et al. 2014), the question arises whether disembodied CAs could be inserted in the broad domain of CASA paradigm. The use of natural language at the human–computer interface elicits anthropomorphism (Brahnam 2009; De Angeli et al. 2001; Epley et al. 2007), thus it is possible that social stereotypes and expectations should be attributed to disembodied CAs as well.

When engaged in a conversation, humans usually take advantage not only of the verbal meaning of the conversation itself, but also of the so-called body language, as well as several different other non-verbal cues. Among the last, language style, voice modulation (which is strictly connected to the emotional state of the speaker), voice gender and regional accent are all cues that could easily induce the mindless application of social cognitive constructs and stereotypes to a CA. Based on this, several studies were focused on the possible influence of linguistic cues (e.g. language style) in anthro-pomorphic attributions to disembodied CAs. The use of linguistic style is often used to induce a perceived "personality" of the CA, which is generally referred to as "tone of voice" (ToV). Existing literature regarding how humans perceive CAs have found that personality can offer a stable pattern to how a chatbot is perceived, and add consistency to the user experience (Smestad and Volden 2018). In a recent study (Araujo 2018) testing whether participants interacting with a human-like agent (i.e. a chatbot with a human name and a linguistic style more similar to humans) will perceive the agent as having stronger levels of social presence in comparison to participants interacting with a machine-like agent, it was found that an informal linguistic style for a customer service chatbot was associated with a higher degree of anthropomorphism and social presence. Also the perceived gender of the CAs seems to play a crucial role. In a study analyzing conversations between Internet users and different gender presentations of a chatbot (Brahnam and De Angeli 2012), it was found that people attribute negative stereotypes to female-presenting chatterbots more often than they do to male-presenting chatterbots, and female-presenting chatterbots are more often the objects of implicit and explicit sexual attention and swear words. Interestingly, it has also shown (Ciechanowski et al. 2019) that when a CA is too human-like (i.e. a human-like avatar), attitudes toward it are more negative as compared with disembodied CA (i.e. a textual chatbot).

Studies on the personality of CAs, as well as books and non-scientific publications dedicated to marketing purposes, are progressively increasing in recent times, together with the increasing amount of CAs developed by the private market for different goals. However, results are controversial in terms of how a CA is capable of eliciting social constructs towards it. Recent results question whether user's satisfaction is more related with the emotional ToV of the CA or rather with the content of the output information (Jenkins et al. 2007). The context in which the conversation takes places seems to have a strong influence on the perceived positive or negative effect of the perceived personality of the CA (Smestad and Volden 2018), which changes with the job it performs, the group of its users and the place where the interaction takes place (which could be virtual, as Facebook, or physical, as a kiosk, a hospital or an office). Given (i) the importance of personality in CA and (ii) the fact that they could elicit different degrees of anthropomorphism depending on several variables, they seem to be the good technology to test for our proposed methodology.

To the best of our knowledge, no study at present has addressed the possibility to investigate the UX with the IAT. By developing a CA with different ToV (i.e. linguistic styles) and gender we could be able to compare implicit and explicit attitudes toward it, with a reasonable expectation of eliciting at least some effects related with CA's perceived personality.

3   Developing Different Versions of a Chatbot with Different Gender and Tone of Voice: An Experimental Study

Chatbots could be inserted in the broader domain of "Conversational Agents", where the conversation could be in written (typed) or oral form (De Angeli and Brahnam 2008). Typically, a chatbot is a conversational agent that allows users to have access to specific data or services through dialogues in natural language (Følstad and Brandtzæg 2017). Thus, chatbots could be defined as programs that mimic conversation using Artificial Intelligence (AI) or, alternatively, that understands users' requests by means of natural language elaboration techniques.

Besides AI, which represents the core functionality of a chatbot and impacts its performance, the design of a chatbot in terms of visual and textual features may convey different messages about the personality of the chatbot itself. For instance, by differentiating the way in which a chatbot asks questions, provides answers and/or its avatar and gender, designers and developers can shape the experience of the interaction according to their specific goals.

The present work aimed at designing the prototype of a chatbot operating for the Human Resources of a private company, which had the fictional goal of pre-selecting and contacting potential candidates for an open position within the company, and fixing the date for the job interview. In addition, we wanted to test the role of different variables related to the chatbot personality (i.e., tone of voice and gender) on UX, measured both explicitly and implicitly. Hence, by means of Dialogflow (powered by Google ML) we developed an interactive prototype in which we specified different possible interactions and consistent expected answers (see Fig. 1). Dialogflow allowed us to test the chatbot in the User Interface of Google Assistant. The conversation was mainly "chatbot-driven", meaning that the chatbot guided the interaction flow, asking users a series of questions and providing options. As mentioned earlier, the goal of the present study was to test the effect of the tone of voice and gender of a chatbot on the User Experience, with both implicit and explicit measures. Thus, we designed different versions of the prototype aiming to convey different chatbot personalities and test their influence on UX. Specifically, we built six versions of the chatbot, as a combination of different tones of voice (formal vs. informal) and genders (male vs. female). The tone of voice was conveyed by either the clothing of the avatar and the linguistic "style" of the bot. Chatbot gender was conveyed by either the avatar and the gender inflections of the bot, which was always referring to itself according to the assigned gender.

Our hypotheses were the following: since the context of Human Resources for which the chatbot was operating is commonly linked to several soft skills (e.g., empathy, warmth) that are stereotypically associated with the female gender (Eagly and Mladinic 1989; Edwards and Spence 1987), and given the fact that female chatbots are more common that male chatbots (Feine et al. 2019) we expected to find a preference towards the female chatbot, in terms of UX both at the explicit and implicit levels. In addition, we expected participants to be more likely to accept and show up at the job interview and to feel more comfortable when interacting with the female version rather than the male one.

Moreover, we expected to find an implicit and explicit preference towards the informal chatbot, as chatbots should be perceived as less formal tools than emails or phone interviews. As a consequence, we hypothesized participants to be more likely to accept and show up at the job interview and to feel more comfortable when interacting with the informal version rather than the formal one.

3.1 Pretest

With the aim to test whether the tone of voice of the chatbot was correctly conveyed and perceived by the participants, we ran a pretest.

Participants. The sample consisted of forty participants (age range: 22–56 years old; M = 30.57, SD = 7.55; female: 19).

Stimuli and Material

Conversations. As for the conversations, we created two different variants of the dialogues. Specifically, the formal linguistic style was obtained by using a refined and mannered language and by the use of the third person. Conversely, the informal version was obtained by either the use of a more friendly and colloquial style, a less rigorous use of punctuation, and by the use of the second person.

Avatars. As for the avatars, we created 6 different versions, by presenting female and male avatars wearing informal, neutral and formal clothes (see Fig. 2 for four of the six tested versions).

Procedure

Participants received an online questionnaire created with LimeSurvey in which they were asked to evaluate an image and a text. Each participant was randomly presented with one out of the six variants of the avatar and one out of the two versions of the text. Next, they were asked to evaluate on a 5-point Likert scale the tone of voice, the level of empathy, the perceived trustworthiness and the general appreciation for both the avatar and the text. Finally, participants' socio demographics information were collected.

Results

Conversations. A series of independent-samples t-tests revealed that the informal version of the conversation was perceived as having a more friendly tone of voice (M = 3.59, SD = 1.01) than the formal one (M = 1.74, SD = .806), t(39) = 6.44, p = .0001, whereas no other differences emerged on the other dimensions (level of empathy, trustworthiness, general appreciation), ps > .34.

Avatars. The analysis of variance on the avatars revealed a significant effect on the perceived tone of voice, F(2, 37) = 16.17, p = .0001, showing that the informal avatars were correctly perceived as more informal (M = 3.47, SD = .99) than the formal (M = 1.50, SD = .94) and the neutral ones (M = 2.82, SD = .87). No differences emerged on the other dimensions (level of empathy, trustworthiness and general appreciation), ps > .44.

Hence, we selected the 4 avatars with more extreme evaluations on the tone of voice dimension, and we validated our manipulation on the conversations.

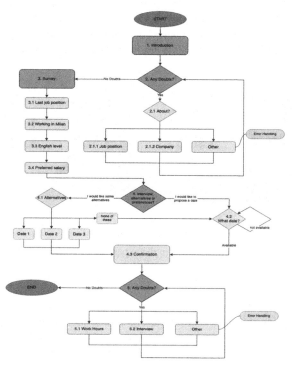

Fig. 1. The conversation flow implemented in Dialogflow for the chatbot used in the study.

3.2 The Experiment

Methods

Participants. Thirty-six participants voluntarily took part in this experiment (age range: 23–46 years old; M = 30.8, SD 6.49; female: 23). They were recruited through word-of-mouth, in order to have a sample balanced in terms of seniority level: 7 participants were graduate students looking for a job, 7 participants were newly hired (entry level), 11 participants were mid-level, 7 participants were senior level and only 1 participant was an executive.

Stimuli and Material

Chatbot. On the basis of the pretest we developed four different versions of a chatbot, in which *gender* (2 levels: male vs female) and *tone of voice* (2 levels: formal vs informal) were manipulated (Fig. 2). Each chatbot was introducing itself to the participant with a different "name" (i.e. Alfa, Beta, Gamma and Delta). The name was deliberately not associated with gender, because we wanted to limit the weight of this dependent variable to the linguistic style of the chatbot, with no other possible confounders (as the possible and not controlled familiarity with a given name). Thus four different versions of the chatbot were developed: (i) Female and Formal (Alfa); (ii) Female and Informal (Beta); Male and Formal (Gamma); Male and Informal (Delta). *Chatbot gender* was conveyed by either a comic-like graphical identity (presented above the conversation) and by the conversation of the bot, which was always referring to itself according to the assigned gender (consider that, according to Italian grammar's rules, adjectives inflect for gender).

Fig. 2. The four comic-like identities used in the experiment to convey chatbot gender and tone of voice.

Chatbot tone of voice was conveyed by either the clothing of the comic-like corresponding identity (i.e. formal vs. informal, Fig. 2) and the linguistic "style" of the bot. Specifically, formal linguistic style was obtained by using a refined and mannered language and by the use of the third person (which in Italian language is considered the formal and polite way to address an unknown person) when referring to the participant. On the contrary, informal linguistic style was obtained by either (i) the use of more colloquial phrasing, (ii) a less rigorous use of punctuation, which was often including exclamation points and (iii) by the use of the second person (which in Italian language is more confidential, and less polite when addressing an unknown person) when referring to the participant.

Manipulation Check. In order to verify whether our manipulation was effective, a brief questionnaire was administered to participants (i.e. Manipulation Check Questionnaire, MCQ) after the interaction with the bot. The MCQ comprised 5 items, in which participants were asked to recall the gender of the bot (i.e. female, male or neutral) and to evaluate on a 5-point Likert scale its (i) tone of voice, (ii) level of empathy, (iii) trustworthiness and (iv) general appreciation.

Explicit Measures: UEQ+. To measure explicit attitudes towards the chatbot, we used the UEQ+ (Schrepp and Thomaschewski 2019), which is a modular extension of the UEQ questionnaire (Laugwitz et al. 2008). The UEQ+ allows to construct a questionnaire which could address any out of 20 (not independent) dimensions possibly involved in UX evaluation. Each dimension is investigated by means of a semantic differential, which is a type of a rating scale designed to measure opinions, attitudes and values on a psychometrically controlled scale, Osgood (1952). Based on both our supposed context of use and on our research questions, we chose to evaluate the following six dimensions, which are the dimensions that better fit UX evaluation (Laugwitz et al. 2008): (i) Efficiency (two scales); (ii) Perspicuity (2 scales); (iii) Stimulation (2 scales);

(iv) Novelty (2 scales); (v) Usefulness (2 scales) and (vi) Quality of Content (3 scales), for a total of 13 semantic differentials.

At the end of the experiments *three additional explicit measures* were obtained by asking participants to rate on a 7-point Likert scale *(1)* the probability for the participant to fix a date for a real job interview *(Efficacy 1)*; *(2)* the probability for the participant to show up at the interview *(Efficacy 2)*; and *(3)* the level of comfort felt during the conversation *(Emotional Experience)*.

Implicit Measures. For implicit measures a single category IAT (Karpinski and Steinman 2006) has been used, designed and programmed with Inquisit Lab©. Differently from the classic IAT, the Single Category Implicit Association Test (SC–IAT) measures association strength with a single attribute category. For each version of the chatbot we presented as target concepts four images (i.e. two images showing the identity of the corresponding bot and 2 screenshots of the chat), while as evaluation attributes we presented six words related with positive and negative semantic attribution. Those words were, specifically: marvelous, love, joy, wonder, pleasure and happiness for the positive attribution, and terrible, disaster, ugly, horrible, death and pain for the negative attribution.

As recommended by Karpinski and Steinman (2006), IAT was administered in four blocks and E and I keys were assigned as response-keys for categorization of positive and negative attributes, counterbalanced throughout the experiment. Target concept was randomly associated with positive or negative categories in blocks 1 and 2, and to the opposite categories in blocks 3 and 4. Blocks 1 and 3 (practice blocks) were composed by 24 trials presented in a 7:7:10 ratio (i.e., in Block 1, 7 positive and 7 target stimuli on leftward response, and 10 negative stimuli on rightward response, resulting in 24 stimuli; in Block 3, 10 positive on leftward response, and 7 negative and 7 target stimuli on rightward response, resulting in 24 stimuli), while Blocks 2 and 4 (critical blocks) were composed by 72 trials each (in Block 2, the same 7:7:10 ratio as in the Block 1 was presented three times, resulting in 72 stimuli; in Block 4, the same 7:7:10 ratio as in the Block 3 was presented three times, resulting in 72 stimuli).

In each Block, after a pre trial pause of 250 ms, stimuli were presented until the correct response was given. According to Greenwald et al. (2003) participants were required to correct error responses.

D-scores have been calculated using the improved scoring algorithm as described in Greenwald et al. (2003). Only trials from test blocks count towards d-score calculation. The final SC-IAT d-score, as in the IAT classic version, ranges between -2 and $+2$, which in this case is an index of the association intensity between target concept and negative (-2) or positive $(+2)$ evaluation attributes.

The association between target concept and evaluation attributes was counterbalanced between participants, with a version of IAT (i.e. IAT 1) starting with the association "positive" and "bot" and a version (i.e. IAT 2) starting with the association "negative" and "bot".

Procedure

The Experiment took place in a well-illuminated and comfortable room, with each participant tested singularly. The entire procedure lasted approximately 15 min.

Upon arrival at the location, participants were asked sociodemographic information, such as gender, age, level of seniority, and their job. Information about participant's job served as an input for the bot to make the interaction more realistic; after collecting such information, the experimenter sent it to the bot, and the bot referred to the real participant's job consistently during the interview, so to help participant in imagine him/herself having a "real" job interview.

Afterwards, participants were told that they were asked to evaluate a chatbot proto-type, developed for the Human Resources (HR) Department of a private company (i.e. AlphaGroup). As mentioned above, the position for which participants have been con-tacted was similar to actual participants' positions (for instance, if participant was a UX designer, the open position in AlphaGroup was for a UX designer). To this aim they were asked to play the role of a candidate interested to work in the AlphaGroup company and to engage with the chatbot, which selected their profile as potentially suitable for the job. Participants were also told that their task was to take an appointment for an interview.

After this introduction, participants were given a smartphone (Samsung Galaxy A40) with Google Assistant showing the version of the chatbot to be evaluated. Then, they were told that they were free to interact with the version of the bot assigned to them. The experiment was between-participants, thus each participant interacted with a single version of the bot.

Once participants fixed the date for the interview, they were asked to fill-out the MCQ.

Afterwards, a brief reminder of the chatbot they interacted with (i.e., a sheet with the comic-like profile and the name of the chatbot they interacted with) was given to participants. Next, the chatbot evaluation session started. Participants were asked to perform the SC-IAT and to fill out the UEQ+ questionnaire. In order to prevent any possible order bias, we counterbalanced the order of presentation of the UEQ+ and the IAT, and the order of presentation of the two SC-IAT versions (as described in the Stimuli Section). Thus, half participants firstly fulfilled the UEQ+ and then were administered with the IAT (version 1 or 2 respectively), while the other half was firstly administered with the IAT (version 1 or 2 respectively) and then fulfilled the UEQ+.

Lastly, they were presented with the three explicit questions relative to Efficacy1, Efficacy2 and Emotional Experience, as described in the Stimuli Section.

At the end, participants were fully debriefed.

Hence, the experimental design consisted of a 2 (chatbot gender: male vs. female) × 2 (tone of voice: formal vs. informal) factorial design, with both factors varying between participants.

Results

Preliminar Analysis We removed data from one participant from the dataset, due to technical problems occurring during the experiment. Prior to the analysis, we reverse scored the negatively worded questions in the UEQ+. Then, we conducted reliability analysis on the responses to the 13 pairs of adjectives (Cronbach's alpha values for each dimension are reported in Table 1). After this analysis we could average the items relative to each dimension in order to obtain a single value relative to each dimension as well as a unique UEQ+ index, for each participant.

Table 1. UEQ+ dimensions measured in the study and the corresponding Cronbach's Alpha

UEQ+ dimensions	Cronbach's Alpha
Efficiency	.60
Perspicuity	.77
Stimulation	.79
Novelty	.80
Usefulness	.82
Quality of content	.82

We also analysed the MCQ, to test, prior to the analysis, whether the two dependent variables were effectively manipulated. To this aim we performed a chi square on the perceived gender and an independent sample t-test on the (i) tone of voice, (ii) level of empathy, (iii) trustworthiness and (iv) general appreciation. Both gender (chi-square = 20.01, p < .001) and tone of voice resulted significant (t(32) = −2.56, p = .016, M = 2.59, SD = 1.06, and M = 3.41, SD = 0.80 for the informal and formal ToV respectively), confirming that our manipulation was effective. No other variables were significant (all ps > .21).

Implicit measures - IAT A 2 (chatbot gender: male vs. female) × 2 (tone of voice: formal vs. informal) between-factors ANOVA was carried out on the individual d-scores of SC-IAT. The analysis revealed a significant main effect of the ToV, (F(3,33) = 4.01, p = .05, ηp2 = 0.12), showing an implicit preference for informal chatbot (M = .21, SE = .081) as compared with the formal one (M = -.021, SE = .081), independently from the perceived gender (Fig. 3). Neither main effect of chatbot gender nor interaction effect were significant, ps > .56.

Explicit measures - UEQ+ A 2 (chatbot gender: male vs. female) × 2 (tone of voice: formal vs. informal) between-factors ANOVA was carried out on the UEQ+ scores. Neither main effects nor interaction effect were significant, ps > .10.

Efficacy 1
A 2 (chatbot gender: male vs. female) × 2 (tone of voice: formal vs. informal) between-factors ANOVA was carried out on the Efficacy 1 scores. The analysis showed a significant main effect of the ToV, (F(3,33) = 7.57, p = .01, ηp2 = .20), revealing that the probability for the participant to fix a date for a real job interview was higher for those who interacted with the informal chatbot (M = 6.42, SE = .22) than for those who interacted with the formal one (M = 5.56, SE = .22). Neither main effect of chatbot gender nor interaction effect were significant, ps > .10.

Efficacy 2
A 2 (chatbot gender: male vs. female) × 2 (tone of voice: formal vs. informal) between-factors ANOVA was carried out on the Efficacy 2 scores. The analysis revealed a significant main effect of the ToV, (F(3,33) = 6.64, p = .015, ηp2 = .18), showing that the

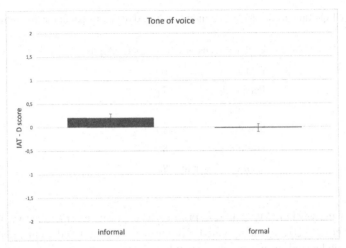

Fig. 3. The main effect of the Tone of Voice on the D scores of the SC-IAT. Error bars represent standard errors.

intention to show up at the interview was higher for participants who interacted with the informal chatbot (M = 6.65, SE = .24) than for those who interacted with the formal one (M = 5.79, SE = .24). Neither main effect of chatbot gender nor interaction effect were significant, ps > .20.

Emotional Experience
A 2 (chatbot gender: male vs. female) × 2 (tone of voice: formal vs. informal) between-factors ANOVA was carried out on the Emotional Experience scores. The analysis revealed a significant main effect of the ToV, (F(3,33) = 6.71, p = .017, ηp2 = .19), showing that the level of comfort felt during the interaction was higher with the informal chatbot (M = 6.71, SE = .17) than with the formal one (M = 6.06, SE = .18). Neither main effect of chatbot gender nor interaction effect were significant, ps > .67.

Discussion
In an experiment aimed at investigating UX with both implicit and explicit measures, we ask participants to interact with one of four possible version of a chatbot, which had the fictional goal of pre-selecting candidates for a job in the "alfa group" of a private company, and to consequently fix the date for the job interview. Each version had a different ToV and gender. Based on previous literature (e.g. Eagly and Mladinic 1989; Edwards and Spence 1987) we hypothesized a preference for (i) the informal ToV and (ii) the female chatbot. Contrary to our expectations, no effect of gender emerged, neither with implicit nor with explicit measures. However, it could be interesting to notice that female chatbot was correctly identified as such by the 76.5% of participants (the remaining 23.5% identified it as neutral), while male bot was correctly identified only by the 52.9% of participants. Other participants mainly identified male chatbot as neutral (41.2%) and only the 5.9% identified it as female. This difference in the (mis)perception of chatbot gender, although not significant, could be due to the well known bias (e.g. Feine et al. 2019) for which the majority of chatbots are females. Although this speculation

deserves further investigations, results regarding a possible preference for a specific gender are weakened by this asymmetry in chatbot gender perception.

Interestingly, results from IAT show a preference for informal ToV (as expected) which was not present in the UEQ +. The same preference found with the IAT was instead found in the three explicit questions asked to participants about (i) the probability to fix a date for a real job interview *(Efficacy 1)*; (ii) the probability to show up at the interview *(Efficacy 2)*; and (iii) the level of comfort felt during the conversation *(Emotional Experience)*.

The preference for the informal ToV is an expected result, confirming and complementing previous findings. Indeed, on the one hand (Araujo 2018) it has been shown that the usage of human-like language or name is sufficient to increase perception of the agent as being human-like, while on the other hand chatbot ToV adds consistency to the user experience (Smestad and Volden 2018). With our findings we show that informal ToV is preferred (at least in HR context) as compared with a formal ToV, being more "comfortable" in terms of emotional experience and reasonably perceived as more close to participants' personality.

The Research Questions guiding this study were (RQ1) whether it is possible to study UX by using IAT as a measure of implicit attitudes towards a chatbot and (RQ2) whether IAT could complement explicit measures of UX. The fact that a result emerged when using the IAT and that the same result was not present with the UEQ+ could be interpreted in favor of one or the other. However, the same result found with the IAT was confirmed by the self-report responses to the three explicit questions presented at the end of the experiment. In our view this concordance is in favor of the IAT as a better index for evaluating both the efficiency of the chatbot in accomplishing its supposed goals (as participants are more inclined to fix a date for a real job interview and to show up at the interview after interacting with the informal chatbot) and the overall emotional experience, which seems to fit nicely with implicit attitudes. Noticeably, if the experiment had been conducted with only a standard measure for UX, as the UEQ+ questionnaire, then no difference would be detected between the two versions of the chatbot: this at least put some doubts on the effectiveness of questionnaires in measuring UX.

We are aware that the use of IAT as a measure for UX needs further studies to be consolidated. Studies on different devices, or with chatbots with different purposes (and possibly different contexts of use), as well as studies comparing IAT with different explicit measures (i.e. different dimensions of the UEQ +, different self-report methodologies) are needed, in order to understand to what degree implicit attitudes could contribute to the overall UX.

However, we think that the results presented in our studies are promising, showing that IAT is an effective tool for measuring implicit attitudes towards a chatbot (RQ1) and that it helps in the understanding of the overall UX, complementing the use of explicit measures (RQ2).

In this study we present the use of IAT, and consequently the measure of implicit attitudes, in the interaction of humans with a technology that, although disembodied, is at least partially human-like, having a behavior (i.e. a conversation) and a comic-like identity, which could be easily associated with humans. We think that the use of IAT could be even more effective in the study of non-human-like products and interfaces, given that it could help in shading light on the effect of different unconscious processes that are proved to influence our behavior. In saying this we are referring not only to emotions, feelings and stereotypes, but also to the controversial role of physical attractiveness in guiding our choices and in perceived usability (e.g. Tractinsky et al. 2000; Tuch et al. 2012). We are actually testing this possibility by developing a protocol combining explicit measures (Capellini et al. 2015) and IAT and by using this protocol in evaluating UX with different non-human-like products.

References

Alexander, M.G., Brewer, M.B., Herrmann, R.K.: Images and affect: a functional analysis of out-group stereotypes. J. Pers. Soc. Psychol. **77**, 78–93 (1999)

Anderson, J.R.: The moderating role of socially desirable responding in implicit–explicit attitudes toward asylum seekers. Int. J. Psychol. **54**(1), 1–7 (2019)

Araujo, T.: Living up to the chatbot hype: the influence of anthropomorphic design cues and communicative agency framing on conversational agent and company perceptions. Comput. Hum. Behav. **85**, 183–189 (2018)

Brahnam, S., De Angeli, A.: Gender affordances of conversational agents. Interact. Comput. **24**(3), 139–153 (2012)

Brahnam, S.: Building character for artificial conversational agents: ethos, ethics, believability, and credibility. PsychNology J. **7**(1) (2009)

Capellini, R., Sacchi, S., Ricciardelli, P., Actis-Grosso, R.: Social threat and motor resonance: when a menacing outgroup delays motor response. Front. Psychol. **7**, 1697 (2016)

Capellini, R., Tassistro, F., Actis-Grosso, R.: Quantitative metrics for user experience: a case study. In: Abrahamsson, P., Corral, L., Oivo, M., Russo, B. (eds.) PROFES 2015. LNCS, vol. 9459, pp. 490–496. Springer, Cham (2015). https://doi.org/10.1007/978-3-319-26844-6_36

Ciardo, F., De Angelis, J., Marino, B.F., Actis-Grosso, R., Ricciardelli, P.: Social categorization and joint attention: interacting effects of age, sex, and social status. Acta Psychologica **212**, 103223 (2021)

Ciardo, F., Marino, B.F., Actis-Grosso, R., Rossetti, A., Ricciardelli, P.: Face age modulates gaze following in young adults. Sci. Rep. **4**(1), 1–7 (2014)

Ciechanowski, L., Przegalinska, A., Magnuski, M., Gloor, P.: In the shades of the uncanny valley: an experimental study of human–chatbot interaction. Futur. Gener. Comput. Syst. **92**, 539–548 (2019)

Cuddy, A.J., Fiske, S.T., Glick, P.: Warmth and competence as universal dimensions of social perception: the stereotype content model and the BIAS map. Adv. Exp. Soc. Psychol. **40**, 61–149 (2008)

De Angeli, A., Brahnam, S.: I hate you! Disinhibition with virtual partners. Interact. Comput. **20**(3), 302–310 (2008)

De Angeli, A., Johnson, G.I., Coventry, L.: The unfriendly user: exploring social reactions to chatterbots. In: Proceedings of the International Conference on Affective Human Factors Design, London, pp. 467–474 (2001)

Dimofte, C.V.: Implicit measures of consumer cognition: a review. Psychol. Mark. **27**(10), 921–937 (2010)

Eagly, A.H., Mladinic, A.: Gender stereotypes and attitudes toward women and men. Pers. Soc. Psychol. Bull. **15**(4), 543–558 (1989)

Edwards, A., Edwards, C., Spence, P.R., Harris, C., Gambino, A.: Robots in the classroom: differences in students' perceptions of credibility and learning between "teacher as robot" and "robot as teacher." Comput. Hum. Behav. **65**, 627–634 (2016)

Edwards, C., Edwards, A., Spence, P.R., Shelton, A.K.: Is that a bot running the social media feed? Testing the differences in perceptions of communication quality for a human agent and a bot agent on Twitter. Comput. Hum. Behav. **33**, 372–376 (2014)

Edwards, V.J., Spence, J.T.: Gender-related traits, stereotypes, and schemata. J. Pers. Soc. Psychol. **53**(1), 146 (1987)

Epley, N., Waytz, A., Cacioppo, J.T.: On seeing human: a three-factor theory of anthropomorphism. Psychol. Rev. **114**(4), 864 (2007)

Etemad-Sajadi, R., Ghachem, L.: The impact of hedonic and utilitarian value of online avatars on e-service quality. Comput. Hum. Behav. **52**, 81–86 (2015)

Feine, J., Gnewuch, U., Morana, S., Maedche, A.: A taxonomy of social cues for conversational agents. Int. J. Hum Comput Stud. **132**, 138–161 (2019)

Følstad, A., Brandtzæg, P.B.: Chatbots and the new world of HCI. Interactions **24**(4), 38–42 (2017). https://doi.org/10.1145/3085558

Greenwald, A.G., Banaji, M.R.: Implicit social cognition: attitudes, self-esteem, and stereotypes. Psychol. Rev. **102**(1), 4–27 (1995)

Greenwald, A.G., McGhee, D.E., Schwartz, J.L.: Measuring individual differences in implicit cognition: the implicit association test. J. Pers. Soc. Psychol. **74**(6), 1464 (1998)

Greenwald, A.G., Nosek, B.A., Banaji, M.R.: Understanding and using the implicit association test: I. an improved scoring algorithm. J. Pers. Soc. Psychol. **85**(2), 197–216 (2003). https://doi.org/10.1037/0022-3514.85.2.197

Haberman, J., Whitney, D.: Rapid extraction of mean emotion and gender from sets of faces. Curr. Biol. **17**(17), R751–R753 (2007)

Hasler, B.S., Tuchman, P., Friedman, D.: Virtual research assistants: replacing human interviewers by automated avatars in virtual worlds. Comput. Hum. Behav. **29**(4), 1608–1616 (2013)

Hung, S.M., Nieh, C.H., Hsieh, P.J.: Unconscious processing of facial attractiveness: invisible attractive faces orient visual attention. Sci. Rep. **6**(1), 1–8 (2016)

Jenkins, M.-C., Churchill, R., Cox, S., Smith, D.: Analysis of user interaction with service oriented chatbot systems. In: Jacko, J.A. (ed.) HCI 2007. LNCS, vol. 4552, pp. 76–83. Springer, Heidelberg (2007). https://doi.org/10.1007/978-3-540-73110-8_9

Karpinski, A., Steinman, R.B.: The single category implicit association test as a measure of implicit social cognition. J. Pers. Soc. Psychol. **91**(1), 16 (2006)

Kim, Y., Sundar, S.S.: Anthropomorphism of computers: Is it mindful or mindless? Comput. Hum. Behav. **28**(1), 241–250 (2012)

Laugwitz, B., Held, T., Schrepp, M.: Construction and evaluation of a user experience questionnaire. In: Holzinger, A. (ed.) USAB 2008. LNCS, vol. 5298, pp. 63–76. Springer, Heidelberg (2008). https://doi.org/10.1007/978-3-540-89350-9_6

Nass, C., Moon, Y.: Machines and mindlessness: Social responses to computers. J. Soc. Issues **56**(1), 81–103 (2000)

Nass, C., Moon, Y., Carney, P.: Are people polite to computers? Responses to computer-based interviewing systems. J. Appl. Soc. Psychol. **29**(5), 1093–1110 (1999)

Nass, C., Moon, Y., Green, N.: Are machines gender neutral? Gender-stereotypic responses to computers with voices. J. Appl. Soc. Psychol. **27**(10), 864–876 (1997)

Nass, C., Steuer, J.: Voices, boxes, and sources of messages: Computers and social actors. Hum. Commun. Res. **19**(4), 504–527 (1993)

Nevid, J.S.: Introduction to the special issue: implicit measures of consumer response—the search for the holy grail of marketing research. Psychol. Mark. **27**(10), 913–920 (2010)

Osgood, C.E.: The nature and measurement of meaning. Psychol. Bull. **49**(3), 197 (1952)

Pickard, M.D., Roster, C.A., Chen, Y.: Revealing sensitive information in personal interviews: is self-disclosure easier with humans or avatars and under what conditions? Comput. Hum. Behav. **65**, 23–30 (2016)

Reeves, B., Nass, C.: The Media Equation: How People Treat Computers, Television, and New Media Like Real People. Cambridge University Press, Cambridge (1996)

Schrepp, M., Thomaschewski, J.: Design and validation of a framework for the creation of user experience questionnaires. Int. J. Interact. Multimed. Artif. Intell. 5(7), 88 (2019). https://doi.org/10.9781/ijimai.2019.06.006

Smestad, T.L., Volden, F.: Chatbot personalities matters. In: Bodrunova, S.S., et al. (eds.) INSCI 2018. LNCS, vol. 11551, pp. 170–181. Springer, Cham (2019). https://doi.org/10.1007/978-3-030-17705-8_15

Talaska, C.A., Fiske, S.T., Chaiken, S.: Legitimating racial discrimination: emotions, not beliefs, best predict discrimination in a meta-analysis. Soc. Just Res. 21, 263–296 (2008)

Tractinsky, N., Katz, A.S., Ikar, D.: What is beautiful is usable. Interact. Comput. 13(2), 127–145 (2000). https://doi.org/10.1016/S0953-5438(00)00031-X

Tuch, N., Roth, P.S., Hornbæk, K., Opwis, K., Bargas-Avila, J.A.: Is beautiful really usable? Toward understanding the relation between usability, aesthetics, and affect in HCI. Comput. Hum. Behav. 28, 1596–1607 (2012)

Verhagen, T., van Nes, J., Feldberg, F., van Dolen, W.: Virtual customer service agents: using social presence and personalization to shape online service encounters. J. Comput.-Mediat. Commun. 19(3), 529–545 (2014)

Wilson, T.D., Lindsey, S., Schooler, T.Y.: A model of dual attitudes. Psychol. Rev. 107(1), 101–126 (2000)

Wittenbrink, B., Schwarz, N. (eds.): Implicit Measures of Attitudes. Guilford Press (2007)

Yan, Z., Schmidt, S.N., Saur, S., Kirsch, P., Mier, D.: The effect of ethnicity and team membership on face processing: a cultural neuroscience perspective. Soc. Cogn. Affect. Neurosci. 14(9), 1017–1025 (2019)

The Ecosystem's Involvement in the Appropriation Phase of Assistive Technology: Choice and Adjustment of Interaction Techniques

Charline Calmels[1], Caroline Mercadier[1], Frédéric Vella[2], Antonio Serpa[2], Philippe Truillet[2], and Nadine Vigouroux[2(✉)]

[1] Fondation OPTEO, MAS La Boraldette, 12500 St Côme d'Olt, France
[2] IRIT, CNRS, UPS, 118 Route de Narbonne, 31062 Toulouse Cedex 9, France
Nadine.Vigouroux@irit.fr

Abstract. Designing assistive technologies for the benefit of a population of multi-disabled users living in specialized care homes involves the implementation of a user-centered approach (UCD). The purpose of this article is to demonstrate how the ecosystem also plays a key role in the codesign and appropriation phases of a augmentative and alternative communication (AAC), mainly in the choice and adjustment of interaction techniques through a case study. Firstly, we present related works on the codesign of assistive technologies. Then, we will describe the SoKeyTo platform used for the codesign by the human-computer interaction team. We will also explain the collaboration between the ecosystem and HCI team during tests (place of the switch and type of scanning). Usability criteria were used to determine these choices. Finally, we will illustrate our approach in the codesign and appropriation activities of layout and interaction modes of the AAC.

Keywords: Codesign · Appropriation · AAC · Ecosystem · Multiple disability

1 Introduction

Designing assistive technologies for the benefit of a population of multi-disabled users living in specialized care homes involves the implementation of a user-centered approach (UCD) of Norman [1] and the ISO, I. 9241 [2]. Guffroy *et al.* [3] have introduced the "*ecosystem*" as the social environment involved in the design of assistive technologies. This ecosystem is made up of family and/or professional careers, friends, and colleagues in relation to his or her professional activity, who are involved in the activities of the person with a disability. For people with communication impairments (little or no written and oral language), the participation of ecosystem members is essential in order to design assistive technologies that takes into account the context of use and the expression of needs, see Guffroy *et al.* [3], Derboven *et al.* [4]. In addition, these disabled persons need assistive technologies to communicate with their caregivers and their family. For them, people's needs and preferences are unique and often complex. As they have difficulties to

© Springer Nature Switzerland AG 2021
M. Antona and C. Stephanidis (Eds.): HCII 2021, LNCS 12768, pp. 21–38, 2021.
https://doi.org/10.1007/978-3-030-78092-0_2

participate themselves in the design activities, our approach is to integrate their ecosystem in UCD activities.

In a first work, Vella *et al.* [5] have integrated clinical data in place of the needs expressed by the end user himself/herself in addition to those given by the ecosystem. The purpose of this article is to demonstrate how the ecosystem also plays a key role in the codesign and appropriation phases of a augmentative and alternative communication (AAC), mainly in the choice and adjustment of interaction techniques through a case study. Firstly, we present related works on the codesign of assistive technologies. Then, we will describe the SoKeyTo platform used for the codesign by the human-computer interaction team. We will also explain the collaboration between the ecosystem and HCI team. Finally, we will illustrate our approach in the codesign and appropriation activities of layout and interaction modes of the AAC.

2 Related Work on Codesign

The UCD approach assumes that end-users are in the best position to express their needs, participate in the design, evaluate and use the interactive system to the satisfaction of the needs and requirements expressed by the users. As a result, these activities encounter implementation difficulties when designing systems dedicated to people with disabilities (communication disorders, motor disorders, cognitive disorders, etc.) according to Antona *et al.* [6]. Indeed, communication and/or cognitive impairments limit the participation of these end-users in codesign.

Kleinsmann [7] defined the codesign as a process in which actors from different disciplines share their knowledge about both the design process and the design content. This is an interesting approach to engage those who will be directly or indirectly affected by the design. Moreover, for Apper [8], there are four principles to consider when designing technologies for people with special needs: "*deep engagement, interdisciplinary, individuality, and practicality, should be reflected upon at the projects' inception and throughout its development cycle*". In a study on codesign in assistive technology, Luck [9] shown that it was critical to engage users in the design process.

Sitbon & Farhin [10] reported that engaging users with intellectual disability in an hour-long codesign workshop with a carer confirm the benefits of digital prototypes, contribute a better understanding of the role of proxies, and suggest a longer engagement to potentially take advantage of co-development.

Hendriks *et al.* [11] raises the question of the positioning of the participants' impairment in the codesign project "*How was the impairment addressed in the interactions during the codesign process? Were the participants involved in the configuration of the codesign process itself?*".

Gibson *et al.* [12] have studied on how to better support adults with mild Intellectual disabilities to engage in codesign. Firstly, they conducted a review literature to identify research techniques that have been employed to codesign. One of their outcomes recommend a variety of experts "*the experts had to have five + years' experience working with or caring for the target population i.e. individuals who adhered to the ID*" [12] be employed within the focus groups to ensure design tasks are approached from different viewpoints and the optimal number of accessibility barriers are addressed before implementation with target stakeholders. Moreover, we think that the entire ecosystem has to be engaged in the design process. We will describe our approach of taking into account the ecosystem and the person with a disability in the codesign of an AAC.

3   The SoKeyTo Platform

We have an interactive SoKeyTo application for designing AAC systems and configuring interaction techniques. It is an editor for the creation of interaction buttons for the AAC codesign team (occupational therapists, psychologists, assistive technology designers). The editor (see Fig. 1) allows to define several features of an interactive button: the morphology of the button (form, size, colour, background, etc.); the representation of the button (image, text and/or sound); the layout and the structure tree of the interface according to topics; the type of feedback (visual and/or sound) and the type of associated function (communication message, running an application; sending messages by means of a text-to-speech synthesis system or sending messages to control domotic connected object in home automation).

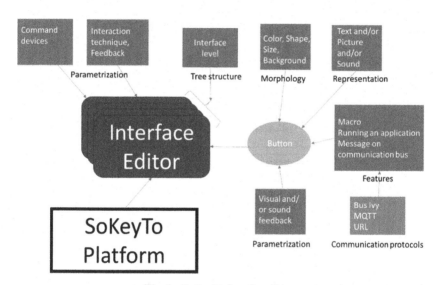

Fig. 1. SoKeyTo functionalities.

The editor also enables to associate to each button the communication protocol required for the button function (for example, the Ivy bus [13] for restoring a voice message, the MQTT network protocol [14]. The editor of the SoKeyTo platform permits to customize not only the AAC interface but also to connect several devices and AAC input interaction modes (scanning system, validation mode, interface return type). Several types of interaction devices (mouse, eyes tracking, joystick, voice recognition, contactor on/off, etc.) are currently supported by the AAC designed with the SoKeyTo platform. The platform also allows setting various validation modes (classic pointing by pressure or by release, timed click, scrolling system) according to the capacities of disabled people. Many options are possible for these control modes.

All these features allow a fully AAC customized codesign for persons with multiple disabled. We used the SoKeyTo platform for the design of AAC for P1 (see Fig. 5).

4   Codesign with the Ecosystem

We are implementing the UCD approach of ISO 9241-210 [2] in which we will demonstrate the role of the ecosystem in the UCD activities to design customized AAC. In a previous article, Vella *et al.* [5] reported the observational methods, including the contribution of both clinical scales and ecosystem expertise. The ecosystem has played an important role in both *Understand and specify the context user* activity and *Specify the user requirements* activity (See Fig. 2). In this paper, we will describe the role of the ecosystem in the codesign and the adaptation of a customized AAC.

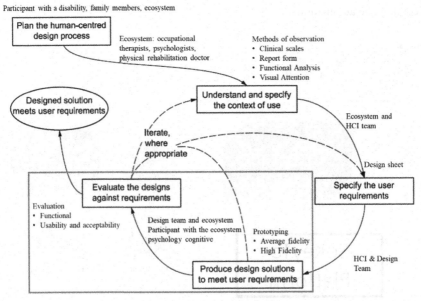

Fig. 2. UCD phases with ecosystem for OUPSCECI design.

The ecosystem and the human-computer interaction (HCI) teams codesigned the AAC interface. The ecosystem has proposed pictogram representations while the HCI team suggested pictogram sizes and contrasts. Both teams have taking into account the perceptive and motor capacities of the person measured by the clinical scales. They also discussed the AAC tree structure to meet user's needs and to be adequate to the intended functions.

This phase has generated many exchanges between the two teams. We codesigned all prototype versions (version 0 for the choice of the most efficient member to control the AAC, version 1 for the place of the control switch (see Sect. 5.3), version 2 for the choice of scanning strategies (see Sect. 5.4). The HCI team designed the AAC by means of the SoKeyTo platform while the caregivers specify or clarify new requirements of AAC functions.

The adaptation of AAC to the functional capacities of the person with a disability is characterized by a very long phase of appropriation and adaptation (several sessions per week for several months, reported by the study of Sauzin *et al.* [15]. In this phase, the ecosystem played an essential role during the following phase: parameterization of the control modes (scanning system, timed click, normal click, etc.), ergonomic placement of the AAC in the environment (place of digital tablet and control switch), validation of pictogram representations (size, validation feedback). The involvement of the ecosystem is also important in the learning phase of the pictograms and the navigation mode in the AAC. We discussed each weekly by videoconference, during 9 months, the adaptation of the AAC. This close collaboration resulted in the addition of a release validation mode, the addition of new pictograms corresponding to new needs, the need to study several scanning strategies.

In the following section, we describe the collaboration of the P1's ecosystem and the HCI team in the design and the appropriation of the AAC.

5   Codesign and Appropriation of the AAC for P1: A Case Study

5.1   P1 Profile

P1 is an adult person with cerebral palsy, without written and oral expression. P1 uses a foot control device, with five switches, to control his electric wheelchair (see Fig. 3). He has athetotic movements in his upper limbs but there are fewer of them at foot level. The only voluntary movements that P1 can control are those of the left foot (better managed on the left (in average 40 times per minute) than on the right (30 times per minute).

The aim is to define the same control device usable by P1 to control his electric wheelchair and his communication notebook. According to Sugawara *et al.* [16] "The strong correlation found between abandonment levels and the simultaneous use of multiple devices should be taken into account by health professionals when prescribing assistive products and providing guidance to users".

5.2   Design of a Customized Communication Notebook

The main P1's needs is that his paper's communication notebook should be integrated into the digital interface. This one will also integrate a home automation part (music management, television control) and some others functionalities (access to his calendar, meteo, etc.) identified by his ecosystem (professional and familial caregivers) [5]. We codesigned two previous version used to measure the acceptance and the use according the cognitive, attentional and motor abilities of P1. The main and described in details in [5].

The main difference between version 1 and 2 (see Fig. 5) of the communication book is the enhancement of the topics and the tree structure in level in a given topic.

The codesign team has structured the interface in three blocks. We chose this layout to allow the user to identify more easily the intention of his/her interaction with the

Right   Left   Down   Up   Useless button

I want to
talk to you

Please grab my
communication
notebook

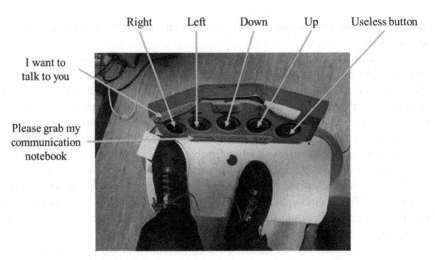

Fig. 3. Foot control of P1's wheelchair. The four grey buttons are used to control the wheelchair and the two yellow markers for "I want to talk to you" and "Please grab my communication notebook" (Color figure online).

interface. So, we defined the set of pictograms to be categorized: 1) navigation inside a set of a topic; 2) navigation inside the pictogram set of communication or automation home; 3) navigation inside the interface or mention of an error. To improve interaction, we chose to put the pictogram "I was mistaken", accessible at all levels of the interface (see Fig. 5).

The communication interface consists of the following components (see Fig. 4). Level 2 offers pictograms to contextualize communication with a caregiver. For example, if P1 wishes to express a problem with his pants. P1 selects the "I have a problem" button, and then the Category interface appears automatically. P1 can then choose the button "clothes" which makes a set of clothes (Level 3) appear, including the pants that P1 can select (Level 4). This contextualization of the level 1 buttons allows: 1) the interlocutor to contextualize the communication and 2) to reduce the production time of the message by P1. The current interface has 23 contextualization buttons which allows P1 to have a good communication register with his professional caregivers.

The interface (see Fig. 5) displayed currently consists of three blocks:

- 1st line (in yellow), navigation pictograms (Previous button: return to the previous interface; Next button: move to the following interface; these two buttons allow to navigate in the set of the same pictogram topic;
- 4th column (in yellow), Topics button: choice of the communication theme; pictogram signifying a choice error; return to the first level;
- The central block composed of 4 lines/3 columns is made up of communication pictograms. The codesign team has added a textual description to facilitate the communication between P1 and her caregivers (family and professional).

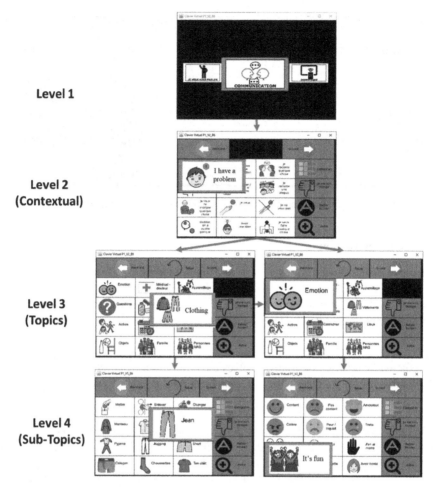

Fig. 4. The different levels of the interface.

The codesign team has moved the navigation pictograms to the first block to optimize the access (saving time) to the navigation buttons. In the V0 version, these navigation buttons were located at the bottom of the interface and P1 needed to scan the whole communication block [5].

Ongoing weekly trial carried out by the occupational therapist show that the representation of the interface is suitable even if the number of items is greater than initially envisaged by the ECP (Polyhandicap Cognitive Skills Rating Scale) [17]; scale (from 9 to 12 for the central block). The codesign team has designed this size of the central block because P1 has shown cognitive capabilities under development.

A red feedback (primary color suggested by ComVor scale [18]) mentions the pictogram block or the current pictogram that P1 can select. It is also possible to activate the audio description by means of a text-to-speech of the pictogram selected.

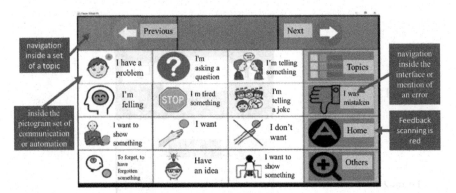

Fig. 5. Communication interface (version 1), level 2. (Color figure online)

5.3   Device Interaction

The ecosystem has carried out a series of tests for the selection of the switch position and validation mode. Real-world trials will be required to define whether pressure or release is used as a validation technique to select a pictogram. Indeed, the muscles involved in each movement (pressure or release) are not the same, so each action does not mobilize the same muscles:

- Validation by release essentially involves the levator muscles of the foot;
- Validation by support requires the mobilization of several muscles and more coordination.

In order to evaluate the position of the switch and the selection, occupational therapists positioned the switch button in 5 different places (see Fig. 6). The test consisted of finding the best position and the best way to perform the validation action by either releasing or pressing the device. To do this, P1 carried out successive presses and releases on the switch under the control of the occupational therapist. It is to be noted that position 5 was not evaluated because P1 was unable to use the switch in this position. We did not perform release testing at switch place 3. This position makes it difficult for P1 to leave the foot on the switch at this location due to parasitic movements. During the exercises, the person made unintentional or too late selections in positions 1, 2 and 3 but also with the foot sliding on the switch for position 2. On position 4, no parasitic and tiring movements were observed. A complementary test was carried out to verify that this position 4 does not limit the driving of the wheelchair.

In addition, the following results show that position 4 is the most optimized. Indeed, Fig. 7 shows the average selection time with the foot to perform the action on the switch, i.e., pressing or releasing. We can see that in position 4, P1 takes the least time to perform the action. Similarly than for position 4, P1 makes many selections per minute (see Fig. 8). These results are even better for the release.

The occupational therapist performed this trial phase alone in several sessions. This highlights the very important role of the occupational therapist in selecting the appropriate AAC switch based on P1's motor skills.

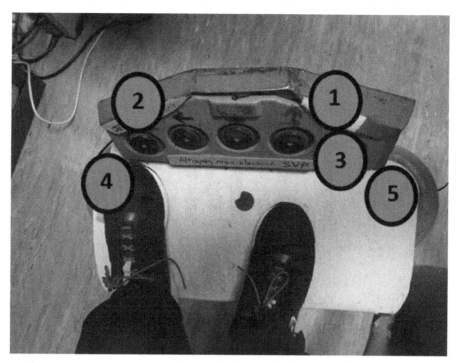

Fig. 6. Various switch positions to control the AAC interface.

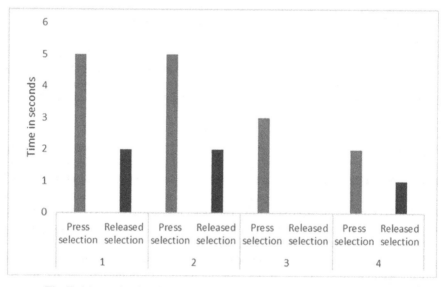

Fig. 7. Mean selection time (including foot movement and selection action).

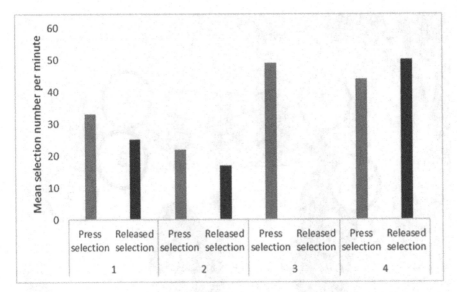

Fig. 8. Mean selection number per minute.

5.4 Scanning Strategies

For P1, the only way to communicate and to control his environment will be with a controlled scanning system operated by a single switch (see above, its place). The main problem with these systems is that the communication process tends to be exceedingly slow, since the system must scan through the available choices. The choice of the type of scanning and the scanning delay are two important parameters, strongly dependent on the motor and attentional capacities of the person with a disability. Several scanning techniques (row/column, circular, group-item and directed scanning, etc.) have been experimented in the field of AAC [19, 20]. Ghedira *et al.* [21] have proposed a method to optimize the scanning delay. White *et al.* [19] reported *"Better accuracy with directed scanning appears to come at the cost of a slower response time. Whereas group-item scanning may be faster, it results in a decreased number of accurate responses"*.

In this context, the interface structure (see Fig. 5) of P1 led us to study the accuracy and efficiency of six scanning systems. These take into account the global layout of the interface (in 2 or 3 blocks) and the topology of the blocks (one row, 3 rows/4 columns, one column). The B1 reference scanning is the classical line/column scanning without taking into account the interface structure. The Table 1 describes the six types of scanning codesigned. In a first time, we estimated the time and the number of clicks to reach the "I tell a joke" button and the "Topics" button (see Fig. 5).

The figure (see Fig. 9) shows the number of actions and the minimum time to access the two communication buttons. If we compare these two parameters, the B1 and B6 scans obtain the best performances.

Firstly, P1's occupational therapist in conjunction with the human-computer interaction team has assessed these six scanning strategies. Figure 10 shows the position

Table 1. Scanning type description

Scanning number	Scanning pattern	Scanning description
B1		one block : scanning row and then column;
B2		scanning through three blocks; first select the block, then inside a given block, scanning key-by-key;
B3		scanning through three blocks; first select the block; then inside the block 1 or block 2, scanning key-by-key; inside the block 3 scanning row and then column;
B4		scanning through two blocks; first select the block; inside these two blocks, scanning key-by-key;
B5		scanning through two blocks : first select the block; then inside the block 1, scanning key-by-key; inside the block 2 scanning row and column;
B6		scanning through three blocks: first select the block 1 or 2; then inside block 1 or 2, scanning key-by-key; if the block 1 or 2 is not selected, the scanning row and column starts automatically in block 3.

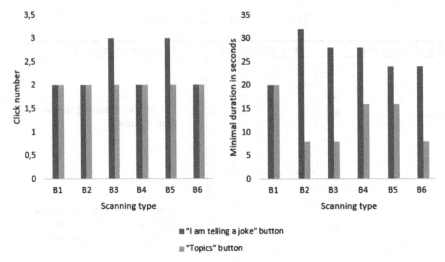

"I am telling a joke" button

"Topics" button

Fig. 9. Theoretical results.

of the left foot at the beginning of each trial. The scanning delay is 4 s. The duration computation starts when the scanning is on the first block of the interface (Fig. 5).

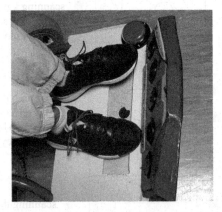

Fig. 10. Positioning of the contactor and the left foot.

In all trials, the B1 and B6 scanning get the best performance and there are no interaction errors. The performance of P1 is very close to the minimum time for scanning strategies B1 and B6. On the other hand, in scanning B2 and B3 (2 Delayed selection), B4 (1 No selection) and B5 (Unintended release), interaction errors occurred. The occupational therapist observed unintentional movements from right foot and arm during the tests of B1, B2 and B3 that may disturb the motor control of his left foot.

We have selected the B1 and B6 scanning and we have carried out a new study of the performance measures by carrying out tests to select a pictogram at various levels of the interface tree structure. The hypothesis was to see if the performances of

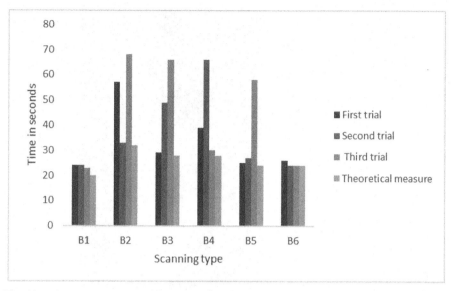

Fig. 11. Effective and theoretical access time to the pictogram "I am telling a joke" for a scanning speed of 4 s.

pictogram selection were similar at different levels of the tree structure of the interface communication block. (Fig. 11).

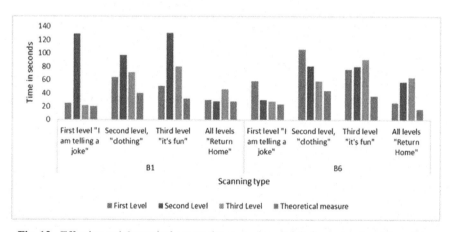

Fig. 12. Effective and theoretical access time to various levels for a scanning delay of 4 s.

The above results (see Fig. 12) show a slightly faster average selection time (62.9 s) with the B6 scanning compared to 64.41 s for B1 for all three-test conditions together. On the other hand, P1 achieves 5 click delays and 2 click anticipation with B6 compared to 4 click delays with B1. Selection errors are mainly due to difficulties in controlling foot

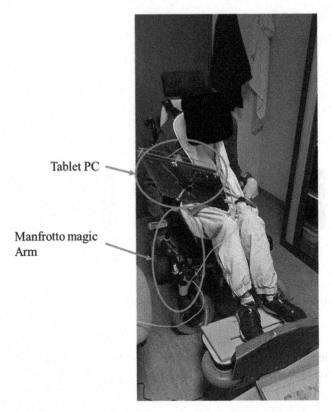

Tablet PC

Manfrotto magic
Arm

Fig. 13. Integration of the interface in the wheelchair environment.

movement. Occupational therapy sessions show that P1 always needs time to control himself in order to limit unintentional movements.

However, the feeling of P1 is that he prefers B6 scanning which allows a faster return to the home page and previous page (when there is no interaction error) and a faster management of selection errors in the communication block. The appropriation of the interface follows with the B6 scanning.

5.5 Discussion

The tests carried out for the place of the switch, the selection mode as well as on the various scanning demonstrate the key role of the occupational therapist in our codesign process. It also highlights the need for close collaboration between the occupational therapy and AAC design teams in the search for an integrated solution that is accessible and accepted by the person with multiple disabilities. This close collaboration resulted in the development of an interface structure and a series of scanning systems to be proposed. After this important codesign and testing phase, the observations of the design and customization choices are very encouraging. Indeed, P1 begins to gain autonomy in the use of her interface by taking the initiative in communication. For instance, P1 has interrogated his occupational therapist, "How is she feeling?".

5.6 Integration of the Interface into the Wheelchair Environment

An important element of the whole setup is the holding system for the tablet fixed on the wheelchair (see Fig. 13). This system must be, at the same time, easy to install and to remove by the stakeholders, sufficiently adjustable to allow an ideal positioning of the screen without obstructing the vision of the participant and safe for him and his entourage if there is a shock when he is moving. We have tested several solutions (see Table 2) to determine the best balance between ergonomic, practical and safety aspects. The table below presents a summary of the envisaged solutions already tested or under test and for each device their pros and cons.

Table 2. Solutions tested.

Setup	Pros	Cons	Status
Manfrotto magic Arm (Articulated arm with centre lever to lock all 3 movements) [22]	When tightened, the arm is strong and stable Can be adjusted using a single lever The positioning of the screen can be precisely adjusted	When the lever is release, the whole arm goes limp, including the ball joints at each end The rigidity of the arm could be dangerous in case of impact with a wall or a person It is difficult for stakeholders to adjust or remove the device without risking dropping the tablet on the participant	Tested
Rigid tube [23]	Easy to install and to remove Strong and stable	The rigidity of the tube could be dangerous in case of impact with a wall or a person The positioning of the screen can't be precisely adjusted	Tested
Semi rigid arm [24]	Easy to install and to remove Easy to adjust The positioning of the screen can be precisely adjusted Can absorb a shock and reduce the risk of injury	The screen is less stable than with rigid setups and may wobble a little bit when the participant is moving	In test
Flexible arm [25]	Easy to install and to remove Easy to adjust The positioning of the screen can be precisely adjusted Can absorb a shock	The screen wobble a lot when the participant is moving Too much flexibility in the arm could be dangerous in case of impact with a wall or a person Screen positioning needs to be adjusted frequently	Tested

The semi-rigid configuration, which is currently in test, seems to be the best solution to hold the tablet. This solution is easy to use and configure by the stakeholders, highly configurable and sufficiently secure and stable.

6 Discussion on the Methodology

Improving understanding of user preferences, the salience of technologies for the user, and personally meaningful outcomes of AT use can contribute to technological solutions that are need-person-centred. For this, we have set up a codesign method. Usually, codesign is performed with end-users. Several adaptations of the codesign tools have been proposed: for instance Gibson *et al.* [12] suggested to take into account the knowledge of "experts" on disabilities; Hendricks *et al.* [11] described research on dedicated methodological approach for involving people living with impairments in codesign projects.

Our approach is different; we have set up a codesign method but with the ecosystem of the disabled person. We have considered members of the ecosystem not only as experts but also as "co-users" of the device (interlocutor customization, use the AAC as a rehabilitation tool). In our case study, the ecosystem involved is composed of a psychologist and an occupational therapist. In Vella *et al.* [5], we demonstrated the pivotal role of caregivers in the clinical evaluation of the motor and communication skills of disabled person. In this paper, we focused on the activity of codesign and evaluation/appropriation of the components of the communication system (communication interface, control modes, ergonomics of the solution in the person's wheelchair environment).

In our approach, it is difficult to measure the contribution of the ecosystem with a reference situation (without the contribution of the ecosystem). We therefore interviewed the HCI team about the configuration proposals that they would have suggested as modalities of interaction without the exchanges with the occupational therapist. The designer team would have proposed the scanning strategy (row/column) B1 and the mode of selection by press. However, the results respectively reported in Sects. 5.3 (Device interaction) and Sect. 5.4 (Scanning strategies) show that these configurations do not achieve the best usability rates. As reported by Fedirici *et al.* [26] "*Abandonment may be due to assignment of inappropriate devices or failure to meet user needs and expectations*". Thus, the ecosystem is the best guarantee that the needs and the best possible configuration of P1's AAC were taken into account.

This study also highlights the impact of associating rehabilitation treatment and assistive technology designer and of following up on users for short- and long-term use. The study also demonstrates the importance of considering the need for reusing assistive products for the environmental.

One challenge in this approach is the balancing viewpoint of the ecosystem and the HCI team. As reported by Hendriks *et al.* [11] equivalence amongst the ecosystem and the HCI team is very important. The various meetings (conducted mainly by videoconference due to the COVID pandemic) have led to the structure of the interface in three blocks, to the proposition of a set of scanning strategies. The ecosystem proposed the set of pictograms (knowledge of the need for communication) while the researchers proposed pictogram sizes, contrasts based on knowledge of accessibility.

The two teams agreed on the importance of supporting collaboration and finding a shared language.

However, this approach, however, raises the time needed to learn and customize the AAC for P1. The whole customization process is very long (more than six months at the rate of one session per week) and requires a very significant involvement of occupational therapists.

7 Conclusion

We described our codesign approach with the ecosystem of a person with multiple disabilities to design his adapted AAC. This is an interesting approach to involve those who will be directly or indirectly affected by the design. However, it raises ethical issues, to the extent that the needs of people with disabilities are respected. Our approach demonstrates the strong interest of collaborating with the ecosystem, on the one hand in the codesign activity but also in the customization and learning phases of the AAC. Indeed, this case study and the results we obtained show us the interest of our approach to design adapted systems. It also show us the interest of undertaking a longitudinal study with more participants. The aim of this future study would be to validate our approach by evaluating the usability and long-term acceptability of the device by the participants and their ecosystems. It could also allow us to assess the contribution of these codesignated devices to improve autonomy, well being and social interactions of the participants.

Acknowledgement. This project is partially supported by "Region Occitanie" and OPTEO Foundation (France). Many thanks also to our P1 participant.

References

1. Norman, D.A.: The Design of Everyday Things: Revised and Expanded Edition. Basic Books (AZ) (2013)
2. ISO, I. 9241: Ergonomic requirements for office work with visual display terminals-Part 11: Guidance on usability. ISO, Geneva (1998)
3. Guffroy, M., Vigouroux, N., Kolski, C., Vella, F., Teutsch, P.: From human-centered design to disabled user & ecosystem centered design in case of assistive interactive systems. Int. J. Sociotechnol. Knowl. Dev. **9**(4), 28–42 (2017)
4. Derboven, J., Huyghe, J., De Grooff, D.: Designing voice interaction for people with physical and speech impairments. In: Proceedings of the 8th Nordic Conference on Human-Computer Interaction: Fun, Fast, Foundational, pp. 217–226 (2014)
5. Vella, F., et al.: Contribution of clinical data to the design of assistive systems. In: Stephanidis, C., Antona, M., Gao, Q., Zhou, J. (eds.) HCII 2020. LNCS, vol. 12426, pp. 144–157. Springer, Cham (2020). https://doi.org/10.1007/978-3-030-60149-2_12
6. Antona, M., Ntoa, S., Adami, I., Stephanidis, C.: User requirements elicitation for uiversal access, chapter 15. In: Stephanidis, C. (ed.) The Universal Access Handbook, pp. 15.1–15.14. CRC Press (2009)
7. Kleinsmann, M.S.: Understanding Collaborative Design. TU Delft, Delft, University of Technology (2006). ISBN 90-9020974-3
8. Alper, M., Hourcade, J.P., Gilutz, S.: Interactive technologies for children with special needs. In: Proceedings of the 11th International Conference on Interaction Design and Children, pp. 363–366. ACM, New York (2012)
9. Luck, R.: Inclusive design and making in practice: bringing bodily experience into closer context with making. Des. Stud. **54**, 96–110 (2018)
10. Sitbon, L., Farhin, S.: Codesigning interactive applications with adults with intellectual disability: a case study. In: Proceedings of the 29th Australian Conference on Computer-Human Interaction, OZCHI 2017, November 2017, pp. 487–491 (2017). https://doi.org/10.1145/315 2771.3156163
11. Hendriks, N., Slegers, K., Duysburgh, P.: Codesign with people living with cognitive or sensory impairments: a case for method stories and uniqueness. CoDesign **11**(1), 1–13 (2015). https://doi.org/10.1080/15710882.2015.1020316

12. Gibson, R.C., Dunlop, M.D., Bouamrane, M.-M.: Lessons from expert focus groups on how to beter support adults with mild intellectual disabilities to engage in codesign. In: The 22nd International ACM SIGACCESS Conference on Computers and Accessibility (ASSETS 2020) (2020). https://doi.org/10.1145/3373625.3417008
13. Buisson, M., et al.: Ivy: un bus logiciel au service du développement de prototypes de systèmes interactifs (French only). In: IHM 2002 Conference. ACM Press (2002). ISBN 1-58113-615-3
14. MQTT (Message Queuing Telemetry Transport). https://mqtt.org/
15. Sauzin, D., et al.: MATT, un dispositif de domotique et d'aide à la communication: un cas d'étude de co-conception. In: Congrès de la SOFMER (SOFMER 2015), Société Française de Médecine Physique et de Réadaptation (2015)
16. Sugawara, A.T., Ramos, V.D., Alfieri, F.M., Battistella, L.: Abandonment of assistive products: assessing abandonment level and factors that impact on it. Disabil. Rehabil.: Assistive Technol. 13(7), 716–723 (2018). https://doi.org/10.1080/17483107.2018.1425748
17. Scelles, R., Evaluation–Cognition–Polyhandicap (ECP), Rapport de recherche, Novembre 2014–Novembre 2017
18. Noens, I., Van Berckelaer-Onnes, I., Verpoorten, R., Van Duijn, G.: The ComVor: an instrument for the indication of augmentative communication in people with autism and intellectual disability. J. Intellect. Disabil. Res. 50(9), 621–632 (2006)
19. White, A.R., Carney, E., Reichle, J.: Group-item and directed scanning: examining preschoolers' accuracy and efficiency in two augmentative communication symbol selection methods. Am. J. Speech Lang. Pathol. 19(4), 311–20 (2010). https://doi.org/10.1044/1058-0360(2010/09-0017). Epub 2 Jul 2010, PMID: 20601623
20. Abascal, J., Gardeazaba, L., Garay, N.: Optimisation of the selection features text input. In: Miesenberger, K., et al. (eds.) Proceedings of the International Conference on Computers Helping Peoplewith Special Needs (ICCHP 2004), pp. 788–795 (2004)
21. Ghedira, S., Pino, P., Bourhis, G.: Conception and experimentation of a communication device with adaptive scanning. ACM Trans. Accessible Comput. (TACCESS) 1(3), 1–23 (2009)
22. https://www.manfrotto.com/uk-en/magic-photo-arm-kit-aluminium-with-locking-lever-143/
23. https://www.rammount.com/part/RAM-VP-TTM12U
24. https://www.rammount.com/part/RAM-B-316-400-202U
25. https://handieasy.com/bras-de-support/63-108-bras-pour-tablette.html#/28-taille-15_cm/30-fixation-pince_metallique_robuste_jusqua_45_mn
26. Federici, S., Meloni, F., Borsci, S.: The abandonment of assistivetechnology in Italy: a survey of National Health Serviceusers. Eur. J. Phys. Rehabil. Med. 52, 516–526 (2016)

Setting Diversity at the Core of HCI

Nana Kesewaa Dankwa$^{(\boxtimes)}$ and Claude Draude$^{(\boxtimes)}$

Gender/Diversity in Informatics Systems (GeDIS), Research Center for Information Systems Design (ITeG), Faculty of Electrical Engineering/Computer Science, University of Kassel, Kassel, Germany
{nkdankwa,claude.draude}@uni-kassel.de

Abstract. The advancing awareness of diversity in HCI is touted as laudable in addressing inequality and the digital divide. This progress however has not been reflected in HCI research. Diversity in HCI has focused on giving underrepresented users voice and confronting homogeneity. By increasing representations, though a diversity affinity is immediately visible, the deconstruction of institutionalized prejudice fails. Additionally, underrepresented voices have the unsurmountable task of representing their group. These approaches to diversity become tokenistic fixes failing to tackle the systemic causes of inequality.

In this paper, we argue for a systemic approach to diversity in HCI. We call for setting diversity at the core of HCI where human realities and experiences are embodied rather than defined by "what users must be" or "what users are not". The paper contributes the following: a detailed overview of diversity in HCI and presents a conceptual framework for diversity driven HCI with three correlated recommendations for setting diversity at the core of HCI.

Keywords: Diversity · Inclusion · Diversity driven HCI · Critical computing

1 Introduction

The advancing awareness of diversity in the field of HCI is heralded as commendable strides in addressing inequality and the digital divide. This increasing awareness has not been evenly reflected in HCI research [3]. Diversity in HCI emphasizes giving voice to underrepresented users and confronting the homogeneity of design and development of technology. This emphasis of HCI has resulted in user categorization/labeling leading to the *othering* of users [8]. Where a representative identity dimension of the user (e.g., race, gender, etc.) is chosen as research focus, highlighting supposed deviation from a "normal" user [4]. There is nearly no consideration for the intersections and complexities of user identity and context in technology design and development.

In increasing representations of for example women, persons with disabilities, the elderly, or black persons in development teams the advocacy for diversity is immediately visible. The deconstruction of established systems of prejudice that keep underrepresented persons out fails to occur [36]. There is then the risk of the endeavor being tokenistic, as persons are not empowered to make changes to organizational structures [1]. In performing research, the choice of the underrepresented group as research-focus

© Springer Nature Switzerland AG 2021
M. Antona and C. Stephanidis (Eds.): HCII 2021, LNCS 12768, pp. 39–52, 2021.
https://doi.org/10.1007/978-3-030-78092-0_3

or inclusion/empathy worthy is a result of power-play [7]. And even then, persons chosen as representative voices face the impossible task of representing a specific group.

We argue that though giving voice to the less heard and confronting homogeneity may increase the awareness of diversity in HCI, the field can benefit from a systemic approach to diversity in HCI. We call for the positioning of diversity as an integral goal in HCI, neither tokenistic (patchworking) nor as a fix. As HCI envisions a future where equal access to information via technology is a primary human right, we anticipate inherent challenges to this vision especially when diversity is pursued as a fix. Futuristic visions of smart cities make the challenges to this vision easily explainable. When cities are designed and developed for the main users and then fixed for the *others*, it bequeaths privilege unto the main users. The main users are often the digitally trained, literate, persons from higher societal hierarchical structures or convenient users (friends and family of researchers/sponsors) chosen to influence the design process [2, 5]. The *others* can get to negotiate their degree of inclusion when deemed design focus. The capability to live or navigate effectively and efficiently in a city is dependent on one's identity dimensions.

The call for the HCI community to set diversity at the core of HCI is based on two main points. First, setting diversity at the core of HCI will bring focus to diversity identity dimensions and intersections hitherto overlooked, placing the user as well as their identities, context of use, and everyday experiences as integral to enabling human- and context-aware technology design [3]. It will represent human realities and experiences rather than classify "what users must be" or "what users are not" [6]. Second, setting diversity at the core of HCI will confront existing systems of oppression, question ways of practice, and empower users, tackling the design and development of computing systems that advance inequalities holistically.

In this paper, we discuss diversity in the context of HCI research. We present an overview of research work on the subject matter in HCI. We define diversity driven HCI (we use this phrase to mean setting diversity at the core of HCI), present our vision, a conceptual framework for setting diversity at the core of HCI. The framework presents three recommendations for consideration. These three recommendations we theme as *confronting the structures*, *questioning the methods*, and *advocating for power*. This paper contributes the following: A presentation of relevant research in HCI on diversity 2. An attempt to define diversity driven HCI and 3. The framework for setting diversity at the core of HCI.

2 Understanding Diversity in HCI

2.1 Meanings of Diversity

Diversity eludes an exclusive definition. We traverse concepts and worldviews of diversity to appreciate a general indication of meaning. Diversity encapsulates issues central to the idea of differentiation or notion of heterogeneity [20]. The term in the natural sciences may refer to discussing variations in population. And for many organizations, diversity objectives address increasing gender and minority representations in the workforce. Audre Lorde highlights diversity as reason for celebration, growth, and not destruction [10]. In computer science, lack of diversity signifies the underrepresentation of women and non-white persons in/completing programs. In the tech industry, diversity means a workforce, representative of diverse persons and team make-up. Diversity highlights the tension between individualization, personal adaptability, and generalization. Diversity can be of use, contexts, and application fields [22]. Adopting a diversity mindset encapsulates mental representations of diversity, representations that capture diversity-related goals and the procedural implications of those goals [9].

Diversity as a term is critiqued as a watered-down concept, a means to avoid addressing the deep causes of exclusion and power imbalance [25, 26]. The term diversity covers up the inherent inequalities faced by specific groups by being a general overarching approach. A result of diversity efforts dwelling on visual representation and not tackling internal structures. In addition, diversity dimensions do not exist independently. There are intersections between for example gender, and race whereby addressing racial inequalities is dependent on gender. Intersectionality, a term coined by Kimberlé Crenshaw, postulates diversity but emphasizes the existence of intersections in social categories [17, 39, 40]. Therefore, markers like age, race, socioeconomic background intersect and produce human identity. These intersections relate to societal power structures and inequalities [23].

In discussing diversity, the emphasis on the intersections of identity dimensions is necessary. No markers of identity can be discussed without relation to other markers of identity. It is impossible to attend to issues of gender without finding intersections to race or culture. That is why addressing, for example, the lack of black women in the field of computing is not remedied by adding more black women [36, 44]. The structures that enforced their absence must first be identified and addressed [44].

2.2 Diversity in HCI

The third wave of HCI has presented broadened use contexts and application scenarios extending the fields' research space and contributions to the design and development of technology [21]. Over the years, there has been increased awareness of the need to extend the field's borders and consider the varying notions of the user, global diversity, and equity in the practice [11]. The field has responded with new HCI perspectives, bringing attention to research gaps, neglected users, and contexts. This has seen an emergence of research and researchers with a dedicated mission to focus on users, contexts, situations, cultures, etc. previously neglected. For example, Queer HCI is by, for, or substantially shaped by the queer community itself and/or queering methods and theory, regardless of application subdomain [18, 27]. Feminist HCI looks at the design and evaluation of interactive computing systems with a feminist lens [14]. These fields facilitate the research, space, recommendations, and committed attention to targeted perspectives. The HCI community has embraced domains such as assistive technologies with the design of useful and technologies dedicated to persons with disabilities and the elderly [41]. Design approaches such as Participatory Design [30], Inclusive Design [31], Positive Design [29], Universal Design [28] are commonplace in the field, focusing on the diversity of users, contexts, etc.

While we in no way wish to deride the ground-breaking work by the community detailed above, we are critical of the ever-increasing categorization of the "other-users".

This generates groups labeled as marginalized, disabled, less heard, etc. These labels segregate, limit influence, and can lead to stigmatization. Until when do the classifications end and the *others* become mainstream with equal power and recognition? Furthermore, though design approaches may learn from and include varying human perspectives, they are adopted when needed, necessary, or permitted. There are structures and stakeholders that exercise power in the choice of study, the design approach, and the study group to include or exclude.

In the following session, we present research work on diversity in HCI. We present agendas and recommendations on embracing diversity in HCI.

2.3 Agendas for Diversity in HCI

In discussing agendas for diversity in HCI, it is impossible to skip subfields such as Critical Race Theory in HCI [43], Gender HCI [42], Feminist HCI [14], Intersectional HCI [11] that espouse diversity. This session is limited to work in HCI over the past two decades [2001–2020] and on the concept of "diversity". We chose literature that presented recommendations, agendas, or steps on how diversity can/should be adopted in HCI. Papers that focused on the concept of diversity for specific groups were excluded. We performed our search on Google Scholar and the ACM Digital Library. Our search revealed a minimal corpus of work on the concept of diversity for the field. This may be due to the field's concentration on dimensions such as gender, race, disability, or diversity in HCI education. We present the following three papers which examine the concept of diversity in HCI.

Diversity Computing
Sue Fletcher-Watson et al. [1] present their vision, Diversity Computing (DivComp) as a framework incorporating innovation in theory, methodology, and technology that embraces diversity and avoids normative ordering. They suggest that as elimination of biases is inevitable and bias can often be useful, DivComp should support people in reflecting on biases, questioning the presumed objectivity, and challenge their negative effects. They refer to diversity as the infinite variety in interpersonal settings, rather than to a set of quantifiable or observable characteristics. Differences between people may operate on known diversity dimensions—for example, gender identity or race—but can also depend on mood, health, recent experiences, and personal goals. DivComp recognizes that everyone is different from everyone, moving away from a stance that one group represents the norm against which others are measured. In DivComp, people with differences come together in an active and reflective sense for a participatory process of meaning making mediated by DivComp tools. The focus is on human-human interaction where a so-called third space is created not to abolish differences but to make sense (meaning) of them. This will lead to disagreements but a DivComp device should serve to support constructive discourse.

As a case example, DivComp in immigration could enable people from different cultural backgrounds to share parts of their life-worlds remotely using DivComp devices. Enabling embodied experiences of everyday activities in personal or public spaces can provide first-person perspectives on what makes up another's sense of identity, including emotional drivers such as anxieties, sense of belonging, or aspirations. These experiences could be shared by connecting directly to other people's bodily responses to experience walking in their shoes almost literally—and combining these with self-annotation. Such DivComp-enabled linkage between communities and individuals would be instrumental in challenging prejudice, building mutual respect, and fostering resilience against fear-driven political manipulation.

DivComp focuses on creating meaning through participatory methodology and digital innovation. This participatory approach assumes an interest in both parties to share their differences and personal experiences. It also assumes a sharing of differences and making meaning of one's preferences or needs may lead to egalitarianism. The possible appreciation of ones' difference may not necessarily lead to a repositioning of one's mindset towards that person or group. It may lead to a change in attitude towards the specific group or not. Additionally, as diversity dimensions seem infinite, how are these differences prioritized for sharing? Are visible differences the focus or all differences existent in these specific groups or people the focus? In the case example of immigrants, how do you share the differences and experiences of immigrants adequately? The experiences of a black female immigrant are different from that of a black male immigrant even from the same African country. How many public space installations or DivComp devices will be necessary to share these divergent experiences? Immigrants may be skeptical of sharing personal stories due to the implications (deportation, legal, trauma, stigmatization, etc.) The role of technology differs for many of different backgrounds, for some freedom for others surveillance.

Diversity Dimensions in HCI Research

Himmelsbach et al. [3] present in their work, a comprehensive content analysis on diversity dimensions in HCI research and make recommendations on identifying relevant identity dimensions and collecting diversity information. They define diversity as social differences with attributed social meaning, that refer to social inequality and are embedded in a historically evolved social and structural context and influence how people live and experience technology. They illustrate the current state and how it has grown historically by analyzing 1,107 articles published in the years 2006, 2011, and 2016. They discover the following: the number of dimensions and the intensity of attention towards certain dimensions has significantly increased, research continues to concentrate on a small number of dimensions and there is still a higher occurrence of research on age, gender, sex, and education.

In their recommendations on how researchers can identify relevant diversity dimensions, they advocate for diversity sensitive analyses. It should be described who is part of the user group(s) and which dimensions cannot be covered. Researchers must ask for the relationship that exists between diversity dimensions and technology usage. Dimensions of relevance should be considered in all stages of research and human-centered design process where researchers and developers must explicitly ask themselves: which characteristics come to our mind when we imagine who we design for – and which characteristics are not reflected by our understanding of "the user(s)". In collecting diversity-sensitive information, they make the following strategy recommendations. Researchers should in user interviews draw attention to users' self-definition and practices instead of providing them predetermined answering options. Diversity sensitive research should be conducted in context, for example considering the physical environment or social status, or geographical location, etc. Researchers should seek creative indirect ways of data collection, explore relevant dimensions in detail, respectively including multiple layers and describing exactly what is intended to capture and explore relationships with concrete technology.

Himmelsbach et al. advocate for critical diversity research that goes beyond mere analysis and toward creative methodological and theoretical implications for diversity-sensitive research. Their work however does not address prejudiced systems integral to undertaking research. These structures can use financial and logistic constraints to impede researchers from conducting research with less heard voices. Working with less heard voices may be more resource-intensive than working with a couple of white male students. It may require an exploration of other methods, resources, and even relevant researchers.

Diversity and Ethics in HCI
Cairn and Thimbleby in their paper "diversity and ethics in HCI" [32] present the value of ethical parallels in HCI taking three schools of ethics: Christian, medical, and Rawlsian justice, and showing how they can help interpret and stimulate diversity in HCI. They argue that by thinking about HCI as a normative and therefore as an ethical science, there is a possibility to adopt from ethics the appropriate framework for the study of good user interfaces.

They recommend privative and complementarity as recommendable practical solutions. Usability as a privative becomes the absence of problems and the researchers and users can specify what usability is achieving. Complementarity in HCI refers to the balance of work done in HCI from different ethical stances, any stance defines and motivates what the work does and does not do. If HCI is big enough to accommodate more than one right way, then an exclusive view of what is right will exclude effective approaches. They ask researchers to consider interpreting and adapting ethics in the practice of HCI for good work. The adaptation of these schools of ethics may be problematic for HCI practices that are not western world centered with alternate schools of ethics or ethical systems.

In the next session, we present our concept of diversity driven HCI and how we envision setting diversity at the core of HCI as the catalyst to designing and developing technology and performing research.

3 Diversity Driven HCI

The ability of technology to advance discrimination and segregation stems from the embodiment of pre-existing individual and societal biases, technical, and emergent biases [33]. Though this process of bias transfer may happen as non-conscious acts, they result in technologies that advance marginalization, digital divide, discrimination, racism [25], and even domestic violence [24]. The computer has evolved, from its invention, dedication to the military, industrial, and technical to domestic, civilian, and even playful contexts and use, with extended application domains, use cases, user groups, and contexts.

The primary notions of what a computer can be and who the user ought to be, have changed. The attempts to design and develop technology for these growing affordances reveal how diverse technology can (or could) be interpreted and used. In HCI, this has triggered the exploration of innovative technology design and development to meet the needs of diverse users, use cases, user groups, and contexts.

The labeling of humans as gorillas by facial recognition algorithms [47], misidentification of citizens as crime suspects [45, 46], sensors failing to detect pulses due to darker skin tones [48], image search results enforcing gender stereotypes [49] are few of the implications of bias embodied technology. Specific groups such as black persons can ultimately be denied opportunities due them, receive unfair treatment, be limited in their capacities, and suffer injustice [33]. In addressing these and future repercussions of bias technology and creating a future of technology that advances egalitarianism, we propose the setting of diversity at the core of HCI, we appeal for a mainstreaming of diversity. This situates all users, regardless of identifiable or non-identifiable traits at the core of research and development. All variances are acknowledged as relevant to the process. Setting diversity at the core of HCI would bring focus to the structural and institutionalized forms of oppression that play key roles in the design and development of technology. This will identify and address biases in the education systems, funding systems, organizational structures, policies, and legal frameworks.

Diversity driven HCI will lead to critical analysis and reconsideration of the methods, knowledge, and practices in the HCI field. The field has adopted methods and practices from social science fields that were set on colonialist ideals. For example, methods and practices that were designed for and primarily used to study persons labeled as objects or subjects of study often indigenous people where the researcher was the learned human [58]. These practices and methods were adopted into the field for the design of technology with users and have been subject over the years to critical reflection by the field [59, 60]. How can diversity be achieved when the inherent biases in these systems of practice and methods are not adequately addressed? Which user experiences and systems of knowledge are advanced and which systems of knowledge are being suppressed by current practice?

Finally, setting diversity at the core will position the design and development of technology as an empowerment movement. Equality is supposedly described as the equal distribution of power. Though the equal distribution of power may take some time, we believe that setting the research and development goal as one of empowerment contributes to advancing equality. We believe that by setting diversity at the core of HCI, we only then begin to address the implications of oppressive technology.

We define diversity driven HCI as the adoption of a holistic approach to HCI design and research which is accomplished by the confronting of structures and institutions that enforce inequality, questioning the methods, knowledge, and practices in the field, and positioning the HCI practice as advocacy for power. Where diversity does not just highlight human diversity, but also diversity in contexts and application fields [50]. A broad understanding thus links diversity to a plurality of people; beliefs, values, norms; methods and approaches; tools; contexts.

In the next session, we present our vision in a framework that sets the three recommendations as integral to HCI.

4 The Framework for Diversity Driven HCI

We illustrate our framework for setting diversity at the core in HCI in Fig. 1 below and explain in detail the three recommendations in the following paragraphs. In the framework, we situate **confront** at the core as confronting existing structural and institutional systems of the HCI practice is key in achieving systemic change. The second approach, **question**, relates to reflecting on the methods, systems of knowledge, and practices of the field and then **advocate**, the third, focuses on the user and researcher roles and relationships and power. These three are not independent of each other but have interdependences represented by the lines that transverse the spheres. The framework acknowledges the existence of external and internal factors such as laws, organizational culture, and even the researcher's internalized prejudices, that will influence its success.

4.1 Confronting the Structures

When inequalities are deeply embedded in structures and institutions, marginalization and racism for example become ordinary, a part of everyday life. Confronting the structures will challenge existing structures and institutions that afford oppression and keep certain persons or groups of people out. It will address this situation in changing or redesigning the systems as suitable [38]. In HCI, example structures and systems would be the educational systems, funding systems, organizations, etc.

For educational systems, we can confront these systems by asking how education policies designed to keep certain groups out can be revised? This will also mean a critical analysis of educational programs and requirements to enter these institutions. How diverse are the programs offered? How can students regardless of their background be positioned to envision computing programs as beneficial to them and their communities? Are programs designed to meet the educational needs of all or designed to cater to the knowing capabilities of the few? For example, in examination structures where memorization is advocated how does this affect students who may have challenges with memorization. Is access to HCI education permitted regardless of a persons' background or identity? Or are persons restricted from access to education due to so-called high standards that fail to consider other contributions of the individuals to the community which is crucial in designing and developing systems for humanity. Again, we need to ask ourselves how and why educational systems are positioned to benefit from limiting others to education in HCI.

In designing HCI or Computer Science programs, why are subjects or topics that cover the implications of computers on society not integrated into the curriculum as compulsory [61]? Why are students not first brought to par with the implications of the systems they design and develop? Why is the focus on coding and mathematics especially for first-year computer science students when it should be on understanding the role of computing in society first and being positioned to think first about the society and then the design and develop systems that advance equality and not oppression [62]? We criticize efforts to bridge diversity gaps by introducing girls and black persons for example to coding. Getting girls to code may be a great thing but it fails to teach them the mindset required to succeed in designing computational futures that advance equality [44].

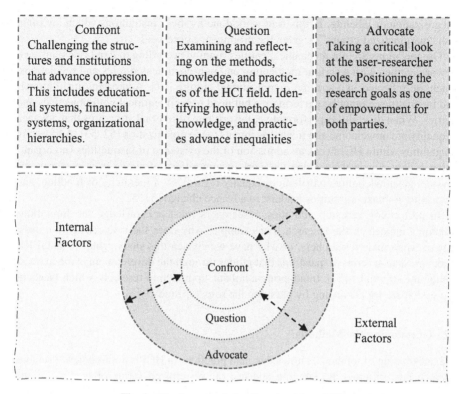

Confront	Question	Advocate
Challenging the structures and institutions that advance oppression. This includes educational systems, financial systems, organizational hierarchies.	Examining and reflecting on the methods, knowledge, and practices of the HCI field. Identifying how methods, knowledge, and practices advance inequalities	Taking a critical look at the user-researcher roles. Positioning the research goals as one of empowerment for both parties.

Fig. 1. The framework for diversity driven HCI

Research in HCI is impossible without funding. Many research institutions are reliant on corporate funding to advance their objectives. Funding bodies decide with research ideas are worthy of funding and which user group deserves inclusion [32]. It is no coincidence that highly funded institutions seemingly tend to present the best results and work in the field. Most of these institutions have had the necessary consistent financial support for decades to support their work. These institutions tend to have their publications highly awarded, can fund an optimum chunk of their annual research goals, purchase the most modern technologies, and pay the highest conference fees. The implications are the association of such dominant work as the only valid or standard approach [32]. Research institutions that may not have similar funding support and are also new to HCI research will be required to meet the standards of these highly privileged institutions. For example, to be accepted to highly accredited HCI conferences, their work will be reviewed against the predefined quality standards of practice instituted by these institutions of privilege. This functions as gatekeeping. How does the HCI community leverage these inequalities by creating the space for other spaces to present their work to the international community? The introduction of international sub-regional conferences does not address this systemic challenge. There must be dedicated structures in the mainstream conferences that support submissions from less privileged institutions without a need for categorization or labeling. In this way work done by these institutions which are often with "marginalized groups" is given the prominence deserved.

Organizations are not mechanical entities running according to fixed rules; instead, they are entities with a certain momentum and non-documented rules and regulations, which are reflected in a specific organizational culture [51]. Addressing institutionalized inequalities cannot be performative but need to be intentional with objectives and metrics. When diversity is performative, the critique of internal structures that advance inequality are unwelcome and treated as threats to the organization [52, 53]. Addressing inequalities within HCI needs an admission of the existence of inequalities (no organization is power-neutral), exalting the work of minorities, refraining from performative allyship, acknowledging contributions equally regardless of hierarchy or function, and advocating to make minorities leaders, to advance change [51, 52].

In performing research activities, researchers must acknowledge the limitations structures impact on the research. For example, why does the research team consist only of white male researchers, or why have we chosen this study group? The GERD model presents a series of questions that guides through the development cycle in questioning the structures [57]. In adopting a holistic approach to research, which facets of oppression are we advancing by pursuing the research study?

4.2 Questioning the Methods

The questioning of methods, knowledge, and practices in HCI is nothing new. Previous research has critiqued the labeling and use of westernized forms of practice as the standard for research even when conducted in other regions of the world with different knowledge systems or practices. Although methods may have no significance to a user group, researchers would use them so that their research is acknowledged as standard by the western world. What are the implications of the use of westernized forms of knowledge gathering in places that have other forms of knowledge gathering [54]? Which methods have been used consistently but require change visible when reflection happens, so it suits others? How are HCI methods and practices furthering oppression and decolonization [59, 60]?

In questioning the methods, we ask researchers to critically reflect on the history of the chosen method and how it perpetuates inequality. What restrictions to expression and knowing are imposed on the users by the application of these methods? One example is the anonymization of names for research, how users' voices are silenced by the anonymization practice that supposedly seeks to protect the user [55]. Michelle Brear, on critically reflecting their work with ten black co-researchers in Swaziland discovered the inherent racism and privilege that exists in the process of replacing participant names with English names [56].

Do the methods we use to consider the diversity of knowledge systems? In questioning methods, researchers may need to explore other ways of knowing and knowledge systems to effectively engage users. Smith et al.'s work reflects the use of westernized practices of information gathering for research which were ignored by their participants who preferred to engage in conversation [34].

4.3 Advocating for Power

The researcher's role is positioned as one inherent with power. The researchers' provision of resources and guidelines for the research project may be the reason for this positioning. However, power relations are not fixed or static. For example, the position of the 'Western' researcher/practitioner in a so-called developing country may be seen as powerful, however, this can be displaced. Power relations are fluid and can be negotiated [35]. In this example, the user or study group holds power in presenting themselves for the study. Thus, power is fully expended when both parties are aware of the power they bring to the table.

In positioning the research as a movement to empower the user, the research project is situated as beneficial to both parties. The user group needs to be aware of the power they herald and how the power of the researcher is only made active dependent on that of the user. Besides, research should be positioned as beneficial, for example in terms of bridging digital gaps (providing technology devices) educationally (imparting skills and training), financially (compensating users with needed funds), etc., Researchers are critiqued as being interested in the users during the contribution to research. There are no follow-ups to access the influence of the research. This even happens with so-called "least heard voices". After the research has folded and the results reported to the major conferences, how does the research continue to empower or influence the lives of the persons involved? Is research positioned to listen and do nothing about the inherent inequalities faced? Can research be positioned primarily to empower users? What necessary resources will be required when research is positioned as an empowerment movement? Which necessary discussions and conversations will need to happen with users to realize this?

5 Conclusion

Diversity set as an integral part of HCI will tackle biases systemically and avoid tokenistic approaches. The further micro-classification of HCI based on facets of identity may contribute to an immediately visible affinity to diversity but fail to address the intersections of identity. Furthermore, the responsibility of diversity in HCI is relegated to the so-called marginalized with the task to represent their identity and group. There is the furtherance of the design for others while the mainstream users remain mainstream.

In this paper, we have called on the HCI community to consider setting diversity at the core of HCI which we term diversity driven HCI. We define diversity driven HCI as the adoption of a holistic approach to HCI design and research which is accomplished by the confronting of structures and institutions that enforce inequality, questioning the methods, knowledge, and practices, and advocating for power. Where diversity does not just highlight human diversity, but also diversity in contexts and application fields [50].

We call on the community to adopt this holistic approach by making diversity mainstream, neither performative nor a fix. We recommend the confronting of structures and systems, questioning of methods, knowledge, and practices, and the advocacy of research activities as an empowerment activity. We hope that this paper will initiate discussions on diversity driven HCI, but most importantly will enable the community to approach diversity holistically and not piecewise.

References

1. Fletcher-Watson, S., et al.: Diversity computing. Interactions **25**(5), 28–33 (2018)
2. Hanson, J.: The inclusive city: delivering a more accessible urban environment through inclusive design (2004)
3. Himmelsbach, J., et al.: Do we care about diversity in human computer interaction: a comprehensive content analysis on diversity dimensions in research. In: Proceedings of the 2019 CHI Conference on Human Factors in Computing Systems (2019)
4. Jensen, S.Q.: Othering, identity formation and agency. Qual. Stud. **2**(2), 63–78 (2011)
5. O'Dell, K., et al.: Inclusive smart cities 28 Aug 2019. https://www2.deloitte.com/us/en/ins ights/industry/public-sector/inclusive-smart-cities.html. Accessed 11 Feb 2021
6. Keates, S., et al.: Towards a practical inclusive design approach. In: Proceedings on the 2000 Conference on Universal Usability (2000)
7. Rothenberg, P.S.: Race, Class, and Gender in the United States: An Integrated Study. Macmillan, New York (2004)
8. Spivak, G.C.: The rani of Sirmur: an essay in reading the archives. Hist. Theory **24**(3), 247–272 (1985)
9. Van Knippenberg, D., van Ginkel, W.P., Homan, A.C.: Diversity mindsets and the performance of diverse teams. Organ. Behav. Hum. Decis. Process. **121**(2), 183–193 (2013)
10. Tate, C., Tate, C. (eds.): Black Women Writers at Work. Continuum, New York (1983)
11. Ari Schlesinger, W., Edwards, K., Grinter, R.E.: Intersectional HCI: engaging identity through gender, race, and class. In: Proceedings of the 2017 CHI Conference on Human Factors in Computing Systems. ACM (2017)
12. Harding, S.G.: The Science Question in Feminism. Cornell University Press, New York (1986)
13. Harding, S.G.: The "Racial" economy of science: toward a democratic future. In: Isis, vol. 86, no. 1, pp. 89–91 (1995). https://doi.org/10.1086/357087
14. Bardzell, S., Bardzell, J.: Towards a feminist HCI methodology: social science, feminism, and HCI. In: Proceedings of the SIGCHI Conference on Human Factors in Computing Systems. ACM (2011)
15. Schiebinger, L.L.: Has Feminism Changed Science? Harvard University Press, Cambridge (1999)
16. Beckwith, L., Burnett, M.: Gender: an important factor in end-user programming environments? In: 2004 IEEE Symposium on Visual Languages-Human Centric Computing, pp. 107–114. IEEE (2004)
17. Crenshaw, K.W.: On Intersectionality: The Essential Writings of Kimberlé Crenshaw. New Press, New York (2017)
18. Spiel, K., et al.: Queer (ing) HCI: moving forward in theory and practice. In: Extended Abstracts of the 2019 CHI Conference on Human Factors in Computing Systems, p. SIG11. ACM (2019)
19. Fletcher-Watson, S., De Jaegher, H., van Dijk, J., Frauenberger, C., Magnée, M., Ye, J.: Diversity computing. Interactions **25**(5), 28–33 (2018)
20. Vertovec, S.: Introduction: formulating diversity studies. In: Routledge International Handbook of Diversity Studies, pp. 19–38. Routledge, London (2014)
21. Bødker, S.: Third-wave HCI, 10 years later-participation and sharing. Interactions **22**(5), 24–31 (2015)
22. Antona, M., Stephanidis, C.: Universal Access in Human-Computer Interaction. Context Diversity: 6th International Conference, UAHCI 2011, Held as Part of HCI International 2011, Orlando, FL, USA, July 9–14, 2011, Proceedings, Part III. Lecture Notes in Computer Science, vol. 6767. Springer, Heidelberg (2016). https://doi.org/10.1007/978-3-642-21666-4

23. Rothenberg, P.S.: Race, Class, and Gender in the United States. Worth Publishers, New York (2009)
24. Dankwa, N.K.: Driving smart home innovation with the gender dimension (2018). http://www.fvt-pp.uk/smartHomeGenderDimension.html. Accessed 04 Feb 2021
25. Noble, S.U.: Algorithms of Oppression: How Search Engines Reinforce Racism. NYU Press, New York (2018)
26. Lawler, K.: Ava DuVernay: I 'hate' the word 'diversity' USA TODAY, January 27 2016. https://eu.usatoday.com/story/life/movies/2016/01/26/ava-duvernay-oscars-academy-awards-diversity/79338066/
27. DeVito, M.A., et al.: Queer in HCI: supporting LGBTQIA+ researchers and research across domains. In: Extended Abstracts of the 2020 CHI Conference on Human Factors in Computing Systems, pp. 1–4 (2020)
28. Goldsmith, S.: Universal Design: A Manual of Practical Guidance for Architects. Routledge, London (2000)
29. Desmet, P.M.A., Pohlmeyer, A.E.: Positive design: an introduction to design for subjective well-being. Int. J. Design, **7**(3) (2013)
30. Muller, M.J., Kuhn, S.: Participatory design. Commun. ACM **36**(6), 24–28 (1993)
31. Clarkson, P.J., Coleman, R., Keates, S., Lebbon, C.: Inclusive Design: Design for the Whole Population. Springer, Heidelberg (2013)
32. Cairns, P., Thimbleby, H.: The diversity and ethics of HCI. Comput. Inf. Sci. **1**(2003), 1–19 (2003)
33. Friedman, B., Nissenbaum, H.: Bias in computer systems. ACM Trans. Inf. Syst. (TOIS) **14**(3), 330–347 (1996)
34. Charlotte Smith, R., Winschiers-Theophilus, H., Paula Kambunga, A., Krishnamurthy, S.: Decolonizing participatory design: memory making in Namibia. In: Proceedings of the 16th Participatory Design Conference 2020-Participation (s) Otherwise, vol. 1, pp. 96–106 (2020)
35. Mainsah, H., Morrison, A.: Participatory design through a cultural lens: insights from post-colonial theory. In: Proceedings of the 13th Participatory Design Conference: Short Papers, Industry Cases, Workshop Descriptions, Doctoral Consortium papers, and Keynote Abstracts, vol. 2, pp. 83–86 (2014)
36. Ahmed, S.: Embodying diversity: problems and paradoxes for black feminists. Race Ethn. Educ. **12**(1), 41–52 (2009)
37. Squires, J.: Diversity mainstreaming: moving beyond technocratic and additive approaches. Femina Politica-Zeitschrift für feministische Politikwissenschaft **16**(1), 11–12 (2007)
38. Rees, T.: The politics of 'mainstreaming' gender equality. In: The Changing Politics of Gender Equality in Britain, pp. 45–69. Palgrave Macmillan, London (2002)
39. Crenshaw, K.: Mapping the margins: intersectionality, identity politics, and violence. Stanford Law Rev. **43**(6), 1241–1299 (1991)
40. Crenshaw, K.: Demarginalizing the intersection of race and sex: a black feminist critique of antidiscrimination doctrine, feminist theory and antiracist politics. u. Chi. Legal f. p. 139 (1989)
41. Abascal, J., Nicolle, C.: Moving towards inclusive design guidelines for socially and ethically aware HCI. Interact. Comput. **17**(5), 484–505 (2005)
42. Beckwith, L., Burnett, M.: Gender: an important factor in end-user programming environments? In: 2004 IEEE Symposium on Visual Languages-Human Centric Computing, pp. 107–114. IEEE (2004)
43. Ogbonnaya-Ogburu, I.F., Smith, A.D., To, A., Toyama, K.: Critical race theory for HCI. In: Proceedings of the 2020 CHI Conference on Human Factors in Computing Systems, pp. 1–16 (2020)

44. Ian, B.: The problem with diversity in computing, June 25 2019. https://www.theatlantic.com/technology/archive/2019/06/tech-computers-are-bigger-problem-diversity/592456/. Accessed 04 Feb 2021
45. Klare, B.F., et al.: Face recognition performance: Role of demographic information. IEEE Trans. Inf. Forensics Secur. **7**(12), 1789–1801 (2012)
46. Garvie C.; Franke J.: The Atlantis, facial-recognition software might have a racial bias problem. www.theatlantic.com/technology/archive/2016/04/the-underlying-bias-of-facial-recognition-systems/476991/. Accessed 10 Feb 2021
47. Lee, W.: How tech's lack of diversity leads to racist software. www.sfgate.com/business/article/How-tech-slack-of-diversity-leads-to-racist-6398224.php. Accessed 10 Feb 2021
48. Hankerson, D., et al.: Does technology have race? In: Proceedings of the 2016 CHI Conference Extended Abstracts on Human Factors in Computing Systems, pp. 473–486. ACM (2016)
49. Kay, M., Matuszek, C., Munson, S.A.: Unequal representation and gender stereotypes in image search results for occupations. In: Proceedings of the 33rd Annual ACM Conference on Human Factors in Computing Systems, pp. 3819–3828. ACM (2015)
50. Akrich, M.: The de-scription of technical objects. In: Bijker, W.E., Law, J. (ed.) Shaping Technology/Building Society. Studies in Sociotechnical Change. Hg.2. Aufl, pp. 205–224. MIT Press, Cambridge (1992)
51. Institutional Transformation European Institute for Gender Equality (2016)
52. Grady, S.D., et al.: Addressing institutional racism within initiatives for SIGCHI's diversity and inclusion. ACM Interactions blog, 11 June 2020
53. Tiku, N.: Google hired Timnit Gebru to be an outspoken critic of unethical AI. Then she was fired for it, Washington Post, 23 December 2020. https://www.washingtonpost.com/technology/2020/12/23/google-timnit-gebru-ai-ethics/. Accessed 10 Feb 2021
54. Suchman, L.A.: Plans and Situated Actions: The Problem of Human-Machine Communication. Cambridge University Press, Cambridge (1987)
55. Dankwa, N.K.: All names are pseudonyms a critical reflection on pseudonymizing names in HCI. In: Extended Abstracts of the 2021 CHI Conference on Human Factors in Computing Systems (2021)
56. Brear, M.: Swazi co-researcher participants' dynamic preferences and motivations for, representation with real names and (English-language) pseudonyms–an ethnography. Qual. Res. **18**(6), 722–740 (2018)
57. Draude, C., Maaß, S., Wajda, K., Zeising, A., Schelhowe, H.: GERD: ein Vorgehensmodell zur Integration von Gender/Diversity in die Informatik. Vielfalt der Informatik-Ein Beitrag zu Selbstverständnis und Außenwirkung **9**, 197–283 (2014)
58. Beier J.M.: Ethnography, ethics, and advanced colonialism. In: International Relations in Uncommon Places. Palgrave Macmillan, New York (2005)
59. Irani, L., Dourish, P.: Postcolonial interculturality. In: Proceedings of International Workshop on Intercultural Collaboration (IWIC 2009), pp. 249–252. ACM Press (2009)
60. Irani, L., Vertesi, J., Dourish, P., Philip, K., Grinter, R.E.: Postcolonial computing: a lens on design and development. In: Proceedings of CHI 2010, pp. 1311–1320. ACM Press (2010)
61. Grosz, B., et al.: Embedded EthiCS: integrating ethics across CS education. Commun. ACM **62**(8), 54–61 (2019)
62. Margolis, J., Fisher, A.: Unlocking the Clubhouse: Women in Computing. MIT press, Cambridge (2002)

A Systematic Mapping of Guidelines for the Development of Accessible Digital Games to People with Disabilities

Taynara Cerigueli Dutra[1] , Daniel Felipe[1] , Isabela Gasparini[1(✉)] ,
and Eleandro Maschio[2]

[1] State University of Santa Catarina (UDESC), Joinville, SC, Brazil
`isabela.gasparini@udesc.br`
[2] Federal University of Technology – Paraná (UTFPR), Guarapuava, PR, Brazil
`eleandrom@utfpr.edu.br`

Abstract. Accessibility is a right for everyone. For this, sets of guidelines are created by authors and organizations with the objective to develop technologies more inclusive. Actually, digital games are one of the most used resources for entertainment, then they need to be inclusive to all people, regardless of their disabilities. This work presents a Systematic Literature Mapping performed to identify the guidelines for digital games aimed at people with disabilities. As a result, 44 papers that propose guidelines were accepted and analyzed. It was found the disabilities, the types of games, and the age range of the target audience covered by the guidelines. With an examination more profound, it was obtained a resulting set of guidelines for the development of digital games aimed at People with Cognitive Disabilities.

Keywords: Guidelines · Accessibility · Digital games · People with disabilities · Systematic literature mapping

1 Introduction

The accessibility of technological solutions has the potential to provide inclusion, but if not applied, it causes the exclusion of People with Disabilities (PwD) [1]. Technological resources allow PwD to have greater autonomy in their lives in general, however, they become a barrier when there are no requirements or items that attend to the needs of their users.

Among these technological resources, there are digital games that have significant importance for the formation of mental structures required for the use of technologies [1]. Video games and computers have conquered an important space in society's daily life and interest in them transcends age, gender, social class, or disability [2]. There are around one hundred million disabled players worldwide [3], who, like anyone, seek digital games as a form of entertainment. However, due to the lack of accessible resources, they usually get a frustrating experience [2].

© Springer Nature Switzerland AG 2021
M. Antona and C. Stephanidis (Eds.): HCII 2021, LNCS 12768, pp. 53–70, 2021.
https://doi.org/10.1007/978-3-030-78092-0_4

In addition to the entertainment factor, games can be used as motivating and engaging tools capable of providing training and education to these people, helping them to overcome difficulties [4]. To create accessible games, developers need to understand the difficulties of their target audience, as well as the necessary adaptations in the process of developing their product. To this end, authors and organizations have established sets of accessibility guidelines for digital games that aim to cover the entire player experience, these need to be followed and implemented in the project.

In order to identify the guidelines for accessible digital games available in the literature, a Systematic Literature Mapping (SLM) was performed based on Petersen et al. [5]. The SLM aims to raise an overview of the area through the quantification and classification of the works obtained. Thus, the SLM described in this paper, aimed to acquire the studies that present the guidelines, as well as to identify the disabilities, the objectives, and the target audience of the games.

The remainder of the paper is organized as follows: Sect. 2 presents the fundamental concepts related to research: digital games, accessibility, guidelines, and People with Disabilities. Section 3 presents works related to the theme of mapping. Section 4 discusses the methodology used and the SLM developed. Section 5, in turn, details the results. Section 6 addresses the risks to mapping validity. Finally, in Sect. 7 is presented the conclusions and future works.

2   Fundamental Concepts

The main themes of this study are digital games, guidelines, and people with disabilities. The concepts are presented in this chapter.

2.1   Digital Games

The term digital game (DG) is often used as analogous to video games or computer games. In this study, it was considered the concept presented by Kerr [6], according to him, DG refers to all arcade games, computer, console, and also mobile games. These games are interactive, based on defined rules and restrictions, in addition to having a clear objective that is usually a challenge [7].

The DG market can be assessed in three main segments: casual and social games, these are played mainly on mobile devices, games for consoles, that are intended for devices developed specifically for high definition games with a connection to the TV, having as examples the Playstation and Xbox and also the games for computers. The DG sector is the fastest growing within the media and entertainment industry. It estimates that the global DGs market generated revenue of approximately 164.6 billion dollars in 2020 [32].

Games have an important space not only with children and teenagers, but also with adults, the elderly, and with PwD. The potential that these games hold outweighs just entertainment, as they can be used for training, skill development, and learning.

Classification of Digital Games. Due to the diversity of their type, execution platforms, genders, and objectives, digital games can be classified in several ways. Focusing on the objective of the game, according to the classification proposed by Derryberry [8], the games can be categorized into: casual games, serious games, and advertising games.

Casual games are entertainment games and can belong to various platforms such as: personal computers, consoles, and mobile. Learning can occur in a casual game, but it is a by-product instead of the main objective of the game [8].

Serious Games (SGs) are considered games that do not have entertainment as their main purpose and include aspects of education, such as teaching, training, and information. According to Hendrix and Backlund [17], SGs are able to engage players and contribute to the achievement of a certain goal other than pure entertainment. These can be applied in different segments, such as the military, government, corporate, health care, and also the educational sector [9].

The purpose of advertising games is to promote products, brands or causes [8].

Accessibility in Digital Games. International Game Developers Association (IGDA) defines accessibility in games as the ability to play despite the restrictive conditions caused by limitations or disabilities [10]. Games are playful tools capable of assisting in the development of cognitive skills and in learning, thus contributing to the improvement of quality of life [11].

In comparison to the movements that value the accessibility of the Web, the conventional games industry took few actions to adapt games to PwD [11]. Therefore, there are still several problems in relation to accessibility elements in games when these games are used by PwD, causing them to experience difficulties in interacting and losing interest in tools like this [16].

In order to change this scenario, games need to be developed considering the accessibility requirements, this way games become accessible for the most diverse audiences to use them. For this, there are researches that seek to propose guidelines to be applied in promoting the accessibility of DGs. Such resources are directed to the game experience, data entry, design, sounds, installation, and configuration of games, as well as, help system, documentation, modes of assistance, and configuration [1].

2.2 Guidelines

Guidelines cover both high-level expressions that can be applied to a wide variety of cases, as well as statements limited to specific contexts [12]. Thus, the recommendations have the goal to guide designers in making decisions for the development of a product/resource.

2.3 People with Disabilities

United Nations (UN) conceptualize PwD as those who have long-term impediments, whether physical, mental, intellectual or sensory, which are able to hinder their full and effective participation in equal conditions in society [13]. The International Classification of Functionality, Disability and Health also proposed a concept for disability, which refers to "an umbrella term for impairments, activity limitations, and participation restrictions. It denotes the negative aspects of the interaction between an individual (with a health condition) and that individual's contextual factors (environmental and personal factors)" [30].

According to Bierre et al. [2] the disabilities that can affect a person's ability to play video games can be divided into four groups: visual, hearing, motor, and cognitive impairments. Visual impairment is characterized by the various conditions that can impact a person's vision to the most varying degrees. Hearing impairment refers to the inability or difficulty to hear or recognize sounds. In relation to motor or physical disabilities, this is the complete or partial change of one or more parts of the human body, which causes the impairment of physical function; it can be caused by injuries, diseases, genetics, or also by old age. Meanwhile, cognitive impairment refers to intellectual functioning below average with limitations related to two or more areas of adaptive skills, such as: communication, personal care, social skills, use of community resources, health and safety, academic skills, leisure, and also work; manifesting before the age of 18 [15]. Lastly, multiple disabilities are the association of two or more disabilities.

3   Related Works

In the work by Pereira et al. [18], a Systematic Literature Review (SLR) was developed to obtain accessibility guidelines in games for people with low vision. Based on the studies obtained, an analysis was performed by the authors together with specialist doctors about guidelines that could be directed to people who have sequelae of Macular chorioretinitis. Through SLR, it was possible to establish criteria for accessible game development to people with visual impairments.

In the SLR presented by Mat Rosly et al. [19], the authors aimed to understand whether exergames could be used as physical activities according to the guidelines by the American College of Sports Medicine and the World Health Organization. As a result, only 10 articles met the stipulated inclusion criteria. The main measures used to analyze the games were energy expenditure, heart rate, and perceived exertion. As final considerations, the authors report that exergames have the potential to promote physical activities of moderate intensity, as recommended by the responsible organizations.

Tomé et al. [20] performed research about design principles capable of promoting accessibility in SGs for people with cognitive disabilities. According to the authors, the possibility of configuring the games to suit the needs of each player is an important resource, as it minimizes the barriers encountered by users who have disabilities. Furthermore, by means of a survey, the most common devices used by serious games were compared in order to help developers in choosing the most suitable for PwD.

The related works address a single disability or a specific type of game. Thus, a Systematic Literature Mapping presented in the next section was conducted with the purpose of gaining a broader view of the literature on the guidelines for the development of DGs more accessible, targeted to all PwD, employing a formal research standard as a methodology.

4 Methodology

Systematic Literature Mapping is a research process to obtain an overview of the area through the classification and quantification of works in the literature. The mapping conducted was based on the process described by Petersen et al. [5]. In order to accomplish this, research questions must be defined, the search for relevant works must be executed (application of the search string in predefined searches) and the selection of papers, for this, inclusion and exclusion criteria are used. After going through the selected filters, the papers that were previously selected must be read in full or parts of it (title, abstract, keywords), then data are extracted and analyzed [5].

4.1 Research Questions

With the intention of obtaining the contributions available in the literature to enable the development of games for PwD, the following primary research question rules this mapping.

– Question 1: What guidelines are available in the literature for developing games for people with disabilities?

To better understand the state of the art, the following secondary questions have been defined.

– Question 2: What are the disabilities addressed by the accessibility guidelines for digital games?
– Question 3: What types of digital games are covered by the accessibility guidelines?
– Question 4: For which age group have the accessibility guidelines for digital games been established?

These questions intend to identify what are the disabilities, the types of games, and the target audience covered by the guidelines available in the literature papers.

4.2 Search Strings

The search for papers is conducted through a search string. To define this, a previous search of primary studies is performed for keyword extraction. Therefore, the search argument defined for this SLM is composed of the keywords that best cover the papers based on the context: (1) Guidelines, (2) Games, and (3) People with Disabilities. Several versions of the search string were tested until it was calibrated. Thus, the SLM was performed based on the articles that match the search argument set out below, in the title, abstract, or keywords section of the paper.

(guide OR recommendations OR principles OR design patterns) AND (games)
AND (disab* OR accessibilit* OR impairment OR deficienc* OR adaptab*)*
(being * equivalent to the wildcard).

For the mapping described, the search engines used were the ACM Digital Library, the IEEE, and the Web of Science. The databases of ACM and IEEE were selected due to proximity to the Computing area and the Web of Science was based on the study of Buchinger et al. [33].

We obtained 466 papers in total, the respective quantity for each search engine can be visualized in Table 1. On the search engine of the ACM, it was necessary to make an adaptation, because it offers the option of filtering in separate sections (abstract, title, author, all the text, among others). Thus, initially, it was searched for papers that contemplated the search argument in the title (4) and then in the abstract (62).

Web of Science search engine covers the most diverse areas of Science. With the purpose of finding results only related to the area of Computing and Education, the filters were used by categories: Education Educational Research (73), Education Scientific Disciplines (19), Education Special (9) - Computer Science Theory Methods (73), Computer Science Artificial Intelligence (51), Computer Science Information Systems (51), Computer Science Interdisciplinary Applications (49), Computer Science Cybernetics (38), Computer Science Software Engineering (28), Computer Science Hardware Architecture (8).

Table 1. Quantity of articles returned by each search engine

Search engine	Quantity
ACM	66
Web of science	244
IEEE	156
Total	466

4.3 Selection Criteria and Process

As Objective Criteria (OC) for the selection of articles, it was established:

- OC1. Unduplicated articles;
- OC2. Be written in English or Portuguese;
- OC3. Be a scientific paper of journals or events.

On the set of papers obtained, the analysis of the information was performed in the title, abstract, and keyword fields, applying the subjective inclusion and exclusion criteria, so that papers are included or excluded from the process. Papers that met all objective criteria and the following Inclusion Criteria (IC) were accepted.

- IC1. Establish guidelines for the development of digital games for People with Disabilities.
- IC2. Papers related to the area of Computing or Education.

During the analysis of the papers, those that met at least one of the Exclusion Criteria (EC) mentioned below were removed.

- EC1. It is not related to the Mapping theme;
- EC2. It is not presented a Digital Game;
- EC3. It is not adapted to People with Disabilities;
- EC4. It is not a primary paper;
- EC5. It is a short paper (less than four pages);
- EC6. The paper is not accessible, considering the availability provided by the Portal of the Coordination for the Improvement of Higher Education Personnel (CAPES/Brazil) or by the free offer on the web.

The first EC aims to exclude papers that do not present guidelines for the development of DG to PwD. In the literature, guidelines are available for the most diverse applications accessible to PwD, whether digital or not. For the purpose of filtering only by those directed to video games, the second EC was used. Through the third EC, papers not directed to the target audience of this mapping, People with Disabilities, were removed. Regarding the fourth EC, primary studies are empirical and investigate a specific research issue, while secondary studies review primary studies based on a specific research question, with the purpose of synthesizing the evidence obtained [21]. As the objective was to obtain the state of the art literature, only primary papers were considered. With regard to the fifth EC, only full papers, which have four pages or more were accepted, because they demonstrate deep research. Finally, with the last EC, it was expected to remove papers that did not have access to the full text free of charge or by CAPES.

In the analyses of the papers, when it is not possible to complete the application of a certain criterion, other sections of the study needed to be read and evaluated, such as the introduction, conclusion, or the whole paper. After the evaluation of ICs and ECs, 44 papers were accepted.

5   Analysis and Results

The papers were analyzed between the months of October and November 2020. The SLM described in this work, had the purpose of investigating in the literature studies that provide guidelines for the development of DGs to PwD. Through the 44 results, it was possible to answer the primary question, noting that there are materials available for the development of DGs, promoting the inclusion of people with specific needs. The list of papers can be found at the following link[1].

---

[1] https://drive.google.com/file/d/19baUEqXfmqEjk0PV-PIcoYlCHHLN3XPI/view?usp=sharing.

DGs are tools, in addition to entertaining, that can be used in the most diverse contexts, such as training, teaching, health, and also favor the acquisition of cognitive skills and the digital literacy of its users. Therefore, when used by PwD it is able to help in different segments of their lives.

The World Health Organization relates that there are about 2 billion people in the world with disabilities, these 1.3 billion have some type of visual impairment, representing about 17% of the world population; 466 million have hearing impairments, 6%; while 200 million have intellectual disabilities, it is equivalent to 2.6% and 75 million need a wheelchair, which represents 1% [22]. Of these, around 100 million are gamers [3]. With a focus on the disabilities that are addressed by the guidelines present in the papers, in greater number are visual and cognitive disability, as shown in Fig. 1. When the disability addressed was not cited, we classified it as "Not Specified".

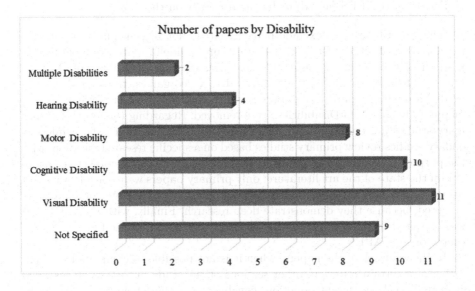

Fig. 1. Disabilities covered by the guidelines

The DGs can be categorized based on several dimensions. According to Connolly et al. [23], when classifying a game, it is important to consider its first function, identifying the initial purpose that was developed, which can be leisure, education, or a serious game. The games were classified according to their objective: casual games, serious games, and advertising games, as proposed by Derryberry [8]. Figure 2 shows the graph with the number of studies found in each category.

In order to emphasize the initial purpose of the game for which the guidelines are intended, within the set of SGs, Educational Games (4 works) were identified as a subset. SGs when developed specifically for Education, being motivators of learning, are called Educational Games (EGs) [17]. These are relevant resources that can be used as a methodological tool to support the teachers in their educational practices. Through the intrinsic characteristics of games, EGs stimulate competition and student engagement for learning content or strengthening skills [31].

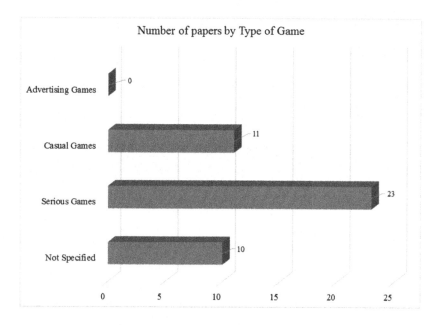

Fig. 2. Game types covered by the guidelines

It is observed that the guidelines were mainly focused on SG (23). Casual games (11) occupy second place, these are games that aim to provide entertainment to their players, through engaging and dynamic activities, making the interest in such leisure games continue to grow [23]. Thus, the guidelines directed to this type of game aims at the development of a tool for PwD fun. No paper was obtained regarding guidelines for advertising games. When there was no mention of the type or purpose of the game, the classification of "Not Specified" was applied.

Regarding the age range addressed by the accessibility guidelines for DG, it was considered: children, adults, and elderly (when not mentioned, the classification of "not specified" was used). The categorization of papers according to the age group can be visualized in Fig. 3. Most of the authors did not specify their target audience. It is noteworthy that people, whether they are disabled or not, at different stages of their lives, have different needs due to their cognitive and physical state, and these need to be considered when idealizing the DG. In a smaller number, guidelines for children were found (13 papers).

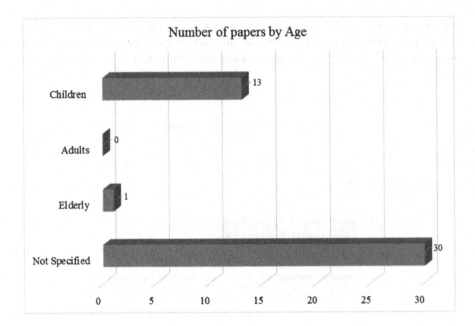

Fig. 3. Age groups covered by the guidelines

As statistical data obtained, there is the distribution of papers by the search engines used and also by the years of publication. Most papers are from the Web of Science, about 59.1% of the final result. Second is ACM and lastly IEEE, with 22.7% and 18.2% respectively. It is believed that the highest percentage of the Web of Science database is motivated by the greater number of results achieved by the search argument, as well as, its greatness in covering several scientific areas, as presented in Fig. 4.

About the publication years of the papers, as shown by Fig. 5, there is a general increase in publications on the topic. It leads to believing that accessibility to DGs is an expanding theme, and much can still be done by both industry and academia to promote inclusion, autonomy and improve PwD lives.

However, despite the availability of guidelines in the literature, the vast majority of commercial games do not yet employ accessibility elements and therefore do not attend to the needs of PwD, as to reach the largest possible number of users with a high level of understanding. As corroborated by Cheiran and Pimenta [1], who state that there is a shortage of accessibility elements in most traditional games, as well as the lack of compatibility with assistive technologies, which makes PwDs not be able to use these resources, causing their exclusion. Thus, it is emphasized that the possibilities provided with the advancement of technology and computing need to be extended beyond the traditional users to become accessible to all [24].

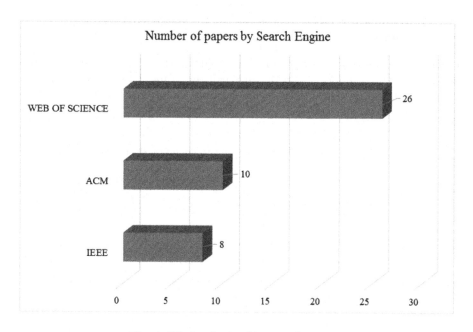

Fig. 4. Works obtained by search engines

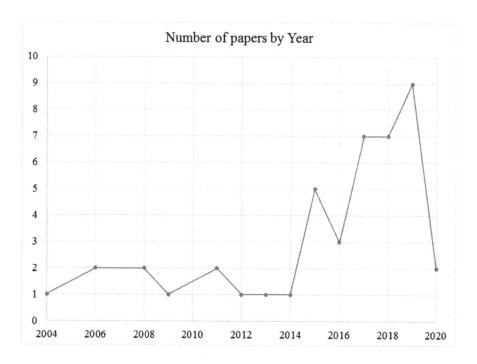

Fig. 5. Works by year of publication

5.1   Guidelines for DGs Accessible to People with Cognitive Disabilities

A more in-depth study in papers aimed at Cognitive Disability made it possible to extract relevant information for this segment. Table 2 presents the papers obtained, identifying the authors, type of game, age group, search engine, and year of publication for each one.

Table 2. Obtained works related to cognitive disability

Id	Title	Authors	Game type	Age range	Search engine	Year
1	Exploring Collaboration Patterns in a Multitouch Game to Encourage Social Interaction and Collaboration Among Users with Autism Spectrum Disorder	Silva, G. F. M., Raposo, A. and Suplino, M.	Serious Game	N/S	Web of Science	2015
2	Designing a Serious Game for Independent Living Skills in Special Education	Tsikinas, S., Xinogalos, S., Satratzemi, M. and Kartasidou, L.	Serious Game	N/S	Web of Science	2019
3	Personalized technology-enhanced training for people with cognitive impairment	Buzzi, M. C., Buzzi, M., Perrone, E. and Senette, C.	N/S	N/S	Web of Science	2019
4	Case Study: A Serious Game for Neurorehabilitation Assessment	Tong, T., Chignell, M. and Sieminowski, T.	Serious Game	N/S	Web of Science	2015
5	Towards a serious games design framework for people with an intellectual disability or autism spectrum disorder	Tsikinas, S. and Xinogalos, S.	Serious Game	N/S	Web of Science	2020
6	Designing effective serious games for people with intellectual disabilities	Tsikinas, S. and Xinogalos, S.	Serious Game	N/S	IEEE	2018
7	Accessibility of Immersive Serious Games for Persons with Cognitive Disabilities	Guitton, P., Sauzéon, H. and Cinquin, P. A	Serious Game	N/S	IEEE	2019
8	The "Malha" project: A game design proposal for multisensory stimulation environments	Castelhano, N. and Roque, L.	Casual Game	Children	IEEE	2015
9	Accessibility Assessment of Mobile Serious Games for People with Cognitive Impairments	Jaramillo-Alcázar, A., Luján-Mora, S. and Salvador-Ullauri, L.	Serious Game	N/S	IEEE	2017
10	Developing a Serious Game for Cognitive Assessment: Choosing Settings and Measuring Performance	Tong, T. and Chignell, M.	Serious Game	Eldery	ACM	2014

N/S = Not Specified

Participatory Design. Based on the analysis of papers focusing on Cognitive Disability, it was observed the mention about Participatory Design (PD), papers 2, 3, 5, 6, and 7, and the convenience of using it in the development of accessible digital games, either at the beginning for requirements gathering or at the end as a means of validation.

PD consists of a design team with access to a set of stakeholders representatives of the target audience. PD is not only up to questioning users about what they want, because often they are not sure about it [25]. It aims to include end-users in the process of developing an artifact, to avoid common problems in projects that do not have access to users, such as the development of features or interfaces as required or do not attend to the end-users needs.

The inclusion of users makes it possible to raise important questions for the developed artifact, that many times would not be thought of by the designer because he did not experience the real tasks [25]. Thus, when developing accessible digital games it is essential to involve PwD, as well as, the professionals who work with them and understand their limitations [26].

Serious Game. It was identified that out of the 10 papers that focused on Cognitive Disability, 8 of these were intended to establish accessibility guidelines for SGs. These, are a tool of great potential when applied to people with cognitive disabilities, as they enable the learning or training of new skills in a playful and engaging way. The paper by Lanyi et al. [27] presents numerous studies that prove that games are able to assist in cognitive rehabilitation, improving deficits such as perceptual disorders, conceptual thinking, attention, concentration, and memory.

Guidelines. Through the analysis of the guidelines proposed in the papers, it was observed that in some studies these were elaborated through bibliographic research, as is the case of papers 2, 6, and 9 or else, through learning provided in the process of development of the game together with stakeholder participation, as is the case with papers 3, 4, 5, and 7. As well as the joining of both, as occurred in paper 1.

In order to identify the most significant guidelines for the creation of games accessible to people with cognitive disabilities, guidelines were extracted which are believed to be fundamental to games aimed at this audience. In addition to that, some of these guidelines were mentioned in more than one study, thus highlighting their essential use. In this way, the suggestions listed in Annex I are extracted and summarized from the papers cited in Table 2. In most cases, these guidelines not only facilitate players' interaction with the game, but also determine whether they can use it or not [28].

Evaluation. Another information obtained is the relevance of the evaluation of the developed game. Tong and Chignell [29] (paper 10) point out as one of the guidelines, the performance of usability tests and the importance of these for validating the product developed with the target audience.

Usability assessments allow designers to identify problems in the game. It is also of great value that sessions are held with the players, so they can test and report their perceptions. In addition, interviews can be conducted with end-users and professionals, in order to identify their satisfaction with the product developed [29]. Of the studies obtained, papers 1, 3, 4, 5, and 10, present tests for the validation of games developed based on the established guidelines.

6   Threats to Validity

To guarantee an unbiased selection process, the research questions, objective criteria, inclusion and exclusion criteria were established before the performed of the systematic mapping. Moreover, the process was performed independently by each author and, when inclusion or exclusion of a paper was controversial, then the decision was made jointly.

In addition, it is possible that relevant studies have not been included yet. To mitigate it, we try taking into account the most important search engines for the area. For the future, we intend to update this scoping study, considering other search engines.

The filters used in search engines can also be a threat. These filters were applied due to most of the results, without filters, it was not related to the theme of this mapping.

Lastly, the classification scheme of this mapping can be a threat to validity. As cited by Pretorius e Budgen [34], determining the best way to categorize the resulting papers is one of the problems of mappings studies.

7   Conclusions and Future Works

The aim of this study was to identify in the literature papers with guidelines for accessible DGs to PwD, through a SLM. In view of this, one primary research question and three secondary research questions were defined. RQ1:

What guidelines are available in the literature for developing games for people with disabilities? RQ2: What disabilities are the accessibility guidelines for digital games addressed to? RQ3: What types of digital games are covered by the accessibility guidelines? RQ4: For which age group were the accessibility guidelines for digital games established?

As result, 44 papers were identified that establish accessibility guidelines **(RQ1)**. There are several disabilities covered by these guidelines, with a greater number of papers aimed at visual and then cognitive impairments, but also the motor, hearing, and multiple disabilities **(RQ2)**. In addition, most of the papers are aimed at establishing accessibility elements for SGs, corresponding to 23 studies, but papers for casual games **(RQ3)** were also obtained. Regarding the age group covered by such guidelines, in most number, this was not stipulated by the authors, but in a smaller amount, there were papers aimed at children and the elderly **(RQ4)**. Regardless of the category assessed, when not specified by the author, the classification "Not Specified" was used.

In addition, based on a formal protocol to obtain and understand papers that encourage the development of accessible digital games, it was possible to conduct an in-depth analysis of the guidelines aimed at people with cognitive disabilities, grouping and classifying them. Thus, this study can also be a reference for developers and designers who aim to develop DGs for people with cognitive disabilities.

As future work, it is suggested to expand the mapping to include other search engines in order to amplify the view on this scenario, maximizing the possibility of obtaining a greater number of guidelines.

Acknowledgments. The authors wish to acknowledge that this work was supported by Santa Catarina State University (UDESC) and Postgraduate Monitoring Scholarship Program (PROMOP) offered by this university. The authors also would like to thank FAPESC (public call FAPESC/CNPq No. 06/2016 support the infrastructure of CTI for young researchers, project T.O. No.: 2017TR1755 - Ambientes Inteligentes Educacionais com Integração de Técnicas de Learning Analytics e de Gamificação), and National Council for Scientific and Technological Development -CNPq (www.cnpq.br.) no. 308395/2020-4. This study was financed in part by the Coordenação de Aperfeiçoamento de Pessoal de Nível Superior - Brasil (CAPES) (www.capes.gov.br.) - Finance Code 001.

Annex I - Guidelines for DGs to People with Cognitive Disabilities

ID	Guideline	Description	Paper
1	Simple interface	The game needs to be attractive, but also effective. Employ a simple interface, eliminating complex animations that can be a distraction factor for users.	[2,6,5]
2	Control buttons	Use game control buttons like "Help" and "Pause".	[2,9]
3	Feedbacks	Provide feedback helps players to remain committed and engaged. It is indicated the use of visual and auditory feedbacks, preferring the positive feedbacks.	[2,5,6,8,9]
4	Customization and personalization	Possibility the configuration of game elements, such as characters, gender customization, name and appearance. This is considered a crucial factor to increase motivation and engagement with the game.	[2,3,4,6,7,8,5,10]
5	Adaptation and progression of difficulty levels	The continuos challenge is important to keep the player engaged and motivated. There may be mechanisms that adjust the difficulty automatically, but it is also necessary that teachers can set the level of difficulty. Thus, different levels of difficulty and the configuration of this levels must be provided. Also, challenges needs advance as each player's skills increase. Keeping the "game flow".	[2, 3,4,5,6,8,9]
6	Monitoring	Providing mechanisms to enable educators to monitor the progress of students within the game and their learning from it. Generate easy-to-interpret data visualizations and graphs of progress.	[2, 4,6]
7	Motivators	It is important to add motivating elements like scores, currencies and also add the mechanics of customization.	[2]
8	Repetition	A characteristic of people with cognitive disability is repetitive behavior. Therefore, the possibility of repeating tutorials or tasks within the game must be offered.	[2,5,9]
9	Time customization	Adapt the ritme of the game and tasks according to the skills and preferences of each player. Avoid limiting time because it can cause anxiety and affect engagement and performance of the player within game.	[3,7]
10	Multimedia contents	Provide content in audio and video format, such as short demonstration videos, showing the necessary interaction. People with Down's syndrome learn through imitation.	[3]
11	Simple language	Use short, clear texts with common and simple words. Providing commands both in the format of sounds and written, avoid only the use of visual information. Also, employ clear and understandable sources.	[2,3,9,7]
12	Accessible assessment tools	Accessible tools should be used in evaluations, as visual Likert scales with few items (three, maximum five).	[3]
13	Technologies usable by the target audience	The technology and platform needs to be considered based on the target audience that you will use and your needs that will need to be met, as well as the context where it will be used.	[4]
14	Simple or real-life commands	People with cognitive disabilities have difficulties in executing new motor controls. Employ simple commands and inspired by real life.	[7]
15	Fail	Failure element is not preferable to be applied in games for this target audience, it can demotivate the players.	[5]
16	Validation	Conduct usability tests to identify problems with the game that that make it impossible for the target audience to use it.	[10]

References

1. Cheiran, J.F.P., Pimenta, M.S.: "Eu também quero jogar!" reavaliando as práticas e diretrizes de acessibilidade em jogos. In: Proceedings of the 10th Brazilian Symposium on Human Factors in Computing Systems and the 5th Latin American Conference on Human-Computer Interaction, pp. 289–297 (2011)
2. Bierre, K., Chetwynd, J., Ellis, B., Hinn, D. M., Ludi, S., Westin, T.: Game not over: accessibility issues in video games. In: Proceedings of the 3rd International Conference on Universal Access in Human-Computer Interaction (2005)
3. Barlet, M.C., Spohn, S.D.: Includification: A Practical Guide to Game Accessibility. The Ablegamers Foundation, Charles Town (2012)
4. Grammenos, D., Savidis, A., Stephanidis, C.: Designing universally accessible games. Comput. Entertain. (CIE) 7(1), 1–29 (2009)

5. Petersen, K., Feldt, R., Mujtaba, S., Mattsson, M.: Systematic mapping studies in software engineering. In: 12th International Conference on Evaluation and Assessment in Software Engineering (EASE), vol. 12, pp. 1–10 (2008)
6. Kerr, A.: The Business and Culture of Digital Games: Gamework and Gameplay. Sage, Thousand Oaks (2006)
7. Wouters, P., van Oostendorp, H.: Overview of instructional techniques to facilitate learning and motivation of serious games. In: Wouters, P., van Oostendorp, H. (eds.) Instructional Techniques to Facilitate Learning and Motivation of Serious Games. AGL, pp. 1–16. Springer, Cham (2017). https://doi.org/10.1007/978-3-319-39298-1_1
8. Derryberry, A.: Serious games: online games for learning (2007)
9. Susi, T., Johannesson, M., Backlund, P.: Serious games: an overview (2007)
10. International Game Developers Association. Accessibility in games: Motivations and approaches (2004). Accessed 16 Jan 2016
11. Fava, F.: Jogando com o ar: o sopro como instrumento de acessibilidade nos jogos eletrônicos. Proc. SBGames **8**, 115–121 (2008)
12. Vanderdonckt, J., Pribeanu, C.: State of the art of web usability guidelines (2005)
13. Training GUIDE: The convention on the rights of persons with disabilities (2010)
14. Amiralian, M.L., Pinto, E.B., Ghirardi, M.I., Lichtig, I., Masini, E.F., Pasqualin, L.: Rev. Saude Publica **34**, 97–103 (2000)
15. Decreto n° 5.296/2004. http://www.planalto.gov.br/ccivil_03/_ato2004-2006/2004/decreto/d5296.htm. Accessed 01 Nov 2020
16. Neves, L.A., Kanda, J.Y.: Desenvolvimento e Avaliação de Jogos Educativos para Deficientes Intelectuais. In: Congreso Internacional de Informática Educativa (Conferência Internacional sobre Informática na Educação-TISE), p. 612 (2016)
17. Hendrix, M., Backlund, P.: Educational games-are they worth the effort. A literature survey of the effectiveness of serious games. In: 5th International Conference on Games and Virtual Worlds for Serious Applications (VS-GAMES), pp. 1–8 (2013)
18. Pereira, A.F.: Game accessibility guidelines for people with sequelae from macular chorioretinitis. Entertain. Comput. **28**, 49–58 (2018)
19. Mat Rosly, M., Mat Rosly, H., Davis OAM, G.M., Husain, R., Hasnan, N.: Exergaming for individuals with neurological disability: a systematic review. Disabil. Rehabil. **39**(8), 727–735 (2017)
20. Tomé, R.M., Pereira, J.M., Oliveira, M.: Using serious games for cognitive disabilities. In: Ma, M., Oliveira, M.F., Baalsrud Hauge, J. (eds.) SGDA 2014. LNCS, vol. 8778, pp. 34–47. Springer, Cham (2014). https://doi.org/10.1007/978-3-319-11623-5_4
21. Dermeval, D., Coelho, J.A.D.M., Bittencourt, I.I.: Mapeamento sistemático e revisao sistemática da literatura em informática na educaçao. JAQUES, Patrícia Augustin; PIMENTEL, Mariano; SIQUEIRA; Sean; BITTENCOURT, Ig. (Org.) Metodologia de Pesquisa em Informática na Educação: Abordagem Quantitativa de Pesquisa. Porto Alegre: SBC (2019)
22. Leite, W.: Disabled people in the world in 2019: facts and figures (2019). https://www.inclusivecitymaker.com/disabled-people-in-the-world-in-2019-facts-and-figures/. Accessed 17 Nov 2020
23. Connolly, T.M., Boyle, E.A., MacArthur, E., Hainey, T., Boyle, J.M.: A systematic literature review of empirical evidence on computer games and serious games. Comput. Educ. **59**(2), 661–686 (2012)

24. Santos, C.P., Stangherlin, V., Ellwanger, C.: Requisitos de Interação para o Desenvolvimento de Softwares Inclusivos para Usuários com Deficiência Intelectual (2014)
25. Nielsen, J.: Usability Engineering. Morgan Kaufmann, San Francisco (1994)
26. Tsikinas, S., Xinogalos, S.: Towards a serious games design framework for people with intellectual disability or autism spectrum disorder. Educ. Inf. Technol. **25**(4), 3405–3423 (2020). https://doi.org/10.1007/s10639-020-10124-4
27. Lanyi, C.S., Brown, D.J., Standen, P., Lewis, J., Butkute, V.: Results of user interface evaluation of serious games for students with intellectual disability. Acta Polytechnica Hungarica **9**(1), 225–245 (2012)
28. Buzzi, M.C., Buzzi, M., Perrone, E., Senette, C.: Personalized technology-enhanced training for people with cognitive impairment. Univ. Access Inf. Soc. **18**(4), 891–907 (2018). https://doi.org/10.1007/s10209-018-0619-3
29. Tong, T., Chignell, M.: Developing a serious game for cognitive assessment: choosing settings and measuring performance. In: Proceedings of the Second International Symposium of Chinese CHI, pp. 70–79 (2014)
30. World Health Organization: International Classification of Functioning, Disability and Health (ICF). World Health Organization, Geneva (2002)
31. Petri, G., Von Wangenheim, C.G.: How to evaluate educational games: a systematic. J. Univ. Comput. Sci. **22**(7), 992–1021 (2016)
32. New Zoo: 2019 free global games market report (2019). https://platform.newzoo.com/. Accessed 15 Nov 2020
33. Buchinger, D., Cavalcanti, G.A.S., Hounsell, M.S.: Mecanismos de busca acadêmica: uma análise quantitativa. Revista Brasileira de Computação Aplicada **6**(1), 108–120 (2014)
34. Pretorius, R., Budgen, D.: A mapping study on empirical evidence related to the models and forms used in the UML. In: Proceedings of the Second ACM-IEEE International Symposium on Empirical Software Engineering and Measurement, pp. 342–344 (2008)

Discount Evaluation of Preliminary Versions of Systems Dedicated to Users with Cerebral Palsy: Simulation of Involuntary Movements in Non-disabled Participants

Yohan Guerrier[1] , Janick Naveteur[1,2] , Christophe Kolski[1]([⊠]) ,
and Françoise Anceaux[1]

[1] LAMIH UMR CNRS 8201, Université Polytechnique Hauts-de-France,
59313 Valenciennes cedex 9, France
{yohan.guerrier,janick.naveteur,christophe.kolski,
francoise.anceaux}@uphf.fr
[2] Univ. Lille, EA 4072 – PSITEC – Psychologie : Interactions, Temps, Emotions, Cognition,
59000 Lille, France
janick.naveteur@univ-lille.fr

Abstract. Simulation of disabled user characteristics can be useful in two cases: (1) during preliminary tests of interactive systems, (2) to train designers and make them understand the difficulties encountered by these users with special needs. This paper describes a case study involving a preliminary user test of a system called ComMob (Communication and Mobility). It is a communication aid for people with motor disabilities of the dyskinetic Cerebral Palsy type. This software is usable in mobility and may be installed on a wheelchair. A preliminary discount evaluation was carried out in the laboratory with non-disabled participants in whom involuntary movements were induced. These movements were characteristic of users with a dyskinetic Cerebral Palsy disability. The paper focuses on the principles of the discount evaluation that was implemented. The first results are promising and show the feasibility of the approach, leading to numerous research perspectives.

Keywords: Disabled user · Discount evaluation · User test · Simulation · Cerebral palsy · Involuntary movement · Communication support

1 Introduction

In the field of disability, there are user profiles (for instance Locked-in Syndrome people, dyskinetic Cerebral Palsy people...) for which it may be difficult to have a large number of participants during the preliminary evaluation stages (user tests, in the sense of Nielsen [1] or Rubin [2]). More, when the system is preliminary and may contain software bugs and basic usability problems, it is often not useful to involve these users and consequently their caregivers. Bad and buggy versions may discourage them, they have no time to loose

M. Antona and C. Stephanidis (Eds.): HCII 2021, LNCS 12768, pp. 71–88, 2021.
https://doi.org/10.1007/978-3-030-78092-0_5

with preliminary versions and it is more relevant to involve them in the evaluation of the next and more advanced version(s) of the system. The envisaged solution involves simulating the characteristics (or rather some of the characteristics) of these disabled users. Such a strategy can also be useful in helping designers better understand the difficulties encountered by disabled users.

This paper is part of a research project aimed at evaluating systems dedicated to the field of disability, with simulation of one or more user characteristics. It describes a step in this context, devoted to a preliminary evaluation of a communication aid called ComMob. Its target users are people with dyskinetic cerebral palsy [3–5]. ComMob was created during the doctoral thesis of the first author of this paper, who has dyskinetic cerebral palsy himself [6]. The software uses pictograms (as in [7] for instance) to allow users to formulate sentences simply and quickly. Figure 1 shows two situations of use of ComMob. Picture (a) shows a use of ComMob in a mobility situation, in a store with a tablet installed on the wheelchair [8]. Picture (b) shows a situation of interaction in the user's home, with control of a virtual keyboard visible on a screen placed on a desk. In both cases, the virtual keyboard is controlled using a joystick installed on the wheelchair. In the context of this paper, we are focused on one of its preliminary (early) versions containing software bugs and basic usability problems.

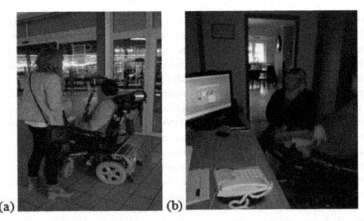

Fig. 1. Use of ComMob (a) in mobility (installed on a tablet), (b) at home (on a personal computer).

The following section is devoted to the background of this research. The paper then describes the principles of a preliminary evaluation of ComMob with simulation of user characteristics, to show the feasibility of such discount evaluation (in the sense of Nielsen [9], Curtis and Nielsen [10], Yao and Gorman [11]). As explained by Maurer and Ghanam [12]: *"While no one explicitly denied the benefits of conducting usability tests prior to releasing products, many did not adopt it due to the commonly perceived fact that it was expensive and time-consuming. In attempt to correct this perception, Nielsen and other usability practitioners coined the term* Discount Usability *in the early 1990s* [13]. *By introducing low-cost and easily accessible usability testing methodologies that value observation and interpretation over complex statistics, and value flexibility of procedure, space and time over expensive test labs and sophisticated experimentation, a new perception of usability engineering has emerged.*" In our case, the difference between the discount evaluation described in this paper and a classical evaluation is that we mechanically and at low cost induce involuntary movements in non-disabled participants. The user test results are provided afterwards. We close the paper by drawing the main conclusions and subsequent research perspectives.

2 Background

This section focuses first on users with dyskinetic cerebral palsy. Then, it deals with the principle of discount evaluation by simulation of disabled user characteristics. Finally, the preliminary version of the system used as a study framework for the proposed discount evaluation is described.

2.1 Users with Dyskinetic Cerebral Palsy

Cerebral palsy (CP) comprises a group of abnormal movement, tone and posture causing activity limitation. Spastic CP, mostly characterized by stiffness in the limbs, is the dominant neurological profile. Dyskinetic CP is less researched but it is one of the most disabling motor types of CP with disorders arising predominantly from a lack of inhibition in motor control [14]. There is evidence for substantial inter-individual differences in the motor profile. The involuntary movements may be associated with both hypertonia and hypotonia. Primitive reflexes persist and spasticity is often present, but not as a dominating feature [15]. About 40% of dyskinetic CP people are in wheelchairs [4]. Additionally, dysarthria [16] causes speech problems that limit speech intelligibility. People with dysarthria pronounce words incorrectly, but they generally have no problem formulating correct sentences. This speech problem has been the subject of much research. Thus, communication aids facilitate simple requests such as "I want to eat" but, in everyday life, each person needs to formulate much longer and more complex sentences to express various requests and feelings. The optimization of communication is also important in various fields such as medicine or justice.

The involuntary movements typical of people with dyskinetic cerebral palsy are due to neurological damage caused by a lack of oxygen at birth, an epileptic seizure or a head injury. These movements vary in amplitude depending on the degree of disability. Other factors (stress, fatigue, environment…) can influence the intensity of involuntary movements in certain circumstances [17]. People suffering from the most serious form of this pathology may have great difficulty (or even find it impossible) to manipulate devices for interaction with computers (in the broadest sense of the term), such as mice, joysticks, or physical keyboards. This is due to their excessive involuntary movements, as well as to a more or less significant lack of precision in the movements.

2.2 Evaluation by Simulation of Disabled User Characteristic

Simulating a motor or sensory problem in non-disabled people is a strategy that has already been implemented to test devices or treatments. Examples include: the use of participants temporarily deprived of vision to test a vibratory guidance device [18, 19] or dragged haptic bumps [20]; the wearing of an ageing simulator by young participants to test a rehabilitation system [21]. The Fig. 2 illustrates a user test with low-cost simulation of blind user interacting with a system.

This approach has its limitations. For example, as Marks points out [22]: "Despite the value of demystifyng impairments, it is important to add a cautionary note regarding certain forms of 'awareness training' and, in particular, 'disability simulation'. Simulation exercices attempt to give non-disabled people an insight into the experience of impairment. This might be done by getting shop assistants to use wheelchairs, attach weights to their arms or wear blindfolds in training sessions in order to increase their appreciation of barriers to shopping. However, such training often fails to capture some of the most difficult aspects of their impairment, such as the effect of cumulative frustration, pain, fatigue or social isolation. On the other hand, simulation can also over-estimate some aspects of difficulties [...]." See also [23] about blindness simulation.

This is why our paper does not try to cover all aspects of a disability: it focuses on a specifically targeted user characteristic (in our case: involuntary movements leading to difficulties in using the user interface).

Fig. 2. Illustration of user test with low-cost simulation of blind user

There is no literature on interactive system evaluation with simulation of user characteristics related to the dyskinetic cerebral palsy profile. As part of a series of preliminary evaluations of the communication support system called ComMob, a first step in this regard is presented in the third section. We present below the HCI principles of ComMob, the system at the heart of the discount evaluation described.

2.3 Presentation of the User Interface of the Tested Preliminary System and Design Principles

The ComMob software mainly allows the user with cerebral palsy to build sentences from pictograms organized by theme and category in a library [24]. The disabled user also has the possibility of preparing a dialogue in advance to make the exchanges with his or her future interlocutor(s) more fluid. An advanced version of ComMob is described in [6].

During the implementation of ComMob user interfaces, we complied with the following rules. Above all, we paid attention to the size of the buttons. Inspired by Fitts' law [25], we determined the size of the buttons by looking for compromises: since a user with dyskinetic cerebral palsy generally has little precision in the movements of the mouse, he or she has difficulty in pointing to a small icon on the screen. However, we could not make the buttons too large because the software must work both on a classic computer and on a small touch tablet installed on the wheelchair (Fig. 3). The pictograms were also designed to be large so that they are easily accessible and also clearly visible. The user must therefore be able to find the desired pictogram easily. We created a tree structure with the different themes grouping all the pictograms. Since, in this study, we focused on public transport (or more generally on mobility), the tree structure does not have a significant depth. This prevents the disabled user from wasting time navigating through the different levels. In addition, we implemented several functions to produce a sentence as quickly as possible: we can cite as an example the display of pictogram proposals in relation to the previously selected pictograms.

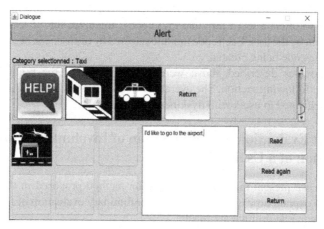

Fig. 3. User interface of the "communication aid" module used to generate sentences from pictograms.

We created a module to prepare a dialogue in advance (see Fig. 4). As a result, the future dialogue should be more fluid. Once the user has finished preparing the dialog, he or she can save it and then open it at the appropriate time and launch a voice-over speech. Another module is called: Reading a prepared dialogue. First, it proposes to choose a theme and then it displays all the dialogues recorded in that theme. Once the dialogue has been selected, the sentences are displayed one below the other. The user can have ComMob read either the entire dialogue or a sentence by placing the pointer on it. The user can modify the dialogue at any time during playback. To create or modify a dialog, the user uses a virtual keyboard (as for the example of sentence visible in Fig. 4). He or she can choose his or her usual virtual keyboard (ComMob does not impose one).

The last module is called: Programming assistance. It helps the user to enter Java code to create software applications. It may be useful for programmers with cerebral

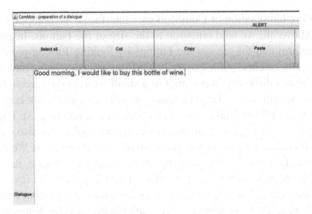

Fig. 4. User interface of the "Preparation of a dialogue" module.

palsy. This module looks like a classic text editor, but pictograms help the disabled user to create the code. It also includes a set of usual functions, i.e. copy-paste, cut-paste, etc. This module also offers a set of reusable Java codes, organized into several categories, which are chosen by the user. Each code module selected by the user can be automatically inserted into the code being created.

All the modules described above were evaluated during the preliminary tests described in the following section. The overall purpose of this evaluation was to improve the modules dedicated to users with dyskinetic cerebral palsy.

3 Discount Evaluation with Simulation of Involuntary Movements: Illustration of a Usable Method

In this section, we present the discount evaluation method proposed in this paper. To illustrate it, we explain how it was used for the preliminary evaluation of the ComMob software, following an original approach.

We had difficulty in recruiting participants with dyskinetic CP so we involved non-disabled people by simulating disability. To this end, we induced uncontrolled movements of the arm in charge of the action on the joystick. The arm was also weighted. This approach is essentially exploratory. The main interest of this user test is to find out if people with disabilities who are not familiar with ComMob can use the device easily.

3.1 Participants

A total of 10 volunteers participated in this preliminary user test, but one of them was discarded for technical reasons. The participants (6 women and 3 men) were all doctoral students in different disciplines. The ages ranged from 23 to 29 years old. One woman and one man were left-handed. The volunteers had varying levels in computing. Their previous expertise in manipulating a joystick was also variable. No participant had extensive theoretical knowledge about cerebral palsy. Each participant signed a consent form. The participants may also be referred to as testers (of the preliminary version of ComMob system) in the following sections.

3.2 Equipment Used for This Discount Evaluation Approach

The equipment included a laptop computer, a joystick installed on the wheelchair, and a device to connect this joystick to the computer (see Fig. 5a). One camera was used to film the computer screen and another was used to record the tester's facial expressions. The other components were designed to simulate a characteristic of cerebral palsy. A 1.5 kg weighted bracelet (see Fig. 5b) made the arm heavier, making it more difficult to move. The bracelet was attached to a rope, itself attached by a hook to a metal pulley structure placed behind the tester's chair. This device was operated by an experimenter who pulled the rope, thereby inducing a lift of the tester's wrist.

3.3 Procedure

The user test takes place in the laboratory. The participant (tester) sits in a seat next to an observer with a dyskinetic CP profile (in this case: first author). The observer can thus observe the interactions, and then give an opinion on them. The observer has also the possibility to observe how the involuntary movements are simulated. The tester handles the joystick with his or her right hand. The joystick is controlled by a box called Easy Rider (from the HMC company) fixed on the wheelchair. This box is the link between the joystick and the computer via infrared technology.

As regards how to pull the rope, it would have been inappropriate to determine a procedure independently of the way the tasks went. As pointed out above, the movement disorders of CP individuals are exacerbated by different factors such as cognitive load, emotions, stress or pain. The prior observation of the first author during his own manipulations of the joystick suggested the occurrence of about ten involuntary movements per minute. However, this ratio was only used as a guidance and was modulated according to the tester behaviour. The rope was pulled preferably when a difficulty was encountered, as deduced from the observation of the computer screen and/or the observation of the tester reactions. The experimenter in charge of the rope was an athlete with a good control and feedback of his own body. These qualities warrant the homogeneity of the procedure. The observer also retrospectively expressed a positive opinion on how the movements were induced, including in terms of amplitude (the hand was rarely raised above the shoulder) and speed (of a large range in order to mimic a choreoathetosis profile). These upward movements with a slight tilt to the left were nevertheless simpler and less diversified than the ones he produces. Several components such as contortion or rotation were missing in order to fit both dystonia and choreoathetosis that are often present in people with CP [26], including the first author of this paper. Nevertheless, the main goal, i.e., to made more difficult to use the joystick, was reached.

The oral instructions given before the user test are reduced to a minimum. He or she was initially informed that arms movements will be induced. The instruction specified that he or she had to perform the tasks at best despite of them, without playing a game of strength against pull-ups. The tester was invited to perform a set of sequential tasks according to a scenario described on a sheet of paper placed next to the computer screen. This scenario was designed to force the tester to perform a set of actions that require the use of almost all the ComMob functions:

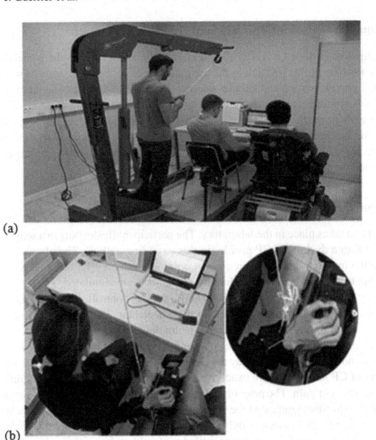

Fig. 5. a) Back view of the experimental station. The participant is in the center, and the experimenter at the back operates the pulley system. b) Position seen from above. A participant activates the joystick on the arm of the experimenter's armchair to her right; in the circle: focus on the weighted bracelet [27].

- The first part is a *communication* task performed with ComMob. First, the tester must create a new theme, then several categories. Then, the tester must insert two pictograms in each theme. Following this action, the tester must prepare a dialogue and then have it read by ComMob. At this point, the tester issues two alerts. This part of the test ends with the deletion of the categories and themes previously created.
- The second part of the test concerns the *Programming assistance* module. It is called *programming* task in the following description. The tester must first create a new document (i.e. program), then insert a *for* loop (control structure) into the document. Then, he or she must insert a code proposed by ComMob. Finally, the tester must search for text in the document and save the document. It is important to note here that the *Programming assistance* module is intended for users with Cerebral Palsy, who are also programmers: code entry can be seen as text entry, with predefined

structures (*while, for, case…*), as here with the *for* loop. It allows to write code faster (in our case essentially *Java* code).

No time constraint is imposed on the participants. The user test ends with a collection of subjective data using a questionnaire. The main purpose is to obtain the tester's opinion on ComMob, and to detect usability problems and software bugs.

The first experimenter (in this case: first author of this paper), called also observer, remains in his wheelchair to the right of the participant during the entire part of the user test involving the use of ComMob. He observes all the manipulations carried out by the participant. At the end of the test, the observer evaluates the test by completing a questionnaire. The evaluations of the tester and the first author are done independently and the results are not compared during the user test.

The second experimenter is always in the background. This experimenter induces involuntary movements by pseudo-randomly (without pre-fixed frequency) pulling the rope and monitors the test to note any problems that may occur during the procedure. As mentioned previously, involuntary movements do not follow a particular standard pattern. Therefore, we decided to induce it mechanically in this way, simply to get closer to reality, to roughly simulate it (*discount* approach).

At the end of the user test, the participant is invited to comment freely on it. He or she receives additional information about the performed evaluation and about cerebral palsy. The total duration of a session was approximately one hour per participant.

3.4 Data Collection and Analysis

From the videos, an analysis of the activity was carried out using the Actogram Kronos software. This tool allows chronological observations of the event code/time stamp type to be processed on the basis of a categorization carried out by the user by defining a description protocol in advance. Thus, the two phases of use of ComMob were analyzed with reference to the different stages of the specifications (scenario of tasks to be performed). A total statement of the number of clicks was also extracted for the entire session, distinguishing in particular between performing clicks (allowing progress in the completion of the task) and non-performing clicks. The clicks are categorized into icon clicks and keyboard clicks; the use of keyboard shortcuts is also quantified. Finally, the movements from the keyboard to the icons and from the icons to the keyboard are collected. The data distribution allowed parametric processing. ANOVA were performed, followed by post-hoc comparisons using the Neuwman-Keuls test. Two-by-two comparisons were made using the Student t-test. Correlations were calculated using Bravais-Pearson's r.

4 Results

4.1 Chronometric Analysis

A chronometric analysis was carried out on the *communication* and *programming* tasks (described in the scenario to be followed by the testers).

Communication **Task.** All the participants successfully completed this task. The completion of the full *communication* task took in average 34 min (±9; range: 23 to 42 min). Figure 6 shows the duration of the different phases of this task. These data were submitted to a one-factor ANOVA with 6 levels corresponding to the 6 phases of the task. A significant effect arose: $F(5.40) = 39.79$, $p < .001$. The completion duration for adding pictograms as well as for dialogue preparation exceeded 10 min. Post-hoc comparisons show that the former was significantly longer that the latter ($p < .05$). These two tasks lasted significantly longer than each of the four remaining phases (all ps < .001) that do not differ from each other (less than 5 min each).

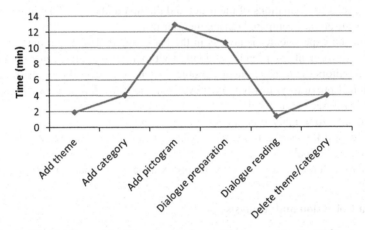

Fig. 6. Average duration of each phase of the *communication* task.

Figure 7 shows the individual chronograms. The overall time profile is found in all participants except three of them for theme/category deletion due to a bug that caused ComMob to stop. It is important to mention/recall that the detection of this bug, occurring only under particular use conditions, is considered as an interesting result in such a user test with a preliminary version of the system.

Programming **Task.** All participants successfully completed this task. The completion of the full *programming* task took in average 7.3 min (±1.5; range: 5.7 to 9.9 min). Figure 8 shows the duration of the different phases of this task.

These data were submitted to a one-factor ANOVA with 5 levels corresponding to the 5 phases of the task. A significant effect arose: $F(4.32) = 7.20$, $p < .001$. With a risk of error inferior to .05, post-hoc comparisons show that participants spent significantly more time opening a new program and inserting codes than searching for characters and saving the file. The durations of the first three phases do not differ from each other but the time taken to insert the "for" loop (control structure) does not differ significantly from the file saving time ($p = .07$), while its difference with the character searching time is significant. Figure 9 shows the individual chronograms for the *programming* task.

Comparison of Total Move Time on the Keyboard and on the Interface. For both tasks together, participants spent a total of 16.8 min (±2.6) on keyboard moves and

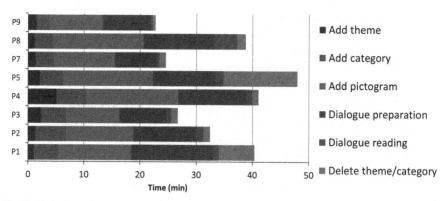

Fig. 7. Duration of each phase of the *communication* task performed using ComMob for each participant (P: participant) with simulated cerebral palsy.

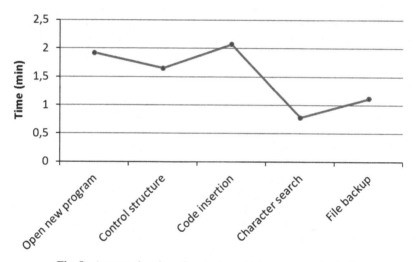

Fig. 8. Average duration of each phase of the *programming* task.

clicks and 26 min ($\pm$5.2) on interface moves and clicks; this difference is significant ($t(8) = 5.74$; $p < .001$).

4.2 Quantification of Clicks

All tasks together, the whole group of participants performed 342 clicks (with an average of 38 clicks per participant), in addition to which 18 keyboard shortcuts were used. Overall, an average of 25.3 unsuccessful clicks was recorded ($\pm$7.3; range: 15–35), so less than 5% of the total number of clicks. Figure 10 summarizes the distribution of the different types of clicks and use of shortcuts.

Although the number of inter-support clicks is a fortiori equivalent on the interface and on the keyboard, the total number of clicks made on the interface tends to be higher

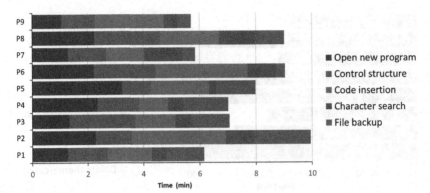

Fig. 9. Duration of each phase of the *programming* task performed using ComMob for each participant (P: participant) with simulated cerebral palsy.

than that made on the keyboard (184.5 ± 19 versus 157.4 ± 23.1; $t(8) = 2.30$; $p = .051$). However, the trend disappears if the use of keyboard shortcuts is associated with this support ($t(8) = 0.87$; $p = .41$).

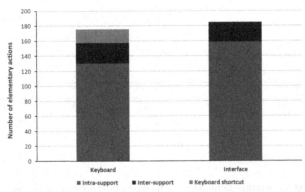

Fig. 10. Number of elementary actions (clicking or using a shortcut) performed on the keyboard and on the interface (clicking on icons) during both tasks (*communication* and *programming*) by participants with simulated cerebral palsy. Inter-support action: from the interface to the keyboard for clicks on the keyboard and vice versa for clicks on the interface.

4.3 Subjective Assessments and Link with the Use of the Device

Placed in a simulated cerebral palsy situation, participants asked to rate the usability of ComMob on a scale from 0 to 10 provided an average rating of 8.77 (± 1.1; range: 7–10). Correlational analysis shows that the participants with the highest usability ratings are those who clicked most on the icons ($r(8) = .71$; $p < .05$; see Fig. 11). It is also interesting to note a positive correlation between the number of icon clicks and the use of keyboard shortcuts ($r(8) = .73$, $p < .05$), even if the direct link between this latter item and the estimated usability of the device was not found (r(8) = .24, ns). No correlation between the usability rating and the duration measures reaches the significance level. When asked to assess the ease of moving the cursor with the joystick without simulating cerebral palsy (during a phase of familiarization with the equipment), and with the simulation of cerebral palsy, the scores provided by the participants were respectively 7.77 (±1.71; range: 6–10) and 6.11 (±2.71; range: 2–10); this difference is significant (t(8) = 2.58; p < .05).

Also asked about the ease of the *communication* task (without simulating cerebral palsy, and with the simulation of cerebral palsy), the observer with dyskinetic CP profile gave average ratings of 7.11 (±1.16; range: 5–8) and 4.66 (±1.41; range: 3–7); the difference is significant (t(8) = 2.67; p < .05). A 2 × 2 ANOVA with combining the data obtained from both the participants and the observer with dyskinetic CP confirms an overall effect of movement induction (F(1/16) = 30.25; p <. 001) but no significant effect of the respondent (tester vs observer, p = .19) or interaction between the respondent and movement induction (p = .31). Overall, participants report that they used the keyboard quite well (average rating: 6.89/10 ± 1.53) and that they had no major difficulties in navigating the tree structure (average rating: 2/10 ± 1.22). Also, when asked about this aspect of the task, the observer gave an average difficulty rating of 3.00 ± 2.06 which was not significantly different from that of the participants (t(8) = 1.34; p = .21).

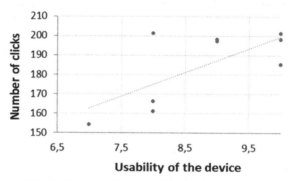

Fig. 11. Judgement of the device's usability according to the number of clicks on the interface icons by participants with simulated cerebral palsy.

As regards the *communication* task proper, 4 participants (see Table 1) reported difficulties (written in the Table in red colour), all concerning the addition of pictograms, but none of them stood out in requiring a longer period to complete this task (see Fig. 7). Table 1 shows that the observer with a dyskinetic CP profile is more critical than the participants regarding the occurrence of difficulties during this task.

In addition, when asked to compare the time taken to complete the task by the tester with the time the observer considers necessary for a user of his/her profile (score from 0 to 10, ranging from an equivalent to a much longer duration), the observer gave an average rating of 3.55 (±2.00; range: 0–6). He therefore suggests that he estimated that the task could require about 23 min (as compared with 34 min recorded during the user test, see above). This evaluation is positively related to the time taken by the participant to add

Table 1. Tasks considered difficult according to each participant (P: participant) with simulated cerebral palsy and the observer with dyskinetic CP profile.

	Point of view of the participant	Point of view of the observer with CP profile
P1	Addition of pictogram	Addition of pictogram
P2	Addition of pictogram	Addition of pictogram
P3	No difficulty	Addition of pictogram
P4	No difficulty	Addition of pictogram
P5	No difficulty	Click
P6	No difficulty	No difficulty
P7	Addition of pictogram	No difficulty
P8	Addition of pictogram	Addition of pictogram
P9	No difficulty	Addition of pictogram

pictograms and to prepare the dialogue (respectively, $r(8) = .73$ and $r(8) = .76$; ps $< .05$). In the *programming* task, no difficulties were reported by the participants, Once again however, the observer with dyskinetic CP profile is more critical. He concluded that there was no difficulty for only two participants. On the other hand, he noted difficulties in entering a file name for one participant, difficulties in inserting a code for two participants and in finding characters for four participants.

5   Discussion

The purpose of this user test was to verify the usability of a preliminary version of Com-Mob through a discount evaluation approach. In the absence of available disabled people (with a dyskinetic CP profile) for such preliminary stage, we recruited non-disabled people and simulated the disability. To this end, we created uncontrolled movements on their weighted arm in charge of actions on the joystick.

With regard to the *communication* assistance module, we found that participants spent the most time adding pictograms and preparing a dialogue. When adding pictograms, the user loses time because he or she has to add the pictograms one by one. Even if the observer with a CP profile (first author) considers himself faster than the participants in these phases, we would like to create a function that allows several pictograms to be added at the same time in the next version of ComMob. Concerning the preparation of a dialogue, each participant had to enter all the words with a virtual keyboard. Subsequently, we would like to establish a direct link between the function "preparation of a dialogue" and the function "formulation of sentences with pictograms". In this way, the user will have the possibility of formulating a dialogue with pictograms.

Concerning the *programming* assistance module, we were able to observe that the *creating a new file* sub-task took a considerable amount of time. We believe that this time is due to the lack of knowledge about the software environment. Indeed, when the participant begins on this new interface, he or she takes the time to look at the position of the specific buttons. And only then does he or she start the action. The obstacle should therefore no longer be present in users who are familiar with the device, but this aspect must be taken into account in familiarization phases. The second longest task is the insertion of Java codes. The user must find their place in the code tree. This action is not obvious *a priori* for a person who is not a computer scientist. However, the test shows that all users successfully completed the task. This module is therefore more easily accessible than initially envisaged.

During the evaluation, the participants who made the most positive judgments about ComMob were those who made the most clicks. This result may seem counter-intuitive because having to perform many manipulations on software often leads to a poor appreciation of it. In this case, however, it is possible that the number of clicks was related to faster progress in the task. Therefore, it made the task more pleasant. This interpretation would require confirmation in future user tests. Through this evaluation method, we have tried to get as close as possible to the conditions of dyskinetic CP disability. In addition to the fact that motor constraints are not integrated into the internal patterns of action in volunteers (participants), modeling has not enough integrated the fact that the involuntary movements of people with dyskinetic CP are strongly linked to emotions. It would have been difficult to include a controlled induction of emotions in the procedure (and this was not one of the goals of such discount evaluation). However, in the first estimate, the pulling of the rope is close to the conditions of occurrence observed in the observer with dyskinetic CP profile. The imposed motor constraints therefore provide a heuristic basis for further user tests of this type with non-disabled people. It is thus possible to gather initial user feedback to improve the system in question. We will then carry out further evaluation campaigns with targeted disabled users.

6   Conclusion

This paper showed the feasibility of discount evaluation approach with simulation of disabled user characteristics. The scope of the study included a preliminary evaluation of a communication support system, called ComMob (Communication and Mobility), intended for users with a dyskinetic Cerebral Palsy profile. A first simulation of dyskinetic Cerebral Palsy disability was implemented through involuntary movements using a pulley system. Participants had to perform a set of tasks with ComMob, while being handicapped by involuntary movements caused by an experimenter. This approach was very useful in collecting initial data (usability problems, bugs) and improving the system, before conducting evaluations with users of the targeted profile. The first results obtained are promising and it is a question of going further into depth in the analysis of the results with a view to modeling involuntary movements and studying their impact in terms of human-machine interaction.

Concerning the preliminary evaluation method that we implemented, with the introduction of involuntary movements, we aim to improve it according to the following stages:

- Work with one or more experts, from the healthcare and/or rehabilitation domains, specialized in Cerebral Palsy disability, to optimize the modeling of involuntary movements.
- Contact several users with dyskinetic cerebral palsy to help this modeling but also to deepen the knowledge of the feelings and the inter- and intra-individual variability of the use limits, with the final objective of categorizing the impacts in terms of accuracy and fatigue. The additional opinions of people present in their ecosystem (in the sense of Guffroy *et al.* [28, 29]) could prove useful to better characterize the situations concerned.
- Carry out user tests following this model by approaching ecological conditions of use, i.e. with situations requiring realistic tasks involving dialogues between disabled people and one or more interlocutors, for example: purchase of a transport ticket, request for information about a product on a store shelf, writing a Java program (only for programmer users), etc.
- Another perspective is to use this principle for the training of interactive system designers in order to raise their awareness of the characteristics of users with disabilities, by facing them directly.
- In the longer term, it would be possible to propose a robot (or a robotic articulated arm), capable of simulating involuntary movements, in order to support such evaluations. To do so, a control model would first have to be developed. This one should be configurable particularly in terms of frequency, amplitude and speed of the involuntary movements. Such an approach would move away from discount evaluation approaches.

Acknowledgment. The authors thank all the participants for giving their time to carry out the various user tests, as well as Jean-Hugues Moreau, Jean-Baptiste Orma and Maxime Wroblewski for their help in the data collection and analysis. They thank Franck Poirier for his contribution to the design of the ComMob system. The authors thank also the anonymous reviewers for their constructive comments.

References

1. Nielsen, J.: Usability Engineering. Academic Press Inc. (1994)
2. Rubin, J.: Handbook of Usability Testing: How to Plan, Design, and Conduct Effective Tests. John Wiley, New York (1994)
3. Rosenbaum, P., et al.: A report: the definition and classification of cerebral palsy. Dev. Med. Child Neurol. Suppl. **109**, 8–14 (2007)
4. GAATES, Asia Pacific Broadcasting Union, et al.: Guideline on Inclusive Disaster Risk Reduction: Early Warnings and Accessible Broadcasting (2016)
5. WHO (World Health Organization): ICD10 (International Classification of Diseases) (2010)
6. Guerrier, Y.: Proposal of a software support for information entry in degraded situations: Application for users with Cerebral Palsy athetosis in transport and daily activities (in french). Unpublished Ph.D. Thesis, Univ. of Valenciennes and Hainaut-Cambrésis, France, (2015)

7. Tuset, P., López, J.M., Barberán, P., Janer, L., Cervelló-Pastor, C.: Designing messenger visual, an instant messaging service for individuals with cognitive disability. In: International Workshop on Ambient Assisted Living, pp. 57–64. Springer, Heidelberg (2011). https://doi.org/10.1007/978-3-642-21303-8_8

8. Guerrier, Y., Naveteur, J., Kolski, C., Poirier, F.: Communication system for persons with cerebral palsy. In: Miesenberger, K., Fels, D., Archambault, D., Peňáz, P., Zagler, W. (eds.) ICCHP 2014. LNCS, vol. 8547, pp. 419–426. Springer, Cham (2014). https://doi.org/10.1007/978-3-319-08596-8_64

9. Nielsen, J.: Guerrilla HCI: using discount usability engineering to penetrate the intimidation barrier. In: Bias, R.D., Mayhew, D.J. (eds.) Cost-Justifying Usability, pp. 245–272. Academic Press (1994)

10. Curtis, B., Nielsen, J.: Applying discount usability engineering. IEEE Softw. **12**(1), 98–100 (1995)

11. Yao, P.N., Gorman, P.N.: Discount usability engineering applied to an interface for Web-based medical knowledge resources. In: AMIA 2000, American Medical Informatics Association Annual Symposium, Los Angeles, CA, USA, 4–8 November, pp. 928–932 (2000)

12. Maurer, F., Ghanam, Y.: Discount Usability Testing. Technical report 2008-06-18T17:44:31Z, University of Calgary (2007)

13. Redish, J.: A bit history of usability testing – and why it's not expensive any more (2007). http://redish.net/writingfortheweb/index.php/2007/06/10/a-bit-of-history-of-usability-testing-and-why-its-not-so-expensive-any-more, 11 November 2007. Accessed by Maurer and Ghanam [12]

14. Minear, W.L.: A classification of cerebral palsy. Pediatrics **18**(5), 841–852 (1956)

15. Himmelmann, K., Hagberg, G., Wiklund, L.M., Eek, M.N., Uvebrant, P.: Dyskinetic cerebral palsy: a population-based study of children born between 1991 and 1998. Dev. Med. Child Neurol. **49**(4), 246–251 (2007)

16. Darley, F.L., Aronson, A.E., Brown, J.R.: Differential diagnostic patterns of dysarthria. J. Speech Hear. Res. **12**(2), 246–269 (1969)

17. Monbaliu, E., et al.: Clinical presentation and management of dyskinetic cerebral palsy. Lancet Neurol. **16**(9), 741–749 (2017)

18. Adame, M.R., Yu, J., Moller, K., Seemann, E.: A wearable navigation aid for blind people using a vibrotactile information transfer system. In: 2013 ICME International Conference on Complex Medical Engineering, pp. 13–18. IEEE (2013)

19. Pietrzak, T., Crossan, A., Brewster, S.A., Martin, B., Pecci, I.: Creating usable pin array tactons for non-visual information. IEEE Trans. Haptics **2**(2), 61–72 (2009)

20. Pietrzak, T., Martin, B., Pecci, I.: Information display by dragged haptic bumps. In: Proceedings of the Enactive conference (Enactive 2005), October, Genoa, Italy (2005)

21. Lambregts, M.C.P., Raijmakers, F.D., Ramselaar, M.S., Toering, T.F.: Continuous monitoring of functional recovery of frail elderly people after treatment of a hip fracture, making use of the data of the monitor devices' Fitbit Charge HR and MOX, in order to optimize the rehabilitation process. Bachelor's thesis, University of Twente, The Netherlands (2019)

22. Marks, D.: Disability. Controversial Debates and Psychosocioal Perspectives. Routledge, London (1999)

23. Silverman, A.M.: The perils of playing blind: problems with blindness simulation, and a better way to teach about blindness section. J. Blindness Innov. Res. **5**(2) (2015). Retrieved from https://nfb.org/images/nfb/publications/jbir/jbir15/jbir050201abs.html

24. Guerrier, Y., Kolski, C., Poirier, F.: Towards a communication system for people with athetoid cerebral palsy. In: Proceedings INTERACT 2013, 14th IFIP TC 13 International Conference. LNCS, Cape Town, South Africa, 2–6 September, pp. 681–688. Springer (2013). https://doi.org/10.1007/978-3-642-40498-6_61

25. Fitts, P.M.: The information capacity of the human motor system in controlling the amplitude of movement. J. Exp. Psychol. **47**(6), 381–391 (1954)
26. Stewart, K., Harvey, A., Johnston, L.M.: A systematic review of scales to measure dystonia and choreoathetosis in children with dyskinetic cerebral palsy. Dev. Med. Child Neurol. **59**(8), 786–795 (2017)
27. Guerrier, Y., Naveteur, J., Anceaux, F., Kolski, C.: Test préliminaire de systèmes dédiés à des utilisateurs IMC, avec induction mécanique de mouvements involontaires chez des utilisateurs non atteints. IHM'2019, Proceedings of the 31st Conference on l'Interaction Homme-Machine: Adjunct, 10–13 December. ACM, Grenoble, France (2019)
28. Guffroy, M., Vigouroux, N., Kolski, C., Vella, F., Teutsch, P.: From human-centered design to disabled user & ecosystem centered design in case of assistive interactive systems. Int. J. Sociotechnol. Knowl. Dev. **9**(4), 28–42 (2017)
29. Guffroy, M., Guerrier, Y., Kolski, C., Vigouroux, N., Vella, F., Teutsch, P.: Adaptation of user-centered design approaches to abilities of people with disabilities. In: Miesenberger, K., Kouroupetroglou, G. (eds.) ICCHP 2018. LNCS, vol. 10896, pp. 462–465. Springer, Cham (2018). https://doi.org/10.1007/978-3-319-94277-3_71

Accessibility Practices for Prototype Creation and Testing

Nandita Gupta[✉] and Carrie Bruce

Georgia Institute of Technology, Atlanta, USA
`Carrie.Bruce@gatech.edu`

Abstract. The paper will share practices and processes followed for the design and prototyping stage of the digital accessibility storytelling collective project that showcased the stories and work done by various technology professionals around the globe working in digital accessibility. By being more inclusive in our processes, we can bring more people into the conversation. Thus, we aimed to bake accessibility into our processes to ensure an inclusive and accessible product. Our specific aims during this phase were: 1) Seek feedback from different users and stakeholders. 2) Ensure documentation and prioritization of accessibility issues. 3) Create an inclusive product through iterative inclusive design. Thus, the goal of this paper is to describe and share the process of building this storytelling product, followed by a discussion of the learnings from integrating accessibility into design.

Our processes led us to various insights that not only helped us improve our product, but also taught us valuable lessons for future processes. It gave us an opportunity to iterate on our product to ensure accessibility errors were documented and prioritized. Feedback sessions with users and stakeholders improved our awareness on our processes. Our later project stages, including evaluation, showed us how these design processes led to an accessible product and allowed us to capture critical issues and errors during this stage.

Keywords: Accessibility · Prototype · Processes · Usability · Human-centered design · Feedback

1 Introduction

Accessibility and inclusive design practices not only provide an enriching use experience, but also create equitable experiences for more users. Creating a good user experience for users extends the objective components of usability to consider more experiential, subjective qualities that emerge after using a digital product [1]. Usability is now the minimum; we need to create accessible user experiences so that large and diverse populations have enjoyable experiences with digital products.

There are numerous barriers for implementing these accessible practices within the workflow, and education and practice are effective tools in reducing these barriers. The lack of documentation on overall processes also leads designers down different paths, and there is a need for more documentation around practical and applied knowledge.

© Springer Nature Switzerland AG 2021
M. Antona and C. Stephanidis (Eds.): HCII 2021, LNCS 12768, pp. 89–98, 2021.
https://doi.org/10.1007/978-3-030-78092-0_6

While there is ample documentation to educate and instruct designers and researchers about accessibility design and compliance requirements, the diverse array of resources may prove overwhelming, especially for novices within accessibility. In some cases, designers and researchers may be unaware of these practices, and it makes it harder to implement accessibility on the back end of the process. In many cases, accessibility is often tied to compliance and this focus on guideline conformance may not consider context of use and provides no direct requirement to consider user experience of people with disabilities [2].

This paper touches on accessibility in multiple facets. One of them is to share accessible design practices that aided the production of an accessible and inclusive product. The other is to share the processes followed for these practices, where accessibility was baked into every aspect of those processes.

2 Background and Related Work

The industry follows various practices to ensure accessibility in their products; research, design, and testing practices, coupled with feedback loops are needed to ensure that accessibility is baked into every process. If accessibility is not included on the front end, reworking designs at a later phase has a significant negative impact on timelines, processes, and budgets. The best approach to accessible user experience is to integrate accessibility into the design and development process [3].

Several researchers have investigated the possibility of this integration within computing processes. Moreno et al. showcases the integration of usability techniques in the whole life cycle of a web application which provided a 'methodological support for the development of accessible web applications' [4]. Their work demonstrates the importance of integrating accessibility throughout various processes. It is imperative to consider accessibility in the overall software life cycle along with user interaction. However, it is important to understand that following accessibility standards does not guarantee complete accessible web applications [4]. Stephanidis et al. presented a 'preliminary collection of design-oriented guidelines and development requirements for accessibility and universal design in HCI' [5]. All these guidelines are valuable implementation-based resources that designers and developers may utilize to create accessible products. A common theme between all this work is the need to bake accessibility into all procedures and process to ensure an inclusive outcome.

Various companies, such as Microsoft and Adobe, have also shared their industry best practices for designing inclusive and accessible products. Microsoft's Inclusive Design toolkit provides different inclusive activities and methodologies that designers may use in their processes [6]. Adobe released their training materials with teachers' guide and practical exercises that demonstrate the benefits of a more inclusive design process [7]. Other companies are using these resources to kick-start their accessibility efforts.

In addition to resources developed by companies, there are other resources available to UX professionals to integrate accessibility into their processes. The Web Accessibility Initiatives Web Content Accessibility Guidelines (WCAG 2.0) are an excellent resource for designers and other implementation professionals. One of their systematic, guidelines-based approach is to map the WCAG 2.0 success criteria to the roles on the product team. The WAI-Engage Community Group is currently exploring this approach on their collaborative wiki where the success criteria are mapped to different project management, research, design, content, and development roles. While this is valuable for establishing primary roles and responsibilities within a project team, care should be taken to treat accessibility as a holistic and shared process across the project team and beyond [8].

In our case, we used these guidelines as metrics throughout the entire project – from research until implementation. We ensured that all the research insights were tied to specific design requirements, with basis in inclusive and accessible practices. Our project was focused on creating an accessible digital platform that would showcase the stories of various professionals within digital accessibility. The features on the platform tied back to those insights and requirements; the overall development and design phase was conducted with accessibility in mind. Continuous documentation of issues and backlogs, with accessibility specific requirements, were essential towards creating an accessible product.

3 Additional Project Background

Our designs were based on previous research and insights, which were then con-verted into design considerations and woven into the design process. This section will provide background on the project insights along with user needs, with additional details on design considerations based on those insights.

3.1 Summary of User Needs

While there are diverse resources available in the industry, there is a need to provide relevant resources and support for UX professionals pursuing accessibility. These resources could be provided in different forms such as interactive guides for accessibility implementation or a social media platform to connect with other accessibility professionals in the field. Currently, platforms like LinkedIn offer limited capacity to connect with likeminded professionals, and other organizations like IAAP require membership to access and connect with other members. These additional support systems and resources would not only motivate other UX professionals to continue working within the accessibility field, but also create a pipeline to introduce other UX professionals to accessibility and inclusive design processes.

3.2 Key Insights

- People: Allies and team members around accessibility influenced people's ability to work on accessibility practices. They found these interactions valuable. Users saw a need for more people-based resources around accessibility.
- Motivation: Negative experiences and detractors around implementing accessibility practices influence people's motivation towards working on accessibility practices.
- Confidence: Users' confidence on integrating accessibility practices into their current workflow was influenced by prior knowledge and practical and educational experiences.

3.3 Design Considerations

These insights led to specific design considerations that would be tied to the design. Here are the Design Considerations that emerged from various user needs:

- Design will enable a diverse audience to interact with the website without accessibility issues. It will achieve WCAG 2.1 AA compliance.
- Design will share knowledge of accessibility practices through storytelling, so as to educate users about accessibility practices and experiences.
- Design needs a way to contact the people in the stories.
- Design will include people with disabilities and their stories.
- Design will include stories from UX Researchers, Developers, Designers and Product Managers
- Design will include stories from Leadership, and other added categories of jobs within accessibility.
- Design will include stories that highlight challenges and detractors and ways to overcome them.
- Design will provide a platform to reach more allies through Storytelling.
- Design will provide a platform to find activities and spaces for accessibility work.
- Design will provide knowledge about accessibility and practices to help improve confidence for users.
- Design will provide knowledge about accessibility and practices to help improve motivation for users.
- Design will provide multiple ways to consume information.

These design considerations played a crucial role throughout the design phase as all trade-offs and decisions were taken with the above considerations in mind.

4 Methods and Processes

This section will highlight the methods used within this design stage, and how these methods were applied with inclusion in mind. We followed methods and processes through different stages of this design process to ensure accessibility was an integral part of the process. There were various pieces that contributed towards the successful creation of the storytelling collective, as seen in Fig. 1. Accessibility played an important role through each piece in this design process.

4.1 Evaluate Tools

We made the decision to evaluate tools upfront, to ensure that accessibility was considered since the early stages of the project. We considered numerous web-hosting platforms, in addition to website-building software products to host this storytelling collective. Based on the design considerations, specifically regarding accessibility support, we decided to pursue WordPress as our primary option. They not only provided various accessibility support features but also supported many templates that promised a speedy

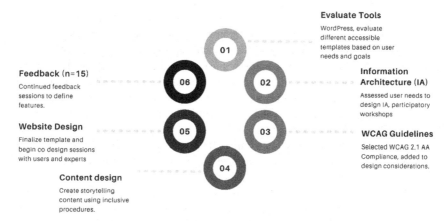

Evaluate Tools

WordPress, evaluate different accessible templates based on user needs and goals

Feedback (n=15)

Continued feedback sessions to define features.

Information Architecture (IA)

Assessed user needs to design IA, participatory workshops

Website Design

Finalize template and begin co design sessions with users and experts

WCAG Guidelines

Selected WCAG 2.1 AA Compliance, added to design considerations.

Content design

Create storytelling content using inclusive procedures.

Fig. 1. Various pieces in the design phase

development process. To select a template, we mapped the features in our design using the Minimal Viable Product (MVP) strategy that enabled feature prioritization for the MVP. This was the overall process:

1. Create a list of design considerations.
2. Brainstorm and map out features that correspond to the design considerations.
3. Finalize the features and now prepare for prioritization.
4. Involve stakeholders in prioritizing these features, and group them into primary, secondary, and tertiary needs.
5. Create a timeline and roadmap of these features and figure out the interdependencies.
6. Evaluate the timeline and document issues.

This strategy was valuable as it helped us prioritize features and manage them throughout the design cycle of this project. It ensured that accessibility was prioritized through various stages, and the tools used during this process, including design and development, were accessible. The final accessible template selection was driven by this process, as we had a clear idea of which important accessibility features were required, for example, based on our design considerations of providing content in multiple accessible formats, there was a need to ensure that the template supported audio, video as well as text formats. WordPress also provided other back-end support for accessibility and those automations were invaluable in terms of time for design and development. These constraints narrowed down our viable options and helped us made informed evidence-based decisions. Evaluating tools upfront also reduced time and effort for design and helped us constrain our design ideas later in the process.

4.2 Information Architecture (IA)

Information architecture formed the backbone of a digital website; before we finalized specific design elements, we wanted to ensure that our accessible template supported a robust information architecture. Based on previous research and user needs, we extracted specific design considerations and features that were critical within this information architecture. In addition to previous exploratory research, we held co-design sessions and participatory design workshops with users and stakeholders to gain a deeper understanding for the IA for this website. The brainstorming helped us understand different options for organizing the storytelling content, and based on the feedback we received, we organized the content with a primary navigation of categories. We provided additional flexibility for users to access content and thus, we added features like 'Search', 'Tags' and 'Recent Posts'. We also added a 'Next' button to suggest additional content. Our feedback indicated that users found all these different methods valuable. Users had unique preferences on how they preferred to consume content and providing this additional flexibility led to a richer user experience.

The design for the IA had specific accessibility considerations and features; for screen reader and keyboard users, we wanted to ensure that the IA was simplistic enough, and thus, content was organized in a structured manner with the use of Headings, so as to enable screen reader users to skip content as needed. We added a complete Site Map. All these features provided additional flexibility for these users to consume the content based on personal needs and preferences. We also removed carousels from the template, as they posed a major accessibility issue for screen reader users. Features such as 'Skip to Content' and 'Skip to Footer' were implemented as they provided flexibility for screen reader users to navigate the website.

4.3 WCAG Guidelines and Accessibility

The Web Accessibility Initiatives Web Content Accessibility Guidelines (WCAG 2.1) are an excellent resource for designers and other accessibility professionals [9]. In our case, we used these guidelines as metrics throughout the entire project – from research until implementation. We ensured that all the research insights were tied to specific design requirements, with basis in inclusive and accessible practices. Our project focused on creating an accessible digital platform that would meet WCAG 2.1 AA compliance. We sought an accessible template through the WordPress platform and pushed for feedback at every stage to ensured that users and several stakeholders were an integral part of the process through co-design sessions. One of the major features of the website was the 'Accessibility' page that included an accessibility statement with detailed information on the specific accessibility elements in this collective. This page also included information on reporting accessibility specific errors that users may face during their experience exploring the content.

We used various automated testing tools such as WAVE, Silktide, and Insights for Accessibility to catch issues during the design interaction process. Silktide is a browser extension that simulates different disabilities and conditions; we used this tool to make inclusive design decisions throughout the design and development phase. This continuous testing and audit processes were invaluable as they reduced our overall design and development time; if these issues were not fixed during these early stages, they would be harder to correct later and would negatively impact the user experience.

4.4 Content Design

Content for this website focused on gathering virtual interviews with different accessibility professionals in the field who worked across various UX roles. These interviews would then be processed into consumable information that would be featured on the website.

To create content, we started with curating a list of questions that would be included within the storytelling collective. The initial questions were created based on previous research and user needs. We also conducted participatory workshops with several experts within the accessibility field, who added their thoughts to these questions based on their expertise. The questions were modified based on the feedback received during these sessions. Even though we had a final draft of questions, during the interviews for content creation with the expert, we followed an overall 80/20 rule where 80% of the questions would be the same across all interviews and 20% would be unique to the person we were interviewing. For example, Leaders would have slightly different questions as compared to Designers, but overall, 80% of the questions were same across all roles.

Once the overall questions were finalized, we followed this process to create content for the website:

- We set up interviews with experts through Calendly or emails, to select a time slot for 45 min.
- The interview was recorded and held through Microsoft Teams.
- Post recording, we requested additional information such as personal website links, photographs etc. that would be added to the collective with their interview.
- We then created subtitles, Video transcriptions, Interview Highlights for each interview and these were then posted on the Shakti Collective Website.

During the overall process to create content, we ensured that tools used were accessible by users. The interviewees were given all the information regarding the interview, questions, format etc. upfront. We utilized accessibility features found in software, such a Microsoft Teams' in-built captions feature, during these interviews and provided additional support and accomodations as needed. For the participatory design workshops, we used accessible tools for experts and engagement.

There were several ways in which we made the content on the website accessible; the virtual interviews were recorded through Microsoft Teams, and each interview was converted into an accessible text transcript. We added closed captions to the videos, and additionally, pulled information from the interviews to provide them in an accessible manner on the website.

4.5 Website Design

The website design process began after content creation had started, as the content drove all the design decisions. After we successfully finalized the accessible template, we used the data from our feedback sessions, as well as co-design sessions with designers to create a prototype. Additionally, we utilized WordPress Accessibility features for their websites, where they automatically implemented navigation features such as 'Skip to Content' for screen-reader users using the website. We did not utilize all default template features, as we found them lacking; although the template was accessible, some features such as carousels, led to a negative user experience for screen-reader users. The colors were modified to ensure an appropriate contrast for users, and color pickers were useful during this stage of the process. We used Headings to create visual hierarchy and additionally used colors to differentiate between elements, as well as to highlight certain aspects on the page; we ensured that the colors and contrast on the page would remain accessible in black and white mode as well. This prototype underwent many iterations, and eventually led to the creation of the MVP.

The WCAG Guidelines not only aided in the design but also development aspects for the website. We utilized specific guidance for WCAG 2.1 AA compliance for website design. We incorporated continued testing using automated tools and wanted to ensure that the website was accessibility through a multitude of platforms and devices.

4.6 Feedback

We sought feedback at every stage and ensured that users and several stakeholders were given the opportunity to co-design on the product. These sessions were conducted every week, throughout the development and design phase of the website. This was imperative as we wanted to prevent designer bias throughout the project life cycle. In addition to automated tools, we invited numerous experts within intersectional fields of Storytelling, User Experience (UX) Research, UX Design, Product Management, and Accessibility Specialist to give us feedback throughout the various iterations of the website. In addition to experts, some of these participants also intersected with the user group. This process ensured that the user needs were front and center throughout the process. We conducted around sixteen informal feedback sessions with different professionals in the fields with varied roles such as designers, storytellers, researchers, developers, accessibility specialists, and many more. We did not ask participants to identify a label for gender. Participants were recruited through previous exploratory research interviews, accessibility-related conferences (e.g., UX Hustle, Disability: IN), social media (i.e., LinkedIn, Facebook), online groups (e.g., a11y), word-of-mouth, and personal referrals.

These sessions were inclusive and accessible to participants. We ensured the use of inclusive language, in addition to accessible tools. These sessions were held virtually, and participants identified numerous issues on the website that were resolved during this iterative design process. Due to the diverse participants in these feedback sessions, we received critical feedback that shaped the iterations for the MVP. Some participants who included people with disabilities, weighed in on specific accessibility features of the design and helped us test the website using various assistive technology devices. All these sessions played a vital role to ensure accessibility throughout the design phase.

5 Discussion

This overall process was valuable as it showed us the gaps and opportunities in our design throughout the iterations. Various users utilized different methods to navigate the website including NVDA screen readers, keyboard, mouse, and touch screen through their personal devices to navigate and explore the website. These diverse methods gave us a deep understanding of overall user interaction and enabled us to enrich their experiences on varied platforms and interactions. We also found certain limitations of the platform, where we were unable to fix those issues and concerns, and thus, chose to completely change the design to eliminate the problem. For example, the template had an in-built carousel which passed the automated accessibility testing requirements but proved to be a screen reader nightmare during user feedback sessions. Another interesting finding through this process was regarding the use of accessible overlays. Even though website overlay solutions have become incredibly popular, they fail to protect website owners from litigation, and fail to serve people with disabilities [10]. We avoided using these overlays and aimed to meet WCAG 2.1 AA compliance or our design. Thus, it was imperative to ensure that user and expert testing was included in addition to automated testing. Each iteration of the product was tested and as the website evolved, we created new interaction patterns based on previous experiences – both negative and positive.

Although we went through rigorous testing and iteration, there were certain issues that our process did not capture. There were certain features that users did not access during the feedback sessions, and these issues emerged later during other stages of the project. For example, Video Headings were not created during the design and development phase as an additional means to navigate the page using a screen reader. Users did not access this feature and thus, as we did not receive input, this was an issue that was undiscovered until later. Thus, this showed the importance of including accessibility through each phase of the project as the issues and challenges would have been far greater by excluding accessibility. Another challenge we encountered was the balance between usability and accessibility; it was imperative to ensure that one does not overpower the other. Even though some features successfully passed the accessibility check, through those feedback sessions, we realized that they did not equate to a pleasant user experience. For example, when we created transcriptions of the video interviews, we added timings before the speaker IDs. While this was not an issue for a visual reader, this became frustrating for screen reader users who heard the name and time with each sentence.

6 Conclusion

While these are various testing resources for accessibility in the market, there is always a need to ensure co-design and continuous feedback mechanisms within the design process through successive iterations. It is easier to make changes during the iterations, as compared to waiting to get feedback in the end after the design has been completed. More companies need to step forward and adopt accessible practices and share their journey and experiences with other industries and companies. As accessibility becomes more prevalent within the technology field, we will see a dramatic improvement within overall usability and user experience of products we use.

All UX Professionals have a responsibility to create inclusive products; in order to do so, we need to incorporate accessibility and inclusive design within all processes. It is imperative to include accessibility in all processes throughout the design and development life cycle, as every stage will have unique challenges associated with it.

References

1. Hassenzahl, M.: User experience and experience design. In: Soegaard, M., Dam, R. (eds.) The Encyclopedia of Human-Computer Interaction, 2nd edn. Aarhus, Denmark. The Interaction Design Foundation (2013). Accessed 20 Feb 2021. http://www.interaction-design.org/encyclopedia/user_experience_and_experience_design.html
2. Sloan, D., Kelly, B.: Web Accessibility Metrics for a Post Digital World. Presented at W3C Web Accessibility Initiative Research and Development Working Group Website Accessibility Metrics Online Symposium, 5 December 2011 (2011). Accessed 20 Feb 2021 http://opus.bath.ac.uk/27541/
3. Horton, S.: Accessibility in Practice: A process-driven approach to accessibility. https://developer.paciellogroup.com/blog/2014/03/accessibility-practice-process-driven-approach-accessibility/
4. Moreno, L., Martínez, P., Ruiz-Mezcua, B.: Integrating HCI in a web accessibility engineering approach. In: Stephanidis, C. (ed.) UAHCI 2009. LNCS, vol. 5616, pp. 745–754. Springer, Heidelberg (2009). https://doi.org/10.1007/978-3-642-02713-0_79
5. Stephanidis, C., Akoumianakis, D., Sfyrakis, M., Paramythis, A.: Universal accessibility in HCI: process-oriented design guidelines and tool requirements (1998)
6. Microsoft Inclusive Design. https://www.microsoft.com/design/inclusive/
7. Adobe Accessibility Resources. https://www.adobe.com/accessibility/resources.html
8. Accessibility Responsibility Breakdown. WAI-Engage Community Group. Accessed 20 Feb 2021. http://www.w3.org/community/wai-engage/wiki/Accessibility_Responsibility_Breakdown
9. Web Content Accessibility Guidelines (WCAG 2.1). https://www.w3.org/TR/WCAG21/
10. Why Accessibility Overlay Solutions Fail to Protect or Serve. https://www.accessibility.works/blog/avoid-accessibility-overlay-tools-toolbar-plugins/

Methods of Usability Testing for Users with Cognitive Impairments

Cathleen Schöne[✉], Ulrike Große, Alexander Wölfel, and Heidi Krömker

Technische Universität Ilmenau, PF 10 05 65, 98684 Ilmenau, Germany
{cathleen.schoene,ulrike.grosse,alexander.woelfel,
heidi.kroemker}@tu-ilmenau.de

Abstract. One challenge of the user-centered development of accessible information systems is the conduction of cognitively impaired persons in usability tests. The paper gathers existing guidelines for the application of usability testing with cognitively impaired people and shows empirical values for modified usability tests based on a case study. In addition, the advantages and disadvantages of on site and remote usability testing are presented in a comparative study. Especially in the context of COVID-19, remote testing has gained in relevance in the present time.

Keywords: Usability testing · Accessibility · Cognitively impaired persons · Remote testing

1 Introduction and Research Question

In the context of this paper, the application of usability testing for users with cognitive impairments was investigated. There are a variety of established methods, but most of them do not consider impaired people. According to the Federal Statistical Office, around 7.9 million severely impaired people live in Germany. This results in a share of 9.5% of the total population. These people often have physical impairments and/or cerebral disorders. Around 13% of the severely impaired people are cognitively impaired, which results in a number of 1.03 million people (see Fig. 1) [1, 2]. Their mental or emotional health is not in balance and must be considered individually. These statistics refer to Germany only, as there are country-specific classification and rating systems for impairments and cognitive impairment. For example in the development of websites or applications, these physical and cognitive aspects have a variety of effects regarding to the requirements in information design. Too little attention is paid to them in order to ensure accessibility of digital information. Not only cognitively impaired people would experience a great advantage from appropriate consideration. The adaptations would mostly also be helpful for other user groups e.g. children or elderly people. There are already guidelines, such as the Web Content Accessibility Guidelines [3], which are an international standard for the accessible design of websites and other web contents. Appropriate websites are thus accessible to people with sensory and motor (and to some extent mental) impairments, e.g. they can grasp the digital information offered and make

M. Antona and C. Stephanidis (Eds.): HCII 2021, LNCS 12768, pp. 99–115, 2021.
https://doi.org/10.1007/978-3-030-78092-0_7

necessary inputs. User-centered development also takes into account the requirements and abilities of the intended target group. By involving the target group, for example in requirements analyses and usability tests, the individual abilities of end users are recognized and taken into account in the development of websites and applications.

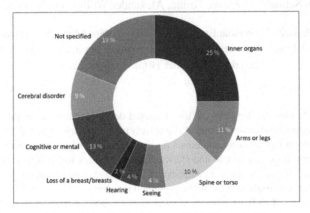

Fig. 1. Types of impairment 2019 Germany [2]

The empirical evaluation of two applications has raised the question of feasible testing methods. It is necessary to investigate how usability testing methods need and can be adapted accordingly to the linguistic, emotional, and cognitive abilities of users with cognitive impairments. Due to COVID-19, part of the tests were conducted as remote tests. Therefore, the possibilities and limitations of remote testing with the target group were also examined in more detail, as this form of testing has gained relevance in times of COVID-19. Therefore, this paper deals with the two research questions:

How must usability testing be modified for cognitively impaired persons?

What are the advantages and disadvantages of on site and remote usability testing for cognitively impaired persons?

The aim of the work is to define and test the modification of usability testing for persons with cognitive impairments. In addition, the application of on site and remote usability testing is compared. It will become evident that it is quite possible to test with cognitive impaired people. Adjustments have to be made to the concept and process of testing. This will be discussed in detail in the course of the paper.

2 Related Work

On the basis of the foregoing explanations, the target group of cognitively impaired persons is first examined in more detail as an important component of testing. There are various procedures as a tool for assessing the competencies of cognitively impaired people. They lead to a better understanding of the user group of cognitively impaired people and are summarized below. In addition, existing work such as studies and guidelines for the use of usability testing with cognitively impaired people will be examined and related to the procedure and aspects of usability testing.

2.1 Analysis of Procedures for the Assessment of People with Impairments

The well-founded definition of the target group is essential for the application of usability testing. Cognitive impairment is defined as a collective term for impairments in external and internal information processing in the brain. Briefly summarized, a cognitive disorder has an impact on a person's thinking, which mainly affects the functions of perception, attention, memory, action planning, judgment, problem solving, and communication [4]. Experts in the healthcare field use various procedures as a tool to assess individuals with cognitive impairment. For a better understanding a short selection is summarized in Table 1. Basically, these are needs-based individualized tests that aim at a holistic assessment of the person and his or her behavior, as well as his or her support needs and requirements for the daily and working routine. In Germany, there is no consensus on which procedure should be preferred.

Table 1. Short selection of tools to assess the abilities of individuals with cognitive impairment

Procedure	What is determined?
Werdenfels Test Battery [5]	This quantitative test procedure allows differentiated statements to be made about cognitive-intellectual abilities of people with impairments. The WTB includes different subtests such as Orientation, Memory, Number Knowledge, Language, Reading/Comprehension or Fine Motor Skills
Competence analysis [6]	The focus of the competence analysis is on cognition, motor skills and social-emotional development. Aspects such as self-assessment, resilience, tolerance situation, conflict ability and independence of the cognitively impaired persons are determined within this framework
CogniFit's cognitive assessment battery [7]	The CogniFit Cognitive Assessment Battery (CAB) is a complete neurocognitive test to identify cognitive impairment in individuals with or without disease. Different items are tested such as Memory, Attention, Perception, Coordination and Logical reasoning
Bochum matrix test [8]	The Bochum matrix test is a language-free procedure for assessing general intelligence and intelligence capacity in the high cognitive performance range. The use of test items based exclusively on shapes and figures allows an assessment of cognitive ability independent of formal educational processes

In addition to cognitive impairment, most people have other disorders. For example, a combination with physical impairments is common. Collectively, people with cognitive impairment can be classified into different levels of intelligence impairment. The

World Health Organization (WHO) defines intelligence impairment as a developmental manifestation, arrested or incomplete development of mental abilities with a particular impairment of skills that contribute to the level of intelligence, such as cognition, language, motor and social skills [9]. These levels describe the intelligence age of a person compared to the age of a child. This shows that a comparison is often made between people with impairments and children.

In Germany, the latest figures from 2016 show that to date 680 workshops belonged to the Federal Association of Workshops for People with Impairments, in which a total of 308.691 people with impairments worked, of whom the clear majority 76% were affected by cognitive impairments (see Fig. 2) [10]. In order to be able to properly assess the abilities of cognitively impaired test users, a longer period of time, expert knowledge and a certain connection with the test users are furthermore needed. This is difficult to achieve as an external person, which is why cooperation with care institutions such as workshops for impaired people is essential. The workshops regularly carry out analyses and tests. As already mentioned, which procedures are used differs from institution to institution, at least here in Germany.

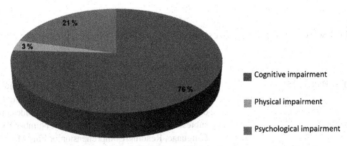

Fig. 2. People with impairments in workshops for people with impairments 2016 by types of impairment [10]

2.2 Analysis of the Procedure and Aspects of Usability Testing

Usability testing is a method in which experiments are conducted with users of an application using specific test tasks in order to identify usability problems. Representative users of the application are given specific and typical tasks to perform with the application. The users are observed while performing the tasks. The aim of usability tests is to obtain feedback from future users at an early stage of product development in order to increase usability and thus customer acceptance through product improvements. The procedure of usability testing can be divided into three main steps - preparation, realization and evaluation. The actions inherent in each of the three steps is shown in Fig. 3.

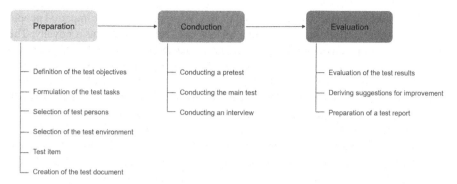

Fig. 3. Own depiction of usability testing procedure based on [11]

Next, related work in the context of usability testing with cognitively impaired persons is discussed. In relation to this specific test user group, different guidelines and studies consider various test recommendations with regard to user requirements and needs. A paper by Imke Niediek [12] deals with questions and supporting techniques in interviews with cognitively impaired people. In addition to the aspect of the question format, Tassé et al. refer in their Guidelines for Interviewing People with Impairments [13] to the relevance of further aspects such as processing time and respondent rapport when conducting interviews and represent a certain interviewer etiquette. Even though the question format is an important part of testing, the usability factor, which means the actual testing of applications or interfaces with cognitively impaired people, is missing in the sources mentioned so far. Mostly, such usability tests only involve elderly people and/or people with learning impairments. An example of this is a usability test of information technology applications with learners with special educational needs conducted by Williams and Nicholas [14]. In the same year Williams published *Developing methods to evaluate web usability with people with learning difficulties* and also provided insights there into "A number of key themes emerged, including the nature of the tasks encountered, engagement, relevance to needs and the role of supporters" [15]. Another test by Williams and Shekhar [16] focuses on testing the usability of a Touch-Screen Interface of Smartphones with people with learning impairments. In view of the current COVID-19 situation, remote tests have regained relevance and can certainly be conducted with cognitively impaired people, as the paper will show in the further course. Conducting remote usability tests with impaired people is by no means new. Already in 2006, Petrie, Hamilton, King and Pavan published an article on this topic, which provides "[…] a set of principles for local and remote evaluations with impaired users […]" [17].

These studies and guidelines show that the inclusion of cognitively impaired people in interviews and usability tests is comparatively rare, but by no means a novelty. The creation and conduction of suitable test concepts brings with it some challenges, but with the right knowledge about the abilities of the user group of cognitively impaired people and the corresponding adaptations to them, it is just as possible as with any other user group. Nevertheless, they are more likely to be involved in interviews, some of which are used to assess their own abilities or to get their opinions on issues. However, the involvement of cognitively impaired people in usability tests is rare and tends to focus on people with learning impairments. Therefore, usability tests with cognitively impaired people who also have severe intelligence impairments seem to represent a research gap. In light of the desired inclusion of people with impairments and the advancement of accessibility, however, this represents an important element in achieving it.

Table 2 lists guidelines and studies on the respective phases of usability testing from which recommendations can be derived. It is shown which abilities of cognitively impaired people can be better taken into account by modifying the procedure of usability testing.

Table 2. Extracted recommendations to the consideration of usability testing with cognitively impaired persons

Preparation		Reference
Definition of test objectives	No modification	
Formulation of test tasks	• for constant motivation, the tasks should be of personal relevance • for constant attention and readiness, no underchallenge should occur • for better understanding test task and assessment must be described in detail and in Easy Language • for consideration of the limited attention span, the frequency of the questioning should be modified	Williams [15] Tassé et al. [13]
Selection of test persons	No modification	
Selection of the test environment	• for better communication and interaction individual assistive tools should be considered (e.g. Talkers) • for feeling of safety a familiar environment should be preferred	Petrie et al. [17] Tassé et al. [13]
Test item	No modification	
Creation of tests documents	• for consideration of a lower frustration tolerance technical equipment and necessary materials are organized, tested and provided in advance (especially with regard to remote tests)	Petrie et al. [17]

(*continued*)

Table 2. (*continued*)

Preparation		Reference
Conduction		
Conducting a pretest	Modifications according to the main test	
Conducting the main test	• for feeling of safety/familiarity and improvement of communication the presence of caregivers and supporters is helpful • for preventing deviations from the test concept caregivers and supporters need to be briefed and prepared • for a smooth test conduction aspects of engagement and motivation should be maintained • for consideration of the limited attention span and combinability, the test procedure should be designed in order to question immediately after the task • for a smooth test conduction the primary form of communication, such as signing, spoken language, pictures, or writing should be maintained	Williams [15] Tassé et al. [13] Niediek [12]
Conducting an interview	• for adequate assessments, the question format should be modified → closed question formats are the easiest to answer e.g. yes/no questions, choice questions or scaled assessment questions → open questions are only partly feasible, as they are more difficult to answer • for adequate assessments, appropriate question wording and techniques for visualization and verbalization are helpful • for consideration of the limited attention span and combinability, the frequency of the questioning should be increased and the time span for answering should be extended • for respect and appreciation it is important to follow an interview etiquette in order to consider people's abilities and limitations without being condescending • for feeling of safety/familiarity and improvement of communication a high level of rapport and trust between the interviewer and the cognitively impaired person positively influences the interview	Niediek [12] Tassé et al. [13]
Evaluation		
Evaluation of the test results	No modification	
Deriving suggestion for improvement	No modification	
Preparation of a test report	No modification	

Based on the information obtained from the Related Works mentioned above, as well as through close cooperation and consultation with caregivers of cognitively impaired test users, test concepts for usability tests with cognitively impaired persons could be developed and conducted. Detailed explanations on this follow in the next sections.

3   Method

In the next step, the paper examines the conduction of the modifications for usability tests with cognitively impaired test users within the framework of its own case study, which were determined on the basis of the analysis of the guidelines and assessment procedures for cognitively impaired people. The case study compares the application in an on site test and a remote test and critically examines the advantages and disadvantages.

3.1   Case Study – Modified Usability Testing

Two usability tests were conducted with cognitively impaired users. The on site test was conducted with 6 test users, referred to below as test group A, and the remote test was conducted with 34 test users, referred to below as test group B.

As already mentioned there are no uniform standards to assess the abilities of cognitively impaired people. Regarding the test groups the assessment was based on competence analysis and the Werdenfels Test Battery (WBT) for measuring cognitive-intellectual abilities of people with impairments (see Fig. 4) [5].

"The WTB includes the following subtests: Temporal Orientation, Spatial Orientation, Auditory Memory, Visual Memory, Episodic Memory, Number Knowledge, Series Formation, Quantity Comprehension, Arithmetic Tasks, Factual Tasks, Articulation Language, Nominative Function Language, Vocabulary, Concept Formation, Situation/Content Comprehension, Task Comprehension, Reading/Comprehension, Visual Differentiation, Consistency and Reflection, Fine Motor Skills" [5].

	Independence	Scheduling	Memory	Self-assessment	Tolerance of frustration	Contact ability	Cooperation	Conflict ability	Tolerance	Punctuality	Reliability	Resilience	Endurance	Flexibility
Test person 1	3,25	3,25	3,75	3,75	3,25	2,75	3	2	2,75	3,5	3	2,5	3,25	3
Test person 2	1,75	1,75	1,75	1,5	1,75	1,75	2,25	2,5	2	2	1,75	2	2	2
Test person 3	2,5	1,25	2,25	1,75	2,25	2,5	2,25	2,25	2,25	2,5	2,25	1,5	1,5	2,25
Test person 4	2,5	1,5	2,5	2,25	4,75	2,5	2,25	3,25	3,25	3	3	2,5	1,75	1,25
Test person 5	2,5	1,25	3,5	1,5	2,5	2,75	1,75	3	3,5	3	2,5	2	2,5	3,25
Test person 6	3,5	1,5	2,5	3	2,5	3,5	2,5	3	1,5	0,75	2	2,5	3,5	4,5
Test person 7	4	3,5	3,5	3,5	4	3,75	3,5	4	3,5	4	3,5	4,25	2,5	4
Test person 8	2,75	1,5	2,75	2,5	2,25	2,75	2,75	3	2	3	2,25	1,5	1,5	2,5
Test person 9	2,5	0,75	3,25	1,5	1	3,25	1,25	0,75	2	1,75	1	1	0,75	1,5
Test person 10	1	1	2,25	1,5	1,75	3,25	1,5	1,25	0,75	1,5	1,5	1	1,5	1,5
Test person 11	3,75	2,25	2,25	3,5	2,5	3,25	2,75	1,75	2	3,25	1,25	2,5	2,5	2,5
Test person 12	3,5	2	4	4	4	4	3	2,5	3,5	3,5	4	4	3	4
Test person 13	2,5	1	3,5	2	2,25	2,25	3,25	2,25	0,75	1,5	2,5	2,5	2,5	3,75
Test person 14	5	3	4	2,75	3,25	3	4	4	3	2,75	3	3	3	4
Test person 15	2,25	1,75	2	1,25	1,5	2	1	1,5	2,25	3	2,75	2,75	2,5	3
Test person 16	2,5	1,25	2,75	1,5	1,25	2,5	1,75	2,5	1,75	2,5	1,5	1,5	1,5	1,75
Test person 17	0,75	0,25	0,75	0,5	1,25	1,25	0,75	1,5	1,5	2,5	0,75	0,75	1,25	0,5
Test person 18	4,25	0,5	3,5	2	1	2	2	0,5	0,75	0,75	1,75	0,75	0,75	3,25
Test person 19	4	3,5	4	4	3,75	3	3,5	3,5	3,25	3,25	3	4,25	3	3,5
Test person 20	5	3,5	4,5	3	2	4	3,5	3,5	4	4	2,5	3	2	3,75
Test person 21	2,25	0,5	0,75	0,75	0,5	1,5	1,25	1,5	1,75	0,5	1	0,5	0,75	0,75

Fig. 4. Extract from the WTB, conducted with one of the test groups (Color figure online)

The test users were selected in close consultation with the caregivers. Based on the cognitive impairments of the test users identified by them, a cross-section of possible cognitive impairments within test groups could be presented. However, the caregivers were not only involved in the selection of the test subjects, but also in the entire test conception and conduction. Only in this way was it possible to modify the tests to suit the test groups. As introductory examples, only two modifications are briefly mentioned here:

The phrasing of the test instructions had to be clear, short, in simple words and unambiguous. In order to achieve this, it was necessary to discuss in advance with the caregivers how Easy Language needs to be applied and what vocabulary needs to be used in the institution.

The phrasing of the test questions also had to be clear, short, in simple words and unambiguous. It had to be clarified in advance with the caregivers what evaluations the cognitively impaired test users are capable of. In this case, it was not possible to go beyond a three-scaled evaluation - good/neutral/bad or yes/maybe/no. In the case that test persons could not speak, symbols (tick, cross, thumbs up, thumbs down, thumbs horizontal) in combination with emoticons (smiling, grumpy, neutral) and color gradations (red, green, yellow) were prepared in advance (to open up a communication channel for the test persons. It was also important to ensure that the symbols were familiar and common, as they can differ from one institution to another.

These two examples already show very clearly that the modifications with regard to the cognitive impairments of the test users are necessary in order to make the conduction of a usability test possible. The following section therefore deals in more detail with the conduction of the modifications in the on site and remote tests carried out as part of the case study.

3.2 Case Study – On Site vs. Remote

In the case study, the modifications for usability tests with cognitively impaired test persons were carried out both on site and remotely, and compared to determine the advantages and disadvantages of the two options.

During the on site test, there were always two persons from the test team, one cognitively impaired test user and a caregiver for the test user in one room. During the remote test, one cognitively impaired test user and a caregiver were on site in a workshop for impaired people. Two persons from the test team were remotely connected. In the scope of both tests the app to be tested was made available to the test user on a tablet. The setup of both tests can be seen in Fig. 5 and Fig. 6.

In accordance with the preparation of the usability testing procedure mentioned under related works, Table 3 lists the modifications that were made to the individual phases of the usability tests on the part of the on site test and on the part of the remote test.

4   Results

After completion of the tests, it becomes clear that usability tests with cognitively impaired people are entirely feasible. There were no drop-outs during the tests, to which

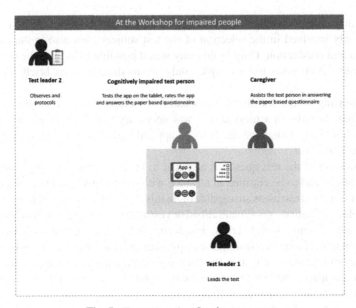

Fig. 5. Test group A – On site test setup

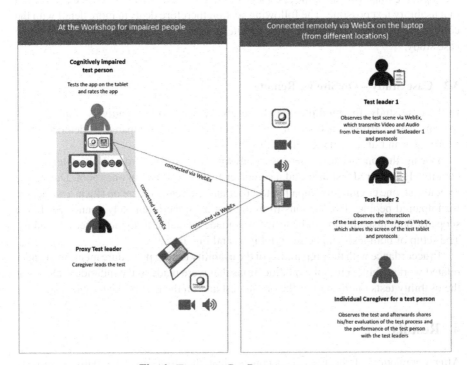

Fig. 6. Test group B – Remote test setup

Table 3. Modifications of usability testing procedure - On site vs. Remote

	On site – test group A	Remote – test group B
Preparation		
Definition of test objectives	Testing an application on effectiveness, efficiency and satisfaction Testing conditions for usability tests with cognitively impaired test users	
Formulation of test tasks	• to gain a better understanding of the abilities and needs, the formulation was realized in close consultation with the caregivers • to ensure the understanding of the test tasks Easy Language was used e.g. short sentences, familiar and short words • not to strain the limited attention span the frequency of the questioning should be modified • to enable a better communication and interaction in case of limited language and reading comprehension, icons and symbols were prepared • to handle non-comprehension at the first attempt, alternative rephrasing were prepared • to take different impairments into account and enable a successful evaluation, different alternatives were offered, which the test persons were allowed to select independently or use in combination e.g. language/communication, ratings by symbols and icons as paper based and digital mean	
	• for constant motivation a playful task was entered into the app	• for constant motivation a task from their everyday life was entered into the app
Selection of test persons	• in consultation with caregivers based on competence analysis of and assessment procedures for cognitively impaired people • 6 test persons - 2 women, 4 men → 2 test persons with a mild intelligence impairment → 4 test persons with a medium intelligence impairment	• in consultation with caregivers based on competence analysis of and assessment procedures for cognitively impaired people • 34 test persons - 13 women, 21 men → 11 test persons with a mild intelligence impairment → 22 test persons with a medium intelligence impairment → 1 test person with a severe intelligence impairment
Selection of the test environment	• to provide a feeling of safety/stability, to avoid distraction and to include test persons, who can't travel a familiar environment was chosen = workshop for impaired people • to test the app, the test persons are given a tablet • to raise motivation/interest and to enable test persons who cannot articulate clearly or at all clickable symbols/icons are provided on the tablet for the evaluation • enable non-speaking people to express themselves verbally assistive technology can be used (e.g. Talkers) • 1 test person • 2 test leader • 1 caregiver as emotional support and, if necessary, to support communication and interaction with the test person	• to provide a feeling of safety/stability, to avoid distraction and to include test persons, who can't travel a familiar environment was chosen = workshop for impaired people • to test the app, the test persons are given a tablet • to raise motivation/interest and to enable test persons who cannot articulate clearly or at all a second tablet with clickable symbols/icons is provided for the evaluation • a laptop is placed in the room as mean of communication and observation for test leaders → WebEx was installed to make this possible 1 test user on site • 1 caregiver as proxy test leader on site • 2 test leader remotely connected • 1 individual caregiver remotely connected just for observation and evaluation after the test
Test item	Testing a prototype of an application	
Creation of tests documents	• in consultation with caregivers • to ease communication and interaction different forms of assistance were prepared - pictures, symbols, other means of communication digital and/or paper based to ensure a smooth test procedure and to avoid disturbance and misguided interference the participation of caregivers were regulated in advance (specify whether, when and how they may interact with the test person and the test item) – checklist • test instructions • test tasks • observation protocols • questionnaire • to enable the planned test persons to take part in the test, their guardians had to sign the consent forms in advance on their behalf	• in consultation with caregivers • to ease communication and interaction different forms of assistance were prepared - pictures, symbols, other means of communication digital and/or paper based • to ensure a smooth test procedure and to avoid disturbance and misguided interference the participation of caregivers were regulated in advance (specify whether, when and how they may interact with the test person and the test item) – checklist instructions for the proxy test leader • test instructions • test tasks • observation protocols • evaluation questions • to enable the planned test persons to take part in the test, their guardians had to sign the consent forms in advance on their behalf

(*continued*)

Table 3. (*continued*)

	On site – test group A	Remote – test group B
Conduction		
Conducting a pretest	Modifications according to the main test	
Conducting the main test	• to provide orientation a brief introduction about the aim of the test, prototype and task was held • to facilitate a smooth test procedure, test leader 1 guides through the test to counteract problems of understanding and to direct attention the test tasks were read aloud slowly and clearly • to better assess the test person and their interaction without distraction, test leader 2 observes and protocols without actively participating in the test (critical incidents are noted in an observation sheet) • to provide emotional support and a feeling of safety a caregiver is present and supports the communication between test leader and test user (under pre-regulated conditions) • to ease communication and interaction and to maintain interest and motivation different forms of evaluation were provided → clickable familiar Emojis combined with familiar symbols and colors were provided on the tablet (yes, no, maybe/good, medium, bad) → familiar Emojis combined with familiar symbols and colors were provided on paper to point at (yes, no, maybe/good, medium, bad) → verbally using simple words and rating levels (yes, no, maybe/good, medium, bad) • to avoid confusion and to save attention for the test no demographic data was collected provided in advance by the caregivers not to strain the limited attention span and memory the frequency of the questioning was shortened	• to provide orientation a brief introduction about the aim of the test, prototype and task was held • to facilitate a smooth test procedure, proxy test leader guides through the test and at the same time provides emotional support and stability due to his dual role as a caregiver • to ensure a uniform performance of tests the proxy test leader adheres to previously agreed and written instructions and formulations • to counteract problems of understanding and to direct attention the test tasks were read aloud slowly and clearly • to capture and assess the test person and their interaction without distraction, test leader 1 observes the test scene via WebEx/Laptop and protocols without actively participating in the test (critical incidents are noted in an observation sheet) • to capture and assess the interaction with the app test leader 2 observes the shared tablet screen via WebEx/Laptop and protocols without actively participating in the test (critical incidents are noted in an observation sheet) • to better asses the performance of the test person their individual caregiver were also remotely connected • to ease communication and interaction and to maintain interest and motivation different forms of evaluation were provided → clickable familiar Emojis combined with familiar symbols and colors were provided on the tablet (yes, no, maybe/good, medium, bad) → familiar Emojis combined with familiar symbols and colors were provided on paper to point at (yes, no, maybe/good, medium, bad) → verbally using simple words and rating levels (yes, no, maybe/good, medium, bad) • to avoid confusion and to save attention for the test no demographic data was collected → provided in advance by the caregivers • not to strain the limited attention span and memory the frequency of the questioning was shortened
Conducting an interview	• to ease the communication and evaluation closed question formats were used • to ease communication and maintain motivation test persons could use digital and/or paper based means to answer and share their opinion • to facilitate the answering of questions, a maximum of 3-part answer options were offered (yes, no, maybe/good, medium, bad) • to ensure stability test leader 1 follows an prepared interview guide • for feeling of safety/familiarity and improvement of communication a caregiver supports the test person in answering under predefined conditions	• to ease the communication and evaluation closed question formats were used • to ease communication and maintain motivation test persons could use digital and/or paper based means to answer and share their opinion • to facilitate the answering of questions, a maximum of 3-part answer options were offered (yes, no, maybe/good, medium, bad) • to ensure stability the proxy test leader follows an prepared interview guide and supports under predefined conditions the test person
Evaluation		
Evaluation of the test results	• evaluation of the answers • evaluation of completed and cancelled tasks • evaluation of critical incidents	• evaluation of the answers • evaluation of completed and cancelled tasks • evaluation of critical incidents • after the test, the remotely connected caregiver was asked to assess the test behavior of the test persons in order to compare whether facial expressions, gestures, emotions and reactions were correctly understood and interpreted by the test administration
Deriving suggestions for improvement	No modifications	
Preparation of a test report	No modifications	

the modifications and the involvement of caregivers contributed decisively. The modifications made regarding the common usability testing procedure have proven to be purposeful, but the qualitative evaluation makes it clear that they still need to be fine-tuned to the needs of the cognitively impaired people.

4.1 Case Study – Modified Usability Testing – Advantages and Disadvantages

Based on the previous explanations of the modifications made to the usability tests, one factor has emerged as crucial - the cooperation with the caregivers. This plays an important role throughout the entire usability test procedure, as only they know the full extent of the test persons' characteristics and abilities. This means that their assessments and support are not only necessary during the preparations, but also during the conduction and evaluation of the tests. Through consultation with the caregivers, the test leaders obtain a comprehensive picture of which cognitive impairments the test persons are subject to and which measures must be taken to compensate them within the scope of the usability test.

With regard to the test preparations, most of the modifications proved to be successful and sufficient. In particular, the formulation of the test instructions and questions in Easy Language with familiar vocabulary and simplified rating options, as well as the reading aloud by the test leader and the decision to conduct the tests in an environment familiar to the test persons, enabled and facilitated the attention and understanding of, as well as the communication with, the test persons. The cognitively impaired test persons were mostly able to understand and implement the test tasks directly at the first attempt. In particular, the use of simplified and familiar terms to make partial aspects of the prototype comprehensible proved helpful (e.g. avoiding Anglicism). However, one aspect that can be better adjusted to the target group is the procedure for obtaining the consent of the test persons to participate in the tests. Although it is correct and obligatory to obtain consent through the legal guardian, it would be motivating for test persons with less severe limitations and, moreover, beneficial for the feeling of independence if they were also given a consent form and had it signed, even if the test persons can only sign with an X. It should be noted here that it must be discussed with the caregiver beforehand which of the cognitively impaired test persons would find this procedure motivating and which would find it rather unsettling.

With regard to the test conduction, it becomes clear that the test leader plays a much more important role than usual in the context of usability tests with cognitively impaired people. For the test leader, a deeper understanding of the test conduction is required, since every aspect, no matter how small, must be taken into account and a multitude of prepared alternatives must be worked with in order to enable interactions and evaluations despite limited communication and combination ability on the part of the test persons. This also includes the decision to allow the presence of caregivers during the usability tests or even make them proxy test leaders. This circumstance encouraged and motivated the cognitively impaired test persons to approach and perform the test tasks without fear. In addition, it gave them enough confidence/safety to openly exchange thoughts with the unfamiliar test leaders. This modification has proven to be a double-edged sword. On the one hand, it simplifies communication and increases the motivation and concentration of the cognitively impaired test persons. On the other hand, despite detailed instructions from the test leader, there is a risk that the caregiver/proxy test leader becomes too involved and unintentionally controls the interaction and assessment on the part of the cognitively impaired test person out of a habit to help him or her. In order to avoid admonishing exchanges between test leader and caregiver/proxy test leader during the test or between the individual tests, gestures or similar should be agreed upon in advance, which test leaders can use to slow down the caregiver/proxy test leader without disturbing the course of the test and the attention of the cognitively impaired test person.

With regard to the technology used in the usability tests, it became apparent that at least the test groups in this case study were very open-minded and interested in any form of technology. This was an advantage with regard to the test object - the prototype - because the cognitively impaired test persons tested it willingly and curiously. However, this curiosity becomes a disadvantage when it is directed towards other technology that is only used to observe the tests. Thus, parts of the technology used can also lead to distraction of the cognitively impaired test persons. The use of technology therefore offers a lot of support in the interaction with cognitively impaired test persons, but must also be precisely adapted to their needs and limitations so as not to appear as a disturbing factor.

4.2   Case Study – On Site vs. Remote – Advantages and Disadvantages

The modifications of usability tests were used in various forms in the on site and remote tests. Based on this, a comparative statement can be made about their advantages and disadvantages.

With regard to the test preparations, the preparations for the remote tests proved to be more extensive and lengthy. Beforehand, ways and means had to be tested to be able to observe the interaction with the tablet on which the prototype of the app was located and to follow the communication between the cognitively impaired test persons and the caregiver/proxy test leader on site. This meant that relevant software had to be installed on the tablets and laptops and the tablets had to be sent to the workshop for impaired people. In order to ensure that the usability tests ran smoothly, the deputy test leader on site had to be instructed in the use of the technology in addition to the test concept.

Even though the preparations for the remote test were more time-consuming, it turned out that the performance of the test persons was much more focussed and consistent than at the on site tests. The remote test offered the advantage that only one cognitively impaired test person and one caregiver/proxy test leader were present in the workshop to guide the test persons through the tests. Since the test persons only held the tablet with the app to be tested in their hands, the laptop via which the scene was remotely connected to the test leader was not noticed at all by the test persons due to a smart placement in the room. In this way, the distraction of the cognitively impaired test persons by the unfamiliar test leaders and by the functioning of the transmission technology, which would have been too complex for the understanding of the cognitively impaired test persons, could be avoided. Thus, at least from the point of view of the cognitively impaired test persons, the test was conducted by only one person, namely a caregiver known to them.

Based on this, the second major difference between the on site test and the remote tests emerges. In the on site test, the test leader was able to guide the cognitively impaired test persons through the usability test themselves, whereas in the remote test, a caregiver from the institution had to act as a proxy test leader (for the reason already mentioned, that the transmission technology in combination with the communication with several strangers would have represented too great a distraction). This gave the on site tests the advantage that the test leader had a direct overview of the scene, could offer interaction alternatives if necessary, and could involve the caregiver sitting in on the test. This was not possible with the remote test. The test leader had to rely completely on the proxy test leader and leave all interaction with the test persons to him. However, even with good preparation of the proxy test leader by the test leader, deviations from the planned procedure occurred from time to time due to inexperience of the proxy test leader (e.g. questions were asked differently or the order was changed). In these moments, the fact that the test leader was not even noticed by the test persons became a disadvantage, as the test leader was not able to draw attention to him/herself and enter into an exchange with the proxy test leader. For the next remote tests, it can be deduced that a communication channel between the proxy test leader and the test leader should be planned via headphones in order to be able to counteract such errors. However, since only one and the same caregiver acted as proxy test leader during the remote tests, the tests became more and more routine. The proxy test leader was a caregiver who was known to all cognitively impaired test persons, even if he was not specifically responsible for them personally. The individual caregivers of the test persons were also remotely connected without the test persons being aware of it. This procedure minimised the effort involved in training a proxy test leader, but nevertheless allowed the assessments of the individual caregivers to be taken into account based on their many years of experience in dealing with the respective cognitively impaired test persons.

In conclusion, it can be said that although the remote tests are more time-consuming to prepare and to conduct, but they cause fewer distractions or uncertainties on the part of the cognitively impaired test persons compared to the on site tests and thus provide a more realistic picture of and assessment on the part of the cognitively impaired persons.

All in all, usability tests with cognitively impaired people are very feasible and also effective. However, compared to usability tests with other user groups, the cognitively impaired test persons could only suggest minimal recommendations or alternatives, as they are not aware of the functional and design potential of the app development. Often, errors in the app are not addressed because they are not perceived as such by the cognitively impaired test persons. They may stumble over the handling, but do not question it. For this reason, the observation of the test subjects and the assessment of their reactions in cooperation with the supervisors is also of great importance for the evaluation of the tests. In this way, the results can be put into perspective. In connection with the closed question formats and the three-point rating scales, which the cognitively impaired test persons were able to take without any problems, it was thus possible to obtain evaluable and interpretable results.

5 Discussion

Due to the diversity of the user group of cognitively impaired people, it is of utmost importance to consider each phase of the usability test in particular and to modify it according to the needs of the user group. Generalizability is only possible to a limited extent, because although the impairments of the test persons can be taken into account in the test design, their emotional stability cannot necessarily be. This means that these challenges can only be overcome with the support of the caregivers - an approach that can only be designed or planned uniformly to a limited extent.

Creating alternatives is an important part of planning and conducting usability tests with cognitively impaired people. On the one hand, these alternatives relate to enabling interaction and communication with the cognitively impaired test persons. On the other hand, they refer to the possibilities offered to them to perform an evaluation and to communicate their opinion. These alternatives can only be tailored to the cognitively impaired test persons in close consultation with the caregivers. In the case of test leader, it can even go beyond mere consultation in that way that the caregivers themselves act as proxy test leaders, as described in the example of remote tests. In this case, the caregiver is briefed in advance by the test leader in order to introduce the cognitively impaired users to the test items and the associated evaluation options as well as to the technology to be used for this purpose.

Contrary to general expectations, the tests (both on site and remote) showed that at least the cognitively impaired test persons in this case study were very open-minded and willing to test the technology provided. It is not perceived as an uncertainty factor but rather as a motivation. Especially in the context of digitalization, the user group of cognitively impaired people should not be neglected. This would make an important contribution to inclusion, which aims at the social participation of all people, regardless of their individual dispositions and starting points [18].

In conclusion, it can be said that usability tests with cognitively impaired people are very feasible if proper modifications are made to the test procedure. Thus, in the sense of user-centered development, usability tests with cognitively impaired people should also become the norm.

Fig. 7. Project and its funding organizations

Acknowledgement. The case study was conducted in the scope of the diBAss [19] project. The project is funded by the German Federal Ministry of Education and Research and the European Social Fund as part of the promotion of inclusion with digital media program (see Fig. 7).

References

1. Destatis, Pressemitteilung Nr. 230 (24.06.2020): 7.9 million severely impaired people live in Germany. https://www.destatis.de/DE/Presse/Pressemitteilungen/2020/06/PD20_230_227.html. Accessed 26 Feb 2021
2. REHADAT Statistik, Statistik der schwerbehinderten Menschen. https://www.rehadat-statistik.de/statistiken/behinderung/schwerbehindertenstatistik/. Accessed 26 Feb 2021
3. Web Content Accessibility Guidelines (WCAG) 2.1. https://www.w3.org/TR/WCAG21/. Accessed 26 Feb 2021
4. Was sind kognitive Störungen? https://www.psychisch-erkrankt.de/kognitive-stoerungen/. Accessed 26 Feb 2021
5. Werdenfelser Testbatterie zur Messung kognitiv-intellektueller Fähigkeiten bei Menschen mit Behinderungen. https://www.testzentrale.de/shop/werdenfelser-testbatterie-zur-messung-kognitiv-intellektueller-faehigkeiten-bei-menschen-mit-behinderungen.html. Accessed 26 Feb 2021
6. Konzept der Kasseler Werkstatt für das Eingangsverfahren und den Berufsbildungsbereich. https://www.sozialgruppe-kassel.de/wp-content/uploads/2016/06/Fachkonzept-KS-Werkstatt.pdf. Accessed 26 Feb 2021
7. Kognitive Bewertung, Testbatterie zu kognitiven Fähigkeiten (CAB). https://www.cognifit.com/de/cognitive-assessment/cognitive-test. Accessed 26 Feb 2021
8. Bochumer Matrizentest Standard, https://www.testzentrale.de/shop/bochumer-matrizentest-standard.html. Accessed 26 Feb 2021
9. Verhaltensauffälligkeiten bei Intelligenzminderung. https://www.asklepios.com/wiesen/experten/psychiatrie/intelligenzminderung/. Accessed 26 Feb 2021
10. BGWforschung, Behindertenhilfe in Deutschland, Zahlen–Daten–Fakten, Ein Trendbericht. https://www.bgw-online.de/SharedDocs/Downloads/DE/Medientypen/Wissenschaft-Forschung/BGW55-83-140-Trendbericht-Behindertenhilfe.pdf%3F__blob%3DpublicationFile. Accessed 26 Feb 2021
11. Rubin, J., Chisnell, D.: Handbook of Usability Testing. How to Plan, Design and Conduct Effective Tests. 2 edn. Wiley (2008)
12. Niediek, I.: Wer nicht fragt, bekommt keine Antworten – Interviewtechniken unter besonderen Bedingungen. In: Zeitschrift für Inklusion-online.net, 4, 2015 (2015). https://www.inklusion-online.net/index.php/inklusion-online/article/view/323/275. Accessed 26 Feb 2021
13. Tassé, M.J., Schalock, R.L., Thompson, J.R., Wehmeyer, M.: Guidelines for interviewing people with impairments: support Intensity Scale. American Association on Intellectual and Developmental Impairments. AAMR, Washington, DC (2005). http://aaidd.org/docs/default-source/sis-docs/sisguidelinesforinterviewing.pdf?sfvrsn=2. Accessed 26 Feb 2021
14. Williams, P., Nicholas, D.: Testing the usability of information technology applications with learners with special educational needs (SEN). J. Res. Spec. Educ. Needs 6(1), 31–41 (2006)
15. Williams, P.: Developing methods to evaluate web usability with people with learning difficulties. Br. J. Spec. Educ. 33, 173–179 (2006)
16. Williams, P., Shekhar, S.: People with learning impairments and smartphones: testing the usability of a touch-screen interface. Educ. Sci. 9(4), 263 (2019)
17. Petrie, H., Hamilton, F., King, N., Pavan, P.: Remote usability evaluations with impaired people. In: Proceedings of the SIGCHI Conference on Human Factors in Computing Systems (CHI 2006), pp. 1133–1141. Association for Computing Machinery, New York (2006)
18. Inklusion in der beruflichen Bildung. https://www.bibb.de/de/697.php. Accessed 26 Feb 2021
19. diBAss project – digital Blended Assistance. https://www.dibass-projekt.de. Accessed 09 Feb 2021

Remote Evaluation in Universal Design Using Video Conferencing Systems During the COVID-19 Pandemic

Joschua Thomas Simon-Liedtke[1]([✉])(iD), Way Kiat Bong[2](iD), Trenton Schulz[1](iD), and Kristin Skeide Fuglerud[1](iD)

[1] Norwegian Computing Center, P.O. Box 114, Blindern, 0314 Oslo, Norway
{joschua,trenton,kristins}@nr.no
[2] University of Oslo, P.O. Box 1072, Blindern, 0316 Oslo, Norway
waykb@uio.no
https://www.nr.no/en/ict

Abstract. Usability and accessibility evaluations with diverse users are an essential part of an iterative universal design process for digital solutions. The COVID-19 pandemic has made it difficult to run traditional local evaluations due to social distancing restrictions to reduce infections. Remote synchronous and asynchronous evaluation methods may be a solution if it can be used by various user groups, including people with impairments. Incorporating video conferencing systems into traditional remote evaluations can be a valuable supplement to—or, given the current situation, alternative to—traditional usability and accessibility evaluations. We present a protocol for remote formative usability evaluations designed with accessibility in mind. The protocol explains how to prepare for an evaluation and its technical setup, how to conduct synchronous evaluations using video conferencing systems, and how to debrief and analyze the collected data. We tested this protocol in a pilot study for an ongoing project where we ran both synchronous and asynchronous remote evaluations. In our pilot, the synchronous evaluation using video conferencing systems provided opportunities for richer qualitative data than the asynchronous evaluation as we ran it. The findings from the pilot study indicate that the protocol is feasible and can be used when having participants with diverse abilities or impairments. We also provide suggestions for others that wish to adapt the protocol.

Keywords: Universal design · Usability · Accessibility · Remote evaluation · Video conferencing · Pandemic · COVID-19

1 Introduction

Universal design (UD) is a design process that makes products and environments usable and accessible to the greatest extent possible by all members of society regardless of level of ability [23]. One of UD's main goals is to promote equality

© Springer Nature Switzerland AG 2021
M. Antona and C. Stephanidis (Eds.): HCII 2021, LNCS 12768, pp. 116–135, 2021.
https://doi.org/10.1007/978-3-030-78092-0_8

and ensure full participation in society for individuals with impairments [23]. UD has been shown to give improved products and services, increased market and customer satisfaction, enhanced community relations and reputation, improved internal processes, increased financial effects, and avoid legal costs and damages [12]. Studies have shown that cross-disciplinarity and participation from user organizations and diverse user groups in the planning, implementation and evaluation stage of the development process is important for achieving a universally designed solution, i.e. a solution that is usable and accessible to as many people as possible [2,3,10,11,13,14,23,26,27].

The COVID-19 pandemic has made the process of involving users with impairments more challenging due to obstacles and challenges related to, for example, health concerns, lockdown measures, and travel restrictions. At the same time, the pandemic has been advancing digitization of the society, and its workflows that may offer new opportunities for people with impairments. Remote evaluations as discussed in several studies [19,27,28] may be a solution for evaluating systems during this challenging time. More people have had to start using a video conferencing solution such as Microsoft Teams, Zoom, or Google Meet on a regular basis. Several of these solutions promote their accessibility features. This could mean that remote evaluation using a video conferencing solution could offer an even more convenient and accessible evaluation setting for people with impairments. Much of the research within remote evaluation, however, was done before these current solutions were available and in common use.

We have investigated possibilities, challenges, and limitations of video conferencing systems in the remote evaluation of usability and accessibility of web applications and present our findings in this paper. First, we review related literature concerned with remote usability and accessibility evaluation. Second, we propose a protocol for using video conferencing systems in remote usability and accessibility evaluation. Third, we implement the protocol in a remote pilot study assessing a web application, CAPABLE, where we tested our methodology with users from different user groups. Fourth, we discuss the observations from the pilot study and its implications. Finally, we conclude with recommendations for running remote usability and accessibility evaluations and our future works.

2   Related Work

A guide for selecting an appropriate strategy for evaluation of design artifacts are outlined by Venable et al. including iterative technical and formative evaluations [37]. One way to include people with impairments in the UD process is by conducting *formative* and *summative* evaluations involving participants with impairments at various stages of the design process. The goal of a formative evaluation is to determine which aspects of the design work well (or not), why, and to propose improvements to the design. The goal of a summative evaluation is to give an overall assessment of a product or service [9].

Both kinds of evaluations reveal barriers, needs, and bottlenecks for different user groups and increase the understanding of these issues by the developers [27,28]. The evaluations are often performed as *local (user) evaluations* where the participant and the evaluator are at the same location, e.g. in a usability lab. These approaches can be resource intensive since they require a dedicated location, an appointment, and can represent an additional burden for people with impairments needing to travel to an unfamiliar location [28]. Some of these burdens could be reduced by having the evaluation at the participant's home or another familiar location of their liking in a *field study* [28]. Here, the evaluators do the travelling, and equipment may need to be transported for the evaluation process. This reduces some of the control of a lab environment with standard equipment and software but expands the diversity of people that can participate.

Consequently, a *remote evaluation*, where the participant and evaluator are not in the same location, may provide a convenient and efficient alternative for both parties [28]. One study with normal-sighted participants found that participants often perceive remote evaluations as more comfortable and convenient than travelling to a local evaluation at a usability lab [6]. At the same time, this study found that participants had difficulties concentrating on the task at hand, and that the collected issue descriptions were less rich. These observations have been confirmed by other studies that showed that remote user evaluation of usability and accessibility give similar quantitative results as a local evaluation, but that qualitative data was less rich. One reason for the lack of qualitative richness was due to participants not recording observed issues thoroughly enough, and the inability for evaluators to observe the participants and ask question where needed [6,7,27].

Remote evaluation methods can be further split into methods where the evaluator and the participant are separated by space alone, i.e., *synchronous*, or by space and time, i.e., *asynchronous* [8]. Studies [6,7,27] showed that synchronous remote evaluation give similar quantitative results as a local evaluation, but the qualitative data is less descriptive for asynchronous evaluations. One study [27] suggested that newer video conferencing systems could increase the richness of the qualitative data compared to asynchronous remote evaluation methods. Another study with blind and visually impaired users found that most of the participants preferred a local test to a synchronous remote test [21]. The main reason for this preference was that the preparations and setup of the remote synchronous test were too demanding. The tests were conducted on an internet phone program, and the authors noted that a web-based application might have been less technically demanding and might have required less setup.

People around the world have met increasing challenges during the COVID-19 pandemic related to health concerns, local lockdown measures, or travel restrictions. These challenges create demands and needs to running evaluations in a remote environment. Some people with impairments may be more vulnerable in a pandemic. For example, a study examining the effects of COVID-19 on people with visual impairment reported that nearly 37% of the 937 respondents have underlying health problems that make them more vulnerable to COVID-19 [30]. Comorbidities such as diabetes I/II, asthma, heart disease, chronic obstructive pulmonary disease (COPD), immunosuppression, arthritis, cancer, and kidney dysfunction in this sample of visual impaired people exacerbated their risk of getting a severe case of COVID-19. Thus, local or field evaluations can be a potential source for infection under the on-going global COVID-19 pandemic. Besides the issues mentioned previously, it may be difficult for people with vision impairments to keep a safe, comfortable distance when they cannot see where other people are. Consequently, safety could be added as an additional benefit of remote evaluation.

Moreover, lockdowns, travel restrictions and other governmental measures for mitigating the pandemic have encouraged people to stay more at home and not have visitors. This has made it difficult for people, with or without impairments, to (1) be willing to travel to a usability lab to participate in an evaluation or (2) have an evaluator visit them for a field study at home.

In contrast, the advancement of the digitization of the workplace and the society has offered new opportunities for remote evaluation. Many types of work have switched to digital forms like home schooling or home office [29] offering new opportunities also in the field of remote evaluation. Similarly, many other tasks that before were carried out in person have moved to digital video conferencing systems such as Microsoft Teams, Zoom and Google Meet during the COVID-19 pandemic [29]. This means that many people, including people with impairments, that had previously not used video conferences have gained experience with these collaboration tools. This and the fact that manufacturers of video conferencing systems claim to have accessibility features [22,40] might open up new opportunities for remote evaluation in UD.

Although video conferencing systems provide promising opportunities for remote user evaluation, we are not aware of any studies examining how these current systems can be beneficial for the remote evaluation of usability and accessibility involving people with impairments. Similarly, there is a need to study how these evaluations compare to more traditional asynchronous remote approaches.

3 Protocol for Remote Evaluation of Usability and Accessibility

We propose a protocol for using video conferencing systems for remotely evaluating the usability and accessibility of a web-based application targeting desktop and mobile devices. The starting point for the protocol is in the Human Risk & Effectiveness evaluation strategy [37] that emphasizes iterative technical and formative evaluations early in the process before progressing to a more rigorous summative evaluation to study the effectiveness, utility, and benefit of the artifact. Specifically, a Human Risk & Effectiveness strategy is recommended when one of the major risks of a design is social or user oriented, and it is a goal to rigorously establish that benefit will continue in real situations and over the long run [37]. This strategy includes iterative testing, starting with formative evaluation in an increasingly more naturalistic setting. The protocol presented here is informed by existing research on asynchronous and synchronous formative evaluation methods [6,7,27,28], but revised for the use video conferencing systems like Microsoft Teams and Zoom, which were not included in previous studies on remote usability and accessibility evaluations [6,27].

3.1 Preparations

Before conducting usability and accessibility testing including people with impairments, it is advisable to remove as many accessibility barriers as possible by ensuring conformance to accessibility guidelines, such as W3C WCAG 2.0 or 2.1 [31,38,39]. This is important to avoid wasting participants' and evaluators' time. Besides, research indicates that conformance to these guidelines will improve usability for users with and without impairments [33,34].

The next step is to decide on the goal of the remote evaluation. What should be found out during the evaluation, how should it be examined, and who (broadly) will be participating? This usually results in several tasks for the potential participants to do.

While defining the tasks, one should also look at the different video conferencing solutions that are available and decide what will be used to make sure that the solutions can support our study. Some options to consider can be the accessibility of the system (both with assistive technology and for potential participants to have access to it); the capabilities of the system (e.g., can it record video? audio? share displays?); and how widely used is the system among the target group that will be tested? These considerations are most important when doing a synchronous evaluation. An asynchronous evaluation will normally have less requirements. One should check information from the video system provider and consult with experts in the impairment community to make sure that participants with a specific impairment can use the system. Additionally, it may be necessary to offer more than one system option to reach all participants. When offering multiple options, one should investigate that there are equivalent functions in all system options to get the data that is needed, and that participants can use at least one of the system options.

Another item to consider under preparations is how the participant can give informed consent and how this can be recorded. At the same time, one should consider if and how to distribute compensation to the participants. It is common to compensate participants in usability studies with money or an item, such as a gift card, to acknowledge their effort and time participating in usability studies [28,36]. For research, the method and value of compensation should be appropriate for the subject population and the research activities. Since the evaluation happens remotely, it may be necessary to investigate alternative methods for compensation such as gift cards that can be delivered digitally, using a mobile payment system, or sending something in the mail. A digital delivery can help with an instant gratification for participation, but it is not strictly necessary. Regardless of what is chosen, it is important that compensation is accessible for the participant. Different places and studies will have different requirements. So, ensure that your evaluation's set-up can satisfy them.

Although obvious, it bears repeating that all the documents that are eventually sent to the participants need to be accessible. As a minimum requirement, the materials should conform to accessibility guidelines such as W3C WCAG. Additionally, one can check that the documents work with different types of assistive devices like screen readers, etc.

3.2 Recruiting Participants

As with other evaluations, one must consider how recruitment should be done. User organizations have traditionally been a good way to get in contact with people with impairments. When contacting the user organization, offer the participants two options including synchronous remote evaluation using video conferencing solutions or asynchronous where participants can do it by themselves when they want. Then, the organization may be able to contact additional chapters and talk to people that might not normally have been a candidate earlier, e.g. because of geographical or mobility barriers.

Once participants are recruited, the next steps depend on whether one is planning on running an asynchronous or synchronous evaluation. For asynchronous evaluations, participants receive two documents. The first document includes information about the evaluation, an informed consent form, and information about how to perform the evaluation. The second document provides all the tasks the participant should attempt to complete and questions to answer. If there are specific kinds of feedback that the asynchronous participant should give, be sure to document how it should be given. One should also schedule a debriefing interview when the participant has finished the activities.

Participants for a synchronous evaluation need to be contacted ahead of time to find an adequate time slot for a video conference. Part of the scheduling includes finding out if a participant is familiar with any of the predetermined video conferencing systems or if additional guidance is necessary. One can, for example, offer to send instructions if necessary. It is advisable to choose the option with which the participant is most familiar, especially if they are using an assistive device. The reason for letting participants choose is to consider ease of use and competency, so any lack of skill in using the video conferencing system would interfere as little as possible with the evaluation task at hand. Participants should focus on problems related to the web application and not struggle with unfamiliar video conferencing systems. During this time the information about the evaluation and informed consent form can be sent to them to read and sign.

3.3 Running Synchronous Evaluations

The participants doing an asynchronous evaluation do the tasks on their own and have a debriefing later. This section focuses on a synchronous evaluation, although the debriefing for an asynchronous evaluation may have similar steps.

Before starting the session with the participant, make sure that the audio and video are working on your end of the video system. This will make it easier to isolate issues if things work on your end. Once the session has started, welcome the participant, and make sure that the audio and video works for the participant as well.

If everything is working, the next step is to start with a short briefing session in which one gives a short summary of the study and its goals, the informed consent form, and the participant's rights. It is important to check if the participant has given consent as a reply to the initial e-mail. If they have yet to give consent, give the participant time to read the informed consent form, offer to read it aloud to them, or provide an acceptable summary. Moreover, the participants should be given time to close any other applications, such as e-mail before sharing their screens etc., to protect the participant's privacy. That way, they are not distracted during the evaluation as well [21]. It bears repeating that it is important that consent is given before asking the participant to share their screen or any recording takes place.

After consent is given, screen sharing recording is started, it is simply a matter of going through the tasks and collecting the data. For a synchronous remote evaluation, this is not much different than a local evaluation.

3.4 Debriefing the Participant

An asynchronous or synchronous evaluation should end with a debriefing where the evaluator thanks the participant and the participant can give any final overall impressions. This may also provide an opportunity for collecting additional qualitative information to unclear issues found, especially for asynchronous evaluations. This may also be one possible point to provide compensation if it was not provided at the start of the session.

At this point, the evaluation session is over. Analyzing the data depends on the data collected and the goals that were set at the beginning of the evaluation.

4 Pilot Study Implementing the Protocol

To see if our protocol is feasible, we used the protocol to pilot an evaluation of a web application that is part of the ongoing CAPABLEproject [17,18]. The aim of the CAPABLEproject is to create a universally designed digital tool that empowers citizens in Norway to actively use their clinical and personal health information to manage their health. The target users are all citizens, including elderly people above 65 years old, citizens who have an impairment, using more than three prescribed medications, or having potential nutritional risks. As one of the earliest iterations in our evaluation strategy for CAPABLE, we conducted a pilot study using our proposed protocol. Feedback from this pilot study is used to adjust the protocol. At the same time, we use discovered usability and accessibility issues in CAPABLEto improve the artifact for a later feasibility study involving more users. The current remote testing is naturalistic in the sense that it is conducted in a place selected by the users and on their own devices, but it does not include real data and a real organizational setting.

In addition to developing the protocol, we are interested in comparing asynchronous and synchronous evaluations, and investigate the benefits and challenges of including video conferencing to the synchronous remote evaluation.

We therefore use our pilot study to prepare investigations of the following questions: (1) What advantages and disadvantages do the participant and evaluator experience with synchronous evaluation with video conferencing compared to asynchronous evaluation? (2) Do both approaches give similar quantitative or qualitative results? (3) Does synchronous remote evaluation with video conferencing improve the subjective qualitative experience compared to traditional methods like asynchronous methods? (4) Finally, are our protocol guidelines enough for the smooth implementation of remote evaluation using video conferencing systems?

4.1   Study Preparation

We identified the central functionality of the CAPABLEweb application and defined tasks around the functionality that the participants would later be asked to complete. Typical tasks were logging into the application, retrieving information, registering, and editing data, etc.

We investigated using several video conferencing systems including Microsoft Teams, Zoom, Google Meet, TeamViewer, and Skype. After trying out all of these with a focus on accessibility and relevant functionality (e.g. screen sharing and video recording), we eventually settled on Microsoft Teams and Zoom as they seemed to have the biggest reach for the groups from which we were recruiting, and with whom we could easily schedule meetings. We also wrote detailed instructions for how to use these systems for our study and ensured that the documents that would eventually be sent to participants were accessible, also for participants using assistive technology. We, for example, made all documents comply to the WCAG 2.1 standard, and tested the readability of the documents for screen readers.

For compensation, we devised a method using a mobile payment service. Initially, we were targeting digital gift cards options. However, it turned out to be difficult to find digital gift card suppliers where the distribution, information and use of the gift card was sufficiently accessible and universally designed. Moreover, we considered issues such as the accessibility of the information about where to use the gift card, how to get information about the value on the gift card, and whether it had sufficient usage possibilities, both geographically and digitally. Instead of using gift cards, we chose to work out a payment routine together with the administration of our research organization using a mobile payment service called Vipps that has broad usage in Norway and has won an award for UD [25]. This routine considered privacy, tax rules, and the accessibility and flexibility of payment method to suit the diverse needs of our potential participants. Participants in the pilot were not compensated as they were participating in the pilot as part of their regular jobs. For the final remote usability and accessibility study, participants will receive 300 NOK (around 30) for their effort.

4.2   Recruitment for the Pilot Study

Participants were recruited through three user organizations: Norwegian Association for the Blind and Partially Sighted (NABP), rheumatics (NRF), and people with heart and lung diseases (LHL). These organizations are partners in the CAPABLEproject and have earlier been involved in needs and requirements elicitation [17,18]. The participants recruited in this pilot study were staff persons working in the user organizations. They are user representatives at the system level, with knowledge of the needs of the group they represent. They were divided into a synchronous and an asynchronous reference group.

Participants were asked about their preferred video conferencing systems. For synchronous evaluations, we also provided a document with technical details about how to start the chosen video conferencing system including screen sharing if needed. With the provided information, we then set up a meeting on the preferred platform and sent the participants additional information about the study and an informed consent form. Participants for the asynchronous evaluation also received additional documents as detailed below.

At the time of writing this article, we have recruited four participants for the pilot. Three participants had the synchronous remote evaluation and one performed the asynchronous evaluation. One of the synchronous participants was a proficient screen reader user. All participants reported above average experience with ICT.

4.3   Running the Synchronous Evaluation

After the briefing session described in the protocol above, we verified that the participant's informed consent had been delivered beforehand or provided the necessary information to obtain informed consent in the briefing. We asked for consent to the study in general, sharing the display, and recording the meeting. Only the first two were necessary for us to proceed. The video recording was not necessary but was meant to aid our analysis after the session. After receiving consent from the participants, we asked them to activate screen sharing, and started recording the meeting if consent was given.

Finally, we explained the think-aloud protocol [4] and how to identify usability and accessibility issues. As suggested by Nielsen [24], we provided a video example for a think aloud session if participants were unfamiliar with the technique.

We started to conduct the evaluation by giving the participant the tasks using CAPABLE. The screen sharing with the video conferencing systems made it possible to observe what the user was doing on-screen, at the same time as we could see their facial impressions through the camera when the camera was activated.

To encourage the participant to talk and minimize influence over the participants' focus and workflow, we used acknowledgment tokens [4] rather than asking too many questions while they were completing the tasks. At the end of each task, we asked the participants about their experience, and investigated more details of problems or challenges they might have encountered during the task. Additionally, we inquired participants about their opinions about pitfalls, challenges, or possible improvements especially in those cases where the participant was a specialist in using assistive devices. We also asked them about their perceived difficulty of the task using the Single Ease Question (SEQ) [32].

4.4   Running the Asynchronous Evaluation

After agreeing to participate, the participants in asynchronous evaluation were provided two documents. The first document described how they should perform the evaluations, from providing us their informed consent to answering the questions regarding to testing tasks and arranging for the debriefing session. We provided instructions and guidance, specifically about what kind of feedback they should provide in the answers.

In the second document, all the testing tasks and questions that the participants were required to answer were presented. These questions were the same as in the think-aloud protocol in the synchronous evaluation. The aim was to have the qualitative data collected in asynchronous evaluation as comparable as possible to those in synchronous evaluation. Following the testing tasks and questions, we had questionnaires about the CAPABLEprototype and the evaluation process.

We ensured that these documents were accessible and universally designed, considering our goal to include diverse users, including participants using assistive technologies in our remote evaluations.

4.5   Debriefing

Finally, we conducted a short debriefing session with synchronous and asynchronous participants. For the synchronous participants, this session followed right after completing the tasks, while we set up a separate meeting through video conferencing or telephone for the asynchronous participant. During the debriefing session we collected additional data by interviewing participants and with the help of questionnaires. Here, we asked about the participant's experience with the artifact and the evaluation process with respect to comfort, ease, memory, concentration, convenience, preference, etc. [6,27]. We also included a SUS questionnaire [5] in Norwegian, and a questionnaire with opinions about the evaluation process. Finally, we asked the participants about their demographic background information related to age and gender, ICT experience, and technical details, such as types and version of assistive device if used, operative system and browser.

4.6   Analysis

The analysis for each participant was based on notes we made of the observations during the sessions, and on the video recording in those cases the participants consented to it. For each participant, two researchers extracted information to account for the evaluator effect [16]. The relevant problems were summarized in a list with description of the identified usability and accessibility issue. Each issue was furthermore categorized as either cosmetic, minor, or critical [1].

We also summarized and evaluated issues related to the evaluation protocol, such as the order and number of tasks, the design of the tasks, and questions for the final evaluation. Although the time used to conduct the evaluation varied between participants, we found that the number of tasks and questions was quite realistic to conduct within the allocated time, which we had set to an hour and a half. Since we found that we needed around 15 min for the debriefing, we stopped when there was 15 min left of the agreed time, even if the participant had not completed all the tasks yet. Therefore, it was also important to put the most important tasks in the beginning of the evaluation. In earlier versions of the protocol, we also recorded the time for each participant. However, since the time difference between participants with and without assistive devices might vary, at the same time as different participants talk sometimes more or less during evaluation, depending on their personality and/or interaction with the evaluators, time is not included as a measure for the analysis.

5   Results and Discussion

We completed several synchronous and one asynchronous evaluation using our protocol. Participants uncovered several usability and accessibility issues. We do not report on these issues since the CAPABLEweb application is in an early stage of development and this was a pilot study. In the following we focus on our experiences with the remote evaluation protocol.

All but one participant completed all the tasks in the time allocated (ninety minutes). In the one case were the participant did not finish, we truncated the remaining tasks so that we had time to complete debriefing interview instead. We observed that using assistive devices like screen readers takes more time, which agreed with our experience from previous evaluations. The asynchronous participant reported significantly less usability and accessibility issues than any of the synchronous participants.

In the following paragraphs, we discuss general impressions of the evaluation procedure including flexibility and social aspects, technical preferences and challenges, richness of the obtained data, and the usability and accessibility of the evaluation protocol. We compare both the synchronous with the asynchronous evaluation, and the fact that we are using video conferencing systems.

5.1   Flexibility in Performing the Evaluation

We observed that participants prefer different evaluation types in terms of synchronous or asynchronous evaluation, and different video conferencing systems.

On the one hand, it was faster to recruit participants for the synchronous evaluation than for the asynchronous evaluation in the pilot study. One reason could be the social aspect of the synchronous evaluation, and the familiarity with the video conferencing systems during the COVID-19 pandemic. All our participants were working from home due to recommendations and regulations from their employer and the local and national government. Thus, meetings on Microsoft Teams and Zoom were familiar for all participants. Besides, participants might have considered the synchronous evaluation easier to perform since the process did not require them to read instructions or write elaborate answers. Another reason could have been that participants recruited for the pilot were doing the evaluation as part of their job during work hours, and it might have been easier to work a synchronous evaluation in as part of the workday.

On the other hand, the flexibility in terms of time provided to participants to complete the evaluation by themselves was one of the assumed advantages for the asynchronous remote evaluation. Hartson et al. [15] pointed out that asynchronous participants can decide where, when, and how they want to do the evaluation. During the recruitment, two participants reported that they had other tasks during the day besides their regular work to do. The asynchronous evaluation was likely more flexible for them since they could perform the evaluation whenever they wanted. Asynchronous evaluation may also have appealed to participants who feel uncomfortable talking to or being observed by a stranger, have social or performance anxiety, etc. Providing the option for an asynchronous evaluation can remove pressure in the social setting and remove competitive aspects in future evaluations.

Moreover, participants preferred different video conferencing systems in the synchronous evaluations. Some participants, for example, chose Zoom and some Microsoft Teams. Likely because of having the option to choose, we did not observe any significant usability or accessibility issues related to participants use of the video conferencing systems. All the participants successfully communicated over audio and video and shared their screen with the evaluator.

One advantage of the proposed protocol is the possibility to reach a wider spectrum of participants. One important aspect in UD is the inclusion of diverse user groups, and remote evaluation can contribute in achieving that. Diversity in user groups means the users have different abilities and/or impairments, socio-demographic background, preferences, etc. Using remote evaluations, participants in a bigger geographical area can be reached, and diverse user groups can be included [35]. Using video conferencing systems can make these remote evaluations feel more natural as the participants can see the evaluator and vice versa. Our investigated systems allowed screen sharing, such that we could easily follow the participants on the screen. When a usability or accessibility issue was detected, we could easily identify them without having to rely on descriptions by the participant alone.

However, it is crucial to keep in mind the downsides of conducting remote evaluations using video conferencing systems, i.e. the challenges that might be faced by participants who have low or no ICT skills in using these systems. Our participants were quite skilled in their usage of video conferencing systems but many people may not have the experience in using video conferencing systems as they do not have access to or need for them in their everyday life. We, therefore, suggest to provide detailed instructions on how to use the video conferencing systems to assist those who need them, and to supplement with local evaluations when possible.

5.2 System Preferences

All the participants chose to use video conferencing on a laptop or desktop PC (hereafter simply "desktop system") instead of a mobile phone or tablet (hereafter simply "mobile system"). This choice was made even though phone and tablet were listed before PC as possible devices during recruitment.

There may have been several reasons for the participants in the pilot preferring to use a desktop system. One could be that the people recruited for the pilot where responding to a meeting during working hours and used the system they normally use at that time. In addition, while most phones now carry cameras and microphones, many laptops do as well, and participants may have had the video conference set-up already to work on their desktop systems.

Another reason could be the amount of time set off to do the study. We set up an appointment that could last possibly an hour and a half. People may have been more comfortable doing this length of a meeting sitting at a desktop system rather than having to hold a device during that time. In addition, using a desktop system also frees up both hands to do things with the interface or better use an assistive technology.

Using video conferencing together with a website may have imposed additional barriers for the participants. That is, the participants might have been aware that they would not only have to complete the tasks, but also set up the video connection to the evaluators. This might have been more demanding on a mobile screen compared to the space available on a desktop screen. Screen sharing in the mobile app versions of these systems includes additional challenges such as not being able to use the camera or having to move the video window to work with the rest of the user interface.

Regardless, further research should examine if this was purely by chance or deliberate, and differences in running a remote evaluation with video conferencing software on mobile versus desktop systems. If there is a preference for one system over another, it may be necessary to find ways to have people choose a particular solution to make sure that different systems are sufficiently covered.

The fact that participants likely use their own equipment does provide the advantage that they are also likely using their preferred assistive technology configured correctly for them—something that may be difficult or require additional time to provide in a lab setting with lab-provided equipment.

5.3 Technical Challenges and Pitfalls

During our pilot study, we noticed possible technical challenges and pitfalls related to the camera setup and internet connectivity.

Before running the pilot, we discussed the possibility of recording both the participant and the screen separately. We ultimately chose only the shared screen as we felt that it was a fair balance between richness of information and requiring additional set-up of the users. This is somewhat mitigated by the fact that most video conferencing systems record both the screen and a thumbnail version of the participants' face when participants choose to have their camera on. However, there could have been richer data recordings of the participants' faces (for example, by filming the participant using additional technologies).

Adding additional cameras requires extra set-up by the participant and knowledge of the software. This might have put additional stress on the participants. In our pilot, some participants in the synchronous evaluations seemed already slightly stressed in the beginning of the evaluation as they needed to perform the evaluation tasks while setting up and managing the conference systems on their own. We could improve this in future protocols by providing a checklist before the evaluation. In addition, it is always good to emphasize (or reemphasize) that the artifact is being evaluated and not the participant in these cases [4]. Using supportive statements and maintaining a calm voice can also relieve some stress from the participant.

Moreover, McLaughlin et al. [20] emphasized the importance of considering suitable hardware and software in a study evaluating medical devices remotely. Connectivity and internet access should also be considered. One issue to keep in mind when running synchronous remote evaluations in this way is that it depends on the participant and the evaluator having a stable internet connection with sufficient bandwidth and corresponding equipment (i.e. a microphone, a camera, and a computing device). While this may be taken for granted in some parts of the world, it is not universal. This may lead to excluding segments of people that should be part of an evaluation. Alternate methods like local evaluations or field studies have to be used in these cases. In the pilot conducted in Norway, we did not observe any interruptions related to the Internet connection during the pilot study.

5.4   Obtaining Informed Consent

One issue that arose during the pilot was how to properly record that someone has given informed consent. Participants would normally sign a paper for documentation in local evaluation studies. Having participants send a certified letter with a signed form via the postal service, however, was impractical and would have defeated the purpose of the participants' convenience of remote evaluation.

Ideally, the participants in the synchronous and asynchronous evaluation would have signed, taken a picture of, and sent back a respective form right after the initial e-mail. However, the participants did not always follow the instruction of providing informed consent before the appointment for the evaluation began. To keep the process simple, we chose to record verbal consent on video where participants consented to both the terms of the study and the video recording. In cases where participants only consented to the study itself, we asked them to send a text message by phone or an e-mail with their consent.

5.5   Richness of Data in Synchronous and Asynchronous Evaluations

Given the small participant sample in the pilot, we cannot draw any general conclusions about the difference in issues between synchronous and asynchronous evaluations. We can, however, discuss what we experienced as increased richness of the data we could collect with screen sharing and recording of video conferencing systems.

From our pilot, the participants in asynchronous and synchronous evaluations could complete the tasks, and we were able to collect data from both types of evaluations. This is positive and means that our documents for the evaluations were written well enough. Generally, we were able to collect richer, more detailed data from the synchronous evaluations than the asynchronous evaluation. Our documents for the asynchronous evaluations allowed participants to write detailed answers to the questions. However, in practice the asynchronous participant would write that there were some problems logging in, but not go into details since the participant eventually were able to log in. Contrast this with a synchronous evaluation where an evaluator could watch the participant struggle with the login interface and detect nuances in the participant's voice, actions, and reactions. Previous research already indicated that the tone of voice in phone evaluations was enough to sense frustration [6], and we did notice that facial expressions could add even more information if a participant allowed sharing of their video camera image. The evaluator could then investigate the participants' thoughts or feelings in synchronous evaluations, which often lead to the discovery of additional usability and accessibility issues.

The recording of the synchronous evaluations provided additional rich data since it was possible to look back and investigate some details more deeply than under the initial evaluation. Also, the shared screen made it easier for evaluators to follow the participants on the screen and back track any possible challenges. This *can* be easier with newer video conferencing systems since recording and screen sharing has become an integrated part of most systems. In lab or field studies, evaluators would either have to install additional software, or be next to or behind a participant (i.e., shoulder surfing), which could feel uncomfortable and intrusive.

That asynchronous evaluations provide fewer and less rich data than synchronous evaluations is consistent with previous findings [27]. One way of improving the data for asynchronous evaluations could be asking the asynchronous participants to also record their sessions and send the recording to the evaluators. This does put more burden on the asynchronous participant and evaluators as it may require installing and learning additional software, having storage space for the recording, and needing a secure way to transfer and store the recording. On the other hand, some video conferencing systems provide the ability to record and share screen in a session of just one person, so the actual recording may become easier over time.

5.6   Use of Questionnaires

During our evaluation, we noticed the importance of the distinction between questionnaires and open-ended questions. In this pilot study, we used a questionnaire about the CAPABLEprototype (perceived safety and security, perceived usefulness, and utility) and the remote evaluation process. In addition to usability and accessibility, answers to such questions are important for the future success of the remote evaluation protocol. However, reflecting upon our current findings, it was unclear whether the participants' answers were based on the current version of the CAPABLE, or a potential future improved CAPABLEsolution. It may also have been difficult, especially for a formative evaluation, to answer these questions by assigning a value. It may make more sense to probe for more qualitative data around these perceptions in future evaluations. Therefore, we will improve the questions in the protocol to clarify these aspects. We will, for example, include more open-ended questions as a good approach to obtain more insights from the participants because they can talk more about their experience and clarify their answers to the questionnaire.

5.7   Limitations

This study was a pilot study with limited reach. An obvious limitation is the small amount of participants, and that not all of the participants were representative end users, i.e. elderly people above 65 years old, citizens who are having an impairment, or using more than three prescribed medications, or having potential nutritional risks. Moreover, we only had one participant using one type of assistive device, i.e. a screen reader. We have not yet investigated the protocol for other assistive devices or other impairments. In addition, the participants in this study were competent users of video conferencing systems. Thus, they might face less challenges when performing the remote evaluations. During future evaluations, we will investigate performances of participants with lower ICT competence or experience, and on other devices like mobiles, etc.

Despite the limitation and some identified issues for improvement, we have verified that the protocol is feasible for future remote evaluations. The documents used and sent to the participants in the remote evaluations were prepared with keeping accessibility and UD in mind. We also identified some usability and accessibility problems of the CAPABLEsolution from the participants' feedback. These issues have been reflected accordingly, to provide a more accessible and inclusive remote evaluation experience to the end users, and a more universally designed CAPABLEfor them in the future.

6   Future Work and Conclusion

In this study, we aimed to investigate the use of video conferencing systems in the remote evaluation of usability and accessibility of web applications by exploring possibilities, challenges, and limitations through our pilot study. Following the protocol, we conclude that conducting remote evaluation of usability and accessibility of web applications is feasible for a wider study involving more participants with different impairments using different assistive devices. The discussed protocol was designed with accessibility and UD in mind, and our findings indicate that it was accessible and universally designed enough to be used for a proficient screen reader user.

We discussed advantages of video conferencing systems in the remote evaluation. The participants could perform the usability and accessibility evaluations in their most natural settings of surroundings and devices. Flexibility is given to participants in terms of choosing to take part in a synchronous or asynchronous evaluation. Those who choose synchronous evaluation, have the freedom to use the video conferencing system with which they are most familiar. For those who are busy during working hours or any other reason, they can opt for the asynchronous evaluation and conduct the evaluation by themselves whenever they want. We observed general advantages of the synchronous evaluation related to the quantity and richness of the observed data. At the same time, video conferencing systems can add an additional layer of richness by allowing the evaluators to follow the user on-screen and being able to read facial impressions and body language. The possibility to record both screen actions and camera images that many video conferencing systems provide can help the analysis afterwards even more. Moreover, conducting remote evaluation with assistive technology users using video conferencing systems can be an advantage when the assistive technology users do not have to bring their assistive devices with them.

Finally, we managed to identify issues related to the evaluation protocol through the pilot study. These issues have been addressed accordingly to ensure iterations of the usability and accessibility evaluations can be conducted in a more feasible way. In addition, a better participants' experience can be provided when the remote evaluation process itself is more accessible and inclusive. Moreover, we identified both strengths and weaknesses in the design of CAPABLEin relations to usability, accessibility, and UD through the remote evaluations. Since we only conducted a pilot study, we did not have sufficient participants for a quantitative analysis of the findings. Future work should therefore focus on conducting iterations of usability and accessible evaluation using CAPABLEwith more diverse participants and improving CAPABLEbased on the participants' feedback.

Acknowledgments. The work with this paper was supported by the Research Council of Norway through the CAPABLEproject (Project no. 281202). We are grateful to the CAPABLEconsortium, the non-governmental organizations, which helped with recruiting participants to our study, and to the participants for their valuable contributions.

References

1. Andreasen, M.S., Nielsen, H.V., Schrder, S.O., Stage, J.: What happened to remote usability testing? An empirical study of three methods. In: Proceedings of the SIGCHI Conference on Human Factors in Computing Systems, CHI 2007, pp. 1405–1414. Association for Computing Machinery, San Jose, April 2007. https://doi.org/10.1145/1240624.1240838
2. Begnum, M.E.N.: Universal design of ICT: a historical journey from specialized adaptations towards designing for diversity. In: Antona, M., Stephanidis, C. (eds.) HCII 2020. LNCS, vol. 12188, pp. 3–18. Springer, Cham (2020). https://doi.org/10.1007/978-3-030-49282-3_1
3. Bonacin, R., Dos Reis, J.C., Baranauskas, M.C.C.: Universal participatory design: achievements and challenges. SBC J. Interact. Syst. 10(1), 2–16 (2019)
4. Boren, T., Ramey, J.: Thinking aloud: reconciling theory and practice. IEEE Trans. Prof. Commun. 43(3), 261–278 (2000). https://doi.org/10.1109/47.867942
5. Brooke, J.: SUS - a quick and dirty usability scale. In: Jordan, P.W., Thomas, B., Werdmeester, B.A., McClelland, I.L. (eds.) Usability Evaluation in Industry, 1st edn., pp. 189–194. Tayler & Francis, London (1996)
6. Brush, A.B., Ames, M., Davis, J.: A comparison of synchronous remote and local usability studies for an expert interface. In: CHI 2004 Extended Abstracts on Human Factors in Computing Systems, CHI EA 2004, pp. 1179–1182. Association for Computing Machinery, Vienna, April 2004. https://doi.org/10.1145/985921.986018
7. Bruun, A., Gull, P., Hofmeister, L., Stage, J.: Let your users do the testing: a comparison of three remote asynchronous usability testing methods. In: Proceedings of the SIGCHI Conference on Human Factors in Computing Systems, CHI 2009, pp. 1619–1628. Association for Computing Machinery, Boston, April 2009. https://doi.org/10.1145/1518701.1518948
8. Castillo, J.C., Hartson, H.R., Hix, D.: Remote usability evaluation: can users report their own critical incidents? In: CHI 1998 Conference Summary on Human Factors in Computing Systems, CHI 1998, pp. 253–254. Association for Computing Machinery, Los Angeles, April 1998. https://doi.org/10.1145/286498.286736
9. World Leaders in Research-Based User Experience: Formative vs. Summative Evaluations, July 2019. https://www.nngroup.com/articles/formative-vs-summative-evaluations/. Accessed 2 Feb 2021
10. Fischer, B., Peine, A., stlund, B.: The importance of user involvement: a systematic review of involving older users in technology design. Gerontologist 60(7), e513–e523 (2020). https://doi.org/10.1093/geront/gnz163. https://academic.oup.com/gerontologist/article/60/7/e513/5644100
11. Fuglerud, K.S.: Inclusive design of ICT: the challenge of diversity. Ph.D. thesis, University of Oslo, Faculty of humanities (2014). https://doi.org/10.13140/2.1.4471.5844. http://publications.nr.no/1418159224/Fuglerud_2014_PhD-Thesis_Inclusive-design-of-ICT.pdf
12. Fuglerud, K.S., Halbach, T., Tjøstheim, I.: Cost-benefit analysis of universal design, January 2015
13. Giannoumis, G.A., Stein, M.A.: Conceptualizing universal design for the information society through a universal human rights lens. Int. Hum. Rights Law Rev. 8(1), 38–66 (2019). https://doi.org/10.1163/22131035-00801006. https://brill.com/view/journals/hrlr/8/1/article-p38_38.xml

14. Halbach, T., Fuglerud, K.S.: On assessing the costs and benefits of universal design of ICT. Stud. Health Technol. Inf. **229**, 662–672 (2016)

15. Hartson, H.R., Castillo, J.C., Kelso, J., Neale, W.C.: Remote evaluation: the network as an extension of the usability laboratory. In: Proceedings of the SIGCHI Conference on Human Factors in Computing Systems, pp. 228–235 (1996)

16. Hertzum, M., Jacobsen, N.E.: The evaluator effect: a chilling fact about usability evaluation methods. Int. J. Hum.-Comput. Interact. **13**(4), 421–443 (2001). https://doi.org/10.1207/S15327590IJHC1304_05

17. Janson, A.L., Moen, A., Fuglerud, K.S.: Design of the CAPABLE prototype: preliminary results of citizen expectations. In: Norwegian Centre for E-health Research og EHiN Research (ed.) Linkping Electronic Conference Proceedings, p. 181. Linkping Electronic Conference Proceedings, No (2019). http://www.ep.liu.se/ecp/161/ecp19161.pdf

18. Janson, A.L., Moen, A., Fuglerud, K.S.: Design of the capable health empowerment tool: citizens' needs and expectations. Stud. Health Technol. Inf. **270**, 926–930 (2020)

19. McFadden, E., Hager, D.R., Elie, C.J., Blackwell, J.M.: Remote usability evaluation: overview and case studies. Int. J. Hum.-comput. Interact. **14**(3–4), 489–502 (2002)

20. McLaughlin, A.C., et al.: Evaluating medical devices remotely: current methods and potential innovations. Hum. Factors **62**(7), 1041–1060 (2020)

21. Miao, M., Pham, H.A., Friebe, J., Weber, G.: Contrasting usability evaluation methods with blind users. Univ. Access Inf. Soci. **15**(1), 63–76 (2016). https://doi.org/10.1007/s10209-014-0378-8

22. Microsoft: Accessibility overview of Microsoft Teams (2020). https://support.microsoft.com/en-us/office/accessibility-overview-of-microsoft-teams-2d4009e7-1300-4766-87e8-7a217496c3d5

23. Miljverndepartementet: T-1468 B/E Universell utforming, November 2007. https://www.regjeringen.no/no/dokumenter/t-1468-universell-utforming/id493083/

24. Nielsen, J.: Demonstrate thinking aloud by showing users a video (2014)

25. Øyvann, S.: Vipps har vunnet Innovasjonsprisen for universell utforming—Computerworld, January 2021. https://www.cw.no/artikkel/utvikling/vipps-har-vunnet-innovasjonsprisen-universell-utforming

26. Persson, H., Ohlsson, K., Petersén, S., Jonsäll, A.: Unexploited resources in interaction design for universal access: people with impairments as a resource for interaction designers. In: Stephanidis, C. (ed.) UAHCI 2009. LNCS, vol. 5614, pp. 145–153. Springer, Heidelberg (2009). https://doi.org/10.1007/978-3-642-02707-9_16

27. Petrie, H., Hamilton, F., King, N., Pavan, P.: Remote usability evaluations with disabled people. In: Proceedings of the SIGCHI Conference on Human Factors in Computing Systems, CHI 2006, pp. 1133–1141. Association for Computing Machinery, Montréal, April 2006. https://doi.org/10.1145/1124772.1124942

28. Power, C., Petrie, H.: Working with participants. In: Yesilada, Y., Harper, S. (eds.) Web Accessibility. HIS, pp. 153–168. Springer, London (2019). https://doi.org/10.1007/978-1-4471-7440-0_9

29. Richter, A.: Locked-down digital work. Int. J. Inf. Manage. **55** (2020). https://doi.org/10.1016/j.ijinfomgt.2020.102157. http://www.sciencedirect.com/science/article/pii/S0268401220308422

30. Rickly, J., Halpern, N., Hansen, M., McCabe, S., Fellenor, J.: Covid-19: the effects of isolation and social distancing on people with vision impairment, September 2020. https://doi.org/10.17639/nott.7074. https://rdmc.nottingham. ac.uk/handle/internal/8608. Accessed 28 Jan 2021

31. Røssvoll, T.H., Fuglerud, K.S.: Best practice for efficient development of inclusive ICT. In: Stephanidis, C., Antona, M. (eds.) UAHCI 2013. LNCS, vol. 8009, pp. 97–106. Springer, Heidelberg (2013). https://doi.org/10.1007/978-3-642-39188-0_11

32. Sauro, J.: A practical guide to measuring usability: 72 answers to the most common questions about quantifying the usability of websites and software. Measuring Usability LCC, Denver (2010)

33. Schmutz, S., Sonderegger, A., Sauer, J.: Implementing recommendations from web accessibility guidelines: would they also provide benefits to nondisabled users. Hum. Factors **58**(4), 611–629 (2016). https://doi.org/10.1177/0018720816640962

34. Schmutz, S., Sonderegger, A., Sauer, J.: Implementing recommendations from web accessibility guidelines: a comparative study of nondisabled users and users with visual impairments. Hum. Factors **59**(6), 956–972 (2017). https://doi.org/10.1177/0018720817708397

35. Schnepp, J., Shiver, B.: Improving deaf accessibility in remote usability testing. In: The Proceedings of the 13th International ACM SIGACCESS Conference on Computers and Accessibility, ASSETS 2011, pp. 255–256. Association for Computing Machinery, Dundee, October 2011. https://doi.org/10.1145/2049536.2049594

36. Sova, D.H., Nielsen, J.: 234 Tips and tricks for recruiting users as participants in usability studies. Technical report, Nilsen Norman Group, January 2003. https:// www.nngroup.com/reports/how-to-recruit-participants-usability-studies/

37. Venable, J., Pries-Heje, J., Baskerville, R.: FEDS: a framework for evaluation in design science research. Eur. J. Inf. Syst. **25**(1), 77–89 (2016). https://doi.org/10. 1057/ejis.2014.36

38. World Wide Web Consortium (W3C): Web content accessibility guidelines (WCAG) 2.0, December 2008. https://www.w3.org/TR/WCAG20/. Accessed 17 Sept 2020

39. World Wide Web Consortium (W3C): Web content accessibility guidelines (WCAG) 2.1, June 2018. https://www.w3.org/TR/WCAG21/. Accessed 17 Sept 2020

40. Zoom Video Communications: Meetings for Everyone (2019). https://zoom.us/ accessibility

A Multidisciplinary User-Centered Approach to Designing an Information Platform for Accessible Tourism: Understanding User Needs and Motivations

Pedro Teixeira[1], Joana Alves[1], Tiago Correia[2], Leonor Teixeira[3]([✉]) [iD],
Celeste Eusébio[4] [iD], Samuel Silva[2], and António Teixeira[2]

[1] Department of Economics, Management, Industrial Engineering and Tourism,
University of Aveiro, 3010-193 Aveiro, Portugal
{pmiguel,joanapimentelalves}@ua.pt
[2] Institute of Electronics and Informatics Engineering of Aveiro, Department of Electronics,
Telecommunications and Informatics, University of Aveiro, 3010-193 Aveiro, Portugal
{tcorreia,sss,ajst}@ua.pt
[3] Institute of Electronics and Informatics Engineering of Aveiro, Department of Economics,
Management, Industrial Engineering and Tourism, University of Aveiro,
3010-193 Aveiro, Portugal
lteixeira@ua.pt
[4] Governance, Competitiveness and Public Policies, Department of Economics, Management,
Industrial Engineering and Tourism, University of Aveiro, 3010-193 Aveiro, Portugal
celeste.eusebio@ua.pt

Abstract. The present work aims to expand knowledge on user needs and the motivations of people with disabilities (PwD) in order to create a technological solution for addressing barriers in the accessible tourism market. For this, a user-centered design was followed, putting PwD at the center of the development process. This was obtained by identifying personas and scenarios contributing to a better depiction of the potential users, clearly describing their requirements and accessibility needs. For obtaining the characterization of personas, a comprehensive study in the area of accessible tourism, involving various tourism stakeholders was performed. The methods applied to collect the data were questionnaires, interviews and two focus groups with PwD. Two personas are presented in this article, illustrating the needs and motivations of two groups of PwD. In addition, two scenarios concerning the personas were also elaborated, showing how a technological solution can help the integration in tourism activities.

Keywords: Accessible tourism · User-centered design · Visitors with disabilities

1 Introduction

Information is a crucial resource in accessible tourism [1], transmitting more security and confidence to people with special needs (PwSN) during decision-making processes

© Springer Nature Switzerland AG 2021
M. Antona and C. Stephanidis (Eds.): HCII 2021, LNCS 12768, pp. 136–150, 2021.
https://doi.org/10.1007/978-3-030-78092-0_9

[2]. According to Darcy and Dickson [3], accessible tourism is a solution that enables people with accessibility requirements (e.g. mobility, vision, hearing, cognitive or other functional limitations) to experience tourism products, services and environments independently, with equity and dignity. Accessible tourism seeks to be an inclusive response for all, including people with disabilities (PwD) or other special needs [4, 5].

For PwD the planning stage of a tourism trip is important to ensure that their accessibility requirements are met. In this context, information has a major contribution, since the greater the accessibility requirements, the greater the need for details of information [6]. Moreover, PwD are not a homogenous group of users [7, 8], as different types of disabilities have different demands and requirements [8]. The difficulty of obtaining information according to the needs of the person may lead to their avoiding vacations or seeking alternative leisure solutions [9]. In order to eliminate information barriers between supply and demand, solutions based on information systems are often proposed [10]. However, the process of developing such applications must consider not only the level of accessibility, but also provide all the necessary information, including that related to accessibility. Additionally, it requires merging several areas of expertise to obtain a holistic view of PwD's needs, their contexts, and how these blend with their expectations and needs for participating in tourism activities.

The adoption of a user-centered design (UCD) approach can facilitate the development of this type of solution, since it fosters a focus on user needs and motivations [11]. In this regard, two important challenges need to be tackled: 1) user diversity needs to be thoroughly understood through methods that continuously include users, bring insight into their contexts, capture their behaviors, and create space for their contributions; and 2) the intrinsically multidisciplinary research team involved needs to find common ground to be able to propose novel solutions for the field. Addressing both these challenges can often pose difficulties, since a thorough characterization of users conducted by domain experts in order to capture their diversity can lead to overly complex and hard-to-grasp data to be considered in subsequent stages of the work. In this regard, the literature has adopted tools such as personas and scenarios to embody the most relevant characteristics, contexts and approaches to be considered to develop tourism information systems for PwD. These help establish the common ground to support the interdisciplinary dialogue towards the elicitation of requirements [12, 13].

In this matter, despite the importance of this field, to the best of our knowledge, both these challenges remain unaddressed, as the literature has yet to provide a systematic account of PwD characteristics, needs and motivations for accessibility information. This, in turn, constitutes an immense barrier for those aiming to propose assistive technologies for this audience. So, aiming to fill this gap, the present work describes the core aspects of a human-centered multidisciplinary effort encompassing: 1) a thorough characterization of PwD and their needs regarding accessible tourism for the Portuguese context; 2) the materialization of the data gathered into representative personas of the different types of PwD; and 3) a proposal of illustrative scenarios regarding how the identified needs can be tackled by technology-mediated solutions. These contributions enable a better depiction of the potential users, clearly describing their requirements and accessibility needs, as well as their travel tourism behavior, so that potential information platforms that address these issues can be more easily developed. In this study, even though the research for the characterization of different groups of PwD has already been performed, only two personas were already developed. They are presented as an illustration of how the obtained data can be materialized in tools that can support the design and development of novel assistive technologies. The two personas represent the most ignored groups of PwD in accessible tourism research: the deaf and those with intellectual disability.

This work is structured in five sections. The present section contains the introduction, explaining the scope and the objectives. The second section presents a literature review in the field of accessible tourism, with a brief characterization of the market and user requirements. Additionally, the importance of a UCD approach for developing accessible tourism information systems is also explained, as well as how the concept of personas and scenarios can enhance the potential of that methodology. The third section clarifies the problem, and the methodology applied to obtain the personas. In the fourth section, two personas and representative scenarios developed in this study are exhibited. The last section contains the main conclusions and describes possible limitations and future work.

2 Literature Review

2.1 People with Disabilities: Relevance, Constraints and Needs

General improvements in people's living conditions and advances in medicine have increased life expectancy. On the one hand, people with disabilities, syndromes and other rare diseases now have a chance of living longer and under better conditions than in the past [14]. On the other hand, people will live longer and will probably lose some abilities during their lifespan and become dependent [15, 16]. The number of individuals who have support needs and special requirements to access environments, services or products has been increased. According to WHO (2020), 15% of the world's population (over 1 billion people) have a disability. In Portugal, about 18% of the population have some disability or impairment [17]. In other words, the number of people with disabilities that can benefit from a tourism experience are already considerable [18] and it is likely to increase in the future as a result of population ageing.

With these changes in demographics, there are PwD in all communities [19]. The definition of disability aggregates very heterogeneous people, with different types of support needs and accessible requirements, as a result of an intersection between biological conditions of the individuals (their body functions—mobility, vision, hearing and cognitive) with characteristics of the physical and social environment [20–23]. Disabilities can be permanent or temporary [5] and vary in degree (e.g. mild, moderate, and severe) [24]. The level of support needs and the adequacy of environmental conditions for PwD's needs affect their participation in social life, including tourism activities, where accessibility of the physical environment and accessible information are of utmost importance in increasing the participation of PwD in tourism activities [25].

Physical disability is characterized by restrictions on people's mobility that may have a temporary or permanent character, depending on whether the restrictions are inherited or genetic [24, 26]. Since physical disability affects people's capacity to move around, physical accessibility to the environments and services are essential for their participation in tourism activities [27–29]. In the same way, people with physical disabilities point out structural constraints (e.g. lack of accessibility in buildings or public transport) as the factors which most inhibit participation in society, including tourism [28, 30].

Beyond the physical, there are other types of disabilities, such as sensory. This type of disability is also heterogeneous, depending on the sense affected. Vision restrictions may result in blindness (when a person cannot see), or in low vision (if the lost vision cannot be corrected by glasses) while hearing restrictions could result in deafness (if a person cannot hear) [31]. The causes of sensory disabilities are multiple (e.g. conditions of diseases, accidents, aging process), and can be genetic or inherited [24]. Regarding access, considering that most information is provided by visual or audio formats [31], information access requirements are essential for people with sensory disabilities [32–35]. Whereas deaf people need visual support (e.g. sign language and/or visual alarms systems) to be able to access information and communicate with others [36, 37], blind and low-sighted people need audio (e.g. screen readers) and tactile support (e.g. braille and/or high relief mockups) to have access to information. In addition, for blind and low-sighted people, physical accessibility is important for their mobility in safety [32, 38, 39]. Due to these characteristics, people with sensory disabilities report different types of constraints regarding access to information and communication barriers: structural (e.g. lack of accessible information), intrapersonal (e.g. inability to access to visual or audio information and/or experiences; orientation in unfamiliar environments) and interpersonal (e.g. dependence of a family member or a friend to communicate with others) [34, 38].

An intellectual disability affects a person's intellectual functions (like learning, reasoning, problem-solving capacities) and adaptive behavior (like conceptual, social and practical skills to learn and perform daily living activities) [40]. Intellectual disabilities also have multiple causes (e.g. genetic conditions, problems during pregnancy and birth, community environmental factors). People with intellectual disabilities have difficulty in processing information and adapting their behavior. In this sense, information and communication access requirements (e.g. pictographic writing, uses of simple language principles) and personal support in daily activities (e.g. personal assistance to help in travel and transports, schedules and routines, use of money, personal care) are the most common access requirements for people with this type of disability [41–43].

All these constraints apart, PwD have the same predisposition as everybody else to participate in tourism experiences. In addition to general motivations, escaping from routine, getting away from the usual care environment, gaining self-confidence and being free are the most common reasons for PwD to engage in a tourism or leisure experience according to the literature [8, 30, 44, 45]. The adequacy of environment, services and products to PwD's needs can directly affect their levels of participation, allowing all people, regardless of the diversity of their accessible requirements, to access and enjoy tourism experiences.

2.2 The Importance of a User-Centered Approach in the Development of Accessible Tourism Information Systems

Due to the complexity of the accessible tourism market and the diversity of accessible requirements, conceptualizing tourism information systems [46, 47] can be a rather difficult task [35]. Some authors [7] point out that the main focus should be accessibility, which may imply broad changes to assessment, testing, and validation processes during the development of information systems [48].

Accessibility is directly connected to users' special requirements and particular needs [49], and failure in the integration of this type of human perspective can lead to failures in the implementation processes of information systems in this area and may lead to unsatisfactory results [50]. In addressing this issue, it is important to understand users' point of view, which can be achieved by applying UCD methodologies. The main focus of UCD is "an approach to design interactive systems development that aims to make systems usable and useful by focusing on the users, their needs and requirements, and by applying human factors/ergonomics, and usability knowledge and techniques" [51, p. 1]. The main objective for applying UCD is to focus on the users by incorporating them into the software development procedure [52, 53]. The intention is to look at the system the same way a user sees it, assimilating usability and software requirements [54], with the user's motivation to use the system. For applying UCD methodologies to develop information systems, it is necessary to i) understand and specify the context of use; ii) specify user and system requirements, and iii) design and evaluate the solution [51].

The application of the UCD implies great knowledge of the context and users. Therefore, for developing user-oriented products, elaborating models which describe the users, based on their behaviors can be a good solution. These user models can be represented through the concept of personas [12]. Adlin and Pruitt [55] define personas as imaginary representations of users and their motivations, allowing a better understanding of the users in a more interactive way. Although they are illustrated as individuals, the intention is for them to represent a group of users with similar requirements, allowing a better representation of patterns of behavior, ways of thinking and motivations.

In the tourism sector, the concept of personas has mainly been used to perform market segmentation studies [56]. However, in the context of accessible tourism, due to the potential to perform an analysis of user needs, it can be a crucial step to perform the characterization of visitors with disabilities (VwD). In this context, personas can help establish profiles of VwD, allowing a better understanding of their particular requirements, such as favorite tourism activities or types of vacations. Thus, due to the nature of the requirements of the accessible tourism market, the development of information systems can benefit from a UCD approach using the concept of personas.

3 Problem Contextualization and Methodology

3.1 Problem and Methodology

This work is part of a research project which aims to create a web-based information system (WBIS), supporting information management and knowledge sharing in the accessible tourism context. The intended information system should work as a mediator between offer and supply in the accessible tourism market, providing knowledge transfer among all stakeholders (consumers, supply agents and institutions for training in tourism), and promoting access to relevant information.

To achieve the intended WBIS, a methodological approach that integrates the principles of UCD will be adopted (Fig. 1). The intention of this interactive procedure is to create the WBIS through different stages, always centered on user needs. Because the accessible tourism market is so different and complex, better recognition and interpretation of the users through the use of personas and scenarios can dictate the success of developing accessible information systems for this type of market. This work intends to explore how the creation of personas and scenarios represents an important addition to UCD procedures. It is important to note that, although the market incorporates different stakeholders, the most important accessibility requirements are gathered from VwD. Therefore, personas and scenarios for VwD were created to simplify the development process and help the transition to design phases. By using these, the complexity of the accessible tourism market can be better explored, thus providing meaningful inputs to develop the solution. However, to develop representative personas, both qualitative and quantitative data collection methods were used, specifically interviews, questionnaires and focus groups.

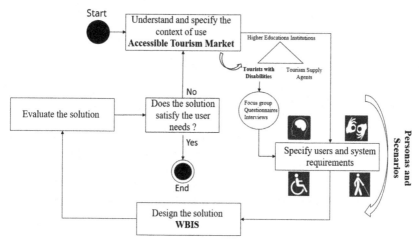

Fig. 1. UCD approached used to develop the WBIS.

3.2 Data Collection Methods

To identify the characteristics, needs, motivations, and requirements of PwD, including needs in terms of information and requirements that should be included in the present system, a mix of quantitative (questionnaire) and qualitative (interviews and focus groups) methods was used in this study.

First, to analyze the perspectives of PwD regarding tourism, a sample of PwD and social organizations (SO) that provide support to this market, especially to persons with intellectual disabilities, were interviewed. Then, to obtain the information required to develop the information system, a questionnaire was administrated to a sample of Portuguese PwD. The scripted interviews and questionnaire were designed based on the literature regarding accessible tourism and international and national laws related to the consumption of tourism products [57–59]. In the interviews, open-ended questions were used to gain insight into the thoughts and experiences of the interviewees about travel behavior, travel planning, travel motivations, accessibility requirements, and information system characteristics (relevance, probability of using, inputs to insert and information to retrieve from it). In questionnaires, the different types of questions (Likert scale, multiple choice, rating scale and open-ended questions) were designed mainly to obtained information about the same themes. Both instruments also included socio-demographic questions, which are important for understanding the profile of the respondents.

Given the heterogeneity of PwD, two focus groups were led to complement and broaden the data obtained in the interviews and questionnaires regarding needs, motivations and information users' requirements. PwD and SO that provide support to PwD participated in the focus groups. The participants were selected with the purpose of achieving contributors from all over the country and with different types and levels of disabilities (mobility, vision, hearing, cognitive). Nine people participated in two focus groups, with a total duration of 5 h and 04 min. Two Portuguese sign language interpreters mediated the participation of a deaf person in the focus group. Table 1 illustrates the process used to collect the data.

Table 1. Data Collection Procedure

Population	Interviews	Questionnaires	Focus Groups
	PwD and SO	PwD	PwD and SO
Sampling approach	Non-probabilistic (convenience and snowballing)	Non-probabilistic (convenience and snowballing)	Non-probabilistic (convenience and snowballing)
Administration method	Face-to-face and online (February and March 2019)	Online and face-to-face (July 2019 to February to 2020)	Online (May 2020)
Language	Portuguese	Portuguese	Portuguese
Sample size	53 interviews (31 PwD and 22 SO)	504 valid questionnaires	9 participants
Data analysis method	Content analysis	Descriptive analysis	Content analysis

After collecting the relevant information to develop personas and scenarios, the most important results concerning travel planning, travel motivations, accessible requirements and interest and characteristics of information system are summarized in Table 2. Owing the heterogeneity of the market under analysis, and despite the data collected including different types of VwD, this article focuses on the main results obtained for visitors with deaf and intellectual disability. The data presented in Table 2 provide relevant insights for exploring the views and needs of the two mentioned types of VwD, providing the necessary inputs to build personas and scenarios, representing those two groups.

Table 2. The most important characteristics of users according to the interviews, questionnaires and focus groups

		Deaf	Intellectual Disability
Travel planning	Person responsible	Oneself; family members	Social organization; family members
	Information sources	Internet	Internet (e.g. social media) and social organization recommendation
	Devices	Mobile phone and computer	Mobile phone and computer
Travel motivations		Have a good time; relax and rest; be happy; and exploring new places	Be happy; have fun; explore new cultures
Travel behavior	Activities	Visit historical places, museums and monuments	Nature tourism; go to the beach
	Travel group	Family and friends	Social organization; family
	Type transport	Car and bus	Bus and airplane
	Accommodation	Hotel	Hotel; family and friends' accommodation
	Type of travel	Independent or with family	Trips organized by social organizations
Accessible requirements		Sign language services; video-guides with sign language; subtitles; visual and sound alarms	Accessible language and information (simple and intuitive); pictograms
System	Interest	Great interest (72%)	Medium interest (46%)
	Characteristics	Information in accessible language; simple navigation; information in sign language	Accessible language and information; simple navigation system

4 Personas and Scenarios

For the work described in Sect. 3 to be useful for creating the intended WBIS, the rich plethora of information collected (Table 2) was then materialized in a family of personas deemed representative of the different characteristics, motivations and stakeholders. In total, and aligned with the data obtained for the Portuguese context of accessible tourism, we are working on four personas, each corresponding to one of the major disabilities (mobility, vision, hearing and intellectual). Below, we report on the two that have already reached a first version as an illustration on how the immense set of characteristics and motivations may be represented. This section presents the developed personas and a set of representative scenarios.

4.1 Personas

One important aspect to note when developing a persona is that it should not be limited to a table with demographic and biographic data. Instead, it should consist of a credible account of a person and avoid using language that is too specific to a particular area (e.g., medical terms) without illustrating how it affects the person's abilities and behaviors. It is this focus on abilities and behaviors, along with other biographical details that fosters both empathy and understanding by the different members of the multidisciplinary team. Additionally, one crucial aspect of the personas presented below is their motivation, since this is the motto by which all design and development options taken need to be assessed: any feature of an assistive technology that does not move the persona closer to fulfilling the motivation should be reassessed.

Considering the abovementioned aspects, two personas were created for characterizing VwD: i) José, a deaf teacher (Fig. 2); and ii) Marta, a bocce player and bartender in a SO, with intellectual disabilities (Fig. 3). These personas were developed based on the information obtained from the users through interviews, questionnaires and the focus groups (see Table 2).

José Alberto Dias[a]

José is a mathematics teacher at António Damásio Secondary School. He is 37 years old, lives in Lisbon and is deaf. He likes to travel with his family and discover new places. He usually makes some national and international trips as part of his work, but sometimes he has difficulties in planning and organizing the trip, and also communicating at the destination. As he is deaf, he needs more accessible information about places to visit and the conditions for deaf people. Even so, he travels because it makes him happy and he likes to meet new people and learn about new settings.

Motivation: José wants to continue travelling for leisure and work and for this to happen he would like to be able to search in an intuitive way (simple language), and when possible access information in Portuguese sign language.

a-Image adapted from: https://thispersondoesnotexist.com

Fig. 2. José, a deaf teacher

Marta Pereira[b]

Marta is a 22-year-old bartender in a social organization for people with intellectual disabilities, where she also practices swimming and bocce. She has an intellectual disability, but likes to travel and usually does it by means of the association's activities, to take part in tournaments. She likes to participate in the decision process of selecting places and destinations to visit. She needs some support to plan trips, getting it from the association and his relatives, but she is also a bit anxious, when unaware of what the routine of his trip will look like.

Motivation: Marta would like to be more participative in the planning and decision of the places to visit and activities to be carried out. For Marta to be part of this process, the language should be displayed accessibly. She would also like to define her travel routine in advance, so that she can consult it.

b-Image adapted from: https://www.flickr.com/photos/so-austria/15093281648

Fig. 3. Marta, a bocce player and bartender with intellectual disabilities

4.2 Scenarios

While the personas are an important resource when proposing novel solutions to support PwD in fulfilling their motivations, they are just the beginning. Next, the team needs to place the personas in their contexts and devise assistive solutions adapted to the characteristics, behaviors and motivations of the personas. To this end, the first level of this effort can be supported with scenarios. In multidisciplinary teams, scenarios are crucial so everyone can be acquainted with the situation and participate in the discussion. Our team is currently working on proposing and discussing different scenarios for the two presented personas and these should, in the long run, yield the requirements for the assistive technology for accessing accessibility information. Below we present two of the proposed scenarios for José and Marta, the two personas described.

JOSÉ SEARCHES FOR A LEISURE ACTIVITY: On his way to the restaurant to have dinner, José noticed a museum dedicated to art on one of the streets near his hotel and thought it might be interesting to visit it the next day. After dinner, when he returned to the hotel room, he decided to get some information about the accessibility conditions of the museum. When entering the system, as he did not remember the name of the museum, he chose an option which allows him to see places of interest in the surrounding area. He found the museum that he was looking for but, unfortunately, it did not offer guided tours in Portuguese Sign Language (PSL). José was disappointed because it seemed like the perfect activity for the following day. Then he noticed that the platform suggested some options that might be of interest: he spotted a theatre play, the day after at 10 am, with PSL interpretation, 10 minutes from his hotel. As José would only attend the afternoon conference on Sunday, he had the morning available to watch this play.

MARTA TAKES PART IN DECISIONS FOR THE TRAVEL PLAN: In order to prepare for the trip, the caregivers and Marta talk about the type of activities she would like to do during the trip. Marta is usually a little anxious about these trips, because she is used to following a routine in her daily basis. All this unpredictability inherent in a trip makes her a little anxious, so she likes to be a more active participant and understand every detail of the trip. So, the caregiver and Marta go through possible activities on the device so that Marta can choose the ones that spark her interest. Marta doesn't like the first activity that she sees, because it involves heights and Marta has a phobia of heights and she "dislikes" the picture of the activity. The second activity seems to be more interesting for Marta and she reacts, on her device, with a "like" for that activity.

One important aspect to highlight, which makes scenarios an important tool to support multidisciplinary work, is that they are not about technical aspects, but about behaviors, actions and context. These scenarios are a depiction of what happens to the personas when using a novel assistive system, along with the when, how and where it happens.

The scenarios above present some underlined text identifying aspects that need to be supported by the system and these, extracted from the full set of scenarios, will be incorporated in the list of requirements to be fulfilled.

5 Conclusion

This study described the development process of an assistive technology (information system) in the accessible tourism context. Due to the characteristics of this market, the development of the information system followed a UCD methodology, integrating the persona and scenario concepts for a better characterization of VwD.

Two of the personas have already been developed and are presented along with two scenarios illustrating how they can be considered to design novel solutions. The creation of the personas provides an overview of the special needs and accessibility requirements of the tourism accessible market. These characteristics reflected the results obtained with data collected using questionnaires, interviews and focus groups. Based on the personas, different scenarios representing the use of the platform in the planning phase and during a tourism trip were defined.

The description of these particular contexts with personas and scenarios is an engaging process supporting elicitation of requirements for the conceptualization and development of accessible tourism information systems. These contributions, encompassing the methodological approach, the personas and the scenarios, provided solid and substantiated grounds to support our ongoing research and are a first step to foster further investigation efforts in the development of information systems, concerning environments encompassing accessible tourism.

Although the study presented a good research basis, some limitations can be pointed out. The study only presents personas and scenarios for two types of PwD and they are only representative of the Portuguese context. Considering this, we believe that in the future, this work can be expanded by creating more types of personas and scenarios concerning other PwD. In addition, the development process needs to produce a solution, whose concept should be tested in order to assess the success of the methodology. This could be achieved by obtaining a prototype and testing it in a real-life environment, as indicated in UCD methodologies.

Acknowledgments. This work was developed in the scope of the research project ACTION - POCI-01–0145-FEDER-030376 - funded by FEDER, through COMPETE2020 - Programa Operacional Competitividade e Internacionalização (POCI), and by national funds (OE), through FCT/MCTES; and supported by Portugal 2020 under COMPETE Program, and the European Regional Development Fund through project SOCA – Smart Open Campus (CENTRO-01–0145-FEDER-000010).

References

1. Michopoulou, E., Buhalis, D.: Information provision for challenging markets: the case of the accessibility requiring market in the context of tourism. Inf. Manag. **50**, 229–239 (2013). https://doi.org/10.1016/j.im.2013.04.001
2. Evcil, A.N.: Barriers and preferences to leisure activities for wheelchair users in historic places. Tour. Geogr. **20**, 698–715 (2018). https://doi.org/10.1080/14616688.2017.1293721
3. Darcy, S., Dickson, T.: A whole-of-life approach to tourism: the case for accessible tourism experiences. J. Hosp. Tour. Manag. **16**, 32–44 (2009). https://doi.org/10.1375/jhtm.16.1.32
4. Liasidou, S., Umbelino, J., Amorim, É.: Revisiting tourism studies curriculum to highlight accessible and inclusive tourism. J. Teach. Travel. Tour. **19**, 112–125 (2019). https://doi.org/10.1080/15313220.2018.1522289
5. McCabe, S., Diekmann, A.: The rights to tourism: Reflections on social tourism and human rights. Tour. Recreat. Res. **40**, 194–204 (2015). https://doi.org/10.1080/02508281.2015.1049022
6. Buhalis, D., Eichhorn, V., Michopoulou, E., Miller, G.: Accessibility market and stakeholder analysis. OSSATE Access Mark Stakehold Anal (2005)
7. Buhalis, D., Michopoulou, E.: Information-enabled tourism destination marketing: addressing the accessibility market. Curr. Issues Tour. **14**, 145–168 (2011). https://doi.org/10.1080/13683501003653361
8. Figueiredo, E., Eusébio, C., Kastenholz, E.: How diverse are tourists with disabilities? A pilot study on accessible leisure tourism experiences in Portugal. Int. J. Tour. Res. **14**, 531–550 (2012). https://doi.org/10.1002/jtr.1913
9. Waschke, S.: Labeling im Barrierefreien Tourismus in Deutschland – Vergleichende Analyse auf Basis Europäischer Beispiele. Thesis. Universität Lüneburg. Universität Lüneburg (2004)
10. Kołodziejczak, A.: Information as a factor of the development of accessible tourism for people with disabilities. Quaest. Geogr. **38**, 67–73 (2019). https://doi.org/10.2478/quageo-2019-0014
11. Teixeira, L., Saavedra, V., Santos, B., Ferreira, C.: Integrating human factors in information systems development: user centred and agile development approaches. In: Duffy, V.G.G. (ed.) DHM 2016. LNCS, vol. 9745, pp. 345–356. Springer, Cham (2016). https://doi.org/10.1007/978-3-319-40247-5_35
12. Cooper, A., Reimann, R., Cronin, D.: About Face 3: The Essentials of Interaction Design. Wiley, New York (2007)

13. Silva, S., Felgueiras, R., Oliveira, I.C.: Geriatric helper: an mhealth application to support comprehensive geriatric assessment. Sensors (Switzerland) **18**, 1–21 (2018). https://doi.org/ 10.3390/s18041285
14. Sánchez, A.S.: Las personas en situación de dependencia, Polibea pp. 32–38 (2002)
15. Alves, J.P.: Cuidar e ser cuidado: Uma análise do cuidado quotidiano, permanente e de longa duração. University of Coimbra (2016)
16. Alves, J.P.: Vidas de Cuidado(s). Uma análise sociológica do papel dos cuidadores informais. University of Coimbra (2011)
17. INE: Resultados Definitivos (2012)
18. Cole, S., Morgan, N.: Introduction: tourism and inequalities. In: Cole, S., Morgan, N. (eds.) Tourism and Inequality: Problems and Prospects. CAB International (2010)
19. Small, J., Darcy, S.: Tourism, disability and mobility. In: Tourism and Inequality: Problems and Prospects, pp. 1–20. CABI Publishing (2010)
20. Oliver, M.: The Politics of Disablement. Macmillan Education, London (1990)
21. Thomas, C.: Sociologies of Disability and Illness. Contested Ideas in Disability Studies and Medical Sociology. Houndmills, Basingstoke (2007)
22. Eisenberg, Y., Maisel, J.: Environmental contexts shaping disability and health. In: Lollar, D.J., Horner-Johnson, W., Froehlich-Grobe, K. (eds.) Public Health Perspectives on Disability, pp. 107–128. Springer, New York (2021). https://doi.org/10.1007/978-1-0716-0888-3_5
23. Froehlich-Grobe, K., Douglas, M., Ochoa, C., Betts, A.: Social determinants of health and disability. In: Lollar, D.J., Horner-Johnson, W., Froehlich-Grobe, K. (eds.) Public Health Perspectives on Disability, pp. 53–89. Springer, New York (2021). https://doi.org/10.1007/ 978-1-0716-0888-3_3
24. ICF: International classification of functioning, Disability and Health. Geneva (2002)
25. Buhalis, D., Darcy, S.: Accessible Tourism Concepts and Issues. Channel View Publications, London (2011)
26. ARUMA: Types of physical disabilities (2019). https://www.aruma.com.au/about-us/about-disability/types-of-disabilities/types-of-physical-disabilities/. Accessed 12 Feb 2021
27. Daniels, M., Rodgers, E., Wiggins, B.: "Travel Tales": an interpretive analysis of constraints and negotiations to pleasure travel as experienced by persons with physical disabilities. Tour. Manag. **26**, 919–930 (2005). https://doi.org/10.1016/j.tourman.2004.06.010
28. Card, J., Cole, S., Humphrey, A.: A comparison of the accessibility and attitudinal barriers model: travel providers and travelers with physical disabilities. Asia Pacific J. Tour. Res. **11**, 161–175 (2006). https://doi.org/10.1080/10941660600727566
29. Ray, N., Ryder, M.: "Ebilities" tourism: an exploratory discussion of the travel needs and motivations of the mobility-disabled. Tour. Manag. **24**, 57–72 (2003). https://doi.org/10.1016/ S0261-5177(02)00037-7
30. Bauer, I.: When travel is a challenge: travel medicine and the 'dis-abled' traveller. Travel Med. Infect. Dis **22**, 66–72 (2018). https://doi.org/10.1016/j.tmaid.2018.02.001
31. ARUMA: Types of sensory disabilities (2019). https://www.aruma.com.au/about-us/about-disability/types-of-disabilities/types-of-sensory-disabilities/. Accessed 12 Feb 2021
32. Small, J.: Interconnecting mobilities on tour: tourists with vision impairment partnered with sighted tourists. Tour. Geogr. **17**, 76–90 (2015). https://doi.org/10.1080/14616688.2014. 938690
33. Loi, K.I., Kong, W.H.: Tourism for all: challenges and issues faced by people with vision impairment. Tour. Plan. Dev. **14**, 181–197 (2017). https://doi.org/10.1080/21568316.2016. 1204357
34. Goss, J., Kollmann, E., Reich, C., Iacovelli, S.: Understanding the multilingualism and communication of museum visitors who are d/deaf or hard of Hearing. Museums Soc. Issues **10**, 52–65 (2015). https://doi.org/10.1179/1559689314Z.00000000032

35. Zajadacz, A.: Sources of tourist information used by deaf people. case study: the polish deaf community. Curr. Issues Tour. **17**, 434–454 (2014). https://doi.org/10.1080/13683500.2012.725713

36. Constantinou, V., Loizides, F., Ioannou, A.: A personal tour of cultural heritage for deaf museum visitors. In: Ioannides, M., Fink, E., et al. (eds.) Digital Heritage. Progress in Cultural Heritage: Documentation, Preservation, and Protection, pp. 214–221. Springer International Publishing, Cham (2016). https://doi.org/10.1007/978-3-319-48974-2_24

37. Zajadacz, A., Śniadek, J.: Tourism activities of deaf poles. Phys. Cult. Sport Stud. Res. **58**, 17–32 (2013). https://doi.org/10.2478/pcssr-2013-0010

38. Devile, E., Kastenholz, E.: Accessible tourism experiences: the voice of people with visual disabilities visual disabilities. J. Policy Res. Tou. Leis. Events **10**, 265–285 (2018). https://doi.org/10.1080/19407963.2018.1470183

39. Small, J., Darcy, S., Packer, T.: The embodied tourist experiences of people with vision impairment: management implications beyond the visual gaze. Tour. Manag. **33**, 941–950 (2012). https://doi.org/10.1016/j.tourman.2011.09.015

40. ARUMA: Types of intellectual disabilities (2019). https://www.aruma.com.au/about-us/about-disability/types-of-disabilities/types-of-intellectual-disabilities/. Accessed 12 Feb 2021

41. Gillovic, B., Mcintosh, A., Darcy, S., Cockburn-Wootten, C.: Enabling the language of accessible tourism. J. Sustain. Tour. (2018). https://doi.org/10.1080/09669582.2017.1377209

42. Gillovic, B.: Experiences of care at the nexus of intellectual disability and leisure travel. University of Waikato (2019)

43. Beart, S., Hawkins, D., Kroese, B.S., et al.: Barriers to accessing leisure opportunities for people with learning disabilities. Br. J. Learn. Disabil. **29**, 133–138 (2001). https://doi.org/10.1046/j.1468-3156.2001.00109.x

44. Kim, S., Lehto, X.Y.: Leisure travel of families of children with disabilities: motivation and activities. Tour. Manag. **37**, 13–24 (2013). https://doi.org/10.1016/j.tourman.2012.12.011

45. Eichhorn, V., Miller, G., Tribe, J.: Tourism: a site of resistance strategies of individuals with a disability. Ann. Tour. Res. **43**, 578–600 (2013). https://doi.org/10.1016/j.annals.2013.03.006

46. Winkler, M., Wöß, W.: Accessibility add-on box enabling barrier-free tourism information systems (TIS). In: Miesenberger, K., Klaus, J., Zagler, W.L., Karshmer, A.I. (eds.) ICCHP 2006. LNCS, vol. 4061, pp. 298–305. Springer, Heidelberg (2006). https://doi.org/10.1007/11788713_45

47. Buhalis, D., O'Connor, P.: Information communication technology revolutionizing tourism. Tour. Recreat. Res. **30**, 7–16 (2005). https://doi.org/10.1080/02508281.2005.11081482

48. Lazar, J.: Integrating accessibility into the information systems curriculum. In: Proceedings of the International Association for Computer Information Systems, pp. 373–379 (2002)

49. W3C: Accessibility (2018). https://www.w3.org/standards/webdesign/accessibility. Accessed 7 Sep 2020

50. Rinkus, S., Walji, M., Johnson-Throop, K.A., et al.: Human-centered design of a distributed knowledge management system. J. Biomed. Inform. **38**, 4–17 (2005). https://doi.org/10.1016/j.jbi.2004.11.014

51. International Organization for Standardization: Ergonomics of human-system interaction—Part 210: Human-centred design for interactive systems (2019). https://www.iso.org/obp/ui/#iso:std:iso:9241:-210:ed-2:v1:en

52. Zhang, J., Patel, V.L., Johnson, K.A., Smith, J.W.: Designing human-centered distributed information systems. IEEE Intell. Syst. **17**, 42–47 (2002). https://doi.org/10.1109/MIS.2002.1039831

53. Teixeira, L., Ferreira, C., Santos, B.S.: User-centered requirements engineering in health information systems: a study in the hemophilia field. Comput. Methods Programs Biomed. **106**, 160–174 (2012). https://doi.org/10.1016/j.cmpb.2010.10.007

54. Zhou, Y.J., Hyvonen, S.L., Louise, S.: Functional requirements and non-functional requirements: a survey (2004)
55. Adlin, T., Pruitt, J.: The essential persona lifecycle: your guide to building and using personas
(2010)
56. Stickdorn, M., Schwarzenberger, K.: Service design in tourism. In: Entrepreneurship und
Tourismus: Unternehmerisches Denken und Erfolgskonzepte aus der Praxis, pp. 261–275
(2016)
57. Morgan, N., Pritchard, A., Sedgley, D.: Social tourism and well-being in later life. Ann. Tour.
Res. 52, 1–15 (2015). https://doi.org/10.1016/j.annals.2015.02.015
58. Yau, Matthew Kwai-sang, McKercher, B., Packer, T.: Traveling with a disability. Ann. Tour.
Res. 31(4), 946–960 (2004). https://doi.org/10.1016/j.annals.2004.03.007
59. Decreto-Lei no 163/2006. Diário da República n.o 152/2006, Série I de 2006-08-08

Accessibility, Usability, User Experience and Technology Acceptance

Users Perceptions of Headphones and Earbuds in Norway and Brazil: An Empirical Study Based on a Kahoot Quiz

Amanda Coelho Figliolia[1,2] , Frode Eika Sandnes[1,3](✉) ,
and Fausto Orsi Medola[2]

[1] Oslo Metropolitan University, 0130 Oslo, Norway
frodes@oslomet.no
[2] Sao Paulo State University (UNESP), Bauru, Brazil
{amanda.figliolia,fausto.medola}@unesp.br
[3] Kristiania University College, 0153 Oslo, Norway

Abstract. Headphones and earbuds are seemingly more popular than ever with the wide availability of smartphones and music streaming services. Such personal audio systems are also essential for many blind and visually impaired computer users that relies on text-to-speech. Few published studies address the users' perceptions of such personal audio output devices. However, past research shows that negative perceptions may lead to device abandonment. General-purpose equipment may therefore be more successful than special purpose assistive technologies for marginalized groups. We therefore set out to gain insight into how users generally perceive headphones and earbuds, and we wanted to base our study in two different cultural contexts. A questionnaire built on a Kahoot quiz was developed involving 12 questions related to headphones and earbuds. A total of 100 participants were recruited in Norway and Brazil. The results show that intuitiveness is the most valued feature of these devices and cost was not. Brazilians expressed skepticism regarding the use of headphones while walking and when travelling on public transport, while Norwegians expressed that headphones were safe to use in such situations. Our experiences showed that Kahoot is a promising platform for conducting such experiments, as it may appear more engaging than regular questionnaires. Moreover, they are relatively easy to set up and allow response times to be measured.

Keywords: Accessibility · Assistive technology · Headphones · Earbuds · Perceptions · Design · Kahoot quiz

1 Introduction

Smartphone technology has drastically changed how people listen to music. The general smartphone has replaced audio specific devices such as stereo systems and portable mp3-players. Internet connectivity allows users to subscribe to and access huge music libraries and audio books via streaming. Such personal audio systems are also an essential tool for

© Springer Nature Switzerland AG 2021
M. Antona and C. Stephanidis (Eds.): HCII 2021, LNCS 12768, pp. 153–165, 2021.
https://doi.org/10.1007/978-3-030-78092-0_10

blind and visually impaired users who use screen readers with text-to-speech [1] as users without vision must rely on audio or haptics instead [2]. Music and other audio contents are highly personal, and most people listen to their audio content via headphones (see Fig. 1) or earbuds (see Fig. 2). Both are seemingly popular. Headphones may be viewed as preferred by music enthusiasts and air-travelers, while earbuds seem to be preferred by joggers and other individuals active in physical sports and exercises. There are also earplugs that are inserted deeper into the ear canal, while earbuds hang on the side of the outside of the ear canal. Occasionally the term earphone is used to refer to such personal audio output devices. Bone conducting headphones and Apple's transparency mode for the AirPods Pro and AirPods Max have also recently emerged as alternatives for users who want to also be aware of their surroundings while listening to an audio source.

Fig. 1. Headphones.

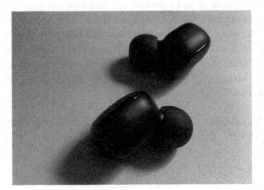

Fig. 2. Earbuds

The headphone and earbud technologies are mostly driven by manufacturers as there is not much academic work on these audio devices. Yet, there is much research that suggests that the physical appearance of devices affect our attitude towards these technologies. Color is one example of a visual attribute that attracts much attention among designers and users [3–6]. This is especially an important factor for assistive technologies as users' perception of these devices are related to the degree in which these devices are used or abandoned [7, 8]. Studies have shown that also visually impaired users are concerned with how the visual aesthetics of the devices they use are perceived by onlookers [9].

In this study we wanted to gain a better understanding about how users perceive these devices according to several dimensions. As the work reported here in is part of a bilateral interdisciplinary Brazil-Norway collaboration project [10–12], we wanted to explore whether these perceptions also are related to culture. We therefore designed a questionnaire that probed participants about 12 characteristics related to both headphones and earbuds. Instead of using a traditional questionnaire we employed a Kahoot quiz (an online game-based learning platform) to make participation more engaging and fun, thereby making it easier to recruit participants. In total we managed to easily recruit 100 participants from Norway and Brazil. Figures 1 and 2 are the authors' own photographs and not the same as the one used in the quiz due to copyright issues.

The rest of this paper is structured as follows. Related work is briefly outlined in the next section, followed by a description of the methodology in Sect. 3. The results are presented in Sect. 4, followed by a discussion of these results in Sect. 5. Concluding remarks are provided in Sect. 6.

2   Related Work

Some of the research efforts into personal audio technology such as headphones and earbuds have explored the dangers that listening to music at high volumes over prolonged times pose to the loss of hearing [13]. The effects of hearing loss due to prolonged headphone use on academic performance has also been studied [14]. However, on a more positive note, low-cost general-purpose earbuds have also been identified as an emerging competitor to special purpose more expensive hearing aids [15]. Bone conducting headphones is a technology that do not obstruct the ear canal and thus allows the wearer to hear all the sounds from the environment [16, 17].

The last decade has demonstrated the emergence of the noise cancellation headphones and earplugs [18] that are highly popular among air travelers. Such noise cancellation technology has also been studied with specific applications in mind. For instance, Kari, Makkonen and Frank [19] studied the effects of using noise cancellation earplugs in open plan offices among software engineers. They did not find that the noise cancellation technology had any effects on stress, strain, or stress recovery. In fact, they found a negative effect on the perceptions on well-being and work performance. Their explanation for these results was that earplugs that are inserted into the ear canal are uncomfortable to wear. Gallacher et al. [20] found more positive results with active noise cancellation headphones in hospitals with noise pollution. The noise reduction helped participants rest and sleep. Bickford, Stanyek, and Gopinath [21] studied how "sharing" of earbuds was an essential part of social interaction and practices among schoolchildren, their role in relationships with friends, networking, and hierarchies. Woods et al. [22] proposed an interesting procedure to test if participants are wearing headphones in remote experiments to ensure a close to constant setup. It works by playing a tone that is phase shifted 180 degrees to the left and the right channel. If played through loudspeakers the sound is difficult to hear as it cancels itself out, while it is easy to hear using headphones as the signal is not canceled due to the phase shifting.

There are also a handful of academic papers related to the design of personal audio output systems [23]. Rogfelt and Lundstrom [24] designed a set of earbuds that aimed at the needs and wants of mobile gamers specifically. Manabe and Fukumoto [25] used earphones as tapping input devices by reversing them as microphones. Xu et al. [26] employed similar ideas but using the built-in microphone currently found on most smartphone earbuds. Young [27] discusses how to design sound for earbuds, as opposed to design sound for loudspeakers.

Reinfelt, Hardish and Ernst [28] studied how the design of headphones affect its use. They conducted a questionnaire study involving 125 participants. They concluded that headphones to some degree are a "hedonic technology" as their use is affected by perceived enjoyment. They recommend that manufacturers consider this during design of headphones. Lin et al. [29] employed a Kansei engineering methodology to find how users perceive headphone designs to identify the optimal characteristics. They conducted an experiment where the participants evaluated 14 different headphone designs and evaluated these using 7-point semantic differentials including the dimensions old-fashioned/fashionable, complicated/simple, ugly/nice-looking, cheap/expensive, bulky/lightweight, uncomfortable/comfortable, difficult-to-use/easy-to-use, and business/casual. Semantic differentials are commonly used to measure perceptions of designs such as assistive technologies [8]. Based on the results the authors conclude on several detailed and specific design choices that are more beneficial than others in terms of users' perceptions of the headphones [29].

3 Method

3.1 Experimental Design

A questionnaire was devised with type of audio-device as within-groups independent variable and cultural affiliation as between-groups independent variable. The audio-device had two levels, namely headphones and earbuds, while the culture had two levels, namely Norway and Brazil. The dependent variables included perceived features described in detail in the following sections.

3.2 Participants

A total of 100 participants accepted to complete the survey. Of these, 44 were recruited in Norway and 56 were recruited in Brazil. The participants were mostly recruited from the authors' respective universities and comprised mostly young adults in their 20s. The participants comprised a balanced mix of both males and females.

3.3 Materials

A questionnaire with 12 questions related to both headphones and earbuds were designed, totaling 24 questions, in addition to a couple of general questions. The questionnaire probed the participants' perception of the respective audio device with regards to price, trendiness, aesthetics modifications, aesthetically pleasing, safe to use on public transport or while walking, robustness, aesthetics, comfort, easy to use and intuitive (see Table 1). Each question was assigned a 4-item Likert scale from 1 to 4. Hence, the participants were forced to indicate a positive or negative direction as there was no neutral option.

Table 1. Questionnaire Likert statements.

Question ID	Likert statements (earbuds/headphones)
Q1, Q13	This product is comfortable
Q2, Q14	The product looks like it is built robustly and will not easily break
Q3, Q15	It is intuitive to use
Q4, Q16	The product aesthetics are pleasing
Q5, Q17	The product aesthetics need some changes
Q6, Q18	I would buy this product because it is easy to use
Q7, Q19	I would buy this product because it looks trendy
Q8, Q20	I would buy this product because it is the cheapest option
Q9, Q21	I would buy this product as I like the design
Q10, Q22	I feel safe to walk outside using the product
Q11, Q23	I feel safe to take the public transportation using the product
Q12, Q24	This product would make me look trendy
Q25	I prefer to use earbuds
Q26	I prefer to use headphones
Q27	In my opinion, I think it is relevant to use Kahoot! in scientific research
Q28	I am more motivated to participate in research using kahoot than regular questionnaires

The questionnaire was implemented in Kahoot, which is a popular online quiz engine which often is used by teachers to engage students in the classroom [30, 31] and has also been used as a platform for controlled experiments [32]. We used a quiz in personal mode. Kahoot has also been used for research projects. Kahoot was chosen over an ordinary questionnaire as it was deemed more fun and engaging and hence thereby increasing the change of acquiring respondents. Another advantage of Kahoot is that it also records the time it takes for each participant to provide the response, which allows the responses also to be analyzed in terms of potential hesitations. The questions were presented in a fixed order, first asking about the earbud characteristics, followed by the headphone characteristics. The Portuguese language version of the questionnaire was translated after the English language version was completed.

3.4 Procedure

The Kahoot quiz was both conducted in several group settings and individually in person or remotely over the internet. The data collection was conducted over a period of two months during the spring of 2020 in both Oslo, Norway and Bauru, Brazil. The Norwegian participants responded to the English-language Kahoot, while the Brazilian participants responded to the Portuguese-language Kahoot.

3.5 Analysis

The responses and timing data were extracted from Kahoot and analyzed using the JASP version 0.12.2.0 statistical software package [33]. The responses to the questionnaire were analyzed using non-parametric tests as the responses were ordinal. Shapiro Wilks test showed that the timing observations did not satisfy the assumption of normality and these were therefore also analyzed using non-parametric tests.

4 Results

4.1 Perception of Audio Device Characteristics

Figure 3 and 4 shows shorted diverging stacked bar graphs [34] of the participants perceived characteristics for headphones and earbuds, respectively. Inspecting the graphs reveal that the participants generally were more positive regarding headphones compared to earbuds as headphones only had 3 characteristics tending towards the negative side while earbuds had 4 of its characteristics tending towards the negative side. Both audio types received the lowest scores related to price and the highest scores related to intuitive.

Wilcoxon signed rank tests reveal that the main differences observed were as follows: Headphones were perceived as more comfortable than earbuds ($W = 208.0, p < .001$), with 55 positive and 45 negative responses for earbuds, and 76 positive and 24 negative responses for headphones. Headphones were perceived as more robust than earbuds ($W = 1435.0, p < .001$), with earbuds: 40 positive, 60 negative, and headphones: 66 positive, 34 negative. Although both were perceived as positive, headphones (91/) were perceived as more intuitive than earbuds (75/25) to use ($W = 165.5, p < .001$). Headphones (83/17) were perceived as easier to use than earbuds ($W = 1604.0, p < .001$) being the 2nd highest ranking headphone feature, with overall neutrally balanced response for earbuds (52/48). Although both headphones (37/63) and earbuds (22/78) received the lowest score on price the earbuds were perceived as more expensive than headphones ($W = 902.5, p < .001$). The headphones (76/24) also received a higher score than the earbuds (57/43) in terms of design ($W = 501.0, p = .018$).

4.2 Cultural Differences

Mann-Whitney U tests were used to indicate any significant differences across cultures and the six characteristics that were significantly different are shown in Fig. 5. The largest differences were observed for the perceived safety of use on public transport ($W = 464.0, p < .001$) and safety of use while walking ($W = 608.5, p < .001$). For both

Headphones

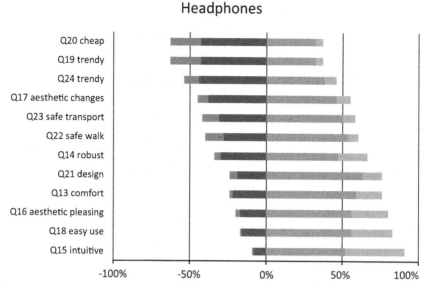

Fig. 3. Diverging stacked bar graph showing perceived headphone characteristics. Likert scale responses are represented by 1 = magenta, 2 = red, 3 = green and 4 = cyan. The gridlines show 50% divisions. (Color figure online)

Earbuds

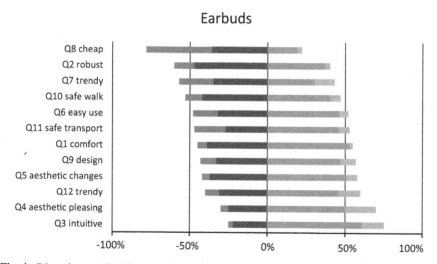

Fig. 4. Diverging stacked bar graph showing perceived earbuds characteristics. Likert scale responses are represented by 1 = magenta, 2 = red, 3 = green and 4 = cyan. The gridlines show 50% divisions. (Color figure online)

dimensions the Norwegian responses were positive (transport 40/4, walking 39/5) and Brazilian responses were negative (transport 18/38, walking 21/35).

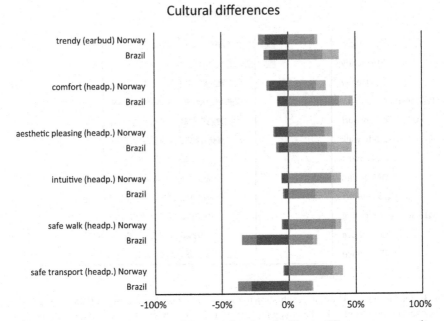

Fig. 5. Diverging stacked bar graph of features flagging significant differences across cultures (Norway vs Brazil). Likert scale responses are represented by 1 = magenta, 2 = red, 3 = green and 4 = cyan. The gridlines show 50% divisions. (Color figure online)

The differences were smaller for the remaining four features and in all cases the Brazilian responses were more positive than the Norwegian responses. Brazilians (52/4) rated the headphones as more intuitive than the Norwegians (39/5) and this difference was significant ($W = 1723.5$, $p < .001$). The Brazilian respondents (47/9) ranked the headphone more aesthetically pleasing than the Norwegian respondents (33/11), also to a level of significance ($W = 1491.5$, $p = .045$). Headphone comfort also triggered a significant difference ($W = 1484.0$, $p = .048$), with more positive responses among the Brazilians (48/8) compared to the Norwegians (28/16). Perceived trendiness was the only earbud characteristic that triggered a culturally related difference ($W = 1547.0$, $p = .019$), also with more positive responses among the Brazilian respondents (38/18) compared to the Norwegian respondents (22/22).

4.3 Response Time

The observations show that the mean response time reduced gradually with the number of questions starting with a mean of 7.1 s for the first question and ending with a mean of 0.7 for the last question (see Fig. 6). It therefore did not make sense to compare the timing for the within factor (audio-device type). However, Fig. 6 reveals that a few questions stand out with higher mean and larger spread than the others, question 6: how easy it is to use the earbuds, and question 13: headphone robustness.

However, we observed the culturally related response time differences (between-group factor) and a series of Mann-Whitney U tests flagged 6 questions. Measured in

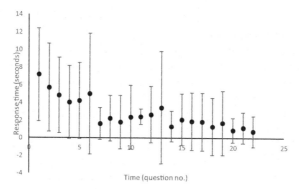

Fig. 6. Mean response times for the sequence of questions. Error bars show standard deviation.

seconds the Brazilians ($M = 4.9$, $SD = 4.4$) responded in nearly half the time as the Norwegians ($M = 8.4$, $SD = 5.8$) on the question related to earbud robustness ($W = 257.500$, $p = .004$). The Brazilians ($M = 1.3$, $SD = 2.8$) responded a bit slower than the Norwegians ($M = 1.2$, $SD = 1.0$) on the question related to earbud trendiness ($W = 320.0$, $p = .035$). In terms of headphone comfort ($W = 661.5$, $p = .015$), the Brazilians ($M = 3.0$, $SD = 3.5$) were nearly three times as slow to respond as the Norwegians ($M = 1.4$, $SD = 1.2$). Although significant the cultural differences related to headphone design ($W = 250.0$, $p = .002$), safety of using headphones on public transport ($W = 212.0$, $p < .001$), headphone trendiness ($W = 252.0$, $p = .002$) were too small to be of any practical significance.

5 Discussions

5.1 Perception of Audio Device Characteristics

The results point in the direction that, from the respondent's perspective, headphones have more beneficial characteristics overall, including better design, better comfort, more robust, more intuitive to use and easier to use. However, these characteristics may also depend on context. Headphones clearly are very suitable when the listener is sitting still, while earbuds are designed for sports and physical activity. It seems that the advertising of earbuds is targeting individuals doing sports and exercise. Especially large headphones may have reduced sound quality while running for instance caused by thumps as the feet hit the ground. Moreover, over the ear headphones may be warm and not allow sweat to dissipate while with earbuds this is not a problem. However, we did not include this element in our study. The perception of comfort and discomfort related to the use of audio-devices is multi-factorial as the interaction encompasses not only physical aspects, but also temperature and sound.

It is also interesting that earbuds were perceived as more expensive than headphones. In fact, it seems that the price range for headphones is much wider than for earbuds. It would have been interesting to probe more deeply into why the respondents provided these answers. We can only speculate that headphones have been around for a long time and there is an established inexpensive high quality headphone, while earbuds is comparatively a younger type of product with some element of fashion and hence the starting price is comparatively higher.

On a different note, headphones are more visible than earbuds, as earbuds sometimes are almost invisible if hidden behind hair and clothing. The visual aesthetics of headphones would therefore seem to be more influential and important than earbud aesthetics when viewed from a social perspective.

Note that this study did not explicitly consider, or compensate, for possible effects of participants' preconceptions, abstract understanding, and experiences related to on-ear versus over-ear headphones and on-ear versus in-ear earbuds. Such effects could have affected the results. The participants were instructed to answer the questions according to their own understanding of headphones and earbuds; the images were just provided as examples.

Moreover, this study did not include cohorts of disabled users. Users with reduced vision (and uncorrected hearing) may be the most relevant cohort to include in this regard. One may speculate that safety in public spaces and ability to be aware of the surroundings would be perceived as important. Technologies such as bone conducting headphones and transparency modes may hold potential. The study of their applicability for disabled users may be fruitful directions for further inquiry.

5.2 Cultural Differences

The most noticeable difference attributed to culture was regarding the safety of use of the headphones on public transport and while walking. One explanation of this result could perhaps be a symptom of differences in the traffic situation in the two countries rather than the audio devices themselves. Norwegian traffic may be comparatively more strongly regulated than the Brazilian traffic situation, and the Norwegian cities are more tailored to pedestrians. Also, one may argue that the Norwegian government has invested more in the public transport in Oslo, than what has been invested in the public transport in Bauru. Therefore, if the walking and public transport situation is viewed as somewhat unsafe in the first place, one may rate the use of headphones lower than when the walking and public transport situation is viewed as safe, in which case the headphone use is also considered safe. If the traffic situation is dangerous the pedestrians need to be careful and able to hear the traffic sounds and probably should not wear headphones to protect their own safety.

It is quite interesting that the Brazilians were generally more positive than the Norwegian respondents in terms of the intuitiveness of the headphones, the aesthetics of the headphones and comfort. This positive perspective can be influenced by the context of use of those products. In Brazil headphones are more frequently used and earbuds are considerably a new product compared to headphones.

5.3 Response Time

Figure 6 shows that the mean response time becomes smaller with each question. This is an indication of a learning curve where the participants learn how to operate within the Kahoot quiz. Once the participants have gained their skills, they are generally able to respond to questions within one second.

However, Fig. 6 also reveals two outliers with larger mean response time and a larger spread than their immediate neighbors. This indicates that the respondents hesitated with these questions, namely how easy it was to use the earbuds, and how robust the headphones were. We can only speculate what the cause for these hesitations were. One explanation could be that the questions were unclear such that the participants needed more time to decipher the intended meaning, or unclear language in the questionnaire or lacking language ability among the participants. For instance, the Norwegian respondents were presented with the quiz in English, yet we did not screen the participants' English abilities. Another explanation may be that the participants had not thought about these aspects before and needed more time to reflect upon the answer. From one perspective the timing of responses can give a clue to the quality of the questionnaire.

The observed differences in response time attributed to culture could probably be explained by language barriers. For instance, the fact that Norwegians needed a mean of 8 s to determine the robustness of earbuds, while the Brazilian participants only needed 4 s. One possible explanation for some of these observations could be that the respondents were asked to answer based on pictures on the screen, and did not have the chance to see, handle and try the products. However, this study aimed to address people's perceptions on the design features of such devices. From the perspective of the practical functions of the products, this research approach can contribute to the comprehension on how the appearance of a product communicates its functions and usage. In the context of global increase of online stores, the use of pictures that best demonstrate the products' features and qualities – thus providing proper estimation of usage - may result in an approximation of the subject's expectation to the experience of use and, ultimately, benefit users' satisfaction with the product.

6 Conclusions

This study measured participants' perceptions of headphones versus earbuds according to 12 dimensions including design, aesthetics, safety, cost, intuitiveness, ease of use, robustness, etc. Participants were recruited in both Norway and Brazil. We therefore explored differences related to culture. Overall, the participants exhibited more positive perceptions of headphones compared to earbuds. Cost was the most negative aspect for both audio devices while intuitiveness was the most positive aspect. In terms of cultural differences, the Brazilians were negative towards using headphones while walking or on public transport while the Norwegians were comparatively positive. We also explored the quality of the questionnaire by analyzing the response times and participant hesitations. Our experiences were that Kahoot is a suitable platform for conducting such types of studies as they are easy to configure, allows responses and response times to be recorded automatically, and may come across as more engaging than a regular questionnaire. It may thus be more easy to recruit participants for an interactive "quiz" than a regular questionnaire.

Acknowledgements. We would like to thank DIKU (project UTF-2016-long-term/10053) for their kind financial support that allowed us to conduct this study.

References

1. Sankhi, P., Sandnes, F.E.: A glimpse into smartphone screen reader use among blind teenagers in rural Nepal. Disabil. Rehabil:. Assist. Technol. **2020**, 1–7 (2020)
2. dos Santos, A.D.P., Medola, F.O., Cinelli, M.J., Ramirez, A.R.G., Sandnes, F.E.: Are electronic white canes better than traditional canes? A comparative study with blind and blindfolded participants. Universal Access in the Information Society (2020)
3. Sandnes, F.E., Zhao, A.: An interactive color picker that ensures WCAG2. 0 compliant color contrast levels. Proc. Comput. Sci. **67**, 87–94 (2015)
4. Sandnes, F.E.: Understanding WCAG2. 0 color contrast requirements through 3D color space visualization. Stud. Health Technol. Inform. **229**, 366–375 (2016)
5. Sandnes, F.E.: An image-based visual strategy for working with color contrasts during design. In: Miesenberger, K., Kouroupetroglou, G. (eds.) ICCHP 2018. LNCS, vol. 10896, pp. 35–42. Springer, Cham (2018). https://doi.org/10.1007/978-3-319-94277-3_7
6. Medola, F.O., Sandnes, F.E., Ferrari, A.L.M., Rodrigues, A.C.T.: Strategies for developing students' empathy and awareness for the needs of people with disabilities: contributions to design education. Stud. Health Technol. Inform. **256**, 137–147 (2018)
7. Hansen, F., Krivan, J.J., Sandnes, F.E.: Still not readable? An interactive tool for recommending color pairs with sufficient contrast based on existing visual designs. In: The 21st International ACM SIGACCESS Conference on Computers and Accessibility, pp. 636–638. ACM (2019)
8. Boiani, J.A.M., Barili, S.R.M., Medola, F.O., Sandnes, F.E.: On the non-disabled perceptions of four common mobility devices in Norway: a comparative study based on semantic differentials. Technol. Disabil. **31**(1–2), 15–25 (2019)
9. dos Santos, A.D.P., Ferrari, A.L.M., Medola, F.O., Sandnes, F.E.: Aesthetics and the perceived stigma of assistive technology for visual impairment. Disabil. Rehabil.: Assist. Technol. (2020)
10. Sandnes, F.E.: What do low-vision users really want from smart glasses? Faces, text and perhaps no glasses at all. In: Miesenberger, K., Bühler, C., Penaz, P. (eds.) ICCHP 2016. LNCS, vol. 9758, pp. 187–194. Springer, Cham (2016). https://doi.org/10.1007/978-3-319-41264-1_25
11. Sandnes, F.E., Medola, F.O., Berg, A., Rodrigues, O.V., Mirtaheri, P., Gjøvaag, T.: Solving the grand challenges together: a Brazil-Norway approach to teaching collaborative design and prototyping of assistive technologies and products for independent living. The Design Society (2017)
12. da Silva, L.A., Medola, F.O., Rodrigues, O.V., Rodrigues, A.C.T., Sandnes, F.E.: Interdisciplinary-based development of user-friendly customized 3D printed upper limb prosthesis. In: Ahram, T.Z., Falcão, C. (eds.) AHFE 2018. AISC, vol. 794, pp. 899–908. Springer, Cham (2019). https://doi.org/10.1007/978-3-319-94947-5_88
13. Villa, A.D., Gayahan, Y.N., Chanco, M.V.V.I., Reyes, J.M., Mariano, L.: An assessment of the potential risk of hearing loss from earphones based on the type of earphones and external noise. In: Arezes, P.M. (ed.) AHFE 2019. AISC, vol. 969, pp. 286–297. Springer, Cham (2020). https://doi.org/10.1007/978-3-030-20497-6_27
14. Fasanya, B.K., Strong, J.D.: Younger generation safety: hearing loss and academic performance degradation among college student headphone users. In: Arezes, P.M.F.M. (ed.) AHFE 2018. AISC, vol. 791, pp. 522–531. Springer, Cham (2019). https://doi.org/10.1007/978-3-319-94589-7_51
15. Dysart, J.: Smart Earbuds: a looming threat to the hearing aid market? Hear. J. **70**(3), 30–31 (2017)

16. May, K.R., Walker, B.N.: The effects of distractor sounds presented through bone conduction headphones on the localization of critical environmental sounds. Appl. Ergon. **61**, 144–158 (2017)
17. Walker, B.N., Stanley, R.M., Iyer, N., Simpson, B.D., Brungart, D.S.: Evaluation of bone-conduction headsets for use in multitalker communication environments. In: Proceedings of the Human Factors and Ergonomics Society Annual Meeting, vol. 49, no. 17, pp. 1615–1619. SAGE Publications, Los Angeles (2005)
18. Liebich, S., Fabry, J., Jax, P., Vary, P.: Signal processing challenges for active noise cancellation headphones. In: Speech Communication; 13th ITG-Symposium. VDE (2018)
19. Kari, T., Makkonen, M., Frank, L.: The effect of using noise cancellation earplugs in open-plan offices on the offices on the work well-being and work performance of software professionals. In: Mediterranean Conference on Information Systems (MCIS). Association for Information Systems (2017)
20. Gallacher, S., Enki, D., Stevens, S., Bennett, M.J.: An experimental model to measure the ability of headphones with active noise control to reduce patient's exposure to noise in an intensive care unit. Intensive Care Med. Exp. **5**(1), 1–8 (2017). https://doi.org/10.1186/s40 635-017-0162-1
21. Bickford, T., Stanyek, J., Gopinath, S.: Earbuds are good for sharing: children's headphones as social media at a Vermont school. In: The Oxford Handbook of Mobile Music Studies (2014)
22. Woods, K.J.P., Siegel, M.H., Traer, J., McDermott, J.H.: Headphone screening to facilitate web-based auditory experiments. Atten. Percept. Psychophys. **79**(7), 2064–2072 (2017). https://doi.org/10.3758/s13414-017-1361-2
23. Huang, C.H., Pawar, S.J., Hong, Z.J., Huang, J.H.: Earbud-type earphone modeling and measurement by head and torso simulator. Appl. Acoust. **73**(5), 461–469 (2012)
24. Rogfelt, J., Lundstrøm, A.: Mobile Gaming Earbud.: Design and functionality investigation of mobile gaming headphones. Master thesis, KTH, Sweden (2019)
25. Manabe, H., Fukumoto, M.: Headphone taps: a simple technique to add input function to regular headphones. In: Proceedings of the 14th International Conference on Human-Computer Interaction with Mobile Devices and Services Companion, pp. 177–180 (2012)
26. Xu, X., et al.: EarBuddy: enabling on-face interaction via wireless Earbuds. In: Proceedings of the 2020 CHI Conference on Human Factors in Computing Systems (2020)
27. Young, M.: Let me whisper in your Earbud: curating sound for ubiquitous tiny speakers. Leonardo Music J. 10–13 (2016)
28. Reinelt, P., Hadish, S., Ernst, C.-P.: How design influences headphone usage. In: Ernst, C.-P. (ed.) The Drivers of Wearable Device Usage. PI, pp. 59–68. Springer, Cham (2016). https://doi.org/10.1007/978-3-319-30376-5_6
29. Lin, H., et al.: A study on the perception of wireless headphone form design based on Kansei engineering. In: Fukuda, S. (ed.) AHFE 2019. AISC, vol. 952, pp. 369–380. Springer, Cham (2020). https://doi.org/10.1007/978-3-030-20441-9_39
30. Zarzycka-Piskorz, E.: Kahoot it or not? Can games be motivating in learning grammar? Teach. Engl. Technol. **16**(3), 17–36 (2016)
31. Licorish, S.A., Owen, H.E., Daniel, B., George, J.L.: Students' perception of Kahoot!'s influence on teaching and learning. Res. Pract. Technol. Enhanc. Learn. **13**(1), 1–23 (2018). https://doi.org/10.1186/s41039-018-0078-8
32. Eide, S.A., Poljac, A.M., Sandnes, F.E.: Image search versus text search revisited: a simple experiment using a Kahoot Quiz. In: HCI International, Springer (2021)
33. JASP Team: JASP (Version 0.12.2) [Computer software] (2020)
34. Heiberger, R.M., Robbins, N.B.: Design of diverging stacked bar charts for Likert scales and other applications. J. Stat. Softw. **57**(5), 1–32 (2014)

Extended Analysis Procedure for Inclusive Game Elements: Accessibility Features in the Last of Us Part 2

Patricia da Silva Leite$^{(\boxtimes)}$ (iD) and Leonelo Dell Anhol Almeida (iD)

Federal University of Technology (UTFPR), Curitiba, Paraná, Brazil
patriciasleite@gmail.com, leoneloalmeida@utfpr.edu.br

Abstract. Implementing accessibility features in digital games is an activity that has been growing over the years. Although these features do not exist in all digital games produced and distributed, some games stand out for their implemented features. In this context, this research involves the game "The Last of Us Part II" (TLOU2), which has more than 60 accessibility features and is considered, by some field experts, as the most accessible game ever produced. Considering the potential consequences that statements like this can represent for the games' industry, this research analyzes the TLOU2 accessibility features with an analysis procedure based on resources and criteria from the community of practice and inclusion principles. From this evaluation, this study proposes an extension and improvement in the analysis procedure adopted, called PANELI, to encompass topics regarding inclusive digital games. Furthermore, we discuss the significance of TLOU2 accessibility features, the relevance of analysis procedure application, and its constant improvement and updates.

Keywords: Analysis procedure · Digital games · Accessibility · People with disabilities

1 Introduction

Game development and playing games are activities that can be present and applied in multiple human knowledge domains, such as health, economics, politics, advertising, entertainment, among others [19]. However, several digital games are still inaccessible to many people, such as those with disabilities [9,18,19].

Towards game accessibility numerous organizations, researchers, and companies contribute to game development that has accessibility features implemented or is more inclusive to people with disabilities. The accessibility features act as a means for people with and without disabilities to adjust game elements to meet their needs or preferences. Through these features, previously insurmountable barriers can be overcome, making the playing experience possible.

© Springer Nature Switzerland AG 2021
M. Antona and C. Stephanidis (Eds.): HCII 2021, LNCS 12768, pp. 166–185, 2021.
https://doi.org/10.1007/978-3-030-78092-0_11

Among the institutions are the *International Game Developers Association (IGDA)*[1], with *Game Accessibility Special Interest Group (GASIG)*[2]; and *The AbleGamers Foundation*[3]. Between researchers are Grammenos, Savidis, and Stephanidis [9]; Yuan, Folmer, and Harris Jr. [19]; Westin, Bierre, Gramenos, and Hinn [18]; Leite, Retore, and Almeida [13], among others.

Within companies engaged in the accessible game's development and actions towards inclusion, *Naughty Dog*[4] is currently in the spotlight with the release of *The Last of Us Part II* (TLOU2)[5] and the accessibility features presented in the game. TLOU2 has more than 60 accessibility features and is considered by some experts in the field as the most accessible game ever produced [8,14].

This research seeks to analyze the accessibility features implemented in TLOU2 through the procedure proposed by Leite and Almeida [12], called PANELI. This analysis intends to reflect the outcomes regarding the features implemented in the game for people with and without disabilities, for the game industry, and for society. We also present reflections regarding PANELI's extension and improvement to include topics not initially outlined. These changes result in the game analysis intended to contemplate the concept of inclusive digital gaming. Besides, PANELI is a live process in constant development, and this research also contributes to the procedure enhancement.

The **A**nalysis **P**rocedure for **I**nclusive **G**ame **E**lements (PANELI) uses resources and criteria from the community of practice and game accessibility concepts in its composition. PANELI encompasses detailed phases and attributes regarding game elements (e.g. technology, goals, rules, mechanics, among others), game selection data, material identification for analysis support, analysis form, and analysis report [12].

Among the research results are 1) the discussion and analysis of main relevant accessibility features from TLOU2; and 2) PANELI's improvement.

Therefore, this study results have the potential to be applied in the game industry to support decisions in the game development process; and in academic research due to the reflections presented on the changes proposed in PANELI, which may serve as a reference for further investigations on this subject.

This research is organized as follows: Sect. 2 presents a summary of the game's launch context and its repercussions, and briefly reviews of related work. Section 3 summarizes the analysis procedure, PANELI, and its initial changes proposed in this research. Section 4 deals with the analysis results of the TLOU2 accessibility features with PANELI's original and new topics. Section 5 presents the discussion regarding the analysis carried out, the potential unfoldings of the TLOU2 accessibility features, and the changes proposed in PANELI. Finally, the last Sect. (6) presents the final considerations of this research.

---

[1] https://igda.org/.

[2] https://igda-gasig.org/.

[3] https://ablegamers.org/.

[4] https://www.naughtydog.com/.

[5] https://www.thelastofus.playstation.com/.

2 Background

2.1 Related Work

Evaluation methods and techniques have several applications, such as to investigate the project status before its release; ensure that the product behaves as expected and meets all requirements; to identify new concepts or to foster ideas; among other objectives. According to Dix et al. [6], evaluations should occur throughout the development process, and the analysis results employed to provide resources for product modifications.

Regarding game accessibility, Fortes et al. [7] propose a literature survey listing researches that perform game accessibility analysis and also present insights related to this subject. Moreover, the authors indicate that even the literature showing extensive studies regarding game usability and software evaluation, these researches do not present detailed methods to perform a game accessibility evaluation.

Considering Fortes et al. remarks, we aim to extend the research of Leite and Almeida [12] that proposes a game analysis procedure incorporating inclusion principles on its approaches. Their study presents the game elements evaluated and contemplate analysis criteria from game review studies and the game accessibility practice community, such as *Game Accessibility*[6], *DAGERS*[7] and *Can I Play That?*[8]. Based on these criteria and sources, Leite and Almeida provide a detailed method to accomplish a game accessibility evaluation.

However, the launch of TLOU2 raise questions about the applicability of procedures such as the one presented by Leite and Almeida and pushes foward the knowledge on game accessibility.

2.2 The Last of Us Part II

Developed by *Naughty Dog*, TLOU2 is an action-adventure game, released on June 19, 2020, exclusively for *PlayStation 4*[9]. Awaited since its announcement, in December 2016, some people criticized the game due to some events that occurred in the game story and for the representation of LGBTQ+ characters. Also, the company was in the middle of discussions and complaints about the poor working conditions of the development team [10].

Despite the problems that occurred before and after its launch [10], TLOU2 is considered, by game accessibility consultants such as Steven Saylor and Courtney Craven, as the most accessible game ever produced [14].

As announced by *Naughty Dog* and *Sony*, TLOU2 has more than 60 accessibility options implemented [8]. The game features contemplate people with hearing and motor disabilities, in addition to presenting resources that support the game experience by people with visual disabilities [8].

---

[6] https://www.game-accessibility.com/.

[7] https://dagersystem.com/.

[8] https://caniplaythat.com/.

[9] https://www.playstation.com/en/explore/ps4/systems/.

In October 2020, *The Game Awards* (TGA)[10] organizers announced a new prize category: *Innovation in Accessibility* [2], and some articles related this category to the TLOU2 accessibility features and efforts in the accessibility gaming community [4]. TLOU2 won this category award and this scenario increase the relevance of this study and discussions regarding game accessibility.

3   Analysis Procedure

The analysis procedure adopted in this study was elaborated by Leite and Almeida [12], and it is based on resources and criteria from the community of practice. PANELI is used in this research due to its attributes, materials, and steps to analyze the game elements regarding the inclusion of people with disabilities perspective. Also, we selected this analysis procedure considering researches such as Leite and Almeida [12] that indicates the lack of academic studies regarding game accessibility analysis procedures, corroborated through analyses such as Fortes et al. [7] that list some papers concerning game accessibility evaluation methods.

The elements analyzed in the PANELI stages are: technology; visual, aural, and haptic elements (V.A.H.Es); narrative; goals; rules; and mechanics. These elements are based on the Artifact-Experience Model (AEM) [13].

In summary, PANELI consists of the following steps and attributes:

1. **Selection and identification of the game to be analyzed**. It consists of selecting the game to be analyzed, and collecting information about it (e.g. reports, developer company, genre, released platforms, among others);
2. **Preparation and separation of material to analysis support**. Involves identifying resources such as the game, published reports, videos, audios, and other materials to analyze the game elements. Thus, the analysis is not limited to the game exploration or experience but also involves document analysis research;
3. **Material examination to construct the review on each of the questions on the analysis form**. Analysis of the game elements regarding the topics presented in the PANELI analysis form;
4. **Writing report and game analysis results**. It involves the game information description and the game elements analysis results.

In addition to the steps and attributes presented by Leite and Almeida [12], this research proposes the use of the concept of "inclusive digital game" as the rationality used in the analysis process. An inclusive digital game is the one designed considering the largest possible number of people so that people with and without disabilities can play and participate in the same environment (physical, social, digital and cultural) and can have the experience that the game offers without discrimination, barriers or harm [11,13]. Also, the inclusive digital

---

[10] The Game Awards (TGA) is one of the most relevant awards in the gaming area/industry.

game considers people with and without disabilities not only as players but also as participants in the game development process [13].

Therefore, the inclusive digital games concept is applied as rationality and a transversal attribute to those already existing in PANELI. Thus, during the analysis, the evaluators undertake to investigate materials indicating the game analyzed goes towards the inclusion of people with and without disabilities. They examine the game elements, considering data collected and information (e.g. game development process, game experience, among other materials), verifying if they provide evidence that the analyzed game goes beyond accessibility and can be considered a game that comprehends the principles and concept of the inclusive digital game.

We propose this change in PANELI for considering accessibility as part of the inclusion process and principles, as presented in the Convention on the Rights of Persons with Disabilities (CRPD) [1]. In this instance, the implementation of accessibility features or the presence of inclusive elements in a game does not guarantee that the game goes towards including as many people as possible, involving people with disabilities, or means an inclusive process. Even these features being relevant and, in some cases, fundamental to people's experience with the game. Thus, inclusion involves comprehensive actions, including accessibility and people participation in the development process.

4   The Last of Us Part II Evaluation

As indicated in PANELI, the evaluator profile is significant, alongside the game information and the analysis results. Thus, this research highlights that the analysis of TLOU2 was performed by a person without disabilities, over 30 years old, right-handed, and familiar with the game genre (action-adventure). Also, the evaluator has technical and theoretical knowledge about accessibility and inclusion of people with disabilities in the digital games field.

The game elements were analyzed using materials released by the *Naughty Dog*, game reviews, and published materials about the game (e.g. game reviews, reports, interviews). Besides, this analysis is also grounded in the TLOU2 playing experience.

4.1   Selected PANELI' Original Topics

Since the PANELI analysis form contains 53 questions[11], we will present the most significant results from the analyzed topics considering the gaming experience and emphasized by the collected materials. Following we present the question of the analysis form, the game element(s) involved, and the used topics description to answer the question.

---

[11] The complete form is available for access in the url (in Portuguese) http://bit.ly/FormularioPANELI.

Can the Controls be Freely Remapped? (Element: Technology): Unusual in console games, TLOU2 allows for complete remapping of game controls. Thus, buttons, directionals, triggers, and touch pad can have their functions changed according to the player's preference or need (Fig. 1). Also, the game features present predefined control schemes such as "left hand only," "right hand only," and "default"; or the option to create custom button layouts. This feature is relevant for taking into account players with physical or motor disabilities that cannot use both hands to hold or use the controller. As a result, this feature can be considered an action towards the inclusion of people with and without disabilities.

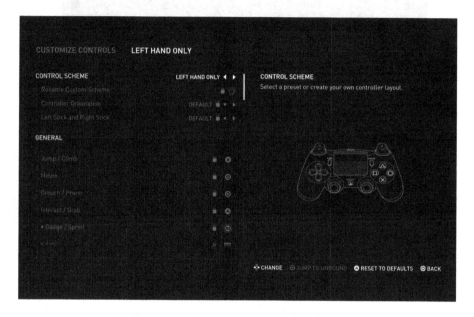

Fig. 1. TLOU2 screenshot of menu options for controls remapping.

Is it Easy to Start the Game and is the Menu Clear? (Element: V.A.H.Es): One of TLOU2's highlights is the way the game starts for the first time. The first menu presented contains options to set up the "text-to-speech," "text language," and "speech language" features (Fig. 2). Present the choice to turn on the text to speech converter, on the first game screen, is important because it considers people with visual disabilities who may need such a resource so that they do not need help from a sighted person to start the game or even avoid the mandatory choice to the player starting the game on standard mode, to configure later the game according to their needs.

After this first menu screen, the game presents menus for screen size and brightness settings. Following are the options for adjusting subtitles, audio, and

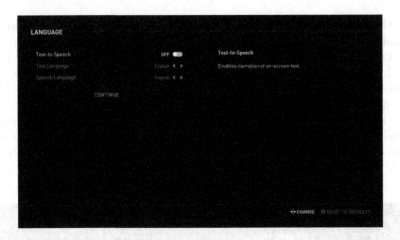

Fig. 2. TLOU2 screenshot of displayed menu on the game starting for the first time.

accessibility presets. Accessibility presets can also be another feature to be high-lighted in the initial TLOU2 configuration. We consider that because these presets represent sets of modifications in the game for people with visual, hearing, or motor disabilities. Thus, players who want or need to use these resources can start the game with them activated. And as in the previous topic, about the text-to-speech, this presets prevents the player from needing to start the game in standard mode and later look for options to meet their needs.

When Applicable, Are There Subtitles During *Cutscenes* and Game Environment? (Element: V.A.H.Es and Narrative): In addition to features usually presented in other games, such as options to enable or disable subtitles, adjust text size, and background color, TLOU2 also present features to 1) display the character's names which are speaking. 2) Display names in different colors. 3) Show an arrow (close to the subtitle) indicating the speaking character's direction that is outside the visible area displayed by the camera. And finally, 4) options to change the subtitles color (Fig. 3-A).

Among the subtitles menu options, the arrow that indicates the direction of the speaking character can be the one that most contribute to people with hearing disabilities to understand the context of a scene in the story or have tips on the location of enemies and allies, without sound dependency (Fig. 3-B). That arrow is displayed close to the subtitle or character's name, and it is shown in all subtitles, being in cutscenes or combat areas. Also, that arrow is displayed in all enemies subtitles, helping the player to identify enemies and allies' position during combat.

According to Morgan Baker [3], one of the consultants who worked on the TLOU2 development, players with hearing disability or deaf may have difficulties distinguishing between combat and story dialogues in games focused on a story. However, she points out that the accessibility features related to TLOU2 subtitles enable a more immersive experience during the game for anyone with hearing

Fig. 3. TLOU2 screenshot of subtitles menu.

disabilities [3]. In addition to the participation of consultants with and without disabilities, in the game development process, the implementation of features such as those presented in the subtitles' menu highlights the actions towards inclusion realized during the TLOU2 development.

In her game review, Courtney Craven [5] highlights the importance of subtitles in all dialogues in which the characters' voices would be audible to the playable character. In this way, all dialogues are subtitled, not just those considered central to the story. As indicated by Morgan Baker [3], the feature to show subtitles in all dialogues commits to players with hearing disability or deaf understand what is happening in a scene, even without the sound.

Are There Texts or Images that Show Essential Information that Acts to be Redundant to Sound Info? (Enemy Footprints or Gun Noise, for Example?) (Element: V.A.H.Es and Mechanics): In addition to the subtitles-related options, the game also presents features to show the direction from where the enemies will attack (or are attacking) the playable character (Fig. 4). Also, the game has features for the controller vibration, applied in specific situations, as redundant resources for sound info. These indicators and options are relevant so that players with hearing disabilities can play without the need for sounds.

Does the Game Have Other Modes, so that the Gameplay Can be Flexible for Different People? (Elements: V.A.H.Es, Rules and Goals): In the PANELI's original analysis form, this question did not consider V.A.H.Es as a game mode resource. However, given the accessibility features presented in TLOU2, this research includes the V.A.H.Es in this question. The reason for that is among the visual accessibility features, TLOU2 presents three high contrast options (Fig. 5), which change the game's V.A.H.Es and act as a mode in the game, in this case, a high contrast mode.

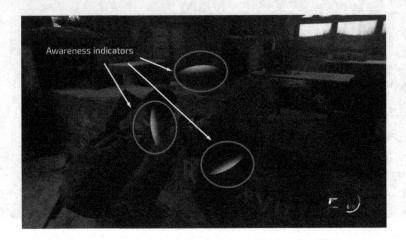

Fig. 4. TLOU2 screenshot of scene with awareness indicators enabled.

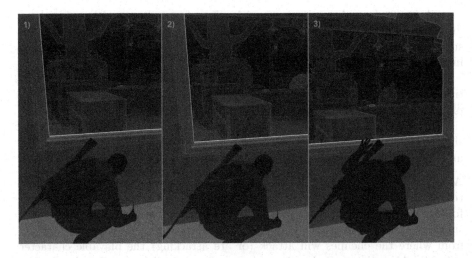

Fig. 5. Game scenes showing the three high contrast options applied.

It is important to note that the first prototypes of the high contrast mode were developed in 2017 [16]. Until the end of the game development, these features were being improved in a continuous testing process and with the consultants' involvement, so that the players' experience becomes consistent [16]. TLOU2's development team demonstrates several inclusive actions through people with and without disabilities' involvement in the game development process and for having started the development of these features since the game project beginning.

Also, TLOU2 presents different modes in the game's difficulty levels, ranging from "very trivial" to "survivor." The game's difficulty options are also noteworthy (Fig. 6), as they present sub-items for a specific configuration of the difficulty related to various elements in the game, listed below.

1. Player (resistance and vulnerability degrees);
2. Enemies (passivity and aggressiveness degrees);
3. Allies (passivity and aggressiveness degrees);
4. Stealth (degrees between absent and vigilant);
5. Resources (between frequently and scarce).

These difficulty level alternatives and options sub-levels are relevant so that players can adjust the different elements of the game according to their preference or need and, as a result, players can build a personalized and particular gaming experience, as stated by researches such as those by Grammenos, Savidis and Stephanidis [9] and game accessibility guidelines.

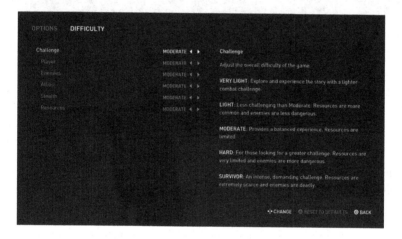

Fig. 6. TLOU2 screenshot of game difficulty level menu.

Is it Possible to Play Without Seeing, that is, Only with Sound and Text (Which Can be Read by Screen Readers)? (Elements: Technology, Mechanics and V.A.H.Es): Since the analysis presented in this research was performed by a person without a disability, the answer to this question is based entirely on the review of players with visual disabilities. And, based on these materials, TLOU2 can be played without seeing. According to *SightlessKombat* [15], the navigation features, sound tips, automatic aiming, sound glossary (Fig. 7), text-to-speech converter, voice acting, controller vibration, among others, allow the game to be fully played without the need for a sighted person to assist the player. *SightlessKombat* highlights the sounds glossary in his review for considering that this is the first time he finds this feature included in a mainstream game, whereas this feature is recurrent in games that have only audio (audio games).

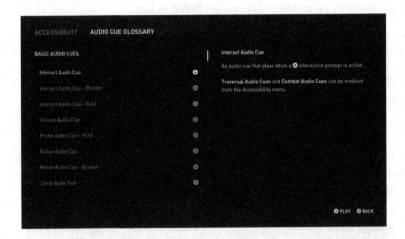

Fig. 7. TLOU2 screenshot of sound glossary screen.

Does the Game Support the Use of Third-Party Hardware or Software? (Element: Technology): Like the console to which it is distributed (*PlayStation 4*), TLOU2 does not support the use of third party hardware or software. This issue is relevant because, although the options related to controls implemented in the game (software) are significant in terms of accessibility, it is noteworthy to highlight that *PlayStation 4* does not have other types of game controller (hardware) besides the standard. Thus, people with very restrictive or severe motor disabilities can experience gaming difficulties or be unable to complete the game.

An example of this issue is presented by Grant Stoner, a player with spinal muscular atrophy and editor of games mobility reviews. In his TLOU2 review, Stoner indicates that even using an alternative controller he was unable to play the game [17]. This points out the relevance of considering game accessibility not only in software terms (systems and digital features) but also in hardware (physical devices). Taking into account the inclusive digital game concept, the lack of support for other controllers, for example, underlines that the game and the platform for which it is distributed can take actions to contemplate players who need these resources to play or who want the possibility of use of third party hardware or software.

4.2 PANELI Extended Topics

During the analysis of the TLOU2 elements, we identified features in addition to the aspects initially addressed in PANELI. Thus, this subsection presents questions that were not in the original analysis form and its related results. We understood the inclusion of these new questions in the analysis form as (1) the extension of the state of the art of accessibility resources, which demands continuous updating of analysis instruments such as PANELI; and (2) the recognition that exists accessibility features specific to some games and which, therefore, go beyond general analysis instruments.

Does the Game Consider Controller Orientation that the Player Prefers or Needs to Use? (Element: Technology): The control orientation refers to the way the player holds or positions the control when playing. The options in TLOU2 are "default," "left," "right," and "upside down" (Fig. 8). Considering the controller orientation is relevant as some people may need to position the controller in a specific way to play and that positioning can, for example, change the direction in which a character walks when the analog stick is pointed forward – doing that in the "upside-down" option would be the same as pointing the analog stick backward, in the "default" option. This question complements the "controls remapping" topic in dealing with the physical layout of the controller and not just the button's functions in the game.

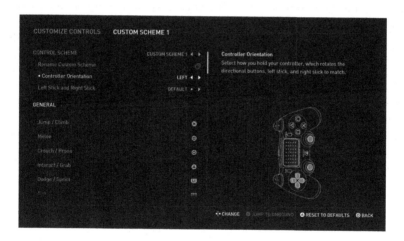

Fig. 8. TLOU2 screenshot of controller orientation menu.

Does the Game Present Grouped Features that Assist its Use or Avoid the Need for Individual Selection of Each Option? (Elements: All): TLOU2 presents three presets for visual, auditory, and motor accessibility (Fig. 9). These presets activate several game features recommended for people with visual, hearing, and motor disabilities. In this way, they act as initial and optional sets presented by the game. It is important to note that even if the players select one of these presets, they can still configure all the game accessibility features individually.

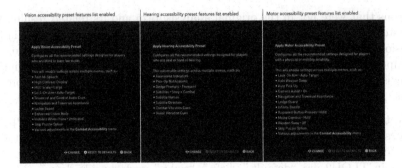

Fig. 9. TLOU2 screenshot of game menus with list of enabled features in visual, auditory and motor presets.

The visual accessibility preset adjusts several game settings to the recommended standards for blind or low vision players. Following are some of the settings enabled in the game with this preset selected.

1. Lock-on aim with auto-target: with this feature, the aim is automatically fixed on nearby enemies;
2. Navigation and traversal assistance: this feature allows the game to indicate where the player should take the character to continue the story, attack enemies, or collect items;
3. Ledge guard: with this feature, the game plays a sound when the character approaches the edge of high places and prevents it from falling from fatal heights;
4. Enhanced listen mode: with this option enabled, the player can search for enemies and items in-game scenes and environments;
5. Unlimited invisibility while prone: in the game there is an action that allows the character controlled by the player, to lie on the floor, making her invisible for a while. However, with this feature enabled, whenever the character is lying down, she becomes invisible indefinitely, providing enough time for the players to decide when to perform their next action.

The hearing accessibility preset adjust game settings to the recommended standards for players with hearing disability or deaf. Following are some highlighted features from that preset.

1. Awareness Indicators: these indicators are displayed when enemies perceive the characters and help to prevent the player from being surprised by enemies (Fig. 4);
2. Dodge prompts frequency: Displayed commands in melee combat.

The motor accessibility preset adjust game settings to the recommended standards for players with physical or motor disabilities. Below are some of the features enabled in this preset.

1. Lock-On Aim with Auto-Target;
2. Auto Pick Up: with this option enabled, the player does not need to press buttons for the character to collect visible items;
3. Camera assist: deals with the camera's automatic rotation in the direction in which the player guides the character. In this way, the player does not need to use the camera control to rotate it in the direction the character is walking;
4. Infinite breath: this feature disables the character's time limit underwater;
5. Change options from press buttons repeatedly to hold;
6. Disable weapon sway.

Does the Game Have Features for Audio Descriptions of Scenarios and Scenes? (Element: Technology): Despite the quantity and quality of TLOU2's accessibility features, the game does not present this option. As indicated by *SightlessKombat* [15], in his game review, the absence of this feature did not prevent him from understanding the game story and the environment in which it takes place. However, we included this question in the analysis to highlight the relevance of this feature, which, in some games, can be essential for understanding the game's environment and story.

Does the Game Have Features of Screen Magnifier or Zoom-In Game Elements (e.g. Interface, Objects and Characters)? (Element: Technology): The game presents a screen magnifier that works for all elements on the screen, such as scene objects, interface, text, among others, and can be useful for people with and without visual disabilities. The console has the same type of feature; however, having this in the game is relevant since not everyone uses this console's feature but may consider it useful during the game.

Figure 10 shows a game scene example without the screen magnifier (on the left) and using the screen magnifier (on the right). The image content on the right side corresponds approximately to the area highlighted on the left.

Fig. 10. TLOU2 screenshot of game scene without the screen magnifier (on the left) and using the screen magnifier (on the right).

4.3   Analysis Overview

TLOU2's more than 60 accessibility options can qualify the game as one of the most accessible ever produced and distributed. However, these features do not prevent the gaming experience from being limited or impossible for some people. In this regard, the main negative points of the game involve the fact that it is exclusive to a platform (*PlayStation 4*), does not have voice commands features, and does not have options for audio-description of scenes and environments.

Another negative point identified in the TLOU2 analysis is the fact that the game does not have support for other devices, particularly controllers, as evidenced by Stoner [17]. Although this limitation also involves the console to which the game is distributed, it is important to note that this issue may represent the exclusion of some people from the experience with the game.

Among the features presented in the game, we highlight some of them below.

1. The displayed menus when the game starts for the first time;
2. Option to enable the text to speech converter on the first game screen;
3. Multiple features related to subtitles;
4. Three presets for visual, hearing and motor accessibility;
5. High contrast features;
6. Screen magnifier and zoom-in features;
7. Accessibility options that work together with others, but also individually.

Features like those listed above allow people with and without disabilities to customize game elements to suit their needs or preferences, without discrimination. These features can still give evidence that *Naughty Dog* considers people with and without disabilities as a game audience and recognize that people have different needs and characteristics.

In addition to the implemented features, we highlight that these features and the game development process involved several inclusive actions, such as the participation of people with and without disabilities, and the planning of these features since the project's beginning [16]. Based on the rationality proposed in this research, for PANELI's use, we consider TLOU2 a game that goes towards the inclusion of as many players as possible. This is because (1) the game considers people with and without disabilities as part of the public since the beginning of the project, (2) provides players means to customize the game elements according to their needs or preferences, and (3) involved people with and without disabilities in the development process.

4.4   Limitations of This Study

This research limitations involve the fact that the game analysis was conducted by only one person supervised by another. Based on usability heuristics evaluation, we acknowledge that including the analysis results of two other reviewers could provide more complex findings to this study. In contrast, we highlight that PANELI's principles and structure recommend using materials from different sources. Thus the current analysis result is also based on multiple experiences.

5   Extended Process and Potential Game Accessibility Improvements

After analyzing the accessibility features of TLOU2 through PANELI, we identified points for potential discussions regarding accessibility in digital games and the analysis procedure used.

5.1   Potential Advancement Initiated with TLOU2 Accessibility Features

With the analysis performed in this research and the accessibility features of TLOU2, it is possible to consider potential developments in (1) the game industry and (2) the gaming community.

According to Steven Saylor and Courtney Craven, TLOU2 is the most accessible game ever produced [14], and the quantity and quality of accessibility features implemented and presented in the game [8] can be used to corroborate the consultants' statement.

In this regard, it is possible to understand that the TLOU2 accessibility options can establish new approaches for other developers to consider implementing accessibility features in their games. Also, TLOU2 settle new quality criteria for gaming accessibility since the game became a benchmark. Therefore, a potential outcome in the gaming industry is the involvement of more people with disabilities in game development processes so that the final products can potentially be more accessible.

Furthermore, the public can pressure the developers to take TLOU2 as an example and thus implement similar or better features in their games, as the players' demand/expectation degree rises. Thus, the accessibility features presented in TLOU2 may represent a new milestone in the digital games accessibility issue, particularly for mainstream companies such as *Naughty Dog*.

Changes in the player's actions concerning the gaming industry may also represent outcomes from TLOU2 accessibility features, particularly by the way that people understand accessibility resources relevance. One possible perspective is that people consider accessibility features as a means for them to personalize their gaming experiences so that their needs, characteristics, and particularities are respected, regardless disabilities.

Another potential consequence of the development of more games with accessibility features is that people with and without disabilities recognize the importance of providing resources so that all people, without distinction, can have the experience with a game. Besides, once people with and without disabilities can play some games together or the same games, they can reject games that do not provide accessibility features.

We highlight that the points previously presented are part of social, political, economic, historical, and cultural contexts. Thus, the decisions made by people regarding game accessibility features occur in power dispute scenarios. Consequently, the development of accessibility features such as those implemented in

TLOU2 does not guarantee changes in the gaming industry towards including people with disabilities as gamers or developers. In this way, results like those achieved by *Naughty Dog* and other companies are part of a continuous movement towards inclusion.

5.2 PANELI Extension and Utilization

The second point to be discussed, based on the analysis of TLOU2 elements, is the PANELI analysis form extension and our proposal to include an attribute related to the rationality used during the analysis process. Also, we highlight potentials benefits using PANELI to increase game accessibility.

The identified lacks in the PANELI analysis form, within the TLOU2 analysis process, might indicate the importance of constantly updating games accessibility analysis methods and procedures. In addition, the need to propose new topics in the analysis form may indicate that the accessibility features of TLOU2 bestow unprecedented or unusual approaches in the gaming area. This highlights the relevance of considering that some games can stimulate different questions or conclusions during an analysis.

Another PANELI change proposed in this research concerns the rationality used for the analysis process. Comprising the concept of inclusive digital game as a principle, the evaluator investigates pieces of evidence that the game goes towards inclusion. Therefore, the game is designed so that people with and without disabilities can have the gaming experience and move forward accessibility features. Furthermore, the concept of inclusive digital gaming highlights the requirement for the participation of people with and without disabilities in the game development process, so investigating these actions contributes to the game analysis and its qualification as an artifact that goes towards inclusion.

Regarding the PANELI uses benefits, we consider that it can be employed as an inspection-based evaluation method, as some listed by Fortes et al. [7], and be applied during the game development process to provide insights and validate data to improve the game accessibility of an ongoing project. Therefore, the main benefits of the use of PANELI are:

1. Low-cost application;
2. Can be employed in the learning or training process of the members of the developer team;
3. Can be used as the baseline for future tests with users;
4. Detailed steps and extensive analysis form;
5. PANELI is grounded on resources and materials of the community of practice and experts;
6. PANELI employs an inclusive rationality that can bring advantages also to the game development process.

Besides, PANELI's application throughout the game development process can prevent the not accomplishment of accessibility features implementation considered a priority to game development. Performing the accessibility evaluation through iterations in the game development process will continuously provide resources to improve the game accessibility features. Also, PANELI's creation involves the gaming accessibility community of practice resources, evidencing that the opinion and requirements indicated and pointed out by the public is considered. We highlight that those community members provide high specialized analysis regarding game accessibility, so the game developers should not disregard their opinions and reviews. Which reinforces the procedure's relevance.

Finally, the use of updated accessibility evaluation methods can contribute to increasing game accessibility when they are considered part of the development process. In this way, evaluation methods, such as PANELI, can offer concrete means to investigate the accessibility features already implemented in the gaming industry and support the evaluation of on-going projects based on structured collected data. Also, these methods can be used by members of development team to understand game accessibility features or with game testers. For this reason, we emphasize the relevance of continuous update on evaluation methods like the performed in the research with PANELI.

6   Concluding Remarks

The implementation of accessibility features in games is an activity that has been more evident over the years. With over 60 accessibility options, TLOU2 is considered the most accessible game ever produced [14].

From the analysis of the game accessibility features, through the PANELI, we presented discussions about these features considering the concept of the inclusive digital game. Among these features, we highlight the autonomy promoted by the game since the first menu screen, allowing players to start the game with features that are essential for their experience, so they do not need to begin the game in a standard mode and later adjust it to their needs.

The analysis carried out in this study can contribute to the investigation of the features presented in TLOU2 and the potential implementation of similar features in games of other developers. Thus, this analysis can be employed as a material for future research or applied in a game development process that goes towards the inclusion of as many players as possible, that is, people with and without disabilities.

Based on the TLOU2 analysis we presented new issues and perspectives related to the PANELI analysis procedure. These issues highlight the diverse resources implemented in TLOU2 and represent the extension of the analysis instrument. Thus, this study presents improvement in academic research and also in the game accessibility features analysis procedure instance.

This research's future works involve the continuous investigation of the consequences of TLOU2's implemented accessibility features in the game industry to understand the features implemented by games launched in the future. Also, investigating the public reactions regarding such resources and the potential connections and comparisons made with the TLOU2 features. Other future work is related to the constant PANELI's improvement and update involving game accessibility community materials and contribution.

Acknowledgments. This study was financed in part by the Coordenação de Aperfeiçoamento de Pessoal de Nível Superior - Brasil (CAPES) - Finance Code 001.

References

1. Convention on the rights of persons with disabilities (CRPD) (2018). https://www.un.org/development/desa/disabilities/convention-on-the-rights-of-persons-with-disabilities.html
2. Innovation in accessibility award added to the game awards (2020). https://thegameawards.com/news/innovation-in-accessibility-award-added-to-the-game-awards
3. Bayliss, B.: The Last of Us Part II accessibility consultants – advancing the industry (2020). https://caniplaythat.com/2020/06/23/the-last-of-us-2-accessibility-consultants-advancing-the-industry/
4. Campbell, K.: The game awards now has an accessibility (aka The Last Of Us 2) category (2020). https://www.thegamer.com/game-awards-accessibility-category-last-of-us-2/
5. Craven, C.: The Last of Us: Part 2 - blind accessibility review (2020). https://caniplaythat.com/2020/06/12/the-last-of-us-2-deaf-hoh-review/
6. Dix, A., Finlay, J., Abowd, G.D., Beale, R.: Human-Computer Interaction. Pearson Education (2004)
7. Fortes, R.P.M., de Lima Salgado, A., de Souza Santos, F., Agostini do Amaral, L., Nogueira da Silva, E.A.: Game accessibility evaluation methods: a literature survey. In: Antona, M., Stephanidis, C. (eds.) Universal Access in Human-Computer Interaction. Design and Development Approaches and Methods, pp. 182–192. Springer, Heidelberg (2017). https://doi.org/10.1007/978-3-319-58706-6_15
8. Gallant, M.: The Last of Us Part II: Accessibility features detailed (2020). https://www.naughtydog.com/blog/the_last_of_us_part_ii_accessibility_features_detailed
9. Grammenos, D., Savidis, A., Stephanidis, C.: Designing universally accessible games (2009). https://doi.org/10.1145/1486508.1486516
10. Hernandez, P.: The Last of Us Part 2 has become a minefield (2020). https://www.polygon.com/2020/6/30/21307200/the-last-of-us-2-controversy-critics-press-naughty-dog-vice-review-leak-sony-ps4-playstation
11. Leite, P.S.: Elementos de jogos digitais inclusivos para gameplay no contexto das pessoas com deficiência sob a perspectiva da interação corporificada. Master's thesis, Universidade Tecnológica Federal do Paraná (2018). http://repositorio.utfpr.edu.br/jspui/handle/1/2892
12. Leite, P.S., Almeida, L.D.A.: Um procedimento de análise de elementos de jogos inclusivos:um experimento com celeste e god of war. In: SBC - Proceedings of SBGames, pp. 296–305. SBC (2019). https://www.sbgames.org/sbgames2019/files/papers/ArtesDesignFull/198040.pdf
13. Leite, P.S., Retore, A.P., Almeida, L.D.A.: Reflections on elements of a game design model applied to inclusive digital games. In: Antona, M., Stephanidis, C. (eds.) HCII 2019. LNCS, vol. 11572, pp. 284–300. Springer, Cham (2019). https://doi.org/10.1007/978-3-030-23560-4_21
14. Saylor, S.: Our The Last of Us 2 discussion on accessibility and blind impressions (2020). https://caniplaythat.com/2020/06/12/our-the-last-of-us-2-discussion-on-accessibility-and-blind-impressions/
15. SightlessKombat: The Last of Us: Part 2 - blind accessibility review (2020). https://caniplaythat.com/2020/06/18/the-last-of-us-2-review-blind-accessibility/

16. Stoner, G.: The Last of Us Part 2 - a conversation with naughty dog (2020). https://caniplaythat.com/2020/06/29/the-last-of-us-part-2-a-conversation-with-naughty-dog/
17. Stoner, G.: The Last of Us: Part 2 - mobility review (2020). https://caniplaythat.com/2020/06/22/the-last-of-us-part-2-mobility-review/
18. Westin, T., Bierre, K., Gramenos, D., Hinn, M.: Advances in game accessibility from 2005 to 2010. In: Stephanidis, C. (ed.) UAHCI 2011. LNCS, vol. 6766, pp. 400–409. Springer, Heidelberg (2011). https://doi.org/10.1007/978-3-642-21663-3_43
19. Yuan, B., Folmer, E., Harris Jr., F.C.: Game accessibility: a survey. Universal Access Inf. Soc. **10**(1), 81–100 (2011). https://doi.org/10.1007/s10209-010-0189-5

Image Search Versus Text Search Revisited: A Simple Experiment Using a Kahoot Quiz

Signe Aanderaa Eide[1], Ana-Maria Poljac[1], and Frode Eika Sandnes[1,2(✉)]

[1] Oslo Metropolitan University, 0130 Oslo, Norway
{s333781,s333745,frodes}@oslomet.no
[2] Kristiania University College, 0153 Oslo, Norway

Abstract. Information search is a common task when interacting with computers. Many studies have investigated the characteristics that facilitate effective search, specifically the use of icons and/or text. This study reports a simple experiment involving Kahoot where the goal was to observe searching performance with images and text. The results show that image search was faster, less error prone and preferred by participants compared to text search.

Keywords: Image search · Text search · Visual scanning

1 Introduction

Visual search is needed when operating graphical computer interfaces, for example to select an option from a menu. Much have been written about visual search both in terms of text and graphical representations, especially icons.

Photographs and photorealistic images are quite different from icons in that they often are rendered as simplified canonical representations of objects while photograph are real representations. The human visual system is trained to perceive and interpret the real world, while on the other end of the scale technical drawings require time to decipher. Icons are often viewed as "user friendly", but as simplified renderings of real objects they need to be learned, especially if they represent abstract concepts such as traffic signs.

On the other hand, text represents a visual coding in which most people have many years of training and experience. Readers tend to recognize entire words instead of individual letters when these are presented using lowercase characters. Trained readers perceive and interpret text at very high rates even though text are advanced sequences of abstract symbols. The question thus arises whether to use text, icons, images, or a combination to facilitate the easy identification of various elements in user interfaces.

This study had two objectives: First, we wanted to collect empiric evidence on the search performance of users when dealing with photorealistic images versus text. Second, we wanted to explore the suitability of using an off-the shelf web-based application Kahoot for setting up and conducting simple experiments.

The rest of this paper is organized as follows. The following section reviews related studies into visual search using text and images. Section 3 presents the methodology.

© Springer Nature Switzerland AG 2021
M. Antona and C. Stephanidis (Eds.): HCII 2021, LNCS 12768, pp. 186–196, 2021.
https://doi.org/10.1007/978-3-030-78092-0_12

This is followed by results and discussion. The paper closes with concluding remarks in Sect. 6.

2 Related Work

Information search is a huge research field and visual search is one part of this. Moreover, semiotics, or the study of symbols, is another established field. More recently, symbols have also been studied in more applied domains such as product design and information technology [1, 2] although Fleetwood [3] in 2002 claimed that there were few studies on icons despite the longevity of graphical user interfaces. Icons have also been studied outside the computing domain, for example the visual search for warning labels on products [4], where it was found that the participants preferred icons and signal words in red.

In one of the early writings on computer icons Byrne [5] claimed that simple icons with clear and few characteristics is the most beneficial, and that complex icons are no better than simple rectangles. Fleetwood and Bryne studied the relationship between search performance and icon quality [3, 6]. Klöckner, Wirschum, and Jameson [7] investigated results lists from search engines and discussed two search list exploration strategies taken by users, namely breadth first and depth first search. Everett and Byrne [8] studied how spacing between icons in a grid affects visual search performance.

Focusing on the visual appearance of icons Arledge [9] compared the effects of icons represented by outlines versus those that are filled. Garcia, Badre and Stasko [10] investigated the level of abstraction of icons and found that context is affecting the understanding of icons. Cho et al. [11] probed senior users' preference for level of realism and level of abstraction. Icon location has also been found to be an important factor in addition to the icon shape [12]. Blankenberger and Hahn [13] claimed that trained users remember where icons are located, that icon design has little effect, and that icon design is more influential for novice users.

Holloway and Bailey [14] compared students and developers' perceptions of icons and found that developers had a different understanding of the icons compared to the students. They concluded that the selection of icons should involve the target audience and not only developers. The involvement of the target audience in icon selection is also echoed by Berget and Sandnes [15] who tested how well students recognized common icons in the public domain. They found that many of the participants did not successfully recognize seemingly common objects such as wrenches and parachutes.

Studies have also addressed the effect of contrast and sharpness for icon search. A study using an eye-tracking methodology [16] found that contrast was more important than sharpness for icons arranged in a grid. Luminance contrast has also been studied extensively for the readability of text in relation to the background [17–19]. Clearly legible text is a prerequisite for visual search [20]. The choice of colors is affected by the color pickers used [21] and different approaches to color pickers have been proposed to facilitate color combinations that ensure enough luminance contrast [22–24]. Huang [25] studied specific figure-ground color combinations for icons as well as outline width and icon shape. It was wound that colors influenced search time. Outline width, border and icon shape was found to have no effect on error rates. The combination of text in visual search has also been explored. In an experiment of visual search with structured layouts Hornof [26] found that the search was more efficient when structured groups were labelled compared to unlabeled. The benefit of redundant coding with icons and text was also observed in menu selection tasks [27]. Although no difference in response time was observed, they did find fewer errors when icons and text were used together.

Icons, images, and text has also been studied in context of disability. For instance, researchers have explored whether icons are more effective than text for users with dyslexia [28] and for users with a diagnosis on the autism spectrum [29].

Juola, Ward and McNamara [30] studied participants' ability to detect absence or presence of letters in strings. Implications of knowledge about search behavior include the manner and order in which search engine results are presented [31].

More recently there has been an interest in icons in connection with the emergence of smartphones and other handheld devices that have limited display real estate. Issues studied includes how users organize their icons [32] and change blindness [33], more specifically how the inability of noticing icon changes communicating status changes is related to the number of icons.

3   Method

3.1   Experimental Design

A controlled experiment with one within-group independent variable and three dependent variables was designed. The within-group variable had two levels, namely search in images and search in text. The three dependent variables included mean search completion time, error rate and preference. The preference variable was dichotomous.

3.2   Participants

A total of 15 participants was recruited randomly from the campus of the authors' university. All the participants were students in the age range of 19 to 25 years with an approximate gender balance. None of the respondents reported any issues related to reduced vision such as color blindness or cognition such as dyslexia [34, 35].

3.3   Materials

A total of 16 tasks were designed of which eight involved image search and eight textual searches. Each task entailed presenting four alternatives of which one was the correct answer. The image search tasks typically comprised identifying the picture with or without a given object, or quantity of objects (see Fig. 1). The images were of varying levels of difficulty such as simple images, stylized cartoons, artistic drawings and for instance an owl camouflaged in its natural habitat. The text search task involved identifying texts with or without a given letter (see Fig. 2) similar to the procedure reported in [30], identifying a specific word or a word denoting a certain concept such as objects that are blue. The text strings were of similar lengths. Instructions were given in Norwegian. Steps were taken to ensure the objects were universally familiar. The tasks were designed to

Fig. 1. Example of image search task (identify the image without a mobile phone).

Fig. 2. Example of textual search task (identify the text with the letter "d").

have varying levels of difficulty. The tasks were presented in increasing level of difficulty alternating between image tasks and text tasks.

The experiment was implemented using Kahoot which is intended as an educational and entertaining quiz tool [36–38]. Kahoot was generally well-known among the cohort of students recruited. Kahoot facilitates four options as images or text and provides time-taking functionality and bookkeeping of correct and incorrect responses.

3.4 Procedure

The participants were first briefed about the experiment before the participants gave their consent to participate. Participation was voluntary and anonymous. No personal information was collected. Participants had the freedom to withdraw from the experiment at any time without having to provide a reason.

The participants were tested individually in an undisturbed meeting room with the two first authors present as facilitators. Each session lasted approximately 15 min. A maximum time limit of 30 s was set for each task and a countdown-timer displayed the remaining time. The participants responded to the quiz using a smartphone but a laptop computer with the same quiz mirrored was also placed in front of the participant. After completing the 16 tasks the participants were asked to indicate their preferred mode of searching.

3.5 Analysis

The median time for each task type was computed for each participant. The errors were analyzed in terms of incorrect responses and number of missing responses within the 30 s window. The observations were checked for adherence to normal distribution using Shapiro-Wilk tests. The results were analyzed using JASP 0.12.0.0 [39].

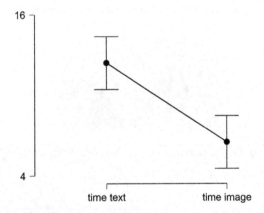

Fig. 3. Mean task complete time in seconds. Error bars show 95% confidence intervals.

4 Results

Figure 3 shows the mean task completion times in seconds for the textual search and image search. Clearly, task completion times are much larger with textual search ($M = 12.4$, $SD = 5.6$) compared to image search ($M = 6.5$, $SD = 1.6$). The two confidence intervals are not overlapping. A paired t-test confirms that the search times are significantly different ($t(14) = 4.54$, $p < .001$, Cohen's $d = 1.173$, 95% CI [0.497, 1.826]).

Figure 4 shows the error rates for the two modes of searching. The error rate is much higher with textual search ($M = 23.3\%$, $SD = 18.2\%$) compared to image-based search ($M = 9.2\%$, $SD = 7.4\%$). A paired t-test shows that the two error rates are significantly different ($t(14) = 3.3$, $p = .032$, Cohen's $d = 0.614$, 95% CI [0.051, 1.159]).

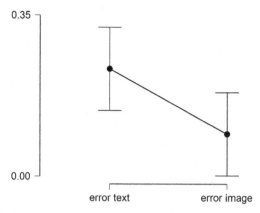

Fig. 4. Error rate. Error bars show 95% confidence intervals.

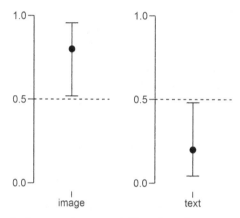

Fig. 5. Preferences for image and text search. Error bars show 95% confidence intervals.

Of the 15 participants a majority of 12 participant preferred image-based search while 3 participants indicated a preference for the text-based search. This 80% preference for image search had a 95% CI of 51.9% to 95.7%, $p = .035$, while the 20% preference for textual search had a 95% CI of 4.3% to 48.1%, $p = .035$ (see Fig. 5). A majority thus prefer image search.

As only three participants preferred text search it was not feasible to conduct further statistical analyses. However, the task completion times for the two search modes were plotted according to preference to get an indication the potential trend (see Fig. 6). The results show that the participants who prefer textual search perform very similar under both conditions, while participants who prefer image search appears to take much shorter time with textual search. Moreover, the 95% confidence intervals reveal that the spread is larger in the least preferred mode compared to the preferred mode for both preferences.

The responses were also analyzed according to question. The results confirm that the questions had different levels of difficulty as intended. The total number of errors, that is, the sum of actual errors and number of missing responses correlated positively and

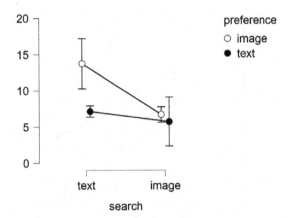

Fig. 6. Task completion time plotted according to preference. Error bars show 95% CI.

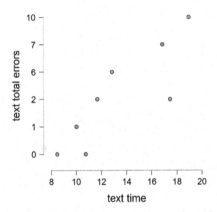

Fig. 7. Scatter plot showing the relationship between the total number of errors and the task completion time.

significantly with the response time for both textual search ($r(16) = 0.778$, $p = .023$, 95% CI [0.163, 0.958]) and visual search ($r(16) = 0.965$, $p < .001$, 95% CI [0.811, 0.994]). Moreover, the number of errors also correlated positively and significantly for both image search ($r_s(16) = 0.756$, $p = .030$, 95% CI [0.110, 0.953]) and text search ($r_s(16) = 0.793$, $p = .019$, 95% CI[0.200, 0.961]). The connection between search time and the number of errors in the textual questions is illustrated in Fig. 7. Only observations for the text tasks are shown since text search were associated with most errors.

5 Discussions

The results show that image search is much faster than text search. In time-critical tasks it is important to facilitate search tasks such that the delay associated with the visual search is reduced. Not only is the search speed critical, but also the error rate. It is not enough for a search to be quick if the result is incorrect. The search needs to be quick and preferably error free. However, the results show that the error rates follow the same trend as the search time. Image-based search was associated with a much lower error rate compared to textual search. These results partially agree with the results obtained when contrasting icons and text where lower error rates were achieved with icons although not difference in search time [27]. This may be because icons are simple not photorealistic representations.

The results give a strong indication that users in general prefer image-oriented search. It is useful from a practical perspective that users' preferences are consistent with performance characteristics, that is, for the types of search studied users prefer the search modes with the shortest task completion times and lowest error rate. Although generalizable, the benefit of image search is not suitable for all users [17, 28, 29]. The convention of redundant coding where image is used together with text and other characteristics seems sensible [26, 27].

The battery of questions was intentionally varied in level of difficulty, and these variations were observed in the results. Difficult search tasks took longer than easier search tasks. The difficult search tasks also associated with more errors and missing responses than easier search tasks.

Kahoot proved itself as a convenient platform for conducting controlled experiments as it was easy to set up experiments. Kahoot managed the stopwatch tasks and tallied correct answers which allowed the answers to be conveniently downloaded into an Excel sheet for subsequent statistical analysis. Kahoot also supports randomization of questions, although we did not exploit this function. The participants provided positive feedback on participating in the Kahoot experiment. It is thus possible that Kahoot may be more engaging than traditional electronic questionnaires. However, it is also possible that the timed tasks were perceived as somewhat stressful. Perhaps the element of competition could have been reduced by not displaying the count down clock during the tasks?

5.1 Limitations

One limitation of this study is the small population size. Hence, it was not possible to conduct detailed analysis of performance according to preference. To perform such analyses a larger sample of participants with a preference for textual search is needed which require pre-screening of the participations. The cohort was also limited. Although the results clearly show distinct trends for image and text searches it is possible that a different cohort would yield different results.

Another limitation of this study is that the presentation order was fixed. Hence, it is possible that there may be some confounding effects. However, attempts were taken to limit this by intertwining the presentation of image-based and textual search tasks.

There was also an issue using the mobile handset with the image search tasks as the display made it hard to see details although a laptop computer also displayed the tasks. For Detail-rich images the experiment should perhaps be employed on experimental setups with a larger display only.

6 Conclusions

A simple experiment was conducted were Kahoot was used to measure users' search performance in images and texts, respectively. The results show that users search time and error rates are smaller with image search compared to textual search. Most participants were in favor of image search. Our experiences revealed that Kahoot was straightforward to configure and is therefore a convenient platform for conducting certain types of controlled experiments.

References

1. Gittins, D.: Icon-based human-computer interaction. Int. J. Man Mach. Stud. **24**(6), 519–543 (1986)
2. Lin, R., Kreifeldt, J.G.: Understanding the image functions for icon design. In: Proceedings of the Human Factors Society Annual Meeting, vol. 36, no. 4, pp. 341–345. Sage, Los Angeles, (1992)
3. Fleetwood, M.D., Byrne, M.D.: Modeling icon search in ACT-R/PM. Cogn. Syst. Res. **3**(1), 25–33 (2002)
4. Bzostek, J.A., Wogalter, M.S.: Measuring visual search time for a product warning label as a function of icon, color, column and vertical placement. In: Proceedings of the Human Factors and Ergonomics Society Annual Meeting, vol. 43, no. 16, pp. 888–892. Sage, Los Angeles (1999)
5. Byrne, M.D.: Using icons to find documents: simplicity is critical. In: Proceedings of ACM INTERCHI'93 Conference on Human Factors in Computing Systems, pp. 446–453 (1993)
6. Fleetwood, M.D., Byrne, M.D.: Modeling the visual search of displays: a revised ACT-R/PM model of icon search based on eye-tracking and experimental data. In: Proceedings of the Fifth International Conference on Cognitive Modeling, pp. 87–92. Universitas-Verlag Bamberg, Bamberg (2003)
7. Klöckner, K., Wirschum, N., Jameson, A.: Depth-and breadth-first processing of search result lists. In: CHI'04 Extended Abstracts on Human Factors in COMPUTING SYSTEMS, p. 1539. ACM (2004)
8. Everett, S.P., Byrne, M.D.: Unintended effects: varying icon spacing changes users' visual search strategy. In: Proceedings of the SIGCHI Conference on Human Factors in Computing Systems, pp. 695–702. ACM (2004)
9. Arledge, C.: Filled-in vs. outline icons: the impact of icon style on usability. Masters thesis (2014)
10. García, M., Badre, A.N., Stasko, J.T.: Development and validation of icons varying in their abstractness. Interact. Comput. **6**(2), 191–211 (1994)
11. Cho, M., Kwon, S., Na, N., Suk, H.J., Lee, K.: The elders preference for skeuomorphism as app icon style. In: Proceedings of the 33rd Annual ACM Conference Extended Abstracts on Human Factors in Computing Systems, pp. 899–904. ACM (2015)
12. Moyes, J.: When users do and don't rely on icon shape. In: Conference Companion on Human Factors in Computing Systems, pp. 283–284 (1994)
13. Blankenberger, S., Hahn, K.: Effects of icon design on human-computer interaction. Int. J. Man Mach. Stud. **35**(3), 363–377 (1991)
14. Holloway, J.B., Bailey, J.H.: Don't use a product's developers for icon testing. In: Conference Companion on Human Factors in Computing Systems, pp. 309–310. ACM (1996)

15. Berget, G., Sandnes, F.E.: On the understandability of public domain icons: effects of gender and age. In: Antona, M., Stephanidis, C. (eds.) UAHCI 2015. LNCS, vol. 9175, pp. 387–396. Springer, Cham (2015). https://doi.org/10.1007/978-3-319-20678-3_37

16. Näsänen, R., Ojanpää, H.: Effect of image contrast and sharpness on visual search for computer icons. Displays **24**(3), 137–144 (2003)

17. Sandnes, F.E.: Understanding WCAG2.0 color contrast requirements through 3D color space visualization. Stud. Health Technol. Inform. **229**, 366–375 (2016)

18. Sandnes, F.E.: On-screen colour contrast for visually impaired readers, pp. 405–416. Routledge (2017)

19. Sandnes, F.E.: An image-based visual strategy for working with color contrasts during design. In: Miesenberger, K., Kouroupetroglou, G. (eds.) ICCHP 2018. LNCS, vol. 10896, pp. 35–42. Springer, Cham (2018). https://doi.org/10.1007/978-3-319-94277-3_7

20. Ling, J., Van Schaik, P.: The effect of text and background colour on visual search of Web pages. Displays **23**(5), 223–230 (2002)

21. Brathovde, K., Farner, M.B., Brun, F.K., Sandnes, F.E.: Effectiveness of color-picking interfaces among non-designers. In: Luo, Y. (ed.) CDVE 2019. LNCS, vol. 11792, pp. 181–189. Springer, Cham (2019). https://doi.org/10.1007/978-3-030-30949-7_21

22. Sandnes, F.E., Zhao, A.: A contrast colour selection scheme for WCAG2. 0-compliant web designs based on HSV-half-planes. In: 2015 IEEE International Conference on Systems, Man, and Cybernetics, pp. 1233–1237. IEEE (2015)

23. Sandnes, F., Zhao, A.: An interactive color picker that ensures WCAG2.0 compliant color contrast levels. Procedia Comput. Sci. **67**, 87–94 (2015). https://doi.org/10.1016/j.procs.2015.09.252

24. Hansen, F., Krivan, J.J., Sandnes, F.E.: Still not readable? An interactive tool for recommending color pairs with sufficient contrast based on existing visual designs. In: The 21st International ACM SIGACCESS Conference on Computers and Accessibility, pp. 636–638. ACM (2019)

25. Huang, K.C., Chiu, T.L.: Visual search performance on an LCD monitor: effects of color combination of figure and icon background, shape of icon, and line width of icon border. Percept. Mot. Skills **104**(2), 562–574 (2007)

26. Hornof, A.J.: Visual search and mouse pointing in labeled versus unlabeled two-dimensional visual hierarchies. ACM Trans. Comput.-Hum. Interact. **8**, 171–197 (2001)

27. Kacmar, C.J., Carey, J.M.: Assessing the usability of icons in user interfaces. Behav. Inf. Technol. **10**(6), 443–457 (1991)

28. Berget, G., Sandnes, F.E.: The effect of dyslexia on searching visual and textual content: are icons really useful? In: Antona, M., Stephanidis, C. (eds.) UAHCI 2015. LNCS, vol. 9177, pp. 616–625. Springer, Cham (2015). https://doi.org/10.1007/978-3-319-20684-4_59

29. Joseph, R.M., Keehn, B., Connolly, C., Wolfe, J.M., Horowitz, T.S.: Why is visual search superior in autism spectrum disorder? Dev. Sci. **12**(6), 1083–1096 (2009)

30. Juola, J.F., Ward, N.J., McNamara, T.: Visual search and reading of rapid serial presentations of letter strings, words, and text. J. Exp. Psychol. Gen. **111**(2), 208 (1982)

31. Hsu, W.H., Kennedy, L.S., Chang, S.F.: Reranking methods for visual search. IEEE Multimed. **14**(3), 14–22 (2007)

32. Böhmer, M., Krüger, A.: A study on icon arrangement by smartphone users. In: Proceedings of the SIGCHI Conference on Human Factors in Computing Systems, pp. 2137–2146. ACM (2013)

33. Davies, T., Beeharee, A.: The case of the missed icon: change blindness on mobile devices. In: Proceedings of the SIGCHI Conference on Human Factors in Computing Systems, pp. 1451–1460. ACM (2012)

34. Berget, G., Mulvey, F., Sandnes, F.E.: Is visual content in textual search interfaces beneficial to dyslexic users? Int. J. Hum. Comput. Stud. **92**, 17–29 (2016)

35. Berget, G., Sandnes, F.E.: Searching databases without query-building aids: implications for dyslexic users. Inf. Res.: Int. Electron. J. **20**(4) (2015)
36. Dellos, R.: Kahoot! A digital game resource for learning. Int. J. Instr. Technol. Dist. Learn. **12**(4), 49–52 (2015)
37. Zarzycka-Piskorz, E.: Kahoot it or not? Can games be motivating in learning grammar? Teach. Engl. Technol. **16**(3), 17–36 (2016)
38. Licorish, S.A., Owen, H.E., Daniel, B., George, J.L.: Students' perception of Kahoot!'s influence on teaching and learning. Res. Pract. Technol. Enhanc. Learn. **13**(1), 1–23 (2018). https://doi.org/10.1186/s41039-018-0078-8
39. JASP Team: JASP (Version 0.12.0) [Computer software] (2020)

Disadvantaged by Disability: Examining the Accessibility of Cyber Security

Steven Furnell[1](✉) ⓘ, Kirsi Helkala[2] ⓘ, and Naomi Woods[3] ⓘ

[1] University of Nottingham, Nottingham, UK
Steven.Furnell@nottingham.ac.uk
[2] Norwegian Defence University College/Cyber Academy, Lillehammer, Norway
khelkala@mil.no
[3] University of Jyväskylä, Jyväskylä, Finland
naomi.woods@jyu.fi

Abstract. Today, we are living in a digitally dependent world. Through the use of digital technologies, life is meant to be easier and streamlined. This includes giving access to services that previously were unavailable to many due to disability. Although technology has evolved immensely over the past few decades, reducing the digital divide, authentication methods have changed very little. Authentication is the forefront of securing users' information, services and technology, yet for many it still poses issues in terms of usability and security, due to specific characteristics of different disabilities. In this paper, drawing upon a literature review, a review of recognized disabilities, and the results of a small questionnaire study, we review the current authentication methods and discuss the potential issues that users with different disabilities face when interacting with these methods. We identify the specific aspects of disabilities that lead users to struggle to authenticate themselves. The results of this study lead to several recommendations, and suggestions for extending the existing inclusive technology framework to the authentication context. Through extending the framework, this could guide the development of future technologies, systems and services, ensuring that they are not only digitally inclusive in their function, but digitally inclusive in their security.

Keywords: Authentication · Disability · Cyber security

1 Introduction

While digital technology offers immense opportunities for improving lives and lifestyles [3, 12, 21, 24], it is recognised that certain aspects can pose challenges for users with disabilities [2, 5, 17]. This applies not only to the primary devices and services that people want to use, but also to the supporting elements – within which we can include cyber security. For many users, the need to handle cyber security is already perceived as an unwanted barrier or overhead [16], and this can be felt even more acutely if it is presented in a manner that is implicitly more difficult for certain users to accomplish.

© Springer Nature Switzerland AG 2021
M. Antona and C. Stephanidis (Eds.): HCII 2021, LNCS 12768, pp. 197–212, 2021.
https://doi.org/10.1007/978-3-030-78092-0_13

This paper examines the extent to which users with disabilities can find themselves potentially disadvantaged by cybersecurity, with particular attention to the issue of user authentication (the frontline element of security that users regularly encounter across a range of devices, systems and services) [19, 28, 36]. As we have focused on security and usability aspects of the authentication methods in our work, we also discuss how the findings of this paper can be used for expanding existing authentication frameworks.

The content draws upon literature review findings, alongside the results of a small questionnaire study that was conducted to assess authentication in everyday life situations among differently impaired people to support the literature search. The discussion begins by setting the scene, with a short introduction to authentication methods currently available, and then continues with a categorization of disabilities. Having established this foundation, the discussion proceeds to consider available authentication methods in the context of different potential disabilities, with the combinations being assessed in terms of whether the disability leads to impacts in terms of security and/or usability. The next section gives the summary of the results of the questionnaire and validates the argumentation given in earlier section. In the later sections, we discuss existing authentication methods in comparison to the existing frameworks and then consider how our findings can be used to expand these approaches.

2   User Authentication and Disability

User authentication methods are commonly categorised into three top-level groups, based upon what they are attempting to assess as the proof of the user's legitimacy [20, 26]. These are outlined as follows (noting that in practice there are many further distinctions that can be made in terms of the underlying technologies and their operation):

- **Something the user knows** (memorised secrets): Knowledge-based methods are based around the user having some form of secret. Various related methods are available and can include traditional passwords and Personal Identification Numbers (PINs), Challenge-Response methods, and a range of graphical approaches. Challenge-response methods can include question and answer techniques, based upon cognitive or associative information [13]. Graphical methods can include recognition- (cognometric), cued recall- (locimetric) and free recall- (drawmetric) based techniques [6, 30]. These techniques varyingly involve recognition of previously selected images, recall of secret points within prior images, or the ability to recall and draw an image-based secret.
- **Something the user has** (tokens): In this context, authentication is based upon the user's possession of a particular object (e.g. a device or token) by which they prove their identity. Such tokens may be user-dependent (in which the user must actively interact with the token during the authentication process) or user-independent (which do not require an active interaction for users to authenticate themselves).
- **Something the user is** (biometrics): This category reflects the use of biometric technologies, which can be based upon physiological or behavioural measurements of the user. The former includes techniques such as face, fingerprint, handprint, iris and retina recognition, whereas behavioural metrics include characteristics such as gait,

signature, typing style and voice. Biometric authentication works by comparing a reference profile established during the registration (or enrolment) phase to later samples provided during the authentication process.

As may be apparent from the descriptions, each type of method carries different expectations and demands in terms of what users will need to do in order to make use of it. These in turn may have potential implications in the context of users with different forms of disability. As such, it is relevant to understand the various forms of disabilities that may be encountered.

Disabled World [7] states that "a disability is defined as a condition or function judged to be significantly impaired relative to the usual standard of an individual or group". They classify disabilities into eight categories: mobility/physical, spinal cord, head injuries, vision, hearing, cognitive/learning, psychological, and invisible. However, the World Health Organization has more detailed categorization for same impairments. Their International Classification of Functioning, Disability and Health (ICF) checklist is employed to measure health and disability at an individual level and a population level [35]. Within this paper, we have selected specific functions from the ICF list, in order to consider whether the impairments would have an impact on the ability to interact, perform and achieve authentication. However, we have excluded some items from the original ICF list on the basis that they are not primary functions or structures needed for participating in the authentication process. This leads to the removal of entries relating to digestive, metabolic and endocrine systems, genitourinary and reproductive functions, and their representative structures, and haematological, immunological and emotional function. As such, the resulting merged ICF list includes the following:

- **Intelligence (I)** relates to a person's intellectual and higher-level cognitive functions, and ability to undertake multiple tasks or a single task and to solve problems.
- **Attention (A)** relates to the capability to hold attention and sleep, energy and drive functions, consciousness, orientation, and capability to undertake multiple tasks or a single task.
- **Memory (M)** relates to capability to remember.
- **Vision (V)** relates to seeing, watching and perceptual functions.
- **Hearing (H)** relates to hearing, listening and perceptual functions.
- **Competence (C)** relates to a person's capabilities to learn to read, write and calculate.
- **Life support (L)** relates to heart, blood pressure, respiration and skin issues.
- **Spoken messages (S)** relates to a person's abilities to communicate with spoken messages, to speak, to have a conversation, knowing a language, and having a voice.
- **Non-verbal messages (N)** relates to a person's abilities to communicate with non-verbal messages, producing non-verbal messages, and knowing a language.
- **Lifting and carrying objects (O)** relates to the capability to lift and carry objects, mobility of joints, muscle power and muscle tone in trunk, head and neck region, shoulder region and in upper extremities. The ability to undertake multiple tasks or a single task, involuntary movements, pain, and vestibular issues.
- **Fine hand use (F)** relates to the capability to undertake fine hand use, mobility of joints, muscle power and muscle tone in trunk, head and neck region, shoulder region

and in upper extremities. The ability to undertake multiple tasks or a single task, involuntary movements, pain, and vestibular issues.

- **Walking (W)** relates to the capability to walk, mobility of joints, muscle power and muscle tone in trunk, pelvis, and lower extremities, involuntary movements, pain, and vestibular issues.

It will likely be evident from this list that the potential disabilities may have varying levels of influence and impact depending upon the type of authentication method in use, and this is consequently explored in the next section.

3   Comparing Current Methods and ICF List Features

In examining the approaches and disabilities together, the discussion now considers the potential implications of different disabilities in the context of individual authentication methods. Specifically, we consider whether the disability is likely to affect usability (U) and/or security (S) perspectives:

- U refers to usability challenges that the authentication method concerned may present for someone with a particular disability – they may find it difficult to use a given method, or they may be rendered entirely inapplicable.
- S refer to achieving less security (or reducing security) for someone with a particular disability – the security of the method may reduce due to the issues that their particular disability present.

The evaluation of the authentication methods is conducted similarly to [14], where security was estimated by the entropy of the authenticator's search space and circumvention difficulties. The usability of the methods was estimated with help of the transaction time and human failure. If a user cannot provide the authentication secret, token or sample, we have taken this as a usability issue, not a security issue, as the security level stays untouched.

It should be noted that we have not sought to calculate any specific security and usability levels for two reasons as the aim at this stage is to more broadly highlight the possible problematic issues, showing where the difficulties might exist and what might be the cause. Progressing beyond this to evaluate the extent of the issue would require wider data collection but could be guided by the preliminary estimations and hypothesis that this paper provides.

Below we discuss how the lack of functions impact the usability and security of different authentication methods. The discussion is based on the literature previously mentioned and additional literature. Table 1 summarizes the discussion and comparison, using the reference letters from Sect. 2 as the shorthand for the relevant ICF list items. However, as none of the authentication methods discussed in this paper are based on non-verbal communication, we have omitted that category from the discussions and Table 1. Similarly, 'lifting and carrying objects' has been left out as it can be merged with 'fine hand use' regarding usage of the authentication methods considered in this paper.

Table 1. Body and cognitive functions vs. authentication methods without assistive technology

Authentication method		ICF functions impairment impact										Total challenges	
		I	A	M	V	H	C	L	S	F	W	U	S
Memorised Secrets	Passwords	US	US	US	US		US			US		6	6
	PIN	US	U	US	US		US			US		6	5
	Challenge – Response	US	U	US	U	U	US			US		7	4
	Graphical – Recognition	US	U	U	U					U		5	1
	Graphical – Recall	US	U	U	U					U		5	1
	Graphical – Drawing	US	U	US	U					US		5	3
Tokens	User-dependent	S	U	US	U					U		4	2
	User-independent	S		US								1	2
Biometrics	Ear							U		U		2	0
	Iris				U			U		U		3	0
	Retina recognition				U			U		U		3	0
	Face recognition				U			U		U		3	0
	Fingerprint recognition				U			U		U		3	0
	Gait							U			U	2	0
	Hand geometry recognition							U		U		2	0
	Typing recognition	S	U	U	U		US	U		US		6	3
	Vein recognition							U		U		2	0
	Voice-Speaker recognition		U	U		U		U	US	U		6	1
	Signature recognition	S	U	U	U		US	U		US		6	3

In general, vision and/or hearing issues could compromise the usability of any of these authentication methods if the method is dependent upon the user following audio or visual prompts/instructions. However, as such, prompts are not an inherent part of any of these methods; and therefore, we have not regarded them as primary issues. There is technology available to assists impaired people. We have not included assistive technology in our discussions as our aim is to emphasise the impact of the impairment.

In the paragraphs below, we expand on the information presented in Table 1, providing further commentary upon the ten ICF functions, and how they are relevant to the usability and security of different authentication methods.

- **Intelligence (I):** This function category handles a person's ability to think, reflect, transfer knowledge from one context to another, solve problems and carry out intellectual tasks. Impairment in this category will have an effect on all memorized secrets. Security of the secrets is based on larger character sets and random-like passwords and drawing. Intelligence impairment might lower the actual search space of characters and drawings lowering the security level of the secrets. In addition, not-sharing the secret might be difficult with intelligent impaired person. Usability is lower, if person does not understand how the authentication methods should be used: when to design secrets and when to provide the memorized secret. Single factor tokens keep the secrets for the user. However, the tokens should not be shared. As with memorized secrets, not sharing might be problematic, lowering the security of the tokens. In case of the biometric, security of typing recognition and signature recognition might be lower due to the simple drawings and typing in the enrolment phase.

- **Attention (A):** Functions in these categories will have effect a person's capability to keep their focus on a task at hand. The usability of the memorized secrets relates heavily to the effort that is put to select the secret. If attention is wrongly placed in enrolment when secrets are enrolled, the usability problems might later occur. In the case of the password, the lack of attention might cause shorter and not random-like passwords lowering the security level. Attention is needed in order to use user-dependent token. Also, typing recognition, signature recognition and text-dependent voice recognition need the user's attention as they have to provide the same sentences or drawing as in the enrolment phase.

- **Memory (M):** A person with a memory difficulty may likely have usability issues with all memorised secrets-based methods and carriable tokens. Security level of passwords, PIN codes, responses to challenges and drawings might be affected, as for compensating the usability issues, the secrets can be made shorter, easy and obvious. Tokens might be easier to steal from persons with memory difficulties, lowering the security of the tokens. In the case of biometrics, the memory difficulties might cause usability issues with text-dependent (passphrase) voice recognition. Typing recognition and signature recognition may also depend on correct spelling, which is affected when correct knowledge of correct symbol-letter and sound-letter combination vanishes [11].

- **Vision (V):** Vison impaired users have usability issues with memorised secrets when the secrets are to be provided. Typing errors are typical when providing passwords and PIN codes. Textual-challenges are problematic also when the challenge cannot be read. Graphical secrets might suffer from the matching errors in drawings and even colour-blinded can have difficulties to recognize objects when colours cannot be seen or are mixed. Security provided by the passwords and PIN codes can be lower due to the earlier discussed reasons: shorter and easier password and codes to compensate the usability issues. With tokens, the usability issue relates to the placement of the token. Small sensors and cameras might cause problems for vision impaired and therefore usability of face recognition and fingerprint recognition might be lower. Typing errors have a usability effect on typing recognition. Similarly, signature recognition might be affected. Regarding iris and retina recognition, some eye diseases can have an effect on recognition matching rate [31]. In extreme cases - a person not having eyes – then iris or retina recognition clearly cannot be used.

- **Hearing (H):** Hearing impairments causes usability issues for audio form challenge-response cases. Also, usability might be a problem with voice-speaker recognition as, a user with a severe hearing impairment, might not be able to control the voice and sound leading to matching errors [27].

- **Competence (C):** In this paper, competence refers to a person not knowing how to read and/or write, and it therefore has an effect on authentication methods that are dependent on textual information. Usability will be therefore be the issue for password, PIN codes, textual challenge-response, typing recognition and signature recognition. Short combination of characters can still be remembered without understanding the meaning of them, meaning that these methods are still somewhat usable. However, this will have an impact to the security level of these methods.
- **Life support (L):** This category contains life supporting body functions such as heart and blood circulation, respiration and skin. The impaired function might affect the usability of all biometrics. The usability issues are therefore related to unreliable or inconsistent biometrics samples.
- **Spoken messages (S):** Voice-Speaker recognition is the only method where speech is needed. The method is inapplicable if a person is unable to produce sound. Usability issues occur, if the voice varies from time to time. Compensating impairment with simple voice samples might create a security issue as simple samples might be easier to mimic.
- **Fine hand use (F):** All methods, except gait and user-independent tokens, are depended hand movements, either for typing, drawing, providing the sample or adjusting the sensors. Impairment in this category will therefore affect usability of these methods. Security level of passwords, PIN-codes, graphical-recognition, graphical-drawing, typing recognition and signature recognition might be lower due to compensating usability problems with using shorter and simpler enrolled samples.
- **Walking (W):** Gait is the only authentication affected by walking style and is inapplicable for persons who are entirely unable to walk. However, the usability is a potential issue if walking style varies on a daily basis.

The above illustrates a variety of challenges that the disability categories would suggest users would encounter in relation to different forms of authentication method. However, in order to consider this beyond a theoretical mapping, the next section introduces some related findings collected from a sample of target users.

4   Validation of User Needs

A small questionnaire containing six questions (see Appendix) was sent to ten people who either have a disability and/or work with people with disabilities. Participants were preselected to receive the questionnaire, as they had been open in discussing their impairments, and were either known to the authors or recommended to the authors by their specific disability association. The age range was also preselected from 30–50 years. The range was chosen to represent people that had lived through the emergence of digitalization and were therefore able to compare situations of before and after digitalized services and smart devices had emerged. Furthermore, the participants included both male and female living in Finland and Norway.

Nine of the ten people responded across the main disability groups, including: mobility disability (n = 2), vision disability (n = 3), hearing disability (n = 2) and cognitive disability (n = 2). The participants were either born with a disability, lived with it most of their lives, or had several years' working experience supporting those with special disabilities. Together participants covered seven out of the 12 ICF list functions, those being: attention, vision, hearing, spoken messages, lifting and carrying objects, fine hand use and walking.

The wording in the questionnaire was slightly adapted for the healthcare personnel in order to allow them to respond on behalf of the disabled group they worked with and not for themselves. Out of the six questions, questions two to five focused on authentication and were utilized in this paper. Questions one and six captured the overall everyday life situation and ICT problem in general.

We contacted the participants either directly or via associated and explained the purpose of the study. Those who were willing to participate, got the questionnaire, as a word-file, by email. The participants were given free choice how to answers to the questions and which form to deliver the answers. Everyone answered in written form, some directly to the word-file, some making a different document. One participant mentioned having another person to read the questions aloud before answering self to them. Others did not mention what kind of, if any, assistance they had used.

4.1 Results of the Questionnaire Study

The responses from the questionnaires provided an insight into the participants' experience and use of authentication methods. The participants reported that passwords were the most used method when logging into devices. With their work computers, they reported to use either passwords or verification cards and/or mobile phone verification. With biometrics, one had also used eye scanning on their work computer. Some protected their home computers with passwords, but often computers and other smart-devices at home were authentication-free as the home was considered as a secure place.

Mobile phones and smart phones gave a wider variety of authentication methods. Passwords were included, but if the phone provided the method, fingerprint and face recognition were popular methods as they could be used (to some degree) without fine motor skills and cognitive burden. Graphical passwords such as pattern recognition and picture-codes passwords (verbally provided for the visually impaired), PIN-codes, and eye-scanning were also mentioned.

With regard to digital services, participants reported the same authentication methods were used as with the devices. In addition, most of them mentioned multi-factor authentication (digital bank ID), where the one-time password solution was specifically named twice (noting that in Finland and in Norway, digital bank ID can be used for several services, not just bank services.)

When asked about the usability of authentication methods, the participants mentioned commonly known issues, such as difficulties in typing long passwords by people lacking fine motor skills, especially on a touch-screen. However, the problems that participants were listing often were not related to the authentication method itself, but to the design of the device or application that was used to capture the authentication sample.

Although, passwords were thought to be a secure method, in addition to the usability issues, cognitive burden was noted to be a problem for people with learning and focus difficulties. Furthermore, cognitive burden was increased if passwords were changed often. However, it was reported that due to passwords and PIN-codes being used for a long time, people were more familiar with them, had grown used to them, and were aware of their pros and cons. Several of the respondents had also mentioned the possible usage of password management applications instead of memorizing the passwords. In addition, it was said that typing a password was not a problem for visually impaired if the assistive technology was compatible with the application where a password is required. However, some felt that typing a password with computer keyboard was easier than typing them on the phone. Passwords can sometimes be copy-pasted, which reduces the amount of typing, but it was noted that not all sites would allow for this (often as a security measure).

The advantage of fingerprint and face recognition is that the required authentication sample is always with the person. Face recognition was found to be easier on the phone, as the device position (camera embedded to the phone) is easier to adjust than a camera position on a computer. However, fingerprint sensors, in general, were found easy to use. Although, sensors on the back side on a phone might cause a problem for a person without fine motor skills. Regarding the motor skills, it was noted that moving a hand (but not fingers) might have been enough for a successful pattern recognition.

Another issue that was noted, was with reference to the booting time of a computer. This might be too long; long enough to distract a person having focusing problems. Therefore, some favoured using services via smart phones, as phone in general, is always on. It was also noted, that a password reset is faster when compared with the time it takes to replace a lost device used for collecting or producing an authentication sample such as phone or code generator.

When asked how to improve authentication methods, the participants' answers were aligned with universal design principles: the layout should be clear with high contrast; sensors should be placed so that everyone can access to them; there should be a more universal design among different brand; and voice commands should be possible. When asked about their ideal authentication method, the participants listed already existing methods, and especially those that require the smallest input from a person such as fingerprint and face recognition. Furthermore, authentication using verification chips placed under the skin were also mentioned. And in addition to ease of use, participants requested that the authentication method was able to provide high levels of security, and that the same method could be used for several services to a larger extent than is currently the case.

5   Existing Frameworks for Accessible Authentication

The accessibility problem has been acknowledged at the governmental level and to improve the situation. Based on the United Nations Convention on the Rights of People with Disabilities [32] and earlier Disability Action Plan the European Union launched the Disability Strategy 2010–2020 [10] to empower equality among people regardless of their impairments or non-impairments. The European Commission with its European Accessibility Act [9] requests that the products are to be built on accessibility principles rather than imposing specific technical specifications. These regulations are also valid for ICT products and services; authentication included.

Røssvoll and Fuglerud [25] worked several years with a project called e-Me where different ICT components were evaluated based on the needs of impaired people. In the end of the project, they gave guidelines and best-practice recommendations to aid ICT projects to deliver accessible and usable solutions [25]. Their main message was to focus on overcoming disadvantages brought by disabilities, from the beginning of the product design. Development stages should therefore include analysis, automated testing, expert testing, and user testing phases. Multiple designs should be tested simultaneously in real user environments with users' own equipment as far it is possible. In addition, the test group should include the main disability categories (vision impaired, hearing impaired, cognition impaired and motor impaired), the combination of those (elderly) and people with low IT skills.

The recommendations of Røssvoll and Fuglerud included several aspects of ICT, not just authentication. However, the guidelines provided by Still, Cain and Schuster [29] and Wang [34] purely focused on accessible and inclusive personal authentication. Both are examples where Universal Design principles [1] are included to the framework.

The human-centered authentication guidelines by Still, Cain and Schuster [29] have six focus areas. First, *Design to be Inclusive,* places focus on authentication interfaces that should consider users' abilities, preferences, experience, social situation, and technological resources. The second, *Avoid Draining Users' Limited Working Memory Resources,* states that the use of authentication should not be too challenging for the user's cognitive capacity. The third, *Inform and Educate Users about Risk,* points out that users should be told, with common everyday language, the risks that are related to breaking the security policy, the authentication they use, or that would come if the method was misused or even bypassed. The fourth, *Eliminate Jargon by Considering Users' Mental Models* emphasizes the use of the correct mental models for different users. Mental models of an authentication process will be different for a security expert compared with a common end-user. The fifth, *Make Appropriate Actions Apparent* reminds us that as authentication is never a user's primary task, the actions to authenticate (as well as other authentication related actions), need to be apparent and intuitive. The last, and sixth, *Provide Users Quick Access Clearly,* guidelines considers the time used to authentication. As the authentication normally happens several times a day, the procedure needs to be fast in order not to take time away from the daily primary tasks.

Wang [34], in his position paper on accessible authentication, also focuses on the user's own capabilities and how the user should be given a chance to choose the most suitable authentication alternative among several methods. The paper lists five goals that need to be fulfilled in order to enable practical authentication for everyone. The first goal, *Secure,* states that the authentication mechanism should be secure against the common security attacks considering search space entropy and circumvention difficulty. The second goal, *Usable,* is that the authentication mechanism should be usable for everyone, considering transaction time, and time delay caused by human error, subjective rating, cognitive load, and physical effort. The third is *Privacy-preserving* including privacy as the authentication mechanism should be able to conceal disability from the host system when considering keystroke patterns, data leakage, and transaction time. The fourth, *Effective,* points out that the authentication mechanism should be effective in accurately logging users into the system, considering rates for identification, false acceptance and false rejection. And the last, the fifth goal, *Reachable/Accessible,* is that the authentication mechanism should work with public terminals considering system and browser requirements.

Comparison of different authentication methods, in general, has existed as long as there has been alternative methods to compare. However, O'Gorman [22] has been one of the first to give a mathematical formula to compare authentication methods across main authentication method categories. There exist many research papers where different authentication methods are compared. The comparison is often based on the security and usability, but in some cases extended to include accessibility, availability, pricing and/or convenience (e.g. [4, 15, 23, 33]). One of the latest, a universal authentication framework [18] is basing its comparison more broadly including security, usability, accessibility, pricing, complexity, privacy and convenience.

Korać and Simić [18] developed a universal authentication framework and created a Fishbone model for evaluating of authentication methods in mobile environment. In their universal authentication framework each authentication method is evaluated by following attributes: *security, usability, accessibility, pricing, complexity, privacy* and *convenience* with labelling them by seven-level scale of descriptive values (fuzzy intervals) from very, very low to very, very high. The Fishbone model uses the universal authentication framework and computes a mathematical score that can be then used to compare authentication methods. Korać and Simić [18] assign the values to each attribute basing them on the existing studies. As these values are changeable, authentication methods can be evaluated based on the more detailed information of the user groups such as, impaired user groups, even though Korać and Simić have not discussed this possibility directly. Similar flexibility is found in the Fishbone model as the weight of the attributes can be changed.

As the universal authentication framework of Korać and Simić [18] is adjustable, the findings of our paper (shown in Sect. 4), can be used to re-evaluate the security and usability attributes of the authentication methods based on the user group.

6 Discussion

Over recent years, the world has become more inclusive towards disabilities through the aid of digital technologies and therefore, assistive technologies [3]. The evolution of technology – devices, systems and services – has meant that those who struggled previously to interact with society (in the online world as well as the offline world), are more capable – narrowing the digital divide [8]. New innovations and technologies are developed with such speed, that one only needs to blink, and current models and systems need updating. However, with all this technological, and societal progress aiming to cater for all of society's needs, one must wonder why the very thing that protects society (authentication) is a relic from the last century. Authentication has barely changed over the last few decades, and more notably, there is little to no differences in the authentication methods provided for impaired users. When asked in this study, all authentication methods referred to by our disabled participants were the exact ones used by non-disabled users. These methods are not tailored for different disabilities, in terms of usability and security, yet the disabled user is expected to gain secure access to their devices, systems and services in an inclusive manner. Our study first, examines the classifications and characterizations of different disabilities.

Disabilities are often divided into four main groups: visual impairments, hearing impairments, motor impairments, and cognitive impairments. As we have shown, the International Classification of Functioning, Disability and Health (ICF) checklist of the World Health Organization [35] can be applied instead. The advantages of using the ICF list is that evaluation of the impact each impaired function have on security and usability aspects of the authentication method become more commonly comprehensive. This also highlights the root causes of the issues, and can therefore be used already as a checklist of functionalities to be taught when a new authentication product is designed.

We have focused on security and usability factors when comparing different authentication methods within each ICF function. The results are shown in Table 1 and can be applied to extend the universal authentication framework of Korać and Simić [18]. However, Korać and Simić did not specifically mention that their framework could be used to compare authentication methods with impaired the user groups. The values used in the framework are adjustable and by using our findings, values of the security and usability attributes can be adjusted to tailor to specific impairments. The ultimate goal, based on the universal design principles, is to have the same score for impaired and non-impaired user groups.

Even though, we have only focused on authentication in this paper, it would be relevant to consider wider use of the ICF list in the context of designing other security and ICT products. The same logic that we have employed when creating Table 1 can be employed to other areas. In addition, temporary impairments can also be included when the ICF list is in use. For instance, normally non-impaired people (e.g., soldiers, fire fighters, medical personnel etc.) while experiencing sleep deprivation, low nourishment, being in a highly stressful situation, or even in extreme hot or cold conditions might have lower functionality in some of the ICF list functions. It is important that the tools work properly even though the user could, for example, be feeling fatigued. Having ensured the consideration of all such eventualities will leave us better positioned to provide all users with authentication that is usable and secure regardless of the context or their situation.

7   Conclusion

With the emergence of digitization, society and the use of technology has changed with society becoming dependent on its use. The forefront a securing users' technology usage, their personal and organization information and devices is the authentication methods. Although society has attempted to reduce the gap in online access and the usability of technologies for disabled people, through considering their needs and consequently adapting technologies; very little consideration or development has occurred to improve authentication inclusivity. Therefore, many users who need to authenticate themselves on a daily basis, struggle to gain access to the systems and services they need.

This paper has reviewed the current authentication methods while considering the usability and security of each method from the perspective of users with different impairments. Our findings have several contributions and implications for practice. First, they bring to light the specific characteristics of different disabilities that cause usability and security issues when engaging with authentication. Through identifying these individual factors and their impact, new solutions can be found to deal with these challenges. Second, the findings extend the existing frameworks used to create inclusive technologies to the authentication context. We also recommend to further use of ICF list for evaluating effects of impairments for other aspects e.g. pricing of the technology and privacy of the user. Through extending the framework, this can be used as a guide to develop and ensure technologies, systems and services consider the impaired users within the authentication process as well as any other function of their product. This will ultimately lead to a more inclusive digital society.

Acknowledgements. The questionnaire is approved by the Norwegian Centre for Research Data and belongs to the project "Digitalisering, autentisering og funksjonshemning" (reference nr. 393208).

Appendix

The information letter, consent form and questionnaire were all originally written in Finnish and Norwegian. The following is a translated summary of the question text, in order to clarify the specific points that were covered.

1. How has digitalization in general affected the quality of your life in the last 10 years? (A few tips: access to services, running things, socializing, working, studying, transport, traveling, etc.)

   a. Positive things
   b. Negative things
   c. Changes in general

2. What «login» methods do you have on digital devices? Why did you choose these methods (many devices have different options)?

   a. Computer (at work and at home)
   b. Telephone (at work and at home)
   c. Other smart device (e.g. tablet, clock)

3. Think of digital services (e.g. banking services, insurance company) and apps (e.g. VR mobile, Teams, Vilma) that you use via computer or phone.

   a. What «login» methods do you have for digital services or apps?
   b. Why did you choose these particular methods (many services and apps have many options)?

4. In Sects. 2 and 3, you listed the identification methods you used. I hope you will now evaluate their practicality for you.

   a. What make them difficult/easy to use?

    b. Are there differences in their use between a computer, phone and/or other smart device?

    c. How could their usability be improved?

5. What is your «dream» identification method? What would it be based on? What would it contain? «Your dream» does not have to be true or even achievable☺

6. Security in the digital world is also enhanced by other methods, such as "are you a robot" questions, warning sounds, various messages and guidance. How practical are these for you? Are there examples of activities that are problematic for you?

Background information:

1. How old are you?
2. What disability do you have?

References

1. Centre for Excellence in Universal Design (CEUD): The 7 Principles of Universal Design. http://universaldesign.ie/What-is-Universal-Design/The-7-Principles/. Accessed 31 March 2020

2. Chadwick, D.D., Chapman, M., Caton, S.: Digital inclusion for people with an intellectual disability. In: Attrill-Smith, A., Fullwood, C., Keep, M., Kuss, D.J. (eds.) The Oxford Handbook of Cyberpsychology. Oxford University Press, UK (2019)

3. Chadwick, D., Wesson, C.: Digital inclusion and disability. In: Attrill, A., Fullwood, C. (eds.) Applied Cyberpsychology. Palgrave Macmillan, London (2016)

4. Clarke, N.L., Furnell, S.M.: Advanced user authentication for mobile devices. Comput. Secur. 26(2), 109–119 (2007)

5. D'Aubin, A.: Working for barrier removal in the ICT area: creating a more accessible and inclusive Canada: a position statement by the council of Canadians with disabilities. Inf. Soc. 23(3), 193–201 (2007)

6. De. Angeli, A., Coventry, L., Johnson, G., Renaud, K.: Is a picture really worth a thousand words? Exploring the feasibility of graphical authentication systems. Int. J. Hum. Comput. Stud. 63(1–2), 128–152 (2005)

7. Disabled World: Types of disability list, Disability World. www.disabled-world.com/disability/types/. Accessed 12 March 2020

8. Dobransky, K., Hargittai, E.: The disability divide in internet access and use. Inf., Commun. (Soc., Spec. Issue: Disabil., Identity, Interdependence: ICTs New Soc. Forms) 9(3), 313–334 (2006)

9. European Accessibility Act (EEA): Directive (EU) 2019/882 of the European Parliament and of the Council of 17 April 2019 on the accessibility requirements for products and services (2019). https://eur-lex.europa.eu/legal-content/EN/ALL/?uri=CELEX:32019L0882

10. European Disability Strategy 2010–2020: A Renewed Commitment to a Barrier-Free Europe (2010). https://eur-lex.europa.eu/LexUriServ/LexUriServ.do?uri=COM:2010:0636:FIN:en:PDF

11. Firger, J.: Handwriting changes can indicate Alzheimer's progression (2013). https://www.everydayhealth.com/alzheimers/handwriting-changes-can-indicate-alzheimers-progression-8042.aspx

12. Foley, A., Ferri, B.A.: Technology for people, not disabilities: ensuring access and inclusion. J. Res. Spec. Educ. Needs **12**(4), 192–200 (2012)
13. Haga, W.J., Zviran, M.: Question-and-answer passwords: an empirical evaluation. Inf. Syst. **16**(3), 335–343 (1991)
14. Helkala, K.: Disabilities and authentication methods: usability and security. In: 7th International Proceedings on Availability, Reliability and Security, pp. 327–334. IEEE Computer Society, Prague, Czech Republic (2012)
15. Helkala, K., Snekkenes, E.: A method for ranking authentication products. In: 2nd International Proceedings on Human Aspects of Information Security & Assurance, pp. 80–93. Plymount, UK (2008)
16. Herley, C., Van Oorschot, P.: A research agenda acknowledging the persistence of passwords. IEEE Secur. Priv. **10**(1), 28–36 (2012)
17. Hoppestad, B.S.: Current perspective regarding adults with intellectual and developmental disabilities accessing computer technology. Disabil. Rehabil. Assist. Technol. **8**(3), 190–194 (2013)
18. Korać, D., Simić, D.: Fishbone model and universal authentication framework for evaluation of multifactor authentication in mobile environment. Comput. Secur. **85**, 313–332 (2019)
19. Ma, W., Campbell, J., Tran, D., Kleeman, D.: Password entropy and password quality. In: 4th International Proceedings on Network and System Security, pp. 583–587. IEEE, Melbourne, Australia (2010)
20. NIST: Special Publication 800-63B, Digital Identity Guidelines: Authentication and Lifecycle Management (2017). https://doi.org/10.6028/NIST.SP.800-63b
21. Norman, K.L.: Cyberpsychology: An Introduction to Human-Computer Interaction. Cambridge University Press, UK (2017)
22. O'Gorman, L.: Comparing passwords, tokens, and biometrics for user authentication. Proc. IEEE **91**(12), 2021–2040 (2003)
23. Ogbanufe, O., Kim, D.J.: Comparing fingerprint-based biometrics authentication versus traditional authentication methods for e-payment. Decision Support Systems. vol. 106, 1–14, (2018). ISSN 0167-9236
24. Ruggiero, T.E.: Uses and gratifications theory in the 21st century. Mass Commun. Soc. **3**(1), 3–37 (2000)
25. Røssvoll, T.H., Fuglerud, K.S.: Best practice for efficient development of inclusive ICT. In: Stephanidis, C., Antona, M. (eds.) UAHCI 2013. LNCS, vol. 8009, pp. 97–106. Springer, Heidelberg (2013). https://doi.org/10.1007/978-3-642-39188-0_11
26. Schneier, B.: Identification and Authentication. Secrets and Lies: Digital Security in a Networked World, pp. 135–150 (2015)
27. Seladi-Schulman, J.: How people who are deaf learn to talk. https://www.healthline.com/health/can-deaf-people-talk#nonverbal-communication. Accessed 09 Sep 2020
28. Song, J., Wang, D., Yun, Z., Han, X.: Alphapwd: a password generation strategy based on mnemonic shape. IEEE Access **7**, 119052–119059 (2019)
29. Still, J., Cain, A., Schuster, D.: Human-centered authentication guidelines. Inf. Comput. Secur. **25**(4), 437–453 (2017)
30. Stobert, E., Biddle, R.: Memory retrieval and graphical passwords. In: 9th International Proceedings of on Usable Privacy and Security, pp. 1–14, Newcastle, UK (2013)
31. Trokielewicz, M., Czajka, A., Maciejewicz, P.: Cataract influence on iris recognition performance. In: 35th International Proceedings on Photonics Applications in Astronomy, Communications, Industry, and High-Energy Physics Experiments, pp. 1–14. IEEE-SPIE (2014).
32. United Nations Convention on the Rights of Persons with Disabilities (UN CRPD) (2008). https://www.un.org/development/desa/disabilities/convention-on-the-rights-of-persons-with-disabilities.html

33. Vapen, A., Shahmehri, N.: Security levels for web authentication using mobile phones. In: Fischer-Hübner, S., Duquenoy, P., Hansen, M., Leenes, R., Zhang, G. (eds.) Privacy and Identity 2010. IAICT, vol. 352, pp. 130–143. Springer, Heidelberg (2011). https://doi.org/10.1007/978-3-642-20769-3_11
34. Wang, Y.n: Universal Authentication: Towards Accessible Authentication for Everyone. https://cups.cs.cmu.edu/soups/2014/workshops/papers/accessible_wang_17.pdf.   Accessed 01 Feb 2021
35. World Health Organization (WHO): International Classification of Functioning, Disability and Health. https://www.who.int/classifications/icf/en/. Accessed 10 Aug 2020
36. Zviran, M., Haga, W.J.: Password security: an empirical study. J. Manag. Inf. Syst. **15**(4), 161–185 (1999)

Web Accessibility and Web Developer Attitudes Towards Accessibility in Mozambique

Suraj Gupta[1]([⊠]) [iD], Terje Gjøsæter[1,2] [iD], and G. Anthony Giannoumis[1] [iD]

[1] Oslo Metropolitan University, Oslo, Norway
gagian@oslomet.no
[2] University of Agder, Kristiansand, Norway
terjeg@uia.no

Abstract. People with disabilities are found to be severely affected by barriers in websites and other web services. This paper aims to study the web accessibility issues in Mozambique and to review the factors that contribute to it. The case study is based on results from 2 perspectives: first, automatic evaluation of five prominent national websites, and second through fieldwork, interviewing and interacting with web developers in Mozambique. The study found that none of the websites are WCAG 2.1 compatible and the web developers, in general, do not consider web accessibility in their products and services. The underlying factors responsible for web inaccessibility are found out to be extrinsic.

Keywords: Web accessibility · Assistive technology · Web (WWW) · Mozambique · WCAG 2.1 · People with disabilities · Web developers

1 Introduction

The essential element of the web is to allow its users, irrespective of any disability, easily access and share the information on it. In this universality lies the power of the web, once said by Tim Berners-Lee, W3C Director and inventor of the World Wide Web [1]. With the growing number of users (including traditionally marginalized groups such as people with disabilities) interacting the web over time, the increased adequacy of web accessibility has become more relevant as to represent all of them [2]. "Web accessibility is the concept of providing web content that is universally accessible to different machines and people with different ages, skills, education levels, and abilities" [3]. However, the prevalence of web accessibility is found to be lacking when it comes to countries in Africa [4], where around 40 percent of the total population suffers from sort of disability, according to the World Health Organization (WHO) [5]. According to the statistics from the National Census in Mozambique [6], the country estimates 727620 of its population to have some sort of disability, representing approximately 2.7 percent of the total population in Mozambique. Not even adequately being able to use the web causes people with disabilities in Mozambique isolated from society, education, health services, and other fundamentals deescalating further in their life [6]. On a similar note,

M. Antona and C. Stephanidis (Eds.): HCII 2021, LNCS 12768, pp. 213–231, 2021.
https://doi.org/10.1007/978-3-030-78092-0_14

this research work presents a case study of Mozambique with an aim to learn, why the web remains inaccessible for these population groups in Mozambique.

The research attempts to analyse the case by empirically basing the undiscovered factors for the analysis. For this, the report chooses different models in the form of research questions to gather information. Since websites, by far, are considered the most prominent exponent form of web services, first research question thus in our report aims to find the level of accessibility in the most used five different purposed websites currently being used in Mozambique. The websites are checked against the WCAG 2.1 guidelines. This follows:

1. To what level do the top five most-used websites in Mozambique meet the web accessibility standards (in particular WCAG 2.1)?
   There exist tools and practical guidelines recommended by W3C through their Web Accessibility Initiative (WAI) on web accessibility. These are responsible for regulating and developing web technologies [7]. These is a widely accepted prerequisite for the web makers, when practicing web accessibility to address the inaccessibility in web for various user groups. The most accepted and recognized website accessibility guidelines in place are WCAG 2.1 [8]. The WCAG v.2 has four principles: Perceivable, Operable, Understandable, and Robust. There are further 12 more specific guidelines under each of these principles. And along with each guideline, there are requirements primarily known as testable success criteria. These success criteria are categorized in three different yet interrelated and dependent conformance levels namely A (lowest), AA (mid), AAA (highest). Thus, satisfying the specific conformance level in the websites fulfils the requirements for the given specific circumstances [8]. There exist design approaches such as User-Centred Design (UCD), User-Sensitive Inclusive Design (USID), Design for User Empowerment (DUE), Ability-Based Design (ABD), Universal Design (UD) to address the accessibility challenges faced by the people with disabilities in web [9].
2. What are the factors that influence the web developers'[1] current practice and approach towards web accessibility in Mozambique?

The second research question aims to understand the knowledge and skills the web developers in Mozambique have in regard with these accessibility specific tools, guidelines, technologies, regional or universal regulations and policies, and design approaches. It also aims to discover their approaches and practices towards web accessibility and what factors drive them, through interviews and interactions.

With the results of above mentioned two distinct research questions our research will learn and analyse the web accessibility situation in Mozambique. Through the combined analysis from these, we shape our discussion part. The methodologies used for these research questions are separately discussed in detail in the methodology section.

---

[1] In this paper we use the term "web developers" to collectively refer to software developers, web developers, web programmers, web designers, webmasters, web makers etc. used as the research participants in this research.

2   Literature Review

2.1   Disability, Web Accessibility and Mozambique

Users with disabilities use various forms of assistive technology to allow them to browse web sites. Assistive technology supplements the reduced ability of the users. These different types of assistive technologies include both hardware and software such as screen readers, voice recognition, alternative pointing devices, alternate keyboards, and refreshable Braille displays [10]. A report work [11] have shown that the use of assistive technologies among people with disabilities[2] in Mozambique is lowest among assistive technologies used in other fields. A similar study by [12], in low-GPD-per-capita countries aimed at blind web users in Nepal, the authors argues that it is challenging to provide access to appropriate assistive technology in low GDP-per-capita countries.

Not all websites are compatible with the usage of Assistive Technology. Only a compatible website with various assistive technology can be used by users with disabilities. A web site that is compatible enough to these assistive technologies is considered an accessible website [13]. There exists a common misunderstanding that accessibility is only for people with disabilities. Leaping beyond this misconception lies the fact that accessible web is very helpful for people without disabilities. The prominent reasons for web accessibility are to create web services that are flexible to meet and address different types of users irrespective of disabilities, their preferences, the situations they are in [14]. The people with disabilities are often hit hard because of inaccessible physical environments, transportation, and information and communications (ICT) systems and are the causes of deprivation to participate in the society [15].

The National Institute of Statistics of Mozambique, INE is also responsible for census reporting [6]. Sida [6], have argued that INE lacks specific instructions and funding to collect information regarding disability and the different studies results reflect the absence of a commonly agreed definition[3] of disability and poor data collection methods. Sida is a government agency working on behalf of the Swedish Parliament and Government to reduce poverty in the world [6]. The new census report of 2017 of Mozambique reads the total country's population as 26,899,105 with 727620 of them suffering from some form of disability, representing 2.7 percent of the entire population [16].

Though the initiative of CRPD along with its optional protocol was first adopted on 13 December in 2006, Mozambique signed the CRPD and its Optional Protocol later on 30 November 2010, and subsequently ratified both on 31 December 2010 [17, 18]. Looking away from CRPD, the provision in the Article 37 of the Mozambican Constitution states that "citizens with a disability shall fully enjoy the rights enshrined in the Constitution, and shall be subject to the same duties, except those which their disability prevents them from exercising or fulfilling." Article 125 and its subsections further explain the

---

[2] The disability or functional limitations, or disablement process is the result produced between the exchange of individual restricted functional abilities with the demands of the society and environment [11].

[3] The definition of disability differs from the social model to the medical model to other models in practice. Neither in this report nor my wider disability research, do I reject the idea that disability is powerfully shaped by social forces.

provisions facilitating people with disability with article 125.3.b especially focusing on the 'creation of appropriate conditions to prevent them from becoming socially isolated and marginalized'[17]. In addition, FAMOD (Forum of the Mozambican Associations for the Disabled) established in 1998 is one of popular organization often functions as an umbrella for other 20 DPOs (Disable people Organizations) in Mozambique. FAMOD, independently or in collaboration with other organizations which work for various types of disabilities and covers all geographical areas in Mozambique, serves people with disabilities [17, 18]. The study also finds that the DPOs implementations often fail in Mozambique because of lack of funding, related recourses, qualified personnel, political will and inept awareness of disability issues in society. Mozambique is seen as not realizing and is often late in embracing Disability rights. It is said that it was DPOs' engagement and involvement that helped the country to achieve the ratification of the CRPD. The authorities in the ministry responsible for addressing disabilities blames unstable country movement and civil war as the key reason for erratic and delayed developments in addressing disability[17, 18].

Universal Design[4] (UD) is sometimes interchangeably perceived as Accessible Design in the field of web. More products will be accessible to and usable by everyone if people with disabilities are routinely included by user experts in usability tests and if Universal design principles are applied by product designers [19]. Universal design benefits everyone. Hence, universally designed web content, websites, and applications not only alleviates the hard experience faced by people with disabilities but also benefit all users [20]. Universal design holds a key for improved accessibility where the needs of all user types can be incorporated as it is inclusive, flexible and cost-effective [21].

2.2 Related Work on National Legislation and Policy Making, Promoting Web Accessibility

Article 9: Accessibility, of UN's CRPD resolution requires its state parties[5] (including Mozambique) to facilitate the measures to identify and eliminate obstacles and barriers to accessibility in Information, communications and other services, including electronic services [22, 23]. The UN refers to Information and Communication Technology (ICT) as an umbrella term to include any information and communication devices, applications or its content [23]. Further, Article 21 in The United Nations CRPD defines access to information, as human rights and specifies responsibilities to the government and related

---

[4] "Universal Design is the design of products and environments to be usable by all people, to the greatest extent possible, without the need for adaptation or specialized design. "Universal design" shall not exclude assistive devices for particular groups of persons with disabilities where this is needed [40]".

[5] A list of state parties to UNCRPD, can be found at https://treaties.un.org/Pages/ViewDetails.aspx?src=TREATY&mtdsg_no=IV-15&chapter=4.

authorities in relation to those rights. Availing accessible web information to people with disabilities[6], therefore, becomes a mandatory aspect on the web.

There have been instances where many nations have acted with national laws for promoting accessibility in ICT. With different practices and approaches, ICT including the web is been addressed with an increasing number of national laws and policies over time [24]. W3C provides a list of laws and policies that some countries have enacted upon [25]. Many European countries have legislation that requires government websites to be accessible [4]. The study from [1] have shown that the Anti-Discrimination Act has improved the accessibility concerns on the web, in South Korea. The successive progression of The American with Disability Act (ADA) over the Rehabilitation act of 1973, to meet the then State's requirement in the United States by addressing and promoting unbiased and equivalent participation of the citizens in programs, activities and services [26].

While many countries have developed their own legislations for accessibility, some developing countries do not have it protecting people with disability's rights [27]. Developing countries in Africa don't have stricter web accessibility legislations mandating governmental websites to be accessible [28]. In the case of Mozambique, the Mozambican government established a national ICT policy commission in 1998. This facilitated the latter in adopting a national ICT policy, simultaneously supplementing its PARPA (Poverty Reduction Strategy Paper), an Action Plan for the Reduction of Absolute Poverty in 2002. In doing so, Mozambique became the first country in southern Africa implementing such act. This was then done mainly to focus on their priority areas of education, human resource development, health, universal access, national ICT infrastructure, and governance to improve and achieve their development goals further [29]. As a gradual realization of ICT policy, currently, many ICT initiatives have taken place in the areas of e-government, e-health, digital divide [30]. Mozambique have shown some promising steps in the field of ICT since then, with major IT project Initiatives throughout the country and African regions which can be found under the URL http://www.ist-africa.org/home/default.asp?page=doc-by-id&docid=5563 [30].

We have found inadequate study indicating the web master's practices in web accessibility[7] in Mozambique. The few peripheral studies in regard to web master's practices in web accessibility are either quite old or represent different geographical locations than Mozambique with different participants/user scope. For example [31] can be referred in a similar context in Uganda.

---

[6] "Disability is an evolving concept and that disability results from the interaction between persons with impairments and attitudinal and environmental barriers that hinders their full and effective participation in society on an equal basis with other" [15]. The current convention proposed by the UN emphasizes to "promote, protect and ensure the full and equal enjoyment of all human rights and fundamental freedoms by all persons with disabilities, and to promote respect for their inherent dignity" [15].

[7] Web accessibility means that people with disabilities can use the Web. More specifically, web accessibility means that people with disabilities can perceive, understand, navigate, and interact with the Web [41].

3 Methodology

This section explains the methodological process involved in achieving the above-mentioned research questions. The evaluation methods of websites using automated tools and interviews and interactions sessions with web professionals in Mozambique. This is a qualitative research work, during the 3 months of fieldwork in Mozambique. The research uses the random sampling technique [32], to study few users as the research subject which represents the whole user group of its kind [33]. The interviews are carried with the web professionals living in Maputo, the capital of Mozambique. The diagram below shows how the report mixes different approaches to illustrate whole process of methodology to derive the discussion (Fig. 1).

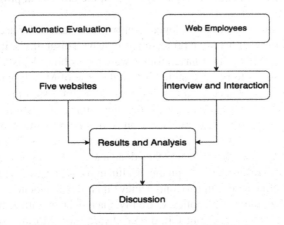

Fig. 1. Methodological approaches of the study.

The research study follows a hybrid assessment approach as it includes automated testing for websites and semi-structured interviews with web developers.

3.1 Website Evaluation (Automatic Testing)

The websites are evaluated against the web accessibility requirements, WCAG 2.1, conformance level AA. Five prominent websites of different categories are chosen from SimilarWeb.com for the Mozambique region. SimilarWeb.com[8] as quoted on its website, it provides "Website ranking, an estimate of a website's popularity among other websites using online competitive intelligence tool that provides traffic and marketing insights for the website". The selected 5 websites of its kind records for highest web traffic and highest popularity in Mozambique. The list of prominent websites used popularly in Mozambique are as follows:

A. http://www.portaldogoverno.gov.mz/ (governmental website.)
B. https://www.olx.co.mz/ (shopping website)

---

[8] https://www.similarweb.com/.

C. https://www.bci.co.mz/ (finance and banking)
D. https://www.movitel.co.mz/ (travel, hotel and accommodation)
E. https://www.mmo.co.mz/ (news and media).

The 3 evaluation tools used in the research to test for the major AA compliance levels in the websites are:

1. Web Accessibility Checker (achecker)[9]: This tool checks the HTML pages of the website for conformance with accessibility standards. With customization, the tool is systemized to match our testing areas of WCAG AA conformance levels. The checks it provides are coding errors (semantic code), standard compliance issues, accessibility problems, missing images, or its alt tags or broken links any many more.
2. SortSite Tool[10]: This web service checks WCAG and Section 508 guidelines. The home website for SortSite reads as the tool, used by federal agencies, Fortune 100 corporations, and independent consultancies.
3. WAVE, Web AIM Online Tool[11]: It checks the inaccessibility of the website and generates the inaccessible web content results.

Table 1 below shows the major AA compliance level, which is at least needed to pass the accessibility benchmark as suggested by WCAG2.1. We check the following guidelines as parameters for each website through the above-mentioned automated tool.

Table 1. Major AA compliance level of WCAG2.1.

WCAG 2.1 (AA conformance level)	Guidelines
1.1	Text alternative
1.2	Time-based media
1.3	Adaptable
1.4	Distinguishable
2.1	Keyboard accessible
2.2	Enough time
2.3	Seizures
2.4	Navigable
3.1	Readable
3.2	Predictable
3.3	Input assistance
4.1	Compatible

---

[9] https://achecker.ca/checker/index.php?lang=eng [42].

[10] https://www.powermapper.com/products/sortsite/checks/accessibility-checks/ [43].

[11] https://wave.webaim.org/ [44].

3.2 Interview and Interaction with Web Developers

Firstly, the companies are selected based on good ratings over the internet, having decent reputation for their work. The web professionals chosen for the research have a job in the role of software developer, web developer, web designer, webmasters. The paper assumes these web developers are supposed to pose more or less knowledge about web accessibility as the nature of their job explicitly requires them contribute to the web development products or services. Interviewing these web developers holds a key to understand what practices they follow for web accessibility and what influences them to follow this. This factor will help us know about their web accessibility approaches they incorporate in their web design and development, which makes the report come closer to fathom the answers to understand if exists any, how their approach is directly or indirectly affecting people with disabilities in Mozambique in web accessibility influences them to follow this. This factor will help us know about their web accessibility approaches they incorporate in their web design and development, which will help the paper to understand if exists any, how their approach is directly or indirectly affecting people with disabilities in Mozambique in web accessibility. A total of fifteen web developers were chosen from six different companies (Table 2).

Table 2. Naming web developers anonymously.

Companies	A	B	C		D			E				F			
Web developers	A1	B1	C1	C2	D1	D2	D3	E1	E2	E3	E4	F1	F2	F3	F4

To investigate the web developer's perception and approach towards web accessibility, a set of interview questions focusing to elicit their knowledge, experiences, and practices were asked. The set of interview questions for web developers are as follows.

1. How old are you in this profession of web technology?
2. What are your academic qualifications in the field of web Technology?
3. Are you aware of any state obligations, regulations and policies put in place for web accessibility?
4. Are you aware of web accessibility and the tools and guidelines for it?
5. Do you practice any approach to make your web products accessible? And how. many projects you have worked with had web accessibility implementation in it.
6. Are you or any other employee in this company is responsible to ensure the. products are designed accessible or review the product for accessibility before. releasing?
7. Do you think implementing web accessibility is important?
8. How important do you think is a topic web accessibility is in regard to the. people with disability in Mozambique?
9. Do you think implementing Web accessibility is a difficult and challenging. task?
10. Do you think the user base for the web products or services would increase. when web accessibility is practiced more frequently?

11. What do you think are the reasons behind web inaccessibility in Mozambique?

Ethical Consideration. Research is a sensitive process. Ethical considerations are vital in research to increase resistance to the false response of the data and encourage the pursuit of valid and reliable data that aids the primary goal of the research [34]. As specific to this research work, all the research participants are signed a pre-written consent form to validate their participation in the interaction and interview process, as an informed consent. A good procedure for the research in attaining consent for the human subject research in low income and rural African settings is obtained from [35]. It explains the importance of consent material in participants home language and parents (guardian, if required) involvement in the consent process, and/or need for community leader or representative approval. However, it is worth noting that, when comprehensively providing proper information to participants in lower income countries, critical challenges can arise in achieving valid consent [36]. All the rights, potential benefits and risks associated with the informed consent form were explained to the participants. To make the process more comfortable and easier the interviewees are entrusted with the right to terminate the interview if they deem at any point of time. The anonymity of the participants is protected to address their confidentiality and to their information at hand. This is done by assigning virtual names namely, participant A, participant B and so on in the report to maintain the confidentiality of the participants. However, it is important to note that the report only analyses the data and information given by the subject but not gathers or processes any personal data.

4   Results and Analysis

As we identify and collect data for results, this section will form the basis for discussion later. The results from each website evaluation tools for all five websites are presented systematically in the Tables 3, 4 and 5 below. Pass (P) and Fail (F) describes the accessibility test of the website and holds true for each conformance level test according to results from the tools. 'N/A' in the table represents the data not available for that section.

Table 3 below shows the results from Achecker website evaluation tool. It shows 4 out of 5 websites utterly failed to pass 1 or 2 accessibility tests for the web accessibility requirement. The only web accessibility guidelines to be achieved were just 3 websites at most, and these were readability and compatibility of the web content. The website that performed the best was www.olx.co.mz with 8 web accessibility guidelines and worst were www.portaldogoverno.gov.mz and www.bci.co.mz with just 1.

Table 3. Table showing the test results of websites from "Achecker" automatic evaluation tool.

WCAG 2.1 (AA)	1.1	1.2	1.3	1.4	2.1	2.2	2.3	2.4	3.1	3.2	3.3	4.1
www.portaldogoverno.gov.mz	F	N/A	F	F	F	N/A	F	F	F	F	F	P
www.olx.co.mz	P	P	F	P	P	P	P	F	F	F	P	P
www.bci.co.mz	F	N/A	F	F	F	N/A	F	F	P	F	F	F
www.movitel.co.mz	F	N/A	F	F	F	N/A	F	F	P	F	F	P
www.mmo.co.mz	F	N/A	F	F	F	N/A	F	F	P	F	F	F

Table 4 below shows the results from SortSite, website evaluation tool. As compared to Achecker tool, SortSite showed many other passes. Except, www.portaldogoverno. gov.mz governmental website all other 4 websites ticked additional web accessibility guidelines requirement. However, the changes for websites, except www.olx.co.mz were still not convincing as more web accessibility guidelines met failed remarks that those met for pass remarks. None of the websites meet the web accessibility guidelines for text alternative, distinguishable and adaptability. During the test, the website that performed best was www.olx.co.mz with 7 web accessibility guidelines and worst was www.portal dogoverno.gov.mz with none.

Table 4. Table showing the test results of websites using SortSite website evaluation tool.

WCAG 2.1 (AA)	1.1	1.2	1.3	1.4	2.1	2.2	2.3	2.4	3.1	3.2	3.3	4.1
www.portaldogoverno.gov.mz	F	F	F	F	N/A	F	F	F	F	F	F	F
www.olx.co.mz	F	P	F	F	P	P	P	F	F	P	P	P
www.bci.co.mz	F	N/A	F	F	P	P	F	F	P	F	F	F
www.movitel.co.mz	F	F	F	F	N/A	F	F	F	P	F	F	P
www.mmo.co.mz	F	N/A	F	F	P	P	P	P	P	P	F	P

Table 5 below shows the test results from the WAVE evaluation tool. It showed all the website's increase in meeting more web accessibility guidelines than those from the tools used for evaluation before. The web accessibility guidelines for readable web content were meet by all the websites whereas the web accessibility guidelines for adaptability of the web content to simpler layout or ways appropriate for the device being used to access web content and navigating or finding the web content were found to fail for all the websites. During the test, the website that performed best was www.olx.co.mz meeting with 10 web accessibility guidelines and worst was www.movitel.co.mz and www.portaldogoverno.gov.mz with just 3.

Table 5. Table showing the website test results of using WAVE website evaluation tool.

WCAG 2.1 (AA)	1.1	1.2	1.3	1.4	2.1	2.2	2.3	2.4	3.1	3.2	3.3	4.1
www.portaldogoverno.gov.mz	F	F	F	F	N/A	N/A	P	F	F	P	F	P
www.olx.co.mz	P	P	F	P	P	P	P	F	P	P	P	P
www.bci.co.mz	F	N/A	F	F	P	P	P	F	P	P	F	F
www.movitel.co.mz	F	F	F	F	N/A	F	P	F	P	F	F	P
www.mmo.co.mz	F	N/A	F	F	P	P	P	F	P	P	F	P

4.1 Summarization of Results from All Three Automatic Testing Tools

For any given website evaluated through different web evaluation tools showed the different results in web accessibility guidelines. This is because each web evaluation tool exhibits a unique benchmark level to evaluate web accessibility guidelines. Some are built with more serious and strictness evaluation benchmark levels and some with loose ones, meaning the website tested through the former can filter for more fails in the web accessibility guidelines than the latter. The pass remarks for any website for a given web accessibility guidelines can be reclaimed with a failure remark with a stronger and strictly built benchmark evaluation tool [37].

Table 6. Summarized results of automated testing

WCAG 2.1 (AA)	Guidelines	High	Medium	Low	Pass percentage
1.1	Text alternative	A	C, D, E	B	13.33
1.2	Time-based media	N/A	N/A	N/A	N/A
1.3	Adaptable	A, B, C, D, E	–	–	0
1.4	Distinguishable	A, C, D, E	–	B	13.33
2.1	Keyboard accessible	D, E	N/A	B	N/A
2.2	Enough time	N/A	N/A	B	N/A
2.3	Seizures	A, C, D	E	B	53.33
2.4	Navigable	A, B, C, D	–	E	6.66
3.1	Readable	A, B	–	C, D, E	66.66
3.2	Predictable	D	C	A, B, E	40
3.3	Input assistance	A, C, D, E	–	B	20
4.1	Compatible	C	A, E	B, D	66.66

The paper reports the collective performance of all the websites, as shown in the above Table 6. In the tables, the columns, 'High', 'Medium' and 'Low', represents the websites which have high to low level of comparative web inaccessibility. The websites in the Table 6 are represented with the alphabets (A, B, C, D, and E) as described in Sect. 3.1.

The column High, Medium, and Low for a website describes the comparative degree of website's suffering or ineptness for a given specific conformance level with respect to other websites. For example, the web accessibility guidelines for A (alphabetical representation for the website 'http://www.portaldogoverno.gov.mz/') are recorded under the column 'High'. This means the website performed worst for the web accessibility guidelines 'Text Alternative' as compared with other websites being used for the evaluation in our research. Similarly, for the same web accessibility guidelines of 'Text Alternative' the website B https://www.olx.co.mz/ in the same row did well as it passed more web evaluation tool's test and thus is placed under the column 'High'. And the websites (C, D, and E) are placed under the 'Medium' column as these websites performed with the results better than 'High' and worse than 'Low'. Classifying the websites in these three columns gives the comparative results among the websites. This shows which website is better or worst compared to the other website for a specific success criterion.

The website A faces the most accessibility issues whereas the website B faces the least. Given that website, A is a governmental website and its importance for the citizens is paramount, the Mozambican governmental website utterly fails to make it accessible to its citizens, and potentially many people with disabilities causing many problems in accessing and using the website.

The pass percentage of any conformance level is the average figure of results from all tools combined over all the websites being evaluated. We define pass percentage to know how well the website has performed overall for a specific conformance level. Mathematically, we calculate it as:

Pass percentage = (number of passes for specific conformance level/total number of fields) * 100.

For Instance, pass percentage for text alternative = (2/15) *100 equals 13.33 percent. This means data for pass percentage depicts all the websites collectively for a given web accessibility guidelines. A total number of fields remains i.e., the denominator or divisor as the total number of fields are 15 as 3 tools times 5 websites. N/A in the table represents the results for that field cannot be obtained because the result was not specified in tools results. Calculating N/A with a known entity would return an infinite or known result.

As can be seen from the Table 6, the combined effort of all the websites, apart from 3 web accessibility conformance levels, Seizures, compatible and readable, the other 9 conformance levels show low to very low pass percentage. Such results are inevitable to cause web accessibility barriers for people with disabilities using it. The results from this prove that the websites do not satisfy the user's needs to access the website if the users are having varied sorts of impairments or disabilities. The overall performance of these websites able to impact to be used by people with disabilities is certainly bleak. This shows that these websites fail to make any prevalence among these group users.

4.2 Results from Interviewing and Interacting with Web Developers in Mozambique

Out of 15 web developers interviewed for the research only 4 of them is found to have less than 4 years of work experience. The average experience of 15 web developers interviewed for the research was calculated to be 5.5 years. The responses from the web developers are categorized in 3 groups, by grouping and differentiating ideas or expressions under specific categories as shown in Table 7.

Table 7. Grouping of web developers' responses into individual, organizational and external factors.

Group of factors	Nature of web developers' responses
Individual factor	Perceiving disability with medical model
	Poor knowledge on the topic of web accessibility
	English incompetency
Organizational factors	Low wages of web employees
	Lack of Internship training
	Organizational/stakeholder requirement
External factors	Customer/client requirement
	State policies and regulations
	Untrendy topic in Mozambique

The Venn-diagram A in the figure number 2 below shows the number of web developers' responses who thinks inaccessibility on the web is due to an individual ineptness or understanding of the topic. The report describes the three nature of responses under individual factor which are responsible for inaccessibility in the web. Several interviewee's responses mentioned under the Medical Model depict disability is an individual condition that limits their ability to use the web. The medical model defines disability located within the individual [38]. Thus, we categories their approach towards people with disabilities under the Medical Model. The response under "poor web accessibility knowledge" means the responses from the interviewee who admitted inaccessibility is due to their poor knowledge on the topic. However, some responses blamed the inadequacy of their level of English. Further, they reported, as most of the mainstream web development environment and applications are in English, sometimes their limited comprehension skills in English do not allow them to advance their work. And thus, they work with a fixed package of workload in their everyday job.

The Venn-diagram B in the figure number 2 below shows the number of web developers' responses who thinks inaccessibility on the web is due to their organizations or company in which they work in. Some of the responses criticized the pay scale for web developers in IT companies being low. According to a few of them, given the nature and level of work in the IT industry, and is called a software developer or web developer, the tag does not justify the payment. While some also feel that, being newly hired in the company, it is the company's responsibility to train them on new or unknown topics. This would make them cognizant of the company's work culture, practice, and trend. Some of the web developers were also noted citing it is not because of them the web products are inaccessible rather it is the project manager's or other stakeholders' requirements that rarely mandates building accessible products. Also, the web developers have hardly been asked to incorporate web accessibility in the projects. There can be many probable inferences to this, including stakeholders' or project master's lack of knowledge on web accessibility. The presumption that the accessible web products can cost more and require more time or being complacent assuming ad hoc solutions satisfies the major customer base.

The Venn-diagram C in the figure number 2 below shows the number of web developers' responses who thinks inaccessibility on the web is due to other factors that are external than those factors mentioned above. Many web developers feel it is due to the State's poor law-making strategy and policy responsible for web inaccessibility to a great extent. They feel the topic is unique and are thus not aware of web accessibility practices because they are not obliged to follow such practices as regulations. They blame the absence of any ICT policies not relating to web accessibility. Also, some responses cited the client, or the customer does not come up with accessibility requirement and as a result, the product must be built based on what they demanded. However, the research also finds some interviewees feel the topic of web accessibility is not ubiquitous in Mozambique and thus untrendy which in effect fails to motivate the web accessibility practice further (Fig. 2).

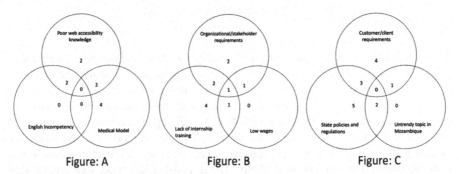

Figure: A   Figure: B   Figure: C

Fig. 2. The three Venn-diagrams A, B and C showing the web developers' responses categorized as individual factors, organizational factors, external factor respectively.

5 Discussion

The paper has explored the web accessibility issues in Mozambique. Analyzing the results from 2 perspectives: evaluation of websites and interviewing and interacting with web developers in Mozambique presented us with a broader understanding of the cause.

The 5 websites evaluated showed basic to major accessibility flaws and none of the websites comply with WCAG 2.1 guidelines to the adequacy to meet web accessibility standards. The governmental website, http://www.portaldogoverno.gov.mz/ is found to have the worst accessibility among the 5 websites. This result is in line with the study [4] where the authors find the Mozambican governmental websites to be very much inaccessible as well, due to failures of HTML elements in the HTML documents. The failures are, missing alt or title attributes on decorative text, some colors being perceived too bright, table captions also being almost inexistent, and no proper connection of some flash objects with textual descriptions [4].

On a disappointing note, this paper studied that no websites showed the satisfactory accessibility level for the conformance level of the web accessibility according to WCAG 2.1 (except www.olx.co.mz). Only 3 web accessibility conformance levels, Seizures and physical reactions, compatible and readable, ranged from 50 to 66.66 pass percentage and the other 9 conformance levels failed to make impressive remarks. Such results of the websites are inevitable to cause web accessibility barriers for people with disabilities, using it. This proves that websites in Mozambique are inaccessible and thus fails to outreach the nation's people with disabilities population.

The approach towards the accessibility in web and inclusive design does not seem a serious practice amongst the web developers. For many (but not all) interviewees, 'accessibility' in the web is a novel and unfamiliar topic. Their responses (around 80 percentage) did not mention web accessibility and thus its scarce experiences among them should not be considered surprising. For remaining interviewees (web developers) showed little knowledge of web accessibility. None of the developers incorporates accessibility measures in all their products and only very few of them practice web accessibility measures at some time. This is to say, there exist, little if any web developers practice web accessibility on their own. The web developers are found to be deeply unaware of the web accessibility guidelines and tools.

The level of understanding and awareness of the web developers in the subject is undoubtedly found to be dearth. However, the other factors buttressing this obvious fact are worth reflecting upfront. Absence of state policies and regulations specific to web accessibility, rudimentary web requirements and apathetic considerations from stakeholders/clients for their products and lack of web accessibility training for web developers are the factors, in the first place, restraining web developers practice web accessibility. These identified extrinsic factors are fairly consistent and can be related to the factors explained in the research [39], where the author urges the simultaneous holistic extension of cultural, political, societal and economic factors for universal ICT access.

Considering that the average job experience for the interviewed web developers exceeds 5 years, the lack of practical experience with web accessibility is hard to fathom. As the web accessibility awareness among web developers is found lacking, this invariably can result in the lack the competencies and demanding skills required in the field of web accessibility. Most of the web developers' responses suggest the need of legislative framework and policies on web accessibility standards for web developers. This study found the similar kind of results, with the study from [31] in the context of Uganda, where web inaccessibility in the country is due to the absence of web accessibility specific regulations and policies. It can fairly be argued that the situations for improved web accessibility in a low-income country like Mozambique largely remains in the hands of the governmental policies.

The field of ICT in Mozambique is at its infancy stage, and certainly needs improvement in ICT policies and regulations relating to web accessibility, which in specific have not taken place before. With the government gradually initiating and developing ICT projects [30] shows the realizations have derived into effect. This research has found evidence on how some nations in the past or recently are able to improve accessibility on the web by amending and enacting the laws. From UN CRPD conventions regulations, web developers' responses, improved history of other nations enacting web accessibility laws, etc. provides enough rationale for Mozambique to act very soon to enact and regulate policies inaccessibility on the web. The UNCRPD article 9: Accessibility, Paragraph 28 of Chapter 3 "Obligations of States parties" presents a suitable case for countries like Mozambique to implement accessibility in ICT by adopting suitable legal framework in the absence of relevant legislation [23].

6 Limitations and Future Work

The coverage of the research participants in the research is narrow. The reliability of the research conducted only in Maputo, to a certain degree can be debatable. This is called error sampling [32]. Nevertheless, as the study was conducted majorly in the capital cities of the provinces (including capita of Mozambique) where it is believed modern technology for web accessibility is provided. Thus, it would not impact the results greatly. This is because the higher value of the range of data would remain the same even though the study had covered more places in the country.

It is worth noting that, few web developers might have falsely responded to some questions favoring accessibility knowledge and practice owning to their dignity, identity, and fear of losing the job. This is because, some hesitancy and reluctancy for some web developer were noticed during interview.

For one of the websites among 5 used for automatic evaluation, the URL for www.olx.co.mz is no longer available. This realization came during the final 2020 self-evaluation before the submission of the thesis. According to local source, the website has been taken down due to security concerns. However, the version of the website evaluated for automatic testing can be traced backdate at https://web.archive.org/web/201901282 20421/https://www.olx.co.mz/ at archive.org.

Future work should include web developers from other various parts of Mozambique to produce more consistent and accurate generalization of the country. Adding people with disabilities as the research subject, user testing and interviewing them could be beneficial in the future study. The results from such study combined with the results of this study should present the overall web inaccessibly situations in Mozambique. This study discovering dearth of accessibility in ICT and web, provides a new opportunity for stakeholders, regulation and policy makers and specially web developers to encompass accessibility/universal design guidelines and principles from beginning. A good reference for such practice can be exercised from widely accepted source of Web

Accessibility Initiative (WAI) of W3C which develops guidelines, widely regarded as the international standard for web accessibility [7].

7 Conclusion

The most used 5 websites in Mozambique being evaluated are found to have major accessibility flaws. Added with, interview and interactions with web developers in Mozambique revealed their inept awareness and skills in web accessibility guidelines and knowledge to perform any web accessibility practices in their web solutions. The fieldwork in Mozambique, helped gather the web developers' responses and subsequently to understand the underneath issues contributing to the web inaccessibility from their individual levels. Our study found that the issues in web accessibility in Mozambique, are more of an extrinsic in nature which is the cause for a functional (technical) issue, inaccessibility flaws on the web. Thus, the extrinsic (non-functional) factors must be addressed to achieve accessible functional (technical) requirements relating to web accessibility. These extrinsic factors are majorly societal, financial, organizational, legislative, and environmental/external factors. These factors contribute to maintaining a gap in the adoption of web accessibility support and services for people with disabilities and practice and awareness among web practitioners. Being one of the members among the state parties to the UNCRPD Article 9 relating to 'accessibility' aiming to improve accessibility for people with disabilities, Mozambique is only slowly progressing, this study finds.

References

1. Noh, K.-R., Jeong, E.-S., You, Y.-B., Moon, S.-J., Kang, M.-B.: A study on the current status and strategies for improvement of web accessibility compliance of public institutions. J. Open Innov.: Technol., Mark., Complex. **1**(1), 1–17 (2015). https://doi.org/10.1186/s40852-015-0001-0
2. Lopes, R., Gomes, D., Carriço, L.: Web not for all: a large scale study of web accessibility (2010). https://doi.org/10.1145/1805986.1806001
3. Kamal, I.W., Alsmadi, I.M., Wahsheh, H.A., Al-Kabi, M.N.: Evaluating web accessibility metrics for Jordanian universities. Int. J. Adv. Comput. Sci. Appl. **7**(7), 113–122 (2016). https://doi.org/10.14569/ijacsa.2016.070716
4. Costa, D., Fernandes, N., Neves, S., Duarte, C., Hijón-Neira, R., Carriço, L.: Web accessibility in Africa: a study of three African domains. In: Kotzé, P., Marsden, G., Lindgaard, G., Wesson, J., Winckler, M. (eds.) INTERACT 2013. LNCS, vol. 8117, pp. 331–338. Springer, Heidelberg (2013). https://doi.org/10.1007/978-3-642-40483-2_23
5. Wright, K.Q.: Disability in Africa | African Studies Centre Leiden (2018). https://www.ascleiden.nl/content/webdossiers/disability-africa. Accessed 26 Mar 2020
6. Sida: Disability Rights in Mozambique, no. December, p. 7 (2014). http://www.sida.se/globalassets/sida/eng/partners/human-rights-based-approach/disability/rights-of-persons-with-disabilities-mozambique.pdf
7. World Wide Web Consortium (W3C): Web Accessibility Initiative (WAI). https://www.w3.org/WAI/. Accessed 10 Dec 2020
8. Web Accessibility Initiative (WAI): Web Content Accessibility Guidelines (WCAG) 2.1. https://www.w3.org/TR/WCAG21/. Accessed 11 Dec 2020

9. Shinohara, K., Bennett, C.L., Wobbrock, J.O.: How designing for people with and without disabilities shapes student design thinking. In: ASSETS 2016 - Proceedings of the 18th International ACM SIGACCESS Conference on Computers and Accessibility, pp. 229–237 (2016). https://doi.org/10.1145/2982142.2982158
10. Paciello, M.: Web Accessibility for People with Disabilities. CRC Press, Boca Raton (2000)
11. Eide, A.H., Kamaleri, Y.: Living conditions of people with disabilities in Mozambique, no. January 2009
12. Sankhi, P., Sandnes, F.E.: A glimpse into smartphone screen reader use among blind teenagers in rural Nepal. Disabil. Rehabil. Assist. Technol., pp. 1–7, September 2020. https://doi.org/10.1080/17483107.2020.1818298
13. Slatin, J.M., Rush, S.: Maximum accessibility: making your web site more usable for everyone. Addison-Wesley Professional (2003)
14. Kurt, S.: The accessibility of university web sites: the case of Turkish universities. Univers. Access Inf. Soc. **10**(1), 101–110 (2011). https://doi.org/10.1007/s10209-010-0190-z
15. United Nations, Toolkit on disability for Africa. Div. Soc. Policy Dev., pp. 1–40 (2016). http://www.un.org/esa/socdev/documents/disability/Toolkit/Intro-UN-CRPD.pdf
16. INE, IV Recenseamento Geral da População e Habitação, 2017 Resultados Definitivos – Moçambique. Inst. Nac. Estatística, Maputo-Moçambique, pp. 16–21 (2019)
17. Lopes, E.C.U.: Mozambique. Afr. Disabil. Rts. YB **1**, 245 (2013)
18. Lord, J., Stein, M.A.: Prospects and practices for CRPD implementation in Africa. Afr. Disabil. Rts. YB **1**, 97 (2013)
19. DO-IT, What is the difference between accessible, usable, and universal design? The Faculty Room (2013). https://www.washington.edu/doit/what-difference-between-accessible-usable-and-universal-design. Accessed 10 Sep 2018
20. Web Accessibility Initiative, Web Accessibility Perspectives: Explore the Impact and Benefits for Everyone | Web Accessibility Initiative (WAI) | W3C. https://www.w3.org/WAI/perspective-videos/ Accessed 10 Dec 2020
21. Fuglerud, K.S., Halbach, T., Tjøstheim, I.: Cost-benefit analysis of universal design. Lit. Rev. Suggest. Futur. Work. Oslo Nor. Regnesentral (2015)
22. Assembly, G.: Resolution adopted by the General Assembly (2007). https://www.ohchr.org/Documents/HRBodies/CRPD/CRPD_ENG.pdf. Accessed: 10 Dec 2020
23. Committee on the Rights of Persons with Disabilities, General Comment no. 2 (2014) on Article 9: Accessibility - CRPD/C/GC/2, vol. 03313, p. 14 (2014)
24. Abuaddous, H.Y., Jali, M.Z., Basir, N.: Web accessibility challenges. Int. J. Adv. Comput. Sci. Appl. **7**(10), 172–181 (2016)
25. World Wide Web Consortium (W3C): Web Accessibility Laws & Policies | Web Accessibility Initiative (WAI) | W3C. https://www.w3.org/WAI/policies/. Accessed 11 Dec 2020
26. Persson, H., Åhman, H., Yngling, A.A., Gulliksen, J.: Universal design, inclusive design, accessible design, design for all: different concepts—one goal? On the concept of accessibility—historical, methodological and philosophical aspects. Univ. Access Inf. Soc. **14**(4), 505–526 (2014). https://doi.org/10.1007/s10209-014-0358-z
27. Sloan, D., Horton, S.: Global considerations in creating an organizational web accessibility policy. In: Proceedings of the 11th Web for All Conference, pp. 1–4 (2014)
28. Kuzma, J., Yen, D., Oestreicher, K.: Global e-government web accessibility: an empirical examination of EU, Asian and African sites (2009)
29. Isaacs, S.: Survey of ICT in Education in Mozambique, pp. 1–12 (2007)
30. IST-Africa, Current ICT Initiatives and projects - Republic of Mozambique. http://www.ist-africa.org/home/default.asp?page=doc-by-id&docid=5563. Accessed 11 Dec 2020
31. Baguma, R., Wanyama, T., Bommel, P.V., Ogao, P.: Web accessibility in Uganda: a study of webmaster perceptions. In: proceedings of the 3rd Annual International Conference on Computing and ICT Research (SREC 2007), pp. 183–197 (2007)

32. Sharma, G.: Pros and cons of different sampling techniques. Int. J. Appl. Res. **3**(7), 749–752 (2017)
33. Taherdoost, H.: Sampling methods in research methodology; how to choose a sampling technique for research. How Choose Sampl. Tech. Res. (2016)
34. David, B., Resnik, J.D.: What is ethics in research and why is it important. Natl. Inst. Environ. Heal. Sci. (2011). https://www.niehs.nih.gov/research/resources/bioethics/whatis/
35. Tindana, P.O., Kass, N., Akweongo, P.: The informed consent process in a rural African setting: a case study of the Kassena-Nankana district of Northern Ghana. IRB Ethics Hum. Res. **28**(3), 1–6 (2006)
36. De. Vries, J., et al.: Ethical issues in human genomics research in developing countries. BMC Med. Ethics **12**(1), 1–10 (2011)
37. Vigo, M., Brown, J., Conway, V.: Benchmarking web accessibility evaluation tools: measuring the harm of sole reliance on automated tests. In: Proceedings of the 10th International Cross-Disciplinary Conference on Web Accessibility. pp. 1–10 (2013)
38. Marks, D.: Models of disability. Disabil. Rehabil. **19**(3), 85–91 (1997)
39. Toks, O.: Universal access wheel: towards achieving access to ICT in Africa. South African J. Inf. Commun., no. 4, (2004). https://doi.org/10.23962/10539/19818
40. United Nations: Division for Social Policy and Development Disability. Article 2 - Definitions | United Nations Enable (2006). https://www.un.org/development/desa/disabilities/convention-on-the-rights-of-persons-with-disabilities/article-2-definitions.html. Accessed: 11 Dec 2020
41. Henry, S.L.: Understanding Web Accessibility. In: Web Accessibility. Apress (2006). https://doi.org/10.1007/978-1-4302-0188-5_1
42. AChecker: IDI Web Accessibility Checker: Web Accessibility Checker. AChecker Web Services (2012). https://achecker.ca/checker/index.php?lang=eng. Accessed 11 Dec 2020
43. SortSite - Accessibility Checker and Validator, "Accessibility Checker: Test WCAG 2.1 & Section 508 Compliance. https://www.powermapper.com/products/sortsite/checks/accessibility-checks/. Accessed 11 Dec 2020
44. WebAIM, WebAIM: WAVE Web Accessibility Evaluation Tool, Webaim.Org (2013). https://wave.webaim.org/. Accessed 11 Dec 2020

Screen Reader Accessibility Study of Interactive Maps

Sayed Kamrul Hasan[1] and Terje Gjøsæter[1,2(✉)]

[1] Oslo Metropolitan University, Oslo, Norway
[2] University of Agder, Kristiansand, Norway
terjeg@uia.no

Abstract. Digital maps have been an integral part of modern life. Whether to venture into an unknown location, check the latest traffic update, update on the weather forecast, we come across digital maps every day. While maps have successfully evolved into digital form from paper and other physical mediums, how much evolution present-day digital maps have observed to ensure accessibility and implementation of universal design principles? Maps by nature have to rely on graphical medium to present their information content. But the users who have temporary or permanent and limited to no visual ability are excluded from reading maps for this reason. In this study, we have conducted a systematic literature review to discover the research gaps of accessibility in digital maps, focusing on map exploration based on screen reader technology. To discover further accessibility issues from users, we conducted semi-structured interviews with participants with varying degrees of visual impairments. The result from these data indicates that interactive maps are not screen-reader accessible at all. There is an apparent research gap in alternative text accessibility in maps and interview participants commonly agreed with multiple accessibility issues on contemporary interactive maps on diverse platforms.

Keywords: Interactive maps · Screen reader · Accessibility · Universal design

1 Introduction

People from all walks of life use digital maps in their daily life for example to find the nearest grocery store, view the public transport map of a city, or understand the severity of a natural disaster of a location. With the ever-rising popularity of smart devices from desktop to handheld, all sorts of maps now can be accessed by the push of a button or tap on the screen as long as the device is on the internet. But throughout all the evolution of maps over the year, questions remain how much work has been done on improving maps, so they can be used by as many people as possible. People with a diverse range of physical, psychological, and socio-economic properties. In other words, how accessible and universally designed today's digital maps are? When it comes to accessibility in using digital maps for navigational purposes, there is a tremendous amount [1] of work has been done to ensure people with various impairments can travel from point A to

© Springer Nature Switzerland AG 2021
M. Antona and C. Stephanidis (Eds.): HCII 2021, LNCS 12768, pp. 232–249, 2021.
https://doi.org/10.1007/978-3-030-78092-0_15

point B conveniently and safely. But when it comes to reading the content of the maps or exploring an interactive map, there is much room for improvement. Maps by nature rely on conveying spatial information through the use of graphical representation. Any point or co-ordinate in a map only makes sense when its physical location can be depicted successfully using relevant surrounding location information like distance, direction, and the elements in between through illustrations. This necessity of presenting spatial information in illustrative form may create barriers for users with a varied level of ability and scenarios. One obvious user group affected by today's digital maps are users with different categories of vision impairments (Corn and Erin 2010). In the digital world, acute vision-impaired users rely on assistive technologies like screen readers and braille displays to interact with electronic devices. So, if the current maps in digital forms cannot be used without or even with assistive technologies, they cannot be considered accessible to visually impaired users. The inaccessibility in maps becomes even more consequential during emergencies. In the event of catastrophic natural disasters like floods or hurricanes, a mass of populations is required to take refuge in emergency shelters. It then becomes crucial to locate the most convenient shelter nearby. If an evacuee must rely on finding that information from digital maps only and unable to use the map due to inaccessibility, in an extreme case it may lead to fatal consequences. In line with accessing meteorological maps, a user might need to use a weather map online to explore critical weather information, imminent and past natural disaster data, or just simply wants to find out the wildfire risk factors of a suburb. If the information is presented only in convention graphical map format without alternative or accessibility options, a user with limited vision might be excluded from accessing the service. In this research paper, we will investigate research gaps and various accessibility issues currently found on digital interactive maps. The research questions investigated in this paper is as follows:

1. How much research has been done so far towards accessible designing of digital interactive maps to accommodate the screen reader user group?
2. What are the common accessibility issues experienced by the impaired user groups in digital maps?

The rest of the paper is organized as follows. Section 2 establishes the theoretical platform for the research through reviews on various sections related to digital maps and their accessibility. Section 3 covers the methodology and Sect. 4 the result of the study. The findings are further discussed in Sect. 5 of the paper with a conclusion.

2 Literature Review

2.1 Accessibility and Design Guidelines

Accessibility is an attribute and the Cambridge Dictionary defines it as the quality of approaching, reaching, obtaining, and understanding something easily [2]. Accessibility is generally associated with people with special needs and their right to independent, equal, and full social living. This includes full access to the physical environment, mobility, information, and communication [3]. The design and development of accessible products and services should cater to all user groups so they can use them with or without a need for assistive technologies. Assistive technology (AT) in turn is an umbrella term for special-purpose devices and services used by persons with limited ability as an enabler to ensure full participation in society [4]. Hearing Aid, Screen reader, or braille display are examples of commonly used Assistive technologies. Universal design is a major focus of this paper. Assistive technology is a dividing factor between Accessibility and Universal Design. Accessibility is achieved through good design and development of a product or service that enables direct (non-assisted) or indirect (assisted) access. Whereas "Universal Design is the design of products and environments to be usable by all people, to the greatest extent possible, without the need for adaptation or specialized design" [5]. So, the design goal of universal design is to ensure the accessibility of as many user groups as possible regardless of their ability while avoiding the need for assistive technology. Universal design principles point out all potential design limitations that need to be addressed to achieve an inclusive design and suggest ways to maximize the usability of any designs under development and indicate affecting variables along the way [6].

In the web technology part of the ICT world, the Web Accessibility Initiative (WAI) taskforce developed accessibility guidelines: Web Content Accessibility Guidelines (WCAG) for creating accessible web content. The latest rendition of WCAG, 2.1 [7] contributes toward legally accepted accessibility for a wide range of impaired user groups: vision, auditory, speech, motor, cognitive, etc. The success of WCAG guidelines resulted in a governmental push for creating accessible web content across the world: the European Union and countries like the United States, Canada, Australia, etc. are also all imposing WCAG conformity laws.

2.2 User Diversity and Visual Impairment

Several factors contribute to the user diversity that engineers and designers must consider while developing universally designed products, services, and environments. According to Story, Mueller and Mace [8], these can be diverse user ability, among-user diversity, situational diversity, technological diversity, etc. Ability based user diversity stem from varying ability in vision, audio, motor, cognition, mental, etc. Even when these physical and mental abilities are not a factor, culture, socio-economic background, education can create further diversity among users. Situational diversity can be triggered by weather conditions, physical location, stressful or emergency state, etc. This paper focuses on screen reader accessibility and alternative text accessibility of interactive maps, so the user diversity based on visual ability is further investigated. The World Health Organization stated in their 2011 world report [9], disability is not an attribute of a person. It is caused when a person with impairment cannot participate in society equally and fully due to environmental and attitudinal barriers. It is important that persons with any level of visual ability are addressed equally and their visual impairment does not characterize their identity. Based on visual acuity, WHO [9], categorizes blindness into the following groups: normal vision $(0.8 \geq)$ moderate low vision $(0.3 \leq)$, severe low vision or legal blindness $(0.12 \leq)$, profound low vision $(0.05 \leq)$ and, near-total or total blindness $(0.02 \leq)$. Aside from visual acuity, there are other variations of impairments like color blindness, photophobia or Light sensitivity, tunnel vision, blind spot, or in severe cases Deaf blindness.

2.3 Maps Design Evaluations

Several papers have attempted to evaluate currently available online maps and maps in web applications. Calle Jiménez and Luján-Mora [10] has uncovered the general barriers that are found on any typical static maps - maps that are presented as an image file. The biggest barriers are the absence of alternative text as well as texts inside the image of the map that cannot be read by a user with low vision and screen reader. Secondly, if the map design did not consider color-blind users, it would have a color combination that cannot be properly read by color-blind users. User exclusion can also be created if the functionality of the map image file presented and the website, in general, cannot be operated by a keyboard. They also indicated if multiple image files are used to represent a single map, it creates a mosaic effect and thus inaccessibility ensues. Medina, Cagnin and Paiva [11] have conducted a thorough investigation to determine the accessibility of a few of the most popular web application maps. Their thorough assessment included heuristic expert evaluation, automated evaluation as well as final user testing with users of limited visual ability. They employed eight experts and evaluated Google Maps, OpenStreetMap, Yahoo! Maps, Bing Maps, and MapRequest using WCAG 2.0 accessibility guidelines. They scoped their evaluation to all the success criteria of Level A conformance level. The expert evaluation revealed Google Maps violated the greatest number of success criteria – 18 out of 24 criteria inspected. On the other hand, OpenStreetMap and MapRequest violated only 4. The other two web maps service scored averagely, abiding by 16 and 14 success criteria, respectively. But according to WCAG, if a website breaks one success criteria under a conformance level, it violates the whole conformance level so none of the evaluated maps conforms to even level A. Their automated accessibility checker tools confirmed the result from expert evaluation to be correct. For maximum accuracy, they evaluated the above-mentioned web maps with 5 different checkers: AChecker, Total Validator, CynthiaSays, TAW, and AccessMonitor. Along with WCAG, these tools also check for accessibility from other guidelines like Section 508, HTML, XHTML, CSS, BITV as well as for spelling errors. From the result of WCAG guidelines, none of the websites met conformance level A criteria. Finally, for the user evaluation, visually impaired users from the Institute for Blind Florivaldo Vargas - ISMAC, located in Campo Grande, State of Mato Grosso do Sul, Brazil volunteered to test only Google Maps for accessibility. Google Maps was chosen due to its popularity and ease of use. Participants were given 9 activities to perform in Google maps. While most activities were performed 100% successfully two activities had a 0% success rate. These are 1) access photos of a given address and read their descriptions; 2) use the zoom feature on the map. switch between "Map" and "Satellite" views using the website tools had only a 50% success rate. So how the digital maps should be designed to accommodate as many user groups as possible? In the paper [12] "Grand Challenges in Accessible Maps", the authors pointed out map data and design is meaningless if the broad users cannot access it. They indicated map interaction functionality should not be limited to keyboards and pointing devices, rather it should also be supported by eye-tracking or one switch interfaces and should incorporate other senses like haptics and olfaction.

3 Methodology

3.1 Research Design Approaches

Action Research. According to Lazar, Feng and Hochheiser [13], research in human-computer interaction is fascinating and complex. They find it fascinating because there are abundant research questions that need to be answered and yet these questions change over time as technologies progress. On the other hand, complexity in HCI research stems from two variable factors. Firstly, the research subject –human beings, who are habitually complex. Secondly, because of the above factors, HCI based research might not rigidly follow conventional frameworks of research approaches. In our HCI research study, we investigate the technological and social gaps left behind during the advancement of digital maps and we try to measure the gap and suggest possible solutions to fill the gap for digital maps designers, implementers, and policymakers. Action research is a research methodology whose root can be traced back to social science [14] and being successfully preferred, revised, and adopted for HCI based research [15] in recent times. Hayes [15] suggested Action research shares common ground with HCI researchers: working with community partners, being involved in fieldwork, and designing and developing a solution in an iterative fashion.

Qualitative Data Collection. Scientific studies rely heavily on quantifiable data from experimental method approaches. But due to the social aspect of HCI based research studies, data might be too subjective to quantify, complex to experimentally manipulate, and challenging to ethically conduct [16]. We might not even have a predictable and assumable research question for our HCI agenda before even starting the research let alone determine quantifiable variables. Also understanding how different user groups individually and collectively perceive and experience usability and accessibility can be very subjective to collect and analyze in a quantitative manner [17]. The answer to our problem is collecting qualitative data in the form of interviews, focus groups, observations, usability testing, accessibility evaluation, media content, etc. which is a norm in social science studies. Lazar, Feng and Hochheiser [13] argued while we are collecting and analyzing subjective data in HCI research, "Qualitative methods do not aim to eliminate subjectivity—instead, they accept that subjectivity is inherent to the process of interpreting qualitative data, and they strive to show that interpretations are developed methodically to be consistent with all available data, and representative of multiple perspectives." In our research, we collected qualitative data through a systematic literature review and interviews.

Thematic Data Analysis. Over the years verities of techniques for analyzing qualitative data have been tested in HCI research namely grounded theory, conversational analysis, discourse analysis, and thematic analysis [16]. At the beginning of our research, we decided to follow the grounded theory technique where data is analyzed as soon as an analyzable amount of data is available [13]. Along with data analysis, grounded theory can be applied to the data collection approach and we believed this is the most appropriate research method for our study as we were uncertain about the accessibility and technology gap in digital maps and had to explore and discover the research gap and formulate research question through systematic literature review. But as we progressed through our research, we realized, the qualitative data collected through the systematic literature review and accessibility guideline evaluation are unconventional. Analyzing such data through the lenses of grounded theory will be complex and time-consuming. During the second phase of our research and onward, data analysis was carried out using the more simplified version of data analysis - thematic technique. The variation of this technique we chose is from Braun and Clarke [18] which is performed in 6 steps respectively: familiarity with data, initial code generation, theme searching, theme reviewing, theme defining, and finally, writing up.

3.2 Systematic Literature Review

A systematic literature review is conducted to seek the answer to the first research question. SLR was designed to explore specifically the state of the study on text alternate and screen reader accessibility of interactive digital maps. A procedural, repeatable, and definite review can be a reference point for future academics and contributors alike. Systematic reviews are fundamentally systematic yet Moher, Tetzlaff, Tricco, Sampson and Altman [19] discovered that only 10% of them truly follow a proper protocol. This systematic review has been designed based on a well-documented and vastly accepted SLR procedure, PRISMA Statement [20]. PRISMA Statement provides a 27-item checklist and four-phase flow diagram to procedurally complete review. To capture the most relevant paper for analysis, the search criteria has been divided into four categories, as illustrated in Fig. 1:

- "Maps" as the primary topic searched with "intitle", to cover all and any work related to maps. Initially, synonyms for maps: cartography, GIS (Geographic Information System), spatial was included within the search parameter of "intitle" but the returned result was beyond a manageable scope. Then, the above-mentioned synonyms were also included as a subcategory for maps as an "intext" search, but the result omitted a large number of relevant results. Eventually, the synonyms for maps were removed completely for this systematic literature review.
- Universal Design, covering Universal Design, design for all, and accessibility.
- ICT covering Web, technology, digital, mobile, smartphone, computer, internet.
- As the primary objective, "textual", "exploration" and "screen reader" keywords have been included "intext" with OR function to capture paper related to map exploration, textual accessibility, or maps that can be accessed using screen readers.

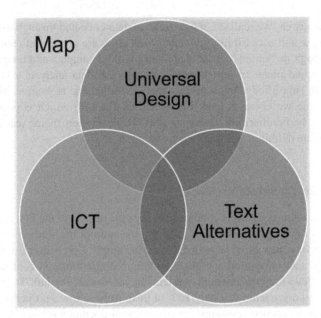

Fig. 1. Venn diagram of SLR search criteria

The paper publication date for the search was kept to the last decade, between 2009 to 2019. The date range 2009–2019 was chosen because WCAG (Web Content Accessibility Guidelines) 2.0 became a World Wide Web Consortium (W3C) recommendation at the end of 2008. Only English papers were searched. Google Scholar (https://scholar.Google.com) was used exclusively for the search database. Following were the exact search keywords used for the search:

intitle:maps intext: "Universal Design" | "Design for all" | "Inclusive Design" | Accessibility | Accessible intext:ICT | Web* | Digital | Mobile | smartphone | Computer | Internet intext:textual | exploration | "screen reader"

3.3 Semi-structured Interview

To obtain end-user perspectives and explore the second research question, semi-structured interviews were conducted with participants of various levels of limited visual ability. According to [13], the Most convincing argument for proceeding with the interview research method is, it allows researchers to "go deep" through asking a wide range of exploratory questions concerning the problem at hand and allowing them to expand on their answers. Based on the responses, interviewers can discover new territories of topics to explore, flexibly discuss interesting and important agendas and acquire an increased understanding that might not be possible with other methods of data collection, namely questionnaires or surveys. The semi-structured interview was chosen because while interviewees have more freedom to answer questions, interviewers have more room for asking structured, probing, and follow-up questions allowing them to have more insight about the topic while maintaining a well-scheduled interview guide [16,

21]. We also considered several challenges [13, 16] of conducting interviews for data collection. The open-ended nature of the responses from the semi-structured interview can be time-consuming to collect and difficult to analyze. When a rapport is built with the interviewer, the interviewee is prone to release sensitive personal data. At the beginning of the interview, we briefed interviewees about the project and what sorts of response we expect from them, so they are more careful about their answers. For extra precaution and ethical consideration, participation identity was kept anonymous and their data highly secured. Also considering the interview is a qualitative approach and qualitative data is subjective, data collection might be prone to the researcher's subjective bias. This issue is dealt with by the researcher's quality and inter-rater validity check during the data analysis period.

Interview Question Selection. Several research goals are expected to achieve from the interviews. The primary goal of the interview is to validate and confirm the claim that, digital maps, in general, lack many aspects of accessibility issues. Considering digital maps rely on conveying information predominantly through visual cues and our selected interview participants have varying degrees of visual impairments, we suspect digital maps' inaccessibility will be mentioned throughout the interviews. We also want to study our interview participants' experience using digital maps – the purpose they use it for, preference on the device they use it on, and preference on the providers of digital maps. Several questions are designed to be asked related to assistive technologies. We want to discover the assistive technologies they use; challenges they may face when using them on digital maps and if they apply any personally learned workaround techniques to mitigate those challenges. Digital maps may offer various accessibility features. One portion of the question sets has been added to learn our participant's familiarity with those accessibility features and how useful they find those in their use of digital maps. The closing portion of the interview focuses on end-user suggestions on designing and developing more accessible digital maps to cater to their ability needs. After designing the interview guide, pilot interviews were conducted and minor adjustments were made after the two pilot interviews. Pilot testing with fellow researchers helped discover new questions and remove a few questions which determined to be trivial for the interview. On the other hand, the second pilot testing helped rephrase the questions by removing jargon and improve the structure of the guide.

Recruitment Process. Considering the emphasis on screen reader accessibility in our research topic, the primary attributes pursued during the recruitment process were participants with severe low vision to total blindness. We also ensured participants have experience using digital maps on a regular basis. Participants were acquired by reaching out to various relevant groups in social media as well as Norges Blindeforbund - a blind and visually impaired interest and service organization in Norway. We got a response from Blindeforbund that they forwarded the interview recruitment invitation letter within their community. The number of participants required for semi-structured interviews depends on the research subject. For semi-structured qualitative studies, recruitment numbers can occasionally be as low as one but commonly 10–12 people [22]. Four interviews were conducted with five participants in total (see Table 1). Three interviews were in a one-on-one setting while the third interview was conducted as a group interview with two participants as per their request. For anonymity and simplicity in referencing, each participant was given the following codes in the table. The participants were arranged according to the sequence the interviews were conducted. Handling of user data was done under the supervision of the Norwegian Centre for Research Data (NSD).

Table 1. Participant list - coded

Participant code	Gender	Age	Visual ability
1M	Female	20	Profound low vision
2S	Female	35	Severe low vision
3T	Male	51	Total blindness
4L	Male	54	Total blindness
5B	Female	26	Profound low vision

Interview Protocol. The preferred location for conducting the interviews was chosen to be within the university campus. But due to the limited ability of our selected participant group, we indicated in the recruitment invitation letter that we can travel to the preferred location of the participants to conduct interviews including their preferred choice of time. Upon request from the interested potential participants, we also sent a summary of the interview question they will be asked. The interview has been designed to last for 30–45 min. Compensation in the form of cash, gift card, or electronic money transfer has been offered. Before starting the interview, participants were explained about the study, the interview process, and what we expect to gain from their participation. We also briefed them about their privacy and the treatment of their data. Notes were taken during the interview then reviewed immediately after the interview while the memory is fresh. This was done to ensure the qualitative data from cryptic shorthand and poor handwriting has been extracted effectively.

4 Results

4.1 Systematic Literature Review

As of Central European Summer, Time 1:41 PM Saturday, May 11, 2019, 1,070 results were presented by Google Scholar. See Fig. 2. Systematic Literature Review PRISMA Flowchart Diagram for an outline of the selection process. All search results have been inspected manually for relevance and authenticity. Initially, the title and the abstract were inspected and if they do not give enough information about the relevancy then the full text of the paper was skimmed through. After going through all search result, in the end, 84 paper was selected for further thorough study. Later, 21 paper was further excluded due to duplications, false-positive maps terms like biology-related maps, heat maps, network maps, historical maps, etc. Finally, 63 papers were eventually selected for the literature review. The quality of the papers was not assessed. All 63 papers were considered as long as they lasted through the filtering process.

Selected papers have been divided into six categories based on the nature of the paper or technology that has been used to present an accessibility option into digital maps. Predominantly, a large portion of the papers is on reflection on the accessibility of maps. These papers can be about literature review [23], accessible map design recommendations [24], barriers in currently available digital maps [10], accessibility assessment [25], challenges in designing accessible maps [12], etc.

When it comes to developing prototype solutions in maps accessibility, 12 papers have been discovered where their solution comes from substituting vision with two other functioning senses: hearing and touch. Solutions were ranging from sonar [26], voice instructions [27], and audio-hepatic feedbacks [28, 29]. One solution from 2013 made use of multisensory interaction with sonification, vibration as well as text to speech technologies [30] while on the other hand Schmitz and Ertl [31] based their prototype mainly on vibration to reach out to the deaf-blind community.

To successfully absorb the information of the maps for exploration, visualization or an alternative solution is necessary. 9 papers were found that suggest alternative processes that can be used to visualize and explore map contents. Aligning with this research, the most compelling solution comes from Afzal, Maciejewski, Jang, Elmqvist and Ebert [32] where they developed a design technique to convert the map element into text. A number of the prototypes under this category cater to the indoor floor plan for navigation, exploration, and emergencies [33, 34]. Sonification is also used under this category to explore weather maps [35] and indoor maps [36].

One set of papers categorized into introductions of an interactive and non-interactive tangible object to create accessibility of maps. Prototypes with swell or raised line paper on interactive touch screen display [37, 38], interactive 3D printed maps [39, 40], with use miscellaneous interactive accessibility objects like WiiMote [41] and Tangible Reels [42] suggested for accessibility.

Involving the end-users with limited abilities who use maps to gather accessibility data and develop accessible maps system in digital form has also been discussed on several occasions. For example, Rice, Jacobson, Caldwell, McDermott, Paez, Aburizaiza, Curtin, Stefanidis and Qin [43] talk about Using crowdsourcing to report obstacles like broken road, uneven curb, or temp closure on road due to construction via various crowdsourcing techniques like social media and then referenced in a crowdsourced mapping system.

Alternative reality like augmented, virtual, or mixed reality has also been observed to be incorporated to create accessible maps. Bujari, Ciman, Gaggi, Marfia and Palazzi [44] developed a system of Combining paper maps and smartphones in the exploration of cultural heritage using augmented reality. Table 2 further shows an overview of the categorization of papers according to their primary study area.

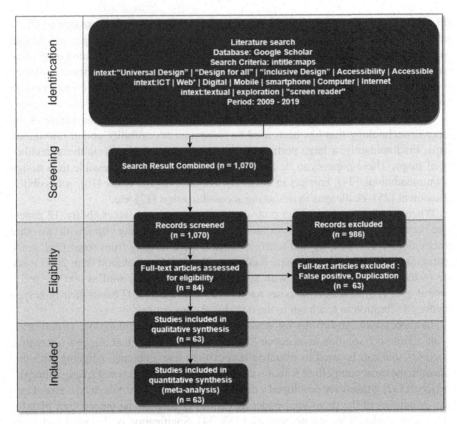

Fig. 2. Systematic literature review PRISMA flowchart diagram

Table 2. SLR papers categorized according to a study area

Area	Papers
Maps accessibility reflections	01–19
Audio - tactile solutions	20–31
Data visualization solutions	32–40
Tangible prototypes	41–54
Crowdsourcing to gather accessibility data	55–59

4.2 Interviews

Purpose and Preferences. We started our interviews by asking our participants about their purposes and preferred platforms of using digital maps, to associate digital maps to their personal experience as well as acquire sample data on digital map trends. Navigation was the primary purpose of using digital maps as answered by all participants. 5B utilizes the Google assistant function also to get traffic updates and approximate travel time and distance to destinations. 3T informed he has experience using digital tactile maps for indoor navigation and wants it to be developed further. Interestingly, Participants 1M and 5B tried using digital maps for "looking around" and "searching for places" respectively which can be considered a map exploration attempt. They expressed their frustration at the very beginning of the interview that trying to explore digital maps is impossible. This is because of their very limited visual ability, their reliance on screen readers, and digital maps not being accessible to screen reader users. 4L quoted: "Digital Maps are not accessible at all".

Asking about which digital maps they use; Google maps was the general answer. Even when the interviewees use Apple devices, which have their own dedicated maps system, they still prefer Google maps. 1M explained, she found Google maps to be comparatively more accessible than apple maps. As more experienced users, 3T and 4L mentioned a few more digital maps they have tried and tested. This includes Taxifix for calling a taxi, iMarka for ski maps, Blindsquare for voice-assisted navigation and exploration, etc. 3T demonstrated, Blindsquare can be used to gather information about the surrounding in the real world. It uses the smartphone's location services and maps data from Foursquare and OpenStreetMap databases. The app also has a rich algorithm to determine and audibly suggest the most relevant point of interest nearby of the user. Arguably, while Blindsquare is 3rd party solution and for exploring a user's surroundings in the real world, these features should be integrated into the most popular digital maps like Google maps and allow users to explore maps on the device itself.

The devices on which the participants use the digital maps turned out to be divisive. Three out of five interviewees have tried to use the Google maps on the desktop, found it completely inaccessible, and exclusively use it on their smartphones. 1M tried using Google maps once on a desktop during a presentation, but her screen reader registered the map just as a "graphics" and she never tried again. 4L informed he rather prefers to search for addresses on his desktop with a braille display, as he can absorb information faster through that, but it hardly ever works. 2S, on the other hand, requires a bigger screen to properly read information, so she mainly uses Google maps on a desktop or laptop, sometimes on her tablet but never on her smartphone.

Accessibility Challenges. In this section of the interview, we asked our participants about the more distinctive difficulties they might have faced when using digital maps. We asked about language accessibility, whether the system can detect and set their preferred language of choice automatically. Most of our participants use English as their preferred language and have reported no issue with language compatibility. Although the group interview revealed, many digital maps are designed exclusively for the English language. 4L informed us that "A problem with these virtual assistants is that much of the features are available in English". Using those maps with the non-English language selected, the screen reader reads out in odd accents. Every language has its unique name for significant locations. They also reported some of the maps do not respect this rule and only display the international name. Asking about the capabilities of apps or browsers to undo mistakes, 5B found it is hard to undo mistakes as a screen reader user. She ordinarily starts the whole process over whatever she was trying to do instead of finding a way to undo it. On the PC, she refreshes the web browser, and on the smartphone, she closes and reopens the app. She also talked about unexpected behavior experienced from Google apps where the app crashed several times or while walking with navigation on, the app took her in the wrong direction. 4L also experienced similar unexpected behavior but he considers these are because of their limited visual ability instead of the apps.

One thing all participants had a positive experience with was the search functionality. Whether on a web browser or as an app, their preferred maps were able to find the specific location they are searching for. If they type the address correctly or say the address clearly, Google maps or apple maps would find the place. Asking about the percentile success rate to one interviewer, she confirmed she was able to find the place 95% of the time. However, the final question we asked all our participants exposed the grim reality that summarizes their user experience. The question "Did you ever felt a lack of control when using maps" was collectively responded with "all the time". Analyzing this response can interpret that while most of these popular digital maps have a rich algorithm to search through the database in the backend when it comes to the accessible and inclusive user interface, there is still a lot to improve.

Personal Suggestions. Before concluding the interviews, we asked the participants for suggestions and recommendations on how we can design more accessible digital maps. Our first interviewee stated screen readers love texts so if there is a way to make an alternative digital map that is text friendly and can be read by screen readers it would be very helpful for her community. She further recommended; the map does not need to be part of the main feature. It can be integrated as an alternative text-friendly layer for screen reader users. 2S has voiced her struggles with the color contrast ratio of the current map design. She feels map elements have a very low color contrast ratio between elements and she finds it hard to distinguish. A significant issue raised by 3T was when Google maps app is opened on the smartphone, screen readers like VoiceOver or TalkBack never speak the current location. Afterward touching on the map returns no feedbacks. 4L suggests that as soon as the app is opened, a screen reader should be able to speak to the current location where the user is. Then, when the user touches on a different location on the smartphone, the screen reader should be able to speak the location name where the user touched. Based on this touch-speak interaction, even a user with impaired vision would be able to draw a mental map of the location. As discussed earlier, 4L also suggested how a keyboard user on a browser can explore the map using arrow keys. Our final interviewee is fond of vibration-based messages that some apps provide. Google maps provide no such tactile feedback functionality. She proposed Google maps to include vibration-sensitive feedback that is only triggered while the screen reader is on. She further clarified it could be one buzz for basic interaction, two buzzes for more specific interactions, and a burst of buzzes for advanced interactions. She gave us another interesting suggestion while we were discussing the redesign challenge that even if a screen reader can read the content of the map, questions remain which element is read and in which direction. She thinks "if even the most basic point of view was readable on the digital maps, we could draw a picture in our mind of the map layout".

5   Discussion

5.1   Systematic Literature Review

When the publication timeline for the papers was investigated, it is apparent most of the research put into making digital maps accessible came from the middle years of the last decade. 2016 has observed the highest number of papers published whereas 2010, 2014, and 2019 have seen only three papers published based on our search criteria (see Fig. 3). This gives insight that accessibility research has received some attention several years ago but now it has lost its research appeal. Also considering a large number of filtered papers reflect on maps barriers, design challenges, literature review, etc. as opposed to generating solutions, it indicates that universal design or accessibility in digital maps is still a new concept that needs further research.

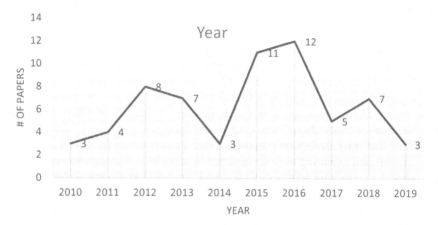

Fig. 3. Number of publications of last one decade

After carefully reviewing all the selected papers in the systematic literature review following noteworthy patterns and research gaps has been revealed:

- Of all the 63 papers, the term "universal design" has been mention once [23], "design for all" was also mentioned once [28], and no mention of "inclusive design" whatsoever in the body of any paper. Although all these terms can be found on a few of the paper's reference list. We can conclude that while accessibility on maps in a digital map is an old concept and actively on research, the concept of universal design has not been applied to digital maps as profoundly as one would expect.
- It was observed during the paper filtering process, numerous papers cover research agendas related to physical accessibility like accessible cities, infrastructures, transports, etc. Moreover, numerous false positives related to the term "accessibility" was filtered upon further study as it was being referred to the study on the inaccessibility of information in the sense of political, privacy, security barrier. This significantly implies that more research on accessibility based on a user's abilities and attributes are essential to close the digital divide gaps.

- The systematic literature review search criteria omitted any keyword related user groups specifically based on their physical and mental ability to find out when researchers work on the accessible digital maps, what user groups do they work on. It was discovered only visually impaired users, limited sighted to totally blind, color blinds, as well as deaf blinds, are the primary focus user groups for accessibility. Other user groups with possible limited abilities like elderly, motor system impairments, minimal educational background, etc. are not considered for universal design in digital maps. Future research can include these diverse user groups.
- Many alternatives and prototype solutions to use digital maps were introduced. Yet, a screen reader accessible solution was not discovered through this systematic literature review. This indicates a significant research gap in the universal design of ICT and digital accessibility.

5.2 Interviews

Based on the interviews it seems that for most participants any interaction with digital maps comes from Google maps. We also discovered that our participants tend to use google maps on their mobile devices as an app. One reason for choosing mobile devices can be Attributed to keyboard inaccessibility. None of the participants seemed satisfied with keyboard interaction with the interactive maps they tried. But even when they are using their preferred maps apps on mobile devices, limitations of what can be done overshadow their expectation. Turns out the only thing it is good for is touch typing an address to search for navigation purposes. Using a touch screen for screen reading the map contents and exploring the map contents is impossible. Participants reported it is also possible to search for addresses with virtual assistants like Google Assistant or Siri. Further analysis shows the underlying reason for being satisfied with the voice input lies in the motivation for using maps. Navigation is the primary purpose of using Google Maps for all interviewees. This does not mean they are not interested in exploring the map content with a screen reader. Some of them tried, failed, and never tried again. Throughout the interview sessions and interview data analysis process a constant theme of dissatisfaction among all participants was observed. Consequently, all participants were able to suggest creative ways to improve interactive map accessibility.

5.3 Limitations

Google Scholar was chosen as the only database source for the systematic literature review. It was decided because Google Scholar has the largest database, 389 million documents as of August 2018 [45] with easy accessibility, convenience, and advanced search query feature. But later study by Gusenbauer and Haddaway [46] showed Google scholar is not the most suitable database for systematic literature review. They reported Google Scholar search algorithm is "more concerned with tuning its first results page", making it more appropriate for the exploratory search for users interested in few initial search results. Yet the biggest issue with Google scholar is retrieval failure. Google Scholar has been found to report duplicate, repeated, and identical search results. This makes any future replication of the SLR search result impossible. Gusenbauer and Haddaway [46] later sympathized with the users of Google Scholar defending, users are usually guided towards Google Scholar for its convenience over strategic consideration, being unaware of its shortcomings.

Another potential criticism point is the decision to include "maps" as a title in the search result. Forcing the database to only show documents with "maps" on the title can be seen as a divisive decision but it was done because having "maps" as intext generates query return in a six-digit number which is not manageable to filter through.

The sample group was limited to individuals with severe low vision to total blindness. This sample group was enough to formulate accessible design suggestions for screen reader users. However, variable visual acuity is not the only user group who interact with digital maps, and including user groups with other visual impairment like color blindness or tunnel vision could have pointed out more accessibility issues with interactive maps and even propose accessibility improvements.

6 Conclusion

The purpose of this paper was to discover the Research gap and accessibility issues of interactive maps. The current study has revealed that despite providing a massive geographical information database with a vast array of features, interactive maps both in websites and mobile app platforms seem to fail in the accessibility department. Not only do these tend to be screen reader inaccessible, but often many visual accessibility requirements also fall short. The investigation indicates that these issues originate from the lack of interest from researchers towards richer digital maps accessibility and map maker's lack of effort towards universal design. Fixing these accessibility issues does not involve "going back to the drawing board and starting from scratch". Minor modification to the existing maps systems or adding a few extra steps for new systems can be sufficient enough to make interactive maps inclusive for substantially more user groups and reduce the gap between user ability and system demand. The Map is a staple artifact of human history that has been used for centuries and continued to be used and evolved with civilization. Cartography is witnessing a major technological migration as we move from physical medium to the virtual medium of information. Subsequently, this is introducing a vast number of diverse users with diverse abilities, environments, and situations. As engineers and researchers, it is our responsibility to ensure that all members of society are included in the technological migration process and not left out with outdated technology. The best way to ensure this is continuous research on map accessibility and adopting universal design in the map's development process.

References

1. Khamgaonkar, S., Vishwakarma, A., Warkar, N., Mishra, S., Selokar, P.R.: Navigation aid for blind people. Int. J. Adv. Res. Innov. Ideas Educ. 6, 152–154 (2020). https://doi.org/10.1007/s10846-011-9555-7
2. Cambridge Dictionary: accessibility. Cambridge Dictionary Online (2013)
3. Lawson, A.: Article 9: accessibility. In: The UN Convention on the Rights of Persons with Disabilities: A Commentary, pp. 258–286 (2018)

4. de Witte, L., Steel, E., Gupta, S., Ramos, V.D., Roentgen, U.: Assistive technology provision: towards an international framework for assuring availability and accessibility of affordable high-quality assistive technology. Disabil. Rehabil. Assist. Technol. **13**, 467–472 (2018)
5. Mace, R., et al.: The principles of universal design. The Center for Universal Design, North Carolina State University (1997). http://www.ncsu.edu/ncsu/design/cud/index.html. Accessed 9 Sept 2005
6. Story, M.F.: Principles of Universal Design. Universal Design Handbook (2001)
7. W3C World Wide Web Consortium Recommendation. https://www.w3.org/TR/WCAG21/
8. Story, M.F., Mueller, J.L., Mace, R.L.: The universal design file: designing for people of all ages and abilities (1998)
9. W.H.O.: World report on disability: World Health Organization. Geneva, Switzerland (2011)
10. Calle Jiménez, T., Luján-Mora, S.: Web accessibility barriers in geographic maps (2016)
11. Medina, J.L., Cagnin, M.I., Paiva, B.M.B.: Evaluation of web accessibility on the maps domain. In: Proceedings of the 30th Annual ACM Symposium on Applied Computing, pp. 157–162. ACM, Salamanca (2015)
12. Froehlich, J.E., et al.: Grand challenges in accessible maps. na (2019)
13. Lazar, J., Feng, J.H., Hochheiser, H.: Research Methods in Human-Computer Interaction. Morgan Kaufmann, Boston (2017)
14. Lewin, K.: Action research and minority problems. J. Soc. Issues **2**, 34–46 (1946)
15. Hayes, G.R.: The relationship of action research to human-computer interaction. ACM Trans. Comput.-Hum. Interact. (TOCHI) **18**, 15 (2011)
16. Cairns, P.E., Cox, A.L.: Research Methods for Human-Computer Interaction. Cambridge University Press, Cambridge (2008)
17. Pace, S.: A grounded theory of the flow experiences of web users. Int. J. Hum Comput Stud. **60**, 327–363 (2004)
18. Braun, V., Clarke, V.: Using thematic analysis in psychology. Qual. Res. Psychol. **3**(2), 77–101 (2006)
19. Moher, D., Tetzlaff, J., Tricco, A.C., Sampson, M., Altman, D.G.: Epidemiology and reporting characteristics of systematic reviews. PLoS Med. **4**, e78 (2007)
20. Moher, D., Liberati, A., Tetzlaff, J., Altman, D.: PRISMA group the PRISMA group preferred reporting items for systematic reviews and meta-analyses. PRISMA Statement BMJ **339**, b2535 (2009)
21. Lazar, J., Feng, J.H., Hochheiser, H.: Automated data collection methods. In: Research Methods in Human-Computer Interaction, pp. 289–299 (2010)
22. Blandford, A.: Semi-structured qualitative studies. Interaction Design Foundation (2013)
23. Kvitle, A.K.: Accessible maps for the color vision deficient observers: past and present knowledge and future possibilities (2017)
24. Hennig, S., Zobl, F., Wasserburger, W.: Accessible web maps for visually impaired users: recommendations and example solutions (2017)
25. Balciunas, A., Beconyte, G.: Research on user preferences for the functionality of web maps. In: Sluter, C.R., Cruz, C.M., Leal de Menezes, P. (eds.) Cartography - Maps Connecting the World, pp. 45–57. Springer, Cham (2015). https://doi.org/10.1007/978-3-319-17738-0_4
26. Kaklanis, N., Votis, K., Moschonas, P., Tzovaras, D.: HapticRiaMaps: towards interactive exploration of web world maps for the visually impaired. In: Proceedings of the International Cross-Disciplinary Conference on Web Accessibility, p. 20. ACM (2011)
27. Lohmann, K., Kerzel, M., Habel, C.: Verbally assisted virtual-environment tactile maps: a prototype system. In: Proceedings of the Workshop on Spatial Knowledge Acquisition with Limited Information Displays, pp. 25–30 (2012)
28. Poppinga, B., Magnusson, C., Pielot, M., Rassmus-Gröhn, K.: TouchOver map: audio-tactile exploration of interactive maps. In: Proceedings of the 13th International Conference on Human Computer Interaction with Mobile Devices and Services, pp. 545–550. ACM (2011)

29. Geronazzo, M., Bedin, A., Brayda, L., Campus, C., Avanzini, F.: Interactive spatial soni-fication for non-visual exploration of virtual maps. Int. J. Hum. Comput. Stud. **85**, 4–15 (2016)
30. Kaklanis, N., Votis, K., Tzovaras, D.: A mobile interactive maps application for a visually impaired audience. In: Proceedings of the 10th International Cross-Disciplinary Conference on Web Accessibility, p. 23. ACM (2013)
31. Schmitz, B., Ertl, T.: Making digital maps accessible using vibrations. In: Miesenberger, K., Klaus, J., Zagler, W., Karshmer, A. (eds.) ICCHP 2010. LNCS, vol. 6179, pp. 100–107. Springer, Heidelberg (2010). https://doi.org/10.1007/978-3-642-14097-6_18
32. Afzal, S., Maciejewski, R., Jang, Y., Elmqvist, N., Ebert, D.S.: Spatial text visualization using automatic typographic maps. IEEE Trans. Vis. Comput. Graph. **18**, 2556–2564 (2012)
33. Paladugu, D.A., Tian, Q., Maguluri, H.B., Li, B.: Towards building an automated system for describing indoor floor maps for individuals with visual impairment. Cyber-Phys. Syst. **1**, 132–159 (2015)
34. Calle-Jimenez, T., Luján-Mora, S.: Accessible online indoor maps for blind and visually impaired users. In: Proceedings of the 18th International ACM SIGACCESS Conference on Computers and Accessibility, pp. 309–310. ACM (2016)
35. Weir, R., Sizemore, B., Henderson, H., Chakraborty, S., Lazar, J.: Development and evaluation of sonified weather maps for blind users. In: Langdon, P., Clarkson, J., Robinson, P., Lazar, J., Heylighen, A. (eds.) Designing Inclusive Systems, pp. 75–84. Springer, London (2012). https://doi.org/10.1007/978-1-4471-2867-0_8
36. Su, J., Rosenzweig, A., Goel, A., de Lara, E., Truong, K.N.: Timbremap: enabling the visually-impaired to use maps on touch-enabled devices. In: Mobile HCI, pp. 17–26 (2010)
37. Brock, A., Truillet, P., Oriola, B., Picard, D., Jouffrais, C.: Design and user satisfaction of interactive maps for visually impaired people. In: Miesenberger, K., Karshmer, A., Penaz, P., Zagler, W. (eds.) ICCHP 2012. LNCS, vol. 7383, pp. 544–551. Springer, Heidelberg (2012). https://doi.org/10.1007/978-3-642-31534-3_80
38. Brock, A., Jouffrais, C.: Interactive audio-tactile maps for visually impaired people. In: ACM SIGACCESS Accessibility and Computing, pp. 3–12 (2015)
39. Taylor, B., Dey, A., Siewiorek, D., Smailagic, A.: Customizable 3D printed tactile maps as interactive overlays. In: Proceedings of the 18th International ACM SIGACCESS Conference on Computers and Accessibility, pp. 71–79. ACM (2016)
40. Simonnet, M., Morvan, S., Marques, D., Ducruix, O., Grancher, A., Kerouedan, S.: Maritime buoyage on 3D-printed tactile maps. In: Proceedings of the 20th International ACM SIGACCESS Conference on Computers and Accessibility, pp. 450–452. ACM (2018)
41. Zeng, L., Weber, G.: Exploration of location-aware you-are-here maps on a pin-matrix display. IEEE Trans. Hum.-Mach. Syst. **46**, 88–100 (2015)
42. Ducasse, J., Macé, M.J., Serrano, M., Jouffrais, C.: Tangible reels: construction and exploration of tangible maps by visually impaired users. In: Proceedings of the 2016 CHI Conference on Human Factors in Computing Systems, pp. 2186–2197. ACM (2016)
43. Rice, M.T., et al.: Crowdsourcing techniques for augmenting traditional accessibility maps with transitory obstacle information. Cartogr. Geogr. Inf. Sci. **40**, 210–219 (2013)
44. Bujari, A., Ciman, M., Gaggi, O., Marfia, G., Palazzi, C.E.: Paths: enhancing geographical maps with environmental sensed data. In: Proceedings of the 2015 Workshop on Pervasive Wireless Healthcare, pp. 13–16. ACM (2015)
45. Gusenbauer, M.: Google Scholar to overshadow them all? Comparing the sizes of 12 academic search engines and bibliographic databases. Scientometrics **118**(1), 177–214 (2018). https://doi.org/10.1007/s11192-018-2958-5
46. Gusenbauer, M., Haddaway, N.R.: Which academic search systems are suitable for systematic reviews or meta-analyses? Evaluating retrieval qualities of Google Scholar, PubMed, and 26 other resources. Res. Syn. Methods **11**, 181–217 (2020)

How Young People Living with Disability Experience the Use of Assistive Technology

Josefin Kristensen[✉] and Jessica Lindblom[iD]

University of Skövde, Box 408, 54128 Skövde, Sweden
jk@datavaxt.se

Abstract. In this paper, we investigate and analyze how young people that have motor impairments experience and have access to various forms of Information and Communications Technology (ICT). The aim is to gain a deeper understanding of how various assistive technologies (AT) mediate between young people and ICT systems, exploring how the user experience is perceived in practice. We apply the lens of the cultural-historical activity theory framework via a series of mainly qualitative explorations in Sweden, studying the user experience of ATs. They obtained findings reveal that there are many breakdowns in the interaction with ICT at the micro level, mainly due to limited fine motor impairments in the hands, which the used ICT - with or without AT - could not handle properly. Still the young adults perceived a positive UX in general. When comparing their parents' view on the access to and experience of ICT a more negative UX of the available ICT systems emerged from a macro level. The parents often mentioned the lack of appropriate ICT and AT as well as relevant support from the education institutions and other authorities. Some identified deficits framed from the perspective of sustainable accessibility are discussed from the societal level. Especially, the need of proper education that is enabled by credible ICT and AT, otherwise disabled young people are hindered to fully participate in society.

Keywords: User experience · Disability interaction · Motor impairment · Disability · Assistive technology · Activity theory

1 Introduction

This study focuses on how young people living with physical disabilities experience and have access to various forms of Information and Communications Technology (ICT), with or without the support of assistive technology (AT). The paper also considers the societal perspective, addressing how this user group is being excluded in society due to insufficient use of ICT.

Various forms of assistive technology (AT) have a fundamental role in the lives of people living with disabilities. Assistive technologies are devices and services that enable people with disabilities to get access to participation in society in general. Holloway [1] explains that currently AT is a neglected area in society. The industry has not systematically investigated, analyzed, developed, and evaluated what solutions that are

© Springer Nature Switzerland AG 2021
M. Antona and C. Stephanidis (Eds.): HCII 2021, LNCS 12768, pp. 250–268, 2021.
https://doi.org/10.1007/978-3-030-78092-0_16

considered suitable, feasible, and favorable for meeting the particular goals and needs of people living with disabilities [1–5]. As pointed out by Cranmer [6], the above described industrial approach has resulted in the production of compensating technologies rather than the development of technological solutions that enable inclusion and acceptance for diversity in society. Therefore, she stresses the need for AT designers and producers to take a much more user-centred perspective in AT design and production [6, 7]. However, Holloway [1] explains that the described way of working in the AT industry seems rather strange. She points out that it is generally acknowledged that if you design a product adapted to people living with disabilities, these products have later on become universal products, being beneficial in people's daily lives at large. Holloway [1] presents two prime examples of universal product that initially were designed for people living with disabilities: the typewriters and the commercial email clients.

Of particular interest in this paper is the development of various forms of ICT systems which have significantly altered the ways humans communicate and interact via the usage of digital artifacts, computers, and services. Hence, the usage of ICT is viewed as an enabler to participate in society. Ravneberg and Söderström [7] point out that this shift is not that evident in disabled people's life, because their access to ICT varies for several reasons. Ravneberg and Söderström [7] argue for the need of a new research approach that combines the perspectives of disability studies with science, technology and society studies. The motivation for such a research approach is to gain a deeper understanding of the complexity of AT, emphasizing the alignment between, AT, disability, and society. Although this take on disability has been around for a while, research on the technological side of the disability aspect has been limited. Some research exists that focuses on the materiality of socio-material practices [7], but we argue that much more work is needed that focuses on enabling people living with disability to use ICT to its full potential, studying to what extent ICT needs to be supplemented with what we here refer to as *digital assistive technology* (DAT), e.g., eye controls, built-in apps, customized computer mice and keyboards, and other kinds of input and output devices.

In the Disability Interaction (DIX) manifesto, it is emphasized that people living with disabilities as a specific user group with certain needs and requirements [1]. The main purpose of the DIX manifesto is to improve accessibility through an innovation process that includes people living with disabilities, developers and other professionals to co-create sustainable solutions to accessibility problems. Holloway [1] has formulated a research agenda consisting of six points, of which two points have inspired the work carried out in this paper. First, the need to "study the problem through in-the-wild studies" is stressed [1]. It is argued that the obtained results from more contextual inquiries can be used to inform innovative models of DIX. By investigating the troublesome usage of ICT for people living with disabilities, some unexplored terrain could be mapped out. Second, the need to "develop new theoretical models of DIX" is stressed. Hence, the obtained results from applying theoretical lenses on DIX could identify and formulate additional research questions and insights, bringing complementary points to the presented DIX manifesto. Moreover, applying the DIX Manifesto may provide relevant answers to the major question why people living with disabilities are excluded to a larger extent in today's society.

By putting these aspects altogether in this paper, we follow in the footsteps of a broadened view on the usage of DAT, inspired by Ravneberg and Söderström [7]. Our work is framed from *sustainable accessibility* perspective [8], investigating and analyzing to what extent the use of DAT has an effect on young adults living with motor impairments, and how their activities and participation in society are accomplished.

In this paper, we study to what extent young adults living with motor impairments have access to and experience various forms of ICT, with or without DAT. Hence, this study aims to gain a deeper understanding of how various DATs mediates between the users and ICT systems, exploring how the user experience of these DAT is perceived in practice. We apply the lens of the Cultural-Historical Activity theory framework (CHAT) via a series of mainly qualitative explorations to gain a deeper understanding of how the perception of disability shapes the positive or negative user experience of DATs [9–11]. The motivations for using CHAT is two-fold. CHAT is one of the most widely used theories in Human-Computer Interaction (HCI) [10] and is nowadays also applied within the User Experience Design (UXD) field [9, 11]. Hence, we argue that it also would be suitable to apply on the DIX manifesto. CHAT has a broadened unit of analysis, focusing on the mediating role of technology use while situating the user at the center of the social and material context. CHAT's focus on studying contradictions during technology mediation provides insights for development. However, the CHAT framework has to the best of our knowledge not been applied to study the user experience of DAT.

The rest of this paper is structured as follows. The background section presents the three areas of research this work builds upon:1) Disability and AT, 2) Sustainability, UXD, and DIX, and 3) the theoretical framework of CHAT. The following method section presents the research approach, the participants, as well as the data collection and data analysis used. Then the major findings are presented in Sect. 4, and the paper ends with a discussion and conclusions section in Sect. 5.

2   Background

2.1   Disability and Assistive Technology (AT)

It has been approximated that 200 million people experience considerable difficulties in their functioning [12, 13]. Moreover, it is anticipated that this number will increase into two billion in year 2050 [13]. It is estimated by the World Health Organization (WHO) that approximately 15% of the world's population are living with some kind of disability [12, 13], meaning that more than a billion humans have to face several challenges in their daily lives. The World Report on Disability [12] states that disability will be an even greater concern in the future because its prevalence will increase in the upcoming years. There are several reasons for this trend, e.g., a constantly ageing population increases the risk of disability in elderly people, the global increase in chronic health conditions, cancer and mental health disorders. It should be highlighted that there is an alarming global trend that people living with disabilities have poorer health outcomes, reach lower education achievements, offer less economic participation, and exhibit higher rates of poverty than people without disabilities [12]. The consequences for this situation are that people living with disabilities experience several kinds of barriers in accessing services and institutions that most persons for long have taken for granted, e.g., health services, education, public spaces and institutions, workplaces, employment, transport, and several kinds of ICT.

It should be pointed out that the concept disability refers to a broad, diverse and varied range of people, meaning that they could not be viewed as a homogenous group. According to the World Disability Report [12], disability is described as being "complex, dynamic, multidimensional, and contested" (p. 4) Ravneberg and Söderström (2017) [7] argue that traditionally disability studies have been dominated from a medical perspective, whereas other researchers have studied it from socio-cultural perspectives. Hence, there has been a shift from how to conceive disability, in which disability has "been recasted from a pathology or a lack, to societal barriers, attitudes and minority issues" (cited in [7], p. 2). During the last decades, the above shift from a more individual and medical perspective to a more structural and social perspective, has resulted in a social model rather than a medical model where people living with disabilities are considered as being disabled by society rather than by their bodies [12]. Hence, the concept of disability is an evolving concept, but instead of presenting a dichotomy of disability as on the one hand viewed as purely a medical condition, and on the other hand, as purely a social condition, it is emphasized that a more balanced view is needed. At the bottom line, persons living with disabilities often perceive problems that originate from their health condition, and therefore a more balanced view of disability is needed that incorporates both sides of the disability coin. In the world report on disability [12], the conceptual framework of disability considers functioning and disability as a dynamic interaction between contextual factors and health conditions, stressing both the individual and environmental perspectives. This so-called bio-psycho-social model embodies a feasible compromise between medical and social models. This means that disability functions as an umbrella term for various impairments, activity limitations, and restriction of participation that altogether refers to the negative aspects of the interaction between an individual (living with a health condition) and that individual's contextual factors (environmental and personal factors). It has been acknowledged that "disability results from the interaction between persons with impairments and attitudinal and environmental barriers that hinder their full and effective participation in society on an equal basis with others" (cited in [12], p. 4). This interactive characterization implies that being disabled is not an attribute of the person himself/herself. Work is carried out to improve the social participation in society for disabled persons. The increased participation can be accomplished by addressing the various kinds of social and physical barriers that persons living with disabilities face in their daily lives.

The International Classification of Functioning, Disability and Health [12] categorizes disability into three interrelated areas: i) impairments that are problems in body function or alterations in body structure such as blindness or paralysis. Of particular interest in this paper are motoric impairments that imply that persons have difficulties using, controlling, balance and coordinate their body as a whole, like the coordination of the head, torso, arms and legs. Impairments are related to ii) activity limitations that denotes several difficulties in executing certain activities, such as walking, writing, clothing, or eating. Finally, iii) participation restrictions refer to problems with various kinds of involvement in any area of a person's life, such as facing discrimination in employment, education, transportation, or public events as well as spaces. In other words, people living with disabilities encounter difficulties in the above areas to various extents.

Independent of being at home, at work, in school, or during play; various forms of *technology* play a crucial role in disabled people's lives; given that technologies affect the ways people consider disability, their experiences with disability and how disability is framed in society at large [7]. Alas, for the massive majority of people living with disabilities around the globe, the access to AT is neither available nor appropriate. An assistive product (AP) is characterized as "any product (including devices, equipment, instruments, and software), either specially designed or produced and generally available, whose primary purpose is to maintain or improve an individual's functioning and independence and thereby promote their wellbeing" [14]. Assistive technology is defined as "the application of organized knowledge and skills related to assistive products, including systems and services. Assistive technology is a subset of health technology" [14]. Throughout this paper, we will use the more common term of AT to refer both AP and AT. Examples of AT range from physical modifications in the built environment, including grab bars, ramps, and wider doorways to enable access to buildings, and physical mobility aids; e.g., wheelchairs, walkers, and prosthetic devices. It also includes hearing aids, cognitive aids, and computer software and hardware such as voice recognition programs, screen readers, gaze following programs, to devices, tools and utensils that help people to perform tasks such as eating, writing, cooking, and getting dressed. It is estimated by the World Health Organization (WHO) that merely 5–15% of people who would require AT in low- and middle-income countries are actually having access to it [12, 13, 15], although the United Nations' Convention on the Rights of Persons with Disabilities (CRPD) addresses many aspects highlighting the importance of AT already in 2006 [16]. To depict the severe situation even worse, the above raised constrains and difficulties are aggravated in less advantaged communities [12]. As pointed out by Khasnabis et al. (2015), CRPD [16] requires its members to commit efforts to promote access to AT, including ICT, which are recognized as *key facilitators* of inclusion and full participation for people living with disabilities in society at large. The origin to this problematic situation partly has its roots in stigma related to AT and partly in the lack of accessibility standards and laws that support the use of AT [1]. As a consequence of this stigma, nearly a third of the available assistive technology is abandoned by disabled people at an early stage of usage [1–3]. Indeed, several disability rights movements use the CRPD [16] to claim access to education, employment, emergency services and healthcare – all of which are enabled by ATs, including DATs.

A recent international initiative is the Global Cooperation on Assistive Health Technology (GATE) [17], launched by the WHO that indicates a larger focus on AT access globally [17]. The GATE's [17] goal is to achieve the articles in the CRPD [16] that deal with AT by increasing access to high-quality and affordable AT. As pointed out by Barbareschi et al. [18], a majority of people living with disabilities will regularly use more than one assistive technology or service in their daily life, although not explicitly mentioned in current research. Harniss, Raja and Matter [19] claim that having access to AT can be conceptualized as a human right, and a means to realize additional human rights.

2.2   Sustainability, User Experience Design, and DIX

In order to decrease the exclusion of people living with disabilities in society there are several European Union and United Nations directives that focus on sustainable development. For example, the 2030 Sustainable developmental Goals [19] aim to achieve long-lasting and better development prospects in order to improve and empower people living with disabilities worldwide. The ultimate goal is to remove the present barriers that to various extent hinder them to fully participate in the community, to increase their wellbeing, the inclusion in society, and to give them a voice in the public sphere. In addition, the 71st World Health Assembly (2018) has recognized the critical contribution of AT to promote inclusion and participation in all areas of society, and currently it is encouraging its members to develop policies, processes, and systems that are being able to provide AT via universal health or social services coverage [14].

A generic path to sustainability is to stimulate humans to change towards more sustainable practices and behaviors. A tentative way of considering sustainability for people with disabilities is to address the concept of *sustainable accessibility* [8]. Mayordomo-Martínez et al. [8] explain that sustainability can be viewed from two complementary perspectives concerning how the usage of ICT has a positive effect on sustainability. They argue that there is a difference between on the one hand "sustainable in ICT", and on the other hand "sustainable by ICT" [8]. The former perspective refers to whether the ICT device itself is sustainable, e.g., a sustainable design process was applied to develop a mobile app, in which the app could be energy-efficient and built from reusable materials having limited environmental impact. The latter perspective refers to whether using the mobile app has a positive effect on sustainability, e.g., the purpose of the app could be to support people living with motor impairments. We will focus on the latter perspective in this paper.

Furthermore, digitalization could be a driving force for enabling sustainable development by focusing on user and societal needs and motives when developing and using ICT. Ravneberg and Söderström [7] point out that the usability of products like DAT are not studied to a large extent, which relates to the field of user experience design (UXD) [20, 21] User experience design considers how to design for a positive user experience (UX) through a human-centered perspective in a product, service or interactive system [20, 21]. Grundgeiger et al. [22] provide several reasons why users' experience should be considered when interacting with technology in general. They emphasize that interaction *per se* is as an ongoing experience, implying that interaction with technology always has an associated UX, which is ubiquitously present whether or not it is explicitly addressed by researchers or designers [22]. Moreover, it is not enough to ensure pragmatic qualities, e.g., error reduction, effective performance, and reduced cognitive load when humans are interacting with technology. Much more focus needs to be put on hedonic qualities, e.g., satisfying humans' motives and psychological needs, including expectations, emotions, and well-being [23].

More recently, Holloway (2019) [1] identifies the need for a new 'undiscipline' within the disability-technology interaction field that goes beyond what currently is possible to achieve with accessibility and AT. She reformulates the disability challenge in her DIX manifesto, in which she views disability as a source of innovation and inspiration, pushing the boundaries of what is possible to achieve. She provides several examples where the challenges faced by disabled people are the driving force for technological developments, e.g., wheelchairs that are becoming part of the Internet of Things as well as the use of artificial intelligence to create a visual assistant for visually impaired humans. This ongoing change of mindset provides the foundation for her vision of AT interactions for disability innovation. She wants to explore what happens when diverse communities of humans are empowered to creatively outline and develop new ways and methods to realize accessibility and inclusion. Following the description of disability as bio-psycho-social model as formulated by WHO [12], the impairment only means that a person encompasses a different spectrum of capabilities than has been satisfied for in the design process. Foley and Ferri [24] stress if AT is only designed to overcome an impairment or a lack of a function, this way of working could unintentionally result in unexpected forms of social exclusion when AT is primarily designed for a disability rather than for humans. Instead, Holloway [1] propose a new lens, in which AT is considered as an extension of the human being, where AT is part of the structural couplings between the users and its material and socio-cultural surroundings. This way of reframing human-technology interaction for people living with disability originates from the more modern approaches for studying human cognition and technology mediated interaction, including embodied interaction and cognition, CHAT, and UXD [23]. Hence, the new paradigm of DIX aims for creating technologies to extend humans' capabilities, rather than specifically designing for coping with impairments. There are five DIX principles that aims at facilitating the creativity of diversity to stimulate a global movement, which will be beneficial for inclusion, innovation, and for the society. The principles range from openness to radically different solutions that are co-created, the acknowledgment that disability inclusion is a wicked problem [1]. A major issue in DIX's research agenda is how to design AT that has a positive impact on users' physical and psychological well-being. The presented roadmap consists of six actions plans that below are slightly modified from Holloway ([1], p. 49):

1. **Learning from what has been done** considers the aim to gain a better understanding of how to release successful technology dissemination to humans around the globe. This could be achieved by gathering disability innovators and global companies that develops inclusive platforms so they jointly could exchange knowledge and experiences to develop a common DIX framework.
2. **Creating a new body of knowledge with disabled people through the exchange of ideas around domain specific knowledge relevant to DIX**. The aim is to collaborate with colleagues from various disciplines such as digital health, neuroscience, international development, medical professionals, and engineering in order to tackle and reduce the knowledge gaps and barriers of DIX via an ongoing learning process from a holistic perspective.
3. **Studying the problem through in-the-wild studies testing co-created solutions with local communities**. The need to design and develop new and available ICT solutions, sensing technologies, as well as novel ways of interacting with technology to investigate and analyze UX in a broader range of contexts of usage. The obtained findings will be used to create new models of DIX.
4. **Developing mission statements from the collective UX for the global community to solve**. The purpose is to form an open-source community of researchers and

innovators that aims to work jointly with disabled people to develop research and design approaches that are based on user-centered interaction design approaches. The outcome could be more detailed empirical methods for assessing the usefulness and usability of newly developed DIX methods.

5. **Co-creating with disabled people curricula for DIX, which can be used globally to train people in how to become creators of new DIXs.** The intention is to create a global community of persons who could provide insights to the development of the curriculum for DIX. This community should be run by disabled persons, and the development of the DIX curriculum should be included into the R&D cycle, continually offering an exchange of acquired theoretical knowledge and empirical findings.

6. **Developing new theoretical models of DIX,** which are based on the pre-DIX disciplines of accessibility, inclusive design, and AT, improved by the theoretical and empirical developments in DIX. The obtained models function as a driving force to identify insights and formulate additional research questions.

To summarize, the DIX manifesto places disability in front of and in the center of the design process with the aim to create accessible new user-centered ICT solutions that will be beneficial and having a positive UX for all users.

2.3   Cultural-Historical Activity Theory (CHAT)

It is acknowledged that the CHAT has since the mid-1990s been widely and successfully applied in human-technology interaction, and it has been stressed that CHAT is the most canonical theoretical foundation for HCI research [10]. The CHAT enables framing of the human-technology interaction within a meaningful context, providing opportunities to better grasp the mutual ways technology affects – and is affected by – individuals and groups, as well as elucidating the underlying meaning of technology usage [10]. Law and Sun [9] view CHAT as specifically promising to shed light onto the understanding of UX by considers the users' motives and needs that are in turn shaped by the socio-cultural context where the users are situated in. The activity system model (ASM) [25] encompasses that the interactions between subject (user), object (context), and community (society level) are mediated by specific kinds of mediational means: mediating artefact and tools/instruments for the subject-object interaction (e.g., ICT, AT), rules (e.g., norms and legislation) for the subject-community interaction, and division of labor for the community-object interaction. Furthermore, the model includes the outcome of the activity system as a whole, namely, the transformation of the object that is generated by the activity in question into a suggested outcome. This way of visualizing highlights the continuous process of transformation and development over a time horizon (Fig. 1).

In the context of DATs for humans living with disabilities, the two seemingly competing motives, i.e., the use of DATs for inclusion in society and the reduction of the various barriers that hinder this participation can be viewed as inconsistencies within the system and discrepancies between the system and its environment. This could be studied from the notion of contradiction in an ASM, which is central part when analyzing an activity system. The search for *contradictions* within the system focuses on identifying any misfit within an element in the system, between elements in the system, or between

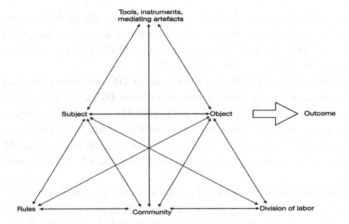

Fig. 1. The activity system model (ASM) modified from Engeström ([25], p. 63).

the current activity system in relation to other activity systems to which it is linked [25]. These contradictions are manifested as problems, interruptions, workarounds, or breakdowns. Therefore, it is of major importance to study contradictions from several perspectives, shifting focus from the actions of the individual to zooming out to the broader activity context and then zooming in again. The analysis of these breakdowns highlights the spontaneous and subjectively experienced problems on a micro level when using DATs for young people living with disabilities when using various forms of ICT in their daily lives. We are influenced by Law's and Sun's [9] view that usability and UX problems often occur when these relations are not well-aligned. The severity and scope of these breakdowns has an impact on the UX. Hence, CHAT can function as a diagnostic tool to identify alterations in UX that have roots in poorly designed AT and/or ICT usage.

3   Methods

3.1   Study Approach

The study included a series of semi-structured interviews and first-hand observations inspired by the "research in the wild" (RITW) approach [26]. The aim was to gain a deeper understanding to what extent young people living with motor impairments have access to and experience various forms of ICT, with or without SDAT. This particular user group was selected as the object of study because they face a situation in their lives when they soon need to act more independently, and where being able to use of ICT seems necessary to take part of society. The study was conducted in Sweden, and mostly qualitative data were collected.

Participants of the study varied depending on the data-collection technique used. For the semi-structured interviews, five (5) informants were recruited either via a survey or approached via a national organization (hereafter denoted 'the organization') that focuses on disability issues in the Swedish context. These informants were 1) a parent couple of a teenager who is in high school and has a motor impairment (referred to as R1 and R2 and they jointly participated in the interview), 2) a younger teenager who is in high school and has a motor impairment (UV1), 3) an older teenager who is in special school and has a motor impairment (UV2), and 4) a person having a management position in the organization (ORG).The youth of the parent couple is living with a disability that has a neurological effect on the whole body, consisting of a major mobility impairment in the legs and therefore uses a wheelchair. The fine motor skills in his fingers are also affected and the teenager has a fairly severe visual impairment that affects how he can use ICT and AT in practice, which makes it more challenging for him using these technologies due to impaired hand-eye coordination ability. Participant UV1 has a physical impairment where mainly the legs are affected (uses a wheelchair) but also the fine motor skills in the hands. He also has a visual impairment that affects how he can use ICT and DAT, which makes it more challenging for him using these technologies due to impaired hand-eye coordination ability. Both participants E1 and UV2 have fine and gross motor impairments that affect the whole body, which means that they use wheelchairs for longer movements. All young people were living at home with their parents.

For the observations carried out 'in the wild', the participants were UV2 and E1. UV2 video recorded four episodes of himself while interacting with ICT through DAT at home while playing a video game. The episodes lasted between 2–8 min. E1 was directly observed in the classroom at an elementary special school. The observation lasted for two lessons and included the interaction between E1 and the iPad via the DAT keyboard. Informed consents were approved for the observations from the parents of E1 and UV2. In the case of E1, an approval was made by the first author to only observe E1 by the teachers at the actual elementary school.

Materials. The interviews were conducted by phone and audio recorded via Mac Book Pro, voice memo. Neither recordings nor photographs were allowed to use for collecting data during observations in the special school. The video recordings in form of "mobile ethnography" performed by UV2 were viewed by the first author only. Sketches and field notes were made by the first author in order to not reveal the identities of the participants UV2 and E1 that were involved in the observations.

Data Collection and Analysis. The data collection was carried out by the first author and was conducted in Swedish. A cover letter including a description of the aim of the study, research ethics principles, and the questions were sent via email a few days before each interview. Prior to the interview with participants under the age of 18 years, written consent was given by the parents after they had received the cover letter. The interviews were conducted by phone and lasted for about 35–50 min each. The questions were framed from the respondent's perspective, focusing on: 1) how the parents experience their child's usage of ICT and DAT, 2) how the young people experience their usage of ICT and DAT, and 3) how the representative from the national organization considers the above issues from a societal perspective. Two additional themes addressed were what challenges the young people encounter when using DAT, and issues concerning sustainable accessibility. The audio-recordings were transcribed for further analysis, and later on translated to English for the included quotes in this paper.

Thematic analysis was carried out primarily by the first author, and the CHAT lens was used as an analytic tool in the interpretation of the collected data with the goal of identifying breakdowns and the perceived user experience of young peoples' usage of ICT and DAT in their daily lives. As the analysis work progressed, the emerging themes, the identified breakdowns, and their impact on the user experiences were repeatedly discussed and formulated among both authors to ensure that the interpretations were credible.

4   Findings

In the current section, the identified themes that emerged as a result from the analysis are presented.

4.1   Young people's Experience of ICT

It was revealed that various forms of ICT systems were used by the young people in their daily lives. They mostly used ICT at school and at home for doing assignments and homework, playing games, surfing on the internet, and keeping contact with family and friends via social media. The access to and the usage of DAT in practice show a somewhat negative picture/outcome, given that many problems occurred in direct interaction with ICTs or when it was mediated through DAT at the micro level. Some selected episodes from E1 and UV2 are described below to illustrate the activities in which many usability problems were identified.

The first episode is from a Swedish lesson, in which E1 did a Swedish assignment (activity) by reading a text on paper and answering as many of the six questions as possible before the lesson ended (action). The assignment was provided by the app called "Skolstil", and E1 used an iPad (object) via the mediating keyboard (DAT) for writing her answers (operations). However, while E1 wrote her answers, several breakdowns occurred. For example, E1 made a "double space" when she pressed a key, because she failed to press the space bar the first time she tried. Her motor impairment means that she is not always able to control how her finger hits the keys. Once when E1 needed support with the spelling, she did not receive any alternative words from the app, even though that function worked for the previous sentence she wrote. She therefore was obliged to ask the teacher for help to continue writing. Hence, E1 tried to get ahead in the activity but had to stop because she encountered a problem with the spelling. For this particular activity, it was of importance that the teacher was able to solve the usability problem caused by highlighted shortcomings in DAT, so E1 could complete her assignment.

The second episode is from the next lesson, in math, where E1 received a paper with 20 math problems that she should calculate with a pen (mediating artefact, AT). It appeared that E1 figured out the math problems effortlessly, but there was a breakdown in manually writing the answers due to E1's fine motor impairments to properly hold the pen. Hence, it took longer for her to write down the answer than solving the math problems. Eventually she became noticeably tired in her hand and shook it a couple of times. When E1 had completed 12 problems, she perceived that it was not possible to continue writing, and therefore she was forced to ask for help. It ended up that the assistant manually wrote down the answers she dictated. This means that the assistant then functioned as the mediating artefact (AT) instead of the pen. It was perceived that the identified breakdown is of high severity, since it may interrupt the activity completely, which means that E1 cannot finalize her math assignments if she continued to use the pen. She was then encouraged to solve some other math problems on her iPad. Since the app called "Nomp" were not supported by the keyboard as an AT, E1 used her fingers to navigate on the touch screen. E1 immediately figured out what to do and correctly calculated all the math problems, despite some noticeable breakdowns. For example, when E1 tried to swipe on the screen, the movement of her finger was not registered, and similarly when she pressed a button. A total of 12 swipes and 11 presses were not registered by the app. The main difference between using the app without DAT and writing with a pen was that she did not get as tired in the hand by pressing on the screen, although she encountered many breakdowns. However, she eventually got annoyed because of the recurrence of the problems. E1 explained that a tentative reason why she initially needed to do the math assignment via a pen, in spite of the fact that she had access to digital aids, was that she suspected that some teachers thought it was easier for them to assess the assignment on a paper-based format instead in a digital format. Her explanation could to some extent be verified when the teacher assessed all pupils' papers immediately at the end of the math lesson.

The third episode is provided by UV2 when he was using the app "Skolstil" sitting on a chair at his desk, using a custom keyboard (DAT), connected to an iPad (see Fig. 2. Left image). To enter the app, UV2 supported his hand on the iPad edge to keep the hand steady while entering the password with his right thumb. When he had opened the app, he wrote a sentence of three short words by the keyboard. To listen to the text, UV2 needed to press an audio symbol at the top right to get his sentence read out.

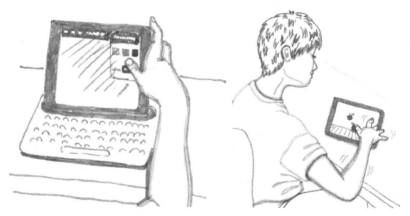

Fig. 2. The left image illustrates how UV2's hand is supported by the iPad's edge, while pressing the selected button with the thumb. The right image illustrates UV2 playing Fungu. (Images made by the first author).

He then deleted the sentence using the keyboard's backspace key, by supporting his hand on the iPad, pressing on the pencil symbol at the top right of the screen. Then a drop-down menu with color, size and guide options appeared. The available options were shown visually in color and a preview of the text size. Still supporting his hand on the iPad, he successfully changed the text size from medium to large, and then tried to select a guide option that was visible at the bottom on the screen, partly covered. He tried to swipe up the menu three times to reach the guides, but nothing happened. He then pressed on a gear symbol for "settings" with his thumb when the menu appeared for a few seconds but then disappeared. He then pressed it twice more while loosened the hand's grip on the iPad's edge. He made another grip with his hand on the right side of the iPad's edge as he clicked off the settings menu by pressing outside the checkbox once. He then rewrote same three-word sentence while a sound was made for each entered letter. In order to listen to the whole sentence, UV2 moved his hand upwards to support it on the iPad's upper edge, and then successfully pressed on the sound symbol, and the whole sentence is read out. He then pressed once on the pen symbol, but nothing happened. He then changed the hand's position and pressed once more, and now the menu was displayed. To reach the size option, which was placed in the center of the screen, UV2 supported his hand with two fingers at the iPad's top edge and with two fingers at the left edge, and then pressed his thumb once on the "small size" option on the screen. When the size menu appeared, he needed to alter his grip on the screen, to select "middle size", and while he changed his grip of the iPad, the hand's unintentionally moved the Ipad to the left side of the keyboard because the recess where the iPad was put is too wide. He then changed the size to "large" and wanted to close the menu and pressed on it, but no response was received since the menu was partly situated outside the screen area. He made another try by clicking outside the menu with his thumb and succeeded. He then placed his hand on top of the iPad, returned to the "settings" by tapping on the menu once with his thumb. His intention was to select the option "reading speed" by swiping twice with his thumb, but nothing happened. The he tried to leave by clicking once with his thumb which missed the correct area, and then he gave up. To summarize, during this interaction, five kinds of breakdowns were identified: 1) the guides could not be accessed under the pen menu, 2) it was not possible to swipe, 3) the option reading speed could not be displayed under the settings menu, 4) the system did not register the pressure made by the thumb, and 5) removal of the menu by thumbprint took place on the "wrong" side and the system did not register the pressure. This means that the breakdowns can be categorized into two types: 1) improperly designed menus that result in unnecessary demand on fine motoric ability, and 2) the lack of registering pressure from the thumb on the touch screen, which could be linked to UV2's fine motor limitation in his hands, which caused the thumb to end up at an angle, and therefore the pressure might not be perceived. It should be noted, however, despite the above breakdowns, UV2 expressed that he has a positive user experience of the system.

The final selected episode, is when UV2 played a game called "Fungu", which is a math app with rather trivial cognitive tasks. However, it requires that the user has well-functioning fine motor skills in their hands because the user should press down as many fingers as there are fruits visible on the screen (see Fig. 2, to the right). He explained that this game is difficult for him to play on the iPad, since it is not mediated by any DAT. To just provide some short excerpts from these major findings of the Fungu interaction, it was revealed that UV2 successfully launched the Fingu app and completed 5 out of 10 tasks at the first level of the game that took 1 min. When he moved the fingers outside the screen play, a hand appeared on the screen twice that he had to click on in order to make it disappear. Then the first game run was over. He replayed the first level of the game, which took 1.5 min. This time, he reached 19 out of 20 tasks and thus succeeds with the actual level. However, at three times he pressed outside the screen and was therefore forced to leave the game, which created a lot of frustration. During the second round, the "hand" appeared six times. When the game session was over, he shook his hand. In total, 17 breakdowns were identified while playing Fungu. Six breakdowns were due to the fine motor impairments in his hand, which hindered him from pressing the correct number of fingers at the same time, even though he knew how many fingers he should use. He uttered *"I get annoyed and angry because when I take five fingers it jumps out of the game."*

UV2's eight breakdowns were caused by him pressing outside the playing field, and therefore a text box appeared depicting a hand that explained that he had pressed outside the playing field, and three severe breakdowns happened because he pushed outside the screen, so the app closed down. This means that many of these breakdowns are due to the fact that the game is designed to be managed via fine motor movements in the hand, but since UV2 has problems with precisely the fine motor movements, many usability problems occur which in the end create a lot of frustration in UV2. He expresses his frustration several times at the end of the second round, when he is thrown out of the game in the middle of the game round. He is noticeably tired in his hand and shook it at the same time as he uttered that he has pain in the hand. He explained that he got stressed because the game should be carried out on time and that his fingers do not act the way he intends. Hence, his negative UX of the game is made very clear.

Zooming out from the detailed micro level, it was revealed that the mobile phone was a popular item to use, to keep in touch with friends and classmates. UV1 explained that she used the mobile phone when she went to school, e.g., being able to visit Instagram, Youtube, Facebook, and Snapchat during breaks, but the screen is too small for her to perceive all the details due to her visual impairment. UV1 said that she uses a Snapchat group, where she could talk to her assistants, but she did not use Snapchat to keep in touch with classmates, since they talk to her when they meet face-to-face. It appeared that her mobile phone was often used without any DAT. For example, she explained that she used her mobile phone a lot at home and where she has a DAT, in the form of a keyboard, but the keyboard is awkward to use in practice if you want to do something quickly, even if it is actually easier to type with it than to use your fingers on the phone. She expressed: *"I prefer to use the phone because it is light and not so big so you can reach all the buttons. I have a keyboard for my phone as well, but I only use it if I have to type something very long. But otherwise, I do not use it. It's easier with buttons like that, but [laughs] you can't bring it out and you take your mobile instead".*

A surprising finding is how often the (human) assistant was used as the mediating AT. Many of the participants provided examples of how convenient it is when the assistant became the assistive device itself. For example, some participants played games. One of them explained that video games are the most difficult device to use because they do not have any DAT for it, instead he uses assistants as a mediating artifact to, e.g., press more buttons simultaneously on the game controller. Another example is when UV1 expressed the needed support from the assistants both at school and at home, uttering: *"They [the assistants] are arms and legs, but not thought"*. Although assistants can be seen as a mediating artifact that provides a positive user experience when using technology and malfunctioning DAT, there are also some negative user experiences associated with assistants as mediating artefacts. An important aspect identified is how to maintain the personal integrity when an assistant "knows everything about oneself". This situation could be especially sensitive for teenagers who strive to free themselves from their parents but who are not sure of "whose side" the assistants are on, whether they are maintaining the young adult's privacy or breaking it and leaking private information to the parents. UV2 explained how it feels having assistants nearby almost all the time, and she sometimes avoided to use ICT for private purposes if she suspected that the assistant can see what she is doing: *"Sometimes it's hard if they are involved and then you have to do one thing, even though I want them not to see what I am doing. If they are not going to see what I do, then maybe I will do it later when they are not working, that I will do it another time"*.

Although young people in general experienced a positive UX, several problems were revealed when using DAT in practice at micro levels that did not last for that long time intervals, although the breakdown several times were of high severity. The negative UX can mainly be explained by the fact that they have a greater physical disability which means that they needed more support from assistants, where feasible DAT was lacking, which made their use of ICT limited. When these usability problems occur, the participants have difficulty coping with the problem on their own. But an assistant is also a person, who works in different ways and has different personalities. Being so close to another person requires that you can familiarize yourself with and respect the personal integrity of the person you serve as assistant to. Thus, there is a risk that the young adult feels that the personal integrity is not fully respected.

4.2   Comparison of Young people's Experience and Their Parents' Experience of ICT Usage

To complement the young people's experienced UX of ICT and AT, some additional data were analyzed from a parent couple and a representative in the management of a national Swedish disability organization. It was revealed that the parent couple focused a lot on the contextual factors, broadening the analysis to the macro level. For example, they pointed out that the ICT used at home generally provided a positive user experience, e.g., when the teenager used an iPad, iPhone, laptop with touch screen and Wii (video games) but also sensor-controlled lights. In the home, the parents have largely been responsible for adaptations that they have sorted out themselves, mostly for entertainment; such as computer games, Wii video games and apps, but also for social media such as Snapchat and Instagram. Additional ICT systems that provide a positive user experience are sensor-controlled lamps and lamps that are voice-controlled via the mobile, which allowed the teenager to move with his wheelchair in the house without having to turn the light on or off by pressing buttons, which makes the teenager more independent. The parents believed that voice control would be a good adaptation in the homes of the future and also that more several technologies can be connected to, for example, turn on the TV. A tentative explanation for why the parents looking more at the contextual factors is that it is difficult for them to imagine what it will be like for their teenager, a few years into the future, when becoming a young adult. One of the parents expressed: *"When the teenager was younger, I wanted to look very far ahead... I probably do not really have that far perspective right now because I cannot really think that far ahead. Because it feels like I have to take what is a little bit closer in time right now first. It can also be defensive on my part."*

A recurring theme is how the perceived lack of effort and resources from the school and habilitation result in negative user experiences. The parents expressed that they have to fight for their child's rights, regarding the identified need of support for their child. The focus is on the gap between their expectations on the support they should receive for the teenager's schooling and from habilitation, compared to how it worked in practice. The recurring problems of ICT and AT that were mentioned included, 1) the difference in the desire to learn about ICT and AT from staff, 2) the amount of available ICT and AT used in schooling, and 3) the gaps not filled by school or habilitation are compensated by the parents themselves. An example was difference in the willingness to learn new ICT and AT among school staff, which means that it is the child's teaching that suffers, and more responsibility to handle the technology and AT is placed on the pupil and the parents. As a consequence, the pupils perceive the pressure to teach the school staff about the technology, while when the responsibility for learning should actually be placed on the staff. The representative from the national organization complements the picture expressed above. He expressed as follows how he views the competence in schools and habilitation: *"There are those people who are real enthusiasts in their professions, but in general I would say that no, it is far too low competence. Crazy too low!"*.

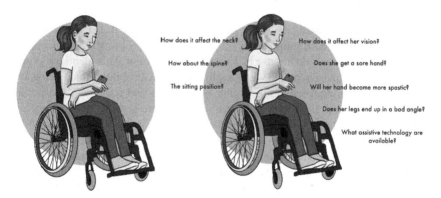

Fig. 3. The left image illustrates how a young person views the use of ICT at the micro level. The right image illustrates how parents view the young person's use of ICT at the macro level. (Images made by the first author).

To summarize, the obtained findings revealed that there are identified problems at both micro and macro levels considering how young adults and their parents experience ICT and AT in practice. Young adults were generally more positive than their parents, which can be explained by parents focusing more on the overall context (macro level) of their child's use of ICT, while the children focus on how it works from their self-experienced perspective (micro level), and therefore experience that it works sat-isfactorily (see Fig. 3). From this perspective, the mediating role of the assistants can partly be viewed as a general compensation of on the one hand, schools' reluctance to learn and use ICT and AT. On the other hand, the available AT is in some cases awkward to use, neither being efficient or effective and does not satisfy the needs of the end-users. IN other words, the assistants try to bridge the shortcomings, which may explain why the young people often perceive a positive user experience of the ICT systems.

4.3 Identified Deficits of Sustainable Accessibility

By zooming out to the societal level, it was revealed there were large differences to what extent the schools' staff provided relevant ICT and AT for young people with motor impairments. This identified problems seemed to start as early as in primary school and continue to follow the children through their education. An illustrative example comes from the representative for the organization: "*What I think happens in school... and it has been told by other parents, ... that you enter the school world with a picture of... you have knowledge of your disability, but you do not always have knowledge of which obstacles it will create for one. ... Instead of [the school] taking the compensatory role seriously and seeing that; Yes, but this is a student with these difficulties, then we will compensate for it as much as possible with these efforts. So, you have given up before you have even tried. It's MY picture... and it's a picture I know I share with a lot of parents who have children with disabilities, you are fighting yourself blue but it does not help*".

If the above picture represents some aspects of the reality in the Swedish context, this may have far-reaching consequences for children having motor impairments due to the increased risk of being excluded from various forms of ICT, but also excluded to fully participate in education. From the interviews and observations, it appeared that especially the schools do not use ICT to a sufficient extent. This identified problem demonstrates the stigma associated with people living with disabilities that Holloway [1] pointed out. As a consequence of this stigma, both parents and young adults experience that it is their responsibility to solve the problems that are actually mandatory for the school and the habilitation systems to handle, especially in Sweden. This means that both parents and young adults are systematically overlooked. The consequence of the identified challenges as well as usability and UX problems that occur at micro and macro levels is that these pupils have a much higher risk of not finishing school and thus not reaching higher education, increasing the risk of not finding meaningful employment.

5   Discussion and Conclusions

We intended to study to what extent young adults living with motor impairments have access to and experience various forms of ICT, with or without DAT. Hence, this study aimed to gain a deeper understanding of how various DATs mediates between the users and ICT systems, exploring how the user experience of these DAT is perceived in practice. The major contributions of this work are a portrayal at both micro and macro levels, which then are addressed to the societal level from an accessible sustainability perspective.

Hopefully, our study provides a promising but small step in contributing to DIX's action plan [1], because we have used CHAT as a theoretical lens to identify UX problems at both the micro level and macro level in practice.

We are aware of the limitations of our study with a rather small sample of observations and interviews, but due to the pandemic situation, we were not allowed to perform the planned research in the wild approach at an organization that runs a daycare centre for young people with motor impairments and other forms of disability.

In our future work we would like to continue on the path set out in this study, by looking at other kinds of ICT systems and DAT. However, it is evident that this is a prioritized research area, and much more research is needed to mapping out the terrain of disability interaction: If the issues and the challenges that we have raised in this paper are addressed, as well as these addressed by Halloway [1] in the DIX manifesto, and we believe that they can be, there is great reason to be optimistic that what we know from this minor study of how DAT and the lack of DAT is experienced can be successfully applied to the DIX manifesto. As a result, DIX will benefit and the young people living with disabilities will benefit even more.

Acknowledgments. The authors wish to cordially thank all the participants for their time and effort that have contributed to our study. Moreover, peers, family, and friends who have provided valuable support during the process. We also want to thank our colleague Erik Lagerstedt for valuable comments on earlier drafts of this paper.

References

1. Holloway, C.: Disability interaction (DIX): a manifesto. Interactions **26**(2), 44–49 (2019)
2. Abascal, J., Nicolle, C.: Moving towards inclusive design guidelines for socially and ethically aware HCI. Interact. Comput. **17**(5), 484–505 (2005)
3. Goggin, G., Newell, C.: The business of digital disability. Inf. Soc. **23**(3), 159–168 (2007)
4. Opie, J.: Technology today. Int. J. Disabil. Dev. Educ. **65**(6), 649–663 (2018)
5. Weber, H.: Providing access to the internet for people with disabilities: short and medium term research demands. Theor. Issues Ergon. Sci. **7**(5), 491–498 (2006)
6. Cranmer, S.: Disability, society and assistive technology. Disabil. Soc. **33**(9), 1539–1540 (2018)
7. Ravneberg, B., Söderström, S: Disability, Society and Assistive Technology. Routledge, London (2017)
8. Mayordomo-Martínez, D., et al.: Sustainable accessibility: a mobile app for helping people with disabilities to search accessible shops. Int. J. Environ. Res. Publ. Health **16**(4), 620 (2019)
9. Law, E.L..-C, Sun, X.: Evaluating user experience of adaptive digital educational games with AT. Int. J. Hum.-Comput. Stud. **70**(7), 478–497 (2012)
10. Rogers, Y.: HCI Theory. Morgan & Claypool, San Rafael (2012)
11. Lindblom, J., Alenljung, B.: The ANEMONE: theoretical foundations for UX evaluation of action and intention recognition in human-robot interaction. Sensors **20**(15), 4284 (2020)
12. World Health Organization: World Report on Disability (2011). https://www.who.int/disabilities/world_report/2011/report.pdf. Accessed 19 Jan 2021
13. World Health Organization: WHO global disability action plan 2014–2021 (2015). https://www.who.int/disabilities/technology/en/. Accessed 19 Jan 2021

14. Smith, R O., et al.: Assistive technology products: a position paper from the first global research, innovation, and education on assistive technology (GREAT) summit. Disabil. Rehabil. Assist. Technol. **13**(5, SI), 473–485 (2018)
15. World Health Organization: Global priority research agenda for improving access to high-quality affordable assistive technology (2017). https://apps.who.int/iris/handle/10665/254660. Accessed 19 Jan 2021
16. United Nation General Assembly: Convention on the Rights of Persons with Disabilities (2006). https://www.un.org/development/desa/disabilities/convention-on-the-rights-of-persons-with-disabilities.html. Accessed 19 Jan 2021
17. World Health Organization: Global Cooperation on Assistive Health Technology (GATE) (2015). http://www.who.int/phi/implementation/assistive_technology/phi_gate/en/. Accessed 19 Jan 2021
18. Barbareschi, G., et al.: Bridging the divide. In: Tiago Guerreiro, T., Nicolau, H., Moffatt, K. (eds.) The 22nd International SIGACCESS Conference on Computers and Accessibility, pp. 1–13. ACM, New York, United States (2020)
19. Harniss, M., Raja, D.S., Matter, A.: Assistive technology access and service delivery in resource-limited environments: introduction to a special issue of disability and rehabilitation: assistive technology. Disabil. Rehabil. Assist. Technol. **10**(4), 267–270 (2015)
20. Hartson, R., Pyla, P.: The UX Book. Morgan Kaufmann, Amsterdam, The Netherlands (2018)
21. Preece, J., Rogers, Y., Sharp, H.: Interactions Design: Beyond Human-Computer Interaction, 4th edn. John Wiley, New York (2015)
22. Grundgeiger, T., Hurtienne, J., Happel, O.: Why and how to approach user experience in safety-critical domains: the example of health care. Hum. Factors: J. Hum. Factors Ergon. Soc. (2020)
23. Lindblom, J., Kolbeinsson, A., Thorvald, P.: Narrowing the gap of cognitive and physical ergonomics in DHM through embodied tool use. In: Hanson, L., Högberg, D., Brolin, E. (eds.) DHM2020: Proceedings of the 6th International Digital Human Modeling Symposium. Advances in Transdisciplinary Engineering, vol. 11, pp. 311–322. IOS Press, Amsterdam (2020)
24. Foley, A., Ferri, B.: Technology for people, not disabilities: ensusring access and inclusion. J. Res. Spec. Educ. Needs **12**(4), 192–200 (2012)
25. Engeström, Y.: Learning by Expanding, 2nd edn. Cambridge University Press, New York (2015)
26. Rogers, Y., Marshall, P.: Research in the Wild. Morgan & Claypool Publishers, San Rafael (2017)

Game Accessibility: Taking Inclusion to the Next Level

Carme Mangiron[✉] [iD]

Universitat Autònoma de Barcelona, Bellaterra, Spain
carme.mangiron@uab.cat

Abstract. This paper provides an overview of game accessibility. It describes what game accessibility is and highlights the need to combine usability and adaptability, as a "one-size-fits-all" approach is not possible due to the interactive and dynamic nature of the video game medium and the array of (dis)abilities different users may have. The main accessibility barriers different groups of users face are also presented. Then, the main focus shifts to the current state of the art in game accessibility, including existing guidelines and research carried out in this field. Finally, future perspectives are outlined, emphasizing the need for a user-centred approach and for collaboration between users, academia, and the industry.

Keywords: Video games · Game accessibility · User-centred design

1 Introduction

Video games have become one of the preferred leisure options for many people around the world, who not only play games to entertain themselves and enjoy new experiences, but also to learn new things, for therapeutic reasons and to socialize with others. The video game industry has also thrived during the global crisis caused by the COVID-19 pandemic [1], as people were forced to be in lockdown and many resorted to games to pass the time, have fun and have social contact with others when playing online. However, video games are still not accessible to persons with disabilities, who account for one billion people, that is, 15% of the world population [2] and who are therefore excluded from this form of entertainment and social phenomenon.

This paper presents an overview of current and future trends in game accessibility. First, a definition of game accessibility is provided, and the main accessibility issues are outlined. Next, the current state of the art in game accessibility is described, including existing guidelines and current research. The paper concludes outlining future perspectives in game accessibility and highlighting the need for collaboration between users, industry and academia.

© Springer Nature Switzerland AG 2021
M. Antona and C. Stephanidis (Eds.): HCII 2021, LNCS 12768, pp. 269–279, 2021.
https://doi.org/10.1007/978-3-030-78092-0_17

2 What is Game Accessibility?

Game accessibility is an emerging field, both from an academic and an industry perspective, although in recent years important advances have taken place, mainly due to the work carried out by the International Game Developers Game Accessibility Special Interest Group, which was established in 2003 with the objective of "making games accessible for all, regardless of impairments or other limitations" [3]. Initially, members of this group defined "game accessibility" as "the ability to play a game even when functioning under limiting conditions. Limiting conditions can be functional limitations, or disabilities – such as blindness, deafness, or mobility limitations" [4]. This definition encompasses not only persons with disabilities, but also those who due to a given situation cannot hear the audio of a game, for example, because they are in a noisy environment and need subtitles to understand the dialogues in an in-game cinematic. The definition also includes younger, older or novice players who may experience difficulties when playing for the first time.

More recently, the Game Accessibility SIG has moved away from the view of disability as a "limiting condition" and instead applies a social model of accessibility by talking about "disabling situations". They refer to accessibility as a means to overcome the unnecessary barriers that sometimes occur when there is a mismatch between a person's ability and the barriers they find:

> Disabling situations occur due to mismatches between a person's abilities and the barriers in what they're interacting with. Many of those barriers are unin-tended, and unnecessary. Accessibility means avoiding these unnecessary barriers [3].

A key difference between game accessibility and accessibility to traditional media, such as movies, series and documentaries, lies in the interactive and dynamic nature of games. In fact, game accessibility shares features in common with web and software accessibility because of its interactive nature and the more active role the user has to adopt. A "one-size-fits-all" approach to game accessibility does not seem possible due to the wide array of different needs players may have when interacting with the game. Therefore, game accessibility should combine usability with adaptability in order to make games available to the widest possible number of users, regardless of their abilities [5]. Game hardware should be compatible with assistive technologies, such as screen reading software, text-to-speech solutions and one-switch controllers, to name but a few. Game software should be designed so that it can be customised to cater for the needs of different users, for example, by including subtitles for all textual assets in the game and audio for all visual and textual elements.

3 Accessibility Issues

Most video games are designed for entertainment purposes, and even games with therapeutic and educational purposes must provide some fun and involve a challenge in order to engage players. According to game accessibility experts, games cannot be fully accessible to everybody, because "the definition of 'game' requires some kind of challenge, which will inevitably exclude someone" [3]. However, game accessibility should contribute to making games accessible to as many people as possible by presenting them with challenges that are fun and can be overcome. It is not a matter of making a game easier or limiting the experience it offers, but a matter of designing a game in a way that it can be customised to provide a different, but equally engaging experience to people with different (dis)abilities [3, 6].

The Accessible Games website [6], powered by the Able Gamers charity, has developed an Accessible Player Experiences (APX) model, addressed to game developers, with the objective of making the experience of playing a video game available to players with disabilities by including a variety of design options. In order to be able to play a game, the first essential step is to be able to access the game, that is, users need to "be able to sense (see/hear/feel) the output of the game and to provide input to the game (click/tilt/speak)" [6]. Once players can access the game, they need to interact with it, by facing the challenges posed by the game, such as climbing a mountain or solving a puzzle. Players need to be able to adapt the game in different ways so that it is not impossible to overcome such challenges [6]. Therefore, developers need to adapt the challenges in a game to different types of users, so that they can all have an engaging experience in their own way. If players can access the game and face the challenges it presents, then they can have an accessible player experience that caters for their needs while providing them with an enjoyable gaming experience [6].

Yuan, Folmer and Frederick [7] identify three main accessibility barriers due to video games interactive nature:

1. Users cannot receive stimuli, be it visual, auditory or tactile. For example, blind users will not be able to process any stimuli that is only presented in visual form, including text and images. Deaf and hard of hearing users, on the other hand, will not be able to receive the output of the game that is only audio-based, such as dialogues, sound effects, music, songs and game tutorials. Users with motor impairments may not be able to feel the haptic feedback provided by the game controller.
2. Users are not able to determine the appropriate response to perform an action required to advance in the game. This can be due to the fact that players do not receive the stimuli from the game or because it is too complex to process, as in the case of cognitive disabilities.
3. No input can be provided to the game once it has been decided what action to perform because the interface device between the player and the video game cannot be manipulated. This mainly affects players with motor disabilities and players with cognitive disabilities, who may not be able to use complex controls.

The following table, adapted from Bierre [8] and Mangiron [5], summarizes the main accessibility barriers different types of users face when playing video games (Table 1).

Table 1. Main accessibility barriers in video games (adapted from Bierre [8] and Mangiron [5])

Types of players	Accessibility issue
Players with cognitive disabilities	Level of difficulty, which leads to comprehension and usability problems Lack of time to read a message or make decisions Lack of a tutorial mode Lengthy tutorials and manuals
Players with hearing disabilities	Audio-only based information, such as dialogues, sound effects, music Solving tasks or playing mini games only based on sound
Players with visual disabilities: Blind players Low vision players Colour-blind players	Information only provided visually, including images and text Small fonts, icons, objects, etc Colour-based puzzles, missions and mini games
Players with reduced mobility	Use of controllers, keyboards Lack of support of alternative input devices High speed of some games

The above-mentioned barriers affect users differently and are also applicable to young and elderly players, as well as novice players. Depending on their (dis)ability, users will have to resort to different strategies to be able to play a game, such as playing with somebody's help or using assistive technology if available. Even if users can play by themselves, if the challenges posed by the game are too difficult, this will result in a reduced gameplay experience, which can also lead to frustration. Another possibility consists of playing games which have been specifically designed for a group of users, such as audio games for blind players or one-switch games for people with mobility impairments. However, users with disabilities should also have the opportunity to enjoy the social aspect of video games, playing mainstream games with their friends and families in order to foster their social inclusion. Therefore, a design which allows a high degree of customization to match an array of users' needs should be the ultimate goal of game accessibility. Access to culture is a human right, and entertainment, such as video games, can be considered culture, so it is therefore essential to try to guarantee game accessibility for all.

4   Current State of the Art in Game Accessibility

Most mainstream games are still largely inaccessible for persons with disabilities, although the situation has improved considerably in recent years. The industry and academia are paying more attention to game accessibility and users are becoming more vocal regarding their needs. There are also specialized blogs, websites and YouTube channels that analyse the accessibility features of mainstream video games, such as Can I Play That?, which is run "by disabled gamers for, disabled gamers" [9] and Game

Accessibility Nexus.[1] The IGDA Game Accessibility SIG, which includes industry and academic members, has a dedicated website, where they include information about resources, events, legislation, etc. There are also events and conferences dedicated to game accessibility, such as the roundtables at the Game Developers' Conference, the Game Accessibility Conference,[2] which is the only industry event exclusively dedicated to game accessibility, and the Fun for All Conference,[3] organised by the TransMedia Catalonia Research Group at Universitat Autònoma de Barcelona, which is the only academic conference dealing with the topic.

There are also a number of guidelines for developing accessible games. For example, the Game Accessibility SIG have developed a series of guidelines addressed to developers, to help them make their games more accessible. The guidelines are available in a stand-alone website and are divided in three levels: basic, intermediate and advanced, based on how easy or difficult they are to implement and how many users they can benefit [10]. The guidelines for each level are divided into six categories: motor, cognitive, vision, hearing, speech, and general [10]. Examples of games which have applied a specific guideline are also provided, so that developers can view how the guidelines have been previously applied in game design.

The basic guidelines are "easy to implement, wide reaching and apply to almost all game mechanics" [10]. There are 30 basic guidelines, which include issues such as:

1. Allowing controls to be remapped and reconfigured (motor).
2. Using simple and clear language (cognitive).
3. Providing high contrast between the text or the user interface (UI) and the back-ground (visual),
4. Ensuring no essential information is provided by sound alone (hearing).
5. Ensuring that speech input is not required and is included only as a supplementary or alternative input method (speech).
6. Offering a wide choice of difficulty levels and information about accessibility features on package or website and in-game (general).

The intermediate guidelines require more planning and resources and are not suitable for all game mechanics, but are beneficial to many people and contribute to "good game design" [10]. There are 65 guidelines, including, for example:

1. Supporting more than one input device (motor).
2. Including in-game help, guidance and tips (cognitive).
3. Using surround sound (vision).
4. Ensuring subtitles/captions can be turned on before any sound is played (hearing).
5. Supporting text chat as well as voice chat for online multiplayer (speech).
6. Including assist modes such as auto-aim and assisted steering (general).

The advanced guidelines require complex adaptations and are only applicable to certain game mechanics. They also require more budget and specialist knowledge and

---

[1] See https://caniplaythat.com and https://www.gameaccessibilitynexus.com.

[2] See https://www.gaconf.com/conference/.

[3] See https://jornades.uab.cat/videogamesaccess/.

are aimed at a specific niche audience [10]. There are 25 different guidelines, that include, for example:

1. Providing very simple control schemes that are compatible with assistive technology devices, such as switches or eye tracking (motor).
2. Providing pre-recorded voice-overs for all text, including menus and installers (cognitive).
3. Using screen reader support, including menus and installers (vision).
4. Providing signing (hearing).
5. Using symbol-based chat, such as smiley icons (speech).
6. Including real time text-to-speech transcription (general).

Some of the guidelines in this level are included in more than one category, as they can be useful for various types of users. For example, providing pre-recorded voice-overs for all text is included both in the cognitive and in the vision categories. Using symbol-based chat is a guideline for the cognitive, speech and hearing categories.

In fact, accessibility features can often benefit more than one group of users and ideally, all options should be made available, so that players can select those that suit them best.

It is important to highlight that in all three levels (basic, intermediate and advanced), in addition to the motor, cognitive, vision, hearing and speech categories there is a "general" category. For the "general category" the emphasis is placed in providing information about accessibility features and in eliciting users' feedback. In the basic category, it is recommended to solicit accessibility feedback from users. In the intermediate category, it is advised to "include some people with impairments amongst play-testing participants" [10], while in the advanced category this is extended to include "every relevant category of impairment (motor, cognitive etc.) amongst play-testing participants, in representative numbers based on age/demographic of target audience" [10]. This user-centred approach to game accessibility is framed within the United Nations approach, summarized in the motto "Nothing about us without us" and it is the best way forward in order to design games that really meet users' needs and expectations. In addition, as stated in the Game Accessibility guidelines, "[g]uidelines provide a very useful base checklist but are a one size fits all. Playtesting with disabled gamers is always enlightening, and gives insights specific to your individual game" [10]. Undoubtedly, testing can provide insights into how different users interact with the game and how this interaction could be facilitated, leading to a more rewarding gaming experience.

Microsoft also has developed the Xbox Accessibility Guidelines (XAGs), using a similar user-centred approach, as they "have been developed in partnership with industry experts and members of the gaming and disability community" [11]. The guidelines are "intended for designers to generate ideas, for developers as guardrails when developing their game and as a checklist for validating the accessibility of their title" [11]. There are 23 accessibility guidelines, which include the following aspects: text display, contrast, additional channels for visual and audio cues, subtitles and captions, audio customization, screen narration, input, game difficulty options, object clarity, haptic feedback, audio description, user interface (UI) navigation, UI focus handling, UI context, error messages and destructive actions, time limits, visual distractions, photosensitivity, speech-to-text/text-to-speech chat, communication experiences, accessible feature documentation, accessible customer support and advanced best practices [11]. For each guideline, Microsoft offers an overview of the issue, implementation guidelines, applicable personas (the types of users it benefits) and additional resources, such as articles and tools expanding on the topic.

As regards hardware, in 2019 Microsoft released the Xbox Adaptive Controller, designed to meet the needs of users with limited mobility. It has two large programmable buttons and 19 ports to which external switches, buttons, mounts and joysticks can be connected [12]. The controller was designed in partnership with several disabled gamers' associations and community members, who provided input about its design, functionality and packaging [12]. In 2019 Microsoft also filed a patent for a controller with Braille inputs and outputs for blind and visually impaired players [13]. Although it is still unknown whether the device is going to be fully developed or not, it shows interest by one of the major gaming companies in promoting accessibility for blind and visually impaired users.

The specialized website Can I Play That? [9] also provides accessibility guidelines, which are classified in six categories:

1. Deaf and hard of hearing accessibility (8 guidelines).
2. Motor/physical accessibility (12 guidelines).
3. Cognitive accessibility (12 guidelines).
4. Blind and low vision accessibility (31 guidelines).
5. Colour-blindness accessibility (10 guidelines).
6. Game PR and marketing accessibility (6 guidelines).

For example, for deaf and hard of hearing players, easy-to-read subtitles, with speaker labels and closed captions or sound visualization for essential sounds should be provided. For players with reduced mobility, full key and button remapping for keyboard, mouse and gamepad should be available and the level of difficulty should be adjustable, among other recommendations. For players with cognitive disabilities, some of the guidelines are providing easy, short and clear instructions, letting players see what controls do at any moment, and making the UI "simple and uncluttered". As regards guidelines for blind and low vision players, they propose guidelines such as the option of changing the font, using scalable fonts, adding screen readers to menus and including audio description (AD). For colour-blindness accessibility, colour should not be the only element used to provide information or a colour-blind mode should be available. Finally, regarding the game PR and marketing guides, they suggest using the right terminology that reflects the social model of accessibility; following the Web Content Accessibility Guidelines (WCAC) when posting information; including alt text for images, and providing transcripts for podcasts, audio and video content. It is beyond the scope of this paper to compare the guidelines, but they include similar issues with different detail and they highlight the growing interest in accessibility by different stakeholders.

All the work on guidelines is starting to bear fruit, as in the year 2020 the game *The Last of Us II* (Naughty Dog, 2020) was released with over 60 accessibility features and it has been considered the most accessible game ever [14]. The game was developed with game accessibility consultants of different disability backgrounds [15]. It includes three accessibility presets with all the recommended settings for vision, hearing and motor accessibility [16]. Some of the features of the vision accessibility preset are text-to-speech technology in menus, high contrast display, traversal and combat audio cues and an enhanced listen mode. In the hearing accessibility preset there are features such as pick-up notifications; subtitles for story and combat; speaker names, and combat vibration cues. The motor accessibility preset includes options such as full control customization, camera assist, automatic weapon swap and automatically locking-on to enemy targets when aiming, to name but a few.

However, despite the numerous accessibility features the game includes, there is no AD in cutscenes, which would be necessary to make the game fully accessible to visually-impaired persons (VIPs). To date, no mainstream commercial game has included AD, although it is mentioned in the three guidelines previously presented. The potential inclusion of AD in video games is currently being studied in the Researching Audio Description: Delivery, Translation and New Scenarios project (PGC2018–096566-B-I00, MICIU/AEI, FEDER, UE) at the Universitat Autònoma de Barcelona (UAB). One of the main objectives of the project is to map the gaming habits of VIPs in Spain, identifying the main challenges they face and their views on the inclusion of AD in games. In order to do so, a questionnaire has been circulated and it will be followed up by interviews with players. Then, with the information gathered from users about their needs and preferences, interviews will be carried out with developers to find out their opinion about the feasibility of including AD in games and the best way to incorporate it. It should be highlighted that although AD is currently not available for video games, recently companies such as Ubisoft have started including AD in their video game trailers, such as the trailer for *Assassin's Creed Valhalla*. In order to do so, the company who was in charge of doing the AD consulted blind users to know what they would like to be described and in what level of detail [17]. Although the ultimate goal of game accessibility should be to include AD in games, this is another step in the right direction.

Another interesting research project related to game accessibility was carried out by Columbia University, who developed a Racing Auditory Display. It is an audio interface for car racing games which allows blind people to compete with the same speed and control as sighted players, providing them with a similar game experience to that of sighted players [18]. The player can listen to the audio-based interface using a standard set of headphones, which can be integrated by developers in almost any racing game [18]. A prototype racing game was built, the display was integrated in it and tested with 15 blind participants. Players responded very positively, as they felt as if they could actually see the track and also stated that it was the first time they could play a video game with realistic vehicle physics, which allowed them to race in a complex racetrack on the same level as sighted players [18]. Due to the scope of this paper, only two research projects have been presented, but as research in this field continues to advance, game accessibility is likely to burgeon in the coming years, as will be further discussed in the next section.

5   Future Perspectives

Many advances have taken place in game accessibility in recent years and the future looks bright if all the stakeholders—industry, academia and users—continue to work together towards an inclusive game design. From an industry perspective, there are currently several design guidelines that can be applied to make video games more accessible. If they are implemented from the conceptual stage of the game, it is easier and less costly. Many solutions are already available and have been used previously in games, often not with an accessibility purpose, but to provide innovative gameplay. However, they can also be beneficial for game accessibility, such as sound radars used in shooter games or sound visualizations like the ones used in *The Sims*. Developers should consult users and accessibility experts and their feedback should be incorporated at the design stage of the game, as was done in *The Last of Us II*, in order to be able to include as many accessibility options as possible. According to game accessibility expert, Ian Hamilton (cited in [15]), there are three key elements to help developers design more accessible games: a) seeking for advice and support from specialists; b) taking into account existing documentation on good practices, and c) engaging the community through social media, user research, forums and beta testing.

A universal, "one-size-fits-all" approach may not be possible for video games due to their interactive and dynamic nature, but the medium also allows for much more flexibility and room for customization, so that different players can tailor their experience by choosing from the different accessibility options. Increasing the degree of customization and the amount of accessibility features available seems like the way forward to promote inclusive design and reach the widest possible audience.

Research is also key to improving game accessibility and it should also adopt a user-centric approach, as has been done in the RAD project from UAB or the Racing Auditory Display project from Columbia University. An area that could benefit from future research is accessibility for cognitively impaired players and how the use of plain, easy-to-read language could facilitate their access to gaming. Existing game accessibility guidelines highlight the need for clear, easy-to-understand language, but they do not specify what this means or how or where to apply it. The EU funded project EASIT at UAB focuses on how to make audiovisual information easy to understand through AD and subtitles. While the project does not address the language in video games, its findings could also be extrapolated to games or become the launchpad for research in this area within the video game context.

Players' active participation has also been key to date to promote accessibility and will continue to be crucial. Gamers are very vocal in social media, specialized blogs and websites and even have dedicated YouTube channels where they play games while reviewing their accessibility features, as Steve Saylor's Blind Gamer channel, which has over 10,000 subscribers.[4] Players should be guiding the industry and letting them know what their preferences and needs are. This, in turn, will also be beneficial for developers, as their potential target market will increase with game accessibility.

Finally, legislation will also play an important role in promoting and enforcing game accessibility, such as the 21st Century Communications and Video Accessibility Act

---

[4] See https://www.youtube.com/channel/UCtWREyqj2spI0KiWHp09Fvg.

2010 (CVVA) in the United States and the EN 301 549 standard for digital accessibility in Europe. The CVVA requires accessibility of all advanced communications services, such as voice chat, text chat, and video chat, including those in game software, gameplay and consoles. The EN 301 549 specifies requirements for information and communications technology to be accessible for people with disabilities, including the technology present in video games. As developers begin to abide by legislation, games will have to include more accessibility options, paving the way towards wide-reaching game accessibility.

6   Conclusions

Game accessibility remains a pending issue for the video game industry, although important advances have taken place in recent years thanks to the growing interest and the joint efforts of industry, academia and users, as well as legislation regulating communication in digital environments. Collaboration between all stakeholders has proven essential to advance in this field and it is undoubtedly the way to go forward to foster game accessibility (and any kind of accessibility). For these reasons, game accessibility can be expected to keep burgeoning, and games are likely to gradually include more accessibility options, following the example of Naughty Dog's *The Last of Us II*. Much of the technology is already available and it is a matter of planning the implementation of accessibility features from the early stages of game design, so that they can be introduced without incurring in delays or high additional costs. A "one-size-fits-all approach" is not likely to work in game accessibility, due to the interactive and dynamic nature of games. A highly customizable approach that caters for the preferences and needs of as many different types of users as possible is necessary to take game accessibility and social inclusion to the next level.

Acknowledgements. This work is supported by the Researching Audio Description project (PGC2018–096566-B-I00, MICIU/AEI, FEDER, UE), awarded by the Spanish Government, the EU project EASIT (2018–1-ES01-KA203–05275) and the project 2017SGR113, funded by the Generalitat de Catalunya.

References

1. The Washington Post. The giants of the video game industry have thrived in the pandemic. Can the success continue? 12 May 2020. https://www.washingtonpost.com/video-games/2020/05/12/video-game-industry-coronavirus/. Accessed 02 Feb 2021
2. WHO. Disability and health. https://www.who.int/news-room/fact-sheets/detail/disability-and-health. Accessed 02 Feb 2021
3. IGDA GASIG. The IGDA Game Accessibility Special Interest Group. https://igda-gasig.org. Accessed 04 Feb 2021
4. Bierre, K., et al.: Accessibility in Games: Motivations and Approaches (2004). https://g3ict.org/publication/igda-accessibility-in-games-motivations-and-approaches. Accessed 04 Feb 2021
5. Mangiron, C.: Exploring new paths towards game accessibility. In: Remael, A., Orero, P., Carroll, M. (eds.) Audiovisual Translation and Media Accessibility at the Crossroads. Media for All 3, pp. 43–59. Rodopi, Amsterdam, New York (2012)

6. Accessible Games. https://accessible.games. Accessed 02 Feb 2021
7. Yuan, B., Folmer, E., Harris, F.C.: Game accessibility: a survey. Univ. Access Inf. Soc. **10**, 81–100 (2011). https://doi.org/10.1007/s10209-010-0189-5
8. Bierre, K. Game Accessibility. Gamasutra, 6 July 2005. https://www.gamasutra.com/view/feature/130754/improving_game_accessibility.php. Accessed 02 Feb 2021
9. Can I Play That? https://caniplaythat.com. Accessed 02 Feb 2021
10. Game Accessibility Guidelines. http://gameaccessibilityguidelines.com/basic/. Accessed 02 Feb 2021
11. Microsoft. Xbox Accessibility Guidelines. https://docs.microsoft.com/en-us/gaming/accessibility/guidelines. Accessed 04 Feb 2021
12. Microsoft Xbox Adaptive Controller. https://www.xbox.com/en-US/accessories/controllers/xbox-adaptive-controller. Accessed 04 Feb 2021
13. Fisher, C. Microsoft designs an Xbox controller with Braille. Engadget. July 07, 2019. https://www.engadget.com/2019/05/07/microsoft-patent-braille-controller/. Accessed 04 Feb 2021
14. Molloy, D., Carter, P. Last of Us Part II: Is this the most accessible game ever? BBC News, June 20 (2020). https://www.bbc.com/news/technology-53093613. Accessed 04 Feb 2021
15. Bayliss, B. The Last of Us Part II Accessibility Consultants — Advancing the Industry. Can I Play That?, 23 June 2020. https://caniplaythat.com/2020/06/23/the-last-of-us-2-accessibility-consultants-advancing-the-industry/. Accessed 04 Feb 2021
16. PlayStation. Accessibility options for The Last of Us II. https://www.playstation.com/en-us/games/the-last-of-us-part-ii/accessibility/. Accessed 04 Feb 2021
17. Wald, H.: How audio description within games could make them more accessible for blind and low vision players. Games Radar, 20 October 2020. https://www.gamesradar.com/how-audio-description-within-games-could-make-them-more-accessible-for-blind-and-low-vision-players/. Accessed 04 Feb 2021
18. Evarts, H.: For Blind Gamers, Equal Access to Racing Video Games. Columbia Engineering. 6 March 2018. https://engineering.columbia.edu/press-releases/rad-blind-video-games. Accessed 04 Feb 2021

Gameography

19. *Assassin's Creed Valhalla* (Ubisoft, 2020)
20. *The Last of Us II* (Naughty Dog, 2020)
21. The *Sims* (Electronic Arts, 2000-present)

E-commerce Usability Guidelines for Visually Impaired Users

Elisa Prati[1]([✉]) [iD], Simone Pozzi[2,3] [iD], Fabio Grandi[1] [iD], and Margherita Peruzzini[1] [iD]

[1] Department of Engineering "Enzo Ferrari", University of Modena and Reggio Emilia, Modena, Italy
elisa.prati@unimore.it
[2] Deep Blue Srl, Rome, Italy
[3] University of San Marino, San Marino, Republic of San Marino

Abstract. The growing diffusion of fashion e-commerce websites shows the appreciation by users, highlighting the importance of offering this service also to users with different disabilities. To this end, e-commerce should be not only accessible - implementing all the technical requirements for accessibility - but also usable, paying attention to the offered user experience.

This study aims to investigate the current e-commerce usability considering visually impaired users' navigation experience and understand which aspects define a good usability level for this target. An expert analysis of a set of fashion e-commerce websites and user testing were conducted, considering five different market segment categories. The analysis highlighted a gap in the consideration of visually impaired users' navigation needs and style, as for instance non-uniformity of layout and page structure. All the findings have been structured in usability guidelines to favor the e-commerce usability improvement, with the goal of offering visually impaired users a better shopping experience.

Keywords: Visually impaired users · E-commerce usability · User experience · Disability and DUXU · Diversity in UX design · Usability guidelines · Branding

1 Introduction

E-commerce marketplaces allow the buying and selling of goods and services on the internet, accelerating the purchase phase and reaching large audiences. In the last few years, the use of e-commerce platforms has grown in a massive way: Internet users who bought or ordered goods or services for private use over a year from 2015 and 2020 increased by 10% [1]. In addition to this trend, Covid-19 pandemic restrictions have accelerated the diffusion of e-commerce purchase, forcing consumers to move online to make purchases normally made in physical stores [2]. Total online spending in May 2020 hit $82.5 billion, up 77% year-over-year [3] and this figure confirms the huge impact of such platforms in everyday life. According to the Eurostat report, most purchases of goods involved clothes, shoes or accessories (64% of e-buyers) [1].

Given the high interest in online shopping, it becomes even more fundamental to take into account access by the entire population, including people with disabilities (e.g.

© Springer Nature Switzerland AG 2021
M. Antona and C. Stephanidis (Eds.): HCII 2021, LNCS 12768, pp. 280–293, 2021.
https://doi.org/10.1007/978-3-030-78092-0_18

vision, hearing, motor, cognitive). The e-commerce accessibility is a fundamental issue to consider [4] but not yet sufficiently implemented [5]. The possibility for people with disabilities to shop online would particularly facilitate them in overcoming difficulties they may have in reaching physical stores [6]. Furthermore, e-commerce websites should provide the same user experience to all users [6].

The principles of accessibility can be applied to different sectors such as environment, architecture, public services and information technology [7]. Mainly it is possible to talk about accessibility in two ways: physical and digital. The physical accessibility definition has undergone changes over the years [8, 9], and it refers to the possibility to reach, enter, use, understand something [10].

Digital accessibility mainly refers to the web world. Multiple definitions have been proposed [11, 12]. In [13] the authors propose an analysis to identify the core concepts used in the definitions present in the literature. From a study it emerged that one of the most recognized definitions is provided by the Web Accessibility Initiative (WAI) [14], which defines web accessibility as the possibility for people with disabilities to "perceive, understand, navigate, and interact with the Web" [15]. Specifically, reference is made to the communication between assistive technologies for disabilities (e.g., screen readers, eye-controller) and the website code. Assistive technologies are hardware or software devices that help overcoming or reducing the constraints of a specific disability (e.g., hearing, physical, motor, cognitive). For example, if a video is not subtitled it constitutes a serious obstacle for a person with hearing impairment, a text with little contrast with the background is very difficult to read for people with visual disabilities, the presence on the screen of elements that blink or moving images can create ailments to people with predisposition to epilepsy. Making web content accessible therefore means eliminating digital barriers within it so that everyone can access information and use the services offered.

The focus of this research is on visual impairment, aiming to analyze how visually impaired or blind users browse online. The visual impairment disability includes many problems (e.g., field of view, color perception, blindness) and it is clearly significantly affected by web design choices [4]. Users with severe visual impairments mainly use screen reading software or Braille displays to access web content. Their use involves specific browsing behavior. When a user accesses a site, he/she first needs to know how the site is set up and to understand what content he/she can find. Sighted people as soon as they access a new site take a quick glance, looking from top to bottom, from left to right, to see what is there. Similarly, visually impaired users also need to explore all the different parts of the site in sequence to be able to compose all the elements into a single mental concept. In case of using screen reader software with voice output, the user moves around the site using only certain keys or keyboard combinations (e.g., to go to the page top, to scroll one by one all contents) by scrolling one element at a time. The same initial exploration process is repeated from page to page.

The order of contents reading by assistive technology follows the order present in the site's writing code, however it does not necessarily coincide with the contents display order on the site. This site exploration process is quite long and cognitively tiring. Moreover, it highlights how much visually impaired users are put to the test every time they log into a new e-commerce site as they have to spend a lot of time understanding how it is set up and how they can navigate it, increasing the likelihood of them leaving the site.

Accessibility is part of inclusive design. There are many approaches to consider people with disabilities during the design process, such as Accessible Design, Inclusive Design, Design for All and Universal Design [16]. According to a user-centered design (UCD) approach, the specific end users' profile is analyzed in order to design a product that meets their needs and desires. Moreover, when it comes to considering users with disabilities in design, Newell [16] suggests increasing the concept of UCD by talking about User Sensitive Inclusive Design.

2 Motivation and Background

2.1 Web Accessibility

Web accessibility has been addressed since the infancy of the World Wide Web [17–19]. In particular, it has spread since 1999 when the World Wide Web Consortium (W3C) [15] launched the Web Content Accessibility Guidelines (WCAG) [20].

The W3C is an international community of companies, organizations and associations with the aim to develop Web standards to ensure access to the web for everyone, with or without disabilities.

Within the W3C there is the WAI (Web Accessibility Initiative) division dedicated to accessibility and responsible for producing guidelines: the Web Content Accessibility Guidelines (WCAG). The WCAG are the first guidelines on web accessibility and are aimed at supporting developers to produce accessible web content. The WCAG consists of 4 parts: principles, guidelines, success criteria, sufficient and recommended techniques. The four principles (perceptible, usable, understandable, robust) are to be considered as the foundations of accessibility and each one contains guidelines whose purpose is to help respect the principle itself. For each guideline, there are success criteria that specifically describe what must be implemented to comply with the technical indication. The characteristics of the success criteria are compliance, verifiability and independence and each of them is organized on 3 levels of compliance (A, AA, AAA).

These guidelines are also considered in the European directive UNI EN 301549:2020 (Accessibility requirements for ICT products and services) [21] and the Sect. 508 of the US rehabilitation Act [22]. However, addressing and respecting accessibility is not enough for an optimal user experience. It is fundamental to consider also usability. In fact, if a site is accessible it does not mean that it is automatically usable and both aspects have a significant influence on the user experience. Good usability level means that users can accomplish their tasks satisfactorily and without difficulties (i.e. effectively and efficiently).

As demonstrated in [14, 23, 24], usability is a key aspect for web design and there are several guidelines, such as the ISO 9241–151 [25] mainly aimed at designers, developers and usability evaluators. Usability has long been considered in the website design process but only considering the navigation by able-bodied users. Also, companies are investing much more effort to improve the usability of their products, especially websites: in e-commerce platforms, usability has a clear impact on sales [26]. A low usability would affect the perception of the site's reliability [6]. However, online shopping websites need to be accessible and usable to all consumers of all ages, including those with disabilities [6].

2.2 Motivation

This research wants to investigate the main factors determining the usability of e-commerce websites for users with visual impairments. At the basis of this research there are questions such as: what is the best way to navigate an e-commerce site for visually impaired users? How do they expect it to be set up? What problems do they meet?

The research goal is to understand the current user experience of e-commerce websites and thereafter understand how to improve the usability of e-commerce websites for blind and visually impaired users.

To this end, an expert analysis of fifteen fashion e-commerce and five user testing sessions were performed to collect users' needs and requirements. Lastly, the findings have been summarized in three principles and corresponding guidelines that help designers to design usable sites for visually impaired users. The goal is to enable visually impaired users to make an online purchase independently, just as a sighted person is autonomous.

3 Methodology

The scope of this research was limited to fashion e-commerce, both at the analysis and design level. The methodology consisted of a first phase of expert analysis followed by a user testing session.

3.1 Expert Analysis

After extensive research of clothing e-commerce sites, fifteen sites were selected and analyzed considering the overall site usability and structure. The selection took into account the width of the catalog, the brand's country and the specific market segment category. Specifically, the expert analysis took into account three sites for each selected market segment category:

– marketplace category: Asos, Yoox, Zalando;
– fast fashion category: H&M, Zara, Mango;
– fashion category: Lacoste, Ralph Lauren, Tommy Hilfiger;
– luxury category: Gucci, Prada, Hermes;
– sport category: Adidas, Nike, Freddy.

A matrix was set up in order to conduct the analysis (Fig. 1). It shows on the rows all the main components of a site (e.g., icons, texts, interaction components) organized by page, and on the columns all the sites taken under consideration, both in the desktop and mobile version. The overall site structure and the position, the appearance and the behavior of each of its components were analyzed.

To carry out the expert analysis, Nielsen's heuristics [27] were considered. Of these, those with better applicability to the dynamics of e-commerce sites were chosen. In particular:

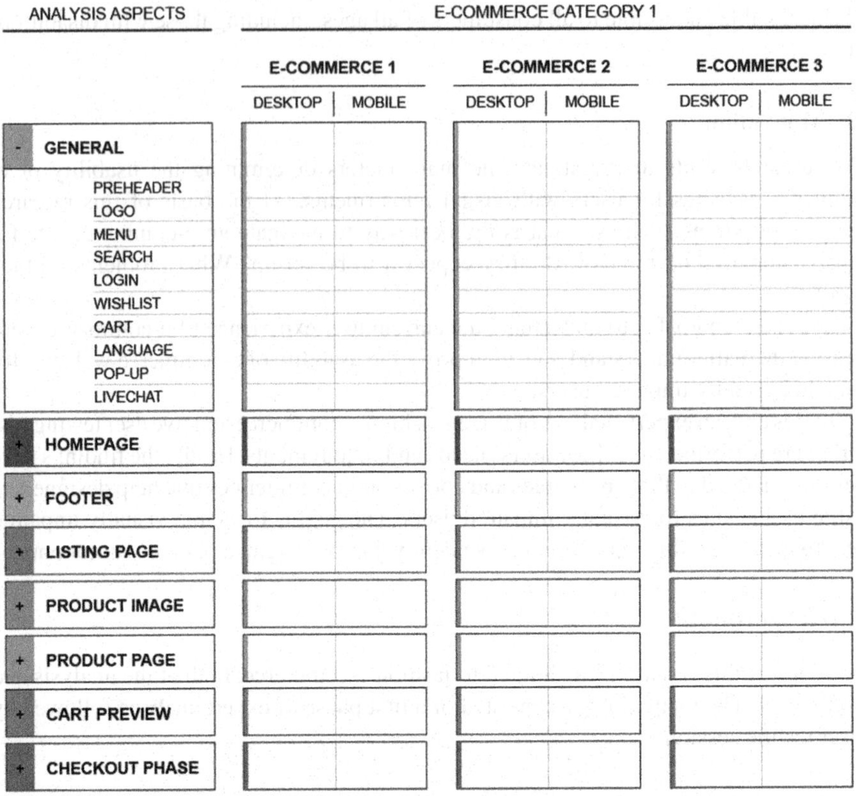

ANALYSIS ASPECTS	E-COMMERCE CATEGORY 1					
	E-COMMERCE 1		E-COMMERCE 2		E-COMMERCE 3	
	DESKTOP	MOBILE	DESKTOP	MOBILE	DESKTOP	MOBILE
GENERAL						
PREHEADER						
LOGO						
MENU						
SEARCH						
LOGIN						
WISHLIST						
CART						
LANGUAGE						
POP-UP						
LIVECHAT						
HOMEPAGE						
FOOTER						
LISTING PAGE						
PRODUCT IMAGE						
PRODUCT PAGE						
CART PREVIEW						
CHECKOUT PHASE						

Fig. 1. Expert analysis matrix. Every category had a number of sub-items. In the figure above, only the "General" sub-categories are presented.

- Visibility of System Status;
- User control and freedom;
- Consistency and standards;
- Recognition rather than recall;
- Help and documentation.

Regarding the first heuristic, specific elements to be analyzed were the notification style, such as pop-up or temporary overlapping windows and the reporting of error messages (e.g., incorrect compilation of edit fields). For the second heuristic, attention was paid to the presence of commands leading to previous pages (e.g., breadcrumbs) and the possibility of returning to the homepage at every stage of navigation, especially during check-out. Regarding the Consistency heuristic, the consistency of the layout of the various pages of the site, the repetition of fundamental components for navigation (e.g., menu, footer) and the choice of components (e.g., checkbox, radio button) were observed. The Recognition heuristic is of key importance as it can significantly speed up the navigation of the blind user, e.g., by pre-filling textual fields. Finally, the online help sections, the frequently asked questions, and contextual help menus were analyzed.

3.2 User Testing

The second part of the analysis consisted of a usability test with users to better understand the real user experience of the specific target. This activity was aimed at bringing out the technical and cognitive obstacles, corresponding respectively to the accessibility and usability of e-commerce. To measure the usability of current e-commerce sites, the technique of formative [28] tests was applied in order to identify the obstacles, discover the causes and resolve them. Given the low number of people involved, the study can be described as exploratory. However, the severity of user experience problems that the subjects encountered clearly indicates a widespread issue.

A sample of 5 users was involved. Despite the small non-representative sample, a number of major usability problems were identified. For example, problems included inability to complete tasks, frustration, misunderstanding. During the selection, attention was paid to taking into consideration people who represented the whole category of users as widely as possible. In particular, were considered:

- man and woman;
- age group between 30 and 65 years;
- different levels of visual impairment;
- different levels of preparation and confidence with the technology;
- different computer operating systems;
- different browsers;
- different levels of familiarity in online browsing;
- level of online purchase interest.

The selection of the site to be considered during the user testing was guided by the expert analysis phase and the execution of pilot tests. The expert analysis led to the identification of the sites that appeared more intuitive, with a well-organized information architecture and an overall good level of usability. The H&M site was considered the most suitable to use during user testing because it was the one that presented less serious obstacles and that didn't affect the navigation.

The tasks to be performed during the tests were defined and associated with descriptive scenarios in order to make the use of the site more realistic and consequently the navigation goal.

At first, nine scenarios and respective tasks were envisaged regarding the e-commerce main pages (e.g., listing page, product page, check-out) and the use of characteristic components (e.g. wish list, size guide tool).

A first user test was performed as a pilot test, to refine the test protocol, identify which site features it was best to focus on, and assess the duration of the test session. This pilot test was also necessary to calibrate the tasks based on the behavior and reactions of people, especially in case of incorrect site functioning, to avoid excessive frustrations for the users. Moreover, the first pilot test was also essential to understand how screen reading software works and how the visually impaired users approach it while using the computer, as well as while browsing online. After the pilot test, the number of tasks was reduced and structured as a linear navigation flow, to simulate a typical navigation of an e-commerce. The rationale of this decision was making the test duration acceptable for the users. Given the low usability of e-commerce websites, performing more tasks and scenarios would have resulted in test sessions lasting more than 2 h. The selected tasks to use during the user testing session are:

- Product research;
- Product information consultation;
- Size guide use;
- Add to wish list and add to cart;
- Filling in the checkout fields;
- Physical store information.

Moreover, as shown in Fig. 2, in each task specific areas were investigated.

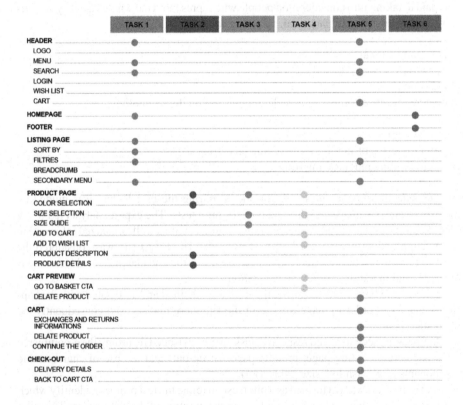

Fig. 2. Mapping of the investigated areas for each task.

The management of a usability test and the correct execution of every single phase that compose it are fundamental to obtain the best results for the purpose of the research. To this end, a test structure was defined.

Mainly the test consisted of three stages:

- welcome and general information collection,
- tasks execution,
- post-test UX evaluation.

Few general questions were asked at the beginning to collect information such as confidence with the technology, frequency of use, devices and assistive technologies used, most visited sites, online shopping experiences. Before starting the users were informed about the purposes of the research and which data would be collected. After receiving their consent, the test started.

During the execution of the tasks, the think aloud technique was adopted to better follow the user's thoughts flow.

At the end of the tasks execution, a user experience evaluation activity was planned, in order to gather qualitative feedback and learn more about the user's perception of the experience. The planned activity is inspired by Microsoft's Product Reaction Cards method [29]. It is adapted to visually impaired users by offering objects to touch, rather than verbal descriptions, to describe the browsing experience. Seven objects with different physical characteristics have been identified (size, shape, material, weight) in order to be able to associate them with a wide choice of the main sensations that the user could have experienced (e.g., stress, confusion, satisfaction) (Fig. 3). Participants were asked to touch the objects one by one, thus they could memorize and study them at will. Subsequently, the user was asked to choose one or two objects that in his/her opinion best describe the browsing experience, motivating and describing the choice.

Fig. 3. Example of objects used for the post-test UX evaluation.

4 Results

4.1 Expert Analysis Results

Very interesting results have emerged from the expert analysis that make it immediately clear how each site uses its own approach in the information architecture setting and adopts its own logic in the choice of contents, their graphics and their behavior. The main analysis results are reported in the Fig. 4.

Examples of each finding are reported below.

FINDINGS	EVIDENCES
1 Information architecture and content inconsistencies between different e-commerce	Different contents and their order in the header
2 Information architecture and content inconsistencies between e-commerce of the same market segment category	Differences in the product page settings, both for the arrangement of the elements and for their hierarchy
3 Inconsistency within the pages of the same site	Multiple product preview layouts in the same listing page
4 Inconsistency between the desktop and mobile version of the same site	The use of different feedback modes to the add to cart action
5 Inconsistencies in pages layout based on different periods of the year (e.g. sales, holiday)	Insertion of new items in the menu

Fig. 4. Expert analysis findings.

Finding 1: an example is the different e-commerce header organization. One of the analyzed e-commerce had: logo, two main navigation menus, search bar, login, wish list and cart icons. Another e-commerce header had hamburger menu, search bar, logo, login, cart, language, find a store and contact us.

Finding 2: on the product pages, one page had two columns with on the left one product image and on the right the product details and possible actions (wish list icon, name, price, colors, size, product details, add to cart button and find a store link); the other page had product images under the same two columns. Another e-commerce product page had: a colored band with product images on the side and in the middle product information (shipping and return information, name, price, size, size guide and add to cart button).

Finding 3: the same website has two versions of the product preview on the listing page, one more expanded (with name, image, price, size selection and add to cart button) and another reduced (image, name, price and colors).

Finding 4: we encountered two different feedbacks to the 'add to cart' action. The desktop version opened a cart summary pop-up, while the mobile version visualized only a temporary pop-up message.

Finding 5: on the same websites, the "sale" voice is displayed on the main menu only in specific months of the year.

These differences and inconsistencies lead to greater difficulty in the e-commerce navigation, resulting in a slowdown in task accomplishment. In the worst cases, the user may feel disoriented, frustrated and thus be led to leave the site because they cannot reach their goal. These observations translate into usability difficulties for able-bodied users, but they become a serious issue of low e-commerce usability for users with visual impairments. The fact that each site has its own logic of organization and behavior of the contents affects the times and quality of navigation with screen reading software.

4.2 User Testing Results

User testing was especially valuable for getting to know users' behaviors, their reactions, their difficulties and needs, as well as identifying the main obstacles currently present on e-commerce sites. These insights can be summarized mainly in two main categories: technical and design problems. The first one includes problems such as incorrect wording in the site code, incorrect browser or coding of assistive technology. A significant problem identified during the user testing was the accessibility difference of the same site using different browsers. Probably these problems can be solved by correctly applying the accessibility guidelines. On the other hand, the second problems category regards the web design, including usability and user experience design aspects. For example, it has emerged that some components and interactions (e.g., mouse over, overlapping layers) facilitate the navigation of sighted users, but could be an obstacle to the navigation of visually impaired users.

The user comments during the tests and the data collected from the UX evaluation activity allowed a deeper understanding of the usability aspects to consider, based on the specific user navigation approach.

(i) Several users agree that if the site has few components (e.g., title, buttons, images), the navigation is faster and easier. Moreover, they have expressed the desire that these components be organized in as many hierarchical levels as possible.

(ii) Another important finding was about the need of orientation inside the e-commerce website. Many users reported that pages title and breadcrumbs are reference navigation points and facilitate orientation. Conversely, having multiple buttons leading to the same page confuses the user. From this, it can be deduced that if the orientation is easy, it is also easier to memorize the website structure logic and to create a mental map.

The users' comments and observations during the tests were then compared with the experience evaluation activity data. For example, one user rated the navigation as flat and cold, and chose two flat objects (one in forex and one in metal) to describe it. Another user to describe the navigation experience chose an object with an irregular and serrated shape because it is an articulated shape that takes time to understand, like the e-commerce. Still another chose the spring because it reminded him of the initial orientation difficulties.

All the findings that emerged during the usability tests were analyzed and classified and led to the formulation of principles and guidelines for improving usability of e-commerce sites for people with visual disabilities.

4.3 Usability Guidelines

The guidelines aim to provide support to brands in the development of an e-commerce site that is not only accessible but also usable by users with visual impairments. The

PRINCIPLES	GUIDELINE EXAMPLES
1 Uniformity and coherence Use of the same information architecture, placement and arrangement of the contents within the page, as well as the same behavior, in all e-commerce. These should be consistent across all breakpoints (adaptation of the page layout to the device resolution).	*Title:* **Reference components: header and footer** *Description:* The same header and footer should be present on all pages. *Purpose:* Ease of navigation *Label:* Generali, Information Architecture *Title:* **Inactive CTA (Call to action buttons)** *Description:* The page CTAs should remain present in the same position even when they are not active. This allows the user to be aware of where to find this information when the user needs it. *Purpose:* Correct presentation of all information on the page *Label:* General, Component specifications
2 Navigation clarity Use clear and organized navigation flows in as many steps as possible, in order to simplify and speed up the execution of the task and the identification of the information sought by the user. Therefore, use hierarchies and categorisations to group the contents in order to reduce the number of items on pages.	*Title:* **Hierarchical subdivision** *Description:* Organize content into hierarchies and steps, from the most generic to the most specific. *Purpose:* To simplify and speed up navigation *Label:* Generali, Information Architecture *Title:* **Product suggestions** *Description:* The product suggestions (e.g. complete the look, similar products) related to the selected product should be contained within an accordion and should not be more than 3 products in order not to create confusion and disorient the user. *Purpose:* Clarity of information *Label:* Product page, Layout of components
3 Logical provisions Place the contents of the site on the most appropriate pages, positioning and ordering them in the most logical way for the navigation of the user with visual impairment.	*Title:* **CTA 'add to wishlist'** *Description:* Enter the 'add to wishlist' CTA after the main product description information (name, description, price, colors) *Purpose:* To provide information in order of importance for consultation *Label:* Page listing, Layout of components *Title:* **Order summary** *Description:* Enter the order summary at the top of the page in the expandable version (accordion). *Purpose:* Clarity of navigation *Label:* Checkout page, Layout of components

Fig. 5. Usability principles.

guidelines help to set the information architecture of the site, to hierarchize and organize the contents, to arrange the components within the various pages and to define their behaviors.

The usability guidelines are divided into 6 categories that refer to the main pages of an e-commerce (homepage, listing page, product page, cart page, check-out page) plus a general category. Each guideline also has a label that defines the topic type (information architecture, component layout, interaction components, component specifics), a title, a description, and the objective. Finally, three general principles have been identified to be considered as the foundation of all the guidelines, in order to ensure the correct usability of e-commerce sites for people with visual disabilities. The three principles are:

1. Uniformity and coherence;
2. Navigation clarity;
3. Logical provisions.

The first principle is about consistency, as a key feature for achieving good site usability. The application of this principle would ensure that users always interact with the "same", predictable interface. For instance, a high degree of consistency in the arrangement and choice of components would avoid that the user has to strive every time to understand where and how to find the information they need. Instead, the objective of the second and third principles is to design navigation flows that follow the user's expectations and prevent disorientation within the sites. The Fig. 5 shows the principles and some related examples of guidelines.

5 Conclusions

The high-level objective of this contribution is contributing to making e-commerce available to all people, in line with the W3C principles.

The research findings highlight a lack of awareness in the e-commerce community of what constitutes good usability and UX for visually impaired users. Addressing accessibility is not enough for removing access and participation barriers. The main lack of current e-commerce sites seems to be the absence of shared design guidelines and standards. Shared usability guidelines would allow designers and developers to better and more easily design user-friendly e-commerce websites for visually impaired users. Furthermore, the research results convey some important values: equality, unification, speeding up, efficiency. The research has allowed us to reflect on the importance of offering anyone the possibility of using this service also in the e-commerce sector. In order to offer a good user experience, it is necessary to pay attention to the theme of accessibility as much as to that of usability, bearing in mind that uniformity between the various sites and within the same site facilitates navigation by users with visual impairment. This aspect together with other small precautions related to the grouping and hierarchization of the site contents would allow faster and more effective navigation, minimizing the cognitive effort.

The present research could be extended by involving a larger number of users, with a variety of assistive technologies. In view of improving the current situation, the most effective action would be engaging with associations of visually impaired users and identify the best approach to address the current gap, whether by dissemination, communication, or by improving the existing regulation.

References

1. S. Explained, E-commerce statistics for individuals, (n.d.). https://ec.europa.eu/eurostat/statistics-explained/pdfscache/46776.pdf
2. Bhatti, A., Akram, H., Basit, H.M., Khan, A.U., Raza, S.M., Naqvi, M.B.: E-commerce trends during COVID-19 pandemic. Int. J. Futur. Gener. Commun. Netw. **13**, 1449–1452 (2020)
3. A. Analytics, Adobe Digital Economy Index, (n.d.). https://www.adobe.com/content/dam/www/us/en/experience-cloud/digital-insights/pdfs/adobe_analytics-digital-economy-index-2020.pdf
4. Lazar, J., Sears, A.: Design of e-business web sites. Handb. Hum. Factors Ergon. **37**, 1344–1363 (2006)
5. Sohaib, O., Kang, K.: The importance of web accessibility in business to-consumer (B2C) websites. In: 22nd Australasian Software Engineering Conference (ASWEC 2013), pp. 1–11 (2013)
6. Sohaib, O., Kang, K.: E-commerce web accessibility for people with disabilities. In: Goluchowski, J., Pankowska, M., Linger, H., Barry, C., Lang, M., Schneider, C. (eds.) Complexity in Information Systems Development, pp. 87–100. Springer International Publishing, Cham (2017). https://doi.org/10.1007/978-3-319-52593-8_6
7. Iwarsson, S., Ståhl, A.: Accessibility, usability and universal design—positioning and definition of concepts describing person-environment relationships. Disabil. Rehabil. **25**, 57–66 (2003)
8. Ingram, D.R.: The concept of accessibility: a search for an operational form. Reg. Stud. **5**, 101–107 (1971)
9. Batty, M.: Accessibility: in search of a unified theory (2009)
10. O. Dictionary, Oxford dictionary, Nd Performance. Accessed (2012)
11. Berners-Lee, T.: W3C leads program to make the web accessible for people with disabilities (press release), Erişim (1997). https://ec.europa.eu/eurostat/web/products-eurostat-news/-/ddn-20210217-1
12. U.S.G.S. Administration, GSA Homepage, (n.d.). www.section508.gov
13. Petrie, H., Savva, A., Power, C.: Towards a unified definition of web accessibility. In: Proceedings of the 12th Web for all Conference, pp. 1–13 (2015)
14. Yesilada, Y., Brajnik, G., Vigo, M., Harper, S.: Understanding web accessibility and its drivers. In: Proceedings of the International Cross-Disciplinary Conference on Web Accessibility, pp. 1–9 (2012)
15. W. WAI, Introduction to Web Accessibility, (n.d.). http://www.w3.org/WAI/intro/accessibility.php
16. Newell, A.F., Gregor, P., Morgan, M., Pullin, G., Macaulay, C.: User-sensitive inclusive design. Univ. Access Inf. Soc. **10**, 235–243 (2011)
17. Brittain, K.D.: Persons with disabilities can and do surf the Net! Color. Libr. **21**, 17–19 (1995)
18. Paciello, M.G.: The web and people with disabilities: cutting edge developments. Florida Libr. **39**(5) (1996)
19. Paciello, M.: Making the World Wide Web accessible for the blind and visually impaired. Florida Libr. **39**(5) (1996)
20. W3C, Authoring Tool Accessibility Guidelines (ATAG) 2.0, (2015). https://www.w3.org/TR/ATAG20/

21. European Telecommunications Standards Institute, EN 301 549 V3.1.1 - Accessibility requirements for ICT products and services, (2019). https://www.etsi.org/deliver/etsi_en/301 500_301599/301549/03.01.01_60/en_301549v030101p.pdf

22. U.S. Government Publishing Office, Vocational Rehabilitation and Other Rehabilitation Services Subchapter V - Rights and Advocacy, (2011). https://www.govinfo.gov/content/pkg/USCODE-2011-title29/html/USCODE-2011-title29-chap16-subchapV-sec794d.htm

23. Waddell, C., et al.: Constructing accessible web sites, Apress (2003)

24. Petrie, H., Kheir, O.: The relationship between accessibility and usability of websites. In: Proceedings of the SIGCHI Conference on Human Factors in Computing Systems, pp. 397–406 (2007)

25. I.O. for Standardization, EN ISO 9241-151:2008, Ergonomics of human-system interaction - Part 151: Guidance on World Wide Web user interfaces (2008)

26. Folmer, E., Bosch, J.: Architecting for usability: a survey. J. Syst. Softw. **70**, 61–78 (2004)

27. Nielsen, J., Molich, R.: Heuristic evaluation of user interfaces. In: Proceedings of the SIGCHI Conference on Human Factors in Computing Systems, pp. 249–256 (1990)

28. Barnum, C.M.: Usability testing essentials, Elsevier (2010)

29. Benedek, J., Miner, T.: Measuring desirability: new methods for evaluating desirability in a usability lab setting. Proc. Usability Prof. Assoc. **2003**, 57 (2002)

Usability Testing on Tractor's HMI: A Study Protocol

Elisa Prati(✉) ⓘ, Fabio Grandi ⓘ, and Margherita Peruzzini ⓘ

Department of Engineering "Enzo Ferrari",
University of Modena and Reggio Emilia, Modena, Italy
elisa.prati@unimore.it

Abstract. The success of a human-machine interface (HMI) heavily depends on its usability. An highly usable interface allows the user to more easily achieve his/her goals and in general have a better User eXperience (UX). In work environments, a structured and ready-to-use usability testing protocol can encourage companies to carry out this type of study and focus on UX from the early design phases. Even though numerous methods to test usability exist, industrial companies still have great difficulties to apply them and choose the best ones for the specific purposes. They should be guided into the analysis by a universal step-by-step approach, which helps also not experienced designers selecting the most reliable and useful methods among the available ones.

In this direction, the paper proposes a structured protocol to focus on UX and guide companies in testing setup, execution and debriefing in an easy and quick way. Checklists are defined to help during user testing and assure its success. As a consequence, end users can be easily involved to give an added value in design problems identification. The novelty of this paper is the definition of a ready-to-use study protocol that can also be used by non-usability experts, in order to make them familiar with UX analysis and extend this practice also in industrial HMI design. As validation, the proposed protocol was applied to the design of interfaces for agricultural tractors during two different stages of the HMI redesign process.

Keywords: Usability · User experience · User testing · HMI · Eye-tracking in user experience research · Universal design

1 Introduction

Usability makes products naturally usable for users: it lets users work without problems and to feel comfortable during the interaction [1]. In particular, a good usability makes an interface easy to learn, easy to use, intuitive, and sometimes also pleasant. The issue of usability acquires greater importance when interfaces are used in work environments for demanding tasks; agricultural machines are an example. In this context, usability testing is not a common design technique, mainly due to time, cost or effort constraints. Moreover, the value of usability testing is greater in the earliest stages of design, but it requires predefined methods to be applied with success due to the poor development of the design itself. Therefore, the level of usability of any interface greatly affects the user's

© Springer Nature Switzerland AG 2021
M. Antona and C. Stephanidis (Eds.): HCII 2021, LNCS 12768, pp. 294–311, 2021.
https://doi.org/10.1007/978-3-030-78092-0_19

perception and, as a consequence, the global user experience. For these reasons, usability issues have to be necessarily included during the design process, taking into account the use' experience along the design phases and not just after the product launch. Nowadays, usability analysis is rather widespread in web design, while it is not a common practice during the design of industrial human machine interfaces (HMI). Contrarily, usability is much more important for industrial HMI where the interface is used to work and user errors could bring negative effects on performance, especially in terms of time, effort and allocated resources. For these purposes, it is necessary to guide the industrial HMI designers and engineers to include usability analysis and understand the users' needs into the real operative context, promoting universal design practices. This research fits into the theme of universal design in two aspects: on the one hand, it provides a ready-to-use protocol able to expand the practice of usability analysis even to non-usability experts; on the other hand, it proposes a structured protocol able to include users' needs in a inclusive way, considering all end-user profiles, even the less known. For example, in the agricultural sector, it is required to consider how older users, accustomed to using agricultural machines with less functionality or without touchscreen displays, can interface with new technological solutions.

The proposed protocol derives from an in-depth study of the existing techniques and methods to test usability. Its knowledge led to the definition of a simple and streamlined method able to guide professional figures, such as engineers and technicians, with a limited knowledge about interface's usability. Actually, the proposed protocol is aimed at non-usability experts, providing a step-by-step workflow and ready-to-use checklists, in order to maximize usability testing.

In the aviation and automotive sectors, usability is frequently included in product validation [2–5]. However, the literature review on this topic indicates the need to consider usability during the design of HMI in relation to the extraordinary type of operative environment, such as a workplace [6]. Indeed, interaction into a work environment has peculiar characteristics: first of all, users have to feel comfortable using the interfaces to be efficient and to avoid errors, which could have also significant repercussions on particular contexts; secondly, an enhanced usability could have a positive impact on user productivity [7], comfort [8] and safety [9].

The agriculture machine sector has recently shown a growing attention to the user comfort by physical ergonomic analysis and seat comfort analysis, in order to improve the operator comfort and visibility in the cab. Recent works provide interesting examples about the design of new commands and armrests, also using digital human simulations tools [10, 11]. Nevertheless, today physical commands are gradually replaced by graphical and digital interfaces, according to the general trend from consumer electronics. However, producing companies rarely have graphical HMI experts in their team or time to dedicate to an intensive, deep user research. As a consequence, the new graphical interfaces are frequently conceived by just digitizing the physical dashboard. It makes tractors' HMI very complex and not logical to navigate and use, due to the lack of a robust usability study. This fact underlines the emergence of HMI usability design practices as well as cabin ergonomics.

The paper is organized as follows: Sect. 2 provides an overview of the most common usability testing methods, Sect. 3 describes the proposed protocol in detail, Sect. 4

presents an application case study and demonstrates the advantages related to the adoption of a participatory design approach focusing on HMI in the tractors' context, Sect. 5 includes conclusions and recommendations.

2 Background

Usability is defined in ISO 9241-11 as "the extent to which a system, product or service can be used by specified users to achieve specified goals with effectiveness, efficiency and satisfaction in a specified context of use" [1]. An interesting research shows that usability and User eXperience (UX) definitions are influenced by geographical and socio-cultural aspects, but they all agree with the ISO definition [12]. According to [13], the usability concept is composed by a set of multiple images *(Universal usability, Situational usability, Perceived usability, Hedonic usability, Organizational usability, Cultural usability)* and not by a unifying concept.

Many techniques to test the usability of an interface have been defined in the last 30 years. As shown by Villani et al. [14], the various techniques to assess industrial interface usability can be grouped into subjective analysis carried out by experts (e.g., heuristic evaluation, cognitive walkthrough, observation) and objective analysis involving users (e.g., user testing, questionnaire).

Among the available methods to verify usability, usability user testing is for sure the main one. Usability testing is characterized by the involvement of end users and the study of their behavior during the interaction with the interface. Usability testing allows listening to the users and learning which aspects of the interface help or fail in supporting task execution, what users appreciate or dislike. Moreover, usability testing highlights if the interface responds to the users' needs and how much the products support them into their goals. These are the reasons why it is important to include usability testing during the design process.

Usability testing can be used for different purposes, like to guide the design process, to conduct a benchmarking, to compare design solutions or to compare competitive products. Moreover, two types of usability testing can be identified as discussed by Barnum et al. [15]: summative testing and formative testing. The former uses usability testing to assess the usability at the end of the development phase and it is useful to test if the requirements met the product and to produce metrics. The latter uses usability testing during the design process to improve the interface and fix problems. A substantial difference between summative and formative testing is the number of the participants. In summative testing a large number of participants are required while in formative testings are involved few people.

Usability tests can also differ according to the place where they are conducted. The place can be an informal environment, like an office or room in general, or a controlled environment like a laboratory dedicated to conducting tests, or also the real contexts of use (i.e., field tests). Tests could be also carried out remotely, on the phone or recently over the Internet, using an insight platform to record the screen (and voice eventually) of test participants as they interact with the interface in their natural environment e.g., at home, in their office, or a specific location. Both physical or web interfaces can be evaluated remotely with several advantages: remote testing is less expensive than in-person testing, it can involve a higher number of participants and from different countries.

The test typology is mainly determined by the type of the interface, the interface status, and the influence of the place of use on the user experience.

Usability testing allows measuring the quality during interaction by a proper set of metrics. The ISO Usability definition highlights three parameters to measure the usability: effectiveness, efficiency, satisfaction. Other definitions include aspects like engaging, error tolerant, easy to learn [16], or others as desirable, credible, findable, valuable [17]. There are many aspects of usability that can be measured and a variety of data that can be collected during a test. Data are mainly divided into two categories: qualitative and quantitative.

Qualitative data allows us to better describe the user feelings, the user perception of the interface and his/her interaction experience. This kind of data helps to adopt the user point of view and see the interface from his/her prospective. For this reason qualitative data suits better in formative testing. This category includes users' comments and facilitator's observations like nonverbal expressions (e.g. body language, facial expressions) or involuntary feedback (e.g. laugh, sigh). In particular, these insights are very precious if the aim of the study is finding out opportunities to improve the product. In this direction, questionnaires usually help to better understand the reason for the users actions, collecting feedback about the user's perception and asking them to express a judgment on the experience. The post-task scenario focused on each single task experience, while the post-test questionnaire focused on overall experience with the interface. Questions could be personalized or standard and in both cases it is important that it is quick and easy. Personalized questionnaire request to pay attention on some aspects like the question construction to avoid influencing the answers [18, 19]. Alternatively, there are many standards questionnaires and they could be used as such SUS (System Usability Scale) [20] or CSUQ (Computer System Usability Questionnaire) [21]. In addition, there are also alternative techniques for collecting user feedback at the end of the experience (e.g. card sorting), but it was considered that for this protocol traditional questionnaires are the most suitable for use by non-usability experts.

Conversely, quantitative data concerns everything that can be measured or counted. This category includes performance measurements like time on task, number of clicks, number of errors, number of success and failure tasks. Furthermore, also questionnaires answers can be included in this category. Generally, quantitative data are more suitable for a developed interface. In particular, this data is useful to support an objective evaluation of the interface and facilitate the comparison with other interfaces (e.g. previous interface version, competitors). Quantitative data can also be collected by measuring users' physiological parameters to objectify the knowledge of the users' status, like the mental workload (MWL) during the interaction [22]. Objective measurements of MWL can be performed by different ways: collecting the Galvanic Skin Response (GSR), measuring the activity of the sweat glands which reflect the intensity of the emotional state [23]; elaborating electrocardiogram (ECG) data, monitoring the electrical activity of the heart, by parameters as the heart rate (HR) and heart rate variability (HRV) [24]; using electroencephalogram (EEG) test to evaluate the electrical activity in the brain, correlating brain waves patterns with state of stress perceived by the user [25]; or by electrooculography (EOG) recording the electrical potential difference between the cornea and the retina of a human eye [26]. A very useful device to be used for usability testing is eye-tracker (ET), using invisible near-infrared light and high-definition cameras to record eyes movements' direction and timing. Different types of ET are available on the market, from screen-based devices directly attachable to monitors, to wearable devices (e.g., glasses) more suitable for field tests. The eye-tracking analysis can be used to support usability testings providing data about the user's visual attention area, mapping eye interaction on the interface layout, and the user's stress level, considering pupil dilatation, saccades/fixations ratio, and fixation duration. Data post-processing creates specific visualizations like heat-map and gaze plot to show in which parts of the interface the user is looking at, for how long, and sequence of looking. However, every time you plan a test, you should consider the users' conditions and the testing place, analyzing the intrusiveness of the adopted devices for human data monitoring, in order to define which are suitable for tests.

From the analysis of the research background, a variety of methods and tools supporting usability testing can be defined. Only the experience and the ability of those who carry out the testing can support the definition of the best testing place, modalities, tools, and data collection strategies. This fact actually limits the adoption of usability practices in companies, where rarely experts in user research are involved in interface design and testing.

3   Proposed Protocol

The proposed usability testing protocol arises from the current limits highlighted by the background review on usability practices, which remark the emergence of ready-to-use guidelines to carry out usability tests during industrial projects. The protocol is for formative scope, thus in support of the design phase to diagnose and fix usability problems. For this reason, the protocol is conceived to perform usability testing quickly and easily, allowing easy inserting this activity within the design cycle. The increasing attention on users' needs during the design stage led to catch usability problems in advance, while traditional practices would detect them only at the end of the design, with an exponential increase in time and effort.

The proposed usability testing protocol is organized into three macro phases, presented in chronological order:

1. Planning;
2. Execution;
3. Debriefing.

The planning phase regards everything it is necessary to define and prepare before to start with the usability testing session, from the goal to equipment set-up. The execution phase is divided into what to do just before, during and after each test. Finally, the debriefing phase guide in the organization of the data collected and in their use to improve the interface design. Figure 1 shows the usability testing protocol flow.

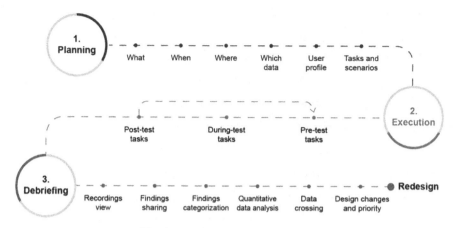

Fig. 1. Usability testing protocol flow

3.1 Planning

The planning of a usability testing begins with the definition of those aspects to explore, considering what it is important to learn from the user experience. This decision is mainly influenced by the test goal, the type of interface (e.g., physical, graphical, web…) and the interface design status (e.g., low fidelity prototype, developed interface). Generally, also budget and time available can influence the definition of the usability testing subject. Figure 2 shows the proposed decision planning guide.

First of all, the planning phase has to define the main interface aspects to test, that we call what to test. The aspects could be considered: concept, information architecture, and visual design. Testings about the project concept are useful to test a new product idea not existing yet or the implementation of new functions. This kind of testing allows understanding if the new proposal meets the user's needs and the project can continue in the intended direction. Testings on the information architecture of the system are probably the most important because they test whether the information architecture responds to the user's expectation. Often, the information architecture is not considered by non-usability-experts but it is the one that causes the most usability problems. The design of the information architecture consists in the organization, subdivision and hierarchization of all the contents of the system. This means that the information architecture goal is to create a system's organization that respects the mental model that users expect. Lastly, usability testings about the visual design test interface aspects that influence the system perception, the contents readability and learnability. Examples of visual design aspects are: screen layout, icons, colours. The definition of what to test supports some subsequent decisions (e.g., if eye-tracking analysis can be useful or not) and the overall test planning.

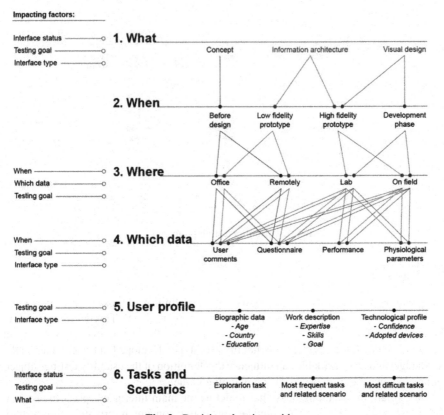

Fig. 2. Decision planning guide

Considering when to conduct a usability study, a first differentiation refers to the project types: redesign or new design. In redesign, usability testing should be carried out at the beginning of the process, in order to evaluate the as-is interface and to better learn how to improve it. Ideally, in a new design project usability testings should be throughout all the design and development phases. Particularly, in which design moment conduct the usability testing depends on the study subject. For example, a completely new information architecture organization probably is better if tested as soon as the wireframes are finished. Conversely, less substantial changes on information architecture could be tested also in a later design stage for example using a high-fidelity prototype.

A further aspect to consider is where to execute the usability testing. There are many locations; the selected place is strongly tied to the testing goal and, in particular, to the interface design status. The location is not relevant when the interface is at a conceptual stage, while acquires greater importance as the tested interface is closer to the final version. Indeed, testing on an advanced prototype or a developed interface requires a great attention to the real user experience, hence the best place for testing is the real using context. The location should also be chosen by considering the influence that the external environment could have on the interaction quality. For example, the context of use of a tractor interface has a fundamental role due to the presence of external factors, such as lighting conditions, noises and dust, or tractor movements. A combination of testing places, at different design phases, can give an overall overview on the user experience, highlighting different issues of the interface usability.

Depending on the goal of the study and on the interface status, it is possible to establish which data to collect. According to usability practice, qualitative and quantitative data can be used to detect important information about the system usability. About quantitative data, user performance (e.g. time, errors) and physiological parameters (e.g. ECG, EOG, GSR) are an example. About qualitative data, questionnaires are used to catch the user impressions. Questionnaire could be post-task or post-test, based on the task and scenario type and interface level of interface maturity. For instance, a wireframe evaluation better supports the exploration of the users' thinking and feeling as qualitative evaluation. Diversely, if the interface status is more advanced, a combination of qualitative and quantitative data could be a good choice. In the planning phase, it is very important to decide which data to collect in order to better guide the following debriefing phase and to organize the testing setup (e.g. camera, eye-tracker).

In addition, the definition of the most proper user profiles is crucial to have reliable usability testing results, according to [1]. Indeed, a specific sample of target users responding to people that really interact with the interface has to be chosen, considering all the characteristics that could affect the interaction process. For example, different uses of the product, different skills and experience about the product use, and different countries should be considered. Surely, the goal and the subject of the testing led the definition of what's most relevant for the study. After the detailed definition of the end user/s profile, also the sample size has to be defined (e.g., how many people engage for testing). For a preliminary, formative study during the early design stages, five users can already lead to most of the discoveries that can be collected in a usability testing session [27–29]. Anyway, to have statistically-relevant analysis more users could be involved. A good practice is to provide a reward for the availability of users.

The final issue to plan is the definition of tasks and scenarios to be performed by users. The tasks are determined by the interface aspects to investigate during the usability testing. They should be prioritized in order to define the order of execution, defining also time required for each task. Generally, the first tasks are more general (e.g., interface exploration, homepage functions) and the following tasks more specific and they could be based on the frequent or difficult tasks. Finally, for a more realistic task execution, it is useful to craft the selected tasks into scenarios. Scenarios should help users to immerse themselves in a real situation of use of the interface and perform the task more naturally. Scenarios contain information about place of use, goal of the interaction, information needed to perform the task (e.g., specific parameter setup). Moreover, it is important that a scenario has simple language and doesn't use specific terminology to avoid giving suggestions to the user and invalidating the test. The scenario could be only one for all the tasks or one scenario per task. The scenario number depends on the type of the tasks. For a better understanding of the tester's actions, it is useful to insert at the end of each scenario an indication to communicate when the user thinks to have finished the task.

When the main issues are planned, it is time to define the last few questions like people involved roles and necessary equipment. A good practice before the beginning of the testing session is to conduct a pilot test. It is useful to test the task-scenario comprehension and it is not strictly necessary to run with an end user.

3.2 Execution

In this protocol, the test is carried out with the presence of one user at a time, one facilitator and the observers. Users are from the user sample, as previously defined, while facilitator or observers usually belong to the design team, the development team and other project stakeholders. Figure 3 presents the execution checklist.

	The day before	Before each test	During the test	Keep in mind	After each test
Facilitator	O Print the tasks-scenarios list for users O Share the tasks-scenarios list with observers O Print the consent format	O Signature concent format O Test mode explanation O Explain that you are testing the interface, not the user O Say to act as much as possible as if he/she were alone, in a real context of use O Explanation thinking aloud pratice O Remind the user to tell when he thinks he has finished a task O Tell if there are any parts of the interface that are not working	O Provide the user one scenario at a time O Read the scenario text together with the user	O Do not give any kind of suggestions (verbal and non-verbal) O Remain neutral in both verbal and non-verbal language O Have always the same positive feedback, whether the user is doing the task well or not O If the user stops thinking aloud, help him with some questions like "what are you thinking?", "what are you looking for?"	O Post-task and/or post-test question-naire O Quick notes reordering
Room technician		O Software and/or hardware setting for audio-video recording O Check the operation of the interface to be tested O Check of the control of software and/or hardware sharing with observers	O At the beginning: device settings	O Don't interact with the users	
Observers			O Take notes on user behavior and comments	O Don't interact with the users	O Quick notes reordering

Fig. 3. Execution checklist

The facilitator conducts the test, so his/her skills directly influence the quality of the results [30]. How shown in Fig. 3, the facilitator has many tasks to perform just before and during the test. Among these, he/she presents the test and what the user has to do. The thinking-aloud practice is preferred: this procedure asks the participant to say what he/she is thinking during the tasks execution. Thinking-along is particularly useful as it highlights the user's intentions and expectations, helping to understand his/her actions and reactions in case of unexpected interface behaviors.

The checklist, as reported in Fig. 3, contains some detailed suggestions to support the usability testing conduction, avoiding invalidating tests.

Diversely, observers don't have to interact directly with the users, without interfering with the test execution. If possible, they should follow the test in another room or remotely, to avoid any disturbance. Observers can include all people that can benefit from the tests, helping to take note of everything that emerges during the tests and to support the facilitator in gathering useful insights.

Lastly, it is good to have a room technician taking care of all the settings. The technician can also be the facilitator himself, or rather one of the observers. The technician must mainly make sure that everything works before starting the test and give support in case of malfunctioning.

The actual testing session begins when the tester arrives. After an initial welcome by the user and an explanation of everything that is necessary to carry out the test, it is possible to begin with the execution of the first task. The moderator provides the user with the scenario text one at a time and after reading it together the user can start performing the task. During the tasks execution both the facilitator and the observers pay attention to the user behavior and take notes on the execution. The facilitator remains alongside the user for the duration of the test and provides support in case of need, always paying attention to the behavioral rules shown in the Fig. 3.

When the user finishes the execution of the task, the facilitator can end the session with the post-test questionnaire. Once the user leaves, it is useful to do a quick notes reordering. This activity allows arranging the notes in a more understandable way and to add notes. This operation also favors better memorization of the emerged findings.

3.3 Debriefing

A fundamental part of the usability testing is the debriefing phase, when all insights collected must be analyzed in a useful way for the design improvement. In this phase, all observers are involved. Debriefing is organized in one or more meetings, physically or remotely, as a round table; everyone shares its findings (e.g. user behaviors or attitudes, thinking-aloud comments) highlighting the most positive interface features and the most frequent problems, also considering the unexpected results.

In order to obtain really useful information for improving the interface, all the findings are grouped in classes and prioritized, according to various criteria, such as general findings or specific pages (e.g., homepage), alternatively using associating labels referring to the type of problem (e.g., terminology, feedback, aesthetics). In this action, the goal of the test could guide the grouping phase. For a deeper analysis and a more accurate user's behavior interpretation, the emerging findings must be crossed with other collected data like responses to post-test questionnaires.

The last part of the debriefing consists in the definition of the design changes with their priority, defined according to different aspects, like problem impact or implementation time. Figure 4 depicts the debriefing guide, focusing on the main actions.

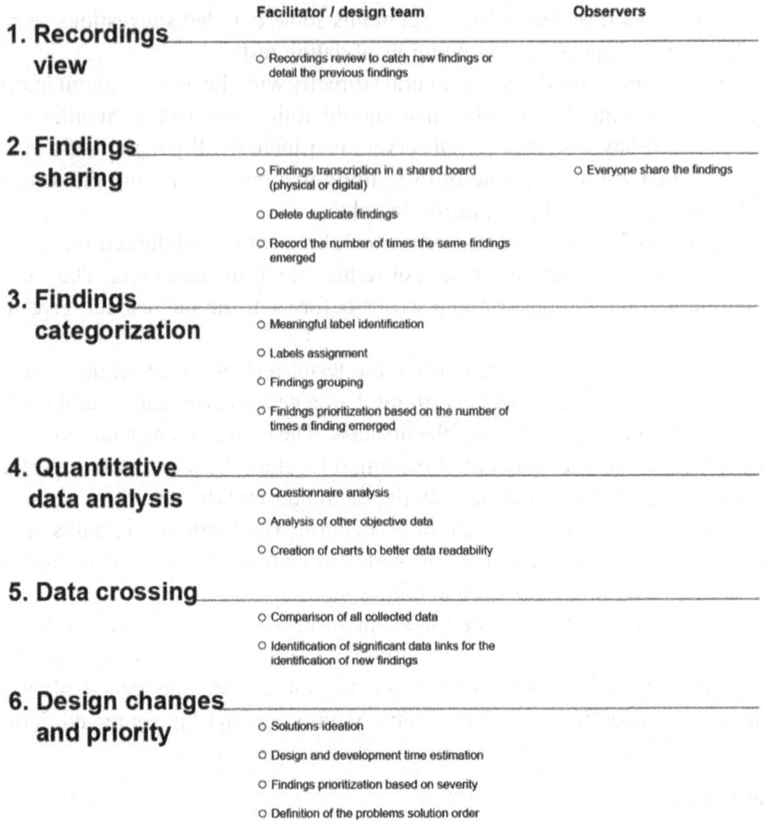

1. Recordings view	Facilitator / design team	Observers
	O Recordings review to catch new findings or detail the previous findings	
2. Findings sharing	O Findings transcription in a shared board (physical or digital)	O Everyone share the findings
	O Delete duplicate findings	
	O Record the number of times the same findings emerged	
3. Findings categorization	O Meaningful label identification	
	O Labels assignment	
	O Findings grouping	
	O Finidngs prioritization based on the number of times a finding emerged	
4. Quantitative data analysis	O Questionnaire analysis	
	O Analysis of other objective data	
	O Creation of charts to better data readability	
5. Data crossing	O Comparison of all collected data	
	O Identification of significant data links for the identification of new findings	
6. Design changes and priority	O Solutions ideation	
	O Design and development time estimation	
	O Findings prioritization based on severity	
	O Definition of the problems solution order	

Fig. 4. Debriefing guide

4 Use Cases

The proposed protocol was applied to agricultural tractors during an HMI redesign process. The considered HMI is designed for small-sized tractors where the interface has two main different functions: visualizing tractor information, and setting of tractor parameters as well as the agricultural implements parameters to achieve the desired performance.

The protocol was applied in two different stages of the redesign process, involving a sample of thirteen users (all male, 30–55 years old, with different levels of experience on this type of interface). Half of users tested a high-fidelity prototype installed on the tractor mock-up in the company Lab, half of users a functional prototype installed on a real tractor and tested on the field. The first analysis aimed at testing the information architecture, detecting the main usability issues and comparing different solutions. The second analysis supported the development phase based on full usability tests where both general UX and performance are investigated. Both usability testings were conducted internally by the company, involving the design and development teams.

4.1   Use Case 1

In the first use case, the protocol was applied to compare two different design solutions of the navigation menu, as conceived during the design phase. The two alternatives provide two different organizations of the system contents and therefore a different information architecture. The goal of the research was to understand which alternative is closer to the users' mental model and better satisfied their needs. This step was mandatory to define the following project steps.

The usability testing session was scheduled on high fidelity prototypes, before the development. The test was conducted in the company lab, because the research focus did not require field tests. For this study, it was considered that a combination of qualitative and quantitative data gives a full understanding of the UX. For this reason, data on task execution time, number of clicks, number of errors were collected. A final questionnaire was prepared to also gather subjective impressions. These data were useful for making a subjective and objective comparison of the two alternatives. Figure 5 shows how the decision planning guide was useful to plan the tests.

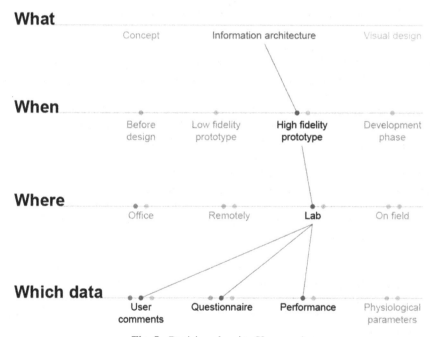

Fig. 5. Decision planning Use case 1

An accurate analysis was made to define the end user profiles to be involved. Of these, six users of different ages, different levels of experience and different use of the tractor were selected.

Based on the usability testing focus, four specific tasks were defined. In particular the used tasks are:

1. Homepage exploration
2. Visualize remotes settings
3. Visualize the cleanliness level of the cabin filter
4. Visualize the worked area
5. Visualize the percentage of engine rpm for automatic rear PTO engagement

These tasks were inserted into two scenarios that describe a real situation of use.

1. Today you have to plow a plot of land using a medium sized tractor. In plowing is essential (2) to visualize the state of valves in order to control plow movements, in particular the percentual flow rate of hydraulic piston in extend and retract. It's summer, so this operation involves raising a lot of dust, so you must (3) check the cleanliness of the cabin filter to prevent it from clogging. At the end of the work shift, you want (4) to view the data related to the worked area to know how extended the plot of land is.
2. Tomorrow morning you plan to carry out a process that involves the use of the mower, which uses the rear Power Take-Off (PTO) to move the cutting blades. You need (5) to check at what percentage of engine rpm the PTO is automatically engaged.

The tests were conducted by the HMI & Ergonomics team leader of the company. Observers belonged to the design team and watched the tests from another room; one of them was also the room technician. The users ran the tests one after the other and filled out the questionnaire at the end of each scenario.

During the debriefing phase all the findings were shared and organized to catch precious insights for the investigation focus. This activity involved the entire design team. The second debriefing activity consisted of watching the test recordings and marking the task duration, the number of errors and the attempts of all tasks for each user. Lastly, the replies to the questionnaires were also combined and schematized. Once all the data of both interfaces had been collected, they were compared to identify the alternative with the best usability for users.

The data collected during the tests highlighted the best alternative from the users' viewpoint, providing useful indications on how to continue the design. An example of finding is "Some users notice that the navigation menu in the Alternative no.2 is redundant" and "Almost all the users said that the Alternative no.1 works more easily and clearly". These comments were reflected also by the evaluation questionnaires. Figure 6 shows the collected quantitative data (execution times per task, number of clicks, and number of errors). The quantitative results were confirmed by the subjective user impressions.

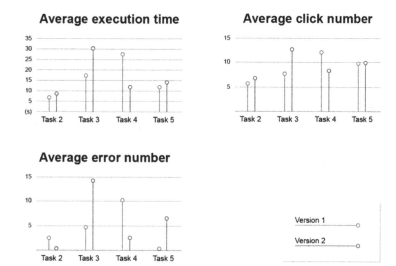

Fig. 6. Quantitative data results

4.2   Use Case 2

In the second use case, the protocol was applied to validate the visual design and the overall UX on field test. The need for the analysis arose from claims from the market (e.g., customers' remarks on the previous interface design). Therefore, the company wanted to guarantee legibility and understanding of the interface visual aspects before the product launch. Indeed, field tests allowed understanding which factors (e.g., tractor vibrations, light conditions) influence the usability of the interface in the real context of use. For these purposes, eye-tracking analysis was used to collect data about eye movements, user's attention area, and level of stress. Moreover, a post-test questionnaire was prepared to collect the user's opinion on the experience. Figure 7 shows the decision planning guide use to plan the tests.

The usability testing involved seven users, not involved in the previous testing, that matched the end users profiles.

The usability testing goal guides in the definition of six specific tasks:

1. Homepage exploration
2. Set remote n1 and n2 flow percentage in extension and retraction
3. Set hitch range of action
4. Set engine rpm
5. Set working lights
6. Clean UREA filter

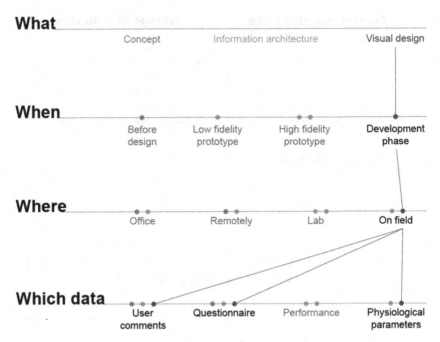

Fig. 7. Decision planning Use case 2

These tasks were inserted into a scenario to help the user perform the tasks more truthfully.

1. This afternoon you have to use the rotary harrow to refine the soil before sowing. Before starting, to move the harrow correctly, you must (2) set the remote number 1 and number 2 respectively with flow percentage values of 60% and 45% in extension and 30% and 45% in retraction. Moreover, you have (3) to set the range of action of the hitch, setting the minimum lift value to 20% and the maximum value to 80%. As a last setting, you have (4) to set the engine rpm value that you want to maintain during the work, setting it to 1600 rpm. At 6 o'clock it starts to get dark, so you want (5) to turn on the lights to better see the processing area around you. At the end of the work shift, you want to (6) clean the UREA filter, in order to have the tractor ready for the next workday.

A tractor was placed outside in a field close to the company and the tests were scheduled at different times of the day to recreate various lighting conditions. Only the user and the facilitator were in the tractor, while the other observers followed the test remotely. In this case also the development team was involved as observers. At the end of the test the users fill in the post-test questionnaire.

The debriefing phase includes the findings reorder, reading the questionnaires and the eye-tracking analysis. In particular, the latter generated heatmaps, gaze plots and provided data on the pupil diameter of the users.

The testing session allowed understanding of the effective UX and visual element visibility, guiding the necessary visual design changes. Results from users' comments and questionnaires' answers provided useful information about the overall experience with the interface. However, two users reported that in the brightest conditions, the icons with lighter colour cannot see properly. This fact focused the attention on contrast and icons design. Lastly, the heat-maps and gaze plots from eye-tracking helped to see if the user's attention focused on the correct area of the interface and the order the user's visual exploration path, as shown in Fig. 8.

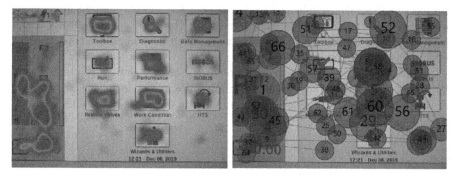

Fig. 8. Heatmap and gaze plot example for the Use case 2

5   Conclusions

Usability is often considered after the design process, when it is usually hard and pretty challenging to make substantial changes. However, a timely consideration of the usability analysis allows the companies to solve usability problems in advance, avoiding modifications after the product launch. The paper proposed a ready-to-use protocol to support usability analysis during industrial projects. This approach allows reducing costs, time and effort required to identify and fix the problems, improving the UX.

From use cases, the study demonstrated that the proposed protocol can be successfully adopted both in the Lab and on the field, and on different types of prototypes, to drive the interface design. The benefits brought by this methodology are manifold: on one hand, the company was able to plan and carry out the campaign test with a reduced time and cost effort; on the other hand, data collection and the subsequent data post-processing provided to the company a set of highly-detailed design guidelines. The first usability testing in the Lab was useful to understand the real users' needs and demands, highlighting the main usability problems and defining the best interface design solution. These feedbacks provide very precious information about how to continue the design. Moreover, the second user testing was useful to understand the level of usability offered by the interface and the related performance, and to review some design aspects during the development phase. In addition, the subjective qualitative data combined with quantitative data and eye-tracking mapping provided reliable feedback on the overall HMI usability.

A significant advantage to spread the usability testing practice even to non-usability experts was linked to the question of interface knowledge. Knowledge of the interface was essential to conduct a usability test and generally for this reason a usability expert needs an initial study of the interface, often long and difficult. Conversely, if the test is carried out by someone who already knows the interface to be tested well, the time needed to prepare for the test is reduced.

The HMI and Ergonomics team in the company reported that, thanks to the proposed protocol, the testing planning was fairly easy thanks to the guided decisions, and observers were able to better understand the users mind while using the interface. Moreover, the proposed approach helped the team to conduct usability testing all along the design process of a tractor cabin for the first time. The company team finally recognized the efficacy of this tool in providing a structured method of data collection and post-processing, overcoming data.

As a conclusion, the application of the proposed protocol validly supported also not-UX experts, designers and engineers from different disciplines, to understand the users' needs and to improve the overall system usability. In this sense, it provides universal access to usability practices.

References

1. International Organization for Standardization: ISO 9241-11: Guidance on Usability (1998)
2. Clamann, M., Kaber, D.B.: Applicability of usability evaluation techniques to aviation systems. Int. J. Aviat. Psychol. **14**, 395–420 (2004)
3. Burkard, E.C.: Usability testing within a Devsecops environment. In: 2020 Integrated Communications Navigation and Surveillance Conference (ICNS), pp 1C1-1. IEEE (2020)
4. François, M., Osiurak, F., Fort, A., Crave, P., Navarro, J.: Automotive HMI design and participatory user involvement: review and perspectives. Ergonomics **60**, 541–552 (2017)
5. Knoll, C., Vilimek, R., Schulze, I.: Developing the HMI of electric vehicles. In: Marcus, A. (ed.) DUXU 2014. LNCS, vol. 8519, pp. 293–304. Springer, Cham (2014). https://doi.org/10.1007/978-3-319-07635-5_29
6. Newell, A.F., Gregor, P., Morgan, M., Pullin, G., Macaulay, C.: User-sensitive inclusive design. Univ. Access Inf. Soc. **10**(3), 235–243 (2011). https://doi.org/10.1007/s10209-010-0203-y
7. Shitkova, M., Holler, J., Heide, T., Clever, N., Becker, J.: Towards usability guidelines for mobile websites and applications. In: Wirtschaftsinformatik, pp 1603–1617. Citeseer (2015)
8. Beul-Leusmann, S., Samsel, C., Wiederhold, M., Krempels, K.-H., Jakobs, E.-M., Ziefle, M.: Usability evaluation of mobile passenger information systems. In: Marcus, A. (ed.) DUXU 2014. LNCS, vol. 8517, pp. 217–228. Springer, Cham (2014). https://doi.org/10.1007/978-3-319-07668-3_22
9. Savioja, P., Norros, L.: Systems usability framework for evaluating tools in safety–critical work. Cogn Technol Work **15**, 255–275 (2013). https://doi.org/10.1007/s10111-012-0224-9
10. Grandi, F., Peruzzini, M., Campanella, C.E., Pellicciari, M.: Application of innovative tools to design ergonomic control dashboards. In: Advances in Transdisciplinary Engineering (2020)
11. Grandi, F., Zanni, L., Peruzzini, M., Pellicciari, M., Campanella, C.E.: A Transdisciplinary digital approach for tractor's human-centred design. Int. J. Comput. Integr. Manuf. **33**, 377–397 (2020)

12. Rajanen, D., et al.: UX professionals' definitions of usability and UX – a comparison between Turkey, Finland, Denmark, France and Malaysia. In: Bernhaupt, R., Dalvi, G., Joshi, A., Balkrishan, D.K., O'Neill, J., Winckler, M. (eds.) Human-Computer Interaction – INTERACT 2017, pp. 218–239. Springer International Publishing, Cham (2017). https://doi.org/10.1007/978-3-319-68059-0_14

13. Hertzum, M.: Images of usability. Int. J. Hum.-Comput. Interact. **26**, 567–600 (2010)

14. Villani, V., Lotti, G., Battilani, N., Fantuzzi, C.: Survey on usability assessment for industrial user interfaces. IFAC-PapersOnLine **52**, 25–30 (2019)

15. Barnum, C.M.: Usability Testing Essentials: Ready, Set... Test! Morgan Kaufmann, Boston (2020)

16. Quesenbery, W.: Balancing the 5Es of usability. Cut. IT J. **17**, 4–11 (2004)

17. Semantic Studios User Experience Design. https://semanticstudios.com/user_experience_design/

18. Fink, A.: How to Conduct Surveys: A Step-By-Step Guide. Sage Publications, Thousand Oaks (2015)

19. Salant, P., Dillman, I., Don, A.: How to conduct your own survey (1994)

20. Brooke, J., et al.: SUS-A quick and dirty usability scale. Usabil. Eval. Ind. **189**, 4–7 (1996)

21. Lewis, J.R.: IBM computer usability satisfaction questionnaires: psychometric evaluation and instructions for use. Int. J. Hum.-Comput. Interact. **7**, 57–78 (1995)

22. Charles, R.L., Nixon, J.: Measuring mental workload using physiological measures: a systematic review. Appl. Ergon. **74**, 221–232 (2019)

23. Nourbakhsh, N., Wang, Y., Chen, F., Calvo, R.A.: Using galvanic skin response for cognitive load measurement in arithmetic and reading tasks. In: Proceedings of the 24th Australian Computer-Human Interaction Conference, pp. 420–423 (2012)

24. Henelius, A., Hirvonen, K., Holm, A., Korpela, J., Muller, K.: Mental workload classification using heart rate metrics. In: 2009 Annual International Conference of the IEEE Engineering in Medicine and Biology Society, pp 1836–1839. IEEE (2009)

25. Seo, S.-H., Lee, J.-T., Crisan, M.: Stress and EEG. Converg. Hybrid Inf. Technol. **27** (2010)

26. Hu, S., Zheng, G.: Driver drowsiness detection with eyelid related parameters by support vector machine. Expert Syst. Appl. **36**, 7651–7658 (2009)

27. Nielsen, J., Landauer, T.K.: A mathematical model of the finding of usability problems. In: Proceedings of the INTERACT'93 and CHI'93 Conference on Human Factors in Computing Systems, pp 206–213 (1993)

28. Virzi, R.A.: Streamlining the design process: running fewer subjects. In: Proceedings of the Human Factors Society Annual Meeting, pp. 291–294. SAGE Publications, Los Angeles (1990)

29. Lewis, J.R.: Sample sizes for usability studies: Additional considerations. Hum. Factors **36**, 368–378 (1994)

30. Dumas, J.S., Loring, B.A.: Moderating Usability Tests: Principles and Practices for Interacting. Elsevier, Amsterdam (2008)

Social Network Behavior, from Information Search to Purchase: The Case of Generation X and Millennials

Célia M. Q. Ramos[1]([⊠]) [iD] and João M. F. Rodrigues[2] [iD]

[1] ESGHT, CinTurs and CEFAGE, Universidade do Algarve, 8005-139 Faro, Portugal
cmramos@ualg.pt
[2] LARSyS (ISR-Lisbon) and ISE, Universidade do Algarve, 8005-139 Faro, Portugal
jrodrig@ualg.pt

Abstract. Generation X and Millennials are very important to marketers, as they are the country's main workforce and consequently have the biggest purchasing power. Social networks enable these consumers to become more informed and direct them toward potential purchases. This study analyzed Generation X and Millennial consumers and their social network behavior while searching for information about commercial products and services, and investigated how these platforms contribute changing a visitor into a buyer. A survey was implemented based on the experience economy theory and was disseminated through social networks. Then a social networks user experience (SNUX) model was developed to study the UX associated with platform use as a medium to find information about products and services with intention to purchase. The data were analyzed via structural equations modeling using SmartPLS 2.0, and the results obtained showed that information disseminated with educational and/or entertainment content was the main variable that influenced purchase intention for these two generations.

Keywords: Social media marketing · Consumer behavior · Technological experience · Generation X · Millennials

1 Introduction

The massive use of the Internet has changed consumer paradigms in three key modes of communication (from-to): Business-to-Consumer (B2C), which allows consumers to get detailed information about products and services quickly; Consumer-to-Business (C2B), which allows business to gather a collection of characteristics about their potential customers; and Consumer-to-Consumer (C2C), which allows consumers to access a massive number of online recommendations, electronic word-of-mouth (e-WOM) reviews, or user generated content [1]. On the Internet, social networking platforms are having a disruptive influence on consumer behavior, contributing in a significant way to the change in consumption patterns. More and more people are using these networks to search for information about products and services, to consult testimonies, and to follow

© Springer Nature Switzerland AG 2021
M. Antona and C. Stephanidis (Eds.): HCII 2021, LNCS 12768, pp. 312–325, 2021.
https://doi.org/10.1007/978-3-030-78092-0_20

the latest trends, all with the main objective of obtaining the best product, according to their preferences, at the lowest price and fees [2].

Social networks help to connect persons with common interests and friends. Considering the growing number of users, brands are actively increasing their presence in these privileged areas of communication—where their potential consumers are—whatever their age and regardless of the generation to which they belong [3]. This means that products and services are being promoted within the medium of social networks to increase purchase intention, and this is encouraged by the fact that the costs associated with social media advertising campaigns are lower compared than for traditional media campaigns.

This paper seeks to determine the effect of social networks used by Generation X and Millennials in their purchase intentions, considering the concepts of the experience economy from Pine and Gilmore [4]. The main contribution is to determine whether or not the consumption of information by these generations on social networks contributes to increasing purchase intention, and if so, what kind of information (variables) are more prone to affecting this behavior. To do so, a survey was implemented based on the experience economy theory; the survey disseminated through social networks. Then, a social networks user experience (SNUX) model was developed to study the UX associated with platforms for finding information about products and services that led to intention to purchase. The data were analyzed through structural equations modeling (SEM) using SmartPLS 2.0.

The present section introduced the context and goal of the paper. Section 2 includes the definition of the investigation hypotheses, the state of the art for consumer behavior, and background information associated with Generation X and Millennials, followed by the concepts of the experience economy as associated with the social networking technological experience. Section 3 defines the methodology used and considers the concept of SEM. Section 4 presents and discusses the results, while Sect. 5 presents the conclusions, limitations, and opportunities for future work.

2   Customer Experience

The definition of *customer experience* has been widely discussed over the years in several scientific areas, such as business, tourism, and marketing. In 1998, Pine and Gilmore [4] presented the first definition "as events that engage individuals in a personal and memorable way", and presented four dimensions of the experience, which influence customer's memories and satisfaction: (a) entertainment, (b) education, (c) escapism, and (d) aesthetics. In accordance with Schmitt [5], consumers are "rational and emotional human beings who are concerned with achieving pleasurable experiences." Schmitt considers consumption as a holistic experience and predicts that there will be a means that allows people and companies to connect with one another at any time, where both can share their experiences, which Schmitt called "the omnipresence of the information technology." In 2010, Palmer [6] mentioned that, compared with Pine and Gilmore [4], there are several other definitions and studies on customer experience, but an academically robust definition that can serve as a managerially useful tool had not yet been presented—and the same remains true now.

To Lemon and Verhoef [7], it is critical that companies understand the customer experience in terms of the customer journey once this experience is increasingly of a social nature, because it contributes to customer satisfaction and loyalty. To Hoyer et al. [8], the customer journey is interactive and dynamic: consumers are increasingly connected, informed, empowered and active in searching for information and in creating their own experiences (while co-creating with companies) once technology transforms the customer experiences over the course of the buying journey. According to Calvo-Porral and Pesqueira-Sanchez [9], "there are differences in the motivations underlying technology behavior in each generational group" – in other words, the way each generation uses and is engaged with technology differs and, as a result, so do interactions with social networks.

2.1 Social Networks Experience and Generations Cohort

Use of social networking platforms has increased dramatically in the last decade as a result of digitalization and interconnected networks that potentiate communication among all the users, contribute to entertainment and allow users to participate in social activities anytime and anywhere while providing an easy way to search for information [9]. Users thus receive a kind of gratification by using these technologies. However, use and engagement with technology differ depending on age, so users can be grouped into generation cohorts. A *generational cohort* can be have different definitions; for instance Llopis-Amorós et al. [10] defined a cohort "as a group of people born in the same time span, united by age and life stage and shaped by the cultural circumstances experienced", while Reisenwitz and Fowler [11] defined it as "a group of consumers with common birth years and shared experiences, attitudes and behaviours" or "are groups of individuals born during the same time, resulting in great similarity in their beliefs, motivations, values and behaviours, giving rise to a generational identity that may be influencing technology usage patterns, engagement and behaviour" [9]. Each generation has unique expectations, experience, lifestyles, values, and demographics that influence their use and engagement with technology, as well as their buying behavior [9, 11]. There is, however, no consensus regarding the years in which a generational cohort begins and ends [10]. The present study focuses on the majority of the workforce, as this constitutes the generations that have more purchasing power. According to Twenge et al. [13], this makes sense for defining the beginning and end of each generation cohort as analyzed in terms of work values. The workforce consists of individuals from four generations: Baby Boomers (Boomers; born 1946–1964); Generation X (GenX; born 1965–1981); Millennials or Generation Y (GenY; born 1982–1999); and Centennials or Generation Z (GenZ; born 2000 until today).

The two generations addressed in this paper are GenX [13], brought up without the internet, social networks, or other information and communication technologies; however, this generation learned how to use these technologies as adults, easily assimilated them into their life. They are also called "digital immigrants" [9, 14]. This generation adopted technology and is one of the most highly educated, as well as being characterized by their skepticism, pragmatism, and an attitude of risk avoidance [9]. The other generation considered in this paper is the Millennial generation [13]. They have been immersed in technology throughout their life and have constantly been in contact with digital media, technologies, and the internet. They are considered "digital natives" [9]. These technologies have been present throughout their lives and influence their behavior, way of thinking, and learning. They also tend to perceive technology in a more positive way than does GenX. Millennials are highly active in the digital marketplace, always connected to social networks by creating and sharing content on blogs and social media sites [15].

Many companies are trying to reach out to different generations customers and trying to understand how to gain the attention of theses diverse buyers in the digital medium [12]. The techniques and strategies to achieve these multi-generational consumers need to be different in a way to appeal to the unique needs of each group, as a personalized offer, to build relationships, gain trust and close business taking in considerations an adequate product and services communication from the moment the need arises and they start looking for information, that is, in the pre-purchase phase.

2.2 Social Network Marketing and Influences on Consumer Behavior

The appearance of Web 2.0 around 2004 made possible bidirectional communication between users, which led to the appearance the social networking sites like Facebook. With this technology, organizations quickly realized that they should bet on strengthening relationships with consumers through social networks, instead of advertising transmitted through other communication technologies [16]. Social networking platforms offered companies greater capacity to reach their audiences than traditional media [10], and consequently, "social network marketing as emerged as one of the most important tools to identify and create marketing strategies" [16].

Social network marketing campaigns "need to be congruent and aligned with the needs of social network users, in this context it is critical to the companies that their marketers identify and understand the needs, motivation and expectations behind the social networks utilization" [17]. The level of personalization is critical: this describes both how a service or product is customized to satisfy individual preferences and how and where communication is carried out. This can be based in the profile or through contact, which can also be personalized or can be broadcast to everyone, as presented in the Social Media Matrix (SMM) in Fig. 1.

Communicating information about a product or service on social networks needs to take consider four elements: (a) relationship, (b) collaboration, (c) self-media, and (d) creative outlets [17]. Relationships can be considered where communications are made to the profile and customized according to customer preferences (e.g., as on Facebook). Self-media should be used for communication based on the profile but that are broadcast to a vast audience (e.g., Twitter). Collaboration is relevant for creating collaborative content, where several users co-create to add value or help others, but that can be customized according to the subject, profile, or question (e.g., forums about a subject). Creative Outlets can be used when companies want to communicate with multiple users based on the creative content made by other users (e.g., YouTube or Instagram).

The different types of social networks can be considered for different audiences or generations to meet specific needs. This provides great opportunities to discover consumer desires while creating a direct communication channel between consumers and business stakeholders where the information about products and services—as well as

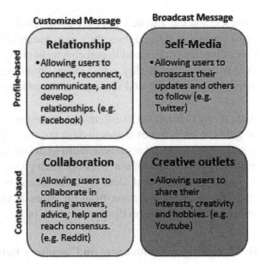

Fig. 1. Social Media Matrix, adapted from Zhu and Chen [17].

questions and testimonials—can be shared [16]. For GenX [12], social network communication should be in an informal style; the word-of-mouth testimonials from other users are very important in the decision-making process. For Millennials it is important to communicate with messages that say the company is contributing to creating a better world, that it has a mission to help the globe, thus enhancing the participation of these users in the company's mission. Images have a role relevant to the decision-making process. Many business stakeholders are defining different policies to reach potential customers in different generations and induce them to consume their products and service. Analysis can lead to greater understanding of how companies can get the attention of these buyers [12] and generate consumer interactions [16].

2.3   The Role of Information Search in the Consumer Purchase Decision Process

The *consumer purchase decision process* is a five-step model [11] that starts with (a) recognition, followed by (b) the information search, (c) evaluation of the alternatives, (d) making a purchase decision, and ending with the (e) post-purchase step. The problem recognition (a) corresponds to the phase when the consumers recognize a problem or need that could be satisfied by purchasing a product or service in the market, motivated by, for example, an insufficient stock of goods, changes in environmental characteristics, changes in financial status, promotional activities, individual development, or the availability of products. After recognition, the consumer will start to search for information (b) and may consult friends and family; however, they will often go to internet in the beginning to find information about products or services, and in the end will go to social networks to discover testimonials and educational information about the items that they may intend to purchase. It is important to stress that the internet is typically the source for search information during the second step and social networks are one of the major points for acquiring information [11]., so e-WOM is a factor that influences the purchase decision process.

When consumers consider that they have sufficient information in hand, they will evaluate the alternative solutions (c) or the choice set, based on attributes, degree of importance, belief in the brand, and satisfaction. The purchase decision (d) is made based on the evaluation supported during the information search. The post-purchase behavior (e) is based on consumer satisfaction (or lack thereof), which is related to the expectations for the perceived performance of the product or service. Users may then share their testimonials on social network sites (among others).

To help marketers understand the generations, McGorry and McGorry [18] suggest creating content that is shared in an entertaining and informative (infomercial) style. With the internet and its associated social media platforms, a new kind of economy has appeared that contributes to consumer behavior changes and to the need to develop new marketing strategies [19]. In parallel, Llopis-Amorós et al. [10] investigated the behavior associated with different ages and the moderating role of the generational cohort in the influence of social media communications on brand equity creation. This also validates the work of Xiang and Gretzel [20], who point out that these platforms serve to provide information about products, brands, and services, because they include a large variety of sources produced and shared by the users themselves, which increases credibility and trust in the shared content, contributing to the development of the social network experience and consumer engagement. In the above context, the first hypothesis of this research is to validate whether the social networking technological experience contributes to the purchase intentions influenced by information search in these sites.

Hypothesis #1(H_1): Does social networks' technological experience contribute to purchase intention, taking into consideration the information sought from these sites?

2.4   Social Networks Technological Experience

The use of social networks to find information contributes to the development of a technological experience in this context; it has also emerged as an important tool to identify and create opportunities to discover consumer's needs [16] and provides a new way to introduce product-associated content and increase consumer engagement. The relationship between the customer experience and the consumer decision-making process is shown in Fig. 2, where customer engagement is associated with all of the steps contributing to their customer and social network experience as they search for information, which in turn contributes to increase the purchase intention. In light of the new economy, the digital economy and the technological experience of social networks can contribute to the business can be analyzed according to economics of experience [4].

Aluri [22] applied the economics of experience theory to the use of the Pokémon GO App to investigate the factors that influence travelers to use the application and its influence on individual experience. Radder and Han [23] examined the experience of visiting a museum through the theory of the "experience economy." Ramos and Rodrigues [3] considered the effect of technological experience, taking into account the concepts of experience economics, to study how information consumption through social networks contributes to the well being of older populations, mainly from the technological experience associated with the use of these platforms. The experience economy by Pine and Gilmore [4], as mentioned in the beginning of Sect. 2, is a concept

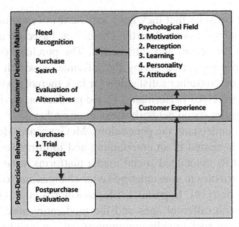

Fig. 2. Customer experience and the consumer decision process, adapted from San and Yazdan-ifard [21].

that unites four main dimensions—*educational, entertainment, aesthetics*, and *evasion*—on a scale from passive to active participation, and feelings of immersion to absorption (for more details see [4]). In terms of the use of social networks, from an information-consumption perspective (in different formats: text, photographs, videos), the dimension of entertainment can be considered in the viewing of videos and photos, communication with others, sharing of comments, and more. The educational dimension is revealed by searches for information regarding products, services, and news. Evasion can be observed while the user is viewing photos and videos. Aesthetics can be measured in terms of the environment provided by the social media interface—that is, whether it is pleasant, beautiful, or intuitive. All of dimensions contribute to the overall experience [4], so we investigate the impact that these four dimensions have on GenX and Millennial users, and consequently how the technological experience of social networks contributes to increasing purchase intention. For this analysis, in addition to H1, the following research hypotheses are considered:

Hypothesis #2 (H₂): Does the social networking technological experience contribute to the consumer evasion (and dreaming) of the generational cohorts?
Hypothesis #3 (H₃): Does the social networking technological experience contribute to the consumer education of the generational cohorts?
Hypothesis #4 (H₄): Does the social networking technological experience contribute to the consumer aesthetics valorization of the generational cohorts?
Hypothesis #5 (H₅): Does the social networking technological experience contribute to the consumer entertainment of the generational cohorts?
Hypothesis #6 (H₆): Does generation/cohort moderate the influence of social networking technological experience on consumer purchase intention?

3   Conceptual Research Model and Methodology

To investigate the objectives presented and the hypotheses formulated, a set of questions was considered for each dimension associated with the concept of the experience economy to assess the experience coupled with the use of social networks. These hypotheses were evaluated through a **research model** called the Social Network User Experience Model (SNUX) [3], as presented in Fig. 3.

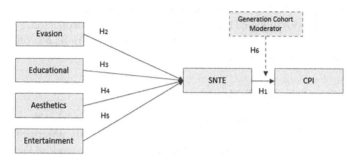

Fig. 3. SNUX model.

The SNUX model evaluates the experience economy dimensions of the *social networking technological experience* (SNTE) [3], where the concepts of the experience economy were considered in the context of the consumption of information and its contribution to consumer purchase intention. The initial model was adapted to reflect how searching for information on social networks influences the behavior of GenX and Millennial users, as measured by the variable *Consumer Purchase Intent* (CPI) and moderated by the variable *Generation.*

After the identification of the research hypotheses, the literature review, and delimitation of the research problem, the proposed study methodology was based on the following steps: (a) construction of the survey, (b) data collection, (c) selection and codification of data, (d) selection of methods and techniques of data analysis, and (e) analysis of the results.

The survey was released in December 2019 and received 1145 survey responses; a total of 215 GenX and 909 Millennial valid responses were obtained. The base sample was social network users between 21 and 54 years of age, using the probabilistic method of convenience sampling, in which the sample was selected based on the availability and accessibility of the population elements. After data collection, responses were codified for analysis by descriptive statistics to characterize the sample, and SEM was applied to evaluate the SNUX model.

4   Results

For sample characterization, the 215 GenX respondents had an average age of 46 years old; most were women (63.3%) and employees (68.8%). In terms of education level, the majority were graduates (41.9%), followed by high school (25.1%). Most of the respondents prefer to use smartphones (54.4%), followed by computers (31.6%), and tablets (13.5%). Most use social networks daily (55.4%), followed by occasionally (25.6%). Of these interviewed users, 97.7% had a Facebook profile, followed by 49.3% on YouTube, 40.9% on Instagram, and 27.4% on Twitter.

For the 909 Millennial respondents, the average age was 24 years; most were women (58.8%) and students (58.6%). In terms of education level, the majority were graduates (45.9), followed by high school (40.9%). Most of the respondents prefer to use smartphones (74.0%), followed by computers (17.9%), and tablets (7.8%). Most used social networks daily (49.3%) followed by are always using social networks (35.5%). Of these interviewed users, 97.8% had a Facebook profile, followed by 83.8% on Instagram, 79.1% on YouTube, and 66.8% on Snapchat.

4.1 Evaluation of the SNUX Measurement Model

SEM was considered for the data analysis because it is the model indicated for overcoming the need to measure multidimensional and not directly observable concepts, also called constructs or latent variables [24]. According to the work of Gefen, Straub, and Boudreau [25], SEM "has become de rigueur in validating instruments and testing linkages between constructs." Here, we used a model founded on variance-based SEM or partial least squares path SEM [26], which permits the construction of the model in an exploratory phase, with a little portion of the sample that can lack normal distribution [27, 28]. It is necessary to analyze the adjustment quality of the model through three steps: (a) evaluation of the measurement model to guarantee the convergent validity, (b) observation of internal consistency values, and (c) assessment of discrimination quality [28].

The measurement model was assessed to guarantee convergent validity by observation of the average variance extracted (AVE) [29], where all AVE values should be more than 0.5. The observation of internal consistency values takes into consideration the values for Cronbach's Alpha (CA) and Composite Reliability (CR), expressed by the *rho* of Dillon-Goldstein, which makes it possible to ascertain whether the sample is free of biases and whether, on the whole, it is reliable. The values for CA should be higher than 0.6, and values of 0.7 are considered adequate. Values of CR should be higher than 0.7, and values of 0.9 are considered satisfactory [27, 28]. Table 1 presents the estimated values for the adjustment quality of the SNUX model. Using the AVE values, it is possible to conclude that the SNUX model will converge to a satisfactory result, as all of the values are higher than 0.5 [29, 30]. The same table also shows that the internal consistency of the model is satisfactory, as values for CA and CR are above the required threshold.

The assessment of discriminant validity permits the investigation of the independence of the latent and other variables. This analysis can be done by observing cross loading, which should indicate the highest factor loadings in their respective latent variables compared with the observed variables, or by the Fornell-Larcker criterion [30], which compares the square roots of the AVE values for each latent variable with the Pearson's correlations between them. The square roots of AVEs should be larger than the correlations between the latent variables.

Table 1. Values of the adjustment quality of the SNUX model.

Millennials				Generation X			
	AVE	Composite Reliability	Cronbachs Alpha		AVE	Composite Reliability	Cronbachs Alpha
CPI	0.513888	0.880542	0.841597	CPI	0.529891	0.899669	0.872019
Aesthetics	0.711794	0.907792	0.864176	Aesthetics	0.733046	0.891705	0.826885
Educational	0.753106	0.92419	0.890870	Educational	0.730116	0.915293	0.877517
Entertainment	0.615180	0.864566	0.790693	Entertainment	0.801500	0.889732	0.755532
Evasion	0.689121	0.869250	0.776144	Evasion	0.656342	0.848260	0.746978
SNTE	0.509505	0.837060	0.756701	SNTE	0.575118	0.842757	0.758525

The cross loadings of the observed variables in one latent variable were always higher than the cross loadings of the observed variables in the other latent variable, which shows that the model has discriminant validity in accordance with the work of Chin [27]. Taking into consideration the values presented in Table 2, the variance identified in the AVE must exceed the variance that the over-served variables share with other latent variables of the model. In practice, discriminant validity exists when the squared root of the AVE of each construct is greater than the correlation values between the latent variables and the observed variables [31]. Table 2 shows that the SNUX model has discriminant validity, as confirmed by the first process, once the values of the square roots of the AVE values, presented in the main diagonal, are higher than the correlation between the latent variables, in accordance with Fornell-Larcker [30]. After guaranteeing discriminant validity in the evaluation of the measurement model (meaning that the adjustments in the measurement model have ended), the next step is the evaluation of the structural model.

Table 2. Values of the correlations between the latent variables and the square roots of the AVE values (on the main diagonal), with A – Aesthetics, Ed – Educational, En – Entertainment and Ev – Evasion.

Millennials							Generation X						
	CPI	A	Ed	En	Ev	SNTE		CPI	A	Ed	En	Ev	SNTE
CPI	0.717						CPI	0.728					
A	0.269	0.844					A	0.244	0.856				
Ed	0.33	0.442	0.868				Ed	0.403	0.539	0.854			
En	0.257	0.553	0.427	0.784			En	0.219	0.285	0.398	0.895		
Ev	0.205	0.366	0.332	0.403	0.830		Ev	0.162	0.304	0.402	0.283	0.810	
SNTE	0.509	0.403	0.478	0.457	0.259	0.714	SNTE	0.514	0.296	0.463	0.34	0.211	0.758

Note: All the values are statistically significant at 5%

4.2 Evaluation of the Structural Model

In the evaluation of the structural model, the first step is the evaluation of the coefficient of determination (R^2) of the endogenous latent variables. In this study there are two endogenous latent variables: CPI with an $R^2 = 25.9$ and SNTE with a $R^2 = 31.6$ for the Millennials and CPI with an $R^2 = 26.4$ and SNTE with a $R^2 = 24.5$ for GenX. These values are moderate and represent the portion of the variance of the endogenous variables that is explained by the structural model [31]. Another aspect to analyze is the model's capacity for prediction, which requires the calculation of the Stone-Geisser indicator (Q^2) and the Cohen indicator (f^2) associated to the effect size [29].

The Stone-Geisser indicator (Q^2) evaluates how close the model is to what was expected; the Cohen indicator (f^2) evaluates how useful each construct is for the model. The Q^2 associated with the endogenous latent variables presents a value higher than zero, which means that both variables have predictive power, and the structural model has predictive relevance, as presented in Table 3.

Table 3. Indicator Values of the Predictive Validity and Effect Size, with EXLV - Exogeneous Latent Variable and ENLV – Endogeneous Latent Variable.

Millennials		Q^2	F^2	Generation X		Q^2	F^2
CPI	ENLV	0.122	0.349	CPI	ENLV	0.122	0.381
Aesthetic	EXLV		0.514	Aesthetic	EXLV		0.443
Education	EXLV		0.574	Education	EXLV		0.539
Entertainment	EXLV		0.355	Entertainment	EXLV		0.361
Evasion	EXLV		0.369	Evasion	EXLV		0.349
SNTE	*ENLV*	*0.157*	*0.278*	SNTE	*ENLV*	*0.125*	*0.303*

The structural model was analyzed, with the individual analysis of the coefficients of the respective model (path coefficients) [30, 31], where it was necessary to analyze the sign, value, and statistical significance, which should be more than 1.96 (bilateral and with a 5% significance level). The model can also be analyzed by its direct effects. Table 4 presents the direct effect, which indicates, by the t-test value of 1.291, that H_0 should be not rejected and the direct coefficient should be zero. This means that the aesthetic dimension does not have an effect on the SNTE. Also, the evasion dimension has a t-test value lower than 1.96, which means that this dimension does not influence the SNTE. However, the educational and entertainment dimension does have an effect on the SNTE and increases the CPI, so it can be concluded that the utilization of social networks contributes to influencing consumer purchase intention if the content is educational and has some entertainment value associated with the products and services that they intend to buy.

Table 4. Direct effects in the structural relationships between the latent variables, with A – Aesthetics, Ed – Educational, En – Entertainment, Ev – Evasion, O - Original Sample, M - Sample Mean, STDEV - Standard Deviation, STERR - Standard Error (STERR) and T - T Statistics = |O/STERR|

Millennials						Generation X					
	O	M	STDEV	STERR	T		O	M	STDEV	STERR	T
A->'SNTE	0.121	0.135	0.094	0.094	**1.291**	A->SNTE	0.047	0.089	0.065	0.065	**0.732**
Ed->SNTE	0.314	0.312	0.099	0.099	3.159	Ed->SNTE	0.366	0.370	0.139	0.139	2.637
En->SNTE	0.253	0.252	0.125	0.125	2.017	En->SNTE	0.181	0.179	0.089	0.089	2.04
Ev->SNTE	0.009	0.068	0.05	0.05	**0.171**	Ev->SNTE	-0.001	-0.092	0.069	0.069	**0.022**
SNTE->AVU	0.509	0.521	0.082	0.082	6.201	SNTE->AVU	0.514	0.534	0.075	0.075	6.866

5   Conclusions

Companies have changed the way they communicate about products by building social networks into their business strategies. Consequently, all stakeholders need to understand consumer behavior and characteristics to achieve their interest and potentiate purchase intention to increase or maintain the sales volumes and increase profitability. It is relevant to analyze GenX and Millennial users' perceptions of the technological experience of using social networks and to study how social networks contribute to influencing the consumer purchase intention. This study investigated this issue by considering the concepts associated with the experience economy from an information acquisition perspective contribute to influence the purchasing intent, which led to considering the research model called SNUX [3], which, after the necessary adaptations, was analyzed through SEM.

In terms of the technological experience associated with the concepts of the experience economy and the use of social networks by GenX and Millennials, the model found no empirical evidence to support a structural relationship between the aesthetic and evasion dimensions and the SNTE. The educational and entertainment dimensions do, however, contribute to the SNTE, which contributes to an increase in consumer purchase intention among GenX and Millennial users. Future work should focus on the analysis of the relationship between the reasons and the dimensions of the technological experience provided by social networks for all the generations, and the results should be compared across generations.

Acknowledgments. This paper is financed by National Funds provided by FCT - Foundation for Science and Technology through project CinTurs (UIDB/04020/2020), CEFAGE (UIDB/04007/2020) and LARSyS - FCT Project UIDB/50009/2020.

References

1. Rose, S., Clark, M., Samouel, P., Hair, N.: Online customer experience in e-retailing: an empirical model of antecedents and outcomes. J. Retail. **88**(2), 308–322 (2012)

2. Ramos, C.M., Matos, N.: Customer experience journey in social networks–analysis of cohorts' behavior. In: International Congress on Engineering and Sustainability in the XXI Century, pp. 1180–1195. Springer, Cham (2019). https://doi.org/10.1007/978-3-030-30938-1_93

3. Ramos, C.M.Q., Rodrigues, J.M.F.: The contribution of social networks to the technological experience of elderly users. In: Antona, M., Stephanidis, C. (eds.) HCII 2019. LNCS, vol. 11573, pp. 538–555. Springer, Cham (2019). https://doi.org/10.1007/978-3-030-23563-5_43

4. Pine, B.J., Gilmore, J.H.: Welcome to the experience economy. Havard Bus. Rev. **76**(4), 97–105 (1998)

5. Schmitt, B.: Experiential marketing. J. Mark. Manag. **15**(1–3), 53–67 (1999)

6. Palmer, A.: Customer experience management: a critical review of an emerging idea. J. Serv. Mark. **24**(3), 196–208 (2010)

7. Lemon, K.N., Verhoef, P.C.: Understanding customer experience throughout the customer journey. J. Mark. **80**(6), 69–96 (2016)

8. Hoyer, W.D., Kroschke, M., Schmitt, B., Kraume, K., Shankar, V.: Transforming the customer experience through new technologies. J. Interact. Mark. **51**, 57–71 (2020)

9. Calvo-Porral, C., Pesqueira-Sanchez, R.: Generational differences in technology behaviour: comparing millennials and Generation X. Kybernetes **49**(11), 2755–2772 (2019)

10. Llopis-Amorós, M.P., Gil-Saura, I., Ruiz-Molina, M.E., Fuentes-Blasco, M.: Social media communications and festival brand equity: millennials vs centennials. J. Hosp. Tour. Manag. **40**, 134–144 (2019)

11. Reisenwitz, T.H., Fowler, J.G.: Information sources and the tourism decision-making process: an examination of Generation X and Generation Y consumers. Glob. Bus. Rev. **20**(6), 1372–1392 (2019)

12. Williams, K.C., Page, R.A.: Marketing to the generations. J. Behav. Stud. Bus. **3**(1), 37–53 (2011)

13. Twenge, J.M., Campbell, S.M., Hoffman, B.J., Lance, C.E.: Generational differences in work values: leisure and extrinsic values increasing, social and intrinsic values decreasing. J. Manag. **36**(5), 1117–1142 (2010)

14. Hill, R.: Embracing digital: key considerations for publishers, marketers and customers. Inf. Serv. Use **37**(3), 349–354 (2017)

15. Noble, S.M., Haytko, D.L., Phillips, J.: What drives college-age Generation Y consumers? J. Bus. Res. **62**(6), 617–628 (2009)

16. Mohamad, M., Zawawi, Z.A., Hanafi, W.N.W.: The influences of social network marketing on student purchase intention in the digital era: the mediating role of consumer engagement. Glob. Bus. Manag. Res. **10**(3), 938–948 (2018)

17. Zhu, Y.Q., Chen, H.G.: Social media and human need satisfaction: implications for social media marketing. Bus. Horiz. **58**(3), 335–345 (2015)

18. McGorry, S.Y., McGorry, M.R.: Who are the centennials: marketing implications of social media use and preferences. In: AMA Procs, pp. 179–181 (2017)

19. Sharma, A.: Consumer behaviour and centennials. In: Shukla, S., Gupta, K., Bhardwaj, P. (eds.) Marketing to Centennials in Digital World, pp. 37–49. Greater Noida: Bazooka (2019)

20. Xiang, Z., Gretzel, U.: Role of social media in online travel information search. Tour. Manage. **31**(2), 179–188 (2010)

21. San, Y.W., Yazdanifard, R.: How consumer decision making process differ from youngster to older consumer generation. J. Res. Mark. **2**(2), 151–156 (2014)

22. Aluri, A.: Mobile augmented reality (MAR) game as a travel guide: insights from Pokémon Go. J. Hosp. Tour. Technol. **8**(1), 55–72 (2017)

23. Radder, L., Han, X.: An examination of the museum experience based on pine and Gilmore's experience economy realms. J. Appl. Bus. Res. **31**(2), 455–470 (2015)

24. Hoyle, R.H.: The structural equation modeling approach: basic concepts and fundamental issues. In: Hoylw, R.H. (ed.) Structural equation modeling: Concepts, issues, and applications, pp. 1–15. Sage, Thousand Oaks, CA (1995)
25. Gefen, D., Straub, D., Boudreau, M.C.: Structural equation modeling and regression: guidelines for research practice. Commun. Assoc. Inf. Syst. **4**(7), 1–78 (2000)
26. Reinartz, W., Haenlein, M., Henseler, J.: An empirical comparison of the efficacy of covariance-based and variance-based SEM. Int. J. Res. Mark. **26**(4), 332–344 (2009)
27. Chin, W.W.: How to write up and report PLS analyses. In: Handbook of partial least squares, pp. 655–690. Springer, Heidelberg (2010). https://doi.org/10.1007/978-3-540-32827-8_29
28. Ringle, C.M., Silva, D., Bido, D.D.S.: Modelagem de equações estruturais com utilização do SmartPLS. REMark **13**(2), 56–73 (2014)
29. Hair, J.F., Hult, T.M., Ringle, C.M., Sarstedt, M.: A Primer on Partial Least Squares Structural Equation Modeling (PLS-SEM). Los SAGE, Angeles (2014)
30. Henseler, J., Ringle, C.M., Sinkovics, R.R.: The use of partial least squares path modeling in international marketing. Adv. Int. Mark. **20**, 277–319 (2009)
31. Bollen, K.A.: Structural Equations with Latent Variables. Wiley, Hoboken (1989)

Citizen Science for All?

Elisabeth Unterfrauner[1]([✉]), Claudia M. Fabian[1], Johanna Casado[2],
Gonzalo de la Vega[2], Beatriz Garcia[2], and Wanda Díaz-Merced[2]

[1] Centre for Social Innovation, Linke Wienzeile 246, 1150 Vienna, Austria
unterfrauner@zsi.at
[2] Instituto de Tecnologías en Detección y Astropartículas (ITeDA), Azopardo 313,
5501 Godoy Cruz, Mendoza, Argentina

Abstract. Citizen science is about democratising access to science for all citizens. A crucial question in this respect however is, whether democratisation of access to research in terms of reaching and involving diverse citizens actually takes place in citizen science projects. Unfortunately, this does not seem to be the case. The EU funded project Reinforce adheres to principles of inclusiveness and monitors and evaluates whether these principles are being met. Safeguarding that citizen science projects are inclusive means addressing technical as well as psychological and sociological aspects. On the technical side, in order for people with visual impairments to participate, the Reinforce Citizen Science projects, which are implemented on the Zooniverse platform, have to be made accessible. The software SonoUno has been developed to transform images into sound signals. A second strand for reaching diverse target groups is the participatory engagement strategy of the project. The applied evaluation process systematically targets quantitative and qualitative methods to evaluate the inclusivity approach of the project. The paper seeks to discuss the inclusivity aspect of citizen science projects in general, to then describe the project Reinforce with its strategies to make citizen scientists projects more inclusive especially for people with visual impairments, technically, psychologically and sociologically. Furthermore, we will share the evaluation framework that has been elaborated to monitor the diversity of participants and inclusivity of the citizen science projects.

Keywords: Citizen science · Accessibility · Inclusiveness · Evaluation

1 Introduction

Citizen Science was firstly introduced to the Oxford English Dictionary in 2014 as "Scientific work undertaken by members of the general public, often in collaboration with or under the direction of professional scientists and scientific institutions" [1]. The number of citizen science projects has constantly been growing in the past years as has the claim for bringing science and society closer together with initiatives such as the SwafS (Science with and for Society) research programmes [2] and the Responsible Research and Innovation framework (RRI) [3, 4] supported by the European Commission. Indeed, citizen science adheres to many of the RRI keys such as public engagement, science education and open access [5–7].

© Springer Nature Switzerland AG 2021
M. Antona and C. Stephanidis (Eds.): HCII 2021, LNCS 12768, pp. 326–335, 2021.
https://doi.org/10.1007/978-3-030-78092-0_21

Citizen science is about democratising access to science for all citizens and broadening participation in science by principles of inclusion [8–10]; it goes beyond informing them about research that goes on in the so-called ivory tower of research but that instead empowers citizens to become citizen scientists themselves and to be involved in a research project as mainstream players; from contributing to a research project to actually collaborating with scientists in the different phases along the process [11–13]. This may comprise involvement already at the stage of generating the research question, developing a theory or hypotheses for being tested, to the actual research undertaken, from data collection, to data analysis and interpretation, and lastly also publications in which individual participants or communities may have a key role. By definition, when citizens do not have an active role in the research process, for instance, if research is making use of citizen data, this is not considered citizen science.

The benefit ideally takes place on both sides. On the one hand, citizens acquire new skills or expand their skills such as scientific literacy and critical thinking, gain new knowledge in the domain of the research project and eventually change their attitude towards science [14]. On the other hand, research benefits from the work that citizens carry out, e.g., by generating new results, by contributing to data classifications that would not be possible otherwise, or by bringing in a new perspective to the research process.

A crucial question in this respect however is, whether democratisation of access to research projects in terms of reaching and involving diverse citizens truly takes place in citizen science projects. Unfortunately, this does not seem to be the case. Studies have shown that the typical (statically normal) citizen scientist is male, white and well educated [e.g. 15].

The paper seeks to discuss the inclusivity aspect of citizen science projects in general, to then describe the project Reinforce with its strategies to make citizen scientists projects more inclusive especially for diverse functional people[1], technically, psychologically and sociologically. Furthermore, we will share the evaluation framework that has been elaborated to monitor the diversity of participants and inclusivity of the citizen science projects.

2 Principles for Inclusivity of Citizen Science

The European Citizen Science Association (ECSA) [17] has published ten principles of citizen science that serve as quality criteria for citizen science projects. These comprise principles such as citizens should have "a meaningful role in the project" and both, citizens and researchers should benefit from their participation in the project, and the project should result in a genuine science outcome. Interestingly, inclusivity in terms of diversity like disability or functional diversity is not mentioned.

The EU funded project Reinforce (REsearch INfrastructures FOR Citizens in Europe) adheres to principles of inclusiveness and monitors and evaluates whether these principles are being met regarding access to information, and aspects of presentation,

---

[1] The term 'disability' has been expanded to definition people' by the World Health Organization (WHO) 'diverse functional to express potential co-morbidity that pertains all disabilities [16] and which integrates the ways people perform as well as their participation in society.

delivery and response to scientific data analysis. Reinforce implements four different citizen science projects on Zooniverse, one of the biggest citizen science online platforms with more than a million contributors. Currently, the platform hosts about 80 citizen science projects, and since it is online people from all over the world can contribute. Projects on Zooniverse typically are data categorisation projects where visual or acoustic data is represented and the participant is asked to categorise the data after he or she has gone through a tutorial explaining how the categorisation has to be performed. Zooniverse seeks to actively comply with accessibility standards and thus should be accessible for diverse functional people but the platform does not safeguard that also the citizen science projects are actually accessible.

The four Reinforce projects are set in the fields of astronomy, particle physics, life in deep sea, and archaeology. Reinforce aims at reaching diverse audiences; among the defined target groups are people with visual impairments and the elderly.

Safeguarding that citizen science projects are inclusive means addressing technical as well as psychological and sociological aspects. The following subchapters describe both the technical as well as the engagement strand of the Reinforce project.

2.1 Technical Strand

On the technical side, in order for people with visual impairments to participate, the Zooniverse projects have to be made accessible, they have to go far beyond the systematised standards defined by the W3C (world wide web consortium) consortium. Reinforce accessibility seeks to equalise access in terms of error recovery, error prevention, and dynamic interactions for peoples with functional diversity (or peoples with disabilities).

The four citizen science projects are data classification projects where data of large Research Infrastructures such as CERN (Conseil européen pour la recherche nucléaire) are shared with citizen scientists who are asked after a short tutorial to classify the presented data and by doing so, to support new discoveries in the field. For doing so, not only the portal, the Zooniverse platform, but also the data has to be accessible. Furthermore, data has to be usable, useful, efficient and effective without submitting the user to physical effort or provoking changes of attention focus that may frustrate them and make it difficult to complete the task. To this end, astronomers have developed a software called SonoUno to transform images into sound signals and to enrich current data analysis techniques with the use of sound for the analysis and perusal of astronomy data. With the SonoUno the space science signals, (which are traditionally displayed using only visual methods) are symmetrically displayed using different sound modalities and visual display. The use of audio in astrophysics and space sciences has been limited to education and people outreach approaches, conveying an auditory image. Through the sonoUNO software, the Reinforce project seeks to go beyond the traditional auditory image approach which ignores temporal build-up and short- and long- term dependencies, which leads and results in non-causal analyses. Reinforce seeks for sonoUno to bring an auditory salience analysis [18] to the loop of identification of events in gravitational wave data. This approach will benefit data analysis approaches, the participation of a wider bandwidth of peoples, and among many factors the facing of the fact that cognition and perceptual processes used for data analysis are not two separate processes. For example, in terms of audio perception the tones we hear every day are not sinusoidal which is an aspect that has been scarcely considered in the literature [19]. In space science and astronomy most of the time it is given the impression that the process of signal identification is determined by recognition of signal and this is not the case. The perception process yields not only to perceive the incoming stimulus but also its interpretation, (conscious or unconscious), in the context of previous experience. Without the later aspect, our perceptual abilities to identify signal is limited.

In the four projects, images can be accessed as signals and people with visual impairments, literally speaking, "can hear the stars" [20]. This additional sensorial representation brings another context, maybe of benefit in general for people, with other contexts of performance and functioning, for peoples that are auditory oriented, for multi-context analysis of information [21] or for the elderly who often do not have the best sight anymore.

The Software SonoUno. The human ability to analyse data through different senses improves the analysis of the information under study. Furthermore, the possibility of analysing the same information in a multi-modal way improves accessibility. Taking the foregoing into account, it is proposed to develop user-centred data sonification software that allows the analysis of the data through visualization and audification. The access to astronomical/scientific performance is an opportunity for multiple learning.

Almost all that we know about the Universe is not in the visible region. In the same way that the Astrophysics multi-wavelength and multi-messenger opened a new window to the Cosmos, a new tool to develop data analysis and data retrieval tools that will permit people with other sensory styles to explore scientific data and make science is proposed, a multimodal approach.

According to that, sonoUno [22] is a sonification software for scientific data based on User Centred Design, the input data must be presented on a table (txt or csv files). The software has been developed based on the study of previous software, such as Sonification Sandbox [23], MathTrax [24] and xSonify [25], and standards of accessibility like the ISO 9241-171:2008 (Guidance on software accessibility) which were taken into account for the design. A preliminary study showed that some of the programmes available to sonify large data sets and symmetrically display the graph are not fully accessible according to the ISO standard. It was identified that those prototypes perhaps lacked high granularity user centred evaluations. This, for instance, threatening to include those users only in terms of intention and theory and for instance, leaves those users out of the loop.

In order to develop an accessible graphical user interface, the sonoUno team initially performed a theoretical framework based on bibliography of user cases focusing first on the comorbidity of blind and visual impairments and conducted focus group sessions with visual impairment people and sighted people.

The develop language is Python and the sonoUno team used modular design, to assure collaborative work. SonoUno is multi-platform, tested on Windows 10, Ubuntu (16.04 and 18.04), CentOS 7, and Mac (Mojave and Catalina); the development team works continuously to maintain this benefit. In order to foster democratisation of data analysis portability, accessibility, and multisensory approach, and data analysis are symmetrical priorities of the team.

SonoUno Main Characteristics. The main goal of sonoUno is to allow the user to open data files (txt or csv extension), show the plot, and sonify the data. This tool was created taking into account:

- The use of sound and visual modalities for data exploration (so far). All sensorial modalities included in the prototype are based on perceptual scientific evidence on its efficiency for astronomy data analysis.
- A user-centred design from the beginning, which allows combining accessible features with the necessary scientific efficiency and I/O (input/output) flow.
- A completely open source and cross-platform tool.
- The need to eliminate the barriers presented by current technologies for people with sensory and motor disabilities.
- Allows improving the work with different styles of data exploration by leading scientists.

Between some of its functionalities, the sonification settings allow to change the pitch, volume, the min and max frequency and the timbre. Also, the sound setting supports modifying the envelope of the sound. Additionally, SonoUno allows to select a specific range of data, mark and save point of interest (picks, special features), apply predefined mathematical functions (for example, logarithm and square), and apply user-defined mathematical states through an GNUOctave interface (c.f. Fig. 1). The user is able to save the plot, the sound, a text file with the marked points on the data, and a csv file with the final plotted data to work offline with the results.

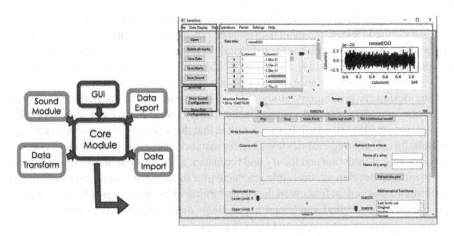

Fig. 1. SonoUno modular software.

2.2 Participatory Engagement Strand

In any public participation initiative as is the case also with citizen science, it has to be kept in mind that the term 'public' to describe the general population is not a monolithic entity [26, 27]. Thus, the public or citizen as such as is challenging to involve in any kind of public engagement undertaking; the 'public' has to be defined: Who should be involved? Who is concerned and which viewpoints are important to have represented?

And where do we find them? And why should they contribute? What is in for them? How to keep them interested and how to motivate those that initially are not pre-disposed?

These tricky questions were taken up in the preparation of the project proposal and led to a second stream of involving the 'public'.

Besides the technical side, this second strand for reaching diverse target groups is the participatory engagement strategy of the project. Science cafés, summer and winter schools, open lab days, open school days, etc. are organised to get people interested and to become aware of the four citizen science projects. It is important to transmit the idea that anyone and everyone actually can become active in science and thus to support active citizenship and to establish the self-concept and the self-efficacy towards citizen science activities. This is especially important for diverse functional people who might not feel empowered to actually contribute to research processes. Research becomes more relatable and tangible when direct contact has been established and exchange between researchers and potential future citizen scientists has taken place in the framework of this above mentioned kind of events.

3   Evaluative Framework for Inclusivity

Whether these two strands of making the project accessible for diverse target groups will be sufficient or whether these two strands have to be further improved is part of the formative and summative evaluation of the project. Formative evaluation will help to identify hints on how to improve the two strands in order to further support inclusion and diversity throughout the project. The evaluation framework is guided by the logic model by Kurz and Kubek [28], which when applied to a citizen science project, safeguards that not only the project processes and the scientific outcomes are evaluated, but also the effects on the participants and the society. Table 1 gives an overview of the three distinct evaluation areas; outputs- the offers of the project and people that are reached; outcomes – what the project wants to achieve within the target group; and impact – the contribution we want to make on the societal level.

Constant monitoring of who participates in engagement activities as well as on the four Zooniverse projects (see box 1b – use of output by target group, Table 1) and continuous feedback by citizen scientists (box 1c- participants' satisfaction) will help to evaluate whether defined target groups are being met and whether the citizen science activities are accessible from different points of view, not only technically but also in terms of the perceived difficulty of the tasks. The geographical distribution of participants as well as indicators for inclusion are part of the continuous monitoring. This information will help to further develop the engagement strategy and to plan additional events to eventually compensate for people underrepresented in the reach of the project. The collected feedback by participants will support the content development of the events and detect additional training needs to empower all participants to contribute to the citizen science projects on Zooniverse.

At the core of the evaluation however is the detection of the actual benefits on participants' side in terms of the above-mentioned areas: knowledge, skills, and attitudes

Table 1. Logic model of Reinforce outputs, outcomes and impacts.

1 OUTPUT	2 OUTCOMES	3 IMPACT
1a - Output	2a - New knowledge, skills, attitudes and awareness	3 - Social and economic impact
Reinforce projects on Zooniverse	Citizen Scientists gain new knowledge, skills and attitudes	Enhancing science literacy of the society
Sonification of projects		
Citizen Science education		
Empowerment of Community	Researchers gain new knowledge	Improving the public understanding of science and critical thinking
Educational resources		
1b - Use of output by target groups	2b - Change actions/behaviour	
Participation in Reinforce projects	Motivation for science career	Economic costs and benefits of citizen science & knowledge
Participation in educational events	Cooperation with researchers	
Participation in community empowerment activities	Exchange of experiences	
Inclusion of diverse target groups	Improving mutual understanding	
1c - Participants satisfaction	2c - Living conditions	
Experience with Reinforce projects	Empowerment & Self-efficacy	Science career motivation
Experience with Reinforce events	Participation even in confinement (COVID-19)	

(c.f. box 2b of Table 1) with a focus on diverse groups. A pre- and post-questionnaire for citizen scientists comprises questions in these three areas as well as questions regarding potential visual impairments and a question regarding whether they feel like a member of a discriminated-against group based on gender, sexual orientation, race, migration history, religion, disability and for other reasons. This information will allow us to comparatively assess the progress of diverse functional people as well as other marginalised groups. Aspects of behaviour change (c.f. box 2b, Table 1) and living conditions (box 2c, Table 1) are also part of the questionnaire in order to detect an immediate impact on people's motivation to participate in science also in the future (questions regarding actions in the future).

Figure 2 gives an overview of the different evaluation instruments in the different phases of the project implementation. In the initial acquisition phase to make citizens aware of the opportunity of contributing to the four citizen science projects and to empower them to do so, in the event monitoring sheet demographic data and information on the functional diversity of participants are collected. The feedback survey helps to identify gaps and to adapt to it accordingly in the engagement strategy. The continuous involvement in the four Zooniverse projects will be monitored through the access data and the Zooniverse experience survey. In order to measure long-term impacts as well as impacts on a societal level (cf. box 3, Table 1), a self-assessment tool developed by Kieslinger et al. [29], will be used to reflect together, the evaluation with the research team. The authors provide a detailed list of questions that can be applied as a self-assessment tool for projects to assess process and feasibility as well as outcome and impact.

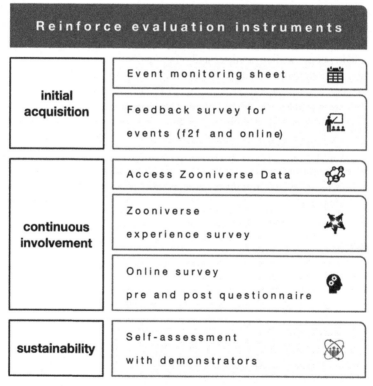

Fig. 2. Evaluation instruments along the different implementation phases of the project

All online questionnaires, i.e. the feedback survey for events, the pre- and the postquestionnaires of all four citizen science projects, have been developed in LimeSurvey[2] and have been tested in respect to accessibility by diverse functional people using

---

[2] https://www.limesurvey.org/.

different kinds of assistive technology. Their feedback has further helped to optimise the evaluation instruments with respect to accessibility.

4 Summary and Conclusion

The paper has identified a gap in citizen science in terms of inclusion and lacking true democratisation of access to science. Reaching diverse people has been neglected in most citizen science projects so far, and studies indicate that the majority of citizen scientists are to be considered privileged as most are white, male and, with a higher educational background.

Part of the achievements of the proposal is connected with the possibility to support organisations to carry out honest assessments, about the gap between what organisations report as achieved and the quality of participation of people with disabilities [30]. On the other hands, this kind of development can help to systematise a report format where national science organisations will have to evidence the UCD (User centred design) development of their prototypes and databases, recognise multi-sensorial exploration as a valid study of the data and stimulate funding agencies to ensure that the proposals funded include people with disabilities and other diversities.

The use of sonification will increase the abilities to identify signatures in the information and as a consequence, the number of scientific discoveries.

The evaluation framework will monitor the reach of diverse groups, their satisfaction with the offer, and the impact their participation has in terms of individual benefits. Whether the two strands, the technical as well as the engagement strands, and how they will have to be improved to support democratisation of access, the projects will learn based on the formative and summative evaluation outcomes. A guide with lessons learned on how to make citizen science projects more accessible will be a crucial future step in this endeavour.

References

1. OED (2016) Citizen science
2. Owen, R., Macnaghten, P., Stilgoe, J.: Responsible research and innovation: from science in society to science for society, with society. Sci. Public Policy **39**, 751–760 (2012)
3. Rip, A.: The clothes of the emperor. an essay on RRI in and around Brussels. J. Respons. Innov. **3**, 290–304 (2016)
4. Smallman, M.: Citizen Science and Responsible Research and Innovation. UCL Press (2018)
5. Bonney, R., Phillips, T.B., Ballard, H.L., Enck, J.W.: Can citizen science enhance public understanding of science? Public Underst. Sci. **25**, 2–16 (2016)
6. Kelemen-Finan, J., Scheuch, M., Winter, S.: Contributions from citizen science to science education: an examination of a biodiversity citizen science project with schools in Central Europe. Int. J. Sci. Educ. **40**, 2078–2098 (2018)
7. Strasser, B., Baudry, J., Mahr, D., Sanchez, G., Tancoigne, E.: "Citizen science"? Rethinking science and public participation. Sci. Technol. Stud. **32**, 52–76 (2019)
8. Solomon, J.: Teaching Science, Technology and Society. Developing Science and Technology Series. ERIC (1993)

9. Irwin, A.: Citizen Science: A Study of People, Expertise and Sustainable Development. Psychology Press (1995)
10. Bonney, R.: Citizen science: a lab tradition. Living Bird **15**, 7–15 (1996)
11. Eitzel, M.V., et al.: Citizen science terminology matters: exploring key terms. Citiz. Sci.: Theory Pract. **2**, 1 (2017). https://doi.org/10.5334/cstp.96
12. Shirk, J.L., et al.: Public participation in scientific research: a framework for deliberate design. Ecol. Soc. **17**(2), 29 (2012)
13. Haklay, M.: Citizen science and volunteered geographic information - overview and typology of participation. In: Sui, D., Elwood, S., Goodchild, M. (eds.) Crowdsourcing Geographic Knowledge, pp. 105–122. Springer, Dordrecht (2013). https://doi.org/10.1007/978-94-007-4587-2_7
14. Bonney, R., et al.: Public participation in scientific research: defining the field and assessing its potential for informal science education - a CAISE inquire group report. Washington, DC (2009)
15. Domhnaill, C.M., Lyons, S., Nolan, A.: The citizens in citizen science: demographic, socioeconomic, and health characteristics of biodiversity recorders in Ireland. Citiz. Sci.: Theory Pract. **5**, 16 (2020). https://doi.org/10.5334/cstp.283
16. World Health Organization: International Classification of Functioning, Disability, and Health: Children & Youth Version: ICF-CY. World Health Organization (2007)
17. Association ECS (10) Principles of Citizen Science. http://ecsacitizen-science.net/sites/default/files/ecsa_ten_principles_of_citizen_science.pdf
18. Anikin, A.: The link between auditory salience and emotion intensity. Cogn. Emot. **34**(6), 1246–1259 (2020)
19. Dobie, R.A., Van Hemel, S., Council, N.R.: Basics of sound, the ear, and hearing. In: Hearing Loss: Determining Eligibility for Social Security Benefits. National Academies Press (US) (2004)
20. TED: How a blind astronomer found a way to hear the stars | Wanda Diaz Merced (2016)
21. Murgia, M., Agostini, T.A., McCullagh, P.: From perception to action: the role of auditory and visual information in perceiving and performing complex movements. Front. Media SA. **10**, 2696 (2020)
22. Garcia, B., Diaz-Merced, W., Casado, J., Cancio, A.: Evolving from xSonify: a new digital platform for sonorization. In: EPJ Web of Conferences. EDP Sciences, p. 01013 (2019)
23. Davison, B.K., Walker, B.N.: Sonification sandbox reconstruction: software standard for auditory graphs. Georgia Institute of Technology (2007)
24. Shelton, R.: NASA MathTrax Homepage (2008). https://prime.jsc.nasa.gov/mathtrax/. Accessed 11 Jan 2021
25. Candey, R.M., Schertenleib, A.M., Diaz Merced, W.L.: Xsonify sonification tool for space physics. Georgia Institute of Technology (2006)
26. Marres, N.: The issues deserve more credit: pragmatist contributions to the study of public involvement in controversy. Soc. Stud. Sci. **37**, 759–780 (2007)
27. Chilvers, J., Kearnes, M.: Remaking Participation: Science, Environment and Emergent Publics. Routledge, London (2015)
28. Kurz, B., Kubek, D.: Social impact navigator. The practical guide for organizations targeting better results. PHINEO gAG, Berlin (2016)
29. Kieslinger, B., Schäfer, T., Heigl, F., Dörler, D., Richter, A., Bonn, A.: Evaluating citizen science-towards an open framework. JSTOR., 81–95 (2018)
30. Shakespeare, T.: Disability: The Basics. Routledge, London (2017)

Design for All Applications and Case Studies

Collaborative Virtual Environment to Encourage Teamwork in Autistic Adults in Workplace Settings

Ashwaq Zaini Amat[1]([⊠]), Michael Breen[1], Spencer Hunt[1], Devon Wilson[2], Yousaf Khaliq[2], Nathan Byrnes[2], Daniel J. Cox[2], Steven Czarnecki[2], Cameron L. Justice[2], Deven A. Kennedy[2], Tristan C. Lotivio[2], Hunter K. McGee[2], Derrick M. Reckers[2], Justin W. Wade[2], Medha Sarkar[2], and Nilanjan Sarkar[1]

[1] Vanderbilt University, Nashville, TN 37212, USA
ashwaq.zaini.amat.haji.anwar@vanderbilt.edu
[2] Middle Tennessee State University, Nashville, TN 37132, USA

Abstract. The employment settings for autistic individuals in the USA is grim. As more children are diagnosed with ASD, the number of adolescent and young adult with ASD will increase as well over the next decade. Based on reports, one of the main challenges in securing and retaining employment for individual with ASD is difficulty in communicating and working with others in workplace settings. Most vocational trainings focused on technical skills development and very few addresses teamwork skills development. In this study, we present the design of a collaborative virtual environment (CVE) that support autistic individual to develop their teamwork skills by working together with a partner in a shared virtual space. This paper described the CVE architecture, teamwork-based tasks design and quantitative measures to evaluate teamwork skills. A system validation was also carried out to validate the system design. The results showed that our CVE was able to support multiple users in the same shared environment, the tasks were tolerable by users, and all the quantitative measures are recorded accordingly.

Note: We are using both identity-first and people-first language to respect both views by interchangeably using the term 'autistic adults' and 'adults with autism' [22].

Keywords: Collaborative virtual environment · Neurodiverse employability · Autism spectrum disorders · Adolescent and adult with ASD · Teamwork · Collaborative skills

1 Introduction

Autism spectrum disorder (ASD) is a range of disorder that can significantly affect a person's ability to socially interact and communicate with others. Based on a new study by Centers for Disease Control and Prevention (CDC), there are approximately 2.21% of adolescents and adults in the USA with ASD [1]. As ASD is considered a

© Springer Nature Switzerland AG 2021
M. Antona and C. Stephanidis (Eds.): HCII 2021, LNCS 12768, pp. 339–348, 2021.
https://doi.org/10.1007/978-3-030-78092-0_22

lifelong condition, there have been growing interest and concern of the challenges faced by individuals with ASD as they are transitioning into adolescence and adulthood [2]. Employability is one of the main challenges as the unemployment rate for individuals with ASD are between 50–85% [2, 3]. For those with employment, majority of them are either underemployed or are unable to retain their position for long [4]. Studies reported that soft skills and communication were the biggest challenges and reasons for unemployment in this population [5, 6]. Despite that, majority of job trainings offered to individuals with ASD are more focused on developing technical skills and rarely on communication and soft skills development [7]. Based on these findings, there is a need for a system that could support soft skills development and encourage social interactions at workplace for autistic individuals.

Stauch and Plavnick combined vocational training with social skills training using video modelling for individuals with ASD [8]. Participants were shown videos of vocational tasks embedded with social skills as part of the intervention while performing the task in real life. Although the study reported improvements in both vocational skills and social skills among the participants, there was limited availability of quantitative measures and the cost to operate such study was quite high. The use of virtual reality (VR) based systems for vocational training has shown potential in recent years. VR training engages the users [9], provides a safe environment for training [10] and provides quantitative measures of the skills they are learning [11]. As a result, several important virtual systems have been explored in the context of vocational training [9–11]. But these systems are not catered for individuals with disabilities. A recent study by Bozgeyikli et al. presented a vocational VR-based training system for individuals with disabilities focused on building technical skills such as cleaning, shelf sorting and point of sale skills [12]. Participants were able to interactively practice on the technical skills within the virtual environment while a job coach supervise their performance. However, these VR-based training systems still lack the support on social skills development, specifically teamwork and collaboration skills.

The use of collaborative virtual environment (CVE) in the last decade has provided autistic individuals the platform to interact with each other or a coach to perform a task together. CVE offers the same advantages as the VR-based interaction with the added ability of sharing the virtual experience with other users, thus expanding on the social interaction experience. iSocial, a distributed learning environment was designed for school students to collaborate and work with each other in virtual settings following a defined syllabus [13]. In one of the tasks, children were asked to communicate with each other to plan a vacation. Zhang et al. designed a CVE system that allowed two children to play collaborative puzzle games with each other [14]. The system was able to promote collaboration and communication between users while quantitatively measure the skills. As can be seen from the examples mentioned, majority of CVE studies focused on social skills development in children with ASD, in support of early interventions creating a gap on the outcome for adult with ASD [15].

In this work, we present a collaborative virtual environment (CVE) where a person with ASD and a neurotypical (NT) partner will interact with each other to complete two designated tasks. The objectives of the CVE are to (i) allow users to work together (teamwork) in a shared virtual space and (ii) encourage communication and collaboration between users through shared tasks. The rest of the paper presents the system architecture, collaborative tasks design, and result of system testing.

2 Collaborative Virtual Environment (CVE) System Design

A collaborative virtual environment (CVE) is a virtual environment that allows multiple users to share the same virtual space where they can interact with other users and the environment itself. In this work, our CVE system was designed for two users to work together as a team to achieve the same goal in each task. In this study we designed tasks within the CVE that simulate workplace environment, even though the system is not limited to only these tasks. The first is a computer assembly task and the second task is a fulfillment center. These tasks were chosen as we wanted a workplace environment that could encourage teamwork and collaboration.

Users access the CVE from two different physical location using their respective computer and join the shared virtual environment by connecting to the same server. In each task, users are presented with a set of instruction that included task objectives, a list and manuals. The users control their movements and interact with the virtual environment by using common computer peripherals such as keyboard keypads, a mouse and or a gamepad. to control movements. Once connected, users can communicate with each other through video and audio streaming component embedded within the CVE. They use the instruction set as reference to navigate within the environment together by collaborating and communicating to accomplish the set goals.

2.1 Tasks Design

The main design criteria we considered for the tasks was they must encourage teamwork and collaboration. Both users need to communicate with each other and synchronize their actions in the virtual space to achieve the goals set in the tasks. Without communicating with each other to perform the task, the users will not be able to proceed with the task. Each task takes between five to ten minutes to complete. When users are unable to proceed with the task, researchers will provide assistance to move to the next step.

Computer Assembly Task. In the computer assembly task, users are working together in a computer workshop room. As shown in Fig. 1, five computer components together with a computer chassis are placed on a table in front of both users. The objective of the computer assembly task is to put together a computer using the provided components. One user plays the role of an assembler while the other user plays the role of a supervisor and has access to the installation manual. The supervisor should provide verbal guidance to the assembler. The assembler then follows the instruction conveyed by the supervisor to put the computer together. Both the assembler and supervisor will take turn to place the component into the chassis as some components are accessible to only either the assembler or the supervisor. To pick up the component, users select the component they want to move with the mouse and use keyboard keypad buttons to move and rotate the component into the right location in the chassis. Both users need to communicate well with each other to fully assemble the computer within a specified time. Throughout the task, the CVE system will continuously monitor interaction and collaborative actions.

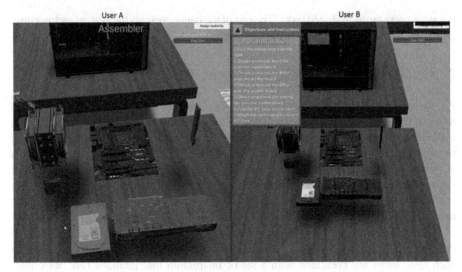

Fig. 1. Users' view of the computer assembly task.

Fulfillment Center Task. The fulfilment center task is set in a warehouse. Users need to drive forklifts in the warehouse to retrieve pallets from the shelves to a collection area. The pallets are color-coded to match them to the different collection area. Figure 2 illustrates the different point of views of both users and overall view of the warehouse with the color-coded collection area. Both users are given a list of pallets they need to pick up from various location in the warehouse. One user is assigned as the trainee while the other user is the supervisor. The supervisor in this task will give directional verbal instruction (e.g., 'Move to the left', 'Move the fork down further') to guide the trainee when picking up and dropping off pallets as the trainee does not have the complete view of the pallet from inside the forklift. This is shown in Fig. 2(a). In this task, a gamepad controller is used to maneuver the forklift and move around in the warehouse. Figure 3 shows the controls used in this task. Additionally, at any time, only one forklift can access the shelves, as such the users have to communicate and coordinate their locations to avoid collision and efficiently transport the pallets. Both users will need to complete the task within a specified time. Similar to the computer assembly task, the CVE system will continuously monitor interaction and collaborative actions.

2.2 CVE Architecture

The virtual environment was designed and developed using Unity, a leading game development software that support interactive play [16]. Figure 4 presents the system interaction diagram and the five main components within the CVE architecture. The Network Communication Module is responsible to set up the shared environment when users start joining. Once connection is established, this module triggers the Player Controller to set up and assign players with their respective roles. At the same time, the module initializes the audio and video streaming component. When users start interacting and performing

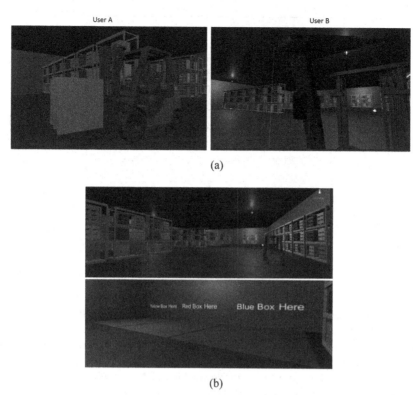

(a)

(b)

Fig. 2. Fulfillment center task views. (a) Point of view of each player. User A can see User B driving the forklift carrying a red pallet. User B's view is from inside the forklift. (b) Overall warehouse view with pallets of different colors and the color-coded collection area.

Fig. 3. Gamepad configurations for forklift user.

a task, the Player Controller trigger events to the Network Communication Module to exchange player data between the users' so that both users' view are synchronized. At the same time, any user interactions with the environment are synchronized through the Environment Controller. Users' data are also stored locally in the Data Collection Module for post-task analysis.

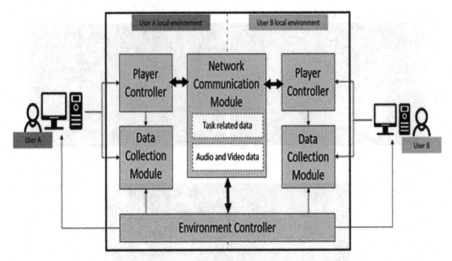

Fig. 4. System interaction diagram

Network Communication Module. The main component that enables a virtual environment to be shared among multiple users is the network component. For our implementation, we used two types of networking interfaces: Mirror [17] and WebRTC [18]. Both are compatible with Unity and purchased through Unity Asset store.

Using similar architecture to Unity Networking (UNet) application that has been deprecated [19], Mirror uses a server-client module. A server connects all the users together and manages data transmission in both server and client. A client is created for each user that is connected to the same environment through the server. In this CVE system, one of the users is connected as a host server which take the role of both a server and client and the other user is connected as client only. The assignment of the server client roles to the users are solely for network configuration and does not influence user experience at all. Mirror is used to exchange environment related data that are dynamically changing such as player actions and objects movements, and periodically exchanging data such as user performance and duration of the task across both user's environments. As our tasks involve moving virtual objects to specific locations and transporting large virtual objects around, we wanted the synchronization to be high but not overload the channel. The default update rate for Mirror was set to 60 messages per second or 60 Hz, which is suitable for high paced game [17]. To stream the audio and video data, we initially used Dissonance, an integration component in Mirror that allow video and audio streaming [20]. Due to incompatibility with other components in the development, we had to use an alternative network interface. We chose WebRTC to stream the user's audio and video data from a webcam and microphone, respectively, in real-time between users while they performed the virtual task. This plugin came with pre-configured network layer that makes establishing connection easy. An event handler within the plugin trigger updates to the receiving user when a new video frame was received, or an audio clip was received. For a smooth video transmission, a frame rate of 30 frame per second (fps) was chosen for WebRTC. In the computer assembly task, we are using both video and audio streaming service, while the fulfillment center uses only the voice streaming service.

Player Controller. The Player Controller configures the user movements within the environment and how they interact with the virtual objects. Within the controller we also defined two different roles for each user to encourage further collaboration and communication between them. The first role defined is of a supervisor, where they need to provide more verbal instruction to the other user and minimal involvement with interacting with the virtual objects. The other role is of a trainee where the user is expected to conduct most of the interaction with the virtual objects and communicate with the other user. The assignment of roles is done randomly and alternately applied between the two tasks. For example, if the first task was the computer assembly task and User A is assigned the supervisor role and User B is assigned the trainee role, then in the fulfillment center task, User A will be assigned the trainee role while User B will take the supervisor role.

This controller is also connected to the Network Communication Module to transmit and receive player's information which include player's location and actions such as moving or picking up virtual objects. Player representation in the shared environment is important to establish a sense of presence of each other and facilitate collaboration and team work better. It is also important to synchronize the players' information to ensure player representation is not delayed that can disrupt the teamwork and collaboration activity they are conducting.

Quantitative Measures. To evaluate the collaborative skills and teamwork, we are using tasks related data and social communication information gathered during the experiment. Task performance data include number of successful collaborative moves, duration of collaborative actions and scores are collected locally for each user in the Data Collection Module. Social communication data include speech and eye gaze data. Within the system we are transcribing the user's speech and including it in the Data Collection Module. Evaluation of speech and conversation are done post tasks where researchers view experiment recording and label the collaborative part of the speech. We then validate it against the transcription and add the label accordingly. The labelling can be used in future study to improve our system. For eye gaze data collection, we are using a TobiiEyeX [21] to track gaze points in the virtual space and specific virtual objects that the user looks at. Similar to speech data, gaze points are analyzed post tasks to obtain the gaze pattern in collaborative settings.

3 System Validation

We conducted system testing with 3 pairs of NT volunteers to validate that the system can support multiple users and allow users to perform the tasks together in the shared environment without any issues. Additionally, through the system testing we can validate that the data are correct and logged in the right format.

After the test, we asked the volunteers to fill out a system usability scale to rate their experience performing the tasks within the CVE. They commonly agreed that the system was tolerable and simple to understand. They could easily understand the instructions and objectives of both tasks. One user did comment that the use of different controllers across both tasks caused a bit of confusion when transitioning over to the other task. We took note of this and will add them into consideration when we revise the system for a user study.

As part of technical verification of the system, we observed two areas of the system: connectivity and recording of quantitative measures. To verify the system connectivity, we tested connecting two computers in the same building but in separate rooms 10 times a day and repeated the same process for five days. We achieved a success rate of 98% where only 1 trial failed to get connected. When testing with the volunteers, they accessed the shared environment six times where each pair connected twice, one time for each task. In all six times, there were no connectivity issues, and they were able to stay connected until they finished the tasks. Our Network Communication Module was robust, where players and all virtual objects in the computer assembly task and fulfillment center task were synchronized with unnoticeable latency. We have yet to test the network performance of this system in different buildings and observe the latency.

To verify the quantitative measures, the researchers reviewed and compared the recorded data against the video recording of the volunteers. As we did not have matching time stamp between the video recording and the log files, we relied on the duration of the task to align the data with the actual video. From the analysis of the 3 sessions with the volunteers, we were able to match the speech transcriptions to the utterances in the videos. Although we did not analytically measure the accuracy of the transcription, the system successfully discriminated the speech coming from both users (e.g.: User 1 Speech, User 2 Speech). As for the eye gaze data, we selected a short clip from the video recording and observe what was the volunteer doing in that clip. We then compared this to the gaze log file and find if there was a match between the object in the video to the object logged in the gaze log file. We found 100% match in eye gaze data against the video recording for the virtual object logging. We did not verify the raw gaze point data as that required more processing time. Both the speech and gaze data can be used to analyze collaborative level of the participants.

With the completion of our system testing, we can validate that our CVE system is tolerable by users, easy to understand, able to support multiple users connected to the same virtual environment and record meaningful quantitative data related to teamwork and collaborative skills. It is ready for user testing where we will analyze the user performance, teamwork skills and the system performance.

4 Conclusion

We designed a CVE that is aimed to support the development of teamwork and collaborative skills of autistic adults in vocational settings. This initial study addresses the design considerations for suitable tasks that would encourage individuals with ASD to communicate and work together with a partner to achieve a common goal. To quantitatively measure teamwork and collaborative performance, our system continuously collects user's actions in the task together with speech and gaze data.

There were a few limitations in our system validation. The main limitation is the system was tested with neurotypical users only. Next, there was not enough variation in the tasks to allow for more collaborative work between users. Also, the current design of the feedback is limited to only acknowledgement of successful attempts but does not prompt the users when they are stuck. Finally, availability of speech data that are labelled with collaborative tags are limited due to the limited number of study participants and shorter tasks length.

Our future work will address the limitations we identified from this round of testing. First, we would conduct a pilot study with autistic adults and NT partners. We will also introduce variations to the tasks. For example, we plan to have three different difficulty level for each task. The basic level will serve as a baseline to evaluate the users task performance while the second and third level introduces ambiguity to the tasks that would drive the users to work together to overcome the challenge. To further improve user experience using the system, a more robust feedback mechanism will be introduced to support users when they are not sure what to do. After the pilot study is finished, we plan to use the speech data to train a machine learning model that could classify the collaborative speech in real-time more accurately. With these improvements in plan, we are confident that our CVE system can benefit individuals with ASD by providing them with the right tool and support to secure and retain employment by preparing them to work better with others.

Acknowledgement. We are grateful for the support provided by NSF grants 1936970 and 2033413 for this research. The authors are solely responsible for the contents and opinions expressed in this manuscript.

References

1. Dietz, P.M., Rose, C.E., McArthur, D., Maenner, M.: National and state estimates of adults with autism spectrum disorder. J. Autism Dev. Disord. **50**(12), 4258–4266 (2020). https://doi.org/10.1007/s10803-020-04494-4
2. Levy, A., Perry, A.: Outcomes in adolescents and adults with autism: a review of the literature. Res. Autism Spectr. Disord. **5**(4), 1271–1282 (2011)
3. U.S. Bureau of labor statistics
4. Brooke, V., et al.: Employees with autism spectrum disorder achieving long-term employment success: a retrospective review of employment retention and intervention. Res. Pract. Pers. Severe Disabil. **43**(3), 181–193 (2018)
5. Hendricks, D.: Employment and adults with autism spectrum disorders: challenges and strategies for success. J. Vocat. Rehabil. **32**(2), 125–134 (2010)
6. Taylor, J., Seltzer, M.: Employment and post-secondary educational activities for young adults with autism spectrum disorders during the transition to adulthood. J. Autism Dev. Disord. **41**, 566–574 (2011)
7. Walsh, L., Lydon, S., Healy, O.: Employment and vocational skills among individuals with autism spectrum disorder: predictors, impact, and interventions. Rev. J. Autism Dev. Disord. **1**, 266–275 (2014)
8. Stauch, T.A., Plavnick, J.B.: Teaching vocational and social skills to adolescents with autism using video modeling. Educ. Treat. Child. **43**, 137–151 (2020)
9. Checa, D., Bustillo, A.: A review of immersive virtual reality serious games to enhance learning and training. Multimed. Tools Appl. **79**(9–10), 5501–5527 (2019). https://doi.org/10.1007/s11042-019-08348-9

10. Norris, M.W., Spicer, K., Byrd, T.: Virtual reality: the new pathway for effective safety training. Prof. Saf. **64**(06), 36–39 (2019)

11. Zhang, L., Warren, Z., Swanson, A., Weitlauf, A., Sarkar, N.: Understanding performance and verbal-communication of children with ASD in a collaborative virtual environment. J. Autism Dev. Disord. **48**(8), 2779–2789 (2018)

12. Bozgeyikli, L., et al.: VR4VR: vocational rehabilitation of individuals with disabilities in immersive virtual reality environments. In: Proceedings of the 8th ACM International Conference on Pervasive Technologies Related to Assistive Environments, pp. 1–4, July 2015

13. Stichter, J.P., Laffey, J., Galyen, K., Herzog, M.: iSocial: delivering the social competence intervention for adolescents (SCI-A) in a 3D virtual learning environment for youth with high functioning autism. J. Autism Dev. Disord. **44**(2), 417–430 (2013). https://doi.org/10.1007/s10803-013-1881-0

14. Zhang, L., Fu, Q., Swanson, A., Weitlauf, A., Warren, Z., Sarkar, N.: Design and evaluation of a collaborative virtual environment (CoMove) for autism spectrum disorder intervention. ACM Trans. Access. Comput. **11**(2), Article 11 (2018)

15. Glaser, N.J., Schmidt, M.: Usage considerations of 3D collaborative virtual learning environments to promote development and transfer of knowledge and skills for individuals with autism. Technol. Knowl. Learn. **25**(2), 315–322 (2020)

16. https://unity.com/

17. https://mirror-networking.com/

18. https://www.because-why-not.com/webrtc/#WebRTC_Video_Chat

19. https://docs.unity3d.com/Manual/UNet.html

20. https://dissonance.readthedocs.io/en/latest/Basics/Quick-Start-Mirror.html

21. https://www.tobii.com/

22. Kenny, L., Hattersley, C., Molins, B., Buckley, C., Povey, C., Pellicano, E.: Which terms should be used to describe autism? Perspectives from the UK autism community. Autism **20**(4), 442–462 (2016)

Image Adaptation Based on Color Saturation and Linear Matrices for People with Deuteranopia-Type Color Blindness

Daniel Delgado-Cedeño[1] and Mario Chacón-Rivas[2]([✉])

[1] Maestría en Computación, Instituto Tecnológico de Costa Rica,
Cartago, Costa Rica
[2] Inclutec, Instituto Tecnológico de Costa Rica, Cartago, Costa Rica
machacon@itcr.ac.cr
http://www.tec.ac.cr/inclutec

Abstract. Around 350 million color blind people in the world and 64% of people indicated that color blindness was their biggest problem and 42% considered it difficult to fully integrate into society. This type of condition is not usually understood as a disability, however it could be the cause of dangerous situations depending on the context in which the person suffering from it is found. Color blindness has various color perception conditions. In this paper, a description of the types of color blindness is presented and the development of an assistive technology that allows deuteronopia-type color blind users to view modified images to mitigate the deficiency is presented. The modification of the images is based on algebraic transformations use of the image, color saturation and linear arrays. The app was tested and validated with color blind people and achieved an 83% approval rating.

Keywords: Assistive technologies · Daltonism · Color-blindness app

1 Introduction

People with color blindness can generally face situations in their daily lives that do not pose serious danger or that threaten their life or that of others. This condition known as color blindness is considered a type of disability that color blind people face, but since it is not visible, it has rarely been given the necessary attention. On the other hand, people with this condition have focused on facing this disability as a very personal issue and generally do not share it. In cases where the condition affects them at the study or work level, they seek to resolve them on their own so as not to feel separated from the group or society.

This investigation is aimed to evaluate thru an *applied research* the viability to design and build an application that can help color blind people to visualize the color range on images where blindness is not let them see those blind spots according to their color blindness type and how the technology can help people

M. Antona and C. Stephanidis (Eds.): HCII 2021, LNCS 12768, pp. 349–368, 2021.
https://doi.org/10.1007/978-3-030-78092-0_23

in any circumstances on their daily lives. This investigation also identifies and compares the color blind type and how those affects people today. During the systematic review of similar technologies and studies, it was possible to identify and to compare different systems, applications, and algorithms to resolve similar problems.

After the contextual research was completed, a usable application was designed based on the user experience of one of the authors. The application is available on url [https://blindspottec.com] and it is free, currently it is only available on iOS Platform and Apple devices. The user will have the option of choosing an image from their device or taking a picture with the camera of their smartphone or tablet. When capturing the image, the system will automatically process the image and apply a base correction filter for deuteranopia (green blindness) color blindness. The system will show the original image together with an adjusted image with the filter applied, using saturation and linear matrices. In addition, a series of features will be displayed on the menu that will allow the user to modify the images in real-time and adjust them according to their color blindness. The application will also show a series of preloaded defined filters, which are not intended for color blindness but may help to visualize in severe cases.

As part of the investigation and experimental process, the system was tested as part of a lab playground with a set of users with Color Blindness in order to show and evaluate the results on accuracy and user experience. As a result, the research showed how precise is the application and the methodology used to modify images and how Color-blind people interact with the system. This information provided recommendations for future work and how to apply this technology in a professional, academic and daily circumstances.

1.1   Context

Color blindness is the inability to see some colors in the normal way. Color blindness occurs when there is a problem with pigments in certain nerve cells in the eye that perceive color. These cells are called cones and are found in the layer of light-sensitive tissue that lines the back of the eye, called the retina [16]. There are several types of color blindness: ranging from total color blindness known as *achromatopsia*, to the condition that affects the perception of some particular colors.

This research presents the study and analysis of the types of color blindness from a perspective of presentation of graphic information by means of digital technologies. Based on this analysis, a systematic search for information on assistive technologies for people with this condition is carried out. Then a tool for IOS devices is designed and developed in order to provide help to people with color blindness so that in an alternative and inclusive way they can view images with adapted adjustments with respect to their color blindness.

The software application compares and displays the perceived differences between two images equal but one normal and the other with the adaptation applied. The adaptation made by the application is based on adjustments that provide an option to people with deuteranopia-type color blindness, this being the reason that one of the authors of this paper presents this condition.

The image adaptation process is based on the use of coloring algorithms with linear matrices and saturation levels.

1.2 Justification

Assistive technologies for people with disabilities seek to eliminate or reduce barriers and in this way provide conditions for equalization of opportunities. However, for people with color blindness, these technologies have hardly been considered at the work or academic level, so that the solutions that are available have not been designed in a comprehensive way for work environments and even less academic.

On the other hand, there are professional or technical occupations that base decision-making on information that is presented in graphic or colored form. In addition, the decisions made could put processes, money, information or even people's lives at risk. Some examples of this are:

- Security drivers for data server traffic: application design can be based on color patterns that identify high risks with colors such as red or its shades.
- Financial risk analyzers: those who must make decisions depending on investment ranges or amounts, in which these ranges are also classified by color.
- Processes that require combination of chemical agents: there are cases in academic evaluations that request the combination of chemical agents until *"produce an intense blue hue"*.
- Researchers who base results and conclusions on statistical information: this is one of the most common cases that present information in pie charts, bars or any other type and the tools for generating graphs do not consider the conditions of color blindness.

Therefore, based on the considerations set out above, adding to the experience lived by one of the authors of this work, this research and its results are highly relevant for a population of professionals and people who see their needs invisible.

To exemplify what has been described, Fig. 1 shows a sequence of 4 images, the first a normal image [2], the second shows how a deuteranopia person perceives said image without correction. The third image shows the transformation made by Visolve [13], where a deuteranopia filter is applied and finally the fourth image shows this applied filter and how it is perceived by a person with deuteranopia-type color blindness.

For a person without color blindness, the four segments of the Fig. 1 can easily display the number 29 in all segments. But for a person with deuteranopia-type color blindness it is impossible to see the number 29 in any of the four segments. Segment 4 shows a slight discoloration in the center of the image that could be interpreted as an "88" or as an "8J".

Imagen Original   Simulación de Deuteranopía

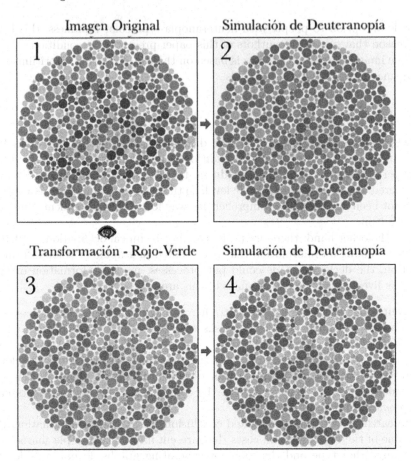

Transformación - Rojo-Verde   Simulación de Deuteranopía

Fig. 1. Natural, colored image sequence and example of differences [13].

2   Problem

There are around 350 million color blind people in the world and 64% of people indicated that color blindness was their biggest problem and 42% considered it difficult to fully integrate into society [11].

One of the authors of this paper, as a person with deuteranopia-type color blindness, has a great interest in providing a method that not only complies with having greater usability in Web sites, images or photos, but also overcomes the failed attempts of different technological proposals that as a user you have tried and have not achieved the expected results. Therefore, it is identified as a problem that *the technology currently available does not facilitate or help to evaluate and improve the different coloring techniques objectively.*

The most important problems of color blindness are shown when making a decision regarding the color that the color blind sees. A clear example of a work-related nature is shown in the Fig. 2 taken from the Sicid (Costa Rican Disability Information System) [15] in the National statistics section, this graphic from the National Census of population and housing carried out in 2011. For a colorblind person, column D and E have the same color, so in a decision-making situation based on the information in the graph, they cannot know to which column the "University" data belongs or the "incomplete Primary". The rest of the columns are seen without any problem.

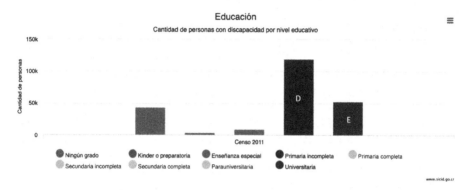

Fig. 2. Deuteranopia color blindness - Column D and E show the same color [15]. (Color figure online)

Not all forms of color blindness are the same. People who suffer from hereditary difficulties in perceiving colors often only realize this after many years of living with this problem. People with normal vision have three different types of cones, each of which is responsible for a certain range of colors: red-sensitive L-cones, blue-sensitive S-cones, and green-sensitive M-cones. L, S and M refer to the area they cover of the color spectrum: L corresponds to "long" wavelengths, S to short wavelengths ("short") and M to "medium" wavelengths [18].

For this research it is known as **blind spots** when a person suffering from partial color blindness who has green color blindness (deuteranopia), in this case there are no functional cones for the color green. As a result, they can only perceive a limited spectrum of colors [18], a part of the sensory cells necessary to perceive colors either does not exist or does not work. The person will not be able to see this color so it is named *blind colors* or *blind spots*.

Many of the applications are based on a methodology and base design of providing people with color blindness the possibility of seeing colors with respect to their RGBA code, or of making a correction using standard base filters or pixel by pixel corrections. What happens with this type of technology is that it is considered not very inclusive or often unwise, in most cases a total change of the image is made and the blind spots are not identified. In addition to the above, even more serious is that when doing it using pixels, the perspective of the image is lost and many times unrecognizable transformations are shown with respect to the original image.

2.1 Color Blind Users

The English naturalist, chemist and mathematician John Dalton (1766–1844) was one of the main people responsible for the study of *achromatopsia*, a disease of a genetic nature and congenital profile that, according to experts, is not progressive. It is an anomaly that affects sight. Due to the valuable contributions of this specialist, over time partial color blindness began to be described as color blindness [9].

When we talk about this genetic problem we have to state that there are several types of it. Specifically, at a general level we can determine that there are three, but for this tool only deuteranopia will be used. Deuteranopia and Deuteranomaly are the most common forms of color blindness.

People with these conditions have cones that are sensitive to medium wavelengths (green), but the end result is similar to protanopia, with the exception that the red ones don't look as dark. Deuteranomaly is less severe of the two conditions. Although individuals with deuteranomaly probably cannot perceive reds and greens in the same way that people without these problems can, they can often distinguish between shades of reds and greens with relative precision [14].

The condition of color blindness in people is commonly due to the fact that by not seeing the nuances of colors, such as red and green in the case of deuteranopia, their daily life is exhausted. It is difficult for this population to be able to paint, read maps, distinguish part of the traffic signs, check the cooking point of food, among others [7].

Currently, color blind people face a series of limitations resulting from the lack of adaptation to the physical environment in which they live, but also from the means offered by new technologies.

For the year 2011, surveyed users with visual disabilities (people with low vision, blind and color blind) indicated that the institutional pages had the following weaknesses [8]:

- Images that do not have alternative text.
- Complex images (eg graphics) that are not adequately described.
- Video is not described in text or audio.
- Frames that do not have "Noframe" alternatives, or do not have names descriptive.
- Shapes lack a logical sequence or they are mislabeled.
- Browsers and authoring tools that lack keyboard support for all commands.
- Browsers and authoring tools that do not use the standard application programming for the operating system on which they are based.
- Use of standard document formats that can be difficult to interpret for the screen reader.

At the same time, among other requirements, the following stand out: "Color blind people require special sheets which, at the discretion of the people in the consulted organizations, are rarely available [8].

In other words, despite the laws that have been drawn up in this regard following international treaties, efforts by government institutions to enforce them remain scarce, where actions in favor of soft visual disabilities such as color blindness are not clear and where it is possible to establish methodologies, agreements and technologies of great help for education, government and public entities having a better reach and accessible inclusion for all the population with color blindness.

Color blindness occurs when there is a problem with the granules (pigments) that perceive color in certain neurons in the eye, called cones. These cells are found in the retina, that is, the layer of light-sensitive tissue that lines the back of the eye [10]. If only one pigment is missing, the individual may have difficulty differentiating between red and green, which is the most common type of color blindness. In Fig. 3 you can see 3 basic examples of color blindness.

If a pigment is missing, you may have trouble seeing blue and yellow. People with blue and yellow color blindness generally have trouble identifying red and green colors as well [10].

The most serious form of color blindness is *achromatopsia*. The person with this rare condition cannot see any color, so everything is seen in shades of gray. Achromatopsia is often associated with lazy eye, nystagmus or poor vision (small jerky movements of the eye), severe photosensitivity [10].

2.2   The Cones

There are three types of cones, responsible for perceiving each of the three primary colors of light (blue, green and red) as can be seen in the Fig. 4. In a person without color blindness, the combination of these three colors allows him to discern a very wide range of intermediate hues. The problem comes when one of these three types of cones is missing or malfunctioning. In such a case, "the disorder" known as color blindness or daltonism will occur. There are several types of color blindness, depending on the type of cone affected [17].

To detect color blindness, the Ishihara [5] (pseudoisochromatic) plates are generally used, which can be seen in Fig. 5. These contain dot-filled patterns made up of primary colors. These dotted patterns represent a symbol that is superimposed on a background of randomly mixed colors. This test can determine certain visual abnormalities related to the perception of colors in a person [17].

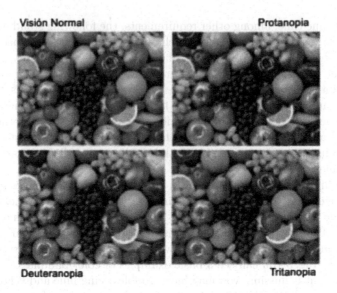

Fig. 3. Example types of color blindness (Color figure online)

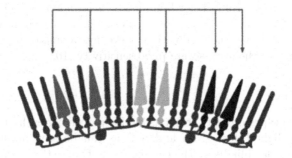

Fig. 4. Cones in the Retina according to Color (Red, green and blue). (Color figure online)

2.3 Technological Principle of Solution

The proposal is to identify the colors that must be highlighted for the person with color blindness, and that those pixels are so close to themselves that when a group of them is transformed, they have a logical composition with respect to the rest of the image so as not to transform pixels in places that will not provide content in the images. The method to be used emphasizes this aspect, which can mark the points where it is not seen. You do not change the colors to be able to see them, but define the viewing areas to establish the blind spots, which helps to identify the various ranges of colors.

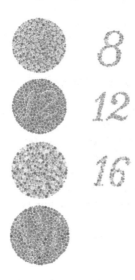

Fig. 5. Ishihara Test [5]

3   Proposal

The application proposal arises from the need to provide help to people with deuteranopia-type color blindness. This is a help tool for daily activities or decision-making activities in which technology help is needed to solve your visual impairment.

The design of the application is based on the principles of usability and user-centered design [4], seeking a tool that is intuitive and that can be offered as free software and included in learning support platforms [1,6]. The application is only available on the IOS platform and you will need an Apple brand device to be able to use it, however it can be adapted for other platforms.

The user will have the option of choosing an image from their device or taking a picture with the camera of their mobile device, be it an iPhone or iPad. When capturing the image the system will automatically process it and apply the preset base correction filter for a color blind type of deuteranopia. Later, the system will show the original image together with an image with the filter applied. In addition, a series of alternatives will be shown in the menu that will allow the user to modify in real time in order to be able to visually adjust the image according to its color blindness, from very mild to very severe. The application will also show a series of previously defined filters, which do not correspond to or help any type of color blindness, but just with the deuteranopia base filter it could help to better visualize the colors.

The creation of this system is extremely important, since it can provide visually impaired users with a quick way to visualize something not perceptible in an illusion rendered on the cell phone screen, with which they can make business decisions, everyday life, or simply not to be excluded from society due to an invisible disability.

3.1 Linear Algebra in Image Manipulation

The matrix representation of multi-color images depends on the color system used by the program that is processing the image. For the purposes of this research, RGB (the most popular) will always be used, where each pixel specifies the amount of red (R), green (G) and blue (B), and each color can vary from 0 to 255. Therefore, in RGB, a pixel can be represented as a three-dimensional vector (r, g, b) where r, g and b are integers from 0 to 255 [12]. In this implementation a 4D vector is used where Alpha is included as the fourth value, having a vector (r, g, b, a).

This System stores a four-dimensional vector as a single integer, using the following function:

$$\mathbf{v = f(r, g, b, a) = r * 65536 + g * 256 + b + a.}$$

Where a (alpha) is always 1. Since the degree of opacity does not need to be modified for this type of correction filter.

The blue color of the image Fig. 6 is represented as the vector rgba (83, 51, 237, 1).

Fig. 6. Royal Blue (Color figure online)

From a linear algebra point of view, filters are applied to each pixel in the matrix using the filter function. The input to this function can be just a pixel like brightness adjustment, or a sub-matrix of pixels like blur, where the order of the sub-matrix will depend on the radius used [12].

Let's consider the matrix M, as the matrix associated with a color image Fig. 7:

$$M = \begin{bmatrix} p11 & p12 & ... & p1n \\ p21 & p22 & ... & p2n \\ ... & ... & ... & ... \\ pm1 & pm2 & ... & pmn \end{bmatrix}$$

Fig. 7. Matrix M

In the simplest case (the filter needs only one pixel as input), the function can be a linear transformation, which transforms a 4D vector (pixel) into another 4D vector, or not.

$$T = \begin{bmatrix} 0.33 & 0.33 & 0.33 & 0.33 \\ 0.33 & 0.33 & 0.33 & 0.33 \\ 0.33 & 0.33 & 0.33 & 0.33 \\ 0 & 0 & 0 & 1 \end{bmatrix}$$

Fig. 8. Convert to grayscale

Some of the filters that use linear transformations are shown in the Figs. 8 and 9:

$$T = \begin{bmatrix} 0.39 & 0.76 & 0.18 \\ 0.35 & 0.69 & 0.17 \\ 0.27 & 0.53 & 0.13 \\ 0 & 0 & 1 \end{bmatrix}$$

Fig. 9. Sepia effect

Although these transformations are very simple, they are not linear transformations, but they use the concept of matrix addition. Examples of this type of transformation are shown in the Fig. 10:

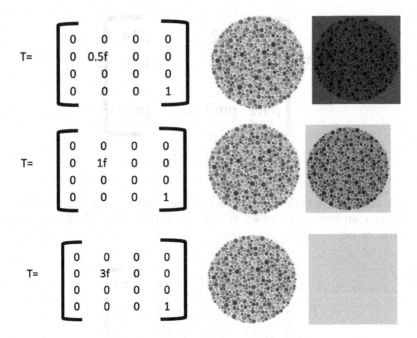

Fig. 10. Green channel setting in **0.5,1 and 3**, Matrix, Base image and Green setting (Left-Right) (Color figure online)

$$\begin{bmatrix} 0.0722f + 0.9278f * s & 0.0722f - 0.0722f * s & 0.0722f - 0.0722f * s & 0 \\ 0.7152f - 0.7152f * s & 0.7152f + 0.2848f * s & 0.7152f - 0.7152f * s & 0 \\ 0.2126f - 0.2126f * s & 0.2126f - 0.2126f * s & 0.2126f + 0.7873f * s & 0 \\ 0 & 0 & 0 & 1 \end{bmatrix}$$

Fig. 11. Base Deuteranopia Matrix

3.2   Matrix Proposal for the Tool

For the tool, it proposes the following correction matrix Fig. 11.

Where **s** is the saturation factor, which can be selected by the user. A factor of 10 is used as the base measure of saturation. Subsequently s is p.

For this base array, they just manipulate the array pointers in the following positions:

$$[0]\ [0],\ [0]\ [1],\ [0]\ [2]$$
$$[1]\ [0],\ [1]\ [1],\ [1]\ [2]$$
$$[2]\ [0],\ [2]\ [1],\ [2]\ [2]$$

The other pointers are static and have no other alteration for the type of color that is required to expose.

As we can see in the position [0] [0] we have a value **0.0722** type float that is added to the multiplication of the same value. **0.0722 * s.** remembering that "**s**" is the saturation level that depends on the user's choice on the main screen, as base saturation the tool would default to **s = 10**.

The purpose of applying this matrix to the original image will have the effect of softening the purity of the red and blue colors; and intensify the purity of greens to the maximum with a hue. The points of the matrix [0] [3], [1] [3], [2] [3], [3] [0], [3] [1], [3] [2], [3] [3] they do not need to be modified since the opacity in the vector [3] does not affect this type of color blindness, as well as the gray colors.

In order to have more control over saturation, all matrix calculations are done with the float data type since the color values have a greater saturation potential when they have an unbalanced proportion of red, green and blue. The saturation slider would have to be increased to very small decimal levels to reflect a highly saturated green or adjacent color in this case.

Image Correction. When choosing the image, the application immediately returns to the main module. There, more functionalities of the application will be displayed where the user can interact with it.

As you can see in the Fig. 12, two images are immediately displayed; the top image is the one that was selected by the user previously. The subsequent image is the image that the tool transformed and where the linear matrix of colors was applied using the aforementioned data.

The tool performs pixel correction using a base saturation value of 10 which corresponds to a float value of 0.10f. as shown in the upper left of the main module.

In addition to showing the before and after image. The tool also offers the ability to modify the saturation of the lower image in real time, using the "−" **or** "+" controls where it can be increased to a maximum of 100, which corresponds

Fig. 12. Saturation level sequence

to 1f at the calculation level. In the correction matrix. The sequence of images in Fig. 12, shows how the level of purity is increased and exalts the colors where the cones of the color blind person with deuteranopia cannot see. This functionality is added to the tool, since not all people with this type of visual impairment have the same level of color blindness, for calculation modes a saturation of 10 is used but the user can change it to their preference.

Color Effects. It can be said that the tool does a good job with just the saturation filter, but there are very acute cases of **poor vision** combined with color blindness. For these special low vision cases, a series of base filters predefined by the Acceleration Framework was implemented. These color filters are opposed to image B, which was previously applied with the correction matrix. The idea is to provide extra functionality when the user has low vision and color blindness. As denoted in Fig. 13, 14, the color filters maintain the deuteranopia pattern in most cases.

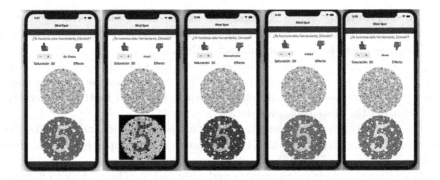

Fig. 13. Color Effects Sequence with Image 1

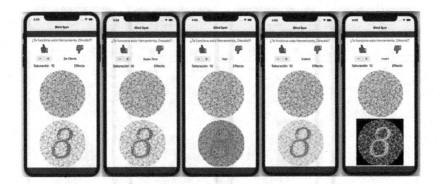

Fig. 14. Color Effects Sequence with Image 2

4   Analysis of the Results

The results capture process is done through a survey with users who have used the Blind Spot technological tool. The first step and one of the most difficult is to find a population that has color blindness and not only that it has color blindness but also wants to participate in the experiment, find, talk and persuade so that this population participates, it is an extremely complicated task and even more so. The year 2020 with the COVID19 pandemic. A campaign was used on the social network Facebook and the messaging application WhatsApp where a publication was made:

Groups and friends were asked to share this publication on their social networks and also in WhatsApp groups. Faced with all uncertainty, some people actually answered that they did not see the number 5 in the image and attached their phone numbers. Although it is clear that it is only an image and it cannot be generalized that all users are colorblind of the deuteranopia type, it is an indication that they all have a visual problem. Remembering that the tool does not determine if a user is color blind or not, but it is a technological aid at hand to visualize colors in a different way.

Ishihara cards are sampled [2] Letters 10, 11, 12, 13, 34, 35. To carry out the experiments always following the same pattern of images and using the same procedure.

For data collection, an online survey is used; This survey is applied only to users who used the Blind Spot tool. This survey is based on six letters from Ishihara cards, Fig. 15, this is to have a technical reference of the type of color blindness the users present and understand if the users are really color blind.

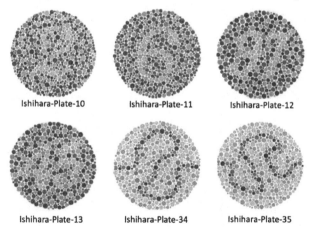

Ishihara-Plate-10   Ishihara-Plate-11   Ishihara-Plate-12

Ishihara-Plate-13   Ishihara-Plate-34   Ishihara-Plate-35

Fig. 15. Ishihara Cards 10, 11, 12, 13, 34, 35 [5]

4.1   Survey summary

In the Figs. 16, 17, 18, part of the survey of 13 questions applied to users of the Blind Spot tool is detailed: [3].

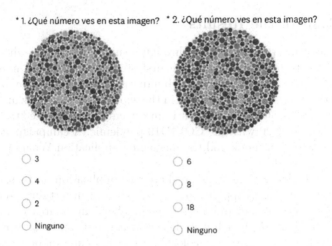

Fig. 16. Blind Spot Survey, Question 1–2

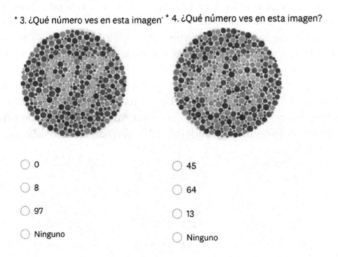

Fig. 17. Blind Spot Survey, Question 3–4

Translation types Text translation Source text 4988/5000 Translation results.

4.2 Final Results

This section presents the results of the analysis of the data obtained based on the tests carried out by users with color blindness and low vision, as well as the results of the evaluation of the survey carried out. The results were submitted individually and some of the users who participated in the Laboratory agreed to use personal information for this research. Those Users who wanted to be anonymous were called, User1, User2, User3, etc.

A total of 8 people carried out the laboratory where 2 of them did not present any type of visual problem, such as color blindness or poor vision; These were random users who were used to test the technical performance of the application and its possible limitations. Some of your answers are going to be used as systematic recommendations and improvements.

The subjects of this research did not perform a conventional test, rather they had to fill out a questionnaire; They used a laboratory where it was evaluated not so much whether the application worked or not, but also whether or not they had a visual problem.

As part of the tests it was observed that users spent between 7 and 56 min on the application with an average use of 25.5 min, and where they used the application at least 2,375 times on different occasions. In addition, it is observed that the subjects used at least 204 h in total using the tool.

Analyzing the results of the survey; the first 6 questions described above are used to categorize which users have visual problems and be as objective as possible to collect information from the tool for users with visual impairments.

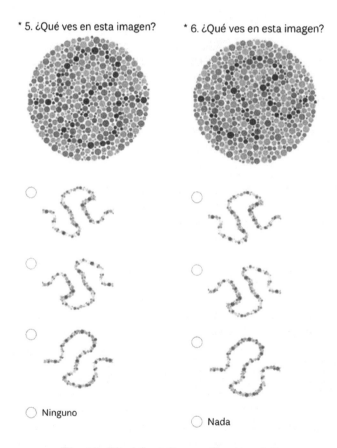

Fig. 18. Blind Spot Survey, Question 5–6

As mentioned above, 2 of the 8 users have no visual problems. The study shows that only users with normal vision were able to see all the images correctly. While the rest of the users have a very high percentage of being color blind. For the most part, prospects were unable to answer most of the initial 6 questions correctly. In this case, the percentage of correct questions from each user is taken to determine if they are colorblind of the deuteranopia type or not.

Once the users are identified, it can be determined that they are color blind according to their answers from a simple point of analysis using the Ishihara charts. Based on the interview, it can be determined that only 80% of the users knew in advance that they were color blind. And 20% of them discovered it from this experiment. It can be thought that older users have a tendency to know that they already suffered from this visual impairment. But as a great exception is the minor individual with a range between 0 and 10 years old, who did not believe that he had a visual impairment but the study totally demonstrates the opposite. Research does not guarantee 100% that a user is color blind or not, but using a scientific method like the Ishihara cards has a very high level of probability.

This case is very important for future studies and the need for the use of these tools for educational or social purposes in children to help the teacher and the family in the inclusion of school technology and that this disability is not exclusive to use the virtual tools that today the school sector uses.

5   Conclusions

Based on the study, experiments, tests and experience, the following conclusions are reached.

- According to the objective analysis of the literature and different studies found, the possibility that technological tools can be created that can change the color of the images through an application of the base color matrices and the manipulation of the pixels not only with the colors is confirmed. Visible, but with saturation levels.
- An appreciation was made of the key concepts of color blindness and how it affects individuals, how it is transmitted from generation to generation and the fundamental role that technological tools play today to close the inclusion gap.
- Based on the experimental application of the tool, the importance of having technological supports that allow the early detection or identification of school students the condition of color blindness was detected. Technological systems must ensure that people with disabilities have the same conditions of quality, opportunity, and rights as the rest of the inhabitants; but they should also be available as early help in identifying color blindness in children.
- A native mobile technology tool was developed that allows people with Deuteronopia type color blindness to correct images in real time in which they cannot see the colors for their color blind type, as a result of the conjugation of theoretical and technological studies used in the investigation. This

development, together with the application study and the survey, makes it possible to verify that the objectives set in the thesis research were met

- The method in which the technology tool corrects the images is a procedure that can be integrated into any computer technology that is to be developed or existing, where it is necessary to add technological inclusion in any type of environment, in education, business and life in general. As demonstrated by the proofs of concept conducted in this research, the technology is shown to work and is accepted by users with color blindness.
- The proposal was created in order to satisfy only one type of color blindness, but the same technology with some modifications can be used for the other types of color blindness. This development is outside the scope of study or research, but the possibility of expansion is evident.
- Color blindness is often not considered a disabling condition in people who present it. However, in some professional or technical occupations this condition could generate a risky condition and in some cases disability, which would lead to problems or difficulties at work, safety or health.

References

1. Chacon-Rivas, M., Garita, C.: A successful OSS adaptation and integration in an e-learning platform: TEC digital. In: Corral, L., Sillitti, A., Succi, G., Vlasenko, J., Wasserman, A.I. (eds.) OSS 2014. IAICT, vol. 427, pp. 143–146. Springer, Heidelberg (2014). https://doi.org/10.1007/978-3-642-55128-4_19
2. Colorlib: Ishihara Test for Color Blindness (2009). https://www.colour-blindness.com/colour-blindness-tests/ishihara-colour-test-plates/
3. Delgado, D.: Survey Monkey. Blind Spot (2020). https://es.surveymonkey.com/r/HPX26FF
4. Delgado-Quesada, G., Porras-Fernández, J., Araya-Orozco, K., Chacón-Rivas, M.: Good practices in usability testing on people with disabilities. In: 2019 International Conference on Inclusive Technologies and Education (CONTIE), pp. 187–1873 (2019). https://doi.org/10.1109/CONTIE49246.2019.00043
5. Ishihara, S.: The Series of Plates Designed as Tests for Colour Blindness, 7th edn. Collection Léo Pariseau, Kanehara & Co. (1936). http://www.dfis.ubi.pt/~hgil/P.V.2/Ishihara/Ishihara.24.Plate.TEST.Book.pdf
6. Garita, C., Chacón-Rivas, M.: TEC digital: a case study of an e-learning environment for higher education in Costa Rica. In: 2012 International Conference on Information Technology Based Higher Education and Training (ITHET), pp. 1–6, June 2012. https://doi.org/10.1109/ITHET.2012.6246061
7. incluyeme.com: Discapacidad por daltonismo ¿Qué es? (2013). https://www.incluyeme.com/discapacidad-por-daltonismo-que-es
8. Jiménez Lara, J.A., Lobo Araya, B.A.: Problemática actual del Acceso a la Función e Información Pública Administrativa a favor de Personas con Discapacidad. Ph.D. thesis, Universidad de Costa Rica Facultad de Derecho (2015). http://repositorio.sibdi.ucr.ac.cr:8080/jspui/bitstream/123456789/2633/1/38415.pdf

9. Porto, J.P.: Definición daltonismo (2008). https://definicion.de/daltonismo/
10. Alulema Defaz, M.Y.: Alteraciones En La Percepcion Cromatica En Estudiantes De Las Unidades Educativas De Las Parroquias Rurales Del Canton Guano, Provincia De Chimborazo, Durante El Periodo Abril - Septiembre 2014. Ph.D. thesis, Escuela Superior Politecnica De Chimborazo Facultad De Salud Publica Escuela De Medicina, Riobamba - Ecuador (2014). http://dspace.espoch.edu.ec/bitstream/123456789/7312/1/94T00319.pdf
11. Neiva, M.: ColorADD (2010). http://www.coloradd.net/why.asp
12. Rodriguez, A.: El álgebra lineal y el procesamiento digital de imágenes. Parte I, September 2016. https://www.nibcode.com/es/blog/1135/algebra-lineal-y-el-procesamiento-digital-de-imagenes-parte-I
13. Ryobi Systems Co., Ltd.: What is Visolve (2020). http://www.ryobi-sol.co.jp/visolve/en/visolve.html
14. Mora, S.L.: Daltonismo (2006). http://accesibilidadweb.dlsi.ua.es/?menu=deficit-visual-daltonismo
15. Sicid: Sicid - Estadísticas Nacionales (2011). https://www.sicid.go.cr/#/statistics/inquests/inquest/type/1
16. U.S. National Library of Medicine: Daltonismo: MedlinePlus enciclopedia médica (2019). https://medlineplus.gov/spanish/ency/article/001002.htm
17. Vélez, V.M.S.: Proceso educativo de los niños de 5 años con daltonismo. Elaboración y ejecución de una guía de ejercicios estratégicos para docentes y representantes legales. Tesis de Licenciatura en Ciencias de la Educación (2014). http://repositorio.ug.edu.ec/bitstream/redug/29370/1/V
18. ZEISS: Deficiencia rojo-verde, daltonismo rojo-verde y daltonismo total (2017). https://www.zeiss.es/vision-care/mejor-vision/entender-la-vision/deficiencia-rojo-verde-daltonismo-rojo-verde-y-daltonismo-total.html

Design of Digital Therapeutic Workshops for People with Alzheimer's Disease

Anne-Marie Dery-Pinna[1]([✉]), Alain Giboin[2], and Philippe Renevier-Gonin[1]

[1] Université Côte d'Azur, I3S, CNRS, Sophia Antipolis, France
`Anne-Marie.PINNA@univ-cotedazur.fr`
[2] INRIA, I3S, Université Côte d'Azur, I3S, CNRS, Sophia Antipolis, France

Abstract. Progressive memory loss is the hallmark of Alzheimer's disease. This memory loss has a profound impact on the activities of daily living (ADL) of people with this condition. ADL exercises are essential for maintaining the skills of people with Alzheimer's disease in order to expand their presence at home. But such exercises require a huge personalization to be adapted to each people with Alzheimer's disease. In this article, we report the approach and the solutions we have adopted to set up digital workshops around ADL by "personalizing" the solutions adapting the content and functionalities of the application to the specific characteristics of each Patient. This solution has been elaborated with the collaboration of caregivers of a day-care center. We put into practice a participatory design process adapted to Patients with Alzheimer's disease. The design effort is essentially at the level of choosing the best possible representation of objects and actions to digitize the workshops.

Keywords: Personalization · Design · Activity of daily activity · Alzheimer's disease

1 Introduction

Progressive memory loss is the hallmark of Alzheimer's disease. This memory loss has a profound impact on the activities of daily living (ADL) of people with this condition. They encounter more and more difficulties in remembering the actions to be performed and the function of the objects necessary for the accomplishment of these essential activities (eating, dressing, taking care of oneself, etc.). ADLs are essential for maintaining the skills of people with Alzheimer's disease in order to expand their presence at home. To ensure this maintenance, therapeutic workshops on ADL are offered by nursing staff (neuropsychologists, psychomotor therapists, occupational therapists, medico-psychological assistants) in a day-care center.

In this article, we present the approach and the solutions we have adopted to set up digital workshops around ADL by "personalizing" the solutions adapting the content and functionalities of the application to the specific characteristics of each user [16].

In the first section, we present how personalization is currently carried out by the nursing staff in a workshop for the recognition of objects of daily life. Then we explain

© Springer Nature Switzerland AG 2021
M. Antona and C. Stephanidis (Eds.): HCII 2021, LNCS 12768, pp. 369–383, 2021.
https://doi.org/10.1007/978-3-030-78092-0_24

in Sect. 3 how we introduce personalization in a digital therapeutic workshop for the activity of tooth brushing. Before concluding we give some feedback relative to our design process and lessons that we learned from our design solutions.

2 Personalization of a Non-digital Therapeutic Workshop for the Recognition of Objects of Daily Life

We work with a day-care center for Alzheimer's Patients moderately affected by the Alzheimer's disease (AD). They are between 70 and 90; they are sufficiently autonomous to live at home but accompanied. The AD is a progressive disease that causes behavioral problems: phases of opposition, agitation, and even aggression can lead to a refusal to engage in activities at any time. Phases of anxiety and withdrawal may occur when the residents encounter difficulties. Moreover, dementia affects them differently, depending on the effects of the AD and the Patient's original personality. This means that each case is unique, and caregivers must deal with each individual case as each Patient reacts differently.

The aim of the day-care center is to support the Patients with AD in maintaining a certain level of autonomy, through specific workshops, especially on activities of daily living (ADL) – e.g. tooth brushing – for which Patients progressively loose their abilities. For the nursing staff who manage these workshops, a main concern is to adapt the workshops' contents to each Patient, a task they experience as very difficult and time-consuming. Briefly speaking, the nursing staff's main concern is Workshop Personalization. To help the nursing staff improve this personalization, we agreed with the daycare center to move to digitizing the workshops. And we decided to begin with digitizing the tooth-brushing workshop.

In this section, we first present the future users of the digitalized version of the workshop, the observations and the activity analysis.

2.1 Alzheimer's Patients and Facilitators

There are two kinds of users of the workshop: the Patients with AD and the Facilitators (i.e. members of the nursing staff), both modelized with personas [1, 2]. We also consider the Patient's close family: they do not directly participate to the workshops, but they have an important role by providing Patients' personal information.

Patients with AD. The aim of the persona technique is to obtain "archetypes" of users of interactive applications to design and consequently adapt these applications to their users. In the case of Patients with AD, it is important to provide information on more specific characteristics of the disease such as: stage of the disease, associated behavioral disorders, possible associated age-related disabilities (vision, motor skills, etc.), positive and impaired ADLs, passions and interests. In other words, we need to design user models that are more specific, more personalized than the classical personas.

About Patients' goals (life, experience or end goals), it can be observed that the Patients show few needs related to their disease, are not always aware of their real difficulties and tend to overlook the subject. This more medical information can be provided by the center's Facilitators or Patients' close family depending on the impact of the illness on the person (e.g., moderate stage with a tendency to aggressiveness, needs to feel reassured about his or her memory skills, needs to maintain autonomy for mealtimes and remember everyday objects related to body care, etc.). A personalized representation of the Patients must be obtained. This requirement for specificity has led us to develop personas that are used to create specific Patient files, illustrated by the Table 1. This information is facilitated by a good collaboration; Patients – caregivers – Facilitators – Patients' close family. The user-centered approach implies that the application customization process is based on this step of information gathering.

Table 1. Example of the Patient file extracted from the Persona.

Name	Peter Holmes
Age	80
Disease Stage	3
Associated behavioral disorders	Anxious and aggressive
Age-related disabilities	Presbiopic
Positive ADL	Eating
Impaired ADL	Personal Hygiene
Passion	Football (Chealsea F.C.)
Center of Interest	Drawings Butcher job

Facilitators. The nursing staff acting as Facilitators are practitioners from different professional fields (psychologists, psychomotor therapists, occupational therapists, medical-psychological assistants, etc.) who have a good knowledge of the pathology and know each Patient very well. These competences allow them to consider the Patients through strengths and not only through difficulties to maintain and use their capacities in moments of social life. The Facilitators offer a personalized support by identifying for each Patient a life project which aims to maintain as much as possible the existing Patients' capacities, focusing on maintaining the activities of daily life. The Facilitators also aim at sharing pleasure with Patients around different activities and at minimizing withdrawal and social isolation.

Engagement in activities can be affected by behavioral problems. In such cases, it is necessary for Facilitators to adapt their behavior so that they do not force the Patients, nor reprimand them. The Facilitators remain reassuring, or even they may distract the Patients. The Facilitators need to be close to the Patients. The Facilitators can also gather information from the Patient's close family.

The Facilitators prepare, conduct and analyze the workshops.

2.2 Observations and Interviews

In order to acquire knowledge on how the existing workshops are managed, we conducted observations and interviews on a workshop involving four Patients, under the guidance of a Facilitator, a psychomotor therapist familiar with the four Patients. The Patients had to recognize everyday objects used for hygiene in order to remain familiar with these objects and their uses.

Any session of a workshop of the day-care center is composed of three steps:

1. *Preparation of the session.* We observed the Facilitator manipulating objects used in the workshop and interviewed her. In Fig. 1, for example, the Facilitator explains the graphic support provided to the Patients when they go to the toilet; she shows the graphic support used to remind Patients of the activity "Wash Hands".
2. *Performing of the session.* If we could interact with the Facilitator as "usual" (with observations and interviews), we couldn't disturb nor interview the Patients. During observations where Patients were involved, we were hidden to film the workshop.
3. *Analysis of the session.* We interviewed the Facilitator about her analysis and lessons she learnt about her Patients.

The observations and the interviews were done in context, in the places where these different workshop steps usually take place.

Fig. 1. Example of a contextual explanation provided by the Facilitator during the preparation phase of a workshop.

2.3 The Workshop Personalization

The collected data allowed us to identify the way in which personalization is carried out by the Facilitators and the related difficulties. Each step of the workshop is concerned by the personalization: (1) predefined personalization prior to workshop facilitation, (2) personalization along the way (or personalization during the workshop) and (3) personalization following the analysis of the workshop.

Personalization During the Workshop Preparation. During the preparation phase of the workshop, the Facilitator carefully chooses the participating Patients according to their affinities and their ability to exercise in order to have a relatively homogeneous group. The Facilitator consults the participants' files in search of new information that may have an impact on the conduct of the workshop. The Facilitator chooses the objects according to the participants' sex, hairstyle, hygiene and aesthetic habits, etc.: shaving foam, razor, hairbrush, toothbrush, toothpaste, deodorant, etc. The objects are few, but they are supposed to be known and recognized by all participants: they know/recognize their properties, the actions they can perform with them, where they can find them, etc.

There is both individual and group personalization. The individual one concerns Patients taken independently (the workshop is adapted to each participant) by selecting specific objects or action representation. The second one is turned towards the group taken as a whole; the Facilitator focuses here on the personality of the group. This personalization is based on the affinities and compatibilities between the members of the group.

Personalization During the Workshop. During the workshop, the Patients and the Facilitator are around a table (see Fig. 2), the objects to be identified are on the table. The Facilitator adapts the exercise to each Patient all along the workshop. The Facilitator always takes care not to create frustration in each of Patient and not to highlight failures when they occur; building trust - associated with empathy - is the golden rule. The Facilitator adapts the instructions, she uses the words that each Patient understands, changing them when they are not understood; when the words are not enough, she uses other modalities or strategies: gesture, questions with two possible answers, mimicking, etc. The Facilitator identifies the involvement of each Patient: when this level drops for one of them, she pronounces words of encouragement. She also has gestures: for example, when the retreat results in a collapse on the chair, she kindly asks the Patient to stand up and brings the chair closer to the table. When a Patient feels in great difficulty, the Facilitator makes the choice to make him/her leave the group rather than continuing so as not to put him/her in too uncomfortable a situation.

In this phase we see a) individual personalization and group personalization as in the previous phase; b) personalization of objects or representations of objects, and personalization of representations of actions; c) personalization of the involvement for each Patient.

Personalization During the Workshop Analysis. During the analysis phase of the workshop, the Facilitator assesses how each participant approached the exercise in order to be able to improve the workshop or to reconstitute the groups differently in the future. This also allows her to identify individual activities that may need to be practiced. The Facilitator takes note of the difficulties of each one and wonders about the choice of objects for the next session. For example, is it necessary to show a given Patient another brand of toothpaste because the Patient did not recognize the used brand? Another example is the case of a Patient who can only recognize his own toothbrush but not another one. There is also the case of Patients who need to associate the word with the object in order to recognize it. There are those who need to read but also those who have vision problems related to their age.

In other words, the Facilitator in this phase evaluates the gap between the anticipated personalization during the workshop preparation phase and the actual personalization

Fig. 2. Configuration of a workshop.

during the workshop, and decides what actions need to be taken to further improve the customizations.

2.4 Users' Needs

For the Facilitators, setting up a workshop is a long operation, especially when they must adapt them to different Patient. In particular, the task is even more laborious when the personalization relating to the objects handled during the workshops does not involve real objects, but rather representations of these objects, such as images: appropriate images must be chosen that are legible but not childish, cut out, laminated, etc.

The "tooth brushing" workshop is representative of the workshops because it encompasses the activity of object recognition and involves recognizing a) the objects necessary to perform the activity; b) the order of the actions to be performed to perform the activity; and c) the room where to locate the objects.

3 Personalization in a Digital Therapeutic Workshop for the Recognition of a Daily Living Activity

In this section, we describe the personalization solutions we proposed to digitize a workshop dedicated to tooth brushing. There are other digital adaptation of ADL workshops, for example the "kitchen and cooking" serious games [10, 14]. As underlined in [15], and according to methods used by the caregivers of the day care center, there is a need of personalization, but in unusual way. Generally, the users parametrize themself the personalization, like in [13]. Here, the caregivers will do instead of the Patients.

3.1 User-Centered Design, Participatory Design and Personalization: Our Design Approach

Our personalization approach falls within user-centered design and participatory design. This is a particular-user-centered design approach, i.e., an approach within which the expectations and characteristics of individual users – and not of generic users – are as much as possible considered at each step of the design process, and where the direct or indirect participation of the individual user (Patient, Facilitator) is solicited.

Considering the particularities of Patient (and more generally of people with dementia) when choosing a design method has been already raised in various ways, for example:

- presenting the Kite Approach, an empathy-directed design approach, Lindsay et al. [9] recommended what they called Personally Tailored Design (i.e., iterative personally tailored design cycles), respecting the experiences of people with dementia (and their accounts of these experiences);
- discussing the challenges in doing participatory design with people with dementia, Hendriks et al. [6] pointed out that "the way in which dementia occurs and affects daily life is different for each person and thus, the [participatory design] method used will also be"; in other words, "participation must be configured";
- providing guidelines for participatory design together with persons with dementia, Hendriks et al. [7] stated that "each chosen (set of) method(s) should be tuned towards the persons' background, interest and specificities of the deficit", e.g. « As the verbal might be a problem, make use of non-verbal elements such as visual stimuli like photos of objects or physical artifacts";
- concerned with co-designing with people with dementia, Wang et al. [18], suggested differentiated tools and recommendations according to dementia stage, as at a mild stage of the dementia, "Select people with dementia who know each other for group discussion, Apply visual prompts", and, at a mild to moderate stage, "Use external memory aids; Use subtle physical prompts".

This individualization of the design method amounts to considering application personalization as a main design concern. This was also expressed in different ways. For example:

- Leorin et al. [8] stated that it is only by allowing people with dementia to be co-designers that a true personalized approach to eHealth and mHealth solutions can only emerge;
- Treadaway [17], presenting the Compassionate Design approach, claimed to prioritize personalization;
- Wolters et al. [19] asserted that "personalization of system is crucial" in the case of people with dementia;
- Nugent et al. [12] observed that people with dementia expressed their need for different forms of personalization in interface design.

In the global participatory design approach, the "Producing design solutions" step is based on the "Understanding users' needs" step.

3.2 Design Solutions and Evaluation According to the Requirements

Design solutions are traditionally illustrated by iterating on mockups evaluated by users (6 iterations with 3 Facilitators). In our case, it is important to present finalized mockups to Patient to put them in an ideal and trust condition. We cannot get feedback from them as from usual users. It is only by observing their usages in real situations and by warm and informal exchanges that we can collect valuable information to improve the solution. Before getting a solution that can be shown to the Patient, we iterated mockups with Patients' family and caregivers.

The experiments took place in a room dedicated to experiments and evaluations in a quiet atmosphere, with a friendly welcome and presentation of the location and of the experiment members (6 patients and 1 Facilitator, for 3 experimentations). Sometimes the psycho-motor therapist observed the workshop to better understand the Facilitator activity. In this case, a designer who observed a psycho-motor therapist in the Day Care Center played the role of the Facilitator.

Design solutions are based on several design choices allowing to establish personalization solutions.

Basic Design Choices. For the Patients to feel familiar with the digitized version of the workshop and to keep one's bearings, we decided to keep the configuration of the Daily Care by selecting as interaction devices an interactive tabletop and a tablet. Patient and the Facilitator sit around the interactive tabletop. The Facilitator acts as a caregiver during the workshop: she can operate the application via the tablet to refine the personalization (changing an image), temper operations (moving on to the next Patient) (Fig. 3).

Fig. 3. A digitized workshop.

So that the personalization choices are well perceived, another important design choice is to digitize the signs of encouragement within the workshop.

Design Choices Related to the Personalization Dimensions. Several personalization dimensions have been taken into account in the design of the digitized workshop. These dimensions are based on Patients and Facilitators' needs that were identified during our observations:

- The Facilitator need to manage the workshop (and thus the personalization) at different steps of the workshop management: during the workshop preparation, during the workshop, during the workshop analysis.
- Patients have different perception/representation modes and preferences (e.g., visual, auditive, kinesthetic modes), depending on the stage of their Alzheimer dis-ease, and other possible disabilities. The Facilitator personalizes the perceptual modalities to each Patient.
- Patients have different action modes and preferences, depending on the stage of their Alzheimer disease, and other possible disabilities. The Facilitator personalizes the action modalities to each Patient.

Design Choices Implementation. The representation of objects and actions must allow to get experience feedback on the advantages and drawbacks of the different modalities (tangible objects vs images or videos, text, sound). Personalization is important to select the appropriate modalities. The following tables, Table 2, Table 3 and Table 4, illustrate how the design choices related to personalization were implemented according to the different steps of the workshop management process.

Table 2. Personalization during the workshop preparation.

	In the file of a Patient, a Facilitator can enter a bank of images associated with the objects of the workshops which can come from photographs provided by the families or from images sought on the Internet, both being more specific and adapted to the Patients
Acquisition of personalized images	
	Before starting the workshop there can be a phase of parameterization of modalities adapted to the Patient who will participate to the workshop: chronological frieze (numbered or not); text or image...
Identification of adapted modalities	

Table 3. Personalization during the workshop.

Assistance to recognition through multimodality	Multimodality is an indirect personalization: each one exploits its primary modality (especially used when making choices in the menus). During the workshop, thanks to her tablet, the Facilitator can decide to choose a modality for a Patient by replacing the image with the text if she realizes that the Patient does not recognize the proposed image. 
Building trust - Taking charge of decision making	The Facilitator can help a Patient to make a choice by zooming in on one of the images offered to him or her. The decision-making process can finally be completely transferred to the Facilitator so as not to leave the Patient facing a difficulty for too long. 
Assistance to action recognition through a video	If the Patient does not seem to understand the action represented in the image, the Facilitator can propose a video illustrating the action. 
Assistance to object recognition through explanations of tangible objects provided by Augmented Reality	Another solution is to offer all Patients tangible objects (non-personalized) to which we associate the possibility to ask for help thanks to augmented reality. At this moment, the Patient being helped can place the object he or she does not recognize on a help zone of the tabletop and an intelligent glass will offer him or her a personalized representation chosen by the Facilitator in the workshop preparation phase. 

Table 4. Personalization during the workshop analysis.

Capitalization of personalization for Patient's behavior analysis or preparation of future exercises	The workshop of each Patient being recorded, it makes it possible to keep the choices made by the Facilitator on the best possible object or action representations for the concerned Patient.  This can be confirmed by replaying the activity individually on a tablet. 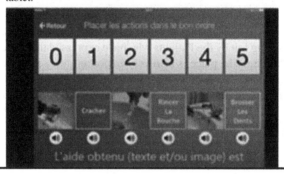

4 Feedback

This section first describes our design process and then the lessons that we can learn from our design solutions.

4.1 Review of the Design Method

In this study, we put into practice a participatory design process adapted to Patients with Alzheimer's disease. The Alzheimer's problems introduce difficulties in communication between users and designers during interviews, focus groups, participatory evaluation… The approach has therefore been adapted according to the social environment of each Patient [4, 5, 11].

To "understand and include the context of use" we observed workshops in day care. We conducted interviews with families to understand the difficulties encountered by AD in their activities of daily living. We then noticed that it is very important to pay attention to the biases introduced by relatives. It is important to compare all points of view to verify the suggestions. We deduced from this that the formalization (using persona) of the information acquired must integrate the personalization criteria to allow the creation of adapted Patient files.

As the workshops focus on the recognition of objects and the sequence of actions related to a daily living activity such as brushing teeth, the choice of the representation of objects and actions is an essential part of the design. It is necessary to integrate them from the first models. The choice of these representations was established with the Facilitators and families by setting up discussion groups including card sorting.

The choice of the modes of interaction and the way of integrating the elements of confidence building are also integrated in the first models. The first models are a mixture of low fidelity for navigation and high fidelity for action and interaction objects.

As written in Sect. 3, to "Evaluate the solutions", it is not possible to present "unfinished" models to Patients; they must be placed as much as possible in a real situation so as not to disturb them. The solution adopted is to have the intermediate models evaluated by relatives: family or caregivers. When evaluating with the Patients, the evaluation team must show empathy and listening. Observation is essential, both factual and behavioral, in order to anticipate the difficulties that may cause behavioral problems.

This approach having been applied in the context of HCI projects carried out by students, we noted that the inter-generational aspect "students - seniors" is clearly favorable to the well-being felt by the Patients who have expressed their interest in traveling to the school for testing. The place is also very important; they must be quiet, surrounded by familar people and comfortably installed.

We also noticed that when we were able to involve the families in the preliminary interviews, the personalization elements made it possible to involve the Patients with even more positivity.

4.2 Feedback on Design Solutions

The design effort is essentially at the level of choosing the best possible representation of objects and actions to digitize the workshops, as underlined in [3].

To digitize everyday objects, we have chosen either images representing them or real-world objects made tangible (toothbrush, toothpaste, etc.). If the use of tangible objects seemed preferable beforehand because they were close to the workshops practiced in day care, their personalization makes the logistics complex for the Facilitators. Indeed, it would be necessary to store and identify many objects per Patient, per workshop, etc. Moreover, when we want to associate other modalities (text, sound or video) with tangible objects, the solutions are not easy because not introduced at the same level. To overcome these difficulties, the use of augmented reality makes it possible to show each Patient a personalized image of the object being manipulated. It turns out that this interaction is too complex for the Patient to do. The Facilitator uses the "smart magnifying glass" if necessary.

The use of tangible objects to represent an action is not natural, it is difficult to find meaningful objects and the solution proposed with a cube with image for representing the action affixed on it did not facilitate the recognition of the action.

The use of images to represent objects and actions associated with activities of daily living has many advantages: (1) the creation of a personalized image bank per Patient facilitating personalization; (2) the association of other modalities (text or sound) (3) the dynamic change during the workshop from one image by another or by another modality.

The Patients welcomed during the workshop can see the personalized representations of objects for each of them on the table (common space) which can disturb them. The choice to have a personal area in front of the Patient on the table partly overcomes this difficulty. However, we have found that it is preferable when to form homogeneous groups for which a common image acceptable to all to which are associated textual designations, videos and a sound. Setting up on-the-fly customization when needed reduces disruption to the operation of the group.

We took the engagement into account by introducing kudos for correct answers and not explicitly flagging errors. We also allow the Facilitator to come to the aid of a Patient in difficulty by changing the representation of an object or an action. She can also decide instead of the Patient. The Facilitators suggest pushing digital assistance further by automatically guiding the Patient to the right answer by limiting the possible choices, for example.

In terms of post-personalization, the Facilitators pointed out that it would be useful to give them the possibility to add annotations in relation to the personalization choices made on the fly or to the difficulties encountered during the exercise. Indeed, they have shown that the loss of a notion by a Patient could be detected more easily thanks to digitalization by recording the errors made by each Patient. The Facilitators could then personalize the following workshops to no longer put the Patient in difficulty by no longer offering this notion (no need to have the toothbrush recognized if it no longer has it in his memory).

Keeping the customizations associated with each Patient is crucial because it allows to have another way of following the course of the disease.

5 Conclusion

Digitizing workshops dedicated to Alzheimer's Patients is complex due to the strong need for personalization and to the importance of building Patient confidence. We have chosen to tackle personalization needs by offering customization tools through the Patient file and in allowing to personalize a workshop at different steps (before the workshop, during the workshop and after the workshop). If we can generalize some lessons of the digitalization of the teeth brushing workshop, current solutions remain ad hoc: workshop by workshop. We did not study how we can automatize the role of Facilitators in building Patient confidence. The Facilitators expressed their needs on tools facilitating creation of individual and group therapeutic workshops. We work now on generating adapted quiz on tablet for a Patient or on tabletop for group of Patients, although the presence of Facilitator during the activity is still necessary. We can apply the design principle relative to images and multi-modality interactions to quiz generation.

References

1. Cooper, A., Reimann, R.: About Face 2.0: The Essentials of Interaction Design. Wiley, Hoboken (2003)

2. Cooper, A., Reimann, R., Cronin, D., Noessel, Ch.: About Face: The Essentials of Interaction Design, 4th edn. Wiley, Hoboken (2014)
3. Guerrier, Y., Naveteur, J., Kolski, C., Poirier, F.: Communication system for persons with cerebral palsy: in situ observation of social interaction following assisted information request. In: Miesenberger, K., Fels, D., Archambault, D., Peňáz, P., Zagler, W. (eds.) Computers Helping People with Special Needs, ICCHP 2014, Part I, pp. 419–426. Springer, Cham (2014). https://doi.org/10.1007/978-3-319-08596-8_64
4. Guffroy, M., Vigouroux, N., Kolski, C., Vella, F., Teutsch, P.: From Human-Centered Design to disabled user & ecosystem centered design in case of assistive interactive systems. Int. J. Sociotechnol. Knowl. Dev. 9(4), 28–42 (2017)
5. Guffroy, M., Guerrier, Y., Kolski, C., Vigouroux, N., Vella, F., Teutsch, P.: Adaptation of user-centered design approaches to abilities of people with disabilities. In: Miesenberger, K., Kouroupetroglou, G. (eds.) ICCHP 2018. LNCS, vol. 10896, pp. 462–465. Springer, Cham (2018). https://doi.org/10.1007/978-3-319-94277-3_71
6. Hendriks, N., Huybrechts, L., Wilkinson, A., Slegers, K.: Challenges in doing participatory design with people with dementia. In: Proceedings of the 13th Participatory Design Conference on Short Papers, Industry Cases, Workshop Descriptions, Doctoral Consortium Papers, and Keynote Abstracts, PDC 2014, vol. 2, pp. 33–36 (2014)
7. Hendriks, N., Truyen, F., Duval, E.: Designing with dementia: guidelines for participatory design together with persons with dementia. In: Kotzé, P., Marsden, G., Lindgaard, G., Wesson, J., Winckler, M. (eds.) INTERACT 2013. LNCS, vol. 8117, pp. 649–666. Springer, Heidelberg (2013). https://doi.org/10.1007/978-3-642-40483-2_46
8. Leorin, C., Stella, E., Nugent, C., Cleland, I., Paggetti, C.: The value of including people with dementia in the co-design of personalized eHealth technologies. Dement. Geriatr. Cogn. Disord. 47, 164–175 (2019)
9. Lindsay, S., Brittain, K., Jackson, D., Ladha, C., Ladha, K., Olivier, P.: Empathy, participatory design and people with dementia. In: Proceedings of the SIGCHI Conference on Human Factors in Computing SystemsMay 2012, CHI 2012, pp. 521–530 (2012)
10. Manera, V., et al.: 'Kitchen and cooking', a serious game for mild cognitive impairment and Alzheimer's disease: a pilot study. Front. Aging Neurosci. 7, 24 (2015)
11. Markopoulos, P., Timmermans, A.A., Beursgens, L., Van Donselaar, R., Seelen, H.A.: Us' em: the user-centered design of a device for motivating stroke patients to use their impaired arm-hand in daily life activities. In: Engineering in Medicine and Biology Society, EMBC 2011 Annual International Conference of the IEEE, pp. 5182–5187. IEEE (2011)
12. Nugent, C., et al.: The development of personalised cognitive prosthetics. In: 30th Annual International IEEE EMBS Conference Vancouver, British Columbia, Canada, pp. 787–790 (2008)
13. Peissner, M., Häbe, D., Janssen, D., Sellner, T.: MyUI: generating accessible user interfaces from multimodal design patterns. In: Proceedings of the 4th ACM SIGCHI Symposium on Engineering Interactive Computing Systems, New York (2012)
14. Robert, P.H., et al.: Recommendations for the use of serious games in people with Alzheimer's disease, related disorders and frailty. Front. Aging Neurosci. 6, 54 (2014)
15. Sarne-Fleischmann, V., Tractinsky, N., Dwolatzky, T., Rief, I.: Personalized reminiscence therapy for Patients with Alzheimer's disease using a computerized system. In: Proceedings of the 4th International Conference on PErvasive Technologies Related to Assistive Environments (PETRA 2011), pp. 1–4, Article 48. ACM, New York (2011)
16. Schade, A.: Customization vs. Personalization in the User Experience. https://www.nngroup.com/articles/customization-personalization/. Accessed 12 Jan 2021
17. Treadaway, C.: Personalization and compassionate design. In: Brankaert, R., Kenning, G. (eds.) HCI and Design in the Context of Dementia. HIS, pp. 49–61. Springer, Cham (2020). https://doi.org/10.1007/978-3-030-32835-1_4

18. Wang, G., Marradi, C., Albayrak, A., van der Cammen, T.: Co-designing with people with dementia: a scoping review of involving people with dementia in design research. Maturitas **127**, 55–63 (2019). https://doi.org/10.1016/j.maturitas.2019.06.003

19. Wolters, M.K., Kelly, F., Kilgour, J.: Designing a spoken dialogue interface to an intelligent cognitive assistant for people with dementia. Health Inform. J. **22**, 854–866 (2016)

Tasteful: A Cooking App Designed for Visually Impaired Users

Yunran Ju[✉], Zhenyu Cheryl Qian, and Weilun Huang

Purdue University, West Lafayette, USA
ju27@purdue.edu

Abstract. Nowadays, more and more visually impaired people want to live independently and cook for themselves. However, cooking independently may bring lots of challenges. This paper provides a better solution by helping visually impaired users locate ingredients quickly and find more ways to cook flexibly. The design is a comprehensive process. After the stage of problem identification, brainstorming, concept development and prototyping, we finally designed an application, Tasteful, that helps visually impaired users better solve the problems encountered in the cooking process.

Keywords: Visually impaired · Cooking app design

1 Introduction

According to the data provided by the World Health Organization in 2012, the number of visual impairment people is estimated at 285 million in the world [1]. The number of visually impaired and blind people will double in the next 35 years in the United States [2]. Visual impairment greatly increases the difficulty of necessary activities of daily living [3], especially when it comes to the cooking experience. Visually impaired people have to spend extra time to purchase, store, allocate, and prepare food [4]. They also have to practice and build a precise system to support their activities in the kitchen. These extra procedures have made blind cooking a time-consuming and laborious job. Due to limited resources and learning frustrations, lots of them would avoid difficult-preparing food and choose a more straightforward diet option such as microwave frozen meals. Long-term consumption of these "easy choices" can lead to nutritional imbalances and even overweight.

On the other hand, the emerging of some technologies has changed the problematic situation. Through voice-in features, visually impaired people would navigate websites and use some applications by themselves [5]. In this research, we adapted the voice-in feature and developed a mobile application "Tasteful" to help visually impaired users' cooking process. The major functions include 1) helping users record, keep track of food, and remind users to quickly consume the expiring materials, 2) suggesting more ways to cook flexibly, 3) making an inventory of cooking by select items they have, and offering some tasteful and healthy recipes. A step by step recipe guidance makes it

© Springer Nature Switzerland AG 2021
M. Antona and C. Stephanidis (Eds.): HCII 2021, LNCS 12768, pp. 384–393, 2021.
https://doi.org/10.1007/978-3-030-78092-0_25

easier and accessible for visually impaired users to follow. The research aims to design a better cooking application for visually impaired users, reduce the difficulty of cooking independently through voice-in features, and prevent errors caused by memory failures.

2 Background of the Study

To better understand our design challenges, we analyzed existing data such as research reports, websites, and related literature during the secondary research. We also studied recent technological, behavioral, and cultural innovations, which helped us create design guidelines. According to the literature, more than 3.4 million (3%) Americans aged 40 years and older are either legally blind or are visually impaired [6]. Rates of blindness will double by 2020. An additional 50,000 people are losing their sight each year [7]. Also, about 90% of visually impaired people who live in the developing world have limited food resources.

Visually impaired people are facing lots of challenges while cooking independently. Bilyk et al.'s 2009 survey [8] has shown that nearly half of the visually impaired participants want to make a healthier choice and prepare their food, even though it means they will face numerous problems from shopping, preparing, and cooking.

With the development of technology, some advanced smart device features, such as VoiceOver and TalkBack Screen Reader, have been released to help visually impaired users to navigate websites and use applications. Taking VoiceOver as an example, it is a screen-reading technology that describes aloud what appears on the smart device screens. Auditory descriptions of onscreen elements help users navigate the screen through the keyboard or gestures [9]. Lots of users with visual disabilities can navigate smart devices with the help of the VoiceOver function.

Based on these features, some cooking applications and websites have been designed for blind and visually impaired users [10], such as Yes, Chef and In the Kitchen. Yes chef is a hand-free cooking application that talks through recipes and answers user's questions. In the Kitchen is a free application for iOS. The VoiceOver feature will read out content and details on the screen, and it is necessary to navigate only with simple gestures. After a survey upon the existing blink cooking apps, we found some problems. For example, few instructions teach cooking step by step, and the app usually speaks way too fast, and users cannot follow. Moreover, the searching and repeating functions can frustrate and confuse the visual impaired users [11].

After analyzing existing products, we realized that most well-designed cooking applications are all intended to solve problems at the cooking stage. However, the pre-cooking experience also comprises other issues existing in the kitchen. For example, it is hard for visually impaired users to locate particular food or items in the refrigerator during the preparation stage and judge their freshness. In this paper, Tasteful focuses not only on the cooking itself but also on solving the problems generated by users in the preparation stage.

3 User Experience Research and Analysis

3.1 Analysis of YouTube Videos

To gain a better understanding of visually impaired cooking experiences, we went through several YouTube videos that recorded the cooking process of blind people and visually impaired people [12, 13]. In the videos, they demonstrated the cooking process and shared their experience with blind cooking. We list every issue that appeared in the video during video reviewing and summarized them into three cooking phases: shopping, preparation, cooking, and cleaning.

- Shopping: when visually impaired users go grocery shopping, they usually need assistance from friends or family or store employees to identify item or shelf locations [4] and avoid running into other customers. Barely being able to read the information on the packaging, most of them would select the same brands for many years. Also, most package food has no special labels designed for visually impaired people.
- Preparation: During the preparation phase, it is hard to locate particular food or item in the refrigerator and judge the freshness without vision. Visually impaired users have to use other senses such as touching and smelling to identify ingredients. They also have to memorize every food package and seasoning bottle with different shapes and sizes, then arrange them according to their own habits. Moreover, if visually impaired users have roommates, this process becomes more complicated since others might change items' location. After find items, users need to washing and slicing the right amount of ingredients. This step is full of risks and dangers. Users without functional sight have to rely on the sense of touching to find slicing tools and start cutting.
- Cooking: After a long preparation phase, more difficulties appeared in the cooking stage. To ensure that the food is fully-cooked, users would use several cooking methods, including frying, baking, steaming, boiling, etc. Since every cooking method requires heat, these methods bring cooking more risk factors. It is also hard to distinguish how well the food has been cooked without sight. Users usually rely on touching or tasting to determine the status, which is easy to get hurt. To measure a small amount of seasoning also full of challenge. Measuring spoon sometimes is helpful, but there is not much effect when it comes to liquid seasoning. Using all kinds of cooking appliances is not easy as well. For the sake of beauty, the buttons on almost all cooking appliances are de\signed to have the same shape and size, such as rice cooker, stove, and microwave. Without letters, raised icons, or Braille instructions, it is difficult for visually impaired users to use them without others' help.
- Cleaning: After cooking, it is usually hard to keep the kitchen clean and tidy. Therefore, the last phase is to clean and reorganize the kitchen and wash dishes. For visually impaired users, they need to use hand to guide positions and determine whether the dishes are clean by touching and feeling.

After observation, we were able to found out user problems and understand how they feel about cooking.

3.2 Empathetic Study to Understand the Experience

Empathic design is a user-centered design approach that pays attention to the user's feelings toward a product. The research approach has been employed in industrial design and user experience design domains to identify and understand the users' real needs through acting in their roles. To verify the existence and accuracy of the above problems we gathered from observation and decide the design direction, we conducted an empathetic study of blind cooking. I used an eye mask to cover my eyes and could not see items during the process, and my team member recorded and observed the whole cooking process. I decided to cook Chinese noodles in the experiment because it was an easy cooking process without complicated steps. The entire cooking plan was: finding ingredients, boiling the water, washing pakchoi, putting raw noodles and vegetables into the pot, seasoning the noodles, and serving the noodles.

During the empathetic study, we first affirmed the problems we found in the video review, then summarized the difficulties I met into three categories: First, for visually impaired users, it is hard to locate items and ingredients in the cabinet or refrigerator; Second, blind cooking is mainly dependent on the user's cognition and memory, whether it is the storage location or the specific buttons of cooking appliances. Third, distinguishing the status of food and ingredients are always challenging. Whether to feel or taste, it is still full of dangerous uncertainties such as burnt or cut or eating undercooked food.

3.3 Summary of User Research Findings

After concluding the analysis outcomes from both YouTube videos and empathetic study, we outlined all the findings and narrowed them down to four key insights.

It is hard for visually impaired users to locate food items
During the video review, every visually impaired user showed difficulty locating items or ingredients during the preparing process. We found that visually impaired users have their storage and memorization habits or methods. For example, condiments are placed in certain drawers and ranged according to the size of the bottles. Users have to remember the order of bottles and every slight difference of each bottle. Also, vegetables or meat products are usually stored in the refrigerator according to the frequency of consumption. They need to feel the shape and texture of vegetables by touching to discover. Visually impaired users also showed frustration during grocery shopping. The user either needs to request a personal shopper from customer service or has someone's company. They cannot shuttle between shelves and identify similarly shaped items or distinguish the same veggie with different colors, such as green pepper and red pepper.

Take advantage of limited food resources
We learned that most people do grocery shopping in the following two ways. First, some users prefer to buying ingredients based on recipes. For example, when users want to cook certain kinds of dishes, they would list every ingredient and do grocery shopping. Second, other people prefer to do grocery shopping regularly, and they usually would select certain items based on habits or food preferences. No matter which way, most users will encounter the situation that there are only a few limited ingredients or items left at home. However, they do not know how to take advantage of these limited ingredients

for cooking. For instance, to cook some unfamiliar dishes or some unusual combinations. Especially for visually impaired users, cooking is complicated and challenging to operate. Most people prefer microwave food or semi-finished products. It is not only unhealthy but also lacks a variety of food choices.

Users always forget food expiration dates
Due to visual impairment, it is difficult for visually impaired users to distinguish foods' expiration dates. For fresh foods like fruits and vegetables, users can identify the freshness by touching or smelling. However, for some packaged foods, such as seasonings, frozen foods, or other semi-prepared foods, it is difficult for users to distinguish whether they are expired without vision. It is also hard for visually impaired users to remember every single item stored in the refrigerator or cabinet. Thus, it becomes impossible for them to recognize which ingredient is expired and which is about to expire.

Hearing, taste, smell, and touch are significant senses used by visually impaired users
During the secondary research, we found out that without sight, the functions of other senses hearing, taste, smell, and touch, are greatly enhanced. Sound is one of the most powerful senses used by visually impaired people. Data shows that visually impaired people can navigate websites and use applications through voice-in features. While touch is also an important information source for visually impaired users, by feeling the shape, texture, temperature, they would be able to identify lots of objects.

4 Design Process

After the research, we decided on four design goals of our application design. First, provide users with various recipes to help them take advantage of their limited food resources. Second, create output accommodating the needs of visually impaired users. Third, design for the short-term memory to prevent errors caused by memory failures. As for looking for inconveniences during cooking for visually impaired users, we tried to take full advantage of Voice-in features to improve the user experience. We also created a user journey map that describes the scenario of after shopping, preparing, and cooking (see Fig. 1). We tried to find pain points continually and solutions by analyzing a typical blind cooking process.

Based on the previous findings and user journey, we want to focus on the pain points of blind cooking and started ideation. After several rounds of brainstorming, we gathered lots of design ideas and narrowed down the final one according to three design goals. Then we started to design the low fidelity user interface (Fig. 2), which shows the overview structure of the application. Next, we created the style guide and applied it to the high fidelity user interface. Finally, we modified several details and made an interactive prototype.

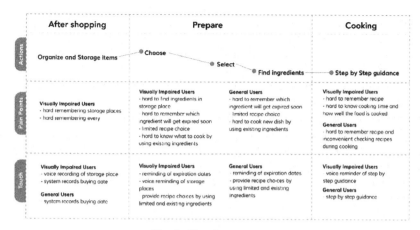

Fig. 1. User journey map

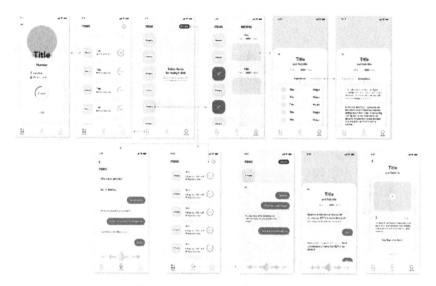

Fig. 2. Low fidelity user interface

5   Final Design

The final version of the Tasteful application contains two main parts: the item page and recipe page. Also, the Voice button is located in the middle of the bottom tab.

5.1   Keep Track of Items

First, by encouraging users to record all items they brought and places they stored, it helps users keep track of items and remind users to consume the expiring materials sooner (see Fig. 3). Users can add items on the items page by clicking the plus icon on the right upper corner, and Tasteful will record the purchase date and storage place by voice instructions. When users try to find items in the refrigerator or the cabinet, they do not need to touch or feel every item to identify the correct one anymore. The application will remind users of the place they stored the item.

While adding the items, the app will find the item's image and set an expiration date to make the process more efficient and keep the list organized. For example, ordinarily, green peppers will keep up for two to three weeks at the proper temperature. Therefore, on the item description window, it will show as the item expires in two weeks. The order of the list will be sorted according to the expiration time of the item. Expiring items are listed from top to bottom, and users can quickly check the status. When some certain item is about to expire, the small alert icon will appear and remind the users to soon consume the expiring ones.

Fig. 3. Keep track of items

5.2 Make Your Inventory

The Recipe page is designed based on accessibility for visually impaired users. This page is divided into the left and right part, which is easy to learn and navigate by closed eyes and using two hands (see Fig. 4). On the left part is the list of items that users have recorded, and the right part is the recipe suggestions. The design means to solve a general problem that lots of users will encounter in daily cooking. When there are only a few ingredients left, they have no idea what kind of dishes can be made with existing ingredients. By merely selecting ingredients, users can receive different food recipe suggestions. For example, when selecting tomatoes, the App will offer basic tomato recipes, such as roasted tomatoes or tomato sauce. Tasteful will also offer users different recipes by selecting different amounts or different types of ingredients. When selecting two or more ingredients, the App will provide a richer selection of recipes based on the different combinations. For instants, when selecting tomato and chicken, the App will offer more recipes such as Skillet Tomato Chicken, Creamy tomato chicken, etc.

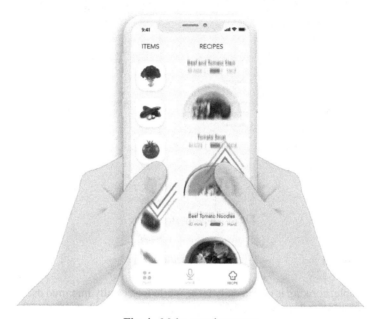

Fig. 4. Make your inventory

5.3 Hands-Free Recipes

Third, Tasteful offers a flexible and accessible cooking experience for visually impaired users by adapting voice-in features. The Voice-in feature makes it easier to add items and allows users to follow the step-by-step voice recipe during the cooking. After selecting a certain recipe, users can check the detailed ingredients, estimate cooking time, difficulty level, and detailed guidance. With a single click or a voice instruction, it will start the step by step cooking instruction and plays the voice guidances slowly and clearly. At meanwhile, the application will also start the timer. When it reached the estimated cooking time, Tasteful will remind the user to check the food status. It solved the problem that visually impaired users always have trouble distinguishing how well the food is cooked. Also, with step-by-step cooking instructions, users do not need to remember which seasoning is already put and which is not (see Fig. 5).

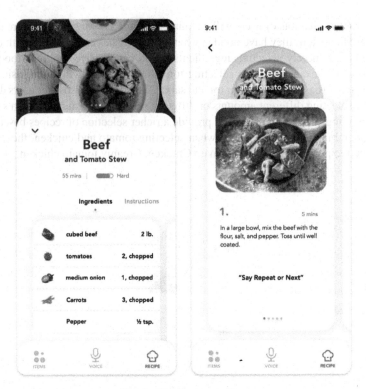

Fig. 5. Step-by-step recipe

6   Conclusion

For most people, cooking is only a daily task. While for visually impaired users, cooking is time-consuming and encountered dangers and challenges. To better solve problems of blind cooking, we designed this cooking application by helping users reducing short-term memory and employing the Voice-in feature. With literature review, user research, and field study of blind cooking, we understood problems encountered in visually impaired people's cooking process. By narrow down several insights, we decided to focus on the preparing and cooking process. We started ideation to study the functionality, understand user behavior, and prioritize interface elements. To better solve problems caused by loss of short-term memory, including forgetting food storage places and food expiration dates, we encourage users to use the voice-in feature to recoding. Other features such as step-by-step cooking instructions, make food inventories also make blind cooking easier.

However, some details of the application design still need to be polished in the future. Also, the voice-in feature requires the users to use it in a real blind cooking environment, and the insufficiency is hard to measure and test with an interactive prototype. The next step of our design will focus on making a more detailed working prototype and conducting an evaluation.

References

1. Maritto, S.P.: Global data on visual impairment 2010. World Health Organization, Geneva (2012). WHO/NMH/PBD
2. Varma, R., et al.: Visual impairment and blindness in adults in the United States: demographic and geographic variations from 2015 to 2050. JAMA Ophthalmol. **134**(7), 802–809 (2016)
3. Welp, A., et al.: "The Impact of Vision Loss." Making Eye Health a Population Health Imperative: Vision for Tomorrow. National Academies Press (US) (2016)
4. Kostyra, E., et al.: Food shopping, sensory determinants of food choice and meal preparation by visually impaired people. Obstacles Expect. Daily Food Exp. Appetite **113**, 14–22 (2017)
5. Oldman, J.: 10 Free Screen Readers For Blind Or Visually Impaired Users. Usability Geek (2012). usabilitygeek.com/10-free-screen-reader-blind-visually-impaired-users/
6. Saaddine, J.B., Venkat Narayan, K.M., Vinicor, F.: Vision loss: a public health problem? Ophthalmology **110**(2), 253–254 (2003)
7. Snelling, S.: Visual Impairment & Blindness in the U.S. to Double by 2050. USC Roski Eye Institute, 7 July 2020. eye.keckmedicine.org/visual-impairment-blindness-prevalence-us-double-2050-study-usc-roski-eye-institute-researchers/
8. Bilyk, M.C., et al.: Food experiences and eating patterns of visually impaired and blind people. Can. J. Diet. Pract. Res. **70**(1), 13–18 (2009)
9. Apple Incorporation: VoiceOver for IOS. Let Our Voice be Your Guide. www.apple.com. http://www.apple.com/accessibility/ios/voiceover/. Accessed 6 Feb 2021
10. Ingber, J.: Accessible Recipes for Holiday Cooking and Entertaining. Accessible Recipes for Holiday Cooking and Entertaining, AccessWorld, American Foundation for the Blind. Web (2016)
11. Appadvice: Yes Chef - Hands Free Recipe Assistant by Conversant Labs. AppAdvice (2017). appadvice.com/app/yes-chef-hands-free-recipe-assistant/1092772390
12. Ha, C.: MasterChef Winner Christine Ha Shows How the Blind Cook (2017). www.youtube.com/watch?v=65gqX2QhVRA&t=5s&ab_channel=ChristineHa. Accessed 9 Nov 2020
13. Edison, T.: How Blind People Cook Food Alone (2012). https://www.youtube.com/watch?v=umiOuVA7PEc&t=2s&ab_channel=TheTommyEdisonExperience. Accessed 9 Nov 2020

Effect of the Peripheral Visual Field Elements of 3D Video Clips on Body Sway

Fumiya Kinoshita[1]([⊠]), Honoka Okuno[1], Hideaki Touyama[1], and Hiroki Takada[2]

[1] Toyama Prefectural University, 5180 Kurokawa, Imizu, Toyama 939-0398, Japan
f.kinoshita@pu-toyama.ac.jp
[2] University of Fukui, 3-9-1 Bunkyo, Fukui 910-8507, Japan

Abstract. It has been pointed out in previous studies that information from the peripheral vision may trigger three-dimensional (3D) motion sickness. In a previous study, the authors created two types of 3D images with different background elements, and determined the regional cerebral blood flow as the 3D images were viewed via functional near-infrared spectroscopy (fNIRS). Accordingly, we verified that the differences present in the background elements of the peripheral visual field region affected cerebral hemodynamics when viewing 3D images. In addition, we reported the possibility of overload in the depth perception-related visual information process that occurs in the dorsal visual pathway when viewing 3D images with complex background elements. In this study, we focused on the background elements in the peripheral visual field region that were added to 3D images, and investigated the effects of the differences in these elements on the body balance function. Consequently, we verified that the difference in the amount of the background element protrusion influences the body balance function.

Keywords: Stereoscopic video clips · 3D motion sickness · Peripheral visual field · Body sway · Stabilometry

1 Introduction

Recently, there have been significant improvements in the display technology of stereoscopic images, which are applied in various fields such as movies, televisions, and games. The concept of binocular stereovision was first proposed by the British physicist Charles Wheatstone in 1832; the development of this concept spans a historic timeline exceeding 150 years [1]. Until the first half of the 20th century, stereoscopic vision almost always implied stereoscopic display technology. However, terms such as "augmented reality" and "virtual reality (VR)" have recently emerged as stereoscopic display technologies [2]. Stereoscopic display technology is actively applied in a wide range of fields such as medical care, education, and entertainment.

© Springer Nature Switzerland AG 2021
M. Antona and C. Stephanidis (Eds.): HCII 2021, LNCS 12768, pp. 394–404, 2021.
https://doi.org/10.1007/978-3-030-78092-0_26

Several studies have investigated diverse methods for presenting stereoscopic video clips. However, the most common methods include the use of binocular stereos that express a stereoscopic effect by presenting two images that primary differ by the parallax of both eyes. Regarding the content of stereoscopic images, the movie "Avatar" was released in 2009, and instantly became a record hit. In 2010, the world's first full high-definition (FHD) three-dimensional (3D) television was launched; this indicated an increasing trend of the use of stereoscopic images. However, 3D televisions were not adopted owing to various reasons, including safety concerns. Based on their image elements and viewing conditions, stereoscopic video clips cause discomfort, such as headache, vomiting, and eye fatigue, to the viewer [3, 4].These symptoms are termed as 3D motion sickness. In 2008, the 3D Consortium published the "3DC Safety Guidelines for the Dissemination of Human-friendly 3D" [5]. Revised versions of these safety guidelines were published in December 2009 and April 2010. However, in these revisions, only a few theories explained the causes of 3D motion sickness, and no significant improvement was achieved [6, 7]. To safely view stereoscopic video clips, it is crucial to verify the effects of stereoscopic video clips on the body.

Conventionally, 3D motion sickness is considered to occur when stereoscopic video clips are viewed, and this is considered the reason for the mismatch between the crystalline lens adjustment function and convergence movement. In normal natural vision, accommodation and vergence reflexes are simultaneously performed owing to near-vision reactions. Conversely, according to the vergence–accommodation conflict theory, while viewing stereoscopic video clips, the crystalline lens adjustment function is fixed onto the screen on which the video clips are presented, whereas convergence is fixed to the protruding virtual object. Therefore, visual fatigue is considered to occur owing to the continuous difference in appearance from natural vision while viewing stereoscopic video clips. The hypothesis of the vergence–accommodation conflict theory is conventionally described as a cause of visual fatigue when viewing stereoscopic images, and it is described in several documents, such as safety guidelines [5]. However, in 2013, Shiomi et al. established a simultaneous measurement method to accommodate crystalline lens and convergence movement while viewing video clips, and compared them with real objects, 2D and 3D video clips [8]. The obtained results confirmed that the crystalline lens adjustment while young individuals viewed stereoscopic images was linked to the pop-out and retraction of the virtual object in a manner similar to the natural vision state. Hence, it was confirmed that there is no discrepancy between the accommodation of crystalline lens and vergence movement [9].

Currently, the explanation provided by the sensory conflict theory is conventionally considered as the mechanism of 3D motion sickness [10, 11]. Spatial orientation becomes unstable when the combination of information input from the visual, vestibular, and somatosensory systems does not correspond with the combination of sensory system information established by previous experience. This triggers symptoms such as headache or vomiting. As a recent trend in the VR field, several research efforts have focused on ascertaining the sensory conflict theory as the root cause of 3D sickness, as well as avoiding sensory inconsistencies by modifying information input to sensory organs. For example, studies have investigated the control of discomfort symptoms by applying a weak current to the head (vestibular system) via vestibular electrical stimulation (galvanic vestibular stimulation; GVS) to impart an inclination or a movement sensation to the user. In addition, some studies have adopted a large simulator to introduce an inclination sensation by rotating the user physically based on given visual information [12, 13]. However, although the aforementioned approaches are effective in increasing the immersion and presence of the user, they are ineffective solutions for 3D motion sickness.

In recent years, the possibility of the effect of peripheral vision information as a 3D sickness trigger has been pointed out. In a previous study, it was reported that the sickness score by a subjective questionnaire and intensity of swaying of the center of gravity significantly increased when the images were viewed with peripheral and follow-up visions [14]. Here, among the visual pathways in the cerebral cortex, the dorsal visual pathway is known to be involved in depth perception, i.e., recognizing visual objects located in space [15]. In other words, by measuring the dorsal visual pathway, it is possible to evaluate the effect of 3D video clips on the peripheral visual function. In this research, we created two types of 3D video clips with different background elements, and measured the regional cerebral blood flow via functional near-infrared spectroscopy (fNIRS) while 3D video clips were viewed [16]. Accordingly, we also verified that the differences in the background elements of the peripheral visual field region affected cerebral hemodynamics. In addition, it was confirmed that visual information related to depth perception in the dorsal visual pathway may be overloaded when viewing 3D video clips with complex background elements.

Therefore, in this research, we proposed the following research hypothesis: "incoming images as visual information are processed by the eye as stereoscopic images in the brain even when the eye is in peripheral vision." In addition, we attempted to develop a technology for reducing 3D sickness by investigating the components placed in the peripheral vision region of the image content. In this study, we focused on the background elements in the peripheral visual field region of the 3D video clips, and investigated the effects that the differences in the background elements exert on the motion of the center of gravity.

2   Experimental Method

In this study, we created three patterns of 3D video clips by altering the background elements in the peripheral vision area. Pattern 1 is the control image, which is a 3D video clip with depth, where a sphere (hereinafter referred to as "sphere-A") moves

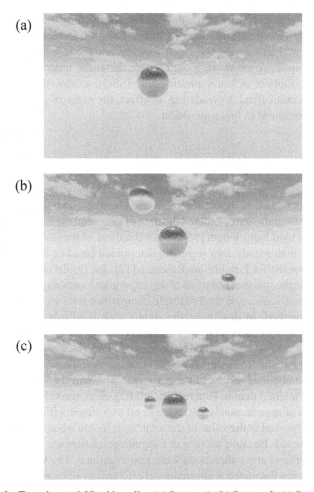

Fig. 1. Experimental 3D video clips (a) Pattern 1, (b) Pattern 2, (c) Pattern 3

around intricately in the screen (Fig. 1a). In Pattern 2, two more spheres were introduced to the image of Pattern 1, and each of the introduced spheres moved about the screen independently. However, the amount of protrusion and depth of the two spheres were set to be the same as the sphere in Pattern 1 (Fig. 1b). In Pattern 3, the initial positions of the two spheres introduced in Pattern 2 were positioned far away from the subject, such that the subject did not feel the amount of protrusion and depth (Fig. 1c). In this experiment, we investigated the effect that the difference in the peripheral visual field region exerts on the body equilibrium function by making the subjects watch sphere-A displayed in all the images with follow-up viewing.

The subjects were 14 healthy young men and women (21.8 ± 1.28 years old). We comprehensively explained the experiment to the subjects and obtained their written consent beforehand. This experiment was conducted after obtaining approval from the Ethics Committee of Toyama Prefectural University. In this experiment, we adopted a center-of-gravity trajectory measuring device manufactured by Takei Scientific Instruments Co., Ltd. with a time resolution of 100 Hz. The measurement time of the center-of-gravity sway was 60 s during the video viewing, and the measurement posture was the Romberg posture. After viewing each video, the visual analogue scale (VAS) for discomfort and simulator sickness questionnaire (SSQ), a subjective questionnaire for sickness, were administered. Considering its effect, the order of presenting the image patterns was randomized in this experiment.

3 Results

Figure 2 illustrates a typical stabilogram sample for the same subject. Here, a change in the amount of sway owing to different background elements can be observed. Next, from the obtained stabilogram, we calculated the area of sway and the total locus length. The area of sway and total locus length are analytical indices of the stabilogram obtained in previous studies; in this study, they were also determined based on the definition formula of the Japanese Society for Equilibrium Research [17]. The results obtained are presented in Figs. 3 and 4. In the statistical analysis of this experiment, one-way analysis of variance (ANOVA) was performed, and then multiple comparison tests were conducted via the Tukey–Kramer method. In this study, the significance level was set at 0.05, whereas the values of the area of sway were approximately $4.0\ cm^2$ in all experiments (Fig. 3). The values of the area of sway tended to be larger in Patterns 2 and 3 with background elements than in Pattern 1, which is the control image. A multiple comparison test was conducted on the obtained results of the perimeter area, and the value increased more significantly in Pattern 3 than in Pattern 1 ($p < 0.05$). Next, the values of the total locus length fluctuated at approximately 240.0 cm in all experiments (Fig. 4). No significant difference was observed in the value of the total locus length when multiple comparison tests were conducted. Because there was a significant difference in the area of sway, the variances of the x- and y-directions were also examined. The value of the variance along the x-direction fluctuated at approximately $0.2\ cm^2$ in all experiments (Fig. 5), and the multiple comparison test for the results of the variance obtained in the x-direction exhibited a more significant increase in Pattern 3 than in Pattern 1 ($p < 0.05$).The value of the variance in the y-direction fluctuated at approximately $0.2\ cm^2$ in all experiments (Fig. 6), and the multiple comparison test for the result of the variance in the y-direction exhibited a more significant increase in Pattern 3 than in Pattern 1 ($p < 0.05$). The results obtained from the subjective questionnaire administered after viewing each video are presented in Figs. 7 and 8. The visual analogue scale (VAS) values were approximately 12% in all experiments (Fig. 7), and the multiple comparison test for the obtained VAS results exhibited a more significant increase in Patterns 2 and 3 ($p < 0.05$) than in

Pattern 1. The total score of the SSQ fluctuated at approximately 12% in all experiments (Fig. 8), and multiple comparison tests performed on the results of the total SSQ score demonstrated that the values of Patterns 2 and 3 increased more significantly than those of Pattern 1 ($p < 0.05$).

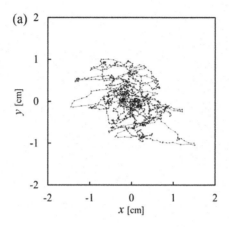

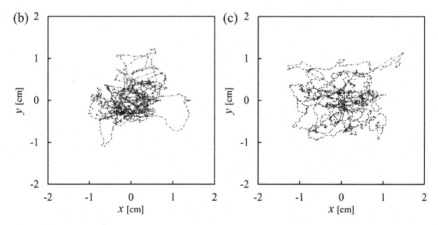

Fig. 2. Typical stabilograms for one participant: (a) Pattern 1, (b) Pattern 2, (c) Pattern 3

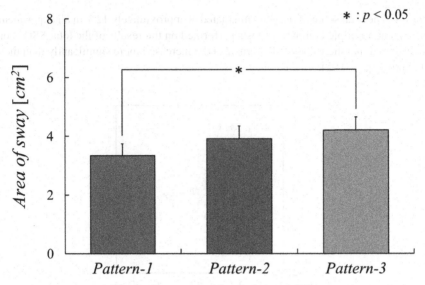

Fig. 3. Average area of sway (mean ± SE)

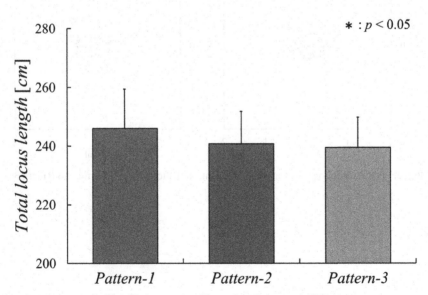

Fig. 4. Average total locus length (mean ± SE)

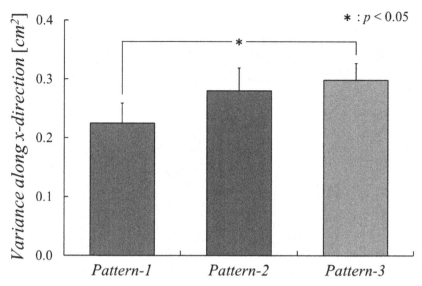

Fig. 5. Average variance along *x*-direction (mean ± SE)

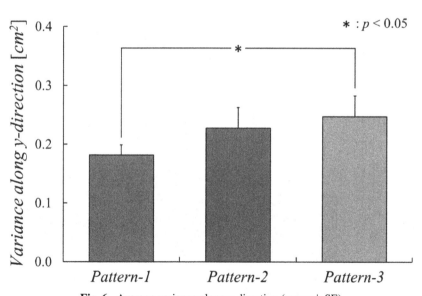

Fig. 6. Average variance along *y*-direction (mean ± SE)

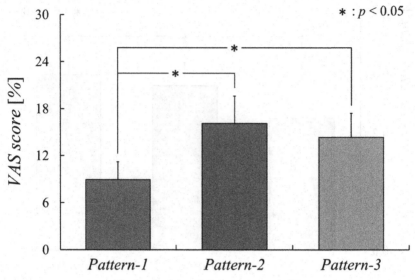

Fig. 7. Average VAS score (mean ± SE)

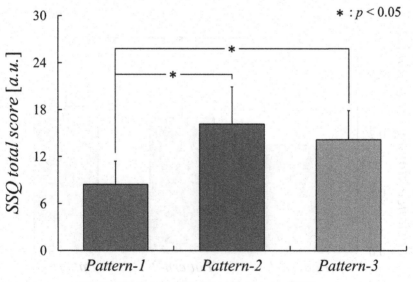

Fig. 8. Average SSQ total score (mean ± SE)

4 Discussion

To view 3D images safely, empirical studies on the effects of 3D images on the body are essential. In this study, we proposed a research hypothesis that "the eyeballs process received visual information as stereoscopic images in the brain even when they are in peripheral vision." In addition, we investigated the effects that the differences in the background elements of the peripheral vision area of 3D images exert on the body balance function. In this study, three types of 3D images with different background elements were adopted, and to investigate the effect that the difference in the peripheral vision exerts on the body balance function, the subjects followed sphere-A, which was displayed in all the images. In the subjective questionnaire on sickness obtained via VAS and SSQ, the sickness values increased more significantly when the background element was introduced than in the control case without the background element. This suggests that the position of moving 3D-objects in the peripheral vision area could increase discomfort. Regarding the area of sway, the variances alomg the x- and y-directions increased more significantly in Pattern 3 than in Pattern 1. It was verified that the effect on the body sway changed depending on the protrusion of the 3D object in the peripheral vision area, although the subject viewed the sphere with tracking vision. In the future, we will determine the characteristic parameters that emerge in the center-of-gravity sway when 3D sickness occurs by examining the experimental data comprehensively using mathematical models [18–20].

Acknowledgements. This work was supported by JSPS KAKENHI Grant Number 19K20620, Tateisi Science and Technology Foundation, and Hoso Bunka Foundation.

References

1. Oguchi, T., Tanishima, M., Haibara, M.: 3D seiki-Kyoi rittai eiga no 100nen to eizo shin seiki-, Borndigital (2012)
2. Tamura, H., Ohta, Y.: Mixed reality. J. Inst. Image Inform. TV. Engnr. **52**(3), 266–272 (1997)
3. International Standard Organization: IWA3: 2005. Image safety-reducing determinism in a time series. Phys. Rev. Lett. **70**, 530–582 (1993)
4. Lambooij, M., Jsselsteijn, W., Fortuin, M., Heynderickx, I.: Visual discomfort and visual fatigue of stereoscopic displays: a review. J. Imaging Sci. Technol. **53**(3), 1–14 (2009)
5. 3D Consortium: 3DC safety guidelines for popularization of human-friendly 3D (2008).
6. Yano, S., Emoto, M., Mitsuhashi, T.: Two factors in visual fatigue caused from stereoscopic image. J. Inst. Image Inform. TV. Engnr. **57**(9), 1187–1193 (2003)
7. Yano, S., Ide, S., Hal, T.: A study on visual comfort and visual fatigue at the point of accommodation response in viewing stereoscopic image. J. Inst. Image Inform. TV. Engnr. **55**(5), 711–717 (2001)
8. Shiomi, T., et al.: Simultaneous measurement of lens accommodation and convergence in natural and artificial 3D vision. J. Soc. Inf. Disp. **21**(3), 120–128 (2013)
9. Miyao, M.: Lens accommodation while viewing 3D Video clips. Stereopsis Hyg. 13–24 (2018)
10. Reason, J.T., Brand, J.J.: Motion Sickness. Academic Press, London (1975)
11. Takeda, N.: Motion sickness and vomiting reflex. Pract. Otorhinolaryngol. Suppl. **41**, 197–207 (1991)

12. Nakayama, Y., Aoyama, K., Kitao, T., Maeda, T., Ando, H.: How to use multi-pole galvanic vestibular stimulation for virtual reality application. In: Proceedings of the VRIC, Laval, France (2018)

13. Nakagawa, C., Ohsuga, M., Takebe, T.: Basic study on autonomic responses of 'sickness' induced by visual and motion stimuli: using four projected screens and a 6-DOF motion base. Trans. Virtual Reality Soc. Japan 6(1), 27–35 (2001)

14. Takada, M., Tateyama, K., Kinoshita, F., Takada, H.: Evaluation of cerebral blood flow while viewing 3D video clips, Universal Access in Human-Computer Interaction. Interact. Tech. Environ. (UAHCI/HCII 2017) **10279**, 492–503 (2017)

15. Kato, T., Kamei, A., Takashima, S., Ozaki, T.: Human visual cortical function during photic stimulation monitoring by means of near-infrared spectroscopy. J. Cereb. Blood Flow Metab. **13**, 516–520 (1993)

16. Kinoshita, F., Okuno, H., Touyama, H., Takada, M., Miyao, M., Takada, H.: Effect of background element difference on regional cerebral blood flow while viewing stereoscopic video clips. In: Antona, M., Stephanidis, C. (eds.) HCII 2020. LNCS, vol. 12188, pp. 355–365. Springer, Cham (2020). https://doi.org/10.1007/978-3-030-49282-3_25

17. Suzuki, J., Matsunaga, T., Tokumasu, K., Taguchi, K., Watanabe, Y.: Q & A and a manual in stabilometry. Equilibr. Res. **55**(1), 296–306 (1996)

18. Kinoshita, F., Miyao, M., Takada, M., Takada, H.: Expression of balance function during exposure to stereoscopic video clips. Adv. Sci. Technol. Eng. Syst. J. (ASTESJ) **2**(1), 121–126 (2017)

19. Kinoshita, F., Takada, H.: Numerical analysis of stochastic differential equations as a model for body sway while viewing 3D video clips. Mech. Syst. Control (formerly Control and Intelligent Systems) **47**(2), 98–105 (2019)

20. Jono, Y., Tanimura, T., Kinoshita, F., Takada, H.: Evaluation of numerical solution to stochastic differential equations describing body sway by using translation error. Forma **35**(1), 27–31 (2020)

An Enhanced Open Source Refreshable Braille Display DISBRA 2.0

Alvaro Boa Vista Maia Bisneto[1]([∞]) [iD], Victor Hazin da Rocha[1] [iD], and Diogo Silva[2] [iD]

[1] CESAR School, Avenida, Cais do Apolo, 77, Recife, PE, Brasil
abvmb@cesar.school
[2] POLI - Escola Politécnica de Pernambuco, R. Benfica, 455 - Madalena, Recife, PE, Brasil

Abstract. A World Health Organization study states that there are 2.2 billion people with some sort of visual impairment. Some of those people are considered blind. A way blind people can communicate is by using a tactile alphabet called Braille. The percentual of blind people that can read Braille in developing countries is very low, about 10%, since the cost of tools for teaching Braille can be high. Additionally, not enough tutors are available to teach the students. Usually, a commercial tactile display costs over 800 dollars ($US), using components that are both expensive and hard to repair. This paper proposes enhancements for the DISBRA, a low-cost, open source, single digit Braille display that is inexpensive and made using cheaper electronical components and 3D printed parts. The DISBRA can be used to train tutors without teacher input, besides being an aid in teaching students. The improvements proposed by this paper eliminate the need for an external control device for the DISBRA, reducing its cost and making it a standalone solution. The DISBRA 2.0 prototype was tested by individuals without visual impairment. After one session of less than two hours they could correctly identify a character using only touch 68.46% of the time. While looking at the Braille the success rate was 86.15%.

Keywords: e-learning and distant learning · Haptic user interface · Interface for disabled and senior people · Accessibility · Refreshable Braille display · Visual impairment

1 Introduction

According to research by the World Health Organization (WHO) published in 2019, 2.2 billion people had serious vision problems [1] and an estimated 200 million people suffered from blindness [2].

People with disabilities face barriers in education and employment. They do not have enough access to basic services such as health, therapies, and computerized tools. Specifically, people with disabilities have difficulties when they need to express their opinions or share ideas. They are left in an unequal position when compared to people who can communicate by normal means. According to the WHO, these barriers are more present in developing countries where there are higher rates of poverty and low levels of success in education [3].

© Springer Nature Switzerland AG 2021
M. Antona and C. Stephanidis (Eds.): HCII 2021, LNCS 12768, pp. 405–417, 2021.
https://doi.org/10.1007/978-3-030-78092-0_27

The segments of the population that normally have most restricted access to eye health include people with less economic means, women, the elderly, people disadvantaged by various disabilities, ethnic minorities and refugees. Consequently, these groups concentrate the largest number of blind people [1].

Also, according to the WHO, investments in assistive technologies are beneficial for these groups. These types of technology provide possibilities for people to return to their homes and communities in order to live independently. This allows them to participate in education, the workforce and enjoy life in public, in addition to reducing the burden of various support services [3].

For all of the opportunities braille offers, paradoxically there is a decline in knowledge and study of the Braille code ("un-braille-ization"). According to the study by Forcelini, García and Schultz [4], 90% of blind people in the USA lacked proper Braille reading skills. A similar proportion is found in Brazil. Some of the main factors for this low level of Braille education, cited by the study, are the lack of instructors, social prejudice and the high cost of Braille teaching technologies.

Studies also denote that there are a large number of reading applications available but emphasize that books in digital audio format known as audiobooks and screen reading software are not proper substitutes for reading information in Braille [4]. Braille literacy for visually challenged people contains the same educational aims as normal literacy methods have for people with vision [5]. In developing countries most of the Braille teachers are visually challenged themselves. Also worthy of note is that the literacy rate for visually challenged people is as low as 3% to 5% in most developing countries. The conventional technique for learning Braille is bulky and requires assistance [5].

DISBRA was created as a way to facilitate learning and spread reading in Braille [6]. This work proposes the enhancement of DISBRA's advantages [6], a low-cost open-source Braille display using cheap electronic parts and 3D-printed components to form Braille characters. DISBRA can be used for teaching Braille without the need for a tutor [6], or train Braille tutors without teacher training. The proposed improvements enhance the initial prototype by adding the following: the possibility of using the teaching or tutor mode without a smartphone; using electronic components to play audio files; and minor improvements for Braille cell alignment issues.

2   Theory

In this section, information about the Braille system, dynamic Braille displays, as well as some notions about the Braille literacy process will be presented, alongside coverage of some relevant issues.

2.1   The Braille System

One of the ways in which a blind person can communicate and learn is through a tactile alphabet, known as Braille. This is the main way of transmitting information through tactile means and it is one of the most common ways of communicating with blind people in our daily lives [2].

There are also studies that indicate the advantage of using Braille reading for learning, since learning by actively reading Braille text leads to a greater understanding of the content by the students when compared to simply receiving the information passively, via audio format [7, 8]. The study by Russomanno [8] also states that for situations where understanding information in a text is the main priority, in settings such as education, reading in Braille should be considered the optimal mode of transmitting information.

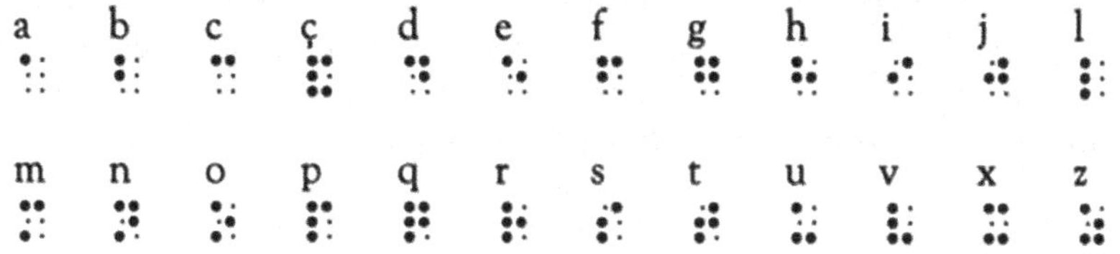

Fig. 1. The Braille alphabet [9]

Text in Braille can be formed in cells of 4 lines by 2 columns of dots or 3 lines by 2 columns of dots. Each cell can represent a letter of the alphabet or a number [7]. In this project, we will use the 3 by 2 format of Braille as shown in Fig. 1.

For the experiments, the Roman alphabet with 26 letters is used. Despite the use of the Portuguese language the tests do not include any accents.

2.2 Braille Displays

There are several devices capable of providing writing and assembling for Braille text on the market. Prices for commercial tactile displays range from 800 to 3000 dollars ($US). The cost will depend on factors such as the number of digits and the fact that, more often than not, the displays are equipped with small piezoelectric actuators. This type of component requires high voltage, around 200 V. The pieces are expensive and difficult to repair [10] and demand costly power supplies. DISBRA uses cheaper stepper motors and drivers [6] and costs about 30 dollars. This difference in cost also resides in the main difference between the commercial aims of the devices. The more expensive device displays text with multiple digits, while DISBRA has only one digit in the use of a single cell for basic Braille education.

2.3 Braille Alphabetization

The literacy process in the Braille system has, as one of its main objectives, the development of reading with the fingers and also the purpose of producing texts manually. When starting to learn the Braille System, the student must have already gone through a preparatory period, aiming at the development of fine motor coordination and tactile perception to discriminate the letter shapes, as the distinctions are very slight [11]. The DISBRA can be used to aid teaching the alphabet in Braille, since its simplified one-digit display can be used in the development of reading skills for individual letters.

Usually, during Braille education, the teacher works with concrete objects whether they are prefabricated or developed in the classroom, showing the idea of the shape of the letters and leading the student to experiment and trace the letters with their fingers. The objects of interest are the representation of the alphabet and alphanumeric Braille made of Ethyl Vinyl Acetate rubber - EVA and / or Medium Density Fiberboard (MDF) [11].

After carrying out the activities that allow Braille cells to be recognized, the clamp and punch are used as a writing instrument. The recognition of the combination of the points will present a letter, which in turn is combined to form words. Braille makes it possible to study raised paintings and read technical books more efficiently [11].

The quality of Braille teaching is decisive for reading Braille and aids in acquiring reading habits. If students are motivated to constantly practice this method of reading and writing, this activity can quickly become more enjoyable and instructive [11].

3   Proposed Solution

The proposed solution is to improve the DISBRA. That is to say, to build a low-cost Braille display with the objective of being a device that is easily replicated by a person with little specialized knowledge in microcontrollers. Originally, the DISBRA was controlled via an application for mobile devices. Its main advantage was that it was inexpensive. In order to create this device with lower costs, a combination of Arduino controller and electronic components with physical components that could be produced using 3D printing techniques was used [6]. The improvements focus on removing one's dependence on an external device, such as a smartphone, to control the DISBRA. With this change, the DISBRA 2.0 becomes a standalone solution for teaching fundamental Braille. We will also see the reduction of Braille cell alignment issues caused by power supply limitations on DISBRA's Arduino board. Each change proposed will be presented below.

3.1   Changes on the Interface and Usability

This new version, DISBRA 2.0, increases DISBRA's flexibility and reduces its cost by removing the need to use an external device, usually a smartphone, to control the display. For this purpose, an audio reproduction system was used. The system was then programmed to provide feedback that enables DISBRA's control menus to provide a solution directly on the DISBRA 2.0. To provide for this functionality, a module for playing MP3 files, the DFPlayer mini along with a small speaker and 4 buttons, were added to the prototype.

In Fig. 2 you can see the DISBRA in Version 1.0. In this version it is a simple display and needs an external controller in order to function. In DISBRA 2.0 the biggest difference for a user that had used the original DISBRA would be a new layout that accommodates 4 buttons and the speaker on the DISBRA 2.0 cover. The DISBRA 2.0 is a standalone solution, which does not need an external controller to properly function.

In Fig. 3, it is possible to see the prototype used to define the positions of the controls and the final positions that were integrated on the DISBRA 2.0 cover. The positioning considered the opinions of the people involved in the DISBRA 2.0 tests. During the tests,

Fig. 2. The DISBRA [6]

Fig. 3. The DISBRA 2.0 cover

the components were connected to the Arduino board and glued to the original DISBRA cover.

The audios used in the tests for the DISBRA 2.0 prototype were recorded in MP3 and stored on a microSD card. The audios represent the equivalent of the solution menus for mobile devices in addition to the letters of the alphabet and the success/error feedback for the question mode. The user could navigate the solution by listening to the menu, using the buttons on the left and right to move forward and backward through the menu options and the buttons above (up) and below (down) to enter and exit the submenus of each option. With these controls and audio files, the researcher reprogrammed the Arduino so the volunteers could use the DISBRA 2.0 solution without needing a smartphone or any other external control device, due to the menus now being presented in audio format. The functionality of connecting to the smartphone, or other Bluetooth devices, was not removed from DISBRA 2.0, but its use is optional. The hardware components for this operation can be removed, to reduce further costs, without affecting usability.

Original Menus versus Audio Menus. The main challenge for this improvement was to replicate the experience of navigating solutions on a smartphone using only audio and buttons to represent and control all menus and interactions needed to navigate the DISBRA 2.0 as a standalone tutor. The original DISBRA used an Android app to display its menus and provide audio feedback to its users.

The main solution (implemented for Android mobiles) was comprised of a teaching, or tutor, mode alongside a question mode.

In the tutor mode there were six divisions, called modules, four of them containing five letters, one containing six letters, and the last containing all 26 letters on the alphabet.

The question mode was also divided into six modules to test the user's ability to read the characters for each module. The app would select a letter from the current module at random, send it to the display, and when the user clicked an answer option it would evaluate and send the proper feedback to the user.

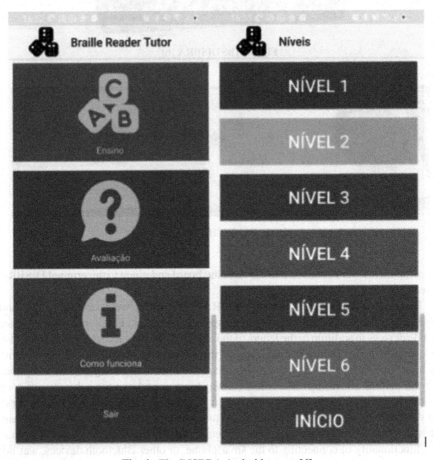

Fig. 4. The DISBRA Android menus [6]

Figure 4 shows the layout and color scheme for the Android solution for the DISBRA in its first version. This was the solution used by volunteers during the test phase for the DISBRA project. They used a smartphone to control the display and process all teaching and question modes.

Figure 5 shows the diagram for the Audio navigation used to display character A in module one during tutor mode for the DISBRA 2.0. Button pressures needed for this action are shown as arrows.

As the user turns on DISBRA 2.0, the speaker announces that the solution at the start, for it to play an MP3 file that would announce "Tutor Mode". It is the first option for the main menu. If he clicks the right button, the state would change, and the speaker

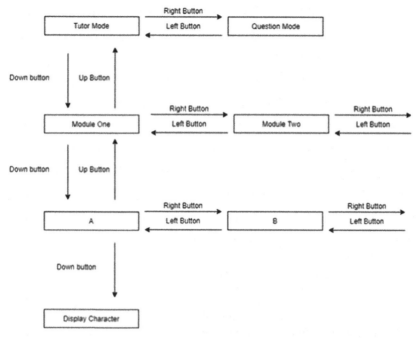

Fig. 5. The DISBRA 2.0 menu navigation diagram for the tutor mode

would announce "Question Mode". If the user clicks the down button, in the state of tutor mode, the solution will change the state and announce that it is now at the "Module One" stage. Again, clicking the left or right buttons would go to the options for this submenu. If the user clicks the down button in the module one state, the system would, again, change its state and announce "A". While at this stage, the left and right buttons could be used to navigate all the letter options for this module. If the user clicks the down button at the letter a stage, the display digits would rotate and the Braille equivalent for letter a would be formed by its dots. This last action does not change the current state for the solution. Clicking the up button at all stages, except in the tutor or question modes, would change the state to the previous upper submenu. Clicking up twice from the letter a stage would bring the user back to the tutor mode stage.

Figure 6 shows the diagram for the Audio navigation used to input the character A as an answer for the question mode of module one on the DISBRA 2.0 display. The button presses needed for this action are shown as arrows. The audio feedback will announce if the user has selected the correct answer for the random character displayed.

As the user turns on the DISBRA 2.0, the speaker announces that the solution is in its start state, so it would play an MP3 file that would announce "Tutor Mode", since it's the first option for this menu. If he clicked the right button, the state would change, and the speaker would announce "Question Mode". If the user clicks the down button, while on the question mode state, the solution will change the state and announce that it is now in the "Module One Questions" state. Again, clicking the left or right buttons would cycle on the options for this submenu. If the user clicks the down button in the module

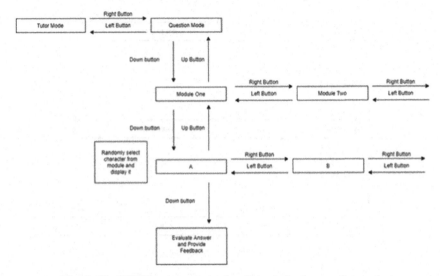

Fig. 6. The DISBRA menu navigation diagram for the question mode

one questions state, the system will randomly select a letter for this module, display it by rotating and aligning the dots on the digits, then change its state and announce "A". While in this submenu, the left and right buttons could be used to navigate all the letter options for this module. If the user clicks the down button in the letter a state, the solution will check if this is the correct answer for the displayed character, then send an audible feedback for the evaluation – correct/ incorrect choice. The system will, again, randomly select a character, display and await new inputs. Clicking the up button on all states, except in the tutor or question modes, would change the state to the previous upper submenu. Clicking up twice from the letter a state would bring the user back to the question mode state.

Table 1. DISBRA modules and letters for the modules.

Module	Letters
One	A, B, D, G, Q
Two	C, F, N, Y, W
Three	E, H, P, O, V
Four	I, J, R, M, U
Five	K, L, T, S, X, Z
Six	All 26 letters on the alphabet

Table 1 shows the letters selected for each module. The number of modules was defined based on the work by [12]. The letters were selected randomly as proposed by [13].

3.2   Reducing the Braille Display Alignment Issues

During the DISBRA tests, a feedback by one of the volunteers was that the display, formed by an extruded octagon formed in 3D printing, had a tendency to sometimes lack alignment. There was a problem with the power supply to the prototype's stepper motor drivers. This problem was fixed for the DISBRA 2.0 by removing the power supply for the stepper motor controllers from the Arduino board and using a direct connection to the external power source that also feeds the Arduino (Fig. 7).

Fig. 7. The Braille cell disks [6]

Figure 5 illustrates the digits used to form the Braille cell. By spinning and aligning the faces of this extruded octagon, the Braille cell is formed. During the longer DISBRA tests the display would often lose its alignment, obliging the researcher to manually realign the cell. Once the new circuit design for the DISBRA 2.0 solved the energy supply problems, the occurrence of alignment problems dropped significantly, greatly improving the readability for the cell during long tests. The test results compare the effectiveness of reading only properly aligned characters in both DISBRA and DISBRA 2.0, comparing only the impacts of removing the use of the smartphone and the use of audio menus. The impact of this improvement for the alignment was not measured since there was no data to compare it to the original solution (Fig. 8).

With the use of two 3D printed extruded octagons, each forming half of a braille cell or digit, it is possible to form combinations of the dot arrangements shown in Fig. 6. These combinations are sufficient to assemble all the characters in Braille used for the Roman alphabet. The main advantage of DISBRA is its cost being approximately 30 dollars. This is not significantly impacted by adding MP3 reproduction and standalone navigation capabilities for the DISBRA 2.0 version. The cost of a DISBRA 2.0 is approximately 36 dollars. If the user decides not to install a Bluetooth module during the assembly, the cost of DISBRA 2.0 is reduced to 24 dollars.

Figure 9 shows a simplified scheme for DISBRA 2.0 electronics. The Braille cell digit for both DISBRA versions is composed of two 3D printed extruded octagons. The 3D model replicates a standard Braille cell. Each dot is 2 mm wide, 0.65 mm tall. The dots are 2.7 mm apart from each other, both vertically and horizontally. Each digit is attached to a stepper motor (model 28BYJ-48) as shown in Fig. 9. Each motor is connected to an Arduino nano ATmega328 for control and to the external power source for power supply. A Bluetooth module (HC-06) can also be connected to the solution to control

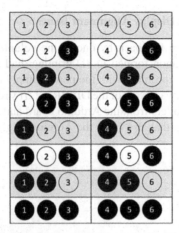

Fig. 8. The Dotted Faces for the Braille Cell [6], the cells filled in black show where the protuberances are on each face of the display digit.

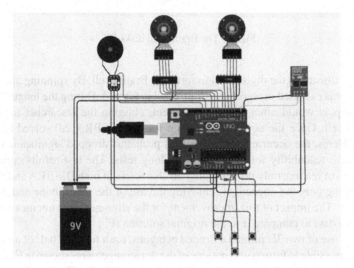

Fig. 9. Simplified electronic scheme for the DISBRA 2.0.

the display remotely and wirelessly. For the new user interface, 4 simple buttons are added, with a pull-down resistor for each. A DFPlayer mini is connected to the Arduino. This module reproduces MP3 audio files stored on a microSD card. The DFPlayer mini module controls a small speaker that is 40 mm wide, 0.5 W and 8 Ω.

4 Analysis

To validate the proposal, initial tests were carried out with 5 volunteers, the same number used in DISBRA tests. None of them had training or knew the Braille alphabet. This was also the setup for the tests using DISBRA [5]. Braille literacy for visually challenged people has the same procedure as normal educational methods have for people with vision [5].

The number of volunteers was based on [14]. The author affirms that 80% of the usability discoveries are found after testing the solution with only 5 volunteers.

Before testing and being evaluated on the DISBRA 2.0, the volunteers studied each module. They could spend as much time as they wanted on this phase. After they studied a module, a smaller test containing only the letters for that module was applied. If the results for this test were above or equal to 80%, the volunteers could advance to the next module. The final results are based on the sixth and final module. The volunteers were tested for all 26 letters in this module.

The volunteers had time to study the characters in DISBRA 2.0 and underwent a test, first with their eyes covered, then being able to see the Braille display. The success rate for character recognition using only touch was 68.46% while using the DISBRA 2.0. The same result for the original DISBRA was 69.23%. With the possibility of seeing the display, the success rate obtained by the volunteers using the new DISBRA 2.0 was 86.15%, results comparable to that of DISBRA. The volunteers for the previous research scored 86.82% of success in this scenario.

The researcher encouraged the volunteers to comment on the process and on their overall impression of DISBRA 2.0. Two of the points for improvement raised by the volunteers were the use of an amplifier in the speaker if the solution was ever to be used in environments with normal background noise, such as on the street; or adding a headphone entry for the purpose of listening more clearly to the menus. They also pointed out the possible use of different material for the elevated dots on the display, possibly metal spheres. Sometimes defects in 3D printing were enough to cause confusion between the characters. When this happened, the disks were re-printed and changed for the tests. They also asked for an adjustment in the distance of the disks that compose the cell, moving them apart a little, to improve readability for beginners. The volunteers had the opportunity to use DISBRA 2.0 during their training and tests, without the necessity of using an external control device. The navigation by audio menus had good feedback. The test results indicate that the teaching capabilities of the DISBRA was not diminished by removing the external component of a smartphone screen to guide the volunteers.

DISBRA 2.0 improves affordability and positively alters the use of DISBRA, becoming a completely standalone solution. This is achieved by reprogramming the Arduino solution to remove the necessity of the usage of smartphones or other external control devices. According to Kavitha, Privadarshini and Saradha [11], this type of solution (where the user has control over the display and receive feedbacks that can be evaluated) in the form of text or audio can be used for teaching Braille even when the tutors are not trained in Braille, or even so that these tutors can learn Braille without the need for extra assistance, enabling people without disabilities to learn Braille using only such a device.

5   Final Considerations

The objective of this research was to implement improvements in the DISBRA system, a low-cost Braille display which can be used in teaching Braille [5]. The enhancements were made in order to improve its viability, giving more freedom to users while also reducing its cost, proposing and implementing a new standalone solution, the DISBRA 2.0. There were also improvements to the prototype's circuit, based on the feedback for the alignment errors received during the tests of Version 1.0. The Braille teaching scenario still shows a deficit in tutors. The number of people with visual impairments will grow [4, 5]. Tools like the DISBRA could be used to help train new tutors.

Based on this observation, this work presented the DISBRA 2.0 with a series of improvements implemented with regard to DISBRA, while promoting a solution capable of teaching the identification of Braille characters and their correspondence to the Roman alphabet without the need for a human tutor. The tests results showed no significant loss of effectiveness in the teaching method by removing external control devices.

For future works, the researcher recommends the development of the improvements suggested during this evaluation, as well as new rounds of testing of the proposed solution with more volunteers. Use of the device for a longer period will allow for further evaluation of results for its use as a major tool for learning Braille.

References

1. World Health Organization: World report on vision (2019)
2. Kim, J., Han, B.K., Pyo, D., Ryu, S., Kim, H., Kwon, D.S.: Braille display for portable device using flip-latch structured electromagnetic actuator. IEEE Trans. Haptics. **13**, 59–65 (2020). https://doi.org/10.1109/TOH.2019.2963858
3. World Health Organization (WHO): Er Health for All Better People Health With for Disability All People With Disability, pp. 1–32 (2015)
4. Forcelini, P.G., García, L.S., Schultz, E.P.B.: Braille Technology Beyond the Financial Barriers, pp. 41–46 (2018). https://doi.org/10.1145/3218585.3218590
5. Wagh, P., Prajapati, U., Shinde, M., Salunke, P., Chaskar, V., Telavane, S., Yadav, V.: E-Braille-a self-learning Braille device. In: 2016 22nd National Conference on Communication, NCC 2016 (2016). https://doi.org/10.1109/NCC.2016.7561162
6. Rocha, V.H., Silva, D., Maia Bisneto, A.B.V, Silva, G.F., de Souza, F.F.: Ensinando a Identificação de Caracteres Braille utilizando Dispositivos Móveis e um Display Braille. Renote **17**, 82–91 (2019). https://doi.org/10.22456/1679-1916.99429
7. Bettelani, G.C., Averta, G., Catalano, M.G., Leporini, B., Bianchi, M.: Design and validation of the readable device: a single-cell electromagnetic refreshable Braille display. IEEE Trans. Haptics. **13**, 239–245 (2020). https://doi.org/10.1109/TOH.2020.2970929
8. Russomanno, A., O'Modhrain, S., Gillespie, R.B., Rodger, M.W.M.: Refreshing refreshable Braille displays. IEEE Trans. Haptics. **8**, 287–297 (2015). https://doi.org/10.1109/TOH.2015. 2423492
9. Brasil: Ministério da Educação. Secretaria de Educação Especial. Grafia a Braille para a Língua Portuguesa, Brasília (2006)
10. Hossain, S., et al.: Text to Braille scanner with ultra low cost refreshable Braille display. GHTC 2018 - IEEE Global Humanitarian Technology Conference, pp. 1–6 (2019). https:// doi.org/10.1109/GHTC.2018.8601552
11. Façanha, A.R., Lima, L.S., Araújo, M.C.C., de Carvalho, W.V., Pequeno, M.C.: Auxiliando o Processo de Ensino-Aprendizagem do Braille Através de Dispositivos Touch Screen (2012)
12. Toussaint, K.A., Scheithauer, M.C., Tiger, J.H., Saunders, K.J.: Teaching identity matching of braille characters to beginning braille readers. J. Appl. Behav. Anal. **50**, 278–289 (2017). https://doi.org/10.1002/jaba.382

13. Scheithauer, M.C., Tiger, J.H.: A computer-based program to teach braille reading to sighted individuals. J. Appl. Behav. Anal. **45**, 315–327 (2012). https://doi.org/10.1901/jaba.2012. 45-315
14. Nielsen, J.: Usability Engineering. Morgan Kaufmann Publishers Inc., San Francisco (1993)

ParkinsonCom Project: Towards a Software Communication Tool for People with Parkinson's Disease

Káthia Marçal de Oliveira[1]([✉]) [iD], Elise Batselé[2] [iD], Sophie Lepreux[1] [iD],
Elise Buchet[2] [iD], Christophe Kolski[1] [iD], Mathilde Boutiflat[2], Véronique Delcroix[1] [iD],
Hélène Geurts[2] [iD], Kodzo Apedo[1] [iD], Loïc Dehon[3], Houcine Ezzedine[1] [iD],
Yohan Guerrier[1] [iD], Marie-Claire Haelewyck[2], Nicolas Jura[3], Philippe Pudlo[1] [iD],
and Yosra Rekik[1]

[1] LAMIH, CNRS, UMR 8201, Université Polytechnique Hauts-de-France,
59313 Valenciennes, France
{kathia.oliveira,sophie.lepreux,christophe.kolski,
veronique.delcroix,kodzo.apedo,houcine.ezzedine,yohan.guerrier,
philippe.pudlo,yosra.rekik}@uphf.fr
[2] Clinical Orthopedagogy Department, University of Mons, 20 Place du Parc,
7000 Mons, Belgium
{elise.batsele,elise.buchet,mathilde.boutiflat,helene.geurts,
marie-claire.haelewyck}@umons.ac.be
[3] Drag'On Slide, Boulevard Sainctelette 39, 7000 Mons, Belgium
{loic,nicolas}@dragonslide.com

Abstract. Parkinson's disease (PD) is the second most prevalent neurodegenerative disease in the world. Impacts of the disease on both quality of life and social participation make it a major preoccupation in terms of public health. This disease is always associated not only to motor but also non-motors symptoms. Among these symptoms, several people with PD report communication impairments that worsen their speech intelligibility, their ability to express affective states and as consequence, their social relations. In order to improve this situation, we have been working on the ParkinsonCom project. This project aims to co-construct and make available a communication support tool for people with PD using a participatory design. To that end a user-centered design has been applied, integrating people with PD as well as their caregivers (family, friends, medical professionals...) in all stages of the development. This paper presents the whole methodology of the project and the results of the first phase related to requirements analysis.

Keywords: User-centered design · Communication · Parkinson disease

1 Introduction

Parkinson's disease is the second most prevalent neurodegenerative disease after Alzheimer disease. Impacts of this disease on both quality of life and social participation make it a major preoccupation in terms of public health. Symptoms of Parkinson

M. Antona and C. Stephanidis (Eds.): HCII 2021, LNCS 12768, pp. 418–428, 2021.
https://doi.org/10.1007/978-3-030-78092-0_28

are classically divided into motor symptoms (the best known) and non-motor symptoms (Sveinbjornsdottir 2016). Among non-motor symptoms, 70% of people with Parkinson (PwP) report communication impairments of speech and voice (Hartelius and Svensson 1994). These impairments most often lead to active or passive social withdrawal and negatively impact patients' subjective well-being. However, if oral communication difficulties are often reported, withdrawal from oral interactions is rarely investigated.

Based on these observations, we have started a project, named ParkinsonCom[1], that aims to develop a communication tool for PwP in order to improve their social participation and inclusion. To address this goal, we were convinced that a centered-design approach should be applied in a way that we should consider the real needs of communication for PwP and those that interact with them (family, friends, medical professional and so on) as suggested by several authors, such as Antona *et al.* (2009) and Guffroy *et al.* (2017, 2018). In this paper we present the methodology we are following for the project and the results of the first phase of requirement analysis performed with the participation of PwP and/or their caregivers. The other phases of the project are planned until December 2022, which is the closing date of the project.

The rest of this paper is organized in four sections. Section 2 briefly presents the background considering the Parkinson disease and some studies about user centered design for Parkinson domain. Section 3 presents an overview of the methodology followed in the project. Section 4 details the results of the first stage of development before the conclusion presented in Sect. 5.

2 Background

2.1 People with Parkinson Disease as Users

Parkinson's disease (PD) is a progressive, multi-system, neurodegenerative disease that mainly affects older people and is an incurable disease that goes through several stages.

Symptoms of PD are divided into two categories: motor symptoms and non-motor symptoms (Sveinbjornsdottir 2016). Motor symptoms have long been central to disease management although non-motor symptoms are often reported to be more bothersome for patients (Azulay *et al.* 2017). Among the motor symptoms, we note in all cases a bradykinesia, that is to say, a slowness in the initiation of voluntary movements with a progressive reduction in the speed and amplitude of repetitive actions (hypokinesia). Non-motor symptoms can start even before the diagnosis of the disease and are often more discreet. These symptoms can be classified into: dysautonomic signs (e.g. disorders digestive system, arterial hypotension, sexual disorders, respiratory disorders), sensory disorders (pain), psychic and cognitive disorders (sleep disorders, memory disorders, fatigue, depression, anxiety, apathy) and speech disorders (Azulay *et al.* 2017).

Speech production is a motor activity. However, the entire motor system is affected by the PD. Therefore, from the onset of the disease, the patient may present with hypophonia, that is to say a loss of the *volume* of the voice. Secondly, the patient may develop

[1] ParkinsonCom (https://parkinsoncom.eu/) is supported by the European Regional Development Fund (Interreg V France-Wallonie-Vlaanderen) and the Agency for a quality life AVIQ (*l'Agence pour une Vie de Qualité*) from Wallonia, Belgium.

parkinsonian dysarthria which degrades intelligibility and affects approximately 70% to 79% patients (Atkinson-Clément et al. 2015; Dupouy et al. 2017; Herd et al. 2012; Schalling et al. 2017; Stegemöller et al. 2018). Dysarthria is estimated to be the most disabling dysfunction in PD by 29% of patients (Atkinson-Clement et al. 2015). A recent study (Schalling et al. 2017) reported that no less than 92.5% of PwP declared having experienced at least one symptom related to a speech or communication disorder. The most frequently reported symptom was weak voice (71%), followed by word search problems (58.6%). More than half of the respondents (55.7%) said they had an imprecise articulation, and 50.1% strayed from the topic when speaking. Finally, in this study, between 27 and 40% of participants said that speech problems had a negative impact on different areas of participation and, mainly, on the ability to socialize with others as before (40%) (Schalling et al. 2017).

It is essential to indicate that there is no "typical" patient. The presentation of the disease and its symptoms can considerably differ from one person to another (Eisenberg et al. 2018; Compagnon and Melhénas 2010). Furthermore, as the disease progresses, there may be an alternation between phases where the symptoms are mostly under control thanks to the treatment and phases where the treatment is no longer having sufficient effect. This is called, an alternation between "ON" phases, the treatment is effective, and "OFF" phases, the treatment does not work (Vizcarra 2019).

2.2 User-Centered Research in the Domain of Parkinson

We can find several works in literature concerning PD. This section presents some of them that follows a user-centered design approach.

Mishra and colleagues (Mishra et al. 2019), for instance, involved 17 PwP and 6 care-givers to understand their need and motivation to use a symptom-tracking tool in order to better live with the disease. They focused their studies on different aspects: current follow-up habits and attitudes towards follow-up, self-monitoring to support planned problem solving, self-monitoring to avoid "forgetting" the disease and on ambiguous symptoms to be traced for care partners. Finally, the care partners were positioned in the self-monitoring system, allowing them to know the specifications of the system. Other monitoring systems are proposed by (Branco et al. 2019) to help the disease specialists to know the fluctuating states throughout the patient's day. They propose to use connected objects to capture information useful to doctors.

Another way, proposed by Vega and colleagues (Vega et al. 2018), is to provide a notebook for the patients to describe their state during the day, the sensations before and after taking the medication, and to test a set of prototypes in order to define the system's specifications related to specific Parkinson's profiles. They collected data on one of the prototypes for 49 days to perform an evaluation over a longer period of time. As a result, they observed that several participants appreciated the fact that the diary could be completed without writing and with as little movement of the hand as possible thanks to the use of questions with ordinal answers and no open-inquires.

Kuosmanen and colleagues (Kuosmanen et al. 2020) followed a user-centered ap-proach to measure symptoms, disease progression and medication by detecting hand movement. They offered both a game to assess movement and a diary to supplement information about medication and how the patient is feeling. The diary is based on the well-known scale for diagnosis of PD (Fahn and Elton 1987). Further work on monitoring the symptoms of PwP is proposed by (McNaney *et al.* 2020) involving users in two phases: 2 days with health and IoT professionals to explore opportunities, challenges and benefits, followed by 4 workshops involving 13 patients and their caregivers. During these workshops, participants reported using a range of technologies: smartphones, tablets, wearables (connected watches) to capture physical activity, training games and online videos. All of them use computers for email and Internet browsing, and some of them also use tools in their work. From 13 participants, 6 have already used IoT such as GoogleHome, and walking metrics. Moreover, even when speech is one of the most serious symptoms, voice assistants (especially Alexa (6) but also Siri (1)) are cited as being regularly used with pleasure. They sometimes use it to make themselves better understood by others or as a reminder system ("don't forget to take the tablet").

More generally, Neate and colleagues proposed a co-creation of personas to involve patients in the definition of their characteristics in order to offer them adapted human-computer interactions (Neate *et al.* 2019).

ParkinsonCom project also use a user-centered design approach with the novelty that we should consider evolutive profile of the final user (that is, PwP). In other words, we are aware that very different requirements may be identified considering the stage of the disease the PwP will have on the moment we interview them in other to develop a tool that can be adapted to each one and evolve according to the stage of the disease they will go through.

3   Project Methodology

As described previously the goal of ParkinsonCom is to develop the interactive communication support tool that consider the evolutive profile of PwP. A user-centric approach will be used for the design, specification and evaluation of the tool following the standard ISO 9241-110 (2020), since end users are the best positioned to define and influence the development of a product. In this way, PwP, as well as caregivers (family, friends, professionals, etc.) will actively participate in the social construction of the software tool. The general methodology for this project is composed of four phases presented below (Fig. 1): requirement analysis, a cycle of co-construction and evaluation, and cross-border training.

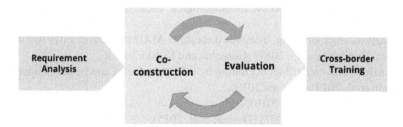

Fig. 1. ParkinsonCom project methodology phases.

3.1 Requirement Analysis

This phase aims to collect the necessary knowledge for the development of the tool related to the PD itself and the identification of the requirements for a communication tool with PwP and their caregivers.

We started this phase by carrying out a literature review about projects in the same domain using user-centered design approaches as well as the symptoms of PD, its evolution, its consequences on communication and the problems of social communication for PwP (a summary of this review is presented in Sect. 2). This review was important not only to know more about PD but also to identify which kind of technology, interaction mode and user centered design approaches were already experimented in this domain.

To identify the requirements for the communication tool we had planned to do face-to-face meetings with PwP and workshops in the Parkinson's volunteer associations from France and Belgium. However, due to the COVID-19 pandemic we had to adapt our plan to perform on line questionnaires and interviews with PwP and caregivers by video-conference. Section 4 presents some initial results from this phase.

3.2 Co-construction

From the results of the previous phase (Requirement Analysis) we start an iterative cycle of co-construction and evaluation (presented in the next section) till a robust version of the tool is obtained. Initially, we plan in detail all activities for the co-construction (such as, requirement specification, context of use definition, design, and coding) establishing the responsible and participants for each one.

The context of use of each user group will be described by specifying:

- the actual characteristics of PwP who will benefit from using the tool,
- the daily tasks that PwP consider important in their daily communication and which will be supported in an evolving way by the tool (communication with the caregiver and/or with the healthcare professional),
- the environment in which the tool will be used (home, hospital, medical office)
- the necessary material resources, and
- communication practices.

Each daily task having a utility to be supported by the tool will be specified according to user requirements using specific methodologies. These methodologies include:

- task analysis and modelling, using for instance K-MAD (Caffiau et al. 2010); see also (Guidini Gonçalves et al. 2017) (Ezzedine and Kolski 2005);
- user analysis and modelling, beginning by a Persona-based approach (Cooper 1999) (Idoughi et al. 2012) (Nielsen 2019);
- Use cases (Jacobson et al. 2016); and,
- Mockups (Coyette et al. 2007) (Dupont et al. 2015).

Testable user interface design alternatives (prototypes) will be developed in conjunction with final users in a participatory design approach (Blomberg and Henderson

1990) (Vandendoren *et al.* 2019) (Geurts and Haelewyck 2020). Thus, PwP, informal caregivers and healthcare professionals will take part in this process. At the end of this phase, an initial version of the software will be developed and submitted for evaluation. The results of this evaluation will allow improvements to develop the final version of this communication tool.

3.3 Evaluation

After the first two phases (requirement analysis and co-construction) the evaluation phase will start in order to continuously improve the developed tool. Particular attention will be paid to the usability of the tool (in terms of effectiveness, efficiency and satisfaction) (Bastien and Scapin 1992, Hartson *et al.* 2001, Ivory and Hearst 2001; ISO/TR 16982 2002; Ezzedine *et al.* 2012), its reliability including compliance with ethical rules and its acceptability (Davis 1989, Venkatesh *et al.* 2003, 2012, Hartson *et al.* 2001). This set of criteria (usability, reliability and acceptability) aim to ensure the quality of the tool produced in this project.

Like in the co-construction phase, we plan to mobilize all the stakeholders (consortium team, PwP, informal caregivers, etc.) so that all of their evaluations can frame the continuous improvement of the tool. This phase focuses on the execution of the different evaluation activities from the definition of an evaluation protocol to the collect and analysis of the results. The associated partners will validate the procedure and the elements defined in this protocol in order to mobilize their networks. After collecting the evaluation data, an analysis and interpretation of the data will be carried out in order to make the information intelligible to all stakeholders in the form of written reports and/or oral presentations.

The techniques used to support the activities of this phase will be those of the human and social sciences, such as focus groups (Krueger and Casey 2014) and questionnaires (Assila *et al.* 2016). Those techniques allow qualitative and quantitative data to be collected. Software measures (Oliveira 2020; Carvalho *et al.* 2018) will also be applied for the evaluation of various usability criteria to ensure the quality of the proposed tool.

3.4 Cross-Border Training

This final phase is closely linked to the previous ones: requirement analysis, co-construction and evaluation. Indeed, it relies on the literature inherent in the social communication's theme of PwP to provide support that responds to evidence-based and practice-based content disseminated using a simple language. In addition, the updated experience of the health and social system contributes to the provision of knowledge promoting rapid and effective ownership of the developed tool. The co-construction of the communication support tool and its validation by users themselves make possible to capitalize on the learning experienced by all the players and the possible solutions associated with the difficulties encountered.

Training is an important phase since it is considered as a lever for both health promotion (improvement of access to information, increased understanding of disorders and their consequences, dissemination of good practices, etc.) and the sustainability of the project, or even to the dissemination of its results on a larger scale (training for

ParkinsonCom project ambassadors). Therefore, we planned to set up training courses for different audiences:

- Psychoeducational training (mainly small groups) for PwP and their close caregivers;
- Training for tool's use with PwP and their close caregivers;
- Communities of practice for experts and practitioners in PD.

Each one of these activities will be provided on both sides of the Franco-Belgian border since this project is supported by European Program of territorial cooperation France-Belgium. The tool will be available both for French-speaking and Dutch-speaking PwP.

4   Requirement Analysis: Creating the Basis for the Next Steps

As described in the previous section, the main goal of this phase was to identify the requirements for the communication tool to be developed. To that end we perform two main actions: a collect of quantitative data using a questionnaire available on web and interviews.

4.1   On-Line Questionnaire

The purpose of the questionnaire was to identify among PwP:

- the impact of the different symptoms on daily functioning,
- difficulties encountered in oral communication,
- the strategies currently used to facilitate daily speech and communication,
- the technologies currently used, and
- the most essential situations to establish a communication.

This questionnaire was available on the website of the project (https://parkinson com.eu) and in different groups related to PD in the social network (facebook and linkedin).

The questionnaire was completed by 56 people: 35.71% men and 64.29% women. On average, the respondents are 58 years old (standard deviation of 11.9).

For these respondents, the physical aspects are considered as the most problematic symptoms in the early stages of the disease. Some other results we highlight from the questionnaire are the following:

- The psychosocial symptoms considered to be the most significant and/or problematic for the respondents are: the difficulties in writing (28.75% of the situations encountered), difficulties in concentrating (25.89%) and variations between the ON and OFF periods (25.71%);
- The most frequent communication difficulties encountered are: a weak voice (71.43%), followed by communication fatigue (60.71%), difficulty finding words (58.6%) and speech too slow or too fast (55.36%).

- The strategies mostly used are: avoiding difficult situations (80.36%), waiting for a more suitable moment to speak (60.07%) and summarizing the information, getting to the point (60.71%).
- The technological tools mainly used by respondents are: the computer (89.29%), instant messaging (85.71%), video conferencing systems (Messenger, WhatsApp, Skype, etc.) (85.71%), the smartphone (83.93%), tablet and touchscreen (66.07%).
- The three most essential situations to establish a communication are: to discuss some subject, make a request, and to express their feelings.

In general, respondents report that their communication disorders impact the way they do their work, their role in the family, participation in leisure activities and socialization.

4.2 Interviews

To perform the interviews, we prepared a set of questions following a specific order covering subjects from the disease's diagnosis to the needs of communication and the ideal communication tool from the PwP point of view.

Those interviews were carried out with 14 people: 71% men (10) and 29% women (4). On average, respondents are 65 years old (standard deviation of 18.4).

The analysis of these interviews highlights the negative perception of the disease by people: constraint and fear are the feelings particularly experienced, especially because of the gaze of society. However, although the disease is present, PwP try to maintain a relatively "normal" life with different activities.

The oral communication difficulties reported during the interviews concern different components of the voice (volume, flow, timbre, articulation), writing, or memory. It is also remarkable that these disorders lead to interpersonal difficulties and negative emotions. To help them communicate orally, participants report mostly calling on paramedical support (speech therapist or physiotherapist).

The use of technologies (computer, smartphone, tablet, telephone, voice assistant) to promote communication is much less mentioned. This is particularly the cause of the difficulties in using these technologies linked to the deterioration of fine motor skills such as having to press small buttons, having a touch screen or a touchpad that is too sensitive or an object too heavy to hold it easily. However, when technologies are used, it appears that it is mainly to communicate and keep in touch with loved ones via various messaging services (emails, SMS, WhatsApp, etc.) or via social networks (such as Facebook or Twitter). Others prefer the oral discussion by video conferencing systems. Then, people also use technology to learn and do research, particularly on PD and its repercussions, but also to consult current events and various subjects. To a lesser extent, people use technology for entertainment through online games or for managing aspects of their daily life (e.g., making purchases, managing their accounts).

In general, different functional requirements were quoted such as: help for preparing a text, supporting a discussion in real time, helping to make a request and to be in touch with other PwP.

5 Conclusion

This paper has presented the ParkinsonCom project that aims to develop a communication tool to help people with PD to interact with their caregivers (family, friends, medical professionals and so on). To that end the project brings together psychologists, educators, doctors, neurologists, engineers, graphic designers, and social workers in a multidisciplinary consortium.

We are currently starting the co-construction phase by performing new interviews in order to specify the functionalities we will integrate in the tool to support communication. Based on that we will perform the design and implementation of the first prototype of the communication tool.

Acknowledgements. ParkinsonCom project is developed with the support of the European regional development fund (Interreg V France-Wallonie-Vlaanderen) and the Agency for quality life AVIQ (*l'Agence pour une Vie de Qualité*) from Wallonia, Belgium, for which the authors are deeply grateful.

References

Assila, A., Oliveira, K., Ezzedine, H.: Standardized usability questionnaires: features and quality focus. Electron. J. Comput. Sci. Inf. Technol. **6**(1), 15–31 (2016)

Atkinson-Clement, C., Sadat, J., Pinto, S.: Behavioral treatments for speech in Parkinson's disease: meta-analyses and review of the literature. Neurodegener. Dis. Manage. **5**(3), 233–248 (2015)

Antona, M., Ntoa, S., Adami, I., Stephanidis, C.: User requirements elicitation for universal access. In: Stephanidis, C. (ed.) The Universal Access Handbook, pp. 15.1–15.14, CRC Press (2009)

Azulay, J.P., Witjas, T., Eusebio, A.: Les signes non moteurs de la maladie de Parkinson. La Presse Médicale **46**(2), 195–201 (2017)

Bastien, J.M.C., Scapin, D.L.: A validation of ergonomic criteria for the evaluation of human-computer interfaces. Int. J. Hum. Comput. Interact. **4**(2), 183–196 (1992)

Blomberg, J.L., Henderson, A.: Reflections on participatory design: lessons from the trillium experience. In: the 1990 CHI Proceedings of Conference on Human Factors in Computing Systems, pp. 353–359 (1990)

Branco, D., Bouça, R., Ferreira, J., Guerreiro, T.: Designing free-living reports for Parkinson's disease. In: Extended Abstracts of the 2019 CHI Conference on Human Factors in Computing Systems. Association for Computing Machinery, LBW1715, New York, NY, USA, pp. 1–6 (2019)

Caffiau, S., Scapin, D., Girard, P., Baron, M., Jambon, F.: Increasing the expressive power of task analysis: systematic comparison and empirical assessment of tool-supported task models. Interact. Comput. **22**(6), 569–593 (2010)

Carvalho, R., Andrade, R., Oliveira, K.: AQUArIUM - a suite of software measures for HCI quality evaluation of ubiquitous mobile applications. J. Syst. Softw. **136**, 101–136 (2018)

Oliveira, K.: Practices to Define Software Measurements. In: Actes du XXXVIIIème Congrès INFORSID, Dijon, France, pp. 77–92 (2020)

Compagnon, C., Melhénas, S.: Livre blanc: Premiers états généraux des personnes touchées par la maladie de Parkinson. France Parkinson (2010)

Cooper, A.: The Inmates Are Running the Asylum. SAMS Publishing, Indianapolis (1999)

Coyette, A., Kieffer, S., Vanderdonckt, J.: Multi-fidelity prototyping of user interfaces. In: Interact'2007, IFIP Conference on Human-Computer Interaction, pp. 150–164 (2007)

Davis, F.D.: Perceived usefulness, perceived ease of use, and user acceptance of information technology. MIS Q. **13**(3), 319–339 (1989)

Dupont, L., Guidat, C., Morel, L., Skiba, N.: The role of mock-ups in the anticipation of the user experience within a living lab: an empirical study. In: 2015 IEEE International Conference on Engineering, Technology and Innovation/ International Technology Management Conference (ICE/ITMC), pp. 1–8 (2015). https://doi.org/10.1109/ICE.2015.7438669

Dupouy, J., Ory-Magne, F., Brefel-Courbon, C.: Autres prises en charge dans la maladie de Parkinson: psychologique, rééducative, éducation thérapeutique et nouvelles technologies. La Presse Médicale **46**(2), 225–232 (2017)

Eisenberg, J.L., Hou, J.G., Barbour, P.J.: Current perspectives on the role of telemedicine in the management of Parkinson's disease. Smart Homecare Technol. TeleHealth **5**, 1–12 (2018)

Ezzedine, H., Kolski, C.: Modelling of cognitive activity during normal and abnormal situations using Object Petri Nets, application to a supervision system. Cogn. Technol. Work **7**(3), 167–181 (2005)

Ezzedine, H., Trabelsi, A., Tran, C., Kolski, C.: Criteria and methods for interactive system evaluation: application to a regulation post in the transport domain. In: Hammadi, S., Ksouri, M. (eds.) Advanced Mobility and Transport Engineering, pp. 183–230, ISBN 978-18482-13777. ISTE-Wiley (2012)

Fahn S., Elton R., Members of the UPDRS Development Committee. In: Fahn, S., Marsden, C.D., Calne, D.B., Goldstein, M. (eds.) Recent Developments in Parkinson's Disease, Vol 2. FlorhamPark, NJ. Macmillan HealthCare Information, pp. 153-163, 293-304 (1987)

Geurts, H., Haelewyck, M.C.: Analyse compréhensive d'une typologie du «vieillir acteur». Gérontol. Soc. **42**(2), 39–55 (2020)

Guffroy, M., Vigouroux, V., Kolski, C., Vella, F., Teutsch, P.: From human-centered design to disabled user & ecosystem centered design in case of assistive interactive systems. Int. J. Sociotechnol. Knowl. Dev. **9**(4), 28–42 (2017)

Guffroy, M., Guerrier, Y., Kolski, C., Vigouroux, N., Vella, F., Teutsch, P.: Adaptation of user-centered design approaches to abilities of people with disabilities. In: Miesenberger, K., Kouroupetroglou, G. (eds.) ICCHP 2018. LNCS, vol. 10896, pp. 462–465. Springer, Cham (2018). https://doi.org/10.1007/978-3-319-94277-3_71

Guidini Gonçalves, T., Oliveira, K., Kolski, C.: The use of task modeling in interactive system specification. Cogn. Technol. Work **19**(2), 493–515 (2017)

Hartson, H.R., Andre, T.S., Williges, R.C.: Criteria for evaluating usability evaluation methods. Int. J. Hum. Comput. Interact. **13**(4), 373–410 (2001)

Hartelius, L., Svensson, P.: Speech and swallowing symptoms associated with Parkinson's disease and multiple sclerosis: a survey. Folia Phoniatr. Logop. **46**, 9–17 (1994)

Herd, C.P., et al.: Comparison of speech and language therapy techniques for speech problems in Parkinson's disease. Cochrane Database Syst. Rev. (8) (2012)

Idoughi, D., Seffah, A., Kolski, C.: Adding user experience into the interactive service design loop: a persona-based approach. Behav. Inf. Technol. **31**(3), 287–303 (2012)

ISO/TR 16982:2002. Ergonomics of human-system interaction—Usability methods supporting human-centred design (2002)

ISO 9241-110:2020 Ergonomics of Human-System Interaction—Part 110: Interaction Principles, ICS 13.180, 2nd edn., ISO 9241-110:2020 (2020)

Ivory, M.Y., Hearst, M.A.: The state of the art in automating usability evaluation of user interfaces. ACM Comput. Surv. **33**(4), 470–516 (2001)

Jacobson, I., Spence, I., Kerr, B.: Use-case 2.0. Commun. ACM **59**(5), 61–69 (2016)

Krueger, R.A., Casey, M.A.: Focus Groups: A Practical Guide for Applied Research, 5th edn. SAGE Publications (2014)

Kuosmanen, E., Kan, V., Visuri, A., Hosio, S. Ferreira, D.: Let's draw: detecting and measuring Parkinson's disease on smartphones. In: Proceedings of the 2020 CHI Conference on Human Factors in Computing Systems. Association for Computing Machinery, New York, NY, USA (2020)

McNaney, R., Tsekleves, E., Synnott. J.: Future opportunities for IoT to Support People with Parkinson's. In: Proceedings of the 2020 CHI Conference on Human Factors in Computing Systems. Association for Computing Machinery, New York, NY, USA (2020)

Mishra, S.R., Klasnja, P., Woodburn, J.M., Hekler, E.B., Omberg, L.K., M., Mangravite, L..: Supporting coping with Parkinson's disease through self tracking. In: Proceedings of the 2019 CHI Conference on Human Factors in Computing Systems. Association for Computing Machinery, New York, NY, USA (2019)

Nielsen, L.: Personas - User Focused Design, 2nd edn. Springer, London (2019)

Neate, T., Bourazeri, A., Roper, A., Stumpf, S., Wilson, S.: Co-created personas: engaging and empowering users with diverse needs within the design process. In: Proceedings of the 2019 CHI Conference on Human Factors in Computing Systems, Paper 650, pp. 1–12. ACM, New York, NY, USA (2019)

Schalling, E., Johansson, K., Hartelius, L.: Speech and communication changes reported by people with Parkinson's disease. Folia Phoniatr. Logop. 69(3), 131–141 (2017)

Sveinbjornsdottir, S.: The clinical symptoms of Parkinson's disease. J. Neurochem. 139, 318–324 (2016)

Vandendoren, B., Geurts, H., Haelewyck, M.C.: Empowerment individuel et grand âge. Gérontol. Soc. 41(2), 213–226 (2019)

Vega, J., et al.: Back to analogue: self-reporting for Parkinson's disease. In: Proceedings of the 2018 CHI Conference on Human Factors in Computing Systems. Association for Computing Machinery, Paper 74, pp. 1–13. New York, NY, USA (2018)

Venkatesh, V., Morris, M., Davis, G.B., Davis, F.D.: User acceptance of information technology: toward a unified view. MIS Quarterly 27(3), 425–478 (2003)

Venkatesh, V., Thong, J., Xu, X.: Consumer acceptance and use of information technology: extending the unified theory of acceptance and use of technology. MIS Q. 36(1), 157–178 (2012)

Vizcarra, J.A., et al.: The Parkinson's disease e-diary: developing a clinical and research tool for the digital age. Mov. Disord. 34(5), 676–681 (2019)

Designing a Consumer Framework for Social Products Within a Gamified Smart Home Context

Juana Isabel Méndez[1]($\boxtimes$) , Pedro Ponce[1] , Othoniel Miranda[1] , Citlaly Pérez[1] ,
Ana Paula Cruz[1] , Therese Peffer[2] , Alan Meier[3] , Troy McDaniel[4] ,
and Arturo Molina[1]

[1] School of Engineering and Sciences, Tecnologico de Monterrey, México City, Mexico
{A01165549,A01652554,A01336766,A01024139}@itesm.mx,
{pedro.ponce,armolina}@tec.mx
[2] Institute for Energy and Environment, University of California, Berkeley, CA 94720, USA
tpeffer@berkeley.edu
[3] Energy and Efficiency Institute, University of California, Davis, CA 95616, USA
akmeier@ucdavis.edu
[4] The Polytechnic School, Arizona State University, Mesa, AZ 85212, USA
troy.mcdaniel@asu.edu

Abstract. The most effective strategy for homes to save energy is by decreasing their electricity consumption. Home Energy Management Systems connect appliances that improve households' energy performance to thermal comfort. These systems need to take into account human behavior regarding saving energy and thermal comfort. This paper proposes a three-step framework that integrates the Smart Residential Load Simulator (SRLS), Adaptive-Network based on Fuzzy Inference System (ANFIS), and a gamification structure to develop an interface designed to reduce energy consumption without losing thermal comfort. Finally, a gamified mock-up for mobile devices is displayed for a household with high energy consumption levels and a temperature setpoint of 23 °C. This proposal integrates the concept of social products to empower the interaction between devices and end-users.

Keywords: Gamification · Smart home · Social products · ANFIS · Gamified homes · Gamified interfaces · HMI

1 Introduction

Household appliances, like televisions, interior lighting, electric stoves, coffee makers, washing machines, geysers, refrigerators, clothes irons, and thermostats, have different energy consumption patterns according to their operating periods, power ratings, and the specific characteristics of each appliance [1]. The Residential Energy Consumption Survey (RECS) conducted by the U.S. Energy Information Administration (EIA) [2] provides data on energy-related characteristics and usage patterns of a representative

© Springer Nature Switzerland AG 2021
M. Antona and C. Stephanidis (Eds.): HCII 2021, LNCS 12768, pp. 429–443, 2021.
https://doi.org/10.1007/978-3-030-78092-0_29

sample of U.S. homes. The most current available survey is from 2015, and it is the 14th edition of the RECS analysis. This database contains 5,686 observations with 759 variables and represents 118,208,250 U.S. homes.

Residential buildings in the U.S. represent approximately 20% of total energy demand and 36% of total electricity consumption [3]. According to RECS, 85% of residential buildings have thermostats in their homes [4]. A growing fraction of these thermostats are connected to the Internet. They offer many features that enable greater information and control. Installation of connected thermostats can reduce energy consumption up to 35% of the peak load and raise overall energy efficiency by 5% through small changes in behavior [3]. Although it is possible to achieve such reductions by interactions between the end-user and the connected thermostat, successful reduction infrequently occurs because users do not entirely accept the connected device, leading to insufficient energy behavior [5–13].

An important parallel trend is the widespread availability of smart household appliances, which has been made possible by the ubiquitous Internet of Things. Such smart appliances can facilitate routine tasks, adjust visual and thermal comfort, and provide building security [3, 14]. In [15], a simulation framework is proposed to manage a smart home's home appliances and lighting systems. Home energy management systems build the interconnection of appliances to manage households' peak power demand and comfort. Research focuses on scheduling optimization of the household appliances to reduce the electricity bill and generation cost; multi-objective optimization models for household electricity consumption and load peak of the utility grid; and analysis of the economic benefit of energy storage [16]. The Smart Residential Load Simulator (SRLS) for Energy Management in Smart Grids is an example of a validated tool. It is based on MATLAB-Simulink-Guide toolboxes that model household appliances, wind and solar power generation, and battery sources based on the ambient temperature and household activity levels in a day [17].

Human factors nevertheless remain a significant determinant in achieving lower energy consumption. Hence, the Universal Thermal Climate Index (UTCI) is a one-dimensional quantity that reflects the human physiological reaction to the actual thermal condition and is categorized as thermal stress [18]. An individual can have no thermal stress within an air temperature range from 9 °C to 26 °C. Therefore, the air conditioner setpoint in a home can be 26 °C without experiencing thermal stress. However, before allowing the temperature to exceed that setpoint, it is essential to understand the three categories of thermal adaptation:

- Behavioral adjustment (personal, technological, and cultural responses).
- Physiological adaptation (genetic and acclimatization).
- Psychological dimension of thermal adaptation: Refers to an altered perception of, reaction, and sensory information due to experience and expectations [19].

The end-users must also be prepared to accept connected products and the operating decisions that they make; this acceptance can be improved by personalizing Human-Machine Interfaces (HMIs) and making social products. Social products come from the S^3 product development reference framework proposed by [20], in which each S means Sensing, Smart, and Sustainable products:

1. Sensing: A system can detect events, gather information, and measure changes throughout sensors that allow the observation of physical or environmental conditions.
2. Smart: The complementary consolidation of physical parts, smart components, and connectivity to make intelligent and accessible products to interface with different gadgets.
3. Sustainable: Social, environmental, and economic elements that create a balanced and optimized performance. The social aspect contributes to the product by gathering people's satisfaction.

Consequently, social products can be supported by understanding the varieties of behavior and usability problems when adopting connected devices, and including household energy users in planning, implementing, and monitoring energy usage [20]. Hence, Ponce et al. [10] recommend including social factors in the design process by implementing a gamification strategy to send stimuli to shape consumer behavior towards energy reduction.

Social products acceptability has the following characteristics [21]:

- Users comprehend that when they buy a connected product, they can leverage its advantages.
- The products align with users' current and dynamic lifestyles.
- The appliances and devices are quick and cheap to acquire.
- The products diminish or eliminate physical demands for operation; users do not require experience, high user-knowledge levels, or regular intervention of experts for installation, troubleshooting, and maintenance.
- The usability of the products considers end-user skills; products do not decay or perform unpredictably.
- The products take into account users' requirements.
- The products take into account privacy and security characteristics, so that users' information is secure and private.

Gamification is developing and creating positive experiences using game mechanics, behavioral economics, and design thinking in non-game contexts to motivate, engage, and educate individuals to solve real-world or productive activities problems [22, 23]. The Octalysis framework proposed by Chou [24] analyzes and builds strategies to make engaging applications. Table 1 shows the extrinsic and intrinsic motivations regarding energy applications [25].

- Extrinsic motivation: People are motivated because they want something they cannot get, and earning it infers outer recognition or even monetary prizes. Includes factors of external control, identification, and integration.
- Intrinsic motivation: The activity is rewarding on its own without a particular purpose to succeed. This motivation considers autonomy, competence, and relatedness [26].

In [8, 11, 27], the authors propose a three-step framework that allows the interface designer to display personalized interfaces to engage, teach and motivate end-users to

Table 1. Gamification elements for extrinsic and intrinsic motivations.

Extrinsic motivation	Intrinsic motivation
Offers, coupons	Notifications
Bill discounts	Messages
Challenges	Tips
Levels	Energy community
Dashboard	Collaboration
Statistics	Control over peers
Degree of control	Social comparison
Points, badges, leaderboard	Competition

save energy at home through a fuzzy logic decision system gamification structure. In [28], a multi-sensory system is proposed on an ANFIS by including Alexa and cameras to track older adults and check their daily status and mood to improve their quality of life by promoting social inclusion and physical exercise.

Conventional analytical mathematical modeling algorithms sometimes encounter problems when dealing with vague or uncertain information. Thus, using linguistic rules (IF-THEN), Fuzzy systems have the strength and ability to reason as humans, without employing precise and complete information. However, a problem arises: transferring human knowledge to a fuzzy logic system and how to tune the fuzzy logic system. Several proposals have been made, such as the combination of artificial neural networks with fuzzy systems. Artificial neural networks can learn and adapt from experience, potentially complementing fuzzy systems. One of the essential techniques is ANFIS, an adaptive neuro-fuzzy inference system proposed by Jang [29]. ANFIS is based on adaptive networks, a superset of feed-forward artificial neural networks with supervised learning capabilities, as Jang stated in [29] and [30].

This paper proposes to use the SRLS simulator to determine the daily energy consumption in Concord, California. Based on the result, ANFIS is used to determine what type of gamification motivation is required to reduce energy consumption without losing thermal comfort.

2 Methodology

The data was collected from the RECS database and analyzed using R Studio. The weather file for Concord, California was analyzed using Energy Plus to obtain the cooling design day. The RECS's exploratory data analysis obtained the characteristics of a typical home in California, and the most common household appliances were analyzed in the SRLS. The information was then fed into the ANFIS, representing input values of energy consumption and temperatures in July. Output is provided as gamified motivation where lower values are related to intrinsic motivation and higher values are related to extrinsic motivation.

3 Proposed Framework

This framework proposes three steps (Fig. 1):

- Knowledge base: Exploratory data analysis of the RECS database and the weather file. Extrinsic and intrinsic motivation of gamification features used for energy savings. SRLS provides insights into daily consumption based on the home and appliances' location and characteristics.
- ANFIS: This step analyzes the energy consumption in a home and the air temperature of a specific location. The output value is related to the gamified motivation that helps the user engage in activities.
- Evaluation: The end-user interacts with the HMI, which provides continuous feedback to the user and the knowledge base to determine whether the user is engaged or if adjustments are required.

3.1 Knowledge Base

RECS Database. The IECC Climate Code [31] classified the country into eleven zones. The mean kWh in the U.S. in 2015 was 11,029 kWh, with a standard deviation of 7,050 kWh. Figure 2 displays different boxplots for each zone and their total site electricity usage in kWh; the blue dashed line represents the average annual electricity consumption for a U.S. residential utility customer. The present work focused on the IECC climate zone 3C and in the Pacific Census Division. This zone 3C has a mean of 5,684 kWh with a standard deviation of 3,171 kWh.

Zone 3C is below the national average; hence, this paper aims to propose a strategy that promotes household reduction. Table 2 displays the type of home's main characteristics and the most common appliances in that zone.

Modeling a Home in California. SRLS was used to simulate and analyze three cases on a typical summer day.

The first case analyzed the most common appliances of Table 1 without any photovoltaic generation. The second case analyzed the appliances that consume less than 3 kWh. The third case considered case 1 with photovoltaic generation to analyze the energy and cost reductions. Table 3 summarizes the characteristics of the household appliances and PV generation used for each case and the type of home in each case.

Besides, Table 2 shows the seven household appliances selected for case 1, the summer season, and the electricity price based on an electricity bill for Concord, California. This SRLS simulator requested the temperature for a single day. July 21st was the cooling design reported at the Statistic Report of the annual weather file (stat file) [32]. Moreover, the tool requested the family characteristics, which were considered in Table 1, with adults' presence during the day, with their dishwasher and clothes washer.

ANFIS and Gamification Structure. Although zone 3C was the lowest zone with total site electricity usage, the present work proposes a gamification strategy to promote energy reduction by promoting the adoption of PV panels and increasing the setpoint to reduce energy consumption without losing thermal comfort. 1 °C can save about 6% of the electricity [33].

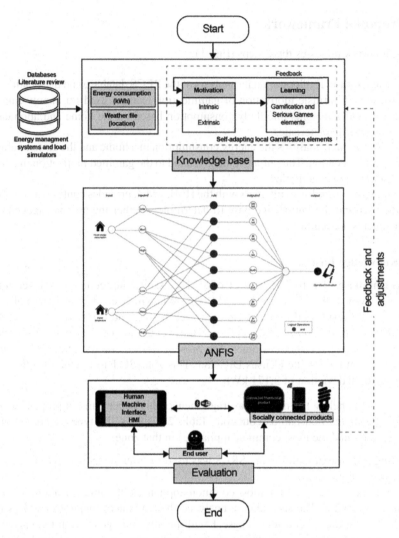

Fig. 1. Proposed framework.

The ANFIS decision system is proposed. There are two input variables, kWh and temperature, and gamified motivation is the output variable. Gamified motivation considers both the intrinsic and extrinsic motivations by following this premise:

- The home that consumes more energy with setpoints based on the outdoor temperature that requires setpoints below 21 °C, requires extrinsic motivation for outer recognition and external rewards. The home that consumes less energy with setpoints above 23 °C can be related to intrinsic motivation as the house uses less kWh than the other in similar conditions. This activity is rewarding on its own. On the other hand, the average home and setpoint below 23 °C and above 21 °C have both motivations. This

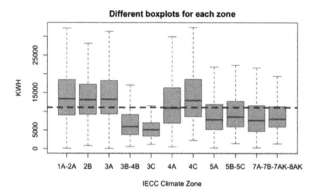

Fig. 2. Boxplots for each IECC Climate Zone and their site electricity usage in kWh.

Table 2. Main characteristics of the type of home and most common appliances in zone 3C

Home characteristics	Most common appliances
Floor area: 165.14 m^2 The average number of rooms: 3 The average number of windows: 34	Stove
Average site electricity usage: 5,864 kWh	Dryer
Average electricity cost: $1,605 USD	Lights (average of 40 CFL)
87% of the homes were built before 1989	Dishwasher
Single-family detached house	Refrigerator
Three household members	Washing machine
Three weekdays someone is at home	Air conditioner and programmable central thermostat

type of home may be motivated by external recognition or autonomy, competence, and relatedness elements.

The ANFIS simulation was done using the Neuro-Fuzzy Designer of the MATLAB toolbox.

Table 3. Characteristics of the household appliances and photovoltaic generation

Household appliances and PV generation	Energy Star	Case 1	Case 2	Case 3
Stove: - General Electric - Size: Two burners of 8" and two of 6" -Morning usage: 7 a.m., 40 min -Noon usage: 2 p.m., 60 min -Night usage: 8:30 p.m., 30 min		x		x
Dryer: - Loads per day: 1 - Minutes of load: 50	x	x	x	x
Lights: - Power (incandescent): 100 W - Power (CFL): 9 W		x		x
Dishwasher: - Miele G 6935 SCi - Number of loads per day: 1 - Minutes of the load: 50	x	x	x	x
Refrigerator: - Blomberg BRFB1045WH - Power: 32.6 W - Dimensions (m): 0.316 * 0.6 * 1.72	x	x	x	x
Washing machine: - LG WM9500H*A - Capacity: 5.8 cu. ft - Annual Energy Consumption: 120 kWh - Number of loads per day: 1 - Minutes of load: 30 - Water temperature: warm	x	x	x	x
Air conditioner: - Capacity: 9000 BTU - Energy Efficiency Ratio: 10		x		x
Photovoltaic Generation				x
Type of home				
Single-family detached house Area: 165.138 m^2 Number of rooms: 3 Size of each room: 7.42 m by 7.42 m Height: 2.75 m Numbers of windows: 34 Height of a window: 0.91 m Thermostat setpoint: 23 °C				

4   Results

Table 4 summarizes the energy (kWh) and cost ($) for the three cases. Case 1 consumed more Energy during Off-peak periods than the other peak loads, whereas Case 2 consumed more Energy during Mid-peak periods. Case 3 reflected the reduction of energy and costs due to the photovoltaic generation. 87.6% of the energy consumption came from the household appliances that consumed more than 3 kWh.

4.1   ANFIS

The result of the SRLS indicates that the home was consuming a significant amount of kWh and above the zone 3C. The ANFIS system suggested that this home required, for

Table 4. Results of each case.

	Case 1		Case 2		Case 3	
	Energy (kWh)	Cost ($)	Energy (kWh)	Cost ($)	Energy (kWh)	Cost ($)
Off-peak	18.34	4.83	1.86	0.49	18.12	4.77
Mid-peak	11.99	3.62	2.84	0.86	9.4	2.84
On peak	9.18	3	0.2	0.06	6.19	2.02
Total (day)	**39.51**	**11.45**	**4.9**	**1.41**	**33.71**	**9.63**

this specific day, an interface with very high extrinsic motivations. Figure 3 shows the ANFIS structure including, in the output, the type of gamified motivation to illustrate better which gamification elements should appear in the gamified interface. Figure 4 displays the Rule viewer, editor, membership function, and surface viewer. Table 5 displays the fuzzy rules for the ANFIS.

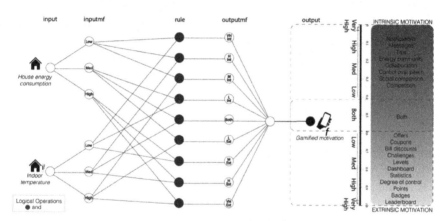

Fig. 3. Proposed ANFIS structure.

Figure 5 shows the HMI for a type of user with a home with high energy consumption and a medium indoor temperature setpoint. An option to reduce energy consumption is by increasing 1 °C, so a 6% of saving can be achieved. Besides, a PV system is included in the section of "My socially connected products" to generate interest to the user and see what is needed to install a PV system. As this type of user requires Very High extrinsic motivations, gamification elements, such as competitions and degree of control elements, are displayed. The degree of control appears as a comparison to others or the weekly savings in electricity and money.

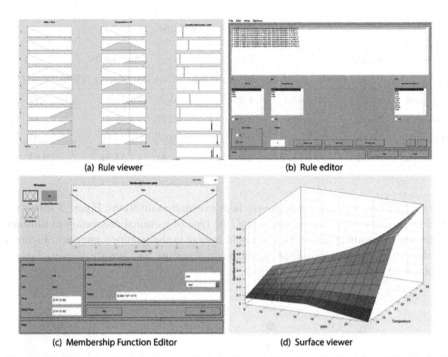

(a) Rule viewer   (b) Rule editor

(c) Membership Function Editor   (d) Surface viewer

Fig. 4. ANFIS results. (a) Rule viewer, (b) Rule editor, (c) Membership Function Editor, and (d) Surface viewer.

Table 5. Fuzzy logic inference rules.

IF		Then
kWh	Temperature	Gamified motivation
Low	Low	Medium Intrinsic
Low	Med	Both
Low	High	High Intrinsic
Med	Low	Low Intrinsic
Med	Med	Medium Extrinsic
Med	High	Low Extrinsic
High	Low	Very High Intrinsic
High	Med	High Extrinsic
High	High	Very High Extrinsic

5   Discussion

The SRLS has limitations in terms of simulating monthly energy consumption; this is probably because this energy management system is designed to be analyzed daily. Moreover, it is impossible to modify the Peak time hour, affecting the total energy consumption in terms of their electricity cost. However, this simulation gives a comprehensive insight into the home and the behavior patterns of the home.

Using this ANFIS system, it is possible to provide the characteristics required to propose a gamified application in terms of motivation. Moreover, ANFIS considers the UTCI values to provide thermal comfort.

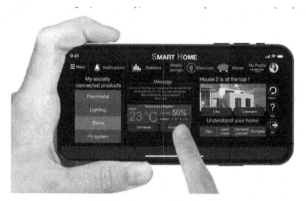

(a) Version for mobile phones.

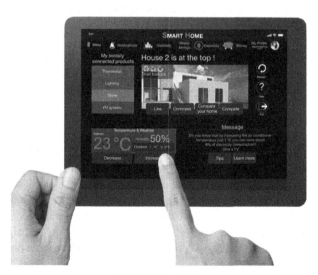

(b) Version for tablets.

Fig. 5. Smart Home interface for a type of home with High energy consumption and Med indoor temperature setpoint.

As the proposal is based on the home, this preliminary analysis shows how it turns into a social product. With this system, it is possible to register and analyze the home's behavior.

The RECS survey demonstrated that the IECC Climate Zone 3C is the zone with low electricity usage compared to the other 10 zones. This low energy demand is due to California, since 1978, proposing the Title 24 to promote efficient buildings and energy codes that reduce consumption in the household. Another fact is that California is one of the states where electricity costs more than the average of the U.S. Besides, that region has a mild climate, and it is not as humid compared to other regions in the country.

Although Fig. 5 displays a mock-up of a gamified application for smart homes and provides tips and messages about increasing the degrees of setpoints, the analysis of thermal comfort must be performed. Further, this interface can be personalized by analyzing the type of user. In previous research, [8], an adaptation for the Octalysis framework was proposed. This adaptation includes the game design elements in [34], the Hexad gamified user, role player, energy end-user segment, and target group.

6 Conclusion

This paper proposed a three-step framework that integrates an energy management simulator, ANFIS, and gamification structure to propose an interface designed to reduce energy consumption without losing thermal comfort.

This knowledge base step analyzes the RECS database to determine the type of home, Climate Zone, energy consumption, and most common household appliances. Based on that, a one-day simulation was performed with the SRLS toolbox. Three cases were analyzed to determine the reduction of energy by adopting renewable sources. 87.6% of the energy consumption in the case belonged to the stove, lights, and air conditioner; by adopting renewable sources such as photovoltaics, a 14.68% energy reduction was achieved. The ANFIS step provides insight into the gamified motivation and the game elements for the interface that the end-user requires to reduce energy consumption. The last step displays the proposed interface based on the ANFIS suggestions, receive feedback from the users and, if it is required, the interface is adjusted to display other intrinsic or extrinsic gamification elements.

Table 5 and Fig. 3 give outcomes regarding which type of gamification structure to use depending on the level of energy consumption and setpoint. However, to improve this gamification structure, it is relevant to monthly simulate the energy consumption so accurate gamified motivations can be tackled. For instance, the end-user may be motivated more by intrinsic elements and other days more in an extrinsic manner.

This framework helps the designer propose interfaces based on data analysis from the thermostat, climate, and electrical consumption. Another relevant aspect of the ANFIS is that depending on the level of consumption and setpoint, it gives insights regarding which type of motivation is needed to propose accurate interfaces that pro-mote energy reduction or energy awareness.

With this proposal, it is intended to profile and know the type of home better to propose an accurate application that promotes energy reduction and improves quality of life without affecting how residents interact in the home. This HMI provides the opportunity to create an atmosphere where end-users can interact with their smart homes in productive and empowering ways.

7 Future Work

We plan to conduct an online survey in Mexico to review any association between a gamified interface and its personality traits. We also plan to consider augmented AI to better understand users to fully leverage them instead of relying on conventional AI that only automates processes.

Acknowledgments. This research project is supported by Tecnologico de Monterrey and CITRIS under the collaboration ITESM-CITRIS Smart thermostat, deep learning, and gamification project (https://citris-uc.org/2019-itesm-seed-funding/), and the National Science Foundation under Grant No. 1828010.

References

1. Alimi, O.A., Ouahada, K.: Smart home appliances scheduling to manage energy usage. In: 2018 IEEE 7th International Conference on Adaptive Science Technology (ICAST), pp. 1–5 (2018). https://doi.org/10.1109/icastech.2018.8507138
2. EIA: Residential Energy Consumption Survey (RECS) - Data - U.S. Energy Information Administration (EIA). https://www.eia.gov/consumption/residential/data/2015/index.php?view=microdata. Accessed on 23 June 2020
3. Cetin, K.S., O'Neill, Z.: Smart meters and smart devices in buildings: a review of recent progress and influence on electricity use and peak demand. Curr. Sustain./Renew. Energ. Rep. **4**, 1–7 (2017). https://doi.org/10.1007/s40518-017-0063-7
4. Huchuk, B., O'Brien, W., Sanner, S.: A longitudinal study of thermostat behaviors based on climate, seasonal, and energy price considerations using connected thermostat data. Build. Environ. **139**, 199–210 (2018). https://doi.org/10.1016/j.buildenv.2018.05.003
5. Iweka, O., Liu, S., Shukla, A., Yan, D.: Energy and behaviour at home: a review of intervention methods and practices. Energ. Res. Soc. Sci. **57**, (2019). https://doi.org/10.1016/j.erss.2019.101238
6. Pritoni, M., Meier, A.K., Aragon, C., Perry, D., Peffer, T.: Energy efficiency and the misuse of programmable thermostats: the effectiveness of crowdsourcing for understanding household behavior. Energ. Res. Soc. Sci. **8**, 190–197 (2015). https://doi.org/10.1016/j.erss.2015.06.002
7. Peffer, T., Pritoni, M., Meier, A., Aragon, C., Perry, D.: How people use thermostats in homes: a review. Build. Environ. **46**, 2529–2541 (2011). https://doi.org/10.1016/j.buildenv.2011.06.002
8. Ponce, P., Meier, A., Mendez, J., Peffer, T., Molina, A., Mata, O.: Tailored gamification and serious game framework based on fuzzy logic for saving energy in smart thermostats. J. Cleaner Prod. **262**, 121167 (2020). https://doi.org/10.1016/j.jclepro.2020.121167
9. Ponce, P., Peffer, T., Molina, A.: Usability perceptions and beliefs about smart thermostats by chi-square test, signal detection theory, and fuzzy detection theory in regions of Mexico. Front. Energ. **13**, 522–538 (2018). https://doi.org/10.1007/s11708-018-0562-2
10. Ponce, P., Meier, A.K., Miranda, J., Molina, A., Peffer, T.: The next generation of social products based on sensing, smart and sustainable (S3) features: a smart thermostat as case study. In: 9th IFAC Conference on Manufacturing Modelling, Management and Control, p. 6 (2019)

11. Méndez, J.I., Ponce, P., Mata, O., Meier, A., Peffer, T., Molina, A., Aguilar, M.: Empower saving energy into smart homes using a gamification structure by social products. In: 2020 IEEE International Conference on Consumer Electronics (ICCE). pp. 1–7. IEEE, Las Vegas, NV, USA (2020). https://doi.org/10.1109/icce46568.2020.9043174

12. Ponce, P., Peffer, T., Molina, A., Barcena, S.: Social creation networks for designing low income interfaces in programmable thermostats. Technol. Soc. **62**, (2020). https://doi.org/10.1016/j.techsoc.2020.101299

13. Peffer, T., Perry, D., Pritoni, M., Aragon, C., Meier, A.: Facilitating energy savings with programmable thermostats: evaluation and guidelines for the thermostat user interface. Ergonomics **56**, 463–479 (2013). https://doi.org/10.1080/00140139.2012.718370

14. Kang, W.M., Moon, S.Y., Park, J.H.: An enhanced security framework for home appliances in smart home. Hum. Centric Comput. Inf. Sci. **7**, 6 (2017). https://doi.org/10.1186/s13673-017-0087-4

15. Avila, M., Ponce, P., Molina, A., Romo, K.: Simulation framework for load management and behavioral energy efficiency analysis in smart homes. In: McDaniel, T., Berretti, S., Curcio, Igor D.D., Basu, A. (eds.) ICSM 2019. LNCS, vol. 12015, pp. 497–508. Springer, Cham (2020). https://doi.org/10.1007/978-3-030-54407-2_42

16. Lu, Q., Zhang, Z., Lü, S.: Home energy management in smart households: Optimal appliance scheduling model with photovoltaic energy storage system. Energ. Rep. **6**, 2450–2462 (2020). https://doi.org/10.1016/j.egyr.2020.09.001

17. Lopez, J.M.G., Pouresmaeil, E., Canizares, C.A., Bhattacharya, K., Mosaddegh, A., Solanki, B.V.: Smart residential load simulator for energy management in smart grids. IEEE Trans. Ind. Electron. **66**, 1443–1452 (2019). https://doi.org/10.1109/TIE.2018.2818666

18. Błażejczyk, K., et al.: An introduction to the universal thermal climate index (UTCI). Geogr. Pol. **86**, 5–10 (2013). https://doi.org/10.7163/GPol.2013.1

19. de Dear, R.J., Brager, G.S.: Developing an Adaptive Model of Thermal Comfort and Preference. Center for the Built Environment, UC Berkeley (1998)

20. Miranda, J., Pérez-Rodríguez, R., Borja, V., Wright, P.K., Molina, A.: Sensing, smart and sustainable product development (S3 product) reference framework. Int. J. Prod. Res. **57**(14), 1–22 (2017). https://doi.org/10.1080/00207543.2017.1401237

21. Hargreaves, T., Wilson, C.: Smart Homes and Their Users. Human–Computer Interaction Series, pp. 1–14. Springer, Cham (2017). https://doi.org/10.1007/978-3-319-68018-7

22. Huotari, K., Hamari, J.: Defining gamification: a service marketing perspective. In: Proceeding of the 16th International Academic MindTrek Conference, pp. 17–22. ACM, New York, NY, USA (2012). https://doi.org/10.1145/2393132.2393137

23. Baptista, G., Oliveira, T.: Gamification and serious games: A literature meta-analysis and integrative model. Comput. Hum. Behav. **92**, 306–315 (2019). https://doi.org/10.1016/j.chb.2018.11.030

24. Chou, Y.: Actionable Gamification Beyond Points, Badges, and Leaderboards. CreateSpace Independent Publishing Platform (2015)

25. AlSkaif, T., Lampropoulos, I., van den Broek, M., van Sark, W.: Gamification-based framework for engagement of residential customers in energy applications. Energ. Res. Soc. Sci. **44**, 187–195 (2018). https://doi.org/10.1016/j.erss.2018.04.043

26. Kappen, D.L.: Adaptive Engagement of Older Adults' Fitness through Gamification (2015). http://dl.acm.org/citation.cfm?doid=2793107.2810276

27. Méndez, J.I., Ponce, P., Meier, A., Peffer, T., Mata, O., Molina, A.: S[4] product design framework: a gamification strategy based on type 1 and 2 fuzzy logic. In: McDaniel, T., Berretti, S., Curcio, Igor D.D., Basu, A. (eds.) ICSM 2019. LNCS, vol. 12015, pp. 509–524. Springer, Cham (2020). https://doi.org/10.1007/978-3-030-54407-2_43

28. Méndez, J.I., Mata, O., Ponce, P., Meier, A., Peffer, T., Molina, A.: Multi-sensor system, gamification, and artificial intelligence for benefit elderly people. In: Ponce, H., Martínez-Villaseñor, L., Brieva, J., Moya-Albor, E. (eds.) Challenges and Trends in Multimodal Fall Detection for Healthcare. SSDC, vol. 273, pp. 207–235. Springer, Cham (2020). https://doi.org/10.1007/978-3-030-38748-8_9

29. Jang, J.-R.: ANFIS: adaptive-network-based fuzzy inference system. IEEE Trans. Syst. Man Cybern. **23**, 665–685 (1993). https://doi.org/10.1109/21.256541

30. Ponce Cruz, P., Ramírez-Figueroa, F.D.: Intelligent control systems with LabVIEW. Springer, London; New York (2010)

31. Heinking, S., Zussman, C.: The science of building codes and climate zones, https://www.pepperconstruction.com/blog/science-building-codes-and-climate-zones. Accessed on 13 Nov 2020

32. Climate One Building: California Climate Zones weather file for building performance simulation, http://climate.onebuilding.org/WMO_Region_4_North_and_Central_America/California_Climate_Zones/index.html. Accessed on 16 Nov 2020

33. Bureau of Energy Efficiency: Energy Conservation in Building Space Cooling through recommended optimum temperature setting, (2018)

34. AlSkaif, T., Lampropoulos, I., van den Broek, M., van Sark, W.: Gamification-based framework for engagement of residential customers in energy applications. Energ. Res. Soc. Sci. **44**, 187–195 (2018). https://doi.org/10.1016/j.erss.2018.04.043

Viva: A Virtual Assistant for the Visually Impaired

Zeeshan Ahmed Pachodiwale, Yugeshwari Brahmankar, Neha Parakh, Dhruvil Patel, and Magdalini Eirinaki$^{(\boxtimes)}$ (iD)

San Jose State University, San Jose, CA 95192, USA
magdalini.eirinaki@sjsu.edu

Abstract. Visual impairment refers to the partial or complete loss of one's ability to see. It is estimated that there are 1.3 billion people in the world with some form of vision loss. In this work, we present Viva, an Android-based virtual assistant aiming to help people with visual impairment. The application provides haptic and voice navigation assistance by detecting obstacles in the user's surroundings and calculating the potential risk. We present the architecture, as well as a proof-of-concept prototype intended to demonstrate a potential use-case for a commercial embedded product that can be integrated into a walking stick or any wearable gadget. This Android application has features such as navigation assistant, object detection, voice-controlled UI and emergency assistant. The navigation assistant analyzes a user's surroundings by detecting and estimating distances from the user to the object. Object recognition mode includes a pre-built object recognition model that can recognize over 100 different common objects. Data collected is then processed by a risk-prediction algorithm to calculate the risk of collision. Feedback is provided to the user whenever there is a potential risk observed. The UI of the virtual assistant is uniquely designed from the ground-up to be intuitive, without the need for any usual aids via voice commands or single point touch control – where the entire screen acts as a soft button. Viva operates in a low-power mode with the screen turned off to efficiently utilize the limited battery resources on mobile phones. Viva is a prototype intended to demonstrate the potential use-cases of this idea. It can be integrated into other IoT devices such as smart walking sticks or wearable gadgets.

Keywords: Navigation assistant · Object recognition · Visually impaired assistance · UI · UX · Haptic feedback · Voice feedback · Android · TensorFlow Lite

1 Introduction

According to the 2019 report from World Health Organization (WHO) [1], there are 2.2 billion visually impaired people worldwide. Over 1 billion people globally suffering from blindness or moderate or severe vision impairment due to cataract, glaucoma, corneal opacities, diabetic retinopathy, trachoma, unaddressed refractive error, and presbyopia [2, 3]. Routine tasks that could seem trivial, could be a real survival concern for people with complete or partial blindness. From doing simple chores to complex activities, visually impaired people are dependent on blind sticks or service dogs or human guidance. One of the biggest challenges, especially to a person with complete vision loss is the ability to navigate around independently. Finding walking routes, crossing streets, and using public transport becomes an almost impossible task, without somebody assisting. Thus, to have a device that can help enhance their ability to function independently would greatly improve their lifestyle. This has been a major motivation for our work.

We propose a cost-effective solution to this problem which can reach users at scale without the need for new infrastructure or manufacturing resources. We introduce Viva, an Android-based virtual assistant that integrates deep learning object recognition techniques and a unique UX designed specifically for the visually impaired. The input to the assistant uses a speech recognition API, that can read the raw voice commands from the user and convert them into text. The feedback from the assistant is delivered using two ways, via voice or haptic feedback.

We experimentally evaluated two state-of-the-art object detection models, SSD (Single Shot Detection) [4] and YOLOv3 [5]. For our proof-of-concept prototype, we selected SSD based on its speed, accuracy, size, and compatibility. SSD can process 41 frames per second on average and has the best performance on Android ecosystem using TensorFlow Lite. In order to train the visual assistant for the prototype implementation, we mainly used the COCO dataset [6, 7] since it has most of the relevant classes required for pedestrian objects' detection, enhanced with our own training data to add classes of objects (e.g., street crossings and trees) not included in COCO. With the implementation of this software solution, the proposed model can be deployed on any embedded device that supports TensorFlow Lite API, hence making it a much cheaper solution than existing options.

The rest of the paper is organized as follows: we review related work in Sect. 2 and provide a high-level overview of the system architecture in Sect. 3. The design of the navigation assistant feature and its core components are detailed in Sect. 4, while the user experience (UX) considerations and interface (UI) are detailed in Sect. 5. In Sect. 6 we discuss our experimental evaluation results, and conclude with plans for future work in Sect. 7. A video demonstrating our proof-of-concept prototype application can be found in [8].

2   Related Work

There exist several virtual assistant devices available in the market. The smart band "Sunu Band" [9] uses SONAR or an echolocation sensor to detect objects. Another mobility device, "iGlasses Ultrasonic Mobility Aid Clear Lens" [10], uses an ultrasonic sensor to detect the existence of any obstacles and alert the user when an obstacle is in proximity. But moving objects are difficult to detect precisely using ultrasonic or echolocation sensors. Ultrasonic & echolocation sensors offer a very limited range and are prone to weather conditions. "LowViz Guide" [11] overcomes few shortcomings of the "iGlasses" and "Sunu Band". It can detect moving object by using installed iBeacons throughout the indoor environment where a person is navigating. But iBeacons restricts usages of the device to indoors, needs special arrangements and makes it costlier. "Eva"

[12] is another advanced product, which is an eyewear voice-controlled device that can be used both indoors and outdoors. This device is comparatively expensive and needs a lot of maintenance. Some research projects have developed navigation assistants for the blind using IoT-based devices [13], smart cane [14], and Android GPS-based navigation assistant [15]. In our work, we aim at incorporating a cost-efficient solution that is not dependent on additional hardware and can run on any mobile device. The camera on the device is used to sense the surrounding environment, estimate risk and help the user navigate safely. It detects indoor and outdoor objects in real time and does not require any special hardware arrangements or maintenance.

Obstacle detection and avoidance is one of the first things to think of when it comes to navigation. Ultrasonic sensors [16] connected in a cascade are usually used for detecting obstacles and measuring their distance from the observer. Data from the sensors are then used to help the user make decisions. However, these sensors are highly unreliable and have a very short range. They cannot be solely trusted to help a person navigate. Apart from object detection and avoidance, object recognition is also a very important aspect of navigation. Road crossings, traffic lights, etc. are a few examples where use of just the ultrasonic sensors is not good enough.

In recent years, due to advancements in deep learning there has been a focus shift into developing models that can detect and recognize objects in each image. Machine learning algorithms and deep learning techniques such as R-CNN [17], Fast R-CNN [18], Faster R-CNN [19], etc. Such techniques have been integrated in different application domains by deploying a deep learning model on a backend server and a frontend UI for capturing the images of the user's surroundings in [20, 21].

For real-time object detection to be reliable, the rate at which the model can detect and recognize objects should be very high. Typically, the deep learning models mentioned above take lots of computational power and time for inference, which is not feasible on an embedded system. Recent developments in deep learning technology have resulted in models that can run on limited resources with good performance. SSD MobileNet [4] and YOLOv3 [5] are two such models considered for this project. Both models yield good accuracy and low inference time. But YOLOv3 works better on systems with high computing power resulting in better results than the SSD model. However, it does not support the TensorFlow Lite rendering it incompatible for the Android ecosystem. The SSD Mobilenet model has comparable results and supports TensorFlow Lite. It also has lesser localization errors compared to the YOLOv3 model. Hence for Viva, SSD (Single Shot Detection) [4] was deemed more compatible.

Our work is inspired by the work of Meliones and Filios on BlindHelper [22]. BlindHelper uses and Bluetooth and WiFi to map the indoor environment and help pinpoint the user's location relative to an obstacle. This paper presents an architecture and proof-of-concept implementation of a virtual assistant for people with complete or partial blindness. Unlike the BlindHelper, Viva can also be used outdoors for navigation. The system is designed for real-time navigation assistance using object detection with support for embedded devices and mobile use cases.

3 System Architecture

As shown in Fig. 1, the core component of our virtual assistant (Viva) is the *navigation assistant*, responsible for detecting obstacles in the user's surroundings and calculating the potential risk to the user. Other key features of the Android application include *object identification*, and *emergency assistance* via an alert system. User experience (UX) is in the center of the application design with haptic and voice interfaces to support smooth and accessible interaction with the system via the *communication assistant*.

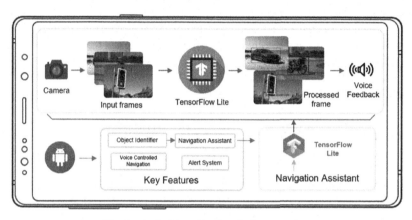

Fig. 1. Android application design overview

The *navigation assistant* is used to help the visually impaired in navigating safely. It uses the device's camera to sense the user's surroundings. Live video feed from the camera is captured and decoded into individual frames. These frames are then cropped and scaled into the right format to be passed to the object detection model. The Tensorflow Lite model identifies a list of objects that, along with context details. This list is passed to the risk prediction algorithm and depending on the prediction, appropriate voice and/or haptic feedback is given to the user.

In order to implement the *object detection* submodule, we evaluated two transfer-learning-based models, namely YOLOv3 [5] and SSD [4]. Transfer learning [23] is the process of using a previously trained model and retraining it using additional training data to detect new objects. The output of this model is a set of objects and their predicted class (i.e., the type of object identified), their prediction confidence level and their location within the image frame. After experimental evaluation, we employed the SSD model for our prototype proof-of-concept implementation due to its lower inference time and better compatibility with TensorFlow Lite API [27].

The *risk prediction algorithm* is another submodule of the *navigation assistant*, used to predict the potential risk to the user from the objects that are in the user's vicinity. The algorithm divides each image into 2 different zones. The central section of the image forms the *critical zone*, representing objects that are considered as potential obstacles. The rest of the image forms the *safe zone*, representing the peripheral view, where objects are away from the user. Objects found in the critical zone are processed first. Each class of object has an associated threat level. For example a dog which can move away from the user is treated to be less risky than a stationary object like a pole or tree. The area of intersection of the object with the area of the critical zone is calculated, and if the intersection value exceeds a threshold, then the object is immediately treated as a threat and reported to the user through vibration of the device followed by a beeping noise.

The user interface (UI) for the mobile application is implemented using the speakers and microphone of the device to provide a *voice-controlled UI* that does not require visual aids for interaction with the user. Viva also has a unique *touch UI*, which utilizes the entire touch screen as an input trigger, so that the user can set the entire screen to act as a button that can be double-tapped to trigger the assistant to start listening for voice commands. We have used Google's Text-To-Speech API [24] to understand the context of the command and recommend a particular action, and the SpeechRecognition [25] API to listen to the user. Viva also includes *emergency assistant*, which calls 911 emergency services upon user's request. Phrases like "Viva, I need help!", "911", "Viva, call 911" can trigger the emergency response.

4   Navigation Assistant

One of the main functions of Viva is the navigation mode, powered through the navigation assistant feature. Using live feed from the device's on-board camera, the assistant can detect objects present in front of the user and notify the user for potential risks. In particular, live feed from the camera is captured, preprocessed and fed to a machine learning model. The model outputs a list of objects that are detected in the image along with their prediction confidence level. It also outputs the boundary vertices of where the object is located in the image. The app uses this information to get awareness of which objects are directly in front of the user and provide alerts if the user is about to collide with an object. For this feature to work, the user is expected to hold the phone so that the camera faces the direction the user wants to move in, as shown in Fig. 2.

Fig. 2. Navigation mode demo interface

The flow of the navigation assistant functionality is shown in Fig. 3. The Camera2API [26] from the Android SDK is used to access the device's camera hardware.

Live video feed from the camera is captured and directed into a buffer implemented in the application. This feed is interpreted as a stream of individual frames with callbacks for each frame. These frames are then cropped and scaled, then fed as image frames (300 × 300 pixels) to the object detection model. These tasks are handled in a parallel thread and the main thread is called when the image is available for processing. The camera feed is typically 60 fps (frames per second), while the model can handle up to 20 fps (depending on the device hardware), which is sufficient enough and does not have a significant impact to the overall working of the *navigation mode*.

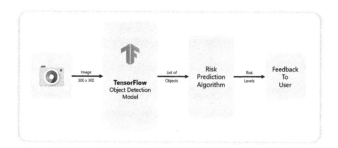

Fig. 3. Information flow

The key design components for the navigation assistant feature are:

1. Objection Detection Model - A TensorFlow Lite implementation of an object detection and object recognition model.
2. Risk prediction model – An algorithm that can predict the level of user's risk of collision with objects that are in the user's vicinity.
3. Feedback UI - A feedback mechanism that can notify the user without a significant lag in response times.

The machine learning-based object detection model, plays a vital role in the functioning of the navigation assistant. Since this is an Android application, the TensorFlow model that serves this purpose needs to be converted to a format compatible for mobile devices. For this, we use the TensorFlow Lite API [27]. Since navigation mode tries to find the safest path for the user, its real-time performance is essential for a reliable experience to the user. Hence, integrating the model offline ensures low latency and relatively higher performance, providing better frame rates. Moreover, local inference makes the app more efficient in terms of battery consumption compared to cloud-based approaches.

4.1 Object Detection Model

One of the core components of the virtual assistant is the *object detection model*. This is a multi-class classifier trained to predict, in real-time, the class of the objects in the image frames passed to it as input. The block diagram in Fig. 4 gives an overview of how the object detection model works. The input frame is pre-processed to detect objects present in the frame using deep learning (*object detection*). The regions of interest are extracted from the image in the form of bounding boxes. The extracted regions go through a pretrained neural network so that the objects can be classified using transfer learning. After the recognition of the objects and prediction of their classes the model will also calculate their locations (*object localization/bounding boxes*) on the image and their estimated distance from the user as well as their predicted classes (*object recognition*).

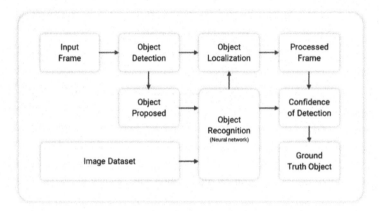

Fig. 4. Block diagram of the object detection model

As mentioned previously, for our system implementation, we considered and evaluated two object detection models, namely SSD [4] and YOLOv3 [5]. One major constraint was compatibility with the Android Tensorflow Lite API. YOLOv3 is a real time object detection algorithm. The algorithm applies a neural network to an entire image. The network divides the image into an $S \times S$ grid and comes up with bounding boxes, which are boxes drawn around images and predicted probabilities for each of these regions. The method used to come up with these probabilities is logistic regression. The bounding boxes are weighted by the associated probabilities. For class prediction, independent logistic classifiers are used. SSD MobileNet is significantly accurate and an efficient model developed to detect real time objects very quickly based on deep neural network. It uses VGG-16 architecture [28] as a base network since it performs well to classify images with great accuracy. During image prediction, this network creates scores for multiple objects present in default bounding boxes. SSD uses multiple small convolutional filters to detect categories and offsets of objects present in these boxes. Furthermore, the base network uses multi-scale feature maps to handle different object sizes. To achieve high prediction accuracy feature maps contribute to detect different scales of objects and classify predictions based on aspect ratio. YOLOv3 works well when tested on systems with high computing power. However, it failed on Android ecosystem due to its incompatibility with the TensorFlow Lite. It also had more localization errors when compared to the SSD model. Hence, for real time object detection, we decided to use the SSD MobileNet model, as it is more compatible and performs well on the Android ecosystem.

The SSD MobileNet model is trained on the COCO dataset [6] which contains most of the relevant classes required for pedestrian objects detection. This dataset has almost 90 classes. However, many of these classes are irrelevant to the street navigation scenario. So, we retrained the model using transfer learning, by removing irrelevant classes and adding a few new navigation-related classes to the dataset (such as traffic lights, pedestrian crossings, trees, etc.), which we manually annotated. More details on the dataset are discussed in Sect. 6.

Figure 5 shows the pipeline for the development of the object detection model needed for the application. TensorFlow framework is used for developing the deep learning model. Training and evaluation is an iterative process. As more and more refined data is obtained, the model is retrained to improve its accuracy. Once the model has reached a satisfactory accuracy level, it is converted to the TensorFlow Lite compatible format. This model is then deployed on the Android device.

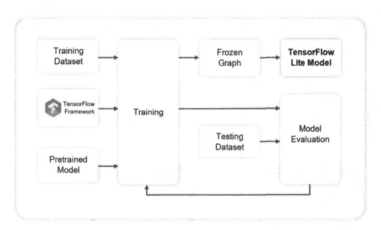

Fig. 5. Pipeline for developing the TensorFlow lite object detection model

4.2 Risk Prediction Algorithm

This submodule is one of the most critical parts of the *navigation assistant* and is responsible for estimating the risk of detected objects in order to promptly notify the user, if necessary. As shown in Fig. 3, it takes as input the output of the object detection model, in the form of a list of objects detected in the frame, along with the respective detection confidence. The confidence factor ranges from 0 to 1 with 1 indicating high confidence. The minimum confidence for an object to be treated as a valid detection is 0.6, whereas any objects with lower confidence levels are disregarded. This threshold is derived after repeated testing.

Each of the entries from the result also include an additional component which includes two points represented in a cartesian plane. These two points denote the bounding boxes around the objects that are detected by the model. The first point indicates the top left corner (*xtop, ytop*) of the bounding box and the second point represents the bottom right corner (*xbottom, ybottom*). An example is shown in Fig. 6.

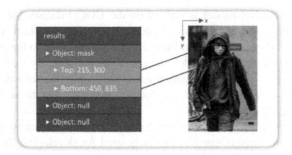

Fig. 6. Example entry of the results obtained from the object detection model

A phone camera typically has a field of view of around 70 to 90 degrees. Each frame is divided into two zones: the critical zone and the safe zone. The *critical zone* covers the center of the frame and the *safe zone* represents the peripheral view of the surroundings. An example is shown in Fig. 7. The first step in the risk prediction algorithm is determining where the object lies. The objects found in the critical zone are processed first – these are objects in front of the user and considered as obstacles in the user's path. Objects in the safe zone are away from the user and can be ignored. As shown in the example, the critical zone includes all objects on the street directly in the user's path. And the safe zone includes the trees that are not in the user's path and don't pose a risk to the user.

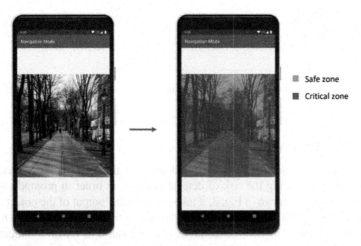

Fig. 7. Camera input divided into zones depending on the priority for response

The input to the risk prediction algorithm comes from the object detection model and a pre-defined database that includes specifications for each object class. The specifications include, risk level (R_L), real height of the object in m (H_R) and a distance threshold in m (d_T) for each object class that the model can predict. The risk prediction algorithm first identifies where the objects are. The area of intersection of the object with the critical zone area is calculated. If the intersection area is larger than d_T, then the object is considered to be a part of the critical zone. Otherwise, the object is still at the edge of the critical zone and is still not a potential threat to the user, and if the object moves into the critical zone, it will be identified in consecutive frames. All other objects that do not intersect the critical zone are considered to be in the safe zone and are disregarded.

The objects that are identified to be in the critical zone are processed further. Using the below mentioned formula, the distance of the object from the user (in meters) is estimated.

$$Object\ Distance = \frac{f \times H_R \times H_I}{H_D \times H_S}$$

In the above formula, f is the focal length of the camera (measured in millimeters), H_R is the real height of the object (measured in meters), H_I is the height of the image captured by the camera (measured in pixels), H_D is the height of the detected object (measured in pixels and calculated as follows: $H_D = ytop - ybottom$), and H_S the width of the camera sensor (measured in millimeters).

Depending on the distance of the object and the predefined risk levels for each class of objects a risk level is decided. Risk levels in the ascending order are LOW, MEDIUM, HIGH. If the distance estimated is:

a) greater than predefined distance threshold (d_T) for that class, then the final risk level is determined by decreasing the predefined risk level (R_L) by one level.
b) less than the threshold d_T, then the final risk level is determined by increasing the risk level by one level (with HIGH being maximum risk).
c) greater than 15 m, then the risk level is set to LOW.

Depending on the risk levels identified for each object, the final risk level is determined by the highest level of risk from all the different detected objects. The result is then fed to the feedback mechanism which implements different feedback methods to notify the user about any potential risk to the user.

4.3 Object Identifier

Another add-on feature that Viva includes is a stand-alone object identifier. This feature allows the user to simply point the camera at any particular object for identification. This is intended to help people with visual impairment understand their surroundings better and get daily tasks done. For example the object identifier can detect public signs helping the user identify between a male and female restroom or a way to distinguish currency bills.

This feature is implemented using an object recognition model that is trained on a larger dataset which can detect more classes. This model is a pre-trained model called inceptionv2 [29] which is trained on the ImageNet dataset [30]. The downloaded model is used for this feature without any modifications and is intended only for offline use cases since the inference times are large. As this does not need to be real time prediction with lowest latencies, the model does not need to be integrated within the app and can be included as an add-on. Hence the model is offloaded to a server. On installation of the application, this model can be downloaded into the device's internal storage. Upon request, the model in imported into memory and requests are served.

5   User Interface

One of the key limitations with any mobile operating system is that the main mechanism for input and output for the system is through the display and its touch controls. The current trend in the smart phone industry is to turn as much of the phone's real estate into display. Android is no different in this regard. This is major limitation for anybody who cannot see what is being displayed on the screen. The project aims at developing a unique user experience tailored to serve the needs of the visually impaired people. It uses different means of input and output which do not require any visual cues to interact with the operating system. To achieve this, the application makes use of voice and single-point touch for input and haptic interactions assisted by audio responses for output. A short video demonstrating the input and output mechanisms of our proof-of-concept application can be viewed in [8].

5.1   Input Mechanism

Voice Input. With this input mechanism, voice commands can be used to interact with the app. For simplicity and fast interactions, the application has all the basic commands pre-built in the form of hard-coded text. These pre-built voice commands are tailored for the in-app features. Simple phrases like "Start Navigation", "Call 911" etc. are pre-defined and do not need additional processing for a response. This is included to remove any latency associated with speech processing, for in-app tasks that are common and frequently used. When a user command does not match any of the pre-defined commands, the user's current command is then processed to extract the context to understand the intention of the command. If the context identified indicates that the user wants to use an app feature, then the user is requested for confirmation before executing the command. This confirmation is not necessary when the command directly matches with the pre-defined commands. Speech Recognition API [25] allows the application to listen to the user (*mic to app interface*). The API also converts the command from speech to text form. Once the assistant is triggered, a callback is sent to the application which then starts listening to the user's command. Upon successfully listening to the command, the command is retrieved by the application in the form of text, which is then compared against compared against the pre-defined set of commands or its context is derived using the same Speech Recognition API. The application then performs an action or provides a feedback to the user as an acknowledgement depending on the purpose of the command.

Touch Input. Most of the virtual assistants today have a trigger phrase which is necessary to be called for them to start listening to the commands (such as "Okay Google" or "Alexa"). In order to avoid this additional phrase every time the user needs to interact with the app, a different approach is used which utilizes the entire touch screen as an input trigger. The application turns the display off (black screen) but keeps the touch screen functional. The entire screen can now act as a button that can be utilized to trigger custom actions on single clicks, double clicks, long clicks and/or even triple clicks. For advanced users, this concept can be taken further ahead by dividing the screen into two halves and with each half of the screen acting as a separate button with all the above-described options available for each of the buttons, essentially doubling the number of actions that can be mapped for ease of access. This makes it more convenient for the user to trigger different functions of the assistant. One such use-case is for triggering the voice input. The user can double tap anywhere on the screen to trigger the assistant to start listening for commands instead of having to say the wake-word before each query. This approach makes the interaction seamless and saves battery that is otherwise spent in keeping the mic powered to detect the triggering phrase. It also avoids the inconvenience that can occur with the assistant not recognizing the wake word when the user doesn't pronounce the wake word in a certain specific way. Another huge advantage of this UI implementation is its remarkable battery savings. Battery is a scarce resource on a mobile device and by far the largest consumer of battery power is the display. By keeping the display off, we could make the last 50% longer. This is especially true for all the modern smartphones that include an O-LED display panel, which can turn off all pixels while keeping the touch screen on.

5.2 Output Mechanism

Voice Feedback. Voice output will be the main form of feedback by the application. The user will get feedback for his actions or replies for his command through voice messages. Text-To-Speech API [24] allows the application to convey messages to the user. The application includes a specific set of responses for different actions related to different features that are included with the app. For more generic responses, the app directs the commands to the Google Assistant which is present on most Android devices. If the google assistant is not present, the user gets a generic error response indicating that Viva cannot process the user's request.

Haptic Feedback. Voice output works best for non-real-time responses. But for critical and time-sensitive feedback (e.g., when a high-risk obstacle is directly in front of the user), the delay with voice feedback is often too high. Hence, we need another form of feedback that can be used alongside voice feedback to address these issues. A very popular form of feedback mechanism in Android devices is the haptic feedback. This uses the vibration motor found on the device. The application makes use of this mechanism to notify the user of certain urgent messages. For example, it is used in the navigation mode to notify the user if an object is directly in front of the user. A short vibration indicates a low risk-factor (far objects or objects with low risk) and a long vibration followed by an audio cue, can indicate a high-risk factor (near objects with high risk factor). The haptic feedback mechanism can also be used for simple messages that do not really need voice confirmation. For example, if the user wants to open the in-app feature through voice command, once the application has successfully identified his command it can give a feedback by subtly vibrating the phone once indicating that the object detection mode is now turned on instead of having the assistant give a voice output each time which may become a frustrating experience.

6 Experimental Evaluation

The project aims at object detection and navigation with high accuracy and fast response time. In this section we give some additional details on the dataset we used to train the object detection model, as well as the experimental evaluation we performed in order to identify the best candidate as the base model for our architecture, both in terms of accuracy and in terms of inference time.

6.1 Data Collection and Preprocessing

There exist several datasets appropriate for training object identification models such as COCO [7], ImageNet [30], Open AI Images [31], etc. These datasets are rich with around half a million images of hundreds of different classes. However, our application is domain-specific and thus the main requirement is for the model to detect certain specific objects such as road crossings, traffic lights, street signs, public display signs, cars, animals, trees etc. We therefore decided to use the COCO dataset for this project because it has most of the relevant classes required for pedestrian objects. This dataset has 90 classes, but not all of them are relevant to this application. Therefore, 20 irrelevant classes were removed and 70 classes were retained.

In addition, we have captured 11 classes such as trees, benches, crossing signs, curbs etc., added to the dataset and created a customized dataset which includes 81 different common objects. The images from the collected dataset came in different shapes and resolutions. Some of the images have multiple objects in them. Also, most of the images have unwanted objects within the frame that we do not intend the model to be trained on. Hence, extensive data pre-processing was needed for creating a clean dataset that was suitable for building our model. Each of the unlabeled images in the dataset was pre-processed and labeled, manually identifying all the objects in a given image and capturing bounding boxes around it. Each bounded box is defined by its corner vertices. This task was a manual, repetitive activity, and the model was retrained multiple times (with a 9:1 training to test data ratio) until we were able to detect all the pedestrian objects with good accuracy. The division also makes sure that each of the classes get distributed evenly to avoid any biases being introduced into the model.

6.2 Object Detection Model Evaluation

In order to evaluate the object detection model, we compare the detected (predicted) bounded box of each object with the actual (*ground truth*) one. For this purpose, we introduce the concept of *Intersection over Union (IoU)*. *IoU* is a measure that is used to identify whether the object detected by the model is considered correct and is defined as the ratio of the overlapping over the union of the predicted and ground truth bounding box areas, as shown in in Fig. 8.

Fig. 8. Example for calculating IoU

We also use *mean Average Precision (mAP)*, a metric commonly used to describe how well a classification model performs. The methodology for calculating *mAP* differs between different contexts, but the basic idea remains the same. For e.g., for COCO images, *mAP* is calculated by varying the *IoU* threshold over a range and calculating average precision for all the classes in the dataset. The mean of these values is then expressed in terms of a percentage metric which is called the *mAP*.

There is always a speed vs. accuracy trade-off [32] in any model when evaluating real-time object detection models. This trade-off needs to be considered when choosing a model for an Android ecosystem, along with other factors such as the model size, software platform, and object size. As previously discussed, considering the compatibility, performance, and the model size issues, we focused our design and evaluation on the YOLO and SSD models. Different versions of these two models were trained on the custom COCO dataset and evaluated. Their performance measures were computed so that the best model could be converted to TensorFlow Lite and deployed on an Android device.

Table 1 summarizes our findings. Experiments were run on a Windows PC with Intel i7 (3.0 GHz, 6-core processor) and an Nvidia GPU (GTX 1060). From the results, it's clear that YOLOv3 worked better than SSD with better accuracy and comparable inference times, when tested on systems with high computing power. However, the main aim of the project was to deploy it on the Android ecosystem using TensorFlow Lite. The biggest problem with YOLOv3 model is that it uses a DarkNet backend which has compatibility issues with TensorFlow Lite version. It also had more localization errors when compared to the SSD model. Hence YOLOv3 was discarded. Also, the ssd_mobilenet_v1_coco performed better than ssd_mobilenet_v2_coco on Samsung Galaxy Note 9 (Snapdragon 855 CPU) running Android 10. In addition, the size of the two models varied significantly as shown in Table 2.

Table 1. Evaluation results

Model Name	mAP	Inference time (ms)
YOLOv2	43	38
YOLOv3	47	22
ssd_mobilenet_v1_coco	23	35
ssd_mobilenet_v2_coco	25	41

Table 2. Model sizes on Android ecosystem

Model	Size (MB)
ssd_mobilenet_v1_coco	73
ssd_mobilenet_v2_coco	256

In summary, SSDv1 proved to be a superior model for our proposed system architecture and prototype implementation as it, a) provides the best accuracy trade-off when compared to other models, b) is small and is compatible with older versions of Android, and c) outperforms other models when it comes to large objects along with support from TensorFlow Lite.

7 Conclusion

The main motive behind the development of Viva is to make the life of visually impaired people less dependent and make their daily tasks easy and risk-free. A navigation assistant, a stand-alone object recognizer, a unique UX that works without any visual cues; all together help achieve this goal to a satisfactory level. The modularized approach to building this application means that different aspects of the application can be improved with over-the-air updates including the most important component – the object detection model. As more data is collected, the model can be refined and deployed to existing users, to make the app usage experience better and more reliable. Moreover, new ideas have been identified to make this product more reliable and faster. The UX can be made more user friendly based on the feedback from users. The application acts like a virtual assistant available at the user's fingertips to help them with daily activities by identifying objects and providing safe navigation.

This application is made adaptable and extensible for future enhancements. Current application can be improved by enhancing the risk prediction algorithm to use additional data from depth-sensing cameras and lidars that are included in some modern phones. This would result in more accurate estimation of the distance between the object and the user. Adding Infrared technology of certain cameras will help to support night-vision with the current application. Integration of the assistant on custom IoT devices that can support TensorFlow Lite can be used to build gadgets like smart walking canes. This will further extend the future scope of this work.

References

1. WHO World Report on Vision 2020. https://www.who.int/publications/i/item/world-report-on-vision. Retrieved on Feb 2021)
2. Bourne, R.R.A., et al.: Global prevalence of blindness and distance and near vision impairment in 2020: progress towards the vision 2020 targets and what the future holds. Invest. Ophthalmol. Vis. Sci. **61**(7), 2317 (2020)
3. WHO fact sheet on blindness and visual impairment. https://www.who.int/news-room/fact-sheets/detail/blindness-and-visual-impairment. Retrieved on Feb 2021
4. Liu, W., Anguelov, D., Erhan, D., Szegedy, C., Reed, S., Fu, C.-Y., Berg, Alexander C.: SSD: single shot multibox detector. In: Leibe, B., Matas, J., Sebe, N., Welling, M. (eds.) ECCV 2016. LNCS, vol. 9905, pp. 21–37. Springer, Cham (2016). https://doi.org/10.1007/978-3-319-46448-0_2
5. Zhao, L., Li, S.: Object detection algorithm based on improved YOLOv3. Electronics **9**, 537 (2020). https://doi.org/10.3390/electronics9030537
6. Lin, T.-Y., Maire, M., Belongie, S., Hays, J., Perona, P., Ramanan, D., Dollár, P., Zitnick, C.Lawrence: Microsoft COCO: common objects in context. In: Fleet, D., Pajdla, T., Schiele, B., Tuytelaars, T. (eds.) ECCV 2014. LNCS, vol. 8693, pp. 740–755. Springer, Cham (2014). https://doi.org/10.1007/978-3-319-10602-1_48
7. COCO dataset. https://cocodataset.org/#download. https://github.com/cocodataset/cocoapi. Retrieved May 2020
8. Pachodiwale, Z.A., Brahmankar, Y., Parakh, N., Patel, D.: Virtual Assistant for Visually Impaired Video (2020). https://youtu.be/fDmqeYOlYWU
9. Smart band, Sunu band. https://www.sunu.com/en/index. Retrieved on Feb 2021
10. Ambutech. iGlasses Ultrasonic Mobility Aid. https://ambutech.com/products/iglasses%E2%84%A2-ultrasonic-mobility-aid. Retrieved on Feb 2021
11. AFB: LowViz Guide: Indoor Navigation for People who are Blind or Visually Impaired. AccessWorld, July (2015). https://www.afb.org/aw/16/7/15437. Retrieved on Feb 2021
12. Extended Visual Assistant "Eva". https://www.eva.vision. Retrieved on Feb 2021
13. Aljahdali, M., Abokhamees, R., Bensenouci, A., Brahimi, T., Bensenouci, M.: IoT based assistive walker device for frail &visually impaired people. In: 2018 15th Learning and Technology Conference (L&T), Jeddah, pp. 171–177 (2018). https://doi.org/10.1109/lt.2018.8368503
14. Hung, D.N., Minh-Thanh, V., Minh-Triet, N., Huy, Q.L., Cuong, V.T.: Design and implementation of smart cane for visually impaired people. BME 2017. IP, vol. 63, pp. 249–254. Springer, Singapore (2018). https://doi.org/10.1007/978-981-10-4361-1_41
15. Nisha, K.K., Pruthvi, H.R., Ashwini, T.S., Hadimani, S.N., Domanal, S., Ram Mohana Reddy, G.: An android GPS-based navigation application for blind. In: The 7th International Symposium on Visual Information Communication and Interaction, pp. 240–241 (2014). https://doi.org/10.1145/2636240.2636878
16. Harish Kumar, N., Deepak, G., Nagaraja, J.: An IoT based obstacle detection and alerting system in vehicles using ultrasonic sensor. In: International Journal of Engineering Research & Technology (IJERT) NCETEIT, vol. 5, Issue 20 (2017)
17. Girshick, R., Donahue, J., Darrell, T., Malik, J.: Rich feature hierarchies for accurate object detection and semantic segmentation. In: IEEE Conference on Computer Vision and Pattern Recognition, Columbus, OH, pp. 580–587 (2014). https://doi.org/10.1109/cvpr.2014.81

18. Girshick, R.: Fast R-CNN. In: IEEE International Conference on Computer Vision (ICCV), Santiago, pp. 1440–1448 (2015). https://doi.org/10.1109/iccv.2015.169
19. Ren, S., He, K., Girshick, R., Sun, J.: Faster R-CNN: towards real-time object detection with region proposal networks. IEEE Trans. Pattern Anal. Mach. Intell. **39**(6), 1137–1149 (2017). https://doi.org/10.1109/TPAMI.2016.2577031
20. Lee, J., Wang, J., Crandall, D., Sabanovic, S., Fox, G.: Real-time, cloud-based object detection for unmanned aerial vehicles. In: First IEEE International Conference on Robotic Computing (IRC), pp. 36–43 (2017). https://doi.org/10.1109/irc.2017.77
21. Beksi, W.J., Spruth, J., Papanikolopoulos, N.: CORE: a cloud-based object recognition engine for robotics. In: International Conference on Intelligent Robots and Systems, IROS 2015, Hamburg, Germany, pp. 4512–4517 (2015). https://doi.org/10.1109/iros.2015.7354018
22. Meliones, A., Filios, C.: BlindHelper: a pedestrian navigation system for blinds and visually impaired. In: Proceedings of the 9th ACM International Conference on PErvasive Technologies Related to Assistive Environments (PETRA 2016). ACM, New York, NY, USA, Article 26, pp. 1–4 (2016). https://doi.org/10.1145/2910674.2910721
23. Transfer Learning in Keras with Computer Vision Models. https://machinelearningmastery.com/how-to-use-transfer-learning-when-developing-convolutional-neural-network-models/. Retrieved on Feb 2021
24. Test-To-Speech API. https://developer.android.com/reference/android/speech/tts/TextToSpeech. Retrieved on Feb 2021
25. Speech Recognizer API. https://developer.android.com/reference/android/speech/SpeechRecognizer. Retrieved on Feb 2021
26. Camera2API package. https://developer.android.com/reference/android/hardware/camera2/package-summary. Retrieved on Feb 2021
27. TensorFlow Lite API. https://www.tensorflow.org/lite/guide/build_android. Retrieved on Feb 2021
28. Simonyan, K., Zisserman, A.: Very deep convolutional networks for large-scale image recognition. arXiv preprint arXiv:1409.1556, ICLR (2015). https://arxiv.org/abs/1409.1556
29. Inception Resnet version2. https://tfhub.dev/google/faster_rcnn/openimages_v4/inception_resnet_v2/1. Retrieved on May 2020
30. ImageNet dataset. http://www.image-net.org/. Retrieved on May 2020
31. OpenAI. https://openai.com/. Retrieved on Feb 2021
32. Huang, J.: Speed/accuracy trade-offs for modern convolutional object detectors. In: 2017 IEEE Conference on Computer Vision and Pattern Recognition (CVPR), Honolulu, HI, USA, 2017, pp. 3296–3297 (2017). https://doi.org/10.1109/cvpr.2017.351

Designing 3D Printed Audio-Tactile Graphics: Recommendations from Prior Research

Emilia Christie Picelli Sanches$^{(\boxtimes)}$ ⓘ, Juliana Bueno ⓘ,
and Maria Lucia Leite Ribeiro Okimoto ⓘ

Federal University of Paraná, UFPR, Curitiba, PR 80060-150, Brazil

Abstract. 3D printed audio-tactile graphics are interactive materials aimed at the accessibility of people with visual impairment. There is not yet a consensus on how to design 3D printed audio-tactile graphics and most publications on this topic follow an empirical approach, experimenting first and learning with the process. However, these research publications show meaningful knowledge that can serve as the base for a set of compiled design recommendations. The goal of this paper is to present recommendations that were analyzed and extracted from 32 publications found in a systematic literature review. In total, 57 recommendations compose the set.

Keywords: 3D printing · Audio-tactile graphics · Visual impairment

1 Introduction

Audio-tactile graphics are interactive and accessible materials for people with visual impairment, especially blind. They can be used as a learning aid, for orientation and mobility, or to enhance access to cultural heritage, for example [15, 19, 30]. Audio-tactile graphics can be defined as a tactile graphic augmented with audio descriptions or feedback. Mixing auditory and tactile senses to assist the blind is not a new concept, though digital fabrications techniques are being explored more recently as a way to fabricate Assistive Technology.

As such, 3D printing is one of technologies being adopted to produce the tactile surface, with an electronic compound to add audio. These are 3D printed audio-tactile graphics. In recent research, other denominations are also used to describe the same material, such as interactive 3D printed model [28], 3D printed interactive small-scale models [8] or audio-responsive tactile templates [18].

Through a systematic literature review on the topic, publications of the last 6 years were analyzed. Most publications follow an empirical approach, meaning that they are inclined to develop prototypes first, then learn with the process. Although every publication is found to be actively important for advancing research on 3D printed audio-tactile graphics, this tends to individualize and scatter information. For example, just on technology alone, choices are varied, from computer vision, to wearables, to touchscreens, to electronic boards. Interaction goes from using touch gestures, to speech commands, to buttons. These are valid findings that could be combined to be used as a resource for future applications.

© Springer Nature Switzerland AG 2021
M. Antona and C. Stephanidis (Eds.): HCII 2021, LNCS 12768, pp. 461–472, 2021.
https://doi.org/10.1007/978-3-030-78092-0_31

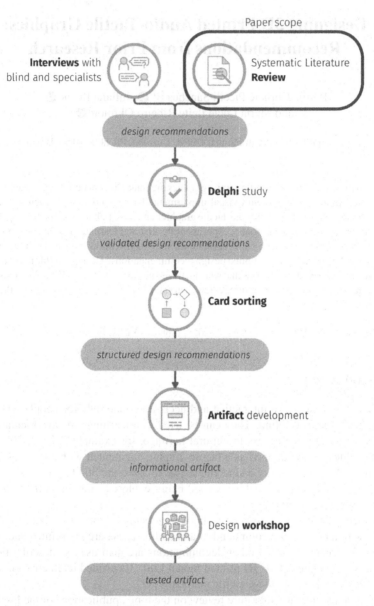

Fig. 1. Doctorate research method.

To address that, a doctorate research is being conducted, which started from the point of view that it is possible and desirable to take a step back and consolidate already published knowledge, before attempting to design new audio-tactile graphics. The doctorate objective is to present a different approach to the matter, proposing that there is space for an auxiliary artifact to help the community design 3D printed audio-tactile graphics, starting from information already published. The objective of this paper, however, is to present initial results.

To give an overall understanding of the research before presenting results, the doctorate method design is explained. It is designed to begin with gathering recommendations or guidelines, then validate them with people with vision impairment and accessibility specialists. Afterwards, the idea is to cocreate an artifact to contain these validated design recommendations. Figure 1 shows the method.

As shown by the figure, six steps are planned to develop the artifact. The goal of this artifact is to empower and help the community (such as makers, educators, and accessibility professionals) develop their own 3D printed audio-tactile graphics. To narrow the scope of this project, the focus is on educational graphics.

As stated before, it starts with learning from already published research. To achieve that, a systematic literature review is proposed. This step was already conducted and will be discussed here.

Interviews with stakeholders (blind, educators, accessibility specialists) was set to be complementary to this set of recommendations. Next, in order to reach consensus among specialists about the set, a Delphi study is proposed. The study works on validating the set of design recommendations on how to develop 3D printed audio-tactile graphics.

To begin developing an artifact, a card sorting is proposed. The aim is to structure recommendations in a significant order and categorization by stakeholders, rather than an arbitrary one made by the researcher. Then, the artifact is designed.

Lastly, to test if the artifact containing all recommendations works, a design workshop is proposed. With the workshop, small groups attempt to develop their own prototypes based solely on the artifact, making suggestions along the way to help improve the artifact.

In this paper, the goal is to present how the systematic literature review was conducted and exhibit its results. To address that, the article s divided in (1) introduction; (2) related work; (3) systematic literature review; (4) recommendations on how to design 3D printed audio-tactile graphics; and (5) conclusions.

2   Related Work

As stated before, publications about 3D printed audio-tactile graphics tend to focus on the technology used, experimenting and prototyping. However, some publications also presented with some guidelines or recommendations about how to design 3D printed audio-tactile graphics, each based on their own experiences.

Four design recommendations were made by [3] for the education of blind children, based on the authors' studies with multi-sensory interactive maps. Another study [15], after testing different compositions of interaction on an audio-tactile map, presents a set of guidelines for 3D printed maps and plans, and also for teaching touch readers how to interact with the map. Other set of guidelines were made to develop the specific part of labelling the audio-tactile graphic [26]. Also, for the education of blind students, a set of ten design guidelines were proposed based on a workshop and an instructional design study using interactive 3D printed models [30].

Lastly, based on the authors' experience and testing, [19] presents guidelines for the reproduction of buildings or large sites, for the accessibility of visually impaired people in cultural sites. This publication was found to be the most thorough, with guidelines descriptions and suggestions for implementation.

All these guidelines and recommendations compose the set here on this paper, along with other publications that did not explicitly propose recommendations, but were also relevant on their findings.

3   Systematic Literature Review

As stated in the introduction, this paper scope is to present recommendations based on the results of a systematic literature review. For transparency, here we present parameters used. One goal was to comprehend the state of the art of 3D printed audio-tactile graphics aimed at people with visual impairment and another was to extract recommendations from publications. First, an overview of all the steps taken is presented in Fig. 2. Then, details about databases, search strings, inclusion and exclusion criteria and reading phases are explained.

Fig. 2. Systematic literature review.

For the search, three major databases were selected: Scopus, Science Direct and Google Scholar. The later was selected as to include paper proceedings, thesis and dissertations as well, so the results would not be restricted to journal articles. The search also was conducted with strings both in Portuguese and English, in order to involve national and international publications (the review was conducted in Brazil).

Both search strings were was followed:

- English: (audio OR auditory) AND (tactile OR haptic) AND (image OR map OR graphic OR model) AND ("visual impairment" OR blindness OR blind OR "low vision") AND ("3D printing" OR "additive manufacturing") AND accessibility.
- Portuguese: *(áudio OR auditivo) AND (tátil OR háptico) AND (imagem OR mapa OR gráfico OR modelo) AND ("deficiência visual" OR cegueira OR cego OR "baixa visão") AND ("impressão 3D" OR "manufatura aditiva") AND acessibilidade.*

Inclusion criteria were:

- Articles, papers, master thesis or doctorate dissertations published between 2015 and 2020;
- Written in English, Portuguese or Spanish;
- Other review publications about audio-tactile graphics;
- Publications with guidelines, recommendations or requirements for the design of 3D printed audio-tactile graphics;
- Publications with prototyping and experimentation on 3D printed audio-tactile graphics;
- Both qualitative and/or quantitative methods;
- Full text available.

Exclusion criteria were:

- Tactile sense is mentioned only for Braille;
- Adaptation of graphics are only for audio descriptions;
- There is no relation to accessibility of people with visual impairment;
- Solely comparisons between blind and sighted perceptions;
- Audio-tactile graphics are not produced by 3D printing;
- Non academic articles, book reviews, opinion articles, abstracts, bachelor dissertations.

As shown by the overview figure, three reading stages were conducted during the review, each serving as a filter for the subsequent stage. In the first reading stage, titles, abstracts and keywords were analysed. In the second reading stage, remained publications had their introduction and conclusion analysed. On the last reading stage, whole publications were read.

In total, 1102 publications were collected through databases and inserted into Zotero, a research and references management software. After that, duplicates (meaning, the same publication appearing in two or three databases) were excluded, resulting in 1058 publications – which were then passed through reading stages.

It is worth noting that this was conducted between January and February of 2020. To keep the review up to date, alerts were set on each database, so the reading process is continued. Table 1 shows quantitative results obtained on each stage.

Table 1. Systematic literature review results for each stage.

Stages	Entry	Output
Database search	–	1102
Duplicates exclusion	1102	1058
Reading of title, abstract and keywords	1058	179
Reading of introduction and conclusion	179	47
Full reading of publication	47	29
Publication from alerts	(ongoing)	3
Total of accepted publications	–	**32**

Table 2 shows publication titles, authorship and the year it was published.

Table 2. Publications from the systematic literature review.

Title	Authorship	Year
Accessible museum collections for the visually impaired: combining tactile exploration, audio descriptions and mobile gestures	Anagnostakis et al. [1]	2016
Multimodal augmentation of surfaces using conductive 3D printing	Brito et al. [2]	2016
MapSense: design and field study of interactive maps for children living with visual impairments	Brule et al. [3]	2016
TangibleCircuits: an interactive 3D printed circuit education tool for people with visual impairments	Davis et al. [4]	2020
Tooteko: a case study of augmented reality for an accessible cultural heritage. Digitization, 3D printing and sensors for an audio-tactile experience	D'Agnano et al. [5]	2015
The cross-sensory globe: co-designing a 3D audio-tactile globe prototype for blind and low-vision users to learn geography	Ghodke [6]	2019
The cross-sensory globe: participatory design of a 3D audio-tactile globe prototype for blind and low-vision users to learn geography	Ghodke et al. [7]	2019
Map learning with a 3D printed interactive small-scale model: improvement of space and text memorization in visually impaired students	Giraud et al. [8]	2017
Empowering low-vision rehabilitation professionals with "do-it-yourself" methods	Giraud and Jouffrais [9]	2016
CapMaps: capacitive sensing 3D printed audio-tactile maps	Götzelmann [10]	2016
LucentMaps: 3D printed audiovisual tactile maps for blind and visually impaired people	Götzelmann [11]	2016
Visually augmented audio-tactile graphics for visually impaired people	Götzelmann [12]	2018
SmartTactMaps: a smartphone-based approach to support blind persons in exploring tactile maps	Götzelmann and Winkler [13]	2015

(*continued*)

Table 2. (*continued*)

Title	Authorship	Year
TacTILE: a preliminary toolchain for creating accessible graphics with 3D-printed overlays and auditory annotations	He et al. [14]	2017
Accessible maps for the blind: comparing 3D printed models with tactile graphics	Holloway et al. [15]	2018
A tangible interface-based application for teaching tactual shape perception and spatial awareness sub-concepts to visually impaired children	Jafri et al. [16]	2015
A tangible user interface-based application utilizing 3D-printed manipulatives for teaching tactual shape perception and spatial awareness sub-concepts to visually impaired children	Jafri et al. [17]	2017
Making 3D laser cut stratigraphic audio-responsive tactile templates	Kolitsky [18]	2019
Design guidelines for an interactive 3D model as a supporting tool for exploring a cultural site by visually impaired and sighted people	Leporini et al. [19]	2020
An interactive multimodal guide to improve art accessibility for blind people	Quero et al. [20]	2018
"Hey Model!" – natural user interactions and agency in accessible interactive 3D models	Reinders et al. [21]	2020
Enabling access to cultural heritage for the visually impaired: an interactive 3D model of a cultural site	Rossetti et al. [22]	2018
Smart cultural site: an interactive 3D model accessible to people with visual impairment	Rossetti et al. [23]	2018
Talkabel: a labeling method for 3d printed models	Shi [24]	2015
Magic touch: Interacting with 3D printed graphics	Shi et al. [25]	2016
Tickers and talker: an accessible labeling toolkit for 3D printed models	Shi et al. [26]	2016
Designing interactions for 3D printed models with blind people	Shi et al. [27]	2017
Markit and Talkit: a low-barrier toolkit to augment 3D printed models with audio annotations	Shi et al. [28]	2017
A demo of talkit++: interacting with 3D printed models using an iOS device	Shi et al. [29]	2018
Designing interactive 3D printed models with teachers of the visually impaired	Shi et al. [30]	2019
Customizable 3D printed tactile maps as interactive overlays	Taylor et al. [31]	2016
Blowhole: blowing-Activated Tags for Interactive 3D-Printed Models	Tejada et al. [32]	2018

4   Recommendations on How to Design 3D Printed Audio-Tactile Graphics

In total, 32 publications from conferences, journals and a master's thesis, published between 2015 and 2020, were found to be relevant. After analysis from each work, information was transformed into a set of 57 recommendations. Recommendations were categorized into (1) Development; (2) Use; and (3) Context.

These recommendations were drawn from explicit stated guidelines /recommendations from other authors, or from authors' procedures and results. Tables 3, 4, and 5 bring them, stating original sources of where they came from.

Table 3. Recommendations from the category development.

Recommendations	Sources
3D printing can be combined with low-cost electronics (examples: NFC tags, capacitive sensors, PIR sensors, Arduino boards, Touch Board, Raspberry Pi, Makey Makey, Lilypad, proximity sensors)	[1–3, 5, 8, 9, 15, 19, 20, 22, 23, 31]
3D scanning is a way to acquire accurate and detailed models of the real object	[1, 5, 22, 23]
Resin can be used as 3D printing material	[5]
PLA or ABS can be used as material for 3D printing	[10, 23, 30, 32]
Conductive material can be 3D printed where there are points of interaction by audio or as a way to integrate an electronic device. An alternative is the use of conductive paint	[2–4, 10–12, 18, 20, 31]
3D printing can be combined with other digital manufacturing processes, such as laser cutting, or even other materials (creating different textures)	[8, 18, 19, 22, 23, 30]
Tablets and smartphones are tools that can be integrated in the development of audio-tactile graphics (apps, touch screens, cameras)	[1, 3, 5, 10–14, 18, 24, 26, 28, 29, 31]
Computer vision can be integrated into the development of audio-tactile graphics (shape recognition, finger position)	[2, 16, 17, 25, 28, 29]
Audios from the graphic must be in accordance with the needs of each blind person (including information in other languages, if necessary)	[5, 22, 23, 30]
Audios are not just verbal. One can make use of music and other non-verbal sounds (sound indicating error or success; playful sounds; ambient sounds; sound effects; animal sounds)	[3, 5, 9, 16, 17, 20, 29, 30]
Audio information can explore levels of complexity or type of information, according to the gesture applied or button pressed (example: one tap, name; two taps: explanation; voice command: more detailed information), avoiding information overload.	[4, 10–12, 15, 19, 22, 23, 27, 30]
Use of tactile/haptic gestures to trigger audio information (pointing, tapping with the finger, scanning with the index finger, scanning with the thumb, pinching, following the edge with the finger, friction with the finger, one tap, two taps, three taps, two taps with two fingers, long press, fast stroke, slow stroke). Similar to those used on smartphones or in natural gestures of tactile exploration	[1, 4, 10–13, 15, 20, 21, 25, 27–30]
Use of typical and familiar movements of tactile exploration to develop the graphic. Five movements are important in tactile exploration. 1. Feel: feel the textures and shape of the graphic; 2. Measure: use of hands to approximately measure the size of tactile elements; 3. Compare: compare two tactile elements to see if they represent the same concept; 4. Count: count the same tactile elements in the graphic; 5. Communicate: indicate, explain or inquire about the graphic. The movement can be to feel the graphic as a whole or elements individually.	[15, 27]
Use of typical and familiar postures of the hand to develop the graphic. Four hand positions are often used in tactile exploration. 1. Grab: hold the graphic with one hand and explore with the other; 2. Stabilize: use one hand to fix the graphic on the table and use the other to explore; 3. Diverge: exploration with two hands in different elements; 4. Converge: exploration with two hands in one element	[27]
To avoid accidental activation of audio by tactile scanning, a time delay for the audio to be released can be added (example: long press for 1 s for the audio to start playing). Activating an audio must be the result of a definitive action	[15, 28]
Buttons (in different formats) can be used as an auxiliary component to obtain audio information, or to have the function on/off	[19, 22, 23, 27, 28, 30]
Use of voice commands to trigger audio information (use of keywords for recognition. Examples: "more information", "distance", "what is that?", "save information")	[11–13, 21, 27–30]
To avoid unintended commands, when using voice command, implement a keyword or a button to be pressed that will trigger the recognition of the command (example: computer, play track 1)	[11, 12]
Acoustic sounds can be used as a way to trigger audios (examples: sound of the finger touching the graphic, acoustic devices)	[24, 26, 32]
Available databases can serve as a tool for the development of tactile map surfaces - automatically or not (example: OpenStreetMap, Google Place, tactilemap.net, GIS data)	[7, 10–13, 31]

(*continued*)

Table 3. (*continued*)

Recommendations	Sources
Audio-tactile graphics can range from only relief to completely three-dimensional models (without a flat base)	[15, 17, 26, 30]
Braille information is replaced by audio recordings. Braille can be used for small markings or labels (example: titles; indication of where to start)	[6, 8, 11–17, 19, 21, 31]
It is necessary to insert markers (easily detectable by touch or computer vision) to indicate points where there are audio responses. They must be designed so that they are not confused with tactile elements of the graphic. These points must not significantly alter or distort the tactile surface	[15, 24–26, 32]
Involve blind individuals and teachers in the process of developing audio-tactile graphics (as users, testers, informants or collaborators). Examples: observations, interviews, diaries, collaborative prototyping, co-design	[3, 6, 7, 9 30]
Colors can be used, as a way of including sighted or people with low vision, also because they have symbolic meanings for blind people	[3, 12, 17, 30]
In addition to touch and hearing, other senses can be stimulated for extra complementary interaction (smell, taste, sight)	[3, 11, 12, 29, 30]
Audio-tactile graphics can be developed from modifications to existing 3D models (examples: found on websites such as thingiverse.com, NIH 3D Print Exchange, Nasa 3D Resources, APH Tactile Image Library, National Library of Medicine Visible Human, terrestrial globes)	[6, 7, 18, 26–30, 32]
Keep the process simple or provide the necessary tools so that even non-specialist people (in 3D printing and electronics) can develop their own audio-tactile graphics	[8, 28, 32]
The audio-tactile graphic can have different shapes, sizes, patterns and textures to accommodate the needs and preferences of each blind person, also to differentiate elements in the tactile surface. The tactile information must be simple, clear and salient, without redundant tactile information or exaggerated details that can confuse the blind user	[17, 27, 30]
The technology used must be robust and relatively inexpensive	[4, 15]
When possible, use iconic or well-established 3D symbols to represent tactile elements	[15]
Make sure there are no sharp edges to avoid discomfort	[15]
Small details and decorations (of the real object or graphic) must be eliminated in the design of tactile elements. If necessary, make a separate audio-tactile graphic on a larger scale to show these details	[19, 22, 23]
Design audio-tactile graphic considering the limitations and characteristics of the available 3D printer (example: maximum print size)	[22]
Maintain consistency across different audio-tactile graphics (example: buttons always in the same position)	[19, 23]
3D printing parameters should be adjusted to prevent imperfections from being confused with textures or tactile components	[30]
Use of three-dimensional representation of tactile elements to be closer to the real object	[4]
In the audio-tactile graphic, greater emphasis is placed on tactile information, with complementary audio to enrich tactile exploration	[19, 21]
The audio-tactile graphic must provide audible intervention in case of errors (for example: a moving part that has been placed wrongly)	[21]
The interaction hierarchy of the audio-tactile graphic is (1) tactile exploration; (2) tactile gestures to listen audios; (3) voice command to hear additional information or confirm understanding	[21]
Divide the digital 3D model into several parts according to the 3D printers available, to facilitate printing	[19]

These recommendations, as stated before, are the basis for and informational artifact. However, they are already useful for other researchers as it helps synthesize prior work for future applications. We hope to continue discussing and exchanging information on the topic.

Table 4. Recommendations from the category use.

Recommendations	Sources
Allow the blind person to use both hands for tactile exploration	[5, 8, 15, 22, 28]
Audio-tactile graphics must be portable	[11, 13]
Interaction must allow the blind person to have control of the information (examples: pause audios, move between categories of information, select, return to the previous audio, turn it on and off)	[1, 15, 19, 21, 23, 28]
Visual, auditory and tactile aesthetic quality is beneficial for the social and cultural inclusion of children	[3]
Use of playful and reflective scenarios for children, together with audio-tactile graphics, can be used to stimulate engagement and access to symbolic representations	[3]
Use of do-it-yourself methods to provide personalizations for children and caregivers (example: students recording their own audios, teachers learning and developing their own 3D prints)	[3, 9, 30]
Use of movable tangible parts to increase the interaction of the blind person with the audio-tactile graphic	[3, 6–8, 17, 21, 30, 32]
All tactile elements must have a compatible size/elevation to be understood by the fingers	[11, 12, 15, 22, 23]
The use of headphones is necessary so that the blind person can focus on the information.	[8, 20]
The audio-tactile graphic can be reused in other contexts just by changing audios at each point of tactile interaction, to personalize information according to the user's perceptual and cognitive skills, or according to the pedagogical objectives	[8, 15, 30]
It is necessary to instruct new users on how to read an audio-tactile graphic, as the dynamics are different from ordinary tactile graphics (example: encouraging to explore the whole graphic, such as sides and base, feeling different heights, etc.)	[15, 19, 30]
The audio information should be easy to add to the tactile model. They must be intuitive and easy to be accessed by blind people	[15, 26, 28]
It is necessary to ensure independence (of use and interpretation of content) for the user	[19, 21]

Table 5. Recommendations from the category context.

Recommendations	Sources
Comments in audio can be added to contextualize the blind person (examples: to position the camera in the correct location, to instruct in the use of the graphic, to exemplify commands, to position the graphic in the correct location, to provide a general context, etc.)	[1, 3, 11, 13, 17, 19, 20, 22, 23, 28, 30]
Audio-tactile graphics can be stored and shared online to other communities	[26, 28, 29]
Contextualize broadly audio-tactile graphics before tactile exploration	[15, 30]

5   Conclusions

The goal of this paper was to present recommendations on how to design 3D printed audio-tactile graphics, from research already published. These recommendations are initial results of an ongoing doctorate research.

To gather relevant publications on this matter, a systematic literature review was conducted in January and February of 2020, with follow ups throughout the same year. Currently, 32 publications were found to be relevant and were analysed. From those, 57 recommendations were drawn and presented here in tables, specifying from which source each recommendation came from.

Even if it is an ongoing research, these findings can already be beneficial for other researchers studying the topic. Going further, updates on this set of recommendations is expected, as it will be validated and tested by experts on accessibility, blind collaborators and educators.

References

1. Anagnostakis, G., et al.: Accessible museum collections for the visually impaired: combining tactile exploration, audio descriptions and mobile gestures. In: 18th International Conference on Human-Computer Interaction with Mobile Devices and Services, pp. 1021–1025. ACM, Florence (2016)
2. Brito, C., Barros, G., Correia, W., Teichrieb, V., Teixeira, J.: Multimodal augmentation of surfaces using conductive 3D printing. In: ACM SIGGRAPH 2016 Posters, pp. 1–2. ACM, Anaheim (2016)
3. Brule, E., Bailly, G., Brock, A., Valentin, F., Denis, G., Jouffrais, C.: MapSense: design and field study of interactive maps for children living with visual impairments. In: Proceedings of the 2016 CHI Conference on Human Factors in Computing Systems, pp. 445–457. ACM, San Jose (2016)
4. Davis, J., et al.: TangibleCircuits: an interactive 3D printed circuit education tool for people with visual impairments. In: Proceedings of the 2020 CHI Conference on Human Factors in Computing Systems, pp. 1–13. ACM, Honolulu (2020)
5. D'Agnano, F., Balletti, C., Guerra, F., Vernier, P.: Tooteko: a case study of augmented reality for an accessible cultural heritage. Digitization, 3D printing and sensors for an audio-tactile experience. In: The International Archives of the Photogrammetry, Remote Sensing and Spatial Information Sciences, pp. 207–213. ACM, Avila (2015)
6. Ghodke, U.: The Cross-Sensory Globe: Co-Designing a 3D Audio-Tactile Globe Prototype for Blind and Low-Vision Users to Learn Geography. OCAD University, Toronto (2019)
7. Ghodke, U., Yusim, L., Somanath, S., Coppin, P.: The cross-sensory globe: participatory design of a 3D audio-tactile globe prototype for blind and low-vision users to learn geography. In: Proceedings of the 2019 on Designing Interactive Systems Conference, pp. 399–412. Canadian Human-Computer Communications Society, San Diego (2019)
8. Giraud, S., Brock, A., Macé, M., Jouffrais, C.: Map learning with a 3D printed interactive small-scale model: Improvement of space and text memorization in visually impaired students. Front. Psychol. **8**, 930 (2017)
9. Giraud, S., Jouffrais, C.: Empowering low-vision rehabilitation professionals with "do-it-yourself" methods. In: Miesenberger, K., Bühler, C., Penaz, P. (eds.) ICCHP 2016. LNCS, vol. 9759, pp. 61–68. Springer, Cham (2016). https://doi.org/10.1007/978-3-319-41267-2_9
10. Götzelmann, T.: CapMaps: Capacitive sensing 3D printed audio-tactile maps. In: Buhler, C., Penaz, P., Miesenberger, K. (eds.) Lecture Notes in Computer Science (including subseries Lecture Notes in Artificial Intelligence and Lecture Notes in Bioinformatics), pp. 146–152. Springer, Verlag (2016)
11. Götzelmann, T.: LucentMaps: 3D printed audiovisual tactile maps for blind and visually impaired people. In: Proceedings of the 18th International ACM SIGACCESS Conference on Computers and Accessibility, pp. 81–90. ACM, Reno (2016)
12. Götzelmann, T.: Visually augmented audio-tactile graphics for visually impaired people. ACM Trans. Access. Comput. **11**(2), 8 (2018)
13. Götzelmann, T., Winkler, K.: SmartTactMaps: a smartphone-based approach to support blind persons in exploring tactile maps. In: Proceedings of the 8th ACM International Conference on PErvasive Technologies Related to Assistive Environments, pp. 1–8. ACM, Corfu, (2015)
14. He, L., Wan, Z., Findlater, L., Froehlich, J.: TacTILE: a preliminary toolchain for creating accessible graphics with 3D-printed overlays and auditory annotations. In: Proceedings of the 19th International ACM SIGACCESS Conference on Computers and Accessibility, pp. 397–398. ACM, Baltimore (2017)
15. Holloway, L., Marriott, K., Butler, M.: Accessible maps for the blind: comparing 3D printed models with tactile graphics. In: Proceedings of the Conference on Human Factors in Computing Systems, pp. 1–13. ACM, Montreal (2018)

16. Jafri, R., Aljuhani, A., Ali, S.: A tangible interface-based application for teaching tactual shape perception and spatial awareness sub-concepts to visually impaired children. Procedia Manuf. **3**, 5562–5569 (2015)

17. Jafri, R., Aljuhani, A., Ali, S.: A tangible user interface-based application utilizing 3D-printed manipulatives for teaching tactual shape perception and spatial awareness sub-concepts to visually impaired children. Int. J. Child-Comput. Interact. **11**, 3–11 (2017)

18. Kolitsky, M.A.: Making 3D laser cut stratigraphic audio-responsive tactile templates. J. Sci. Educ. Stud. Disabil. **22**(1), 5 (2019)

19. Leporini, B., Rossetti, V., Furfari, F., Pelagatti, S., Quarta, A.: Design guidelines for an interactive 3D model as a supporting tool for exploring a cultural site by visually impaired and sighted people. ACM Trans. Access. Comput. **13**(3), 1–39 (2020)

20. Quero, L., Bartolomé, J., Lee, S., Han, E., Kim, S., Cho, J.: An interactive multimodal guide to improve art accessibility for blind people. In: Proceedings of the 20th International ACM SIGACCESS Conference on Computers and Accessibility, pp. 346–348. ACM, Galway (2018)

21. Reinders, S., Butler, M., Marriott, K.: "Hey Model!" – natural user interactions and agency in accessible interactive 3D models. In: Proceedings of the 2020 CHI Conference on Human Factors in Computing Systems, pp. 1–13. ACM, Honolulu (2020)

22. Rossetti, V., Furfari, F., Leporini, B., Pelagatti, S., Quarta, A.: Enabling access to cultural heritage for the visually impaired: an interactive 3D model of a cultural site. Procedia Comput. Sci. **130**, 383–391 (2018)

23. Rossetti, V., Furfari, F., Leporini, B., Pelagatti, S., Quarta, A.: Smart cultural site: an interactive 3D model accessible to people with visual impairment. IOP Conf. Ser.: Mater. Sci. Eng. **364**, 1–8 (2018)

24. Shi, L.: Talkabel: a labeling method for 3D printed models. In: Proceedings of the 17th International ACM SIGACCESS Conference on Computers and Accessibility, pp. 361–362. ACM, Lisbon (2015)

25. Shi, L., McLachlan, R., Zhao, Y., Azenkot, S.: Magic touch: interacting with 3D printed graphics. In: Proceedings of the 18th International ACM SIGACCESS Conference on Computers and Accessibility, pp. 329–330. ACM, Reno (2016)

26. Shi, L., Zelzer, I., Feng, C., Azenkot, S.: Tickers and talker: an accessible labeling toolkit for 3D printed models. In: Proceedings of the Conference on Human Factors in Computing Systems, pp. 4896–4907. ACM, San Jose (2016)

27. Shi, L., Zhao, Y., Azenkot, S.: Designing interactions for 3D printed models with blind people. In: Proceedings of the 19th International ACM SIGACCESS Conference on Computers and Accessibility, pp. 200–209. ACM, Baltimore (2017)

28. Shi, L., Zhao, Y., Azenkot, S.: Markit and Talkit: a low-barrier toolkit to augment 3D printed models with audio annotations. In: Proceedings of the 30th Annual ACM Symposium on User Interface Software and Technology, pp. 493–506. ACM, Québec City (2017)

29. Shi, L., Zhang, Z., Azenkot, S.: A demo of talkit++: Interacting with 3D printed models using an iOS device. In: Proceedings of the 20th International ACM SIGACCESS Conference on Computers and Accessibility. pp. 429–431. ACM, Galway (2018)

30. Shi, L., Lawson, H., Zhang, Z., Azenkot, S.: Designing interactive 3D printed models with teachers of the visually impaired. In: Proceedings of the 2019 CHI Conference on Human Factors in Computing Systems, pp. 1–14. ACM, Glasgow (2019)

31. Taylor, B., Dey, A., Siewiorek, D., Smailagic, A.: Customizable 3D printed tactile maps as interactive overlays. In: Proceedings of the 18th International ACM SIGACCESS Conference on Computers and Accessibility, pp. 71–79. ACM, Reno (2016)

32. Tejada, C., Fujimoto, O., Li, Z., Ashbrook, D.: Blowhole: blowing-activated tags for interactive 3D-printed models. In: Proceedings of the 44th Graphics Interface Conference, pp. 131–137. ACM, Toronto (2018)

Adaptive Augmentative and Alternative Communication Systems for People with Neuromuscular Pathologies

Jhon Fernando Sanchez Alvarez[1]([⊠]), Gloria Patricia Jaramillo Alvarez[2]([⊠]), and Claudio Camilo Gonzalez Clavijo[1]([⊠])

[1] Universidad Nacional Abierta y a Distancia, MDE, Bogotá 050036, Colombia
Jhonf.sanchez@unad.edu.co
[2] Universidad Nacional de Colombia, MDE, Bogotá 050010, Colombia

Abstract. Augmentative and alternative communication systems are devices that seek to solve communication problems in people who require it. People with neuromuscular diseases benefit from these systems, however, there is a growing need to develop systems that adapt to people with these types of diseases due to their degenerative nature. In this paper, a development method based on fuzzy logic is presented to identify the stage of the disease based on heuristic rules whose purpose is to provide a unique and usable system throughout the disease until the death of the person.

Keywords: ACC · MND · Adaptive

1 Introduction

The theory of communication has four basic elements: source, sender, message and receiver. Normally, the sender is the one who issues the message, the message can be transmitted orally or textually, among others, the message is received by the receiver. This process is particularly complex in people with Motor Neurone Disease. An example of this is people with Amyotrophic Lateral Sclerosis (ALS), some studies show that 50% of patients die 18 months after being diagnosed. Likewise, they lose the ability to communicate in the fourth month after diagnosis. Generating symptoms not specifically related to ALS such as depression or dementia. In order to communicate with their environment, Augmentative and Alternative Communication (AAC) is used, which provides the possibility for the patient to express wishes, thoughts and ideas with their environment (Ravits and La Spada 2009).

Some recent studies show that 1% of the entire population has some disease that causes loss of ability to speak (García-Méndez et al. 2018a). This loss is generally due to neuromuscular diseases or other non-paralyzing diseases generating a barrier with the world. The goal of an augmentative and alternative communication (ACC) system is to improve its ease of use for all users, regardless of their abilities and educational level. ACC systems are designed primarily for people with Neuromuscular Diseases (MND)

© Springer Nature Switzerland AG 2021
M. Antona and C. Stephanidis (Eds.): HCII 2021, LNCS 12768, pp. 473–481, 2021.
https://doi.org/10.1007/978-3-030-78092-0_32

such as amyotrophic lateral sclerosis or Duchenne Muscular Dystrophy who share some symptoms (Stephanidis 2001). By general nature, MNDs are neurodegenerative, which means that the effects on the body of the users of these systems are progressive, therefore it is impractical to develop a non-adaptive system (Ball et al. 2012).

Adaptive systems have been proposed as possible solutions for the challenging needs of users with neuromuscular pathologies. Indeed, adaptive software uses the available information to dynamically change its environment to improve its behavior. That is, the software has the ability to adapt to the user needs (García-Méndez et al. 2018b).

The system's ability to adapt generates an important usability characteristic because the bodily functions of people with neuromuscular diseases regress over time (Matos et al. 2016). As a result of this regression, an individual's needs will change over time.

2   Background

Relevant work in this field is focused on adaptive keywords, see, e.g., (Baldassarri et al. 2014; Henzen and Nohama 2016; Simion and Stan 2014) designed a multimodal system that offers various methods to acquire the signal that activates the event to register the desired character by the user:

– Control by buttons
– Movement of the head
– Eye tracking

However, it is not clear how the user chooses the hardware that best suits.

Other studies focus on optimizing text input times by means of relative frequencies of letters or words according to a long text. Otros usan redes bayesianas para predecir las entradas por medio de prefijos. (Higger et al. 2019; Krak et al. 2017).

Neuromuscular diseases are a group of pathologies whose basic characteristics are loss of control and muscle atrophy. The most important are:

Amyotrophic lateral sclerosis, or ALS, is a progressive disease of the nervous system that affects nerve cells in the brain and spinal cord, causing loss of muscle control. ALS is often called Lou Gehrig's disease, after the baseball player who was diagnosed with the disease. Doctors generally do not know why ALS occurs. Some cases are hereditary.

ALS often begins with muscle twitching and limb weakness or trouble speaking. Eventually, ALS affects the control of the muscles needed to move, speak, eat, and breathe. There is no cure for this deadly disease. (Ravits and La Spada 2009).

Duchenne Muscular Dystrophy it is a form of muscular dystrophy that gets worse quickly. Other muscular dystrophies (including Becker muscular dystrophy) get worse much more slowly). Duchenne muscular dystrophy is caused by a faulty gene for dystrophin (a protein in the muscles). However, it often occurs in people with families with no known history of this condition. The condition most often affects children because of the way the disease is inherited.

The sons of women who are carriers of the disease (women with a defective chromosome but no symptoms) each have a 50% chance of having the disease, and daughters each have a 50% chance of being carriers. On very rare occasions, a woman can be affected by the disease. Duchenne muscular dystrophy occurs in about 1 in 3600 males. Because it is a hereditary disorder, risks include a family history of Duchenne muscular dystrophy (Ball et al. 2012)

Myotonic Muscular Dystrophy it is a slow and progressive hereditary muscle disease that usually manifests itself in adulthood. It is characterized by:

– Myotonia or difficulty in muscle relaxation. There is a sustained contraction of the muscle.
– Slow but progressive muscle atrophy.
– Systemic manifestations.
– The earlier the disease occurs, the greater its degree of severity (Ball et al. 2012).

Spinal Muscular Atrophy is a genetic disease that attacks nerve cells called motor neurons found in the spinal cord. These neurons communicate with voluntary muscles, that is, those you can control, such as those in your arms and legs. As muscles lose neurons weaken. That can affect your ability to walk, crawl, breathe, swallow, and control your head and neck. SMA has a family tendency. Parents do not usually have symptoms, but they carry the gene. If the disease runs in your family, genetic counseling is important. (Lefebvre et al. 1995).

These four diseases are the ones with the highest proportion and require active intervention of ACC systems.

3 System Development

The ACC system was developed in C#, based on the design of an old cell phone keyboard with an indirect access method: directed scanning. the system performs a shift every N time from left to right; the user must produce an event when the system reaches the grouping of characters where the desired one is found, and another event when the system reaches the desired character. The event is captured by three different methods of mechanical interaction, touch or vision (Table 1), the methods will be selected according to the adaptation analysis. Additionally, the time intervals range from 1 s to 12 s (Fig. 1).

Development stages of neuromuscular diseases are classified diffusely because two people with a disease are not uniform in symptoms over time. In other words, in practical terms it is not very feasible to determine the stage of advancement versus time with traditional methods. Fuzzy logic adapts to what is desired when classifying the stages of a neuromuscular disease; one of the uses of fuzzy logic is when you have to use the experience of experts to classify something imprecise (Torres and Nieto 2006).

Table 1. Table of interaction methods

Vision method	Mechanical method	Touch method
Vision methods, such as eye observation, eye tracking, and head-pointing devices, have been widely reported in literature (Adjouadi et al. 2004; Hansen and Ji 2010; Townend et al. 2016) Eye gaze technologies work by using the principle of tracking a user's eye movements to determine the direction of gaze (Townend et al. 2016). In the context of ACC, non-invasive eye tracking methods are better suited to address the daily needs of users who lack motor skills.	Mechanical and electromechanical ACC devices have applications for direct and indirect selection access methods. Direct selections offer users sets of options and require voluntary input selection of the desired messages by the user. This usually involves the coordination of voluntary controls using a part of the body, such as the hand or fingers, or a pointing device, to select a message (Muller 1998)	With the escalation of touchscreen developments, touch-enabled ACC applications are commonly used with ACC direct select triggering. Touch screen technologies comprise several types, including resistive, capacitive, surface acoustic wave, and optical/infrared touch screens. Resistive and capacitive touch screens are predominantly used with smart devices (Arif and Stuerzlinger 2013). Resistive touchscreens depend on the production of a force or pressure using the user's fingers, while capacitive touchscreens are activated using the electrical charge present on the user's finger (Qin et al. 2017)

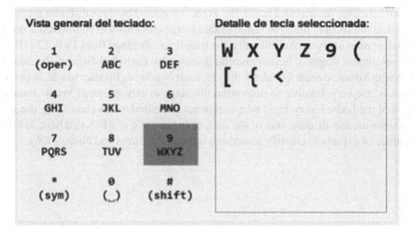

Fig. 1. ACC System Interface

The linguistic variables as well as their interpretation are given by a neurologist with a subspecialty in movement disorders. The stages of neuromuscular diseases are given by three triangular functions defined by the linguistic variables (initial, middle and advanced) (Fig. 2).

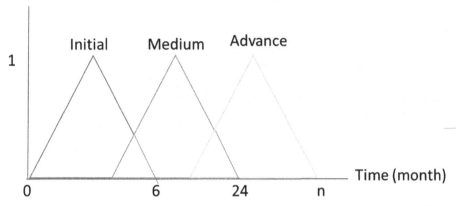

Fig. 2. Diffuse logical function of the stages of neuromuscular diseases

The membership functions are given as a function of the linguistic variables defined by:

M (initial) = triang (x, 6, 3)
M (medium = triang (x, 9, 12)
M (advance) = tfriang (x, 15, 24)

The underlying domain is determined by an average life span up to the crisp (n) value, the latter is the maximum age of life from the onset of the disease that features a very large variance from one person to another.

In fuzzy sets there are three overlaps generating two fuzzy sets where it is the intersection of the sets that is relevant and complex to determine. In terms of symptoms and with the help of an expert preferably with specialty in neurology and subspecialty in movement disorder.

3.1 Heuristic Rules for Determining the Stage of the Disease in the System

When starting the system, the user must carry out four tests once to classify the stage of the disease (Table 2) and generate the best combination between the interaction method and the time of the event:

Two metrics are used to classify users:

Table 2. Tasks performed by users

Task 1	Press "H" key
Task 2	Press at the top left of a Touch screen
Task 3	Make a sound with the mouth
Task 4	Wink twice in a second

Time used: Seconds it takes the user to perform a task determined by the system.
User error: One or more mistakes made involuntarily by the user in the system.

The inference system was designed using a conditional that takes the previous metrics to define the fuzzy set that best suits the user (Table 3). The four tests are averaged based on independent metrics; in case they do not coincide in their two metrics the intermediate linguistic variable is used

Table 3. Fuzzy inference metrics

Mistakes	Time	Linguistic variable
0–1	0,5seg-1seg	Initial
2–3	1,1seg-2seg	Initial and medium
3–5	2,1seg-4seg	Medium
6–8	4,1seg-6seg	Medium and advanced
9–12	6,1seg-10seg	Advanced

Fuzzy sets are specified in Table 4.

Table 4. Methods of interaction associated with the stage of the disease

Neuromuscular diseases	Stage	Interaction methods
	Initial	Mechanical
		Touch
	Initial and medium	Mechanical
		Touch
	Medium	Mechanical
		Touch
		Vision
		Touch
	Medium and advanced	Touch
		EGG
		Vision
	Advanced	EGG
		Vision

The observation window to classify the user in the linguistic variable does not close until the variable 'Advanced' is reached and it adapts to the interaction method suggested by the system.

It should be noted that the user can deactivate the adaptability system.

4   Usability Evaluation

The evaluation of the software was done following the method in (Alvarez et al. 2017), which proposes a heuristic method to evaluate the usability in terms of four characteristics (efficiency, effectiveness, learning capacity and satisfaction). The main feature of this method is that it does not require involving users to evaluate the usability. Two experts evaluated the software to determine the presence of the heuristics and obtained the following results (Table 5):

Table 5. Heuristic evaluation

Efficiency 90%
Effectiveness 100%
Learning capacity 90%
Satisfaction 80%

The overall usability of the software is 88%. These results contrast with those obtained in Alvarez et al. (2017) where the average usability of the software packages evaluated was 66%.

The results provided above are quite obscure, how are different results compared? It would be rather simply said:

The evaluation of the software was done following the heuristic method proposed in Alvarez et al. (2017). The idea is to evaluate the usability in terms of four characteristics (efficiency, effectiveness, learning capacity and satisfaction) and to rely on experts to carry on such an evaluation. The actual evaluation conducted on the proposed software produced very good results, specifically in: efficiency 90%; effectiveness 100%; learning capacity 90%; satisfaction 80%; overall usability 88%).

5   Conclusions

It is necessary to develop individualized ACC systems for each person diagnosed with Neuromuscular Diseases that incorporate means to communicate basic medical messages, as well as new information for daily conversation; a way to "chat" or simply interact; a means of accessing and using the telephone; options for calling attention to assistance; and ways of expressing affection, humor and emotions. The ACC system must change as the disease progresses, with system components ranging from the basic alphabet to symbol tables. A key indication for the use of ACC is that "functional communication is an essential component to improve life quality of people with severe physical limitations, such as those experienced by people with neuromuscular diseases.

In addition, research in communication of people with neuromuscular diseases should be prioritized as well as innovate in systems that facilitate the acquisition of more comfortable events for them.

References

Adjouadi, M., Sesin, A., Ayala, M., Cabrerizo, M.: Remote eye gaze tracking system as a computer interface for persons with severe motor disability (2004). http://link.springer.com/chapter/10. 1007/978-3-540-27817-7_113

Alvarez, J.F.S., Jaramillo, C.M.Z., Builes, J.A.J., Sánchez-Álvarez, J.F., Zapata-Jaramillo, C.M., Jiménez-Builes, J.A.: Heuristic assessment of software usability to facilitate computer use for people with motor disabilities. Revista EIA **14**(27), 63–72 (2017). https://revistas.eia.edu.co/index.php/Reveiaenglish/article/view/1205

Baldassarri, S., Rubio, J.M., Azpiroz, M.G., Cerezo, E.: AraBoard: a multiplatform alternative and augmentative communication tool. Procedia Comput. Sci. **27**, 197–206 (2014). https://doi.org/10.1016/J.PROCS.2014.02.023

Ball, L.J., Fager, S., Fried-Oken, M.: Augmentative and alternative communication for people with progressive neuromuscular disease. In: Physical Medicine and Rehabilitation Clinics of North America,, vol. 23, Issue 3, pp. 689–699. Elsevier (2012). https://doi.org/10.1016/j.pmr.2012.06.003

García-Méndez, S., Fernández-Gavilanes, M., Costa-Montenegro, E., Juncal-Martínez, J., Javier González-Castaño, F.: Automatic natural language generation applied to alternative and augmentative communication for online video content services using simpleNLG for Spanish. In: Proceedings of the 15th Web for All Conference : Internet of Accessible Things, W4A 2018 (2018a). https://doi.org/10.1145/3192714.3192837

García-Méndez, S., Fernández-Gavilanes, M., Costa-Montenegro, E., Juncal-Martínez, J., Javier González-Castaño, F.: Automatic natural language generation applied to alternative and augmentative communication for online video content services using simpleNLG for Spanish. In: Proceedings of the 15th Web for All Conference : Internet of Accessible Things, W4A 2018 (2018b). https://doi.org/10.1145/3192714.3192837

Hansen, D.W., Ji, Q.: In the eye of the beholder: a survey of models for eyes and gaze. IEEE Trans. Pattern Anal. Mach. Intell. (2010). https://doi.org/10.1109/TPAMI.2009.30

Henzen, A., Nohama, P.: Adaptable virtual keyboard and mouse for people with special needs. Fut. Technol. Conf. **2016**, 1357–1360 (2016). https://doi.org/10.1109/FTC.2016.7821782

Higger, M., Quivira, F., Erdogmus, D.: User-Adaptive Text Entry for Augmentative and Alternative Communication. http://arxiv.org/abs/1910.01216 (2019)

Krak, Y.V., Barmak, A.V., Bagriy, R.A., Stelya, I.O.: Text entry system for alternative speech communications. J. Autom. Inf. Sci. **49**(1), 65–75 (2017). https://doi.org/10.1615/JAutomatInfScien.v49.i1.60

Lefebvre, S., Bürglen, L., Reboullet, S.: Identification and characterization of a spinal muscular atrophy-determining gene. Cell (1995). http://www.sciencedirect.com/science/article/pii/0092867495904603

Matos, A., Filipe, V., Couto, P.: Human-computer interaction based on facial expression recognition: a case study in degenerative neuromuscular disease. ACM Int. Conf. Proc. Ser. 8–12 (2016). https://doi.org/10.1145/3019943.3019945

Muller, A.: Handbook of Augmentative and Alternative Communication. Folia Phoniatrica (1998)

Qin, H., Cai, Y., Dong, J., Lee, Y.S.: Direct printing of capacitive touch sensors on flexible substrates by additive e-jet printing with silver nanoinks. J. Manuf. Sci. Eng. Trans. ASME (2017). https://doi.org/10.1115/1.4034663

Ravits, J.M., La Spada, A.R.: ALS motor phenotype heterogeneity, focality, and spread: deconstructing motor neuron degeneration. Neurology **73**(10), 805–811 (2009). https://doi.org/10.1212/WNL.0b013e3181b6bbbd

Simion, E., Stan, E.: Augmentative and alternative communication-support for people with severe speech disorders selection and peer-review under responsibility of EPC KTS and Guest Editors-Dr Cristian Vasile, Dr Mihaela Singer and Dr. Procedia-Soc. Behav. Sci. **128**, 77–81 (2014). https://doi.org/10.1016/j.sbspro.2014.03.121

Stephanidis, C.: User Interfaces for All: New perspectives into Human-Computer Interaction. Lawrence Erlbaum Associates (2001)

Torres, A., Nieto, J.J.: Fuzzy logic in medicine and bioinformatics. J. Biomed. Biotechnol. **2006** (2006). https://doi.org/10.1155/JBB/2006/91908

Townend, G.S., Marschik, P.B., Smeets, E., van de Berg, R., van den Berg, M., Curfs, L.M.G.: Eye gaze technology as a form of augmentative and alternative communication for individuals with rett syndrome: experiences of families in The Netherlands. J. Dev. Phys. Disabil. (2016). https://doi.org/10.1007/s10882-015-9455-z

Multimodal Tactile Graphics Using T-TATIL, A Mobile Application for Tactile Exploration by Visually Impaired People

Leonardo Zani Zamprogno[1]([✉]), Bruno Merlin[1]([✉]), João Ferreira[2]([✉]),
Heleno Fülber[1]([✉]), and Allan Veras[1]([✉])

[1] Federal University of Pará, Tucuruí-PA, Brazil
leonardo.zamprogno@ifpa.edu.br
[2] Federal Institute of Pará - Campus Tucuruí, Tucuruí-PA, Brazil
joao.ferreira@ifpa.edu.br
http://www.camtuc.ufpa.br/, http://www.tucurui.ifpa.edu.br

Abstract. Graphic contents are important resources to communicate information and their use is fundamental in the teaching process. Visually impaired people do not have easy access to this resource owing to their impairment. They mainly use tactile graphics to explore visual contents. In this article, we propose the development of a tool for tablets intended to aid visually impaired people in interpreting tactile graphics. After studying different exploration strategies of tactile graphics adopted by visually impaired people, we propose an application that utilizes the benefit of multimodal interactions. Through a case study, three blind students tested the prototype of the application, demonstrating that the solution is a promising approach to aid in the exploration of tactile graphics.

Keywords: Assistive technologies · Visually impaired · Blind · Tactile graphics · Tactile feedback · Audio feedback · Touch screens · Audio-tactile

1 Introduction

The graphical contents that comprise images and maps are effective in transmitting a considerable amount of information in a small space, allowing better organization of series of data and information so that they become easily understandable. They are widely used in the teaching process at all levels of education. The sense of vision enables a comprehensive and quick understanding of graphic content. While visually impaired students do not have easy access to this type of content, the use of other sensory subsystems, such as hearing and haptics (touch and kinesthetic), can help in the interpretation of these visual contents.

Supported by Federal Universty of Pará and Federal Institute of Pará.

M. Antona and C. Stephanidis (Eds.): HCII 2021, LNCS 12768, pp. 482–498, 2021.
https://doi.org/10.1007/978-3-030-78092-0_33

Tactile graphics are mainly used to help visually impaired students explore graphic representations. To access tactile graphics, the visually impaired (VI) require the support of a person with vision (seeing person) to provide the initial information such as the general message transmitted by the tactile drawing and to guide the individual in the step-by-step reading of the drawing [7]. The absence of this person makes it impossible for the VI to use tactile graphics [16].

Full sound description of the content is an alternative to tactile exploration to access graphic content, and audio is preferred in tasks of exploration and navigation [11]. However, studies showed that the VI tend to prefer tactile presentations to audio exclusively. This shows that the combination of responses of various sensory systems–for example, by combining a tactile sensory response for graph exploration and an auditory response for obtaining complementary information–can have a greater effect on the transmission of graphical information to the VI.

The Brazilian legislation, since the constitution of 1988 [4], established in its articles 205 and 206 that education is a universal right, and that education must be provided based on the principle of equality of conditions for access and permanence in schools. The Law of Guidelines and Bases of National Education, published in 1996 [5], in its article 59, agrees with the view of the constitution on the right to education of disabled people. It also states that education systems must provide specific curricula, methods, techniques, educational resources, and organization to learners with special needs in order to satisfy their needs.

In fact, the entire Brazilian legislation on the inclusion of disabled people is relatively ambitious regarding the promotion of inclusion. However, institutes face many difficulties, especially regarding the budget and the training of personnel to support disabled students and to provide them with the necessary support for good educational development. Some authors state that "there is a contradiction between speech and reality, because the visually impaired, who depend on public resources for their education, face many barriers and challenges" [14].

Assistive technologies (AT) "are resources that enhance the functional abilities of disabled people" [3] and, therefore, can be used to fill the gaps in teacher training and the lack of specialized material. AT can help in several challenges imposed by the presentation of graphic content, helping in the development of correctly prepared tactile graphics and enabling the VI to read tactile graphics on their own. Thus, this work presents an application for tablets designed to help the VI in reading tactile graphics. After studying different strategies for the exploration of tactile graphics adopted by VI people, we propose an application that utilizes the benefit of multimodal interactions. A printed tactile graphic is superimposed on the screen of the device. During the tactile exploration of the graphic, the application provides enlightening auditory information about the area explored by the VI through vocal synthesis. The objective is to supply the assistance given by a seeing person, providing full autonomy to the VI in the reading and interpretation of tactile graphics. The interactions were implemented in order not to impact the strategies of tactile exploration of the graphic.

2   Related Works

Several solutions and approaches can help the VI in the exploration and interpretation of graphic content. First, we can cite the main items presented by related works: TTT (Talking Tactile Tablet) [13] and IVEO Touchpad [8]. Both solutions allow the overlap of tactile graphics on a touch-sensitive hardware connected to a personal computer, via USB, that runs the software allowing the tactile graphics to become interactive. Touching the tactile graphic triggers audio information, which allows more information to be transmitted to the VI.

Although the connection to a computer provides TTT and IVEO Touchpad with considerable processing and flexibility, it limits its portability as the device needs to be physically connected. However, the main limitation of these devices is that they rely on specific hardware, which is not only bulky, but also used exclusively for a certain task (reading tactile graphics printed and overlapped on a touch-sensitive hardware). Another aspect to be highlighted is the high commercial value of these devices, which makes them unacceptable in terms of economic realities with no considerable investment in accessibility for people with disabilities (Fig. 1).

a)   b)

Fig. 1. a) IVEO Touchpad (Source: reproduction/viewplus.com). b) Talking Tactile Tablet (Source: reproduction/ITD Journal

In contrast to the use of specific hardware, we can find solutions that aim at helping the VI in the task of reading and interpreting tactile graphics and that are based on common hardware, i.e., the hardware can be used to perform other tasks such as Internet browsing, reading books, and accessing multimedia content. Two of these solutions are GraVVITAS [10] and Figure Perceiving Tools [6]. Both solutions allow the VI to access graphic content using a touch screen tablet and can provide audio and haptic feedback of the graphic information displayed on the screen.

There is a small difference between these two solutions on the generation of haptic feedbacks. In GraVVITAS, these feedbacks are provided through vibration motors placed in a glove designed specifically for this purpose. Whenever the user touches any graphic object on the touch screen, the system provides haptic feedback by activating the vibration motor in the glove. The Figure Perceiving Tools, in contrast, do not require the use of a glove. Haptic feedbacks are provided by the vibration of the tablet itself (Fig. 2).

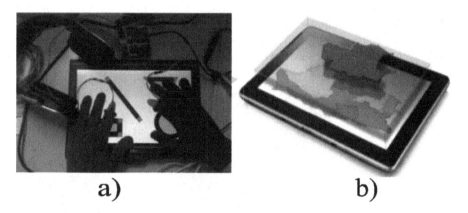

Fig. 2. (a) GraVVITAS (Source: reproduction/[10]). b) Figure Perceiving Tools (Source: reproduction/[6]

However, in a tactile exploration with both hands and several fingers, it is difficult to distinguish at which point the graphic object displayed on the screen is being touched. This prevents tactile exploration with both hands and multiple fingers, which is not a natural way for the VI to explore tactile graphics [1,11]. Another aspect hinders the tactile interpretation of the graphic through vibrations only: the finger simultaneously perceives several points of the printed tactile graphic, which gives a notion of continuity and direction of lines and intersections and allows differentiating lines by size and areas by textures. Vibrations only provide information regarding the presence or absence of the finger at a point and, even if we imagine semantics of the design of vibration that allows differentiating lines or areas (by the intensity of the vibration), it appears challenging to transcribe the perception of continuity or intersections only through this feedback.

3   Comments on Tactile Exploration Without Technological Resources

To develop a solution that satisfies the real needs of a VI student, it is necessary to consider a participatory and user-centered design, because "this approach prevents an engineering trap, with development being driven by computational efficiency and assumptions of designers, often wrong, without considering feedback from the end user" [9]. For this purpose, three observational studies were conducted to analyze the strategies of the VI individual used to explore the graphic content printed in relief.

These studies were conducted during real classes with the VI accessing graphic content (as shown in Fig. 3). One student was a high-school entrant, one student was a high-school graduate, and the third was an engineering graduate. Consequently, the three individuals had very different experiences with tactile graphics. The first admitted having had little contact with this resource owing to the lack of adapted material during his elementary school. The other two students were more familiar because they had attended institutions that sought to use this resource in the best possible way.

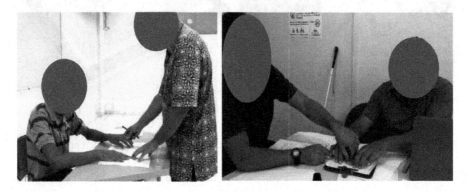

Fig. 3. Observation of how the VI explore graphic content with the help of teachers during the classes

At this stage, we sought to identify: (i) how the VI explores the tactile graphic (use of hands, successive stages of exploration), (ii) what information is provided by the seeing person, and (iii) when and why these descriptions are provided to the VI. The main points observed in this study are highlighted below.

a) In the initial phase of tactile exploration, teachers provided general information on the tactile drawing, explaining the main subject addressed and the spatial organization of the content. At the same time and/or in sequence, the VI devoted time to a general exploration of the tactile drawing. This first general stage of "recognition" was performed with one or two hands. The use of one or two hands appears to be related to the level of experience of the student with tactile graphics;

b) During the tactile exploration, the students were guided by the seeing persons (teachers) on how to explore the tactile drawings and which way to go, with many of them directing the students' hands;

c) As the students explored the tactile image, the seeing person informed them about the explored area and the VI could simultaneously explore the tactile graphic details of that given area.

d) In the second stage of graphic exploration, the participants tended to continue using one or two hands according to the strategy used in the first stage.
In some moments, one hand served as a spatial reference for measuring the
distance between the objects.

Here, we highlight some prerequisites to an AT to be naturally integrated in
the exploration of tactile graphics by the VI without requiring that they change
their methodology of work. Thus, the technology must: (i) be resilient to interaction with both hands; (ii) provide general information on the graphic at the
beginning or when requested by the VI; and (iii) allow the VI to request complementary information on the graphic without the information polluting the
printed graphic. The observation also revealed that the directing of the VI's
hand during exploration could be relevant in certain circumstances, but further
evaluations are required. This feature would hardly be enabled without the use of
a specific device. Another point observed during these studies, and confirmed by
one of the participants, is that tactile drawings with many subtitles and many
details can complicate tactile exploration, and hence, it is recommended that
everything is well organized and with as few subtitles and details as possible,
so that the VI can understand the drawing more quickly and effectively. Some
authors agree with this observation [12,15].

4   Application Development

T-TÁTIL involves the use of a common tablet with an application installed to
detect the gestures of tactile exploration by the VI (Fig. 4.a), with a printed
tactile drawing positioned on the screen of the device (Fig. 4.b) allowing conventional tactile graphics (without audio) to become multimodal tactile graphics
with sound feedback, which connect sound and touch to improve the exploration
of the tactile drawing (Fig. 4.c).

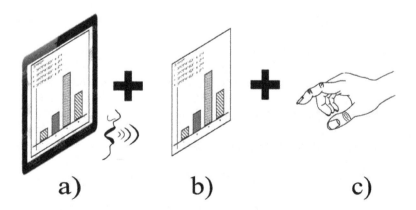

Fig. 4. Application functioning model

The application associates the printed tactile drawing (Fig. 5.a) to a previously created file in SVG format. The SVG contains forms and textual content associated with forms that describe the areas of interest of tactile drawing (These areas and descriptions are inherent to each drawing). The shapes drawn in the SVG file are converted to clickable areas in the application interface (Fig. 5.b). Thus, during the tactile exploration of the graphic superimposed on the tablet (Fig. 5.c), the user can activate the sound descriptions to request additional information. The text content associated with the activated area is read through voice synthesis. A general description can be accessed by clicking an area located in the lower right corner of the interface.

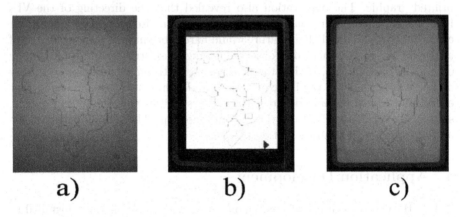

a)   b)   c)

Fig. 5. Use of T-TÁTIL

4.1   Technical Considerations of the Project

The use of touch screen devices was essential for the development of this solution. This technology allows the interaction of users with electronic systems only using a touch screen, activated either by the finger or a special pen, without requiring the use of another peripheral device such as a mouse and keyboard. Currently, two types of touchscreens are most commonly found in devices on the market: resistive screens and capacitive screens. Capacitive screens operate from an electrically charged capacitive layer positioned over the screen. By touching the screen, some of these electrons are transmitted to the finger, and hence, the device understands this small discharge of electricity, calculates the coordinates and then translates it to a command, either a touch or a specific gesture. The resistive screens, in contrast, function by means of pressure exerted on the screen that changes the electric field and allows identifying the location of the touch or gesture on the screen (Fig. 6).

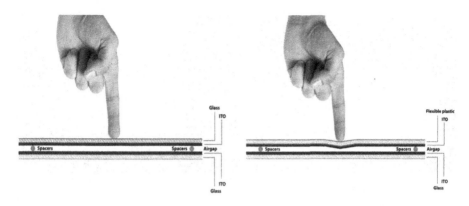

Fig. 6. Representation of capacitive screens (left) and resistive screens (right) (Images: reproduction/Techtudo).

Based on this information, it was necessary to test whether capacitive touchscreens can detect gestures and touches even with the paper positioned on the screen of the device. This problem does not exist a priori in devices that use resistive screens because the operating principle is the pressure exerted on the screen. However, in capacitive screens, which are most widely used, a printed tactile graphic could act as an insulator and prevent the transfer of the electric charge.

To validate the functioning of capacitive and resistive screens, a small experiment was conducted, in which a printed tactile graphic was superimposed on the touch screen of several devices[1] found in local institutions and shops in the region. As illustrated in Fig. 7, the Paint Free application[2] was used to determine whether finger pressures were detected through the paper . The lines of each shape of the drawing were followed only once (Fig. 7.a). The experiment was conducted with Braille paper and flexi paper, both easily found in Brazil.

The results confirmed that, regardless of the type of paper used and the device tested, the drawings made in the "paint free" tool using the tool in conjunction with the paper were correctly reproduced. With the "undo" functionality, it can be observed that there was no discontinuity in the interaction (Fig. 7.b). Consequently, we infer that the touches and gestures performed were correctly detected through the papers.

---

[1] Tested devices. *Tablets*: Positivo YPY-AB10E, Apple iPad mini 4, Samsung Galaxy Tab 7, Multilaser M10A, Samsung Galaxy Tab A, Tablet Positivo T1060; *Smartphones*: Motorola Moto G5S Plus, Motorola Moto G6, Motorola Moto X4, Motorola Moto Z2 Play, Samsung Galaxy J4, Lenovo K8 Plus, Apple iPhone 6S, Apple iPhone 7 plus.

[2] https://play.google.com/store/apps/details?id=com.ternopil.fingerpaintfree.

a)   b)

Fig. 7. Touch recognition test with overlapping tactile drawings on the screen of the device

4.2 Paradigm of Interaction Resilient to the VI's Methodology of Work

From the observational studies mentioned above, it was possible to identify several forms and methodologies of tactile exploration by VI people. Thus, it is possible to define an interaction model for the application that does not harm such methodologies and thus interferes as little as possible in the form of tactile exploration of each user of the application.

a) We observed that the VI individuals used several fingers when performing tactile exploration, even using both hands simultaneously, and rarely using only one finger. This considerably complicates the detection of the area of interest that could be used to play the sound information automatically. Thus, the audio description must be activated by demand, i.e., when the VI request it through a specific interaction (for this application, we have implemented the double touch functionality in the area of interest).

b) Similarly, there must be a way to interrupt the sound descriptions if the user wishes. To this end, we have implemented a simple touch screen interaction that immediately ceases the description being reproduced. This type of interaction does not hinder tactile exploration because it generates sliding events with one or several pointers on the screen, and not simple touch events. Further updates will allow for improvements, as demonstrated in the discussion and future works sections.

5   Case Studies

5.1   Method

To assess whether VI people can use the proposed approach, and to obtain qualitative feedback, we conducted a study with end users of the application.

To evaluate the usability of the application, a low-cost Android tablet (Positivo "YPY-AB10E with 10" screen) was used with the tactile application installed.

With the help of a professional with vast experience in the elaboration of adapted materials, currently working at the Federal Institute of Education, Science, and Technology of Pará with more than 10 years of experience in supporting students with special needs during academic life, we projected seven tactile drawings in several categories of teaching: a line graph (LG), a shark (S) and its main characteristics, a genogram (GN), a representation of the Holy Supper (HS), a floor plan (FP), a soccer field (SF), and a map of Brazil (MB) divided into regions. An extra element that allowed us to include a general description of the image was added to all drawings. This element is represented by the symbol of "play" (an arrow pointed to the right direction), which is in the lower right corner of all drawings. Each participant was informed of the existence of this element and that it could be triggered while the tactile drawing was explored.

The files can be downloaded at https://drive.google.com/drive/folders/1nEEpHeW5Vd9OsTNXh8PPaaOTqsftiADK?usp=sharing.

Three VI individuals were recruited to participate in this case study; details of the participants can be found in the next section. Each study session lasted approximately 2 h. Initially, each participant received a brief explanation about how the application worked, how to obtain the sound feedback from the clickable areas, and how to interrupt the descriptions if they desired. They then had the opportunity to explore a test drawing and were instructed to perform all tactile exploration tasks and obtain the sound feedback from the several clickable areas (Fig. 8).

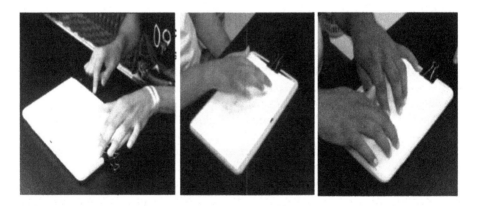

Fig. 8. Testing the prototype of the application with the three participants

After this introductory stage, the testing of the prototype of the application started. Each participant had as much time as they deemed necessary for tactile exploration of the drawing and to obtain the sound feedback from the clickable areas. After exploring each image, as soon as the VI reported having understood the drawing, a questionnaire was provided to determine whether the participant could fully understand the tactile drawing. In case of doubt, the VI could query the graphic before responding. These questionnaires helped support the qualitative results of this study and provided some quantitative results too.

Immediately after exploring and responding to the questionnaires, the participants received a second questionnaire that surveyed qualitative data including the participants' opinions about the experiment, tactile drawings, application, and use of technology.

The questionnaires can be accessed at https://drive.google.com/file/d/1Ys5D9CCF_SlIIbPh4Ei3v9RCdskh9H2z/view?usp=sharing.

5.2   Description of Participants

The first participant, P1, is a student at a high school integrated with technical education in information technology (22 years old). He has been completely blind since he was 3 years old. The participant reported having average braille and tactile drawing skills. He uses braille material every day at school and tactile drawings 2–3 times a week. The participant reported having a good experience using smartphones and computers every day. When asked if he has ever used any technological resource to access graphic content, the participant informed that he uses only tactile drawings printed on braille paper or flexi paper.

The second participant, P2, is a student who has just finished elementary school (15 years old). He has been completely blind since birth. The participant reported having average braille reading skill. He uses braille material 2–3 times a week. He reported that he had almost no skills in tactile drawing because he had used this resource rarely during his school education because according the participant "(Tactile drawings) were not worked on in the municipality where I live." The participant reported that he had no experience at all in using mobile devices and that he had attempted to use a computer and smartphone before but without success. When asked if he has ever used any technological resource to access graphic content, the participant informed that he uses only tactile drawings printed on braille paper or flexi paper.

The last participant, P3, is a sanitary engineering student (25 years old). He has been completely blind since he was 7 years; however, he was born with a disability in one eye and had only partial vision in the other. The participant reported that he has good braille reading and tactile drawing skills, and that he uses these resources every day at the university. The participant reported having significant experience using smartphones and computers every day. When asked if he had used any technological resource to access graphic content, the participant informed that he uses smartphones to access graphic content such as pictures, photos, and audio description, in addition to tactile drawings printed on braille paper or flexi papers.

5.3   Qualitative Results

Opinion on Tactile Drawings. All the participants indicated that tactile graphics are very important for the teaching and learning process in schools. P3 said that "With tactile drawings, it is easy to understand the relationships between objects and figures, which allows you to create this relationship mentally." The participants said that the tactile drawings used in the experiments were easy to understand and that the textures and organization were well ordered so as not to confuse tactile exploration. When asked if they had preference for some of the drawings, P1 indicated the "genogram," the "floor plan", and the "Last Supper." P2 liked the "shark" and P3 the "genogram."

Opinion on T-TÁTIL. All three participants agreed that T-TÁTIL could help in the exploration and understanding of tactile drawings, making them faster to understand and better organized as fewer Braille subtitles are required to explain the details of each drawing. Regarding one of the drawings, P1 said that "it is even faster to obtain the information from the drawing and if subtitles were added, the presentation of this information would require many pages." The participants said that they would like to use the system mainly for activities at school, during class, and some activities at home.

The participant P3 raised a point of interest regarding this technology; according to him, "the blind community, today, talks about a future problem, that is to pay more attention to virtual technologies and forget physical technologies," and hence, it is interesting that an application integrates physical elements with virtual elements, and "this project does the opposite. It encourages the visually impaired to have physical accessibility through the analysis of tactile drawings, combining information technology with the use of a tablet."

Use of the Application. Most of the participants reported not having faced major difficulties in the use of the application, as a few different functionalities had been implemented in order not to confuse the participants in this initial test. We could evaluate the usability and acceptability of the T-TÁTIL.

Although a few instructions are required to use the application, P2 had some difficulties in triggering and stopping the sound descriptions with the gestures provided in the introduction of the tests. We believe that this is due to the participant's limited experience in using mobile devices and computers.

Errors Verified. During the case studies conducted, it was possible to observe some errors and opportunities for improvements to be implemented in the next updates of the application. The interaction model chosen for the application, which was believed not to have major problems, ended up revealing that modifications need to be made as, for example, when the element of general description of the drawings was activated and a general exploration was performed by the VI individuals, the application sometimes detected a false simple click and interrupted the sound description. Although this problem occurred sometimes, after a certain period of adaptation, the VI participants could trigger the descriptions and explore the drawing simultaneously without the "false single click" being triggered.

Another problem occasionally detected was that, even with the tactile drawings attached to the screen of the device, at times, at the moment of exploration, the paper moved slightly. Consequently, the physical object was no longer perfectly superimposed on the corresponding clickable area, making it difficult to activate the sound descriptions. Another paper positioning mechanism should be implemented to prevent the occurrence of this error in an uncontrolled environment.

5.4   Quantitative Results

The time required for each participant to explore the tactile drawings is illustrated in Fig. 9. It is believed that the reason why P2 required a considerably longer time to explore tactile drawings is because he had no experience in exploring tactile drawings. In general, the time taken by the other two participants varied from one image to another, considering only the time required for the application to reproduce the requested sound descriptions so that the VI could understand the details of the tactile drawing.

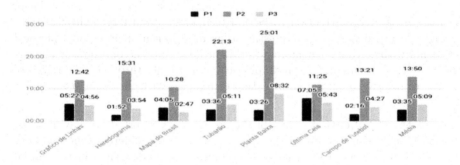

Fig. 9. Graph showing the time spent exploring the tactile drawings

The number of correct answers to the questions are shown in Fig. 10. We also showed the number of times the VI queried the tactile drawing/application to answer the proposed questions.

We believe that, while answering the questions, most of the queries were made because of the amount of information that was presented in the audio descriptions–for example, for all participants (2 queries for 3 questions), the highest number of queries were made to the map of Brazil drawing divided into regions and including audio information informing which states formed the region, the total area, population, and demographic density. Other drawings commonly queried by P2 were that of the Holy Supper (2/3) and soccer field (2/3). We observed that the queries were usually made for the tactile drawings having more tactile and sound information and this may have required a greater cognitive load, making it difficult to memorize this information completely. P1, in exploring the map of Brazil, said, "I seem to have answered more than three questions. I think it is because of the amount of audio information I had to search for answering the questions."

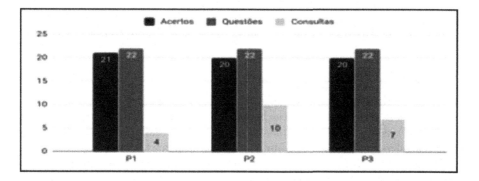

Fig. 10. Correct answers and queries for tactile drawings questions

6   Discussion

This study supports the claim that tactile drawings are very important for VI students. The lack of use of this type of resource can negatively influence the school education of VI people, making it even more difficult to include them in school curricula. Participants reported that tactile drawings are not always ready in time for use in class and they need support from a seeing person (usually the teacher) to understand the details of the tactile drawing. Hence, in this regard, T-TÁTIL can be even more useful for VI students when they are reviewing tactile drawings after their application in classroom.

This evaluation stage emphasized that, regardless of the tool, the tactile graphic/audio needs to be meticulously developed. Although we observed that the tool helped the VI significantly in the task of tactile exploration, describing the drawing in detail through audio in a timely manner, we realized that, even for more experienced VI individuals, the use of a great amount of sound information, sometimes unnecessary, ends up impairing the understanding slightly. This corroborates the statement of [15] that "it is difficult to add information, such as captions or braille notes, without making a tactile graphic excessively complicated." The same applies to audio information. This information needs to be clear and directed to the objective of the tactile drawing.

We believe that the solution proposed in this work can help VI individuals at all levels of education and with different levels of skill in braille reading and tactile drawing. This is demonstrated by the participant P2 who, despite having almost no experience in tactile drawing exploration, could accomplish the tasks and obtain satisfactory results in addition to providing positive feedback regarding the solution.

This study aimed at evaluating whether a tablet could help VI individuals in the task of exploring tactile drawings on their own and to establish whether the sound descriptions added to the tactile drawings help in this task. All the participants indicated that T-TÁTIL is useful and provided examples of how and when the application can help in the exploration of tactile drawings. As the prototype has been evaluated and established, further studies evaluating a larger number of participants can be conducted to develop a more complete solution.

6.1 Future Works

In future works, we intend to (i) include other types of sound feedback (e.g., recording of descriptions by a real person, sounds of certain objects or animals, music, etc.) using different gestures for each type of audio feedback; (ii) implement a mechanism that allows coupling the physical chart with its representation in clickable areas on the tablet without having to use menus (initially, the idea is to use QR codes but new possibilities can be analyzed); (iii) create a mechanism for positioning the tactile impression on the tablet screen without the support of a seeing person; initially, we conceived the idea of a base for the tablet with some locks to hold the paper, but there is also the possibility of marking the printed paper so that, as soon as the VI person touches the markings, the application positions the digital file according to these markings; (iv) adjust the form of interaction to interrupt the audio descriptions (simple touch) in order to avoid "false" events generated by tactile exploration; and (v) develop versions for other mobile platforms.

7 Conclusion

The T-TÁTIL was developed by confirming that the participants could interact with the usual screens through the papers used for relief printing, and based on observational studies and related works, both presented throughout this work. The tool, implemented for mobile devices (for now, only mobiles using the Android platform), enhances printed tactile drawings, providing sound descriptions of the drawing according to the desire of the VI.

Thus, we achieved the objective of proposing a solution that helped VI in the reading and interpretation of tactile drawings based on low-cost mobile devices widely used in society. The tool and the services provided by it do not require specific hardware, unlike the alternative solutions proposed in the past. Moreover, the interaction with the device was resilient to the interaction with both hands even though small, simple adjustments can be made to improve this aspect further. Consequently, the tool was naturally integrated by the participants (who were different from each other) into the tactile drawing exploration methodologies without a learning cost.

Although the evaluation performed does not have the statistical significance that allows us to state that the tool, in its current state, provides complete autonomy to the VI in the task of reading and interpreting tactile drawings, the elements raised in this work show that a significant step was taken in this direction.

Acknowledgment. We thank the participants who volunteered to participate in the experiments to test this prototype, the CTI, ASCOM and NAPNE of the IFPA Tucuruí Campus for their technical support in preparing and performing the experiments, and all those who have contributed in any way to the development of this work.

References

1. Bennett, D.J., Edwards, A.D.N.: Exploration of non-seen diagrams. In: Proceedings of the 5th International Conference on Auditory Display (ICAD98), [s. l.], pp. 1–6 (1998)
2. Braille Authority of North America: Guidelines and Standards for Tactile Graphics (2011). Retrieved from 12 Feb 2018. http://www.brailleauthority.org/tg
3. Brasil. Subsecretaria Nacional de Promoção dos Direitos da Pessoa com Deficiência (2009). Comitê de Ajudas Técnicas. Tecnologia Assistiva (CAT). - Brasília: CORDE
4. Brasil. Constituição da República Federativa do Brasil de 1988 (1988). Retrieved from 21 May 2018. http://www.planalto.gov.br/ccivil_03/constituicao/constituicaocompilado.htm
5. Brasil. Lei n° 9.394, de 20 de dezembro de 1996 - Lei de Diretrizes e Bases da Educação Nacional (1996). Retrieved from 21 May 2018. http://www.planalto.gov.br/ccivil_03/LEIS/l9394.htm
6. Costa, L.C.P., et al.: Accessible educational digital book on tablets for people with visual impairment. IEEE Trans. Consum. Electron. **61**(3), 271–278 (2015)
7. Fusco, G., Morash, V.S.: The tactile graphics helper: providing audio clarification for tactile graphics using machine vision. In: Proceedings 17th International ACM SIGACCESS Conference on Computing and Accessibility (ASSETS '15) (2015)
8. John, G., Vladimir, B.: Scientific diagrams made easy with IVEO. In: ICCHP - International Conference on Computers Helping People with Special Needs (2006)
9. Giudice, N.A., et al.: Learning non-visual graphical information using a touch-based vibro-audio interface. In: Proceedings of 14th International ACM Conference on Computer and Accessibility (ASSETS '12) (2012)
10. Goncu, C., Marriott, K.: Gravvitas: generic multi-touch presentation of accessible graphics. In: Proceedings of the 13th International Conference on Human-Computer Interaction (IFIP '11) (2011)
11. Goncu, C., Marriott, K., Hurst, J.: Usability of accessible bar charts. In: Proceedings of the Sixth International Conference on Diagrammatic Representation and Inference (2010)
12. Götzelmann, T.: Visually augmented audio-tactile graphics for visually impaired people. ACM Trans. Access. Comput. **11**(2), 2 (2018)
13. Landau, S., Russel, M., Erin, J.N.: Using the Talking Tactile Tablet as a Testing Accommodation. Rev.: Rehabilitation and education for blinds and Visual Impairments (2017)

14. da Silva, C.C.M., Turatto, J., Machado, L.H.: Os deficientes visuais e o acesso àÂ informação Rev. Biblioteconomia em Santa Catarina (2002)
15. Suzuki, R., et al.: FluxMarker: enhancing tactile graphics with dynamic tactile markers. In: Proceedings of the 19th International ACM SIGACCESS Conference on Computer and Accessibility (ASSETS '17) (2017)
16. Zebehazy, K.T., Wilton, A.P.: Straight from the source: perceptions of students with visual impairments about graphic use. J. Visual Impairment Blind (2014). https://doi.org/10.1177/0145482X1410800402

An Evaluation of Eye-Foot Input for Target Acquisitions

Xinyong Zhang$^{(\boxtimes)}$

Renmin University of China, No. 59 Zhongguancun Street, Beijing, China
x.y.zhang@ruc.edu.cn

Abstract. The multimodal interaction technique that combines eye and foot input not only provides a great opportunity for the user with busy hands or hand disabilities to interaction with computer, but can also overcome the drawbacks when using dwell time to solve the "Midas Problem" of gaze input. However, the user's capability of eye-foot coordination was still unclear. At the same time, the human performance in the basic task of target acquisitions by eye-foot input was also uncertain, and especially a proper performance model was lacking. Motivated by this situation, an eye pointing and foot tapping task experiment had been carried out to fill these gaps. A low-cost eye tracker and a USB foot pedal switcher were used as the input devices from different modalities. The experimental results indicated that the user was soon able to coordinate her/his foot with the eyes for target acquisitions, and that the user could respond fast to tap the foot pedal to finish a task trial in the level of 600 ms. The main performance measures of eye movement time (EMT) and eye pointing time (EPT) under the eye-foot multimodal input condition were significantly increased with the increase of saccadic amplitude A and/or the decrease of target width (size) W, and vice versa. Regression analysis shown that the ID_{eye} model was more suitable than the standard Fitts' law to model the human performance in this multimodal interaction context.

Keywords: Gaze input · Foot input · Multimodal interaction · Eye-foot coordination · Performance modeling

1 Introduction

With respect to dwell-based gaze input, the dominant task of target acquisition can be easily separated into two cascaded phases, eye pointing and dwell selection, which involve the eye movements of saccades and fixations, respectively. Unfortunately, the user is still suffering the drawbacks of gaze input. For example, the user is able to very quickly switch his/her gaze to the desired target via only one rapid and ballistic saccade in general, and then steadily stare at the target for a given duration to make the final decision of target selection. At the same time, the mechanism of dwell time for target selection could be occasionally disabled by jittery fixations, even if the accuracy of tracking is good enough,

© Springer Nature Switzerland AG 2021
M. Antona and C. Stephanidis (Eds.): HCII 2021, LNCS 12768, pp. 499–517, 2021.
https://doi.org/10.1007/978-3-030-78092-0_34

because two kinds of sub-movements, involuntary tremors and micro-saccades, will take place in fixations. The former is due to the inherent physiological control of visual perception to keep the image of the interested object on the fovea of the eyes, and the latter is probably triggered by fixation error, neural noise, insufficient retinal motion, and/or visual adaptation. That means that the accumulation of dwell time could be canceled before reaching the predefined threshold to finally confirm selections, pro-longing target acquisition.

In order to overcome the drawback of dwell-based gaze input or provide a substitute for the mechanism of dwell time to confirm target acquisition, there are a number of techniques that integrate gaze input with an additional modality, such as manual input, foot input, speech input, head motion, facial electromyogram and even electroencephalogram. However, there is still lack of a deep evaluation of eye-foot input for the dominant task of target acquisitions, especially without an effective performance model for this situation. Therefore, this work carried out an experiment to evaluate the human performance in target acquisition task that was performed using the two input modalities of eye and foot. In brief, the gaze input was used to move the cursor and indicate the desired target, and the foot input via a USB pedal, as Fig. 1d shows, was directly used to generate click events like a mouse so as to confirm and finish the final selection.

2   Related Work

Although hand is the most dominant modality in human-computer interaction (HCI), foot and eye are also two kinds of useful and sometimes very important modalities. We can find a lot of foot-based applications [54], gaze-based interactive systems [16], and multimodal interaction techniques that integrate foot and/or eye to accommodate to the conditions of some specific circumstances or to fulfill the needs of special users. Because of the related topic in this paper, this section will provide a brief review about the multimodal techniques that integrate the eye gaze or the foot modality with the others, and especially those including the two modalities of eye gaze and foot at the same time.

2.1   Integrating Gaze Input with Other Modalities

Eye gaze had been looked as a promising input modality for HCI nearly 4 decades ago, and there already had been a number of gaze-based applications that employed gaze input as an alternative to traditional manual input to perform different tasks, such as eye typing [29] and target selection [43]. Gaze input provides a great opportunity to make interactive systems accessible for people with disabilities or users who probably need to do concurrent tasks, but unfortunately its user experience is still not comparable with that of manual input due to the typical issues of "Midas Touch" problem [15], systematic [12] and local [5] errors of gaze estimations, and calibration drift [14].

Researchers had proposed a number of multimodal interaction techniques that integrated eye tracker with other manual input devices, such as mouse, keyboard, and touch screen. With respect to the quotidian device of mouse, Zhai et al. proposed the pioneer technique of MAGIC [62], which can automatically warp the mouse cursor to the position at which the user is fixating and then can click the mouse to quickly and accurately confirm the selection after a micro-adjustment if the cursor is not appropriately warped on the target. Regardless of the limited accuracy of eye tracking, the desired target is near the estimated position of the user's fixation and the warping behavior does not appear to be abrupt due to the inherent hand eye coordination in target selections [46]. Drewes and Schmidt modified this technique by using a touch mouse to explicitly activate the warping action [2], while Hild et al. employed the right mouse button to do so for moving target acquisition [9]. Fares et al. introduced a dynamic local calibration algorithm into this technique to warp the cursor as accurate as possible [4], and Lischke et al. further verified the effectiveness of MAGIC pointing in the environment where the user acquires the targets on a large high-resolution displays via a head mounted eye tracker [25].

Regarding the traditional keyboard, there were also a kind of techniques that combined it with eye tracker to perform the tasks in different contexts, such as desktop applications [22,58] and web browser [60]. Wang et al., for example, designed a Chinese input approach that used the user's eye gaze to highlight the desired Chinese character or word from a number of homophonic candidates and consistently used the spacebar, instead of different number keys, to confirm the selection [58]. Kumar et al. developed a practical technique that integrated eye gaze with keyboard input for daily tasks. With this technique, the user could press a pre-defined function key to open a sub window after she/he had steadily looked at the desired target, subsequently the user could focus on the magnified target again and then release the key to finally execute the function [22].

With the popularity of touch-based interactions, researchers explored the feasibility of combining gaze and touch together for different scenarios. Using a hand-held device to manually confirm the desired target, Stellmach et al. designed several gaze-supported techniques, such as Fisheye lens and MAGIC, to facilitate target selection [47] and positioning [48] on a remote display. Turner et al. combined gaze input with touch to "move" targets between a small hand-held touchscreen and a large remote display, which the user cannot directly touch but look [52], or to make it possible to indirectly rotate, scale and translate targets on a remote display as directly on a multitouch screen [51]. Voelker et al. explored the feasibility of transferring multitouch gestures from tabletop surface to vertical display, where the desired target is not convenient for touch but natural for look [55]. Pfeuffer et al. carried out a similar work [36], and they further evaluated the effectiveness of extending target manipulations from direct to indirect contact on the same surface of large multitouch screen [34] or small tablet [37], and even in pen-based interface [35]. The combination of gaze and touch input modalities was also used to facilitate text entry in desktop applications [21] or mobile devices [39]. Regardless of the concrete hardware configurations (e.g. head mounted [55] vs. remote [36] eye trackers) in these work, we can find that the touch modality was generally used to manipulate the target in different ways, while the modality of gaze input was mainly used to indicate which is the desired target or where the target needs to be placed.

Besides being combined with the dominant modalities of manual input as mentioned above, gaze input could also be combined with the supplementary modalities from other body parts, such as head and foot. Although head could be independently utilized to perform different tasks in user interfaces [17,19], it generally was used to support other input modality. Špakov and Majaranta investigated the effectiveness of five simple head gestures used to replace the tedious dwell time for target selection and reported that the subjects preferred to the gesture of nodding more than the others (turning left/right and tilting left/right) [57], and they further designed an algorithm to coordinate the gaze cursor with head movements so that its location could be consciously corrected if necessary [56]. Kurauchi et al. extended the idea of MAGIC pointing by replacing the mouse with a video-based head tracking device to finely adjust the cursor when it was not accurately located on the target that the user was looking at [23], while Jalaliniya et al. implemented this idea in smart glasses to alleviate the ergonomic problem of head pointing [18]. Kytö et al. developed and evaluated a series of refinement techniques, such as combining the primary gaze input with the secondary head input, to realize the accurate selection of small targets in head-worn augmented reality (AR) environments [24]. Recently, based on the inherent coordination of eye and head movements, Sidenmark and Gellersen proposed three novel interaction techniques for target acquisitions in virtual reality (VR) environments [44]. Cooperating with other colleagues, they further developed a technique, which could detect gestural head movement, to automatically switch between gaze and head input modes to seamlessly refine eye pointing [45]. This was not like the idea of MAGIC pointing, in which the different input modalities are cascade and explicitly switched to refine eye pointing.

Speech is also an important input modality, and there exist a number of multimodal techniques that combine it with gaze input for hand-free interactions. Tan et al. for example, made use of eye gaze to determine which field the recognized data from speech should be filled in a specific form [50], while Beelders and Blignaut utilized these two modalities to simulate a pointing device and applied it to general text entry [1]. With respect to the typical problem of ambiguities in speech recognition, Zhang et al. differentiated the desired one from the n-best candidates of speech recognition by the criterion that which was the nearest to the user's gaze on the screen [63]. With respect to the typical problem of inaccuracy in gaze input, Miniotas et al. used speech command to indicate which of the colored targets around the user's gaze position was the needed one so as to facilitate the selection of closely arranged small targets [32].

With the advancements of psycho-physiological sensor techniques, the signals of muscle or brain activities, which can be monitored with electromyography (EMG) or electroencephalography (EEG) respectively, could also be used as input modalities. Surakka et al. made use of voluntary frowning action to simulate mouse click event when the user needed to acquire the target that he/she was fixating on [49], realizing a hand-free input method by gaze and EMG, while

Mateo et al. implemented a similar work and shown comparable performance in pointing tasks, in terms of throughput, completion time and error rate, to that by the means of gaze-mouse input [30]. Recently, Pai et al. extended this idea in VR and further verified its effectiveness in a VR game they designed [33]. In brain-computer interfaces (BCI), the EEG input modality provides an opportunity for the system to "understand" the user's intentions. However, the system has to be trained to classify the user's brain activities in every possible scenario. In order to reduce the training time and increase the flexibility of BCI, researchers proposed a number of multimodal techniques that combined gaze with EEG for target selection [61], cursor control [13], "wish mouse" design [42].

2.2 Integrating Foot Input with Other Modalities

In the field of HCI, the modality of foot input had been used in a variety of unimodal interactive systems [54], such as foot pointing, foot-based gestures, mobile interactions, text entry, standing foot input, interactions under the desk or in head-mounted display. At the same time, it had also been combined with other input modalities to extend the capabilities of HCI.

One main combination we can find in the literature is the hand-foot input methods in different environments. Schöning et al. designed an intuitive input approach by feet from a Wii balance board to indirectly pan, tilt or zoom geospatial map on a large-scale multitouch wall so that the hands could be mainly used for precise input with less possibility to reposition [41]. Sangsuriyachot and Sugimoto developed a novel foot platform that could sense the pressures and gestures of the feet when the user was standing on the platform, thus the foot gestures, which they designed to cooperate with the hand gestures on a tabletop screen, were extracted from not only explicit foot movements but also implicit pressure distributions [40]. In handheld devices, the combination of hand and foot input was able to achieve a fast coordination of all four limbs of the user in HCI, especially in mobile games [28]. Besides the hand gestures on different multi-touch surfaces, foot input could also be combined with mid-air hand gestures to manipulate, for example, 3D virtual objects [26] without touching. In order to appropriately evaluate the effectiveness of foot input, with which users are generally less experienced, Garcia and Vu investigated and highlighted the significance of training by four different word-processing tasks when a foot mouse was used as the secondary input device to cooperate with the primary device of keyboard [6].

Another important combination we can find is the methods based on the two hand-free input modalities of foot and eye. That is to say, not only those modalities as reviewed above but also the foot input modality could be combined with gaze input due to the maturity of eye tracking technology in recent years. For zoomable interfaces, Klamka et al. proposed different multimodal interaction techniques that utilized gaze input to indicate the interested area of zooming in/out or the direction of panning, and designed different foot input devices, including foot pedals, foot joystick and foot rocker, to synchronously control the speed of zooming or panning [7,20]. Similarly, Çöltekin et al. proposed a gaze-foot input approach to zoom and pan in geospatial map while using a Wii balance board to detect foot gestures [27]. To acquire moving targets, Hild et al. found that the method of tapping a foot pedal when the user was fixating on the target was comparable to the traditional method of pressing the ENTER-key [10]. Instead of using dwell time to remove the "Midas Touch" problem for general tasks in GUI environments [38], Rajanna et al. developed a wearable quasi-mouse, which was able to simulate most of the standard mouse events by foot on a flexible pressure pad. Using a mobile eye tracker and a tactile floor, Hatscher et al. developed a multimodal technique for physicians to manipulate medical images [8].

As can be seen, there was still a lack of work that comprehensively evaluated the approach of eye-foot input for target acquisitions while the approaches independently based on the modality of eye gaze [31,64–66] or foot [3,11,53] and that based on the MAGIC technique [62] had been done. This situation motivated us to carry out an experiment as described below.

3   Experiment: Eye Pointing and Foot Tapping

The purpose of this experiment was to evaluate the human performance when acquiring targets by the two hand-free modalities of eye and foot. This experiment allows us to examine which model is suitable for this task and how fast the user can response to press the foot pedal when looking at the target, i.e. how well the user can coordinate foot-eye movements.

3.1   Apparatus and Subjects

A low-cost remote eye tracker, *theEyeTribe* (see Fig. 1c), was used as the gaze input device. It worked at the sampling rate of 60 Hz. The tasks were presented on a 24-inch LED display at 1920 × 1200 resolution. As Fig. 1d illustrates, the foot input device was a USB pedal switcher, which can produce click event when treading the pedal. A group of 14 able-bodied subjects (including 10 females and 4 males), with the average age of 24.5, voluntarily took part in this experiment. They were recruited in the campus and had normal or correct-to-normal vision, without color blindness.

3.2   Task and Procedure

At the beginning, the experimenter had the subject naturally sit in front of the display and emphasized the requirement that she/he needed to adjust the chair's position and/or height so as to be able to look straight ahead at the center of the screen. The display was placed on a desktop, keeping a distance of about 70 cm to the subject's head. After a 9-point calibration, the subject was asked to perform eye pointing and foot tapping task, which was to acquire a square target by tapping the foot pedal when the subject was looking at it. As Fig. 1e shows, for each trial, there was a trial-start button randomly appearing

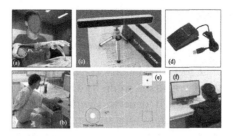

Fig. 1. (a) and (b) the users who can benefit from the method of eye-foot input; (c) and (d) the devices used in this work; (e) and (f) the experimental task and environment.

at one of the predefined positions on the screen. At first, the subject needed to look at the button for a very short time to explicitly begin a trial so that the target immediately appeared in the diagonal direction, with the concurrent disappearance of the trial-start button. Then, the subject was asked to fixate on the target as soon as possible and tap the pedal with her/his preferred foot at the same time to "click" it. If the gaze cursor was hovering on the target when the click event took place, a correct trial was recorded, otherwise an error trial was recorded. If the gaze cursor was not able to enter the effective area of the target within 5000 ms after the trial was started, an error trial would also be recorded. For each of the unsuccessful trials, it could be repeated for 5 times at most before the experimenter suspended the experiment to recalibrate the eye tracker. At the end of each trial, the start button reappeared at a different position for next trial, with the target disappearing again.

Note that the positions of the trial-start button and the target in each trial were symmetrical about the center of the screen, and were in the diagonal lines.

3.3 Design

This experiment employed a repeated measures within-subject factorial design. The independent factors (variables) were target size, i.e. width W (80, 120 and 160 pixels), gaze movement distance, i.e. saccadic amplitude A (500, 750, and 1000 pixels). A fully-crossed design of $3W \times 3A$ resulted in 9 combinations. For each combination, there were 4 trials repeatedly presented in the 4 diagonal directions, respectively, leading to 36 trials per block to cover the whole task conditions. These trials were presented in a given random order, but the trial-start button would not appear at the position where the target had just been placed in the last trial. The subject finished all task blocks within one session of about 30 min.

3.4   Measures

There were 4 main measures defined to reflect the performance as follows.

- Eye movement time (EMT). It denotes the duration from the trial beginning to the time when the gaze cursor enters the target area at the first time.
- Foot response time (FRT). It denotes the duration from the moment when the gaze cursor enters the target area to the moment when the desired target is "clicked" as soon as possible. This measure reflects users' capability of eye-foot coordination.
- Eye pointing time (EPT). It denotes the time that is spent to acquire the desired target after the trial begins. Ideally, $EPT = EMT + FRT$.
- Average cursor distance (ACD). When the gaze cursor was inside of the target area, its positions were sampled at the rate 25 Hz. ACD means the average distance from the sampled cursor positions to their center during the time of FRT.

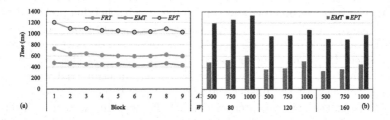

Fig. 2. (a) Learning effects; (b) the averages of EMT and EPT by combination of (A, W).

3.5   Results

This experiment generated more than 5.1 thousand trials, with more than 83 thousand sampled gaze points. We excluded the errors and the outliers (8.4% of the data) from the following repeated measures ANOVA.

Learning Effects. Grouped by task block, the total averages of EMT, FRT and EPT were 449.9 ms, 626.7 ms and 1076.6 ms, respectively. As implied by Fig. 2a, The measure of EPT included a learning effect ($F_{8,104} = 2.127, p < .05$), while both EMT ($F_{8,104} = 1.105, p = .366$) and FRT ($F_{8,104} = 1.813, p = .083$) did not include learning effects. Post hoc pair-wise comparison tests indicated that the learning effect in EPT was mainly due to the significant differences ($p < .05$) between the 1st block and each of the 2nd, 6th, 7th and 9th blocks. There was no significant difference within any pair of the other blocks. Therefore, the first block was further excluded from the following ANOVA.

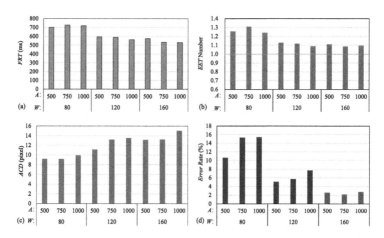

Fig. 3. The averages of (a) FRT, (b) EET, (c) ACD and (d) *Error Rate* by combination of (A, W).

Eye Movement Time (EMT) and Eye Pointing Time (EPT). The factor of W had significant main effects on both EMT ($F_{2,26} = 83.05, p < .0005$) and EPT ($F_{2,26} = 58.16, p < .0005$); and the factor of A also had significant main effects on both EMT ($F_{2,26} = 27.98, p < .0005$) and EPT ($F_{2,26} = 11.66, p < .0005$). While the interaction effect of these two factors on EMT ($F_{4,52} = 0.49, p = .744$) as well as EPT ($F_{4,52} = 0.74, p = .566$) was not significant. As Fig. 2b shows, both EMT and EPT were generally increased with the increase of A but with the decrease of W. The total averages of EMT by W were 545.0, 418.2, 383.3 ms, and those by A were 395.3, 426.3, 524.9 ms. The total averages of EPT by W were 1265.1, 1001.3, 932.0 ms, and those by A were 1021.9, 1045.8, 1130.8 ms. Post hoc pair-wise comparison tests revealed that there was no significant difference of EMT ($p = .081$) or EPT ($p = .292$) only between the two A levels of 500 and 750 pixels.

Foot Response Time (FRT). The measure FRT was significantly affected by W ($F_{2,26} = 24.91, p < .0005$) but not by A ($F_{2,26} = 0.901, p = .418$). The interaction effect of $A \times W$ on FRT was also not significant ($F_{4,52} = 1.50, p = .214$). Figure 3a shows that FRT was decreased with the increase of W. The total averages by W from 80 to 160 pixels were 720.1, 583.1 and 548.7 ms, respectively, being successively and significantly decreased, while the total averages by A were 626.6, 619.5 and 605.9 pixels, without significant differences among them.

Average Cursor Distance (ACD). Only the factor of W had significant main effect on ACD ($F_{2,26} = 22.34, p < .0005$), while both of the main effect of A ($F_{2,26} = 2.03, p = .151$) and the interaction effect of $A \times W$ ($F_{4,52} = 0.82, p = .520$) were not significant. As Fig. 3c shows, ACD was generally increased with the increase of W. The total averages of ACD by W were 9.4, 12.6, 13.8 pixels, and those by A were 11.2, 11.8, 12.8 pixels. Post hoc pair-wise comparison tests revealed that the ACD difference between the two W levels of 120 and 160 pixels was not significant ($p = .061$). The grand mean was about 12.0 pixels, and it could be directly used in performance model fitting.

Error Rate. The factor of W had significant main effect on error rate ($F_{2,26} = 20.89, p < .0005$). Similar to the effects on FRT and ACD, the factor A also had no significant main effect ($F_{2,26} = 3.31, p = .053$) and interaction effect with W ($F_{4,52} = 2.18, p = .084$) on error rate. As Fig. 3d shows, error rate was significantly increased with the decrease of W, and slightly increased with the increase of A. The total averages of error rate by W were 12.8%, 5.9%, 2.4%, and those by A were 5.6%, 7.2%, 8.3%. Post hoc pair-wise comparison tests revealed that the difference of error rate between every pair of W levels as well as that between the two A levels of 500 and 1000 pixels ($p = .023$) was significant.

3.6 Performance Model Fitting

There were different models used to describe foot movement times. As the first work to investigate the performance in reciprocal foot tapping tasks, Drury further modified the Welford's version [59] of Fitts' law (see Eq. 1) to take account of the size of the subject's shoe as expressed in Eq. 2 [3].

$$MT = a + b \log_2 (2A/W) \tag{1}$$

$$MT = k \log_2 \left(\frac{A}{W} + 0.5 \right) \Rightarrow MT = a + b \log_2 \left(\frac{A}{W + S} + 0.5 \right) \tag{2}$$

where k is a constant in Welford's model; a and b are two regression coefficients; and A, W and S denote movement distance, target width (size) and shoe size, respectively. Although the original model of Fitts' law already had very good fit ($R^2 > .95$) to the data of Drury's experiments, the accuracy of the model could be further improved when taking into account the factor of show size in foot tapping tasks. Hoffmann carried out three experiments to compare the movement time of hand and foot in different conditions [11], verifying the effectiveness of Eqs. 3 and 4 for visually controlled and ballistic tasks, respectively.

$$MT = a + b \log_2 (2A/W) + c \log_2 (W) \tag{3}$$

$$MT = a + b\sqrt{A} \tag{4}$$

Especially, when the factor of target size W was fully crossed with task ID, Eq. 3 had better fitness to the data of foot movement ($R^2 > .98$). In the field of HCI, Velloso et al. investigated the fitness of the standard Fitts' model (see Eq. 5) when foot movement was used to perform the 1D and 2D pointing tasks as specified in ISO 9241-9 [53]. According to their experimental results, however, the standard Fitts' model was not robust under different conditions. Fitts' law was also used to evaluate the gaze-based pointing tasks either in a traditional desktop display [66] or in a head-mounted display [31]. Unfortunately, the fitness of Eq. 5 to the data of eye pointing was absent.

$$MT = a + b \log_2 (A/W + 1) \tag{5}$$

On the contrary, Zhang et al. proposed a new model, instead of extending Fitts' law, for eye pointing tasks as Eq. 6 expresses [65].

$$MT = a + b \times ID_{eye} = a + b \times \frac{80e^{\lambda A}}{W - \mu} \tag{6}$$

where the symbols λ and μ are two empirical constants that are directly related to the rapid saccades and jittery fixations, respectively. Zhang et al. pointed out that it was good enough, in practice, to set $\lambda = 0.001$ to reflect the actual contribution of saccadic amplitude, and that μ could be replaced using the size of the area where the gaze points distribute when the user was fixating on a object [64]. In other words, μ is a measurable constant by sampling gaze points. The fraction term is defined as the index of difficulty for eye pointing task (ID_{eye}). Note that the purpose of using a multiplier of 80 in the fraction is to make ID_{eye} comparable with Fitts ID in terms of quantity.

Table 1. Results of model fitting.

Model		a		b		c		R^2
		Estimate	Std. Err.	Estimate	Std. Err.	Estimate	Std. Err.	
Equation 6	EMT	207.30	25.32	153.97	15.28	$\lambda =$	$\mu = 0$	**.936**
	EPT	**722.62**	35.46	165.53	15.87	0.001	$\mu = 24$	**.940**
Equation 7	EMT	334.10	317.19	135.93	28.64	-38.253	37.37	.911
	EPT	**2322.78**	463.17	116.33	41.82	-230.90	54.56	.934
Equation 5	EMT	-37.59	62.53	168.95	21.45	—	—	.899
	EPT	312.784	1169.32	261.05	58.09	—	—	.743

The effectiveness of Eq. 6 had been verified under different dwell time conditions, but not in a multimodal interaction environment like the configuration in this experiment. To fill this gap, it had been fitted to the data of EMT and EPT in this experiment. According to the measure of ACD, the constant μ can be set to 24 (pixels) for EPT, and 0 for EMT. At the same time, the standard Fitts model and a new variation like Eq. 7, inspired by Eq. 3, were also used just for comparisons. Table 1 summarizes the results of model fitting. As can be seen, Eq. 6 got the best fits to the data of EMT and EPT. The regression lines of EMT and EPT based on ID_{eye}, as well as those based on Fitts ID, are all plotted in Fig. 4.

$$MT = a + b \log_2 (A/W + 0.5) + c \log_2 (W) \tag{7}$$

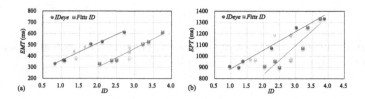

Fig. 4. Regression lines of the ID_{eye} model and Fitts' law.

4 Discussion

In order to accommodate the limited accuracy, precision and output frequency of the low-cost eye tracker used in this experiment, the targets were relatively larger than those in Zhang et al.'s experiments [65], in which a professional head-mounted eye tracker was used as the gaze input device, but the results indicated that the main effects of A and W on the performance measures of EMT and EPT were consistent with those they reported. Therefore, it is believable that the gaze data collected in this experiment also properly reflected the performance in the process of eye pointing.

From the experimental results, we found that saccadic amplitude A had no significant main effect and interaction effect with W on the three measures FRT, ACD, and error rate at the same time. In other words, these three measures were significantly affected only by the factor of W. According to the result to FRT, it seemed as if the user's inherent capability of eye-foot coordination would change with target size, and the user seemed to be slower to respond to smaller target. We further checked the behavior of the gaze cursor and found that it could repeatedly enter and exit the area of the target especially when the target was small. After counting the cursor events of entering target (EET), we found that the EET number increased with the decrease of target size, as shown in Fig. 3b. This was not because of the user's intentional gaze input but the limitations of eye tracking technology or unconscious eye jitters. Therefore, the prolonged FRT most likely resulted from the measurement error on small targets. Ideally, FRT could be accurately measured when EET was just 1. According to the results shown in Fig. 3a and b, it can be inferred that the real average of FRT should be close to 500 ms.

As mentioned above, this experiment employed large targets to overcome the limitations of the gaze input device, but on the other hand the utilized saccadic amplitudes were also relatively large in order to make the distribution of ID_{eye} wide enough. Comparing the levels of A with those in Zhang et al.'s experiments [65], we believe that this experiment did not exactly reveal the main effect of A on ACD and error rate. It just implied that the variations of A on high levels will not result in significant changes of ACD and error rate.

Comparing the results of model fitting in Table 1, we can find that the modified Fitts model (Eq. 7) also achieved good fits to the data of EMT and EPT. However, it is difficult to explain the connections between the corresponding regression coefficients for EMT and EPT. For example, the coefficient a for EPT was extremely larger than the counterpart for EMT, and their difference was even far beyond the maximum of EPT. It means that Eq. 7 is not able to capture the underlying features of eye-foot input, and the improvements of model fitting, compared with the standard Fitts model, is likely due to the fact that the predictive and descriptive ability of a model often can be enhanced mathematically with a supplementary variable. On the contrary, it is easy to explain the coefficients in the ID_{eye} model. The estimates of b for EMT and EPT are close to each other, and the difference of the estimates of a is about 515 (ms). According to the discussion above, this is consistent with the real average of FRT. Therefore, the the ID_{eye} model can properly capture the underlying features of eye-foot input, especially being able to correctly reflect the relationship that $EPT = EMT + FRT$.

With respect to the standard Fitts model, it provided poor fits to the data not like those results in previous work [3,11]. One important reason is that the foot was only used to tap the pedal switcher without moving to control the cursor in this work. Another is that the important feature of scale independency in Fitts' law does not hold true for gaze input. As depicted in Fig. 4, there are three unfilled markers used to plot the identical Fitts ID value (i.e. 2.858) of the three combinations of A and W, i.e. (500×80), (750×120) and (1000×160), respectively. It is clear that the corresponding observations of EMT and EPT are obviously different from each other, resulting in the biggest errors of the Fitts models. However, the corresponding ID_{eye} values determined by those combinations have obvious linear correlation with the observations of EMT and EPT. In other words, ID_{eye} is more accurate than Fitts ID to describe the performance in the context of eye-foot input.

5   Conclusions

Instead of clicking mouse button to confirm the selection after accurately pointing the cursor at the desired target, the user can tap a foot pedal as quickly as possible to confirm the selection just when looking at the target in a multimodal interaction environment with eye-foot input. The eye-foot input provides a great opportunity for the users with busy hands or hand disabilities to interaction with computers. The eye pointing and foot tapping task experiment indicated that the user was soon able to coordinate her/his foot with the eyes for target acquisitions. The experimental results also indicated that the user could respond fast to finish the task in the level of 600 ms from the moment when the gaze cursor just entered the area of the target to the time of pressing the foot pedal down, while a method to measure foot response time more accurately is necessary in the future work.

Similar to the results in dwell-based eye pointing task experiments, the main performance measures of eye movement time (EMT) and eye pointing time

(EPT) under the eye-foot multimodal input condition were also significantly increased with the increase of saccadic amplitude A and/or the decrease of target width (size) W, and vice versa. The ID_{eye} model that was specifically proposed for dwell-based eye pointing task could also be fitted good enough ($R^2 > .935$) to the data of EMT and EPT, and it got better fitness than the de facto standard model of Fitts' law in the field of HCI. Technically, a new modified version of Fitts' law could improve the fitness, but it could not properly uncover the underlying features of eye pointing. For example, the typical feature of scale independency implied in Fitts' law is not true for eye pointing.

References

1. Beelders, T.R., Blignaut, P.J.: Gaze and Speech: Pointing Device and Text Entry Modality, pp. 51–75. Springer, New York (2014). https://doi.org/10.1007/9783-319-02868-2_4

2. Drewes, H., Schmidt, A.: The MAGIC touch: combining MAGIC-pointing with a touch-sensitive mouse. In: Gross, T., et al. (eds.) Human-Computer Interaction - INTERACT 2009. INTERACT 2009. Lecture Notes in Computer Science, vol. 5727. Springer, Berlin, Heidelberg (2009). https://doi.org/10.1007/9783-642-03658-3_46

3. Drury, C.G.: Application of fitts' law to foot-pedal design. Hum. Factors **17**(4), 368–373 (1975). https://doi.org/10.1177/001872087501700408

4. Fares, R., Fang, S., Komogortsev, O.: Can We Beat the Mouse with MAGIC?, pp. 1387–1390. ACM (2013). https://doi.org/10.1145/2470654.2466183

5. Feit, A.M., et al.: Toward everyday gaze input: accuracy and precision of eye tracking and implications for design. In: Proceedings of the 2017 CHI Conference on Human Factors in Computing Systems, pp. 1118–1130. ACM (2017). https://doi.org/10.1145/3025453.3025599

6. Garcia, F.P., Vu, K.P.L.: Effectiveness of hand- and foot-operated secondary input devices for word-processing tasks before and after training. Comput. Hum. Behav. **27**(1), 285–295 (2011). https://doi.org/10.1016/j.chb.2010.08.006

7. Göbel, F., Klamka, K., Siegel, A., Vogt, S., Stellmach, S., Dachselt, R.: Gaze-supported foot interaction in zoomable information spaces. In: CHI '13 Extended Abstracts on Human Factors in Computing Systems, pp. 3059–3062. CHI EA '13, ACM (2013). https://doi.org/10.1145/2468356.2479610

8. Hatscher, B., Luz, M., Nacke, L.E., Elkmann, N., Müller, V., Hansen, C.: Gazetap: towards hands-free interaction in the operating room. In: Proceedings of the 19th ACM International Conference on Multimodal Interaction, pp. 243–251. ICMI '17, ACM (2017). https://doi.org/10.1145/3136755.3136759

9. Hild, J., Gill, D., Beyerer, J.: Comparing mouse and MAGIC pointing for moving target acquisition. In: Proceedings of the Symposium on Eye Tracking Research and Applications, pp. 131–134. ACM (2014). https://doi.org/10.1145/2578153.2578172

10. Hild, J., Petersen, P., Beyerer, J.: Moving target acquisition by gaze pointing and button press using hand or foot. In: Proceedings of the Ninth Biennial ACM Symposium on Eye Tracking Research and Applications, pp. 257–260. ETRA '16, ACM (2016). https://doi.org/10.1145/2857491.2857535

11. Hoffmann, E.R.: A comparison of hand and foot movement times. Ergonomics **34**(4), 397–406 (1991). https://doi.org/10.1080/00140139108967324

12. Hornof, A.J., Halverson, T.: Cleaning up systematic error in eye-tracking data by using required fixation locations. Behav. Res. Meth. Instrum. Comput. **34**(4), 592–604 (2002)

13. Huang, B., Lo, A.H.P., Shi, B.E.: Integrating EEG information improves performance of gaze based cursor control. In: Proceedings of the 6th International IEEE/EMBS Conference on Neural Engineering, pp. 415–418 (2013). https://doi.org/10.1109/NER.2013.6695960

14. Huang, M.X., Bulling, A.: Saccalib: reducing calibration distortion for stationary eye trackers using saccadic eye movements. In: Proceedings of the 11th ACM Symposium on Eye Tracking Research and Applications. ACM (2019). https://doi.org/10.1145/3317956.3321553

15. Jacob, R.J.K.: The use of eye movements in human-computer interaction techniques: what you look at is what you get. ACM Trans. Inf. Syst. **9**(2), 152–169 (1991). https://doi.org/10.1145/123078.128728

16. Jacob, R.J.K., Karn, K.S.: Eye tracking in human-computer interaction and usability research: ready to deliver the promises. In: Hyönä, J., Radach, R., Deubel, H. (eds.) The Mind's Eye, pp. 573–605. North-Holland, Amsterdam (2003). https://doi.org/10.1016/B978-044451020-4/50031-1

17. Jalaliniya, S., Mardanbeigi, D., Pederson, T., Hansen, D.W.: Head and eye movement as pointing modalities for eyewear computers. In: 2014 11th International Conference on Wearable and Implantable Body Sensor Networks Workshops, pp. 50–53 (2014). https://doi.org/10.1109/BSN.Workshops.2014.14

18. Jalaliniya, S., Mardanbegi, D., Pederson, T.: MAGIC pointing for eyewear computers. In: Proceedings of the 2015 ACM International Symposium on Wearable Computers, pp. 155–158. ACM (2015). https://doi.org/10.1145/2802083.2802094

19. Kjeldsen, R.: Head gestures for computer control. In: Proceedings of the IEEE ICCV Workshop on Recognition, Analysis, and Tracking of Faces and Gestures in Real-Time Systems (RATFG-RTS'01), pp. 61–67. RATFG-RTS '01, IEEE Computer Society (2001)

20. Klamka, K., Siegel, A., Vogt, S., Göbel, F., Stellmach, S., Dachselt, R.: Look and pedal: hands-free navigation in zoomable information spaces through gaze-supported foot input. In: Proceedings of the 2015 ACM on International Conference on Multimodal Interaction, pp. 123–130. ACM (2015). https://doi.org/10.1145/2818346.2820751

21. Kumar, C., Hedeshy, R., MacKenzie, I.S., Staab, S.: Tagswipe: touch assisted gaze swipe for text entry. In: Proceedings of the 2020 CHI Conference on Human Factors in Computing Systems, pp. 1–12. CHI '20, ACM (2020). https://doi.org/10.1145/3313831.3376317

22. Kumar, M., Paepcke, A., Winograd, T.: Eyepoint: Practical pointing and selection using gaze and keyboard. In: Proceedings of the SIGCHI Conference on Human Factors in Computing Systems, pp. 421–430. CHI '07, ACM (2007). https://doi.org/10.1145/1240624.1240692

23. Kurauchi, A., Feng, W., Morimoto, C., Betke, M.: HMAGIC: head movement and gaze input cascaded pointing. In: Proceedings of the 8th ACM International Conference on PErvasive Technologies Related to Assistive Environments. PETRA '15, ACM (2015). https://doi.org/10.1145/2769493.2769550

24. Kytö, M., Ens, B., Piumsomboon, T., Lee, G.A., Billinghurst, M.: Pinpointing: precise head- and eye-based target selection for augmented reality. In: Proceedings of the 2018 CHI Conference on Human Factors in Computing Systems, pp. 1–14. ACM (2018). https://doi.org/10.1145/3173574.3173655

25. Lischke, L., Schwind, V., Friedrich, K., Schmidt, A., Henze, N.: MAGIC-Pointing on large high-resolution displays. In: Proceedings of the 2016 CHI Conference Extended Abstracts on Human Factors in Computing Systems, pp. 1706–1712. CHI EA '16, ACM (2016). https://doi.org/10.1145/2851581.2892479

26. Lopes, D., Relvas, F., Paulo, S., Rekik, Y., Grisoni, L., Jorge, J.: Feetiche: Feet input for contactless hand gesture interaction. In: The 17th International Conference on Virtual-Reality Continuum and Its Applications in Industry. ACM (2019). https://doi.org/10.1145/3359997.3365704

27. Çöltekin, A., Hempel, J., Brychtova, A., Giannopoulos, I., Stellmach, S., Dachselt, R.: Gaze and feet as additional input modalities for interacting with geospatial interfaces. In: ISPRS Annals of Photogrammetry, Remote Sensing and Spatial Information Sciences, pp. 113–120 (2016). https://doi.org/10.5194/isprs-annals-III-2-113-2016

28. Lv, Z., Halawani, A., Feng, S., Li, H., Réhman, S.U.: Multimodal hand and foot gesture interaction for handheld devices. ACM Trans. Multimedia Comput. Commun. Appl. 11(1s) (2014). https://doi.org/10.1145/2645860

29. Majaranta, P., Räihä, K.J.: Twenty years of eye typing: systems and design issues. In: Proceedings of the 2002 Symposium on Eye Tracking Research & Applications, pp. 15–22. ETRA '02, Association for Computing Machinery, New York, NY, USA (2002). https://doi.org/10.1145/507072.507076

30. Mateo, J.C., San Agustin, J., Hansen, J.P.: Gaze beats mouse: Hands-free selection by combining gaze and EMG. In: CHI '08 Extended Abstracts on Human Factors in Computing Systems, pp. 3039–3044. CHI EA '08, ACM (2008). https://doi.org/10.1145/1358628.1358804

31. Minakata, K., Hansen, J.P., MacKenzie, I.S., Bækgaard, P., Rajanna, V.: Pointing by gaze, head, and foot in a head-mounted display. In: Proceedings of the 11th ACM Symposium on Eye Tracking Research and Applications. ETRA '19, ACM (2019). https://doi.org/10.1145/3317956.3318150

32. Miniotas, D., Špakov, O., Tugoy, I., MacKenzie, I.S.: Speech-augmented eye gaze interaction with small closely spaced targets. In: Proceedings of the 2006 Symposium on Eye Tracking Research & Applications, pp. 67–72. ACM (2006). https://doi.org/10.1145/1117309.1117345

33. Pai, Y.S., Dingler, T., Kunze, K.: Assessing hands-free interactions for vr using eye gaze and electromyography. Virtual Reality 23(2), 119–131 (2019). https://doi.org/10.1007/s10055018-0371-2

34. Pfeuffer, K., Alexander, J., Chong, M.K., Gellersen, H.: Gaze-touch: Combining gaze with multi-touch for interaction on the same surface. In: Proceedings of the 27th Annual ACM Symposium on User Interface Software and Technology, pp. 509–518. UIST '14, ACM (2014). https://doi.org/10.1145/2642918.2647397

35. Pfeuffer, K., Alexander, J., Chong, M.K., Zhang, Y., Gellersen, H.: Gaze-shifting: direct-indirect input with pen and touch modulated by gaze. In: Proceedings of the 28th Annual ACM Symposium on User Interface Software and Technology, pp. 373–383. UIST '15, ACM (2015). https://doi.org/10.1145/2807442.2807460

36. Pfeuffer, K., Alexander, J., Gellersen, H.: Gaze+touch vs. touch: what's the trade-off when using gaze to extend touch to remote displays?. In: Abascal, J., Barbosa, S., Fetter, M., Gross, T., Palanque, P., Winckler, M. (eds.) Human-Computer Interaction - INTERACT 2015. INTERACT 2015. Lecture Notes in Computer Science, vol. 9297. Springer, Cham (2015). https://doi.org/10.1007/978-3-319-22668-2_27

37. Pfeuffer, K., Gellersen, H.: Gaze and touch interaction on tablets. In: Proceedings of the 29th Annual ACM Symposium on User Interface Software and Technology, pp. 301–311. UIST '16, ACM (2016). https://doi.org/10.1145/2984511.2984514

38. Rajanna, V.D.: Gaze and foot input: toward a rich and assistive interaction modality. In: Companion Publication of the 21st International Conference on Intelligent User Interfaces, pp. 126–129. IUI '16 Companion, ACM (2016). https://doi.org/10.1145/2876456.2876462

39. Rivu, R., Abdrabou, Y., Pfeuffer, K., Hassib, M., Alt, F.: Gaze'n'touch: Enhancing text selection on mobile devices using gaze. In: Extended Abstracts of the 2020 CHI Conference on Human Factors in Computing Systems, pp. 1–8. CHI EA '20, ACM (2020). https://doi.org/10.1145/3334480.3382802

40. Sangsuriyachot, N., Sugimoto, M.: Novel interaction techniques based on a combination of hand and foot gestures in tabletop environments. In: Proceedings of the 10th Asia Pacific Conference on Computer Human Interaction, pp. 21–28. APCHI '12, ACM (2012). https://doi.org/10.1145/2350046.2350053

41. Schöning, J., Daiber, F., Krüger, A., Rohs, M.: Using hands and feet to navigate and manipulate spatial data. In: CHI '09 Extended Abstracts on Human Factors in Computing Systems, pp. 4663–4668. CHI EA '09, ACM (2009). https://doi.org/10.1145/1520340.1520717

42. Shishkin, S.L., et al.: EEG negativity in fixations used for gaze-based control: Toward converting intentions into actions with an eye-brain-computer interface. Front. Neurosci. 10, Article 528 (2016)

43. Sibert, L.E., Jacob, R.J.K.: Evaluation of eye gaze interaction. In: Proceedings of the SIGCHI Conference on Human Factors in Computing Systems, pp. 281–288. CHI '00, ACM (2000). https://doi.org/10.1145/332040.332445

44. Sidenmark, L., Gellersen, H.: Eye & head: synergetic eye and head movement for gaze pointing and selection. In: Proceedings of the 32nd Annual ACM Symposium on User Interface Software and Technology, pp. 1161–1174. ACM (2019). https://doi.org/10.1145/3332165.3347921

45. Sidenmark, L., Mardanbegi, D., Gomez, A.R., Clarke, C., Gellersen, H.: Bimodalgaze: Seamlessly refined pointing with gaze and filtered gestural head movement. In: ACM Symposium on Eye Tracking Research and Applications. ACM (2020). https://doi.org/10.1145/3379155.3391312

46. Smith, B.A., Ho, J., Ark, W., Zhai, S.: Hand eye coordination patterns intarget selection. In: Proceedings of the 2000 Symposium on Eye TrackingResearch and Applications, pp. 117–22. ACM (2000). https://doi.org/10.1145/355017.35504

47. Stellmach, S., Dachselt, R.: Look and touch: gaze-supported targetacquisition. In: Proceedings of the SIGCHI Conference on Human Factors inComputing Systems, pp. 2981–2990. CHI '12, ACM (2012). https://doi.org/10.1145/2207676.2208709

48. Stellmach, S., Dachselt, R.: Still looking: Investigating seamless gaze-supported selection, positioning, and manipulation of distant targets. In: Proceedings of the SIGCHI Conference on Human Factors in Computing Systems, pp. 285–294. ACM (2013), https://doi.org/10.1145/2470654.2470695

49. Surakka, V., Illi, M., Isokoski, P.: Gazing and frowning as a new human-computer interaction technique. ACM Trans. Appl. Percept. 1(1), 40–56 (2004). https://doi.org/10.1145/1008722.1008726

50. Tan, Y.K., Sherkat, N., Allen, T.: Eye gaze and speech for data entry: a comparison of different data entry methods. In: 2003 International Conference on Multimedia and Expo. ICME '03. Proceedings (Cat. No.03TH8698), vol. 1, pp. 41–44 (2003). https://doi.org/10.1109/ICME.2003.1220849

51. Turner, J., Alexander, J., Bulling, A., Gellersen, H.: Gaze+rst: integrating gaze and multitouch for remote rotate-scale-translate tasks. In: Proceedings of the 33rd Annual ACM Conference on Human Factors in Computing Systems, pp. 4179–4188. ACM (2015). https://doi.org/10.1145/2702123.2702355

52. Turner, J., Alexander, J., Bulling, A., Schmidt, D., Gellersen, H.: Eye pull, eye push: moving objects between large screens and personal devices with gaze and touch. In: Kotze, P., Marsden, G., Lindgaard, G., Wesson, J., Winckler, M. (eds.) Human-Computer Interaction - INTERACT 2013. INTERACT 2013. Lecture Notes in Computer Science, vol. 8118. Springer, Berlin, Heidelberg (2013). https://doi.org/10.1007/9783-642-40480-1_11

53. Velloso, E., Alexander, J., Bulling, A., Gellersen, H.: Interactions under the desk: a characterisation of foot movements for input in a seated position. In: Abascal, J., Barbosa, S., Fetter, M., Gross, T., Palanque, P., Winckler, M. (eds.) Human-Computer Interaction - INTERACT 2015. INTERACT 2015. Lecture Notes in Computer Science, vol. 9296. Springer, Cham (2015). https://doi.org/10.1007/978-3-319-22701-6_29

54. Velloso, E., Schmidt, D., Alexander, J., Gellersen, H., Bulling, A.: The feet in human-computer interaction: a survey of foot-based interaction. ACM Comput. Surv. **48**(2) (2015). https://doi.org/10.1145/2816455

55. Voelker, S., Matviienko, A., Schöning, J., Borchers, J.: Combining direct and indirect touch input for interactive workspaces using gaze input. In: Proceedings of the 3rd ACM Symposium on Spatial User Interaction, pp. 79–88. SUI '15, ACM (2015). https://doi.org/10.1145/2788940.2788949

56. Špakov, O., Isokoski, P., Majaranta, P.: Look and lean: accurate head-assisted eye pointing. In: Proceedings of the Symposium on Eye Tracking Research and Applications, pp. 35–42. ETRA '14, ACM (2014). https://doi.org/10.1145/2578153.2578157

57. Špakov, O., Majaranta, P.: Enhanced gaze interaction using simple head gestures. In: Proceedings of the 2012 ACM Conference on Ubiquitous Computing, pp. 705–710. UbiComp '12, ACM (2012). https://doi.org/10.1145/2370216.2370369

58. Wang, J., Zhai, S., Su, H.: Chinese input with keyboard and eye-tracking: an anatomical study. In: Proceedings of the SIGCHI Conference on Human Factors in Computing Systems, pp. 349–356. CHI '01, Association for Computing Machinery (2001). https://doi.org/10.1145/365024.365298

59. Welford, A.T.: Fundamentals of Skill. Methuen, London (1968)

60. Yeoh, K.N., Lutteroth, C., Weber, G.: Eyes and keys: an evaluation of click alternatives combining gaze and keyboard. In: Abascal, J., Barbosa, S., Fetter, M., Gross, T., Palanque, P., Winckler, M. (eds.) Human-Computer Interaction - INTERACT 2015. INTERACT 2015. Lecture Notes in Computer Science, vol. 9296. Springer, Cham (2015). https://doi.org/10.1007/978-3-319-22701-6_28

61. Zander, T.O., Gaertner, M., Kothe, C., Vilimek, R.: Combining eye gaze input with a brain-computer interface for touchless human-computer interaction. Int. J. Hum.-Comput. Interact. **27**(1), 38–51 (2010). https://doi.org/10.1080/10447318.2011.535752

62. Zhai, S., Morimoto, C., Ihde, S.: Manual and gaze input cascaded (magic) pointing. In: Proceedings of the SIGCHI Conference on Human Factors in Computing Systems, pp. 246–253. CHI '99, ACM (1999). https://doi.org/10.1145/302979.303053

63. Zhang, Q., Imamiya, A., Go, K., Mao, X.: Resolving ambiguities of a gaze and-speech interface. In: Proceedings of the 2004 Symposium on Eye TrackingResearch and Applications, pp. 85–92. ACM (2004). https://doi.org/10.1145/968363.968383

64. Zhang, X., Feng, W., Zha, H.: Modeling dwell-based eye pointing at two-dimensional targets. In: CHI'12 Extended Abstracts on Human Factors in Computing Systems, pp. 1751–1756. ACM (2012). https://doi.org/10.1145/2212776.2223704

65. Zhang, X., Ren, X., Zha, H.: Modeling dwell-based eye pointing target acquisition. In: Proceedings of the SIGCHI Conference on Human Factors in Computing Systems, pp. 2083–2092. ACM (2010). https://doi.org/10.1145/1753326.1753645

66. Zhang, X., MacKenzie, I.S.: Evaluating eye tracking with ISO 9241 - Part 9. In: Jacko, J.A. (eds.) Human-Computer Interaction. HCI Intelligent Multimodal Interaction Environments. HCI 2007. Lecture Notes in Computer Science, vol. 4552. Springer, Berlin, Heidelberg (2007). https://doi.org/10.1007/9783-540-73110-8_85

Emotion and Behavior Recognition
for Universal Access

Affective Guide for Museum: A System to Suggest Museum Paths Based on Visitors' Emotions

Alex Altieri[1], Silvia Ceccacci[1(✉)], Luca Giraldi[2], Alma Leopardi[1], Maura Mengoni[1], and Abudukaiyoumu Talipu[1]

[1] Department of Industrial Engineering and Mathematical Sciences, Università Politecnica Delle Marche, Ancona, Italy
{a.altieri,s.ceccacci,a.leopardi,m.mengoni,
t.abudukaiyoumu}@univpm.it
[2] Cherry Merry Lab Srl, Ancona, Italy
info@cherrymerrylab.com

Abstract. This paper introduces a new recommendation system for museums able to profile the visitors and propose them the most suitable exhibition path accordingly, to improve visitors' satisfaction. It consists of an interactive touch screen totem, which implements a USB camera and exploits Convolutional Neural Network to perform facial coding to measure visitors' emotions and estimate their age and gender. Based on the detected level of emotional valence, the system associates visitors with a profile and suggests them to visit a selection of five works of art, following a specific itinerary. An extensive experimentation lasting 2 months has been carried out at the Modern Art Museum "Palazzo Buonaccorsi" of Macerata. Results evidence that the proposed system can create an interactive and emotional link with the visitors, influencing their mood in the Pre-Experience phase and in the subsequent Post-Experience phase. In particular, they highlight that the proposed system, which aims at acting as emotional leverage, has been able to improve the positiveness of the emotions experienced by the visitors.

Keywords: Emotion recognition · Facial expression recognition · Affective computing · Cultural heritage

1 Introduction

In the last decade, museums had to face the increased competition in an economy defined as the "experience economy" [1]. The ultimate goal is to make every museum visit unique, staging experiences that meet the visitor desires [2]. To this end, museums started to apply new technological solutions to manage their exhibitions in a more open, inclusive and creative way to make every visit unique, and increase the affective impact of the visiting experience on the audience and emotionally involve them [3].

It is well known that a museum visit, just like any other experience, generates cognitive and emotive reactions that impact the level of satisfaction of the visitor to differing

© Springer Nature Switzerland AG 2021
M. Antona and C. Stephanidis (Eds.): HCII 2021, LNCS 12768, pp. 521–532, 2021.
https://doi.org/10.1007/978-3-030-78092-0_35

degrees [4]. Visitors who experiment positive emotions are more satisfied [5]. So to measure visitor satisfaction in a museum, emotional aspects are at least as important as cognitive ones, although [6] suggested that emotions are more significant than cognitive aspects in shaping visitors' satisfaction. In fact, it has been observed that segmentation based on emotions could be very useful for determining the type of experience the visitor is expecting and why [7]. This can explain why the conceptualization of the emotion construct as a segmentation variable has received considerable theoretical support [5, 8, 9].

In the past, several adaptive interfaces for museum guides have been proposed to personalize the information provided about each artwork, based on visitors' emotions, in order to better match visitors' expectations and to stimulate their attention and improve learning and enjoyment (e.g., [10–12]). However, based on the best of our knowledge, no systems have yet been proposed to suggest to visitors the exhibition path that could best meet their expectations, based on their emotions. Providing personalized paths, can play an important role in improving visitors' satisfaction. In fact, [4] demonstrated that not only the artworks, but also exhibit arrangement can influence those emotions that prior research identifies as determinants to visitors' satisfaction and much of their behavior.

In this context, this paper introduces a new system able to profile the visitors, based on their emotions detected from facial expressions, and propose them the most suitable exhibition path.

2 Research Background

Recent studies have shown that designing for emotion is a valid form of learning; by integrating emotion with learning goals, museums can create a more personal experience that can increase repeat intent and encourage word-of-mouth [13].

Several guide systems have been yet proposed, to personalize the information provided, according to interest shown by the visitor. Most of them are based on the acquisition of feedback directly provided by visitors through an interface (e.g., [10, 13, 14]). Only a few studies (e.g., [11] and [15]) proposed automatic solutions to detect visitor's engagement, based on their emotion and interests. Such systems provide interesting insights to increase the level of attention during the visit. However, based on the best of our knowledge, no systems have been proposed for personalized exhibition paths, as an emotional leverage to increase people's motivation and attitude towards visiting.

Several technologies can be used to perform emotion recognition. Most of them are based on the acquisition of biofeedback signals, facial expressions, or speech. Obviously, the use of invasive instruments based on biofeedback sensors, (e.g., ECG or EEG, other biometric sensors) can affect the subjects' behavior and in particular it may adulterate his/her spontaneity and consequently the emotions experienced by them [16]. Consequently, in the last years, several efforts have been made to improve non-intrusive emotion recognition systems, based on voice and facial expression analysis. As it is well known, systems based on voice analysis can provide faster temporal resolution than systems based on facial expression recognition. However, sing audio as an input to detect Ekman's six basic emotions yields less accurate results than using video [17]. There have been several models that have been proposed for analyzing emotions from facial expressions. However, the majority of them, such as [18] and [19], allows to recognize the Ekman & Keltner's primary emotions (i.e., anger, fear, disgust, surprise, joy and sadness) [20], as most of the databases of facial expressions currently available are based on these emotions. They use Convolutional Neural Networks (CNN) that take in input different kinds of pictures and make predictions according to the trained model.

3   The Proposed System

3.1   Hardware and Software Architecture

The proposed system integrates different technologies and is characterized by the physical design and the architecture reported in Fig. 1. The totem is a DIGITall Light 32" Touchscreen indoor by iTEC Group [21], characterized by a self-supporting structure in anodized aluminum, and a base with feet, made in steel. On its front side, it implements a 32" LED 16:9 Portrait FullHD 1080 × 1920 - Multitouch monitor with PCap technology and a wide-angle HD Webcam in portrait mode and an internal multi-socket. On the rear side, in a compartment closed by a lockable hinged door for inspection, it houses a PC laptop computer equipped with an Intel Core i7 processor and 16 GB of RAM, running Windows 10 Professional, that controls the system.

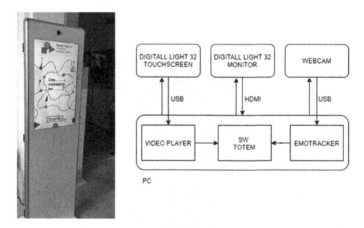

Fig. 1. Hardware and software architecture

The webcam has been connected via USB to the PC to stream the video that is processed frame by frame by the software, to perform both emotion recognition and to estimate users' age and gender. To this end, the software implements two Convolutional Neural Network (CNN). The first one, described in [22], allows to recognize the six basic Ekman's emotions [23] (i.e., happiness, surprise, sadness, anger, disgust and fear) plus the neutral expression, and measure the level of emotional valence (i.e., index of positivity or negativity of emotion from 0 to 100) and engagement (i.e., index of emotional involvement from 0 to 100. The second one, described in [24], performs age and gender estimation. The touchscreen monitor is connected to the PC via USB and

HDMI, respectively to enable the collection of the input data stream from the touchscreen and allows the GUI visualization on the monitor.

3.2 The Graphical User Interface

When in standby, the system display visualizes the screen reported in Fig. 2A. It attracts the visitor to approach it, asking a question: "What kind of visitor are you?". To activate it, visitors must tap the button "Discover it". Once started, the system takes about 30 s to profile the group of people (one or more) in front of it through the analysis of their age, gender and emotions.

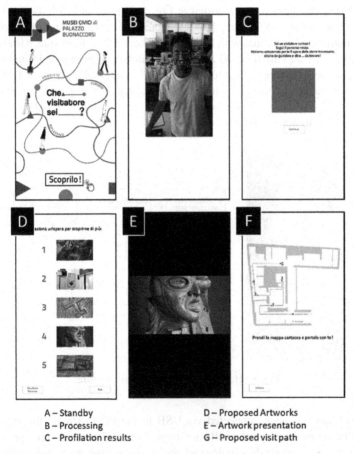

A – Standby   D – Proposed Artworks
B – Processing   E – Artwork presentation
C – Profilation results   G – Proposed visit path

Fig. 2. The graphical user interface

In the case more people are detected, these data are aggregated using appropriate algorithms, so as to obtain a weighted average value, characteristic of the group. The system then associates the group, to one of three profiles, based on the level of valence detected. In particular, the assigned profile is:

- Bored, when the level of valence is between 0 and 33;
- Reflected, when the level of valence is between 34 and 66;
- Curious, when the level of valence is between 67 and 100.

During this time, the user is shown the video image captured by the camera on the screen, where visitors can see their image (just like in a mirror) and the results of the processing of their faces, i.e., detected face segments, recognized emotion, estimated age and gender (Fig. 2B).

The system then shows the profiling result (i.e., on the screen appears the message "You are a [curious/reflexive/bored] visitor!") and proposes a visiting path (Fig. 2C). Each path is associated with a color (i.e., red-curious, blue-reflective, green-bored) and exhibits a total of 5 works of art. By tapping on the button "Continue", the visitors can visualize the list of photos of proposed attractions (Fig. 2D). By tapping on each of them visitors can start the display of videos (about 1 min long) providing details on the author and the artwork (Fig. 2E). Otherwise they can choose to display the proposed path (Fig. 2G) or return to the home screen (Fig. 2A). To make the system always ready to use even if the experience is interrupted, if the system does not detect any interaction for 30 s, the system automatically returns to the home screen (Fig. 2A).

Once finished the digital experience through the totem, the visitor can take a paper flyer where he can find the map with the three proposed paths (Fig. 3).

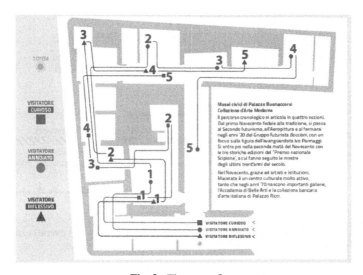

Fig. 3. The paper flyer

4 Experimentation

4.1 Preliminary Testing

A preliminary test has been carried out at the Cherry Marry Lab's headquarter, in order to assess the level of quality of the experience perceived by the users during the interaction with the Totem, in terms of usability, user experience and museum experience.

Materials and Methods. A total of 6 people (4 males and 2 females, aged between 31 and 40) has been involved. participants were asked to interact with the Totem (they were asked to imagine using it before starting the visit of the museum exhibition) and to answer three questionnaires. In particular, the level of usability was measured using the System Usability Scale [25], the quality of the user experience was evaluated using Attrakdiff2 Questionnaire [26], while the questionnaire proposed in [27] was adapted to assess the museum experience.

Results and Discussion. Overall, the proposed user interface has demonstrated an excellent level of usability: the SUS Score of the interface was 87.5 out of 100. Based on the results of [28, 29], this score falls within the fourth quartile: it falls within the 'acceptable' range, according to an acceptability scale, and it corresponds to an excellent level of overall perceived usability, measured on the seven-point, adjective-anchored Likert scale (Fig. 4).

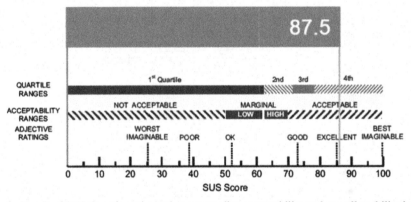

Fig. 4. Result of SUS Questionnaire and corresponding acceptability and overall usability level, according to [28, 29]

The results of the Attrakdiff2 Questionnaire show that the user experience was also positively evaluated (Fig. 5). In particular, the score related to the attractiveness dimension (ATT = 1.86) is higher than the others, demonstrating that the system has been able to attract the users who participated in the test and to arouse curiosity. Slightly lower is the score related to the Pragmatic Quality (PQ = 1.52), which represents a measure of the handling and usability of the product. This is mainly because users perceived the system as more "technical" than "human". This can be due to the webcam, which may be perceived as invasive. The scores collected for Hedonic Stimulation (HQS = 1.48) and Hedonic Identification (HQI = 1.43) are slightly lower, as the users did not find the system very professional and challenging.

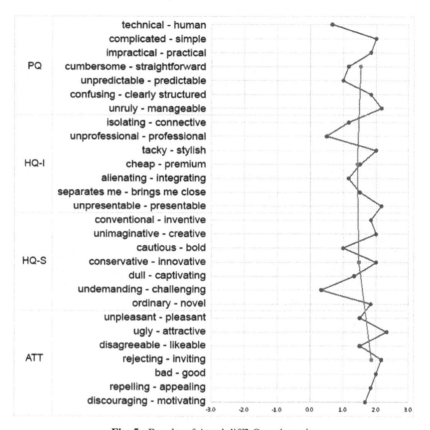

Fig. 5. Results of Attrakdiff2 Questionnaire

Finally, the results related to the perceived quality of the Museum Experience are reported in Fig. 6. As it can be observed, the results highlight the importance of the totem as an interactive guide. In fact, both the metrics 'Meaningful experience' (MD = 5.70) and 'Knowledge/learning' (MD = 5.67) obtained higher scores compared to the other two metrics 'Engagement' (MD = 5.50) and 'Emotion/connection' (MD = 4.80). This suggests how the proposed solution can effectively improve the visitor's understanding about the artworks.

4.2   Testing in Real Setting

An extensive experimentation has been carried out at the Museum of Modern Art of Palazzo Buonaccorsi of Macerata.

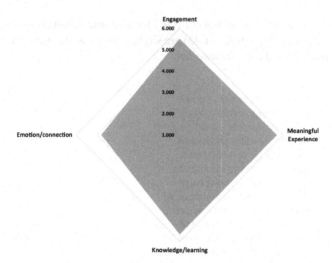

Fig. 6. Results of Museum Experience Scale (MES)

Materials and Methods. The totem was placed at the entrance of the rooms that host the exhibition of Modern Art of Palazzo Buonaccorsi. The application was available to visitors for 2 months, during which the experimentation was carried out. A total of 1,976 experiences, related to one or more people, has been analyzed. Overall, the recorded experiences involved 42% females and 58% males from three age ranges: 18–24 (20%), 25–34 (35%) and 35–over 65 (45%). The objective of the experiment was to evaluate the impact of the service offered by the Totem, in terms of variation in the mood of visitors. To this end, for each group the system recorded:

- The group profile predicted during the pre-experience phase (e.g., period of initial interaction, in which they are the group is profiled);
- The group profile predicted during the post-experience phase (e.g., period of time in which users read the result of the profiling and eventually watch the videos);
- The overall interaction time.

Results and Discussion. Results evidenced that only 44% of the total (876 groups) used the totem to view one or more in-depth videos and the corresponding recommended museum route. The factors that may have influenced this choice are many: other users waiting in line to try the totem, the suboptimal position of the totem at the door of the room, the preventive measures due to the health situation requiring the use of gloves to interact with the totem, finally the interest only in the museum and not in the works of modern art.

The average interaction time between the groups and the system was about 1:26 min (i.e., the duration of one video) while the maximum interaction time recorded was 9:51 min (i.e., time required to view all the proposed videos). This was influenced by the particular time slot and a no-queue situation, which allowed users to interact more with the totem.

By analyzing and comparing between the emotions recorded during the pre-experience and post-experience phase, it can be observed that, in the pre-experience phase, 4% of the groups were 'bored', 80% were 'reflected' and 16% were 'curious'. This suggests how a mixture of curiosity and amazement was aroused in visitors as they saw their faces reflected and covered by a series of face segments while the system was analyzing their facial expression and emotion. A different attitude was recorded in the post-experience phase, in which the number of 'curios' decreased (7%), while the number of 'reflected' increased (84%), and the number of 'bored' remained unchanged (7%) (Fig. 7).

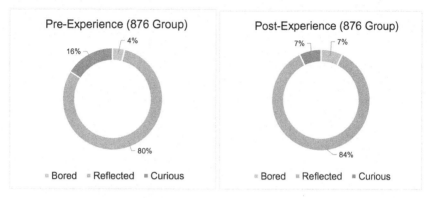

Fig. 7. Results of pre-experience and post-experience

In particular, groups that were 'bored' in the pre-experience changed their attitude to 'reflected' in the post-experience (79%). This suggests that the videos and descriptions proposed for the 'bored' profile was able to lead the visitors to change their attitude to 'reflected'. Another change in profile can be seen in the cluster of 'curious' in the pre-experience, who were more 'reflected' (88%) after the interaction with the totem. This could mean that the enthusiasm and curiosity generated by the first impact with the totem, have been turned into interest and attention by the explanatory videos related to the proposed works of art. A further aspect that needs to be analyzed is the age of the user groups. A high reduction in the percentage of 'curious' profiles between the pre- and post-experience can be noted for all the age ranges, i.e. 18–24 (−14%), 25–34 (−16%), 35–over 65 (−12%). This is a predictable result, considering the first impact of curiosity that the totem provokes. However, while it can be seen that there was an increase in the percentage of 'reflected' profiles: 18–24 and 25–34 (+18%), 35–over 65 (+12%), which could be explained by an increase in the attention of visitors, while watching the videos, the percentage of 'bored' profiles increased for the oldest visitors, 18–24 (−4%), 25–34 (−2%), 35–over 65 (+4%) (Fig. 8).

Overall, there are no differences in attitude change between men and women. For both men and women in the post-experience there was an increase in the number of 'reflected' (+18%) and a corresponding decrease in the number of 'curious' (F − 19%, M − 17%).

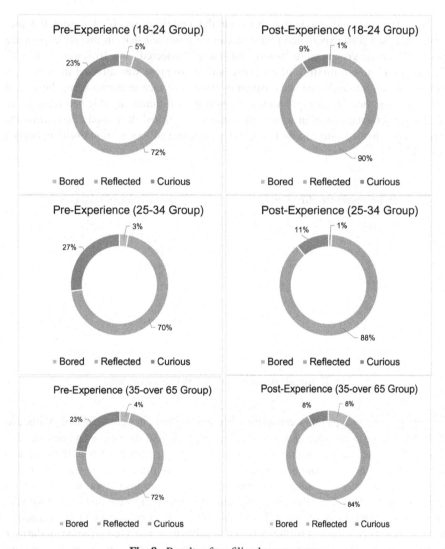

Fig. 8. Results of profiling by age group

5 Conclusion

Results evidence how the Totem has worked in order to create an interactive and emotional link with the groups, positively influencing their mood in the Pre-Experience phase and in the subsequent Post-Experience phase. In particular, they highlight that the proposed system, aimed at acting as emotional leverage, has been able to improve the positiveness of the emotions experienced by the visitors.

From the analysis of the results it can be stated that a different atmosphere was created inside the museum between the visitors and the works. Thanks to the Totem, which guided the exploration of the works of art before they could be seen, visitors were able to appreciate the details more easily and orientate themselves within the museum according to a visit path designed for them.

In addition, the innovative character of the Totem generated a lot of curiosity among visitors, attracting also age groups that would not normally be attracted to visit the modern art exhibition. Nevertheless, the older age groups were not excluded, but were encouraged to interact with it, thanks also to its simple structure, demonstrating the perfect integration of the proposed application with the totem in the museum context. Future studies should be conducted to better understand the actual impact of the proposed solution on the visitor path within the exhibition and visitor experience.

Acknowledgement. We thank the Musei Civici di Macerata, and in particular the director, Dr. Giuliana Pascucci, for her support in the experimentation at Palazzo Buonaccorsi. This work is supported by the Marche Region under the POR-FESR 2014–2020 program, project C.O.M.E., involving the companies Cherry Merry Lab, Marchingegno and Grottini Lab.

References

1. Pine, B.J., Gilmore, J.H.: Welcome to the experience economy. Harv. Bus. Rev. **76**, 97–105 (1998)
2. Neuburger, L., Egger, R.: An afternoon at the museum: Through the lens of augmented reality. In: Schegg, R., Stangl, B. (eds.) Information and communication technologies in tourism 2017, pp. 241–254. Springer, Cham (2017)
3. Leopardi, A., et al.: X-reality technologies for museums: a comparative evaluation based on presence and visitors experience through user studies. J. Cult. Herit. (2020). https://doi.org/10.1016/j.culher.2020.10.005
4. Legrenzi, L., Troilo, G.: The impact of exhibit arrangement on visitors' emotions: a study at the Victoria & Albert Museum. In: Proceedings of AIMAC, pp. 1–14 (2005)
5. Bigné, J.E., Andreu, L.: Emotions in segmentation: an empirical study. Ann. Tour. Res. **31**(3), 682–696 (2004)
6. Del Chiappa, G., Andreu, L., Gallarza, M.: Emotions and visitors' satisfaction at a museum. Int. J. Cult. Tourism Hospital. Res. **8**(4), 420–431 (2014)
7. Thyne, M.: The importance of values research for nonprofit organisations: The motivation-based values of museum visitors. Int. J. Nonprofit Voluntary Sector Market. **6**(2), 116–130 (2001)
8. Bigné, E., Gnoth, J., Andreu, L.: Advanced topics in tourism market segmentation. In: Tourism Management: Analysis, Behaviour and Strategy, pp. 151–173 (2008)
9. Hosany, S., Prayag, G.: Patterns of tourists' emotional responses, satisfaction, and intention to recommend. J. Bus. Res. **66**(6), 730–737 (2013)
10. Goren-Bar, D., Graziola, I., Rocchi, C., Pianesi, F., Stock, O., Zancanaro, M.: Designing and redesigning an affective interface for an adaptive museum guide. In: International Conference on Affective Computing and Intelligent Interaction, pp. 939–946, October 2005
11. Benta, K.I.: Affective aware museum guide. In: IEEE International Workshop on Wireless and Mobile Technologies in Education (WMTE 2005), pp. 53–55, November 2005
12. Lim, M.Y., Aylett, R.: An emergent emotion model for an affective mobile guide with attitude. Appl. Artif. Intell. **23**(9), 835–854 (2009)

13. Alelis, G., Bobrowicz, A., Ang, C.S.: Exhibiting emotion: capturing visitors' emotional responses to museum artefacts. In: Marcus, A. (ed.) Design, User Experience, and Usability. User Experience in Novel Technological Environments: Second International Conference, DUXU 2013, Held as Part of HCI International 2013, Las Vegas, NV, USA, July 21–26, 2013, Proceedings, Part III, pp. 429–438. Springer Berlin Heidelberg, Berlin, Heidelberg (2013)

14. Rocchi, C., Stock, O., Zancanaro, M.: Adaptivity in museum mobile guides: the Peach experience. In: Proceedings of the Mobile Guide, p. 6 (2006)

15. Abdelrahman, Y., Hassib, M., Marquez, M.G., Funk, M., Schmidt, A.: Implicit engagement detection for interactive museums using brain-computer interfaces. In: Proceedings of the 17th International Conference on Human-Computer Interaction with Mobile Devices and Services Adjunct, pp. 838–845, August 2015

16. Ceccacci, S., Generosi, A., Giraldi, L., Mengoni, M.: Tool to make shopping experience responsive to customer emotions. Int. J. Autom. Technol. **12**(3), 319–326 (2018)

17. Karyotis, C., Doctor, F., Iqbal, R., James, A.E., Chang, V.: Affect aware ambient intelligence: current and future directions. In: State of the Art in AI Applied to Ambient Intelligence, vol. 298, pp. 48–67. IOS Press (2017)

18. Bernin, A., et al.: Towards more robust automatic facial expression recognition in smart environments. In: Proceedings of the 10th International Conference on Pervasive Technologies Related to Assistive Environments, pp. 37–44. ACM, June 2017.

19. Salunke, V.V., Patil, C.G.: A new approach for automatic face emotion recognition and classification based on deep networks. In: 2017 International Conference on Computing, Communication, Control and Automation (ICCUBEA), pp. 1–5. IEEE, August 2017

20. Ekman, P., Keltner, D.: Universal facial expressions of emotion. Calif. Mental Health Res. Digest **8**(4), 151–158 (1970)

21. Totem multimediali DIGITall Light. https://www.gruppoitec.com/totem-multimediali/dig itall-light (n.d.). Accessed 4 Nov 2020.

22. Talipu, A., Generosi, A., Mengoni, M., Giraldi, L.: Evaluation of deep convolutional neural network architectures for emotion recognition in the wild. In: 2019 IEEE 23rd International Symposium on Consumer Technologies (ISCT), pp. 25–27. IEEE, June 2019

23. Ekman, P.: An argument for basic emotions. Cogn. Emot. **6**(3–4), 169–200 (1992)

24. Generosi, A., et al.: MoBeTrack: a toolkit to analyze user experience of mobile apps in the wild. In: 2019 IEEE International Conference on Consumer Electronics (ICCE), pp. 1–2. IEEE, January 2019

25. Brooke, J.: SUS: a retrospective. J. Usability Stud. **8**(2), 29–40 (2013)

26. Hassenzahl, M.: The interplay of beauty, goodness, and usability in interactive products. Hum. Comput. Interact. **19**, 319–349 (2004)

27. Othman, M., Petrie, H., Power, C.: Engaging visitors in museums with technology: scales for the measurement of visitor and multimedia guide experience. In: Campos, P., Graham, N., Jorge, J., Nunes, N., Palanque, P., Winckler, M. (eds.) Human-Computer Interaction – INTERACT 2011, pp. 92–99. Springer Berlin Heidelberg, Berlin, Heidelberg (2011). https:// doi.org/10.1007/978-3-642-23768-3_8

28. Bangor, A., Kortum, P., Miller, J.: Determining what individual SUS scores mean: adding an adjective rating scale. J. Usability Stud. **4**(3), 114–123 (2009)

29. Rauer, M.: Quantitative Usability-Analysen mit der System Usability Scale (SUS). Seibert Media. Online verfügbar unter https://blog.seibert-media.net/blog/2011/04/11/usablility-ana lysen-system-usability-scale-sus/ (2011). zuletzt geprüft am, 19, 2016

2D and 3D Visualization of Eye Gaze Patterns in a VR-Based Job Interview Simulator: Application in Educating Employers on the Gaze Patterns of Autistic Candidates

Michael Breen[1]([✉]), James McClarty[1], Caleb Langley[1], Jamshid Farzidayeri[2], Kyle Trevethan[2], Brandon Swenson[2], Medha Sarkar[2], Joshua Wade[1,3], and Nilanjan Sarkar[1,3]

[1] Robotics and Autonomous Systems Lab, Vanderbilt University, Nashville, TN 37212, USA
michael.breen@vanderbilt.edu
[2] Computer Science, Middle Tennessee State University, Murfreesboro, TN 37132, USA
[3] Mechanical Engineering, Vanderbilt University, Nashville, TN 37212, USA

Abstract. Employment of autistic individuals is strikingly low in relation to the skill level and capabilities of this population. Roughly 65% of autistic adults are either unemployed or underemployed relative to their abilities but there is increasing recognition that this number could be greatly improved through empowering autistic individuals while simultaneously providing a boost to the economy. Much of this disparity can be attributed in part to the lack of awareness and understanding among employers regarding behavior of autistic individuals during the hiring process. Most notably, the job interview—where strong eye contact is traditionally expected but can be extremely uncomfortable for autistic individuals—presents an unreasonable initial barrier to employment for many. The current work presents a data visualization dashboard that is populated with quantitative data (including eye tracking data) captured during simulated job interviews using a novel interview simulator called Career Interview Readiness in Virtual Reality (CIRVR). We conducted a brief series of case studies wherein autistic individuals who took part in a CIRVR interview and other key stakeholders provided lived experiences and qualitative insights into the most effective design and application of such data visualization dashboard. We conclude with a discussion of the role of information related to visual attention in job interviews with an emphasis on the importance of descriptive rather than prescriptive interpretation.

Keywords: Eye gaze · Autism · Inclusive employment · Job interview

1 Introduction

In the United States, the employment rate among autistic[1] adults is unacceptably low. An estimated 5.4 million autistic individuals are of working age, yet upwards of 65% remain

---

[1] We have chosen to use identity-first language (e.g., *autistic person*) as opposed to person-first (e.g., *person with autism*) because recent surveys of autistic self-advocates suggest a preference for identity-first language [13].

© Springer Nature Switzerland AG 2021
M. Antona and C. Stephanidis (Eds.): HCII 2021, LNCS 12768, pp. 533–544, 2021.
https://doi.org/10.1007/978-3-030-78092-0_36

unemployed or underemployed (i.e., employed but earning an income that is insufficient to support independence) [1]. Researchers estimate that an employed autistic adult would contribute upwards of $50,000 per year to the US economy [2], representing a staggering loss to the US gross domestic product and, far more importantly, untold societal cost from the opportunities lost by not engaging these individuals in the workforce. What accounts for this massive employment disparity? One major factor is that many autistic job candidates struggle to get past the interview phase of the job search [3]. This is often attributed to differences in social communication within this population, such as inconsistent eye contact or otherwise not engaging in "neurotypical" styles of communication [4]. Additionally, autistic individuals may give literal responses to questions that neurotypical individuals would interpret and respond to differently, leading to potential confusion on the part of the interviewer. To borrow an adapted example from [3], an employer may ask "Can you tell me about X?"—X being a placeholder for any topic—and the autistic candidate may respond simply with, "Yes" or "No" without elaborating.

Fortunately, there is now growing recognition—already quite strong among autistic self-advocates but increasingly so among employers—that simple accommodations in the workplace setting (including in job interviews) can significantly lower barriers to employment for this population [2, 3, 5]. Critically, we believe there is an opportunity to educate employers about issues related to effective and equitable approaches to interviewing autistic individuals. In this context, the current work is concerned with the characterization of visual attention patterns of autistic individuals during simulated job interviews. Our objective in this regard is to show that information about autistic individuals' visual attention (a) should be regarded as *descriptive* rather than *prescriptive*, and (b) can be meaningfully presented through visualizations and metrics that are of practical interest to autistic individuals and to other key stakeholders in the autism employment ecosystem, such as job coaches and career counselors (e.g., with colleges and universities). We emphasize here that information related to the visual attention patterns of autistic individuals is not meant in any way to change the autistic individual or to shape their gaze in the mold of their neurotypical peers. Instead, this information is made available to autistic individuals to be evaluated in any way they deem useful.

To test whether this kind of information is in fact valuable, we conducted a brief series of case studies wherein autistic individuals participated in a simulated job interview using a Virtual Reality-based job interview simulator called Career Interview Readiness in Virtual Reality (CIRVR) [6]. CIRVR is unique among tools for practicing job interviews because it combines speech-based interaction with elements of affective computing to create semi-naturalistic interview scenarios in which the virtual interviewer is "aware" of and sensitive to the interviewee's level of stress. This job interview simulator features (a) natural language-based communication between the interviewee and the virtual interviewer that is currently enabled by Microsoft Azure cloud services; (b) real-time stress detection as measured by the Empatica E4 (https://www.empatica.com/research/e4/)—a small, wrist-worn physiological sensor that measures heart rate variability and electrodermal activity; (c) eye tracking to capture visual attention patterns with current support for devices from both Tobii and Fove; (d) facial expression detection to periodically measure expressions from the set of universally-recognized emotions define in [7]; and

(e) options for immersive VR interaction as well as non-immersive, desktop-based interaction with current support for head-mounted displays from both Fove and Vive. Figure 1 presents visuals from the CIRVR system.

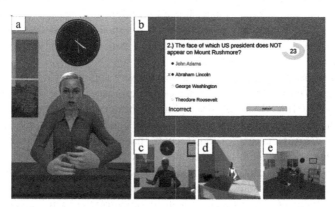

Fig. 1. Career Interview Readiness in Virtual Reality (CIRVR) job interview simulator: (a) interviewer asking a question while using contextually-relevant hand gestures and lip movements; (b) a "whiteboard" feature used to capture interviewee responses to knowledge- and experience-oriented questions; (c) another example of an interviewer avatar gesturing towards the interviewee; (d) a receptionist avatar seated in the lobby of the virtual office environment; and (e) the simple layout of the interviewer's office.

CIRVR is neither the first nor the only technology to be applied in this space. Virtual Interview Training for Transition Age Youth (VIT-TAY) was used by Smith and colleagues in a randomized controlled trial transition age autistic individuals and found evidence of reduced anxiety and improved interview performance post-training [8]. VIT-TAY is a job interview simulator comprised of highly structured, pre-recorded video clips that allow users to practice applying job interview skills. In the commercial arena, Virtual Speech is a VR product that allows users to practice soft skills such as public speaking and provides quantitative measures of progress and performance over time (https://virtualspeech.com/). HireVue is popular example of a commercial product in this space (https://www.hirevue.com/). HireVue's platform allows real-world job candidates to pre-recorded videos of themselves taking part in a job interview that is then quantitively analyzed by HireVue for candidate assessment (but, importantly, not candidate training or practice). While each of these technologies is quite innovative and has shown promise for each of its target populations, only CIRVR and its accompanying dashboard application were designed from the ground up with the singular objective of lowering barriers to employment for autistic individuals.

The remainder of the paper is organized as follows: Sect. 2 provides a brief overview of the data visualization dashboard; Sect. 3 describes the gaze data visualization methods; Sect. 4 presents the results of a small set of case studies; and Sect. 5 concludes the paper with a discussion of the results as well as planned future work.

2 Data Visualization Dashboard

Here we describe the data visualization dashboard that accompanies CIRVR, our novel job interview simulator. While this paper focuses on metrics pertaining to the interviewee's visual attention patterns, the dashboard prototype also features a range of other visualizations and tables related to the interviewee's spoken responses and experienced stress. Validation of these latter features remains part of ongoing work and are not discussed here.

The data visualization dashboard is a React.js web application that houses an array of components, each of which communicates a unique aspect of the interviewee's experience using the CIRVR system. A sampling of these components is given in Fig. 2. Currently, the data presented characterize several signals including physiological and self-reported stress, facial expressions (neutral, happy, surprise, sad, angry, fear, contempt, disgust), speech (from both the interviewee and interviewer), and eye gaze. A variety of interactive visualization methods are used, including time series graphs, scatter plots, heat maps, and tables. The dashboard and CIRVR were each developed with the direct involvement of autistic individuals to maximize the agency and participation of autistic people through inclusive design practices. This involvement included, for example, design decisions at the conceptual level, software implementation, and months of iterative feedback through beta testing and in-depth discussion.

The major aims of the dashboard application and research are two-fold. The first is to provide quantitative information to autistic individuals and support personnel (e.g., job coaches) that could provide insights into, for example, more effective management of anxiety in relation to challenging questions. An autistic user, for example, may be interested in knowing how their visual attention patterns changed during the course of the interview, perhaps due to uncomfortable eye contact or after an ambiguous prompt such as "Tell me about yourself." Likewise, a job coach could identify interview questions that resulted in the greatest stress responses in order to share strategies for managing stress when encountering similar questions in the future. The second major aim is to provide insights to employers about the types of interview questions that do and do not work well in understanding the skills and qualifications of autistic individuals.

Direct and consistent eye contact during a job interview has been traditionally regarded as evidence of a candidate's strength, but eye contact can be quite uncomfortable for many autistic individuals [3]. We reiterate that the visual attention information captured by the eye tracker is *not* designed to prescribe patterns of visual attention such as extending the amount of eye contact demonstrated by the interviewee. Rather, this information is hypothesized to be valuable in and of itself as a means of understanding one's own behavior and our hope is that this work raises the level of awareness of employers that, although some autistic individuals may not make consistent eye contact, this should not be taken to mean that she/he is not paying attention or is any less qualified.

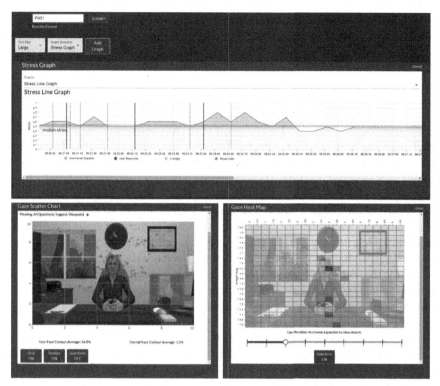

Fig. 2. Example components from the data visualization dashboard: (top) time series plot of stress signal with respect to event markers such as questions and response, (bottom left) a scatter plot of the interviewee's gaze data, and (bottom right) a heatmap-style presentation of the interviewee's gaze data.

3 Visualization Methods

Data collected from the simulated interviews were de-identified and recorded in a SQL database accessible to the dashboard application. The database schema was designed in such a way that the table containing eye tracker data was agnostic to the particular eye tracking device used to collect this data. This allowed the dashboard to query gaze data and to populate 2D or 3D visualizations in a uniform way using any of the supported devices, which, at the time of this writing, includes devices from manufacturers including Tobii, Fove, and Vive. By "2D visualizations," we refer to the non-immersive condition in which the user interacts with CIRVR using a keyboard, mouse, and monitor with a remote eye tracker such as the Tobii X3-120. By "3D visualizations," we refer to the immersive VR condition in which the user interacts with CIRVR using a head-mounted display system with embedded eye tracker, such as the Fove or Vive Eye.

Support for a 3D condition was pursued as a system feature because evidence in other contexts supports an association between increased naturalism/immersion and ecological validity [9]. However, tolerance of head-mounted displays is not universal and must be considered on an individual basis as some people respond negatively to immersive VR experiences. As such, the 2D condition was essential to be inclusive of individuals who would not tolerate the 3D experience. That being said, there is some evidence to support that autistic individuals may generally tolerate immersive VR experiences well and, in fact, may find these experiences quite enjoyable [10].

3.1 2D Visualizations

Gaze data captured while the user takes part in the non-immersive version of the simulated interview were obtained using the Tobii 4C, which has a sampling frequency of 90 Hz, a tracking accuracy $<1°$, and an operating distance between 50 and 95 cm. As these data are recorded, fixations are computed in real-time based on a moving window analysis coupled with a hybrid velocity- and dispersion-based algorithm adapted from [11]. The adaptation simply extends the velocity-based threshold algorithm by introducing statistical parameters to characterize fixations in the context of the simulated interview. Using a moving window conservatively set at 150 ms in length (or roughly 14 samples) [12], we tracked the change in velocity of points within the window in the first pass, then in the second pass these velocities are compared against a threshold, and if the change in velocity is sufficiently small, then the window is labeled as a probable fixation. As fixations are found, they are subsequently recorded in a csv (comma-separated values) file following the format *fixation centroid X, fixation centroid Y, fixation radius, fixation onset time, and fixation offset time,* followed by a list of the names of objects intersecting with the fixation point in the virtual environment (e.g., the virtual interviewer, the clock on the wall, etc.).

After a user has completed a simulated interview and their fixation data have been collected and stored in the SQL database, the data can then be retrieved via their anonymized PID (Participant ID) in the dashboard application. Once retrieved, a user interacting with the dashboard can view the visualized fixation data as either a scatter plot of fixations or as a heatmap of quantized regions within the interviewee's field of view (see Fig. 3). For the scatter plot, made using the provided scatter plot in the Recharts library (https://recharts.org/), the provided fixation points are plotted based on the fixation positions with radii proportional to the fixation duration. The points are placed against a still image representative of what the user would have seen during the simulated interview. For the heatmap, we used the heatmap implementation from Nivo (https://nivo.rocks/heatmap/) and specified the color intensity of individual cells based on the frequency of fixations that intersect them, the color being based on a grey-red gradient where grey corresponds to low fixations and red corresponds to many fixations. For both visualization approaches, a user interacting with the dashboard can view the data over a variety of intervals, including the entire interview or on a question-by-question basis.

3.2 3D Visualizations

Gaze data captured while the user takes part in the immersive VR version of the simulated interview were obtained using the Fove head-mounted display, which has a sampling frequency of 120 Hz and a median tracking accuracy of 1.15°. To capture the location of the participant's gaze, the Fove utilizes Unity's built-in raycasting system, which essentially calculates the intersection(s) of a ray cast in the direction of the user's gaze

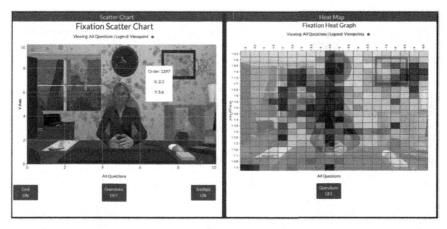

Fig. 3. The 2D approach to gaze data visualization: (left) scatter plot of fixations with radii proportional to their fixation durations and (right) gaze heatmap for quantized regions relative to the interviewee's field of view.

with one or more objects in the path of the ray. To record the times series gaze data from the Fove in this manner, both the direction of the ray, and the origin point in 3D space of the ray were recorded. This information, along with timestamps and the names of viewed objects, were written to the csv files and later transferred to the SQL database.

Once these data are collected in the database, they can then be retrieved and displayed using a Unity WebGL build and a WebGL player component separate from the dashboard itself (in the future, we aim to embed the WebGL player directly in the dashboard application). In the WebGL player, the user can select from among four different 3D visualization methods (see Fig. 4). In each method, a ray is cast from the origin point of the interviewee's eyes in 3D space in the direction of the interviewee's gaze at that point in time. When a ray collides with another object in the scene, that is the point in space where we predict the interviewee's gaze ultimately landed. After all of these points in space have been predicted, we are finally able to plot the points accordingly. The first 3D visualization method simply displays a green sphere that moves over time in relation to the previously noted raycast collision predictions (Fig. 4a). The other visualization methods present variations on this theme (Fig. 4b, 4c, and 4d). With these methods, the dashboard user can choose to view fixation data plotted sequentially (as if by playback in real time) as well as presented as a complete distribution all at once. In the case of the latter, the sequential portion is displayed in green while the static components are presented in a contrasting color.

4   Case Studies

We hypothesized that (a) capture of both 2D and 3D gaze data within CIRVR would be feasible and suitable for visualization within the dashboard tool; (b) autistic individuals and other key stakeholders would find initial value in the visual attention components of the dashboard; and (c) qualitative feedback from autistic individuals and other key

Fig. 4. 3D visualization of fixation data: (a) real-time playback of scan paths; (b) real-time playback of scan paths overlaid onto entire distribution of fixations shown as flattened objects; (c) simple real-time playback of current fixation; and (d) real-time playback of scan paths overlaid onto entire distribution of fixations shown as spheres. (Color figure online)

stakeholders would reveal new insights with respect to more effective and valuable ways to present information about visual attention. To test each of these hypotheses, we conducted a small series of case studies with individuals from each of these target groups as described below. The research was approved by the Institutional Review Board (IRB) at Vanderbilt University and all participants provided informed consent or assent in accordance with the requirements set forth by the IRB. Personnel conducting the sessions had several years of experience performing human subjects research involving autistic individuals and were well-equipped to address accommodations that might have arisen during the sessions. Autistic participants were compensated for their time and travel to take part in the simulated interview. Employer participants were not compensated for their time and did not travel to take part in the study.

4.1 Feedback from Autistic Individuals

Four autistic individuals took part in the study. The reader should note that two of these individuals were also involved in the development of the dashboard application and are co-authors of this work but had not previously taken part in a simulated interview using CIRVR. As such, all of the received feedback is regarded as valid within the scope of the testing performed for the current stage of qualitative evaluation of the technology. Autistic participants were invited to take part in a roughly one-hour session in the university laboratory. Due to the COVID-19 pandemic, appropriate precautions were taken to ensure the safety of both the participants and researchers[2]. After providing consent/assent, the participants completed an approximately 20-minute simulated interview using the CIRVR system. All participants experienced the non-immersive implementation of CIRVR, and the two participants form the development team also experienced the immersive implementation of CIRVR while wearing the Fove head-mounted display. After the simulated interview portion of the study, a researcher and the participant engaged in a brief qualitative interview to discuss the user's experience with the system as well what kinds of information the participant might like to see and learn from based on their experience. All participants completed the study without any adverse events or loss of eye tracker data.

Following the simulated interview using CIRVR, participants were asked to share their thoughts about their experiences and about the potential benefit of seeing the data extracted during the simulated interview. Participants reported largely positive experiences overall, only citing some sections of the interviews as eliciting stress, with some noting a particular interest in seeing how much eye contact they made with the virtual interviewer. Another participant said that he would like to see a general review of his interview performance but was not interested in the eye tracking data. Cumulatively, the data collection and feedback support the hypotheses that data collection of this kind is feasible and that data regarding visual attention during simulated interviews may be of value to some, but perhaps not all, autistic individuals.

4.2 Feedback from Employers

Three representatives from two different corporations (one a small business and the other a major technology company, which we will refer to as Company A and Company B, respectively) participated in in-depth, qualitative discussions about the dashboard tool and the proposed visualizations of visual attention information. Both organizations had active hiring initiatives for neurodiverse[3] and autistic talent with strong endorsement of neurodiversity within the workplace. Participant interactions were accomplished entirely remotely using video conferencing software. Audio of the conversations were recorded with the consent of the participants and then transcribed automatically using the Otter transcription service (https://otter.ai/) for offline qualitative analysis.

After initial formalities at the start of the video calls, participants were shown a brief (i.e., ~5 min) introduction to the full employer dashboard via screenshare, during which time each visualization component was described in some detail. Anonymized data were shown for some of the participants in the study as well for one neurotypical member of the development team. Data were also presented for both immersive and non-immersive VR conditions. After viewing the data, participants were asked questions from a predefined list of questions and were also invited to provide open-ended feedback of their own. The discussions covered all of the dashboard components, but we focus here on the feedback concerning the visual attention-related visualizations.

---

[2] Precautions related to COVID-19 included a symptom pre-screening 24 h before the scheduled session, follow-up symptom prescreening the day of the session, mandatory face coverings, and minimum 6-feet social distancing at all times during the sessions.

[3] See [2] for a definition of neurodiversity.

Two individuals from Company A provided feedback about the dashboard, both of whom served in administrative positions at the organization but regularly engaged in activities related to job coaching with autistic and other neurodiverse individuals. Feedback from these participants tended to focus on topics related to equitable employment practices in relation to the value of eye tracking information. On the subject of eye contact, one of the participants noted that "some people just can't do it, and … that's up to the employer, not to the candidate to have to make that eye contact or even worry about it. The employer needs to know that [eye contact] has no bearing at all on the interview." Building on this, the other participant added that "if you showed some of these results to someone you know, who has gone through the simulation, it's less a matter of you need to do this, you need to that [but instead] making them aware that these are the behaviors and therefore, in an interview situation, you also may have to self-advocate for yourself." Continuing down this line, the first participant added "that's why I was like, so excited … that you're also educating the employers, because that's where I think—it's not on our folks—it's the employer who needs to be educated."

A hiring manager from Company B provided feedback. When asked about the potential utility of the gaze data visualizations, this participant noted that the 2D and 3D fixation data might be particularly useful for a job coach to review but might also be useful for a hiring manager if "there are specific insights that you can feed [to] the hiring manager." Following this point, the participant further suggested that a variety of distinct *user views* might be helpful (i.e., the interviewee view, the job coach view, etc.) and that the order of content presentation on the web page might be accordingly tailored to the particular view. Another general point of feedback was that a "less is more" strategy regarding data presentation may be most effective and that "simplifying towards different [user] roles and what they need to see" could improve the utility of the presented information. Additionally, Company B also noted opportunities to enhance the accessibility of the dashboard through simple user interface modifications.

5   Discussion and Conclusion

Cumulatively, the feedback from autistic individuals and stakeholders largely supported our hypotheses, but with some important nuances. First, we successfully demonstrated that gaze data could be feasibly captured and then visualized in a meaningful way using both immersive VR (3D) and non-immersive (2D) conditions. In the future, we will continue to refine this strategy and will integrate the 3D visualization directly into the React.js web application.

Second, we learned from autistic individuals and job coaches about aspects of the gaze data visualizations that were seen as practical for review. Some of the autistic individuals expressed interest in being able to review gaze data collected during the simulated interviews in order to analyze things like the proportion of eye contact that she/he made with the virtual interviewer. However, some autistic individuals were not particularly interested in being able to review their gaze data. As such, this feature could be regarded as optional in a final version of the tool (i.e., the feature could be enabled or disabled based on the preferences of the individual). The job coaches that we heard from echoed the potential value of being able to review such gaze data with autistic individuals. Importantly, the job coaches also confirmed that a measure of eye contact should not be communicated to the interviewee in the context of changing patterns of visual attention. Finally, we learned from a hiring manager about some ways in which the dashboard could be extended to present information tailored to the type of dashboard user (e.g., interviewee or job coach) and that additional insights may actually emerge from less complex presentation strategies, such as relating changes in visual attention to the real-time stress measurement. This individual also emphasized that, in general, our future work should focus on identifying key insights that can be presented to each type of dashboard users without overwhelming the users with an overabundance of data.

Noted areas of improvement for the current dashboard application include a need to strike a greater balance between raw data and clear insights, the addition of user roles (e.g., interviewee, job coach) in which information is optimally presented for that particular role, and generally improved accessibility (e.g., optimal color schemes and extending the visual presentation to include other modalities for individuals with visual impairment). Additionally, because of the amount of gaze data being presented, the dashboard can sometimes take nearly 10 s to fully load and prepare all the data. Future work should seek to optimize gaze data queries by, for example, transitioning to a time series database solution such as InfluxDB.

Acknowledgement. This project was funded by a Microsoft AI for Accessibility grant and by the National Science Foundation under awards 1936970 and 2033413. The authors would like to thank the participants for their time and generous feedback.

References

1. Shaw, K.A., Maenner, M.J., Baio, J.: Early identification of autism spectrum disorder among children aged 4 years—early autism and developmental disabilities monitoring network, six sites, United States, 2016. MMWR Surveill. Summ. **69**(3), 1 (2020)
2. Austin, R.D., Pisano, G.P.: Neurodiversity as a competitive advantage. Harv. Bus. Rev. **95**, 96–103 (2017)
3. Booth, J.: Autism Equality in the Workplace: Removing Barriers and Challenging Discrimination. Jessica Kingsley Publishers, London (2016)
4. American Psychiatric Association, et al.: Diagnostic and statistical manual of mental disorders (DSM-5®). American Psychiatric Pub (2013)
5. Scheiner, M., Bogden, J.: An Employer's Guide to Managing Professionals on the Autism Spectrum. Jessica Kingsley Publishers, London (2017)
6. Wade, J.W., et al.: Career Interview Readiness in VR (CIRVR): Feasibility of an AI-Driven Platform for Employers and Neurodiverse Talent (2020)
7. Ekman, P.: Are there basic emotions? Psychol. Rev. **99**, 550–553 (1992)
8. Smith, C., et al.: Virtual interview training for autistic transition age youth: a randomized controlled feasibility and effectiveness trial. Autism 1–17 (2021). https://doi.org/10.1177/1362361321989928
9. Parsons, T.D.: Virtual reality for enhanced ecological validity and experimental control in the clinical, affective and social neurosciences. Front. Hum. Neurosci. **9**, 660 (2015)

10. Newbutt, N., Sung, C., Kuo, H.J., Leahy, M.J.: The acceptance, challenges, and future applications of wearable technology and virtual reality to support people with autism spectrum disorders. In: Brooks, A.L., Brahnam, S., Kapralos, B., Jain, L.C. (eds.) Recent Advances in Technologies for Inclusive Well-Being. ISRL, vol. 119, pp. 221–241. Springer, Cham (2017). https://doi.org/10.1007/978-3-319-49879-9_11
11. Salvucci, D.D., Goldberg, J.H.: Identifying fixations and saccades in eye-tracking protocols. In: Proceedings of the 2000 Symposium on Eye Tracking Research and Applications, pp. 71–78 (2000)
12. Delerue, C., Laprévote, V., Verfaillie, K., Boucart, M.: Gaze control during face exploration in schizophrenia. Neurosci. Lett. **482**(3), 245–249 (2010)
13. Kenny, L., Hattersley, C., Molins, B., Buckley, C., Povey, C., Pellicano, E.: Which terms should be used to describe autism? Perspectives from the UK autism community. Autism **20**(4), 442–462 (2016)

Development of an Index for Evaluating VIMS Using Gaze Data

Kazuhiro Fujikake[1]($\boxtimes$), Rentaro Ono[2], and Hiroki Takada[2]

[1] Chukyo University, 101-2 Yagotohonmachi, Showa-ku, Nagoya 466-8666, Japan
fujikake@lets.chukyo-u.ac.jp
[2] University of Fukui, 3-9-1 Bunkyo, Fukui-shi, Fukui, Japan

Abstract. The benefit of using a non-contact eye-tracking system is that it is considered as a low-burden method for measuring biological signals. The goal of this study was to develop a visual induced motion sickness (VIMS) evaluation index that uses a non-contact eye-tracking system for driving simulator (DS) experiments. The participants included nine elderly people who had visual and balance functions that did not interfere with their daily life. The gaze data of the participants were measured at rest—both before and after DS trials. The simulator sickness questionnaires (SSQ) were conducted before and after the experiment. The participants were divided into two groups based on their SSQ results. One group experienced VIMS during the DS trial (four people, with an average age of 79.0 years), whereas the other group did not experience VIMS during the DS trial (five people, average age: 71.2 years). The results of VIMS symptoms were confirmed: data concerning the locus of eye-tracking were lengthened, whereas the eye-tracking data were diffused. Moreover, in the group which experience VIMS, the regularity of gaze data during the DS trials was increased. This experiment demonstrated the usefulness of sparse density and the regularity of evaluation as a quantification index for eye-tracking data in evaluating VIMS. Regarding the application of the findings of this study, it is believed that if an eye-tracking data-based VIMS evaluation index can be used, it will be easier to detect VIMS which is caused by DS operations, thus permitting the detection of the symptoms.

Keywords: Visually induced motion sickness (VIMS) · Gaze data · Rotational eye movement · Driving simulator (DS) · Elderly people

1 Introduction

With the increasing number of elderly drivers on roads, the prevention of accidents involving elderly drivers has become a serious challenge. Research on elderly drivers includes studies on their visual and cognitive functions as well as their driving characteristics to help them to drive more safely. While research on elderly drivers primarily involves actual vehicles on ordinary roads, several studies using driving simulators (DSs) exist. The merits of experiments using DSs include a low risk of accidents or other operational problems, easy setting and reproduction of specific conditions and situations, and the ability to adjust the experimental conditions. In contrast, the demerits of using DSs

© Springer Nature Switzerland AG 2021
M. Antona and C. Stephanidis (Eds.): HCII 2021, LNCS 12768, pp. 545–554, 2021.
https://doi.org/10.1007/978-3-030-78092-0_37

include the occurrence of Visually induced motion sickness (VIMS), lack of a sense of reality, and high cost. In recent years, the performance of DS hardware has improved and its cost has decreased; thus, the reality and cost problems are gradually being resolved, but an effective VIMS prevention measure has not yet been developed. Inversely, as the field of view expands, the symptoms of VIMS are intensified. Therefore, as display screens become larger, the risk of VIMS may also increase. When a DS experiment is performed, it is necessary to detect VIMS precursors promptly before the symptoms become severe.

The use of a non-contact eye-tracking system is considered as a low burden method for measuring biological signals. The goal of this study was to develop a VIMS evaluation index that uses a non-contact eye-tracking system for DS experiments.

As rotational eye movement is caused by unsteadiness resulting from VIMS, the following hypotheses are presented.

Hypothesis 1: VIMS symptoms occur; the locus of the eye-tracking data lengthens.

Hypothesis 2: VIMS symptoms occur; the eye-tracking data are diffused.

Hypothesis 3: VIMS symptoms occur; the eye-tracking data becomes more regular by rotational eye movement.

2   Visually Induced Motion Sickness (VIMS)

VIMS is considered as a type of agitation illness that is thought to be caused by the disharmony between visual information and the vestibular system, such as the tricuspid canal. Therefore, the eye movement control system is expected to be involved. The physical symptoms of VIMS include feeling unwell, nausea (upset stomach), dizziness, and vertigo when standing up. The indices used to evaluate VIMS are the results of simulator sickness questionnaires (SSQs), which are the main evaluation method, and measurements of the gravity center sway of the participants while standing [1, 2]. It is also known that if motion sickness causes unsteadiness, rotational eye movement will occur in the direction opposite to the unsteadiness, so that the individual's eyes do not tilt the field of view [3]. This rotational eye movement can be used as a physiological index of VIMS, and evaluations have been carried out based on electromyographic data from near the eyes. Furthermore, a method for evaluating nausea based on EGG measurements is currently being studied as a new physiological index. However, studies using physiological indices have not obtained consistent results for the complex changes that occur with the progression of motion sickness. As electrodes must be attached to test participants and specialized equipment must be used to obtain electromyograms or EGGs, these options are only feasible in limited circumstances. Although SSQ-based introspective reports permit evaluations with a considerable amount of liberty, in certain cases where the symptoms of VIMS have progressed to the point of subjective assessment, such symptoms persisted for approximately a week.

3   Rotational Eye Movement

Eye movements can be categorized as saccade (saccadic eye movement), smooth pursuit eye movement, vergence (convergence and divergence) eye movement, optokinetic nystagmus (OKN), vestibulo-ocular reflex (VOR), and rotational eye movement [4, 5].

Rotational eye movement is the movement of the eye as it rotates around a gaze axis. It is generated by two types of stimuli: those from the vestibule (especially the otolithic organ) and visual stimuli.

Rotational eye movements that are generated by vestibular stimulation are referred to as vestibular counter-rolling (vestibular torsional counter-rolling). When the body (head) is tilted in either direction, the eyeball rotates in the opposite direction to that of the body (head) tilt, thereby preserving the vision [6].

Rotational eye movements are also a reflection of linear acceleration from the otolithic organ.

It has been suggested that ocular torsional counter-rolling occurs in motion sickness, whereas a postural wobble occurs as a physical symptom of motion sickness [3].

4 Measurement of Eye Movement

With the development of information technology, the accuracy and performance of measurement instruments for biological signals have improved, and new analysis methods have been presented [7]. Such measurement instruments are used extensively in research and medical settings. For example, techniques such as electroencephalography, functional MRI, and near-infrared spectroscopy (NIRS) are used in the field of brain physiology [8–10]. Electrocardiograms (ECG) and electrogastrograms (EGG), which measure action potentials in the body, are also carried out using specialized equipment [11, 12]. Moreover, eye movements are an important type of biological signal data [13].

The eye perceives light energy from the outside world through the photoreceptors of the retina. The received information is transmitted through the nervous system to the brain center, where it is perceived as vision. Two types of photoreceptor cells exist in the retina: rods and cones. The rods are a function of high sensitivity to light and operate while observing objects in the dark. The cones operate in bright areas and respond selectively to different light wavelengths. The three types of human cone cells are classified as the L-cone, M-cone, and S-cone, based on the longer light wavelengths that they absorb. Furthermore, an area of concentration of cones exists, which is known as the central fossa. Therefore, for a human to obtain a clear view of an object, the object must be captured in the central fossa. Six external eye muscles, namely the external rectus, internal rectus, superior rectus, inferior rectus, inferior oblique, and superior oblique, move the eye to capture an object in the central fossa. Thus, eye movements occur based on the structure and function of the eye [4, 5].

The modern scientific observation and measurement of eye movements are believed to have started with Muller [14, 15]. The two methods used at the time were the direct observation method, which allowed the naked eye to observe the iris pattern in the cornea (black eye) and the movement of capillaries on the sclera (white eye), and the after-image method, which quantitatively measured the movement of the after-image generated on the retina by projecting it onto a screen. Subsequently, Huey covered the eye up to the sclera with a plaster contact, and used a technique that mechanically magnified the movement of the bar connected to the contact by using a lever and recorded the movement on paper [16]. At present, methods used to measure eye movements include the magnetic search coil method, pupil center corneal reflection (PCCR) method, limbus tracking method, image analysis method, and electro-oculography (EOG).

In PCCR, a light source is shone onto the cornea to identify the light reflection point and pupil on the cornea, and the eye direction is calculated based on the light reflection point and other geometric features [13, 17, 18]. The PCCR method has been used for a long time owing to its large amount of reflected light, and it remains the most widely used method. In principle, when the cornea is irradiated by a light source, four reflection images (the first to fourth Purkinje images) appear. These images are reflected at the anterior surface of the cornea, posterior surface of the cornea, anterior surface of the lens, and posterior surface of the lens. Among these, the reflectivity of the anterior surface of the cornea is large, at approximately 2.4%, making it the brightest reflection image. Compared to the reflected image on the anterior surface of the cornea, the other reflected images are darker and therefore negligible in the measurement of eye movement.

5   Methods

The participants were nine elderly people who had visual and balance functions that did not interfere with their daily life. The gaze data were measured at rest before and after DS trial (five minutes of driving, five trials). The resting gaze data were obtained by the participants gazing at the center of the DS screen for 1 min during the measurement. Gaze data were also collected during DS operation (first and fifth runs, about five minutes each). SSQs were conducted before and after the start and end of the experiment.

The instrument used for measuring the gaze data and the analysis software were the Tobii Pro X2-30 (sampling rate: 60 Hz) and Tobii Pro Studio (ver. 3.3.2), respectively. The gaze data were plotted corresponding to the resolution (640 × 480 pixels) of the scene camera (Logitech HD Webcam C270).

The participants were divided into two groups based on the SSQ results. One group experienced VIMS during the DS trial (four people, average of 79.0 years old). The other group did not experience VIMS during the DS trial (five people, average of 71.2 years old) (Figs. 1 and 2).

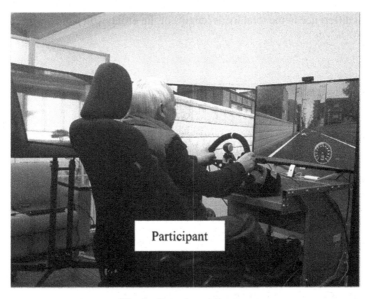

Fig. 1. Experimental setup.

Fig. 2. Measurement device (Tobii Pro X2-30).

6 Results

Figure 3 presents the calculation results of the total locus length for each participant based on the eye-tracking data at rest to determine the average for each case of "no previous or previous experience" of VIMS before and after (pre-/post-) DS trial. The total locus length results indicate that, for both the pre-DS and post-DS trial, the total locus length data were longer for those with than for those without previous experience of VIMS. A corresponding t-test for the value of the total locus lengths among those who did not experience VIMS showed no significant difference. However, there was a significant difference in the total locus lengths of the group which did experience VIMS (p < 0.1).

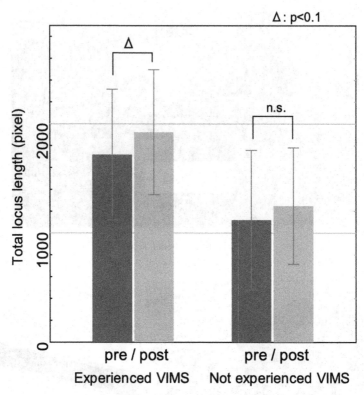

Fig. 3. Total locus length of gaze.

Similar to the total locus length, the sparse density was calculated based on the eye-tracking data to obtain the average for each set of experimental conditions, as illustrated in Fig. 4. The sparse density is a quantification index that is represented by a scatterplot of the data on a plane, and the diffusion of the data increases its value. In the sparse density results, the post-trial value was higher than the pre-trial value for both the participants with and without experience of VIMS. A corresponding t-test for the value of the sparse density among those who did not experience VIMS showed no significant difference. However, there was a significant difference in the sparse density of the group which did experience VIMS (p < 0.01).

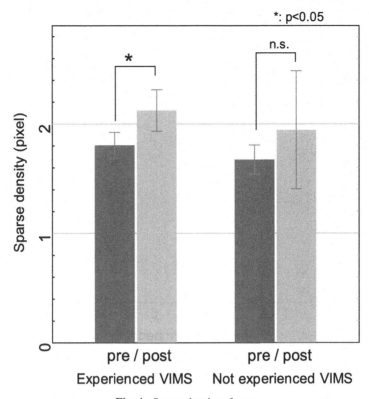

Fig. 4. Sparse density of gaze.

To verify the regularity of the gaze data collected during DS operation, data concerning the vertical gaze during the first and fifth operations were analyzed via the Double-Wayland method. The results of the group with no experience of VIMS are shown in Fig. 5, and the results of the group that experienced VMIS are shown in Fig. 6. The Translation Error (E_{trance}) obtained from the analysis conducted via the Double-Wayland method indicates that the lower the observed value, the higher the regularity. In the group that did not experience VIMS, there was no significant change in the regularity between the first and fifth DS operation. In the group that experienced VIMS, however, the regularity increased in the fifth DS operation (when compared to that of the first). Furthermore, when the corresponding t-test was conducted for the values of each embedding dimension among the non-VIMS group, no significant difference was found. However, when the corresponding t-test was conducted for the values of each embedded dimension in the group that experienced VIMS, significant differences were observed in the second, third, and fourth dimensions (all, $p < 0.05$). Therefore, for the gaze data collected from the VIMS group, the regularity increased significantly in the fifth session compared to that of the first.

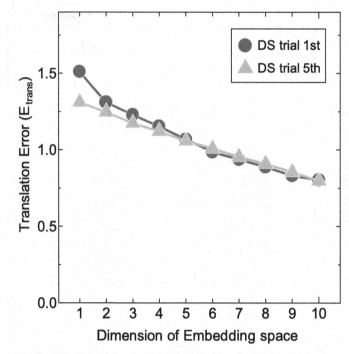

Fig. 5. Gaze of not experienced VIMS (longitudinal line-of-sight data).

7 Discussions

The hypotheses of VIMS symptoms were confirmed: data concerning the locus of eye-tracking were lengthened, whereas the eye-tracking data were diffused (Fig. 3 and Fig. 4). Moreover, in the group which experience VIMS, the regularity of gaze data during the DS trials was increased (Fig. 6). This experiment demonstrated the usefulness of sparse density and the regularity of evaluation as a quantification index for eye-tracking data in evaluating VIMS. Regarding the application of the findings of this study, it is believed that if an eye-tracking data-based VIMS evaluation index can be used, it will be easier to detect VIMS which is caused by DS operations, thus permitting the detection of the symptoms.

Regarding the application of the findings of this study, it is believed that if an eye-tracking data-based VIMS evaluation index can be used, it will be easier to detect VIMS caused by DS operations, thereby permitting detection of the symptoms while they are still at the developmental stage. Furthermore, by coding the VIMS evaluation index algorithm into a program, it will be possible to develop a real-time automatic VIMS detection system to help to reduce the load on participants after viewing stereoscopic motion images or while wearing head-mounted display devices. Moreover, the findings will not be limited to VIMS; they can also be applied to the treatment of disorders relating to rotational eye movements (nystagmus).

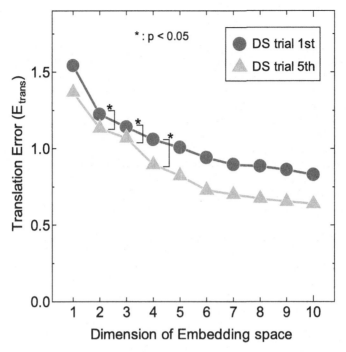

Fig. 6. Gaze of experienced VIMS (longitudinal line-of-sight data).

8 Conclusions

In this study, we investigated the development of the evaluation index of VIMS using eye gaze data. The results of VIMS symptoms were confirmed: the loci of the eye-tracking data were lengthened and the eye-tracking data were diffused. Moreover, the experiments demonstrated the usefulness of sparse density as a quantification index for eye-tracking data in evaluating VIMS. The evaluation of the regularity of the gaze data was shown to be effective for the real-time VIMS. From the results of this study, if an eye-tracking data-based VIMS evaluation index can be used, it will be easier to detect VIMS caused by DS operations.

Acknowledgment. This work was supported by JSPS KAKENHI Grant Number 20K11905.

References

1. Golding, J.F.: Phasic skin conductance activity and motion sickness. Aviat. Space Environ. Med. **63**(3), 165–171 (1992)
2. Wan, H., Hu, S., Wang, J.: Correlation of phasic and motion sickness-conductance responses with severity of motion sickness induced by viewing an optokinetic rotating drum. Percept. Mot. Skills **97**(3), 1051–1057 (2003)
3. Hoshino, K., Ono, N., Tomida, M., Igo, N.: Measurement of rotational eye movement with blue light irradiation. In: Proceeding of ICBBE, pp. 50–54 (2017)

4. Leigh, R.J., Zee, D.S.: The Neurology of Eye Movements. Oxford University Press, Oxford (2015)
5. Klein, C., Ettinger, U. (eds.): Eye Movement Research. SNPBE. Springer, Cham (2019). https://doi.org/10.1007/978-3-030-20085-5
6. Howard, I.P.: Human Visual Orientation. John Wiley & Sons Ltd, Hoboken (1982)
7. Tanimura, T., Jono, Y., Hirata, T., Matsuura, Y., Takada, H.: Trial on low-pass filter design for bio-signal based on nonlinear analysis. FORMA **34**(1), 13–20 (2019)
8. Takada, H., Miyao, M., Takada, M., Kinoshita, F., Tahara, H.: Development of sports vision training system using virtual reality for prevention of mild cognitive impairment. Descente Sports Sci. **40**, 97–109 (2019). (Japanese)
9. Bohning, D.E., et al.: BOLD-fMRI response to single-pulse transcranial magnetic stimulation (TMS). J. Magn. Reson. Imaging **11**, 569–574 (2000)
10. Tanimura, T., Takada, H., Sugiura, A., Kinoshita, F., Takada, M.: Effects of the low-resolution 3D video clip on cerebrum blood flow dynamics. Adv. Sci. Technol. Eng. Syst. J **4**(2), 380–386 (2019)
11. Mincholé, A., Rodriguez, B.: Artificial intelligence for the electrocardiogram. Nat. Med. **25**, 22–23 (2019)
12. Kinoshita, F., Fujita, K., Miyanaga, K., Touyama, H., Takada, M., Takada, H.: Analysis of electrogastrograms during exercise loads. J. Sports Med. Doping Stud. **8**(2), 285–294 (2018)
13. Young, L.R., Sheena, D.: Methods and designs: survey of eye movement recording methods. Behav. Res. Methods Instrum. **7**, 397–429 (1975)
14. Mueller, J.: Zur vergleichenden physiologie des gesichtssinnes des menschen und der thiere. Cnobloch (1826)
15. Mueller, J.: Handbuch der Physiologie des Menschen, Verlag von Hoelscher (1840)
16. Huey, E.B.: Preliminary experiments in the physiology of reading. Am. J. Psychol. **9**(4), 575–586 (1898)
17. Cornsweet, T.N., Crane, H.D.: Accurate two-dimensional eye tracker using first and fourth Purkinje images. J. Opt. Soc. Am. **63**, 921–928 (1973)
18. Crane, H.D., Steele, C.M.: An accurate three-dimensional eye tracker. Appl. Opt. **17**, 691–705 (1978)

The Analysis of Brainwaves to Measuring Music Tone Impact on Behavior of ADHD Children

Chalakorn Juiter[✉] and Ko-Chiu Wu[✉]

National Taipei University of Technology, Taipei, Taiwan
Kochiuwu@mail.ntut.edu.tw

Abstract. This study aims to measure music tone impact on the behavior of ADHD Children in 3 kinds of behavior attention, relaxation, and concentration related to 3 kinds of brainwave 1.Theta wave - Attention 2. Alpha wave - Relaxation 3. Beta - Concentration. In the experiment, we controlled study employing 30 students with ADHD and 30 students without ADHD (total 60 students) ranging in age from 7 to 9 years in Thailand, participated in music listening sessions of comparison design in two different tones of music by the piano melody that was composed for this research in C tone (major key) and G tone (minor key) which is the tone is lower than C tone. In the experiment, all 60 students wear the macrotellect brain-link lite EEG headset V2.0 device meanwhile 3 brainwaves 1. Theta wave 2. Alpha wave 3. Beta was collected from them. The results showed that the music tone has impacted the behavior of ADHD children because the experiment found that the brain waves score of ADHD children collected from the 3 kinds of brainwaves were changed significantly.

Keywords: ADHD · Special education · Tone impact · EEG · Brainwave

1 Introduction

1.1 Background and Motivation

Attention-Deficit/Hyperactivity Disorder (ADHD) is a chronic condition including attention difficulty, hyperactivity, and impulsiveness caused by abnormalities of the brain symptoms that are easy to notice such as lack of concentration, impulsive, nausea, and restlessness, all of which will affect learning, working, and socializing.

In Thailand, 3–5% of school-age children are found. ADHD symptoms in children can separate into two groups, 1. Lack of concentration: found that children will, Unable to complete tasks that the teacher or parents asked, No concentration while working or playing, Looks like they do not listen much when others speaking with them, Not intended to listen shortly and can keep a few details causing frequent mistakes, Disorderly, Avoiding tasks that require thought or concentration, Frequently distracted, Loss of personal or necessary items for work or school, Forgetful. 2. Mischievous, unsteady and low self-control: found that children will, they can't sit for a long time, often walk while at home or in the classroom, Like to climb, Talk too much, can't stop talking,

© Springer Nature Switzerland AG 2021
M. Antona and C. Stephanidis (Eds.): HCII 2021, LNCS 12768, pp. 555–566, 2021.
https://doi.org/10.1007/978-3-030-78092-0_38

Stay alert or always looks excited, Not pay attention to listening to the question, Always interrupt others when others are speaking. Causes of attention deficit hyperactivity disorder are caused by the defects of some important chemicals in the brain with hereditary being an important factor in parenting factors or the environment are just factors that make symptoms or disorders better or worse.

Approximately 20–30% of ADHD in children has a chance of disappearing when entering adolescents. They can study or work without medication but the majority of ADHD children still have impaired attention. Which will affect education to work and socializing with others. Therefore, according to the impact of ADHD children in education to work and socializing with others. The purpose of this study is to measuring music tone impact on the behavior of ADHD Children in 3 kinds of behavior attention, relaxation, concentration which are related to 3 kinds of brainwave 1. Theta wave - Attention 2. Alpha wave - Relaxation 3. Beta - Concentration (Fig. 1).

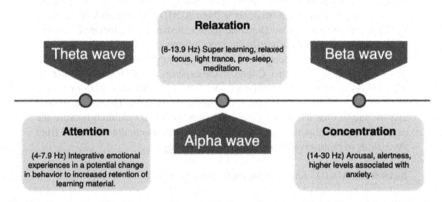

Fig. 1. Categories of brainwaves patterns with the explanation of how they relate to behavior

2   Literature Reviews

2.1   Attention Deficit Hyperactivity Disorder (ADHD)

ADHD is a biological disorder (most probably of genetic origin). The primary symptoms of this disorder are hyperactivity, impulsivity, and distractibility. A person can have certain of these symptoms and not others. This disorder affects 3–5 percent of all children and adults in the United States (and presumably the world). ADHD can be assessed in many ways, or in a combination of ways: a medical history; observations of the child in a variety of contexts; the use of rating scales to document these observations; performance tasks to assess such traits as vigilance; and psychological tests to assess memory, learning, and related areas of functioning. The most effective approaches for treating ADHD are medications and behavior modification. Many children will continue to have ADHD throughout their lives. A child can have ADHD and also have other disorders, such as learning disabilities and anxiety or mood disorders The symptoms of people with attention deficit hyperactivity disorder may persist as well as into adolescents and adults. The pattern of the symptoms may change slightly according to age and according to the treatment that the patient receives or may still have some symptoms that remain and affect the daily life. There are two main types of behavioral problems of ADHD lack of concentration or concentration and being restless and impulsive in which children may have any form of behavior but both behaviors tend to appear together, which will be obstacles that result in difficulties in daily life, work, schooling, socializing and interpersonal relationships [1].

For long term outcomes of ADHD people, recent follow-up studies of children with ADHD show that ADHD persists from childhood to adolescence in 50%–80% of cases, and into adulthood in 35%– 65% of cases [2]. 32.2% of students with the combined type of ADHD drop out of high school, compared to 15% of teens with no psychiatric disorder. Between 2% and 8% of college students are estimated to have ADHD. The National Center for Education Statistics [3]. estimates that there were 20,642,819 students enrolled in college in 2012. If 2%–8% of this population is estimated to have ADHD, then between 412,856 and 1,651,425 students with ADHD enrolled in college in 2012. A 2011 review of research studies on ADHD in prisoners found the rate of ADHD ranged from 10% to 70%. A 1994 study found ADHD in 25% of prisoners in the US. A study of 3,962 male and female adult prison inmates (3,439 men and 523 women, mean age 33.6 years, ages 17–73) found an overall ADHD prevalence rate of 10.5%. The prevalence rate for female inmates was 15.1% while for male inmates it was 9.8%. [4].

2.2 Music Learning for Children

Described in the earliest cultural records, enacted throughout the development of infants, evidenced from cognitive scientists, and utilized by innovative teachers and therapists, the deep and profound relationship between music and language supports their discriminate, concurrent use to improve outcomes for language acquisition. Melodic recognition, contour processing, timbre discrimination, rhythm, tonality, prediction, and perception of the sight, sound, and form of symbols in context are required in both music and language. Like supportive sisters, they comprise "separate, though complementary systems of structured communication… language primarily responsible for content and music evoking emotion". Music positively affects language accent, memory, and grammar as well as mood, enjoyment, and motivation. Language teachers and music therapists alike should encourage the conjoined study of these natural partners, because communicating through a musical medium benefits everyone [5].

2.3 Function of Brainwaves

When stimuli in any modality are presented to a normal human subject electric response appear over wide regions of frontal cortex. However, these responses decline after about 50 repetitions of the stimuli are monotonous and given at regular intervals, a phenomenon generally referred to as "habituation". Any change in the character of the stimulus may restore the responses and the most effective change is to associate them with some other event, such as a subsequent stimulus in another modality. When this is done there is gradually established "contingency" between the stimuli, that is, the probability of association between them grows steadily with the repeated pairing. In such conditions, the brain responses to the first of each pair of stimuli tend to recover their original size and extent while those to the second tend to decline. This effect has been called contingent amplification and contingent attenuation. Such effects suggest that the brain responses reflect a probabilistic analysis of the stimulus situation in terms of its information content. Habituation may be considered as indicating the steady reduction in information conveyed by a monotonous stimulus which becomes increasingly probable. Conversely, contingent amplification is the effect of increasing probability of association, that is the accretion of meaning when the occurrence of the first stimulus always implies the arrival of the second [6].

Brain functioning involves the transferring of electrical signals, leading to the emergence of electromagnetic waves called 'brain waves.' Exploring them involves the use of an Electroencephalogram (EEG), which measures and records the electrical activity along the scalp resulting from changes in these electrical currents. It converts this data into four different types of brain waves. If brainwave functioning is brought to a lower frequency, such as in the Alpha state, one will become a more calm and cheerful person with a creative mind and high concentration, memory and intelligence levels. This is usually found in priests, Buddhist monks or those regularly practicing meditation. Adjusting your brainwaves first involves being in a peaceful environment away from electromagnet fields such as those from a microwave, electrical wiring, transformers, and computers. Recent reports from Germany, Russia, and Switzerland are indicating that a microwave has highly negative impacts on brainwaves. Therefore, it should not be used for preparing a baby's food (i.e. heating the water in a feeding bottle).

Listening to or creating music, especially classical such as that of Mozart together with practicing meditation, doing yoga and even getting in touch with natural environments – helps with producing Alpha brainwaves. Re- search is also revealing that sound waves created from the base and drums stimulate areas of the brain stem and spinal cord related to one's ability to balance. Whereas, instruments such as the flute, guitar, and violin stimulate brain functioning related to the limbic system, which is located in the central part of the brain and related to our emotions. Stringed instruments with high-pitched tones (including the harp, organ, and bell) stimulate the functioning of the neocortex, directly related to one's intelligence. And sounds from the popular, piano stimulate all parts of the brain equally [7].

3   Methodology

3.1   Research Objects

In this study, we controlled study employing 30 students with ADHD and 30 students without ADHD (total 60 students) ranging in age from 7 to 9 years in Thailand, participated in music listening sessions of comparison design in two different tone of music by the piano melody that was composed for this research in C tone (major key) and G tone (minor key) which is the tone is lower than C tone. In the experiment, all 60 students wear the macrotellect brain-link lite EEG headset V2.0 device and meanwhile 3 brainwaves score 1. Theta wave 2. Alpha wave 3. Beta wave were collected from them (Figs. 2, 3, 4 and 5).

Fig. 2. The macrotellect brain-link lite EEG headset V2.0

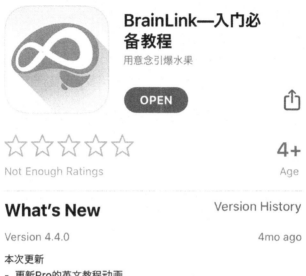

Fig. 3. BrainLink application on app store using with the Macrotellect brain-link lite EEG headset V2.0

3.2 Experiment

30 ADHD students and 30 without ADHD students (total 60 students) listened to music tones by the piano melody in C tone (major key) and G tone (minor key) which is lower than C tone. The song time is around 1 min per each song and preparing time around 1 min, therefore, each experiment will take around 3 min per children (Fig. 6).

Juicy little Duck

Fig. 4. "Juicy little duck" a song was composed in 2 different tones for this study - C tone (major key)

Juicy Little Duck

Fig. 5. "Juicy little duck" a song was composed in 2 different tones for this study - G tone (minor key) which is the tone is lower than C tone.

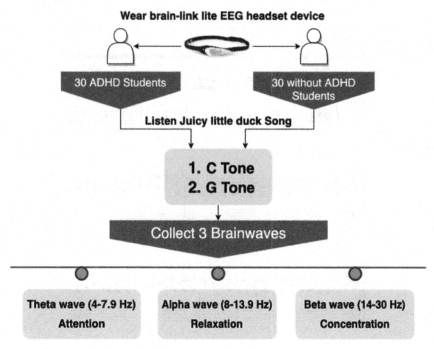

Fig. 6. Research experiment structure

4 Data Analysis

4.1 Analysis Method

The brainwaves were collected by using the Brainwave-Reading Headset device and BrainLink application. The data that will be analyzed is the highest (peak) Hz score on each wave in each student (Fig. 7).

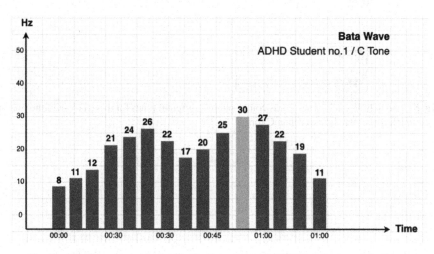

Fig. 7. A brainwaves analysis chart in Beta wave of ADHD student no. 1 in C tone

4.2 Raw Data

See Tables 1 and 2.

Table 1. The below table is showing the data of Peak Hz score of 30 ADHD students in C and G tones in total and average

Peak Hz score of 30 ADHD students						
Student number	Theta-attention		Alpha-relaxation		Beta-concentration	
	C	G	C	G	C	G
1	6	5	8	8	30	19
2	4	6	10	12	14	14
3	7	6	8	10	27	15
4	6	6	10	8	14	14
5	5	5	9	8	21	18
6	6	4	10	11	19	20
7	5	6	8	13	15	20
8	5	5	8	11	14	16
9	7	6	10	8	30	20
10	6	6	8	9	30	14
11	5	4	9	13	28	18
12	7	6	9	13	14	14
13	6	6	10	10	16	18
14	7	6	10	9	21	20
15	6	4	10	11	14	14
16	4	6	8	12	25	16
17	5	5	10	8	24	20
18	4	7	9	13	20	15
19	5	7	9	8	16	14
20	5	6	9	11	19	18
21	4	4	9	13	30	14
22	4	4	8	9	27	19
23	7	5	8	12	25	14
24	6	7	9	10	23	17
25	4	5	10	13	26	16
26	5	7	9	9	14	19
27	6	7	10	9	18	19
28	7	4	8	12	22	19
29	5	5	10	8	24	20
30	4	5	10	12	18	19
Total	163	165	273	313	638	513
Average	5.43	5.55	9.10	10.43	21.26	17.10

Table 2. The below table is showing the data of Peak Hz score of 30 students without ADHD in C and G tones in total and average

Peak Hz score of 30 students without ADHD						
Student number	Theta-attention		Alpha-relaxation		Beta-concentration	
	C	G	C	G	C	G
1	5	5	10	12	25	28
2	6	4	9	12	30	30
3	4	4	10	9	26	27
4	7	5	8	13	14	19
5	7	4	11	12	15	27
6	7	6	11	8	26	30
7	7	5	8	10	28	15
8	5	5	11	12	21	26
9	4	5	10	13	14	18
10	6	6	11	11	24	22
11	5	5	8	10	29	29
12	7	5	9	8	30	18
13	7	6	11	11	28	16
14	4	4	8	8	15	15
15	7	6	9	9	22	20
16	5	6	9	11	30	26
17	7	4	11	8	17	23
18	5	6	9	12	14	17
19	4	5	10	10	14	24
20	7	6	11	12	30	18
21	5	4	9	10	27	27
22	4	5	9	10	17	26
23	4	5	9	8	21	19
24	5	5	8	9	19	28
25	6	4	9	13	19	17
26	7	5	10	12	26	28
27	4	5	11	10	24	26
28	5	5	10	8	15	22
29	7	4	10	13	28	19
30	6	4	11	11	24	22
Total	169	148	290	315	672	682
Average	5.63	4.93	9.66	10.50	22.40	22.73

5 Result and Conclusion

5.1 Result

See Tables 3 and 4.

Table 3. The below table is showing the result of total Hz score of 30 ADHD students in C and G tones in average score

Tone	Theta-attention average score	Alpha-relaxation average score	Beta-concentration average score
C	5.43	9.10	21.26
G	5.55	10.43	17.10
Result	G tone is bit higher	G tone is higher	C tone is higher

Table 4. The below table is showing the result of total score of 30 students without ADHD in C and G tones in average score

Tone	Theta-attention average score	Alpha-relaxation average score	Beta-concentration average scores
C	5.63	9.66	22.40
G	4.93	10.50	22.73
Result	C tone is higher	G tone is higher	G tone is a bit higher

5.2 Conclusion

The Conclusion of the Experiment Found that
Theta wave - Attention, the result shows that whether it's low or high tones ADHD children are also interested in music but they have slightly more attention in the lower tones because the result shows that the average score of theta wave in C tone and G tone is not much different but in G tone score a little bit higher, which means we should use lower tone music in order to get attention from ADHD students from any activities. Meanwhile, for students without ADHD, the result shows that the theta wave score in C tone is higher than G tone, which means we should use normal tone music in order to get attention from students without ADHD.

Alpha wave - Relaxation, the result shows that the alpha wave score in G tone is higher than C tone in both ADHD students and students without ADHD, which means we should use lower tone music in order to make both ADHD students and students without ADHD can be more relaxed.

Beta wave - Concentration, the result shows that the alpha wave score in C tone is higher than G tone in ADHD students but in student without ADHD the result shows that the average score of beta wave in C tone and G tone is not much different but in G tone score a little bit higher, which means we should use the normal tone of music in order to make ADHD students be more concentrated and use lower tone in order to make students without ADHD be more concentrated.

6 Discussion and Future Work

However, in this study, the authors chose to compare only two tones in one song, a normal tone (C Tone Major key) and a lower tone (G Tone Minor key) because we wanted to start from the factor that can be applied easily with many activities in the classroom and not too complicated for ADHD students such as singing class or dancing class. Therefore, according to the result of this study that the students cooperated well with the experiment, in future research, there could be more experimentation with different tones, such as normal tone compare to higher tone or another variable in the composition of the song may also be used in future experiments, such as comparisons between instruments for example string instruments compare to woodwind instruments or tempo, volume, etc. in order to apply to music activities for ADHD children in the classroom to help teachers determine how to choose the correct tone of music that suitable to be used in teaching and learning based on situation and objectives. For example, activities that require a lot of attention to the child, such as dance lessons or physical activities. It is important to choose a song that is consistent with the results of the theta waves that increase student's attention and activities that can make the children be more relax, such as handicraft or painting. It is important to choose music that is consistent with the results of the alpha waves that increase the relaxation of the student. Last one, thoughtful activities, such as problem-solving activities or role-plays. The teacher needs to choose music that is consistent with the results of beta wave experiments that increase student concentration.

References

1. Armstrong, T.: ADD/ADHD Alternatives in the Classroom. ASCD, Alexandria (1999)
2. Owens, E.B., Cardoos, S.L., Hinshaw, S.P.: Developmental progression and gender differences among individuals with ADHD (2015)
3. Xu, G., Strathearn, L., Liu, B., Yang, B., Bao, W.: Twenty-year trends in diagnosed attention-deficit/hyperactivity disorder among US children and adolescents, 1997–2016. JAMA Netw. Open 1(4), e181471–e181471 (2018)
4. Cahill, B.S., Coolidge, F.L., Segal, D.L., Klebe, K.J., Marle, P.D., Overmann, K.A.: Prevalence of ADHD and its subtypes in male and female adult prison inmates. Behav. Sci. Law **30**(2), 154–166 (2012)
5. Jourdain, R.: Music, the brain, and Ecstasy: How Music Captures Our Imagination. HarperCollins Publishers, New York (1997)
6. Walter, W.G.: Slow potential waves in the human brain associated with expectancy, attention and decision. Arch. Psychiatr. Nervenkr. **206**, 309–322 (1964)
7. Methee, W.: https://www.healthtodaythailand.in.th. Accessed 2014

Contextual Cues: The Role of Machine Learning in Supporting Contextually Impaired Users

Martin Kinch[1]([⊠]) [iD] and Simeon Keates[2] [iD]

[1] University of Greenwich, Medway Campus, Chatham Maritime M4 4TB, UK
m.w.kinch@greenwich.ac.uk
[2] University of Chichester, College Lane, Chichester PO19 6PE, UK

Abstract. This paper explores the theoretical aspect of providing context to contextually impaired individuals and offers some considerations on how a machine learning system can be adapted to learn contextual clues and then provide these to users. Context itself, is the clarifying component of a situation and helps people to understand what is happening and why. Some people struggle to understand the situations that they are in, due to several issues, particularly those with sensory or social impairments, such as autism. These impairments can be interpreted as form of contextual blindness, where a lack of awareness of certain contextual clues render communication or understanding of it difficult. These clues can be as simple as a person's current location, to the more nuanced impact of a conversational partner's body language. Since awareness of the current context of a situation can help to clarify its meaning, it is expected that provision of contextual information to contextually impaired individuals will be beneficial; by giving them a point of reference for the tone of the situation they are in and supporting them to react accordingly. The results presented demonstrate the impact of contextual information in a specific social situation (dating), giving an indication of the benefits of both context and contextual awareness, which provide the basis for further investigation.

Keywords: Context · Machine Learning · Contextual support · Autism support · Contextual information processing

1 Introduction

This paper explores the concept of providing contextual information to contextually impaired individuals and whether utilising Machine Learning (ML) would provide additional benefit. Since ML is capable of discerning patterns in data, it has the potential to be trained to recognise context. Providing this context to a user would give them some insight into the situation that they were experiencing, with users being able to use this information to help reduce social anxiety by making them aware of details that they may not be able to detect themselves. It is expected this will be most beneficial for those who find it hard to react accordingly to complex social interactions and behaviors. Machine learning systems would need to be designed to function in a specific application domain,

© Springer Nature Switzerland AG 2021
M. Antona and C. Stephanidis (Eds.): HCII 2021, LNCS 12768, pp. 567–579, 2021.
https://doi.org/10.1007/978-3-030-78092-0_39

such as monitoring body language, locational clues, or audio clues. These systems may also be trainable for specific social situations, like dating, co-worker communication or general conversation.

The work presented in this paper focuses on how contextual information can help users in general, using analyses of how contextual information affects human dating. The analysis uses a custom dataset that was created from several episodes of the Channel 4 television programme First Dates [1]. The creation of which is described later in this paper. This approach was used as it provided a specific scenario, with a restricted set of contexts, allowing for analysis of the effect contextual information had on predicting the success of the interaction.

The contextual information that is present in a date, such as body language, adds significant value to the communication and makes it considerably easier to determine an individual's reaction to certain social stimuli. For instance, a look of disgust or joy related to a comment, can clearly indicate to most people whether the comment was received well. However, a contextually impaired individual, for instance an individual with autism, could easily be unaware of a conversational partners' emotional reactions or any potential atmosphere. This could lead to a possible worsening of the atmosphere if a comment was taken badly and the affront was not addressed. Providing contextual information to a contextually impaired individual, at this point, gives them an opportunity to change their approach and hopefully redress the situation in their favour. It may also be useful for situations where a contextually impaired individual is at risk and they are unaware of threatening, misleading, or dangerous behaviour from another, allowing them to retreat from the situation safely, after being warned of such behaviour.

Recognising a context is also useful for a "situationally impaired" user, such as those driving or on a train. These users may be unable to use their computerised communication systems in a safe manner, due to the situation they are in and recognition of their context may not be useful for supporting them socially. Instead, the context can be passed to other software perhaps on a user's phone, which can then adjust its settings to suit their situation and support the user. For instance, automatically routing phone calls to voice mail while driving, a feature present in some modern mobile phone operating systems, is a good example, which could be adapted to more varied applications.

The benefits are dependent on recognising a context automatically and then effectively and subtly passing this recognition either to the end user or another software process. Which if used effectively, offers users the benefit of being more aware of the context they are in, how a situation is progressing and by potentially providing clues to how that situations outcome can be improved. This helps bridge the gap between contextually impaired individuals and those for which context is ubiquitous.

2 Background

There is a body of work that indicates how important context is to human interaction, specifically regarding communication [2] and cognition [3]. The focus is nominally on how context impacts learning and human memory [4–6], which seems key to how humans handle new information. Context is also helpful in ensuring that humans can infer information, even when they are unsure of an answer [5]. While it is clear that humans benefit from context, there is some limitation in our understanding of specifically what context is and how it can be utilised effectively. For example, there are several descriptions and explanations for context offered in the literature [7–9], although there is no single accepted definition. Context has been used in applications from active phone routing [10] in office buildings, to more recently speech recognition using large datasets [11]; although the use of context is far from common in a computational setting. For the benefit of this work, it is sufficient to view context as a clarification of what is occurring in a situation, undoubtedly important to both machine and human alike. Context can be anything from a location to a time, all the way to an emotional response.

Interestingly, for contextually impaired users, such as those who are autistic; they may struggle to process certain contextual information [12] e.g., body language. This can put them at a significant disadvantage in a social interaction (such as a date) compared to a non-impaired person, who is likely to be able to process emotional context readily [13]. This provides a basis for consideration of how context could prove useful for contextually impaired users, if it is provided in an understandable manner.

While research into contextual information and dating is limited, especially that which links to ML, there has been a study into reviewing the dating goals of daters [14], which considers what daters intended from the date and tracked the contexts (gender, etc.) that impacted these choices. The work presented in this paper attempts to build on this by providing a breakdown of dating success based on more nuanced contexts, such as emotion.

The basis of the emotional recognition used in this study draws inspiration from Argyle [15], who offers an overview of how humans communicate via non-verbal means. While work from Ekman and Friesen provide the basis for the six "universal" basic emotions [16, 17], which were derived from Darwin's original work on emotions and mankind [18]. These six emotions (Happy, Sad, Anger, Surprise, Disgust and Fear) have been used to categorise the emotional responses in this paper.

Despite the use of manual emotion detection in this work, there is growing body of work that provides emotion recognition for non-impaired [19] and impaired users [20]. Supporting the notion that further research could use automatic means to recognise emotions/contexts and provide these to a contextual support system. There is also work that has considered the connection between both context and facial reactions [21] and considered the idea of using facial emotion recognition to support autistic users [22]. It is highly likely that providing additional context beyond facial emotions, may prove useful for such as system. This provided the basis for testing whether contexts, such as the emotional responses of daters or intonation of the voice, provided a significant indication of success in the date and thus would prove beneficial to daters, in a contextual support system.

The dataset created was derived the First Dates television program [1], using sources including All 4 [23] and Learning on Screen [24]. All data collected was not distributed and followed the appropriate copyright legislation.

3 Creating the First Dates Dataset

To create the First Dates dataset, the subtitles from the programme were processed into transcriptions, using the subtitles provided when aired. The subtitles were aligned so that for each sentence there was only one entry in the dataset, including the related contexts. The subtitles provided by the program were normally highly accurate, however while reviewing and aligning the set, some minor errors were corrected. Due to the corrections, the dataset may deviate slightly from the subtitles in the interest of accuracy. These transcriptions were not considered in this work but were used to ensure the proper alignment of identified contextual information.

The contextual information in the dataset was manually collected by annotating the content of the programme on a sentence per sentence basis, ensuring the identified contexts were time dependent and linked to each phase of the interaction. Due to this, each row in the dataset was built from a sentence and its associated contexts. The dataset collection represented 2 episodes (E1 and E3) from season 2 of the program covering 12 couples, 11 of the couples were heterosexual, and 1 couple was homosexual. Some couples have been omitted as they did not generate enough data for processing. Each couple's data represents a significant portion of an individual date between the couple, although it is not clear what parts of the date were missing due to editorial bias. It is likely the key or most interesting parts were the focus of the programme, with less interesting parts removed, which means the dataset is likely to represent the most important parts of the date. On a full date, it is likely some sections would provide minimal benefit and it is expected that focus would need to be on more important sections to provide a benefit.

The second season was chosen to provide the data for the dataset as the program was well established at that point and there was a more consistent flow to the program and format, making collection of the contexts and subtitles more efficient. The dataset represents each couple by ID and by male/female identifiers for the speaker, along with their speech target, contexts also focused on their apparent emotional state when delivering and receiving communication, based on facial and bodily reactions.

During processing each reaction was recorded and appended to the nearest sentence in the conversation, this kept timings relevant to most interactions. The most dominant exhibited emotion was recorded, where there may have been any overlap. The annotation of the dataset was conducted after the annotator had spent time reviewing Argyle's work on non-verbal human communication [15]. Furthermore, they reviewed emotional responses that occurred in the previous season of First Dates, to help inform the recognition/recording process for the dataset, as well as training their emotional recognition and annotation ability. The support of this approach is that a human of normal social ability will be able to determine most emotions naturally, especially when looking for them. Thus, only minimal training would be required to recognise and record the emotions used in the dataset and to align these to the transcriptions effectively and accurately. The contextual types in this work and their different clarifiers/options are described in Table 1.

The five types of context covered a range of different interactions present in the First Dates program between the dating individuals. The gender type indicates who was speaking at the time, either a male or female participant. The other option denotes a person other than the daters, whether this was a family member via a phone call or a staff member at the restaurant. These speakers have been de-gendered to ensure that the dataset does not become overly complex.

Table 1. The contextual types used in the first dates dataset.

Contextual type	Possible options
Gender	Male, Female, Other
Speaker emotion	Anger, Happy, Sad, Surprise, Fear, Disgust, Neutral
Listener emotion	Anger, Happy, Sad, Surprise, Fear, Disgust, Neutral
Speaker intonation	Sarcasm, Hesitation, Joking, Flirting, Nervous, Confident, Neutral
Speaker target	Date, Other, Booth, End, Date_M, Date_F

Speaker and listener emotions represent one of the six mains types of universal emotions. They cover the speaker's emotion and the listener's reaction to the utterance or behaviour of the speaker. The neutral option is used for when a speaker or listener did not exhibit a discernable or significant emotional response at that point.

Speaker intonation covers the way in which the speaker spoke. This included a set of intonations which were commonly present in the program and offer an extra layer of context to the transcripts. The speaker target indicates who someone was speaking to. Date implies the person they were on the date with. Other is a staff member, or another person not on the date, such as a family member on a phone call etc. Booth and end relate to parts of the program where either the daters speak alone (booth) about their experience, or where they meet at the end and decide whether to meet again. Date_M/F refers to when a person who is not on the date is talking to either the male or female dater, such as a staff member, if the speakers is a dater, then they would have spoken to another daters date rather than their own.

Every entry in the dataset contains a value for each contextual type presented in this paper, based on what was observed. These types would potentially be listed as neutral, where applicable, if no particular emotion or context was exhibited or discernable for that contextual type, during that sentence/entry.

4   Analysis of the First Dates Dataset

The analysis utilised the full dataset with all couples and entries included. Each sentence by default links to several pieces of contextual information and each date contained an average of 160 sentences in the full set. The sentences themselves were not processed, as the focus of the research was on whether the context alone could be used to monitor the success of a date, rather than the content of the speech.

What is termed as a successful date is this work, is an outcome where both daters consent to a second date and wish to meet a second time. While there is an element of bias towards those who like or dislike a suitor purely on outward appearance or any other number of factors. It is considered that something as simple and non-committal as a second date is unlikely to be hugely impacted by this bias. Thus, an indication can be drawn on the basis of presented emotions, which could change the outcome of the date or that may result/occur in more positive or negative dates.

The speaker and listener alternate throughout the date to represent the dater who is speaking at the time. Each step of the analysis has considered different sections of the dataset, firstly as a whole, then with samples removed to focus on more specific aspects of the dataset. Where this has occurred, it is described in the analysis. The analysis starts with an overview of the emotions/contexts present throughout the whole dataset, contrasting between the positive and negative outcomes.

4.1 The Successful Date

The results from analysing the dataset contained some interesting trends. It seems that several emotional responses perceived during a data are likely to influence the overall dates outcome. For example, in Table 2 there is a sharp contrast between happy emotions in the speaker and the listener, with 11% difference between a speaker who had a successful date and one who had an unsuccessful date. While a listener had a difference of 16.32% between positive and negative outcomes. Cleary, a positive date is well indicated by a set of happy responses throughout the date, between both daters, whether they were speaking or listening. This is not beyond expectations, nor is it unusual that the addition of sad emotions caused by potentially discussing negative life events, also occurs more often in unsuccessful dates. Other emotions present did not seem to vary to significantly, however this may be due to the number of neutral interactions during the date. It seems that these encompass at least 50% of a date, with the listener normally reacting less that the speaker. In negative dates, listeners spent almost 70% of their time showing no distinct emotion, clearly an inability to draw an emotional response, weakens a dates chance of success.

Table 2. Emotional responses throughout dates, including both male and female speakers.

Emotional types	Speaker positive	Speaker negative	Listener positive	Listener negative
Neutral	46.17%	47.49%	58.94%	67.72%
Happy	39.18%	28.16%	33.39%	17.07%
Sad	3.24%	11.49%	0.17%	6.47%
Surprise	6.30%	3.96%	6.30%	4.29%
Anger	0.51%	3.56%	0.00%	1.05%
Disgust	1.70%	3.40%	1.02%	2.51%
Fear	2.90%	1.94%	0.17%	0.89%

The data in Table 2 contains conversation through all stages of the date, including all "Targets" as described in Table 1. As such, there may be emotions not presented to both daters, thus Table 3 shows the average emotions presented when only the daters are talking. Immediately, it is clear that speakers who reacted in a positive manner, had better outcomes in the date and that the percentage of happy emotions were higher by 15.41% and 17.93%, for speakers and listeners respectively in successful dates. Being angry however, did not seem to help the date. Although, being nervous did not seem to differ much between speakers in either outcome, which must be overlooked by dating partners as par for the course. Being sad clearly impacted the date negatively, while being surprised seemed to have no major impact on the date. Neutral emotions are also exhibited more in the listener of an unsuccessful date.

Table 3. Emotional responses throughout dates, focused only on interactions between daters.

Emotional types	Speaker positive	Speaker negative	Listener positive	Listener negative
Neutral	43.28%	49.15%	49.73%	56.57%
Happy	42.20%	26.79%	39.52%	21.59%
Sad	1.61%	8.45%	0.27%	8.71%
Surprise	8.33%	5.46%	8.60%	6.76%
Anger	0.27%	4.29%	0.00%	1.69%
Disgust	2.15%	3.64%	1.61%	3.51%
Fear	2.15%	2.21%	0.27%	1.17%

Finally, Table 4 presents the data when the neutral emotions are stripped away, leaving only discernable emotions in the set. The difference between positive and negative emotions becomes ever more pronounced. Happy and sad emotions are around 20% higher in positive and negative outcomes, respectively. Clearly showing that interpreting and responding to a dating partner in a positive manner, massively increases the chance of successful date. Emotions such as anger seem to only present in dates that fail and disgust seems to cause an almost equal reaction between speaker and listener, it is likely that dates with a significant amount of offence (anger, disgust) caused, are more likely to fail. Being nervous as a speaker seems to be harmless, while causing a listener to become nervous, causes some negative impact. Surprise seems common in the discussion and having a healthy amount of this seems to be unimpactful. This is probably due to both people not knowing each other; thus, they would naturally have some surprise within their discussion. Overall, it seems that reacting and promoting a positive set of emotions in a dating partner, increases the chance of success. Thus, being able to interpret and react to these emotions, is likely to be a distinct advantage.

Another factor that seems to have some impact on the success of the date is the intonation with which the daters speak. Table 5 indicates that there is a marked difference between the types of emotion present in the date and how successful it was. Dates which contained fewer neutral emotions and those with more flirty or jokey overtones, where more likely to succeed, while overconfidence seemed to be a negative factor. Hesitation rather than nerves, also seemed to be a negative factor, being nervous seemed ubiquitous to the experience and thus did not negatively impact the date.

To further investigate the role of intonation in the date's success, the same data was analysed, this time without the neutral values. As can be seen in Table 6, there is a vast difference between the types of intonation present, for example, positive dates had over 15% more flirtatious interactions and almost 13% more joking interactions between

Table 4. Emotional responses throughout dates, with neutral responses removed.

Emotional types	Speaker positive	Speaker negative	Listener positive	Listener negative
Happy	74.41%	52.69%	78.61%	49.70%
Sad	2.84%	16.62%	0.53%	20.06%
Surprise	14.69%	10.74%	17.11%	15.57%
Anger	0.47%	8.44%	0.00%	3.89%
Disgust	3.79%	7.16%	3.21%	8.08%
Fear	3.79%	4.35%	0.53%	2.69%

Table 5. Speaker intonation, only including conversation in the date.

Intonation	Positive	Negative
Neutral	61.83%	70.35%
Flirting	13.17%	5.72%
Joking	16.13%	8.71%
Confident	4.84%	8.45%
Sarcasm	0.00%	0.52%
Hesitation	0.27%	3.25%
Nervous	3.76%	2.99%

daters. Over confidence was a significant indicator of a poor date, with just under 16% more confident statements in the negative set. Hesitation was also a negative indicator, although this may have been a slight deviation, due to a person with a stutter in the dataset which potentially inflated this result. Regardless, is likely that direct speaking is more likely to achieve a positive reaction. Nerves again seem to be par for the course. Removing neutral statements did not provide any real deviation for intonation, instead it more clearly highlights the benefits and negatives.

Finally, Table 7 describes the ratio of where each dater was focusing their conversation. The date target covers the person with whom they are attending the date, and expectedly this is the highest value. The booth target is a small interstitial section where the dater will comment on their date, without the knowledge of the other dater, this happens after the date and is unlikely to affect the date. It is, however, a good indicator of how the date went. The end is the section of the show, where both daters indicate if they wish to have another date. Other will often refer to a family member on a phone or possibly a member of the waiting staff or a guest, a slightly higher other target seems to have a little effect, possibly due to daters ordering more to prolong the date, but there is not significant data to prove this point. Date_M or Date_F normally includes speaking to another dating couple, this rarely occurs but does not indicate a good date is underway,

Table 6. Speaker intonation, only including conversation in the date with neutral emotions excluded.

Intonation	Positive	Negative
Flirting	34.51%	19.30%
Joking	42.25%	29.39%
Confident	12.68%	28.51%
Sarcasm	0.00%	1.75%
Hesitation	0.70%	10.96%
Nervous	9.86%	10.09%

this may be due to the daters looking for a distraction. Talking to another person's date seems to be a negative effect, unsurprisingly.

Table 7. The target of each speaker's speech, based on the whole dataset, excluding other speakers.

Target	Positive	Negative
Date	63.37%	62.22%
Booth	17.55%	19.17%
End	9.03%	8.66%
Other	10.05%	7.36%
Date_M	0.00%	2.35%
Date_F	0.00%	0.24%

5   Discussion

The results presented in this paper, demonstrate that there is a clear distinction between the emotions present in a positive or negative social interaction. Clearly, being aware of these emotions exhibited during a social situation can make the difference between a situation progressing in an intended manner or not. It is also unsurprising that positive emotions, occurring more often, generally mean that an interaction went better than one with more negative emotions. For people who suffer from a social impairment, reading these signs can be a challenge and certainly being better aware of the mood being displayed by a conversational partner can only be of benefit. Thus, therein lies the question of how this understanding/awareness of the emotions or context can be provided to a contextually impaired user, to improve their understanding, or that or their conversational partner.

5.1 Contextual Support

Providing a means for context to be passed to a contextually impaired user can be achieved simply enough. Most users will own some form of smart device and assuming they use this for normal communication, it should be accessible for them. Context can be passed directly to the user, through any number of means (text, video, audio) for them to be able to act on the context. The problem thus lies in three areas, firstly identifying the context, secondly, how to provide the context in a useful manner and thirdly providing some guidance on what the context means and how to react to it.

It is likely that identifying the context can be achieved via the use of ML. This technology is good at detecting patterns and would be able, after significant training, to be able to process the data provided by a smartphone. Once a context is identified, this can be processed into a format that is useful for the user. The use of ML, or indeed any computational tool, will require significant investment in time to construct, however it is likely that once the set-up is complete it will be a viable method to process an incoming context.

Whilst producing a context may prove challenging, it is not impossible. However, what to do with that context is as important as producing it. A contextually impaired users, by definition lacks the ability to recognise the context and most likely will not know what to do even if they are presented with the context. In the example of a socially impaired user, for instance someone with autism, they can lack awareness of how to act in a certain social situation. The context of that situation can be provided to them through several means, but what they need is an explanation of what they need to do with that context.

To simplify the process, a context could be passed as an identifier e.g., a pop-up message on a smartphone app. Alongside this pop-up, a small description of the context and how to proceed can be provided. The key will be to provide several options or separate reactions tailored to different intentions. If the user wishes to continue a discussion, a topic change may be suggested, if they wish to leave the discussion then a suggested exit line could be provided. The reactions need not only fit the situation the user is in, but also provide them with the options to change that situation if it is not progressing as intended. Knowing the contextual information can also warn a user when their behaviour is being taken the wrong way or if the contextually impaired user is currently at risk and should retreat from the situation.

Of course, the above relies on the situation fitting into one of several pre-established situations and that the user responds positively to the suggestions. Although, this is not always guaranteed. However, having this extra information can provide benefits in many day-to-day interactions. How can one be aware they are boring someone, or that something meant in jest was taken offensively? These little hints provided by the context can aid a user to manage social interactions more easily, whether they are on a date or just doing their day job.

Furthermore, it is also possible that the contextual support system could provide information to the non-impaired conversational partner. This could be useful for ensuring that both the contextually impaired and non-impaired user can communicate more freely, without either misunderstanding each other. It is no unreasonable to assume that a non-impaired user, may have trouble understanding an impaired user and thus providing contextual information to them, may also prove beneficial.

5.2 Dating Support

The work presented in this paper demonstrates the differences between a positive and negative date, helping to make a case for context being valuable in measuring the effectiveness of that date. The topic was focused upon as it provided a social interaction that contained a significant amount of body language. However, it is also true that most human communication is achieved via non-verbal means, making the benefits somewhat ubiquitous to human communication.

Nevertheless, there is also potential that the contextual support described in the previous section could be applied quite readily to dating. Providing both daters with an idea of the emotional state of the person that they are on a date with. While perhaps not useful for most unimpaired daters, those who struggle socially, may find the information particularly insightful and could contribute to a more positive dating experience, regardless of the date's outcome. It is likely that such a system may prove useful for those who are socially impaired.

6 Conclusion

The results presented in this paper indicate at the type of emotions and contexts that exist in a date and to what effect these have on the success of the date. It is clear that positive emotions lend themselves to more positive dates and that presenting these emotions or being able to react to negative emotions from a conversational partner is likely to improve the success of the interaction.

Due to the effect that the context seemingly has on social interactions, such as dating. This work considers the view that providing context to an individual, who may have some form of social/contextual impairment, could help them to interact more easily in both dating and more varied social interactions.

A computational system that can inform users of the context of an interaction and offer tailored support to communicate more effectively is likely to improve their ability to communicate significantly and is worthy of further research. It is hoped that this work offers a new way to consider social interactions for socially impaired users and how best to support them in social situations. In a manner, the provision of context to a contextually impaired user, works in a similar manner to a translator, helping to support them in complex interactions. The crux of the benefit would be a two-way support structure, especially for those who are autistic, having a computer that can inform both the user of what the context is and how to react positively, as well as informing a conversational partner by alerting them to possible changes in mood of the user; could help a number of contextually impaired individuals to reduce stress and better manage their social interactions.

There is also some scope to the provision of contextual information directly in a dating paradigm, where more nervous users may find benefit in being better informed of their conversational partners mood. This could form a separate focus on the overall system, which could also consider the impact contextual support could have for situationally impaired users (being on a train, etc.).

This work recommends that future work considers the positive impact that contextual provision could have on contextually impaired users and that an integration of this to a computational provision may prove useful, to provide such contextual information. Further to this, describing the meaning of that contextual information, with several optional responses for users, would prove beneficial. The provision itself could be provided via ML or other computational methods, depending on the application domain.

References

1. Moraes, A.d.: First Dates. Twenty Twenty/Channel 4, UK, First aired (2013)
2. Kinch, M.W., Melis, W.J., Keates, S.: The benefits of contextual information for speech recognition systems. In: 10th Computer Science and Electronic Engineering (CEEC), Colchester, UK (2018)
3. Smith, S.M., Vela, E.: Environmental context-dependent memory: a review and meta-analysis. Psychon. Bull. Rev. **8**, 203–220 (2001)
4. Smith, S.M.: Background music and context-dependent memory. Am. J. Psychol. **98**(4), 591–603 (1985)
5. Ng, S., Payne, B.R., Stine-Morrow, E.A., Federmeier, K.D.: How struggling adult readers use contextual information when comprehending speech: evidence from event-related potentials. Int. J. Psychophysiol. **125**, 1–9 (2018)
6. Godden, D.R., Baddeley, A.D.: Context-dependent memory in two natural environments: on land and underwater. Br. J. Psychol. **66**, 325–331 (1975)
7. Dey, K., Abowd, G.D.: Towards a better understanding of context and context-awareness. In: Proceedings of the 1st International Symposium on Handheld and Ubiquitous Computing (1999)
8. Ryan, N.S., Pascoe, J., Morse, D.R.: Enhanced reality fieldwork: the context-aware archaeological assistant. In: Computer Applications in Archaeology (1998)
9. Kinch, M.W., Melis, W.J., Keates, S.: Reviewing the current state of machine learning for artificial intelligence with regards to the use of contextual information. In: The Second Medway Engineering Conference on Systems: Efficiency, Sustainablity and Modelling, Medway, UK (2017)
10. Want, R., Hopper, A., Falcao, V., Gibbons, J.: The active badge location system. ACM Trans. Inform. Syst. **10**, 91–102 (1992)
11. Williams, I., Kannan, A., Aleksic, P., Rybach, D., Sainath, T.N., Contextual speech recognition in end-to-end neural network systems using beam search. In: Interspeech 2018 (2018)
12. Baron-Cohen, S.: Mindblindness: An Essay on Autism and Theory of Mind. The MIT Press, Cambridge, USA (1995)
13. Baron-Cohen, S., Wheelwright, S., Hill, J., Raste, Y., Plumb, I.: The "Reading the Mind in the Eyes" test revised version: a study with normal adults, and adults with Asperger syndrome or high-functioning autism. J. Child Psychol. Psychiatry **42**(2), 241–251 (2001)
14. Mongeau, P.A., Serewicz, M.C.M., Therrien, L.F.: Goals for cross-sex first dates: identification, measurement, and the influence of contextual factors. Commun. Monogr. **71**(2), 121–147 (2004)
15. Argyle, M.: Bodily Communication. Routledge, New York, USA (2013)
16. Ekman, P., Sorenson, E.R., Friesen, W.V.: Pan-cultural elements in facial displays of emotion. Science **164**, 86–88 (1969)

17. Ekman, P., Friesen, W.V.: Constants across cultures in the face and emotion. J. Pers. Soc. Psychol. **17**(2), 124–129 (1971)
18. Darwin, C.: The Expression of the Emotions in Man and Animals. John Murray, London (1872)
19. McDuff, D., Mahmoud, A., Mavadati, M., Amr, M., Turcot, J., El Kaliouby, R.: AFFDEX SDK: a cross-platform real-time multi-face expression recognition toolkit. In: Proceedings of the 2016 CHI Conference Extended Abstracts on Human Factors in Computing Systems, New York, USA (2016)
20. Rudovic, O., Lee, J., Dai, M., Schuller, B., Picard, R.W.: Personalized machine learning for robot perception of affect and engagement in autism therapy. Sci. Robot. **3**(19), 1–11 (2018)
21. El Kaliouby, R., Robinson P., Keates, S.: Temporal context and the recognition of emotion from facial expression. In: HCI International, Crete (2003)
22. El Kaliouby, R., Robinson, P.: The emotional hearing aid - an assistive tool for autism. In: HCI International, Crete (2003)
23. Channel 4, All 4. https://www.channel4.com/
24. Learning on Screen. https://learningonscreen.ac.uk/ondemand

Design and Validation of a Stress Detection Model for Use with a VR Based Interview Simulator for Autistic Young Adults

Miroslava Migovich[✉], Alex Korman, Joshua Wade, and Nilanjan Sarkar

Robotics and Autonomous Systems Lab, Vanderbilt University, Nashville, TN 37212, USA
miroslava.migovich@vanderbilt.edu

Abstract. Studies show that young autistic adults are under- or unemployed, with almost half never holding a paying job in their 20's. Unemployment within this population leads to decreased personal growth and increased dependence on caregivers. Research suggests that the interview process is one of the largest barriers to employment for this population. Autistic individuals often struggle with emotion regulation, which can be exacerbated by the interview process. To address this, we propose the use of a stress detection model in conjunction with a virtual reality interview simulator. This combination will allow for the interview to adapt to the state of the participant to improve the skills and engagement of the user and positively influence their comfort level. Data regarding negative affective responses to categories of questions can also be used to inform employers on better interviewing techniques. A model was designed using data obtained from neurotypical participants completing a modified Computerized Paced Serial Addition Task (PASAT-C) and evaluated on a dataset obtained from Autistic participants who took part in a simulated interview. Agreement between the model and ground truth was compared based on Pearson correlation coefficients. It was found that was $r(289) = 0.28$, which was statistically significant ($p < .001$; CI: 0.17 to 0.38). Our preliminary results provide evidence for the validity of observer-based labeling of data captured using a wrist-worn physiological sensor.

Keywords: Emotions in HCI and design · Stress-detection · Physiological response · Machine learning

1 Introduction

It is estimated that over half of autistic[1] adults are unemployed or underemployed. This percentage is higher in comparison to adults with other developmental disabilities [1, 2]. It is also documented that one of the largest impediments to the employment of autistic individuals is the interview process and the associated stress of this process [3,

---

[1] In accordance with recent surveys that suggest a preference for identity-first language by autistic self-advocates, we have chosen to adopted identity-first language (*autistic person*) instead of person-first (*person with autism*) language [23].

© Springer Nature Switzerland AG 2021
M. Antona and C. Stephanidis (Eds.): HCII 2021, LNCS 12768, pp. 580–588, 2021.
https://doi.org/10.1007/978-3-030-78092-0_40

4] due the differences in social communication and behavior that is common in autistic individuals. Autism Spectrum Disorder is a neurodevelopmental condition that is most often characterized by difference in social communication and social behavior, and repetitive/restrictive patterns of behaviors/interests [5]. Often, the individual possesses the required experience and job skills, however they are unable to interview well by "neurotypical" standards. There is limited information regarding emotional regulation of autistic individuals, however it is known that ASD is associated with heightened emotional responses and poor emotion control, which leads to difficulties with the interview process [6]. The inability to regulate emotions effectively has been linked to all core features of ASD, including social and communication functioning [7].

The unemployment of this population adds to the growing cost of caring for autistic Americans, which was found to be $268 billion annually in 2015 [8]. Autistic self-advocates have expressed that accommodations in job interviews can reduce barriers to employment [9]. These accommodations can be integrated, in part, by the use of a virtual reality interview simulator that allows autistic adults the opportunity to practice interview skills and receive feedback in a virtual environment. The information from the virtual interview can be used to inform potential employers on how to better interview the population and provide the user with information regarding their interview performance. With the virtual interview process, it is possible to mitigate the level of stress and allow the participant to practice interview skills in a lower-stress environment by developing a real-time stress recognition module based on physiological responses and machine learning. Such a module would allow the system to dynamically recognize stress and adapt to help individuals manage their stress response and improve their performance.

Previous work has shown that physiological features are significantly correlated with one's affective state, and therefore can be used to approximate stress levels using machine learning. Autistic individuals often experience emotional stress without external expression and therefore implicit measures such as physiological signals are used to determine stress levels without external expression [10]. Physiological signals are the preferred method for emotion recognition because physical signals such as speech, facial expressions, and posture can also be manipulated by the individual and reliability cannot be guaranteed [11]. The autonomic nervous system uses sensory and motor neurons to operate between various organs and the central nervous system. Physiological signals are the body's method of response to these systems. The Cannon-Bard theory states that emotions and physiological responses are simultaneous [12]. Because the central nervous system and the autonomic nervous systems are involuntarily stimulated, physiological responses to stress cannot be as easily manipulated by the individual [11, 13]. While the relationship between individual physiological signals and emotions have been explored [14, 15], it is preferable to use multiple signals in conjunction for more in-depth correlations between stress and physiological signals [11].

There is a paucity of literature concerning the performance of stress models in autistic individuals and, to our knowledge, this is the first exploration of the use of stress detection in an interview setting for autistic individuals [16].

2 System Design

2.1 System Architecture

The proposed stress model was used in conjunction with a Virtual Reality-based interview simulator called Career Interview Readiness in Virtual Reality (CIRVR) [17] in order to inform and adjust the interview based on the individuals' perceived stress levels. CIRVR uses natural language-based interactions coupled with real-time stress measurements to create a semi-naturalistic interview experience. The CIRVR system features five key components: (1) a natural language-based communication module largely enabled by Microsoft Azure cloud services such as LUIS, Speech-to-text, and Text-to-Speech[2] (2) a real-time stress-detection module described in detail in this paper; (3) an eye-tracking module used to track visual attention patterns (e.g., using Tobii eye trackers and the Fove head-mounted display); (4) a facial expression detection module used to measure facial expressions based on universally-recognized emotions which are detailed in [18]; and (5) support for both immersive—e.g., Fove or VIVE head-mounted displays—and non-immersive interaction modalities (Fig. 1).

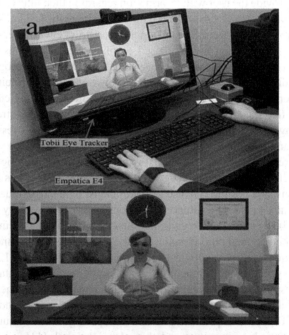

Fig. 1. CIRVR job interview simulator: (a) desktop-based interaction setup with Tobii eye tracker and the Empatica E4 physiological-sensing wristband; (b) desktop-based interaction view of the interviewer

During the interview, stress data will be collected and processed before being sent to the model to be classified. The stress values generated by the model will then be used

---
[2] https://azure.microsoft.com/en-us/services/cognitive-services/.

by to inform the interviewer avatar of the interviewee's stress level and allows them to adjust question types in order to reduce discomfort in the user. This closed-loop system allows for real-time adjustments to take place within the interview scenario. Adjustments include rephrasing of the question, moving onto a new question, or introduction of multiple-choice questions. The adjustments deescalate the stress level of that user so that they are able to gain valuable interview practice in a low-risk environment. The data will also be used to inform future employers on interview techniques for neurodiverse individuals (Fig. 2).

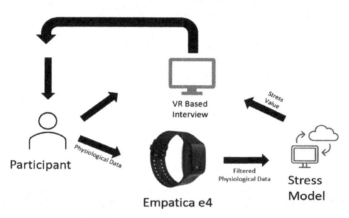

Fig. 2. Interaction of system components

2.2 Training Data Procedure

Training data were obtained from N = 20 neurotypical participants by trained research assistants. The research was approved by the Vanderbilt Institutional Review Board (IRB) and all participants provided informed written consent or assent as required by the IRB. The neurotypical participants were not compensated and training data collection took place before the COVID-19 pandemic.

In order to collect training data, a modified version of the Computerized Paced Serial Addition Task (PASAT-C) [19] was used along with an Empatica E4 sensor (www.emp atica.com) to gather physiological signals. The code for the PASAT-C task was originally developed by Millisecond Software and was modified to include a baseline timer, clear distinction between the three levels, and a Likert scale self-report of perceived stress by the participant. To begin, the participant was asked demographic questions, such as age, weight, if they have exercised or drank caffeine, if they feel sick, and their dominant hand. These are characteristics that affect how the body expresses stress physiologically and should be taken into consideration. The E4 device was then placed on the non-dominant wrist. The computerized task begins with a 3-min baseline during which the participant is asked to sit still and keep their non-dominate hand steady. Following the baseline, a set of instructions is presented. The task is designed to show a series of single digit numbers that the participant is expected to sum and use the mouse to press the box which correlates with the sum. The possible answers are 1 through 18 and are shown in a clockwise manner. Once the next number is shown, the participant continues to compute the sum of only the last two digits shown, not the running total. If the participant chooses the wrong sum, an error noise is played. The task begins with 11 practice trials. This is followed by level one. Level on is three minutes long with three seconds between each digit presentation. Level two is five minutes with two seconds between digits and level three is ten minutes with 1.5 s between the digits. After each level, the participant was asked to rate their stress level in context of the game on a 1–10 Likert scale. Before level three, there is a 45 s pause in which the participant is informed that the digits will be presented faster than before, and they are given the option of a "QUIT" button during the third level to terminate the task prematurely.

After completing the PASAT-C (Fig. 3), open ended questions were asked to gather qualitative data about the participants experience and perceived stress levels.

From the E4, the heart rate, inter-beat interval, blood volume pressure, and acceleration is extracted as individual excel files. These files were then pre-processed before being used in the model to synchronize time stamps across the metrics.

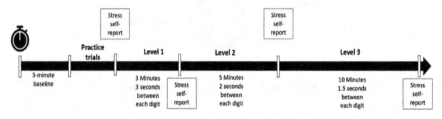

Fig. 3. Timeline of PASAT-C

2.3 Design of Models

The physiological data were processed into separate readings: heartrate, inter-beat interval, blood volume pulse, skin conductance level (SCL), skin conductance response (SCR), and acceleration in the x, y, and z direction.

The dataset was divided into training, testing, and validation sets. Each set was composed of the participant's entire dataset, as opposed to choosing random instances. Four models were initially compared, however the K-nearest neighbor classifier performed better than the support vector machine, neural network, and the random forest models. Pior research has shown this model has high accuracy classifying emotional states [20] K-nearest neighbors classification is based on classifying an unknown sample based on the known classification of neighbors [21]. The training data were segmented into five second intervals and trained according to perceived stress values, with the practice level and level one of the PASAT-C corresponding to a low stress level (labeled 0) and levels two and three corresponding to higher stress (labeled 1). The self-reported stress levels during the PASAT-C were not used due to lack of consistent grading across participants. Task data in the test set were averaged across 5 s increments with a stress value output for each segment. Hyper-parameters were finetuned on the validation set. The KNN had a Mean accuracy of 73.06 and a F1 Score of 77.26.

2.4 Testing Procedure

Five autistic participants took part in the study, leading to a sample size of n = 289 observations. Due to COVID-19 regulations and restrictions, the sample size was limited. Autistic participants were recruited to take part in one-hour sessions at the university lab. Appropriate precautions, such as symptom pre-screening 24 h before the session, follow-up prescreening day of, mandatory face covering, social distancing and disinfection of all materials, were taken to ensure safety of all involved. Written consent/assent was obtained in accordance with Vanderbilt Institutional Review Board (IRB) and then the participant completed a 20-min virtual interview using the desktop version of the CIRVR system. The interview is split into multiple sections, such as introductions, past work experience, technical experience, technical questions on a whiteboard, education, education questions on the whiteboard, and open ended/personal questions. This allows for exploration of patterns of stress during different portions of a typical interview. After the interview, the researcher led the participant through a brief qualitative interview to gain insight on the user's experience and what type of information the user would like to receive from the system. One participant was unable to complete the full interview due to system failure, however no observational data was lost. The autistic participants were compensated for their time and travel.

Video recording of the participant from the waist up were used to determine ground truth stress ratings by a researcher trained in behavioral assessment. Stress was graded on a scale of 1–10 with the participant's demeanor upon arrival set at baseline. The ground truth ratings were then paired with the outputs of the model using timestamps. As the model output a stress rating every 5 s, three model ratings were averaged and compared to the ground truth.

3 Results

Because only one rater was involved in data labeling, we decided to estimate agreement between rater observations and the E4 output using the Pearson correlation coefficient. Statistical analyses were conducted using MedCalc statistical analysis software (version 19.5.3) with default parameters [22]. In the future, other indices of agreement (e.g., kappa and concordance correlations) will be applied. Based on a sample size of n = 289, the Pearson correlation coefficient was $r(289) = 0.28$, which was statistically significant ($p < .001$; CI: 0.17 to 0.38). This result provides preliminary support for the validity of the observer-based rating approach. Next, in order to identify the optimal cutoff score for prediction of the E4 output based on rater observations, we conducted a Receiver Operating Characteristic (ROC) Area Under the Curve (AUC) analysis. As shown in Fig. 4, a statistically significant AUC of 0.604 was found ($p < .01$; CI: 0.55 to 0.66). The Youden Index was used to determine the optimal cutoff score of >5 (i.e., rater observations of 6 correspond to high stress according to the E4 output).

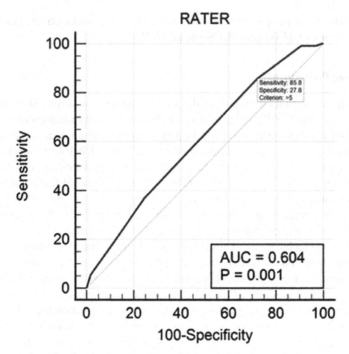

Fig. 4. Receiver operating characteristic curve analysis

4   Discussion and Conclusion

Our preliminary results provide evidence for the validity of observer-based labeling of data captured using a wrist-worn physiological sensor. While encouraging, a number of limitations must be addressed in future work. The performance of the model could be improved by a change in the labeling structure. The training data were labeled as either "stressed" or "not stressed" depending on the level of the PASAT-C. However, this assumes that the participants are less stressed during the first two levels and that their stress increases during the task. More rigorous data collection with additional tasks would help to improve the labels. While the general physiological response is predicted to be similar between the two groups, it is possible that certain physiological patterns exist within autistic physiological data that are not concurrent with neurotypical data. It is necessary to train models using autistic datasets and the observer ratings as labels for training data in order to further investigate the possible differences in physiological responses to stress between the groups.

Future work includes to integration of the model into the real-time system using Microsoft Azure's Machine Learning Studio and Azure Web Services as well as an in-depth exploration of trends of stress during the interview process with autistic participants. This information will then be used to inform both interviewees and possible employers on accommodations that can made to improve the interview experience.

Acknowledgements. This project was funded by a Microsoft AI for Accessibility grant, by the National Science Foundation under awards 1936970 and 2033413 and by the National Science Foundation Research Traineeship DGE 19-22697. The authors would like to thank the participants for their time.

References

1. Autism U.S. Department of Labor. https://www.dol.gov/agencies/odep/topics/autism. Accessed 28 Oct 2020
2. Chen, J.L., Leader, G., Sung, C., Leahy, M.: Trends in employment for individuals with autism spectrum disorder: a review of the research literature. Rev. J. Autism Dev. Disord. **2**(2), 115–127 (2014). https://doi.org/10.1007/s40489-014-0041-6
3. Burke, S.L., Li, T., Grudzien, A., Garcia, S.: Brief report: improving employment interview self-efficacy among adults with autism and other developmental disabilities using virtual interactive training agents (ViTA). J. Autism Dev. Disord. **51**(2), 741–748 (2020). https://doi.org/10.1007/s10803-020-04571-8
4. Mazefsky, C.A.: Emotion regulation and emotional distress in autism spectrum disorder: foundations and considerations for future research. J. Autism Dev. Disord. **45**(11), 3405–3408 (2015). https://doi.org/10.1007/s10803-015-2602-7
5. Diagnostic and statistical manual of mental disorders: DSM-5 (2013)
6. Mazefsky, C.A., et al.: The role of emotion regulation in autism spectrum disorder. J. Am. Acad. Child. Adolesc. Psychiatry **52**, 679–688 (2013). https://doi.org/10.1016/j.jaac.2013.05.006
7. Samson, A.C., et al.: Emotion dysregulation and the core features of autism spectrum disorder. J. Autism Dev. Disord. **44**(7), 1766–1772 (2013). https://doi.org/10.1007/s10803-013-2022-5
8. Leigh, J.P., Du, J.: Brief report: forecasting the economic burden of autism in 2015 and 2025 in the United States. J. Autism Dev. Disord. **45**(12), 4135–4139 (2015). https://doi.org/10.1007/s10803-015-2521-7
9. Booth, J., McDonnell, J.: Autism Equality in the Workplace (2016)
10. Lahiri, U., Welch, K.C., Warren, Z., Sarkar, N.: Understanding psychophysiological response to a virtual reality-based social communication system for children with ASD (2011). https://doi.org/10.1109/ICVR.2011.5971841
11. Shu, L., et al.: A review of emotion recognition using physiological signals. Sensors (Switz.) **18**(7), MDPI AG, 1 July 2018. https://doi.org/10.3390/s18072074
12. Friedman, B.H.: Feelings and the body: the Jamesian perspective on autonomic specificity of emotion. Biol. Psychol. **84**, 383–393 (2010). https://doi.org/10.1016/j.biopsycho.2009.10.006
13. Hagemann, D., Waldstein, S.R., Thayer, J.F.: Central and autonomic nervous system integration in emotion. Brain Cogn. **52**(1), 79–87 (2003). https://doi.org/10.1016/S0278-2626(03)00011-3
14. Kim, H.G., Cheon, E.J., Bai, D.S., Lee, Y.H., Koo, B.H.: Stress and heart rate variability: a meta-analysis and review of the literature. Psychiatry Invest. **15**, 235–245 (2018). https://doi.org/10.30773/pi.2017.08.17
15. Xie, J., Wen, W., Liu, G., Chen, C., Zhang, J., Liu, H.: Identifying strong stress and weak stress through blood volume pulse. In: Proceedings of the 2016 IEEE International Conference on Progress in Informatics and Computing, PIC 2016, June 2017, pp. 179–182 (2017). https://doi.org/10.1109/PIC.2016.7949490
16. Dijkhuis, R.R., Ziermans, T., van Rijn, S., Staal, W., Swaab, H.: Emotional arousal during social stress in young adults with autism: insights from heart rate, heart rate variability and self-report. J. Autism Dev. Disord. **49**(6), 2524–2535 (2019). https://doi.org/10.1007/s10803-019-04000-5

17. Wade, J.W., et al.: Career Interview Readiness in VR (CIRVR): Feasibility of an AI-Driven Platform for Employers and Neurodiverse Talent. INSAR. https://insar.confex.com/insar/2020/meetingapp.cgi/Paper/35598

18. Ekman, P.: Are there basic emotions? Psychol. Rev. **99**(3), 550–553 (1992). https://doi.org/10.1037/0033-295X.99.3.550

19. Lejuez, C., Kahler, C., Brown, R.: A modified computer version of the Paced Auditory Serial Addition Task (PASAT) as a laboratory-based stressor. Undefined (2003). Accessed 25 Oct 2020

20. Fan, J., et al.: A step towards EEG-based brain computer interface for autism intervention. In: Proceedings of the Annual International Conference of the IEEE Engineering in Medicine and Biology Society, EMBS, November 2015, pp. 3767–3770 (2015). https://doi.org/10.1109/EMBC.2015.7319213

21. Cover, T., Hart, P.: Nearest neighbor pattern classification, pp. 21–27, January 1967. https://ieeexplore.ieee.org/stamp/stamp.jsp?tp=&arnumber=1053964. Accessed 27 Jan 2021

22. Schoonjans, F., Zalata, A., Depuydt, C.E., Comhaire, F.H.: MedCalc: a new computer program for medical statistics. Comput. Methods Programs Biomed. **48**(3), 257–262 (1995). https://doi.org/10.1016/0169-2607(95)01703-8

23. Kenny, L., Hattersley, C., Molins, B., Buckley, C., Povey, C., Pellicano, E.: Which terms should be used to describe autism? Perspectives from the UK autism community. Autism **20**(4), 442–462 (2016). https://doi.org/10.1177/1362361315588200

A Study of Classification for Electrogastrograms Before/After Caloric Intake Using Autoencoder

Kohki Nakane[1], Keita Ichikawa[1], Rentaro Ono[1], Yasuyuki Matsuura[2], and Hiroki Takada[1][(✉)]

[1] University of Fukui, 3-9-1 Bunkyo, Fukui-shi, Fukui, Japan
`takada@u-fukui.ac.jp`
[2] Gifu City Women's College, 7-1 Hitoichiba Kitamachi, Gifu-shi, Gifu 501-0192, Japan

Abstract. There are few reports to compare gastrointestinal motility in a seated posture and that in a supine posture for the evaluation of the severity of the motion sickness. It is difficult to distinguish between postural differences by using nonlinear analysis of the electrogastrograms (EGGs) of healthy individuals. The purpose of this study was to determine the feasibility of applying a complex dynamic analysis method to the EGGs of healthy young individuals between in a seated posture caloric intake and those in a supine posture after caloric intake. We analyzed EGGs by using artificial intelligence (AI) and compared mathematical models of EGGs in the seated posture with those in the supine.

Keywords: Electrogastrography (EGG) · Caloric intake · Artificial Intelligence (AI) · Seated posture · Supine posture

1 Introduction

A myriad of activities are performed in a seated posture, including office work and driving, and fatigue accumulates if this posture is maintained for long periods. People usually rest and sleep in a supine posture. Likewise, sick people and those affected by motion sickness take rest in the supine posture. Moreover, humans hardly get motion sickness while maintaining a supine posture [1]. In contrast, a seated posture can lead to experience both motion sickness, especially in moving cars, trains, and ships, and visually induced motion sickness that occurs while watching visual contents such as stereoscopic and virtual reality movies. Still, few studies have compared gastrointestinal (GI) motility in seated and supine postures to evaluate the severity of induced motion sickness.

Like regular motion sickness, the development of visually induced motion sickness can be explained by the sensory conflict theory [2] as follows. The equilibrium system receives information from the visual, vestibular, and somatosensory systems. When the combination of this information concerning body motion is inconsistent with previously established combinations obtained through experience, spatial localization of self becomes unstable and produces discomfort. Input into the vestibular nuclei located in the brainstem from the visual and somatosensory systems and the cerebellum, in addition

M. Antona and C. Stephanidis (Eds.): HCII 2021, LNCS 12768, pp. 589–598, 2021.
https://doi.org/10.1007/978-3-030-78092-0_41

to the vestibular system itself, has been reported [3], suggesting that the nuclei physiologically integrates this sensory information. Moreover, close anatomical and electrophysiological relationships between the vestibular and autonomic nervous systems have been reported [4], strongly suggesting that the equilibrium system is associated with the symptoms of motion sickness and providing a basis to quantitatively evaluate motion sickness based on body sway, an output of the equilibrium system. Furthermore, when rotation sickness was induced in rats, the histamine level in the hypothalamus and brainstem increased, being possibly associated with vomiting during motion sickness [5].

Psychological measurement methods, such as subjective evaluation, and physiological measurements, such as those of autonomic nerve activity, are used to evaluate the influence of visually induced motion sickness on the body. The best-known psychological method to evaluate visually induced motion sickness is the simulator sickness questionnaire [6]. On the other hand, physiological evaluation of visually induced motion sickness has been conducted using parameters such as the heart rate and its variation (RR interval), the low- and high-frequency components of heart rate volubility, blood pressure, respiratory rate, number of blinks, electrogastrography, skin resistance, and sweat rate [7–9].

Percutaneous electrogastrography allows to noninvasively examine human gastrointestinal activity. Human gastric electrophysiological activity cannot be measured by any other conventional method such as magnetic resonance imaging or gastro-fiberscopes. An electrogastrogram (EGG) is usually evaluated by comparing the mean frequency and its power to those derived from the spectrum analysis of previous EGG studies. However, the information retrieved by this analysis is limited, and EGGs are not as usual as electrocardiograms, electroencephalograms, and other biosignal measurements, thus compromising their development.

In 1921, Alvarez [10] was the first to report EGGs obtained from humans. In an EGG, the electrical activity of the stomach is recorded by placing electrodes on the surface of the abdominal wall. The stomach is endowed with a pacemaker located on the side of the greater curvature and generating electrical activity at a frequency of 3 cycles per minute. This electrical signal is reflected to the pylorus area [11]. Gastric electrical potentials are generated by the interstitial cells of Cajal [12], as shown in Fig. 1. These cells are pacemakers that spontaneously depolarize and repolarize at 3 cycles per minute and exhibit low-amplitude, rhythmic, and circular contractions if the electrical potential is above a threshold.

Previously, it was difficult to measure this electrical activity given the EGG signal low-frequency components and higher-frequency noise from electrical activity of the diaphragm and heart. However, the accuracy of EGG measurements has recently improved, and the gastroenteric motility can now be evaluated through spectrum analyses of the EGG signals [13].

Many previous studies on electrogastrography have been conducted but have been mostly related to the clinical field [14]. For instance, hormone, drugs, and motion sickness effects on EGG have been evaluated. Likewise, EGG has been used to study the effects of warm compresses on both GI activity [15] and the epigastric region for relieving constipation [16], and to characterize the intestinal activity in patients with chronic constipation [17]. However, studies on clinical applications mainly consider patients, and hence scarce research is available on the EGG dynamics of healthy subjects.

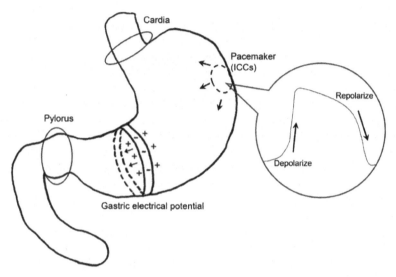

Fig. 1. Wave traveling through gastric potential.

Moreover, diseases associated with abnormal GI activities, such as constipation and functional dyspepsia (FD), have emerged as critical issues, which may cause lifestyle-related diseases. In particular, constipation is considered as a common complaint among patients with latent FD and elderly individuals, and this topic is also of interest with respect to hygiene.

Since EGG can be performed noninvasively and without restrictions, compared with other tests of the GI motor function, such as gastric-emptying and internal pres-sure measurement methods, measurements obtained in a state close to the physiolog-ical condition or over long durations of time are possible. In this chapter, therefore, the methods for the measurement and analyses of EGG are outlined. Further, the latest research trends in EGG evaluations using artificial intelligence (AI) are described, and the future prospects are discussed.

2 Autoencoder

In recent years, the technological developments in AI have achieved remarkable progress, and deep learning has attracted substantial attention as it is particularly good for classifications of complex data. In this study, an example of the application for an Autoencoder (AE) [18], which is one of the deep-learning models, is demonstrated for classifying states.

AE is one of the deep-learning models that excels in information compression, consisting of two types of networks: Encoder and Decoder. Since the Encoder compresses some information x so that it can be reconstructed by the Decoder, the compressed information retains the main features that make up x. It is thought that the main features of the information are preserved in the compressed information. Geoffrey Hinton, a researcher in computer science and cognitive psychology at the University of Toronto, and his colleagues proposed AE. They argued that dimensional compression using AE preserves more information than the compression using principal component analysis [18].

AE can also be used as a generative model. For example, assume that we can compress some data, say A and B, into the latent variable space, and then restore it to the original A and B again. In this case, by inputting a value that is the midpoint of A and B in the latent variable space as a point where the original compressed data does not actually exist into the Decoder and restoring it, data with intermediate characteristics between A and B can be generated.

Most neural network models, which are widely used in tasks such as classification and prediction, require teacher labels to be paired with the input data. AE, on the other hand, does not require teacher labels because it learns to compress and reconstruct the input data so that it can output the input data again. The prepared data can be compressed into a feature space, and tasks such as classification and prediction can be performed by clustering the compressed data (see Fig. 2).

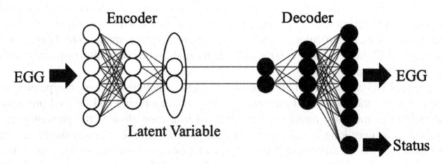

Fig. 2. Schematic diagram of AE

3 Methods

3.1 Experimental Procedure

The subjects were 8 healthy people (8 females) aged between 19 and 24 years. Informed consent was obtained from each subject prior to the experiment. The individuals was approved by the Ethics Committee, Nagoya City University Graduate School of Natural Sciences.

The experimental design as follows Fig. 3. The order of application of the experiments to the subject is randomly set.

Experiment A (Control)

Seated posture (A-1) 30 min	Seated Posture (A-2) 10 min	Seated posture (A-3) 90 min	Supine posture (A-4) 90 min

Experiment B (Caloric Intake)

Seated posture (B-1) 30 min	Caloric Intake (seated posture) (B-2) 10 min	Seated posture (B-3) 90 min	Supine posture (B-4) 90 min

Fig. 3. Experiment

Measurement was performed in a sound-insulated (40 dB) experimental room without windows. The room temperature was between 20–24 °C, humidity was 40–55%, and the air current was below 0.1 m/s. The chair had a seating surface of 55 cm in width and 55 cm in length, a back of 55 cm in width and 58 cm in length, and the angle between the seating surface and the back was 100°. Subjects were told to finish their meals 2 h beforehand so that measurements were not affected by the presence of food. Measurement was started between 14:00 and 15:00 for all subjects to avoid the influence of the circadian rhythm (circadian change).

EGGs were obtained at 1 kHz by an A/D converter (AD16-16U (PCI) EH; CONTEC, Japan). The EGGs were amplified using a bio-amplifier (MT11; NEC Medical, Japan) and recorded using a tape recorder (PC216Ax; Sony Precision Technology, Japan).

EGG electrodes were pasted by using 11 disposable ECG electrodes (Vitrode Bs, Nihon Kohden, Tokyo, Japan) as shown in Fig. 4. Pasting was performed after confirming sufficient reduction of skin resistance by using Skin Pure (Nihon Kohden).

3.2 Calculation Procedure

The recorded EGG was A/D converted at 1 kHz to obtain time-series data. A low-pass filter for a 0.15 Hz treble cutoff frequency was applied to the data obtained to remove electronic noise from the incorporated EMG and electronic devices, and resampling was performed at 1 Hz to remove noise.

The EGG time series with noise removed were extracted for a 32-s interval whose onset was set be every one second.

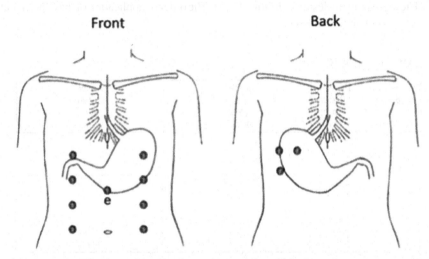

Fig. 4. Position for electrodes passed on the body surface.

We used AE to classify the EGGs of 90 min in the seated posture (A-3, B-3) and those of 90 min in the supine posture (A-4, B-4) before and after caloric intake. The EGG data of 11 channels recorded in the experiment were used for machine learning in the AE, where the latent variable was set to be two variables for each channel. The similarity if the original EGGs could be visualized by representing the EGGs embedded in the pair latent variables and measured the distance on the metric plane. At the same time, if the embedded EGGs form multiple sets, they can be classified in accordance with meaning of the metric plane. In this study, we created a learning model in which the EGG time series is given as inputs of the Encoder, and the output of the Decoder recovers the caloric intake condition embedded in the latent variable, so that the metric plane makes the caloric intake condition as an important meaning. We drew straight lines on the metric plane for the embedded EGGs before and after caloric intake and evaluated the results of linear separation for the condition of before and after caloric intake. The straight line drawn on the metric plane was obtained using linear Support Vector Machine (SVM) (Appendix).

4 Results

EGGs in the seated (experiment A) and supine (experiment B) posture of healthy women were herein analyzed over 5 min from the beginning of measurements. A large amplitude and unstable fluctuations could be found in the EGGs in seated posture (Fig. 5a), whereas (Fig. 5b) shows regular variations as an EGG in the supine.

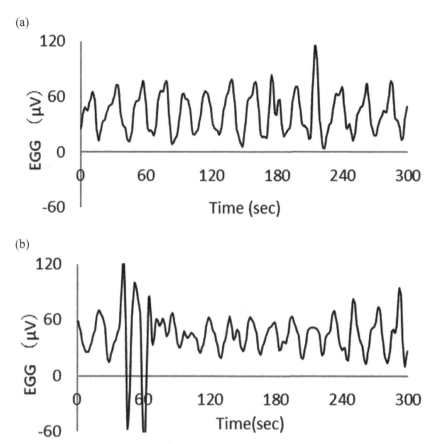

Fig. 5. Typical examples of EGG measured with seated posture: in (A-3) (a), after caloric intake (B-3) (b).

We herein conducted the leave-one-out method in which one case of measurement data for each subject was removed for each measurement state, in order to classify EGGs into those before and after calorie intake. The mean and variance of F1-measure were calculated along with the increase of sample size of the EGG classification (Fig. 6), where F1-measure is the harmonic mean between the precision and the recall (Appendix). The mean value of F1-measure was obtained as 0.65 for 32 s, which is the minimum sample size of the EGGs to determine the caloric intake state in this classification. It was the lowest value in Fig. 6, where F1-measure was evaluated. In addition, the standard deviation was about 0.15, which was the highest value. As the side notes, both these statistical indices did not change remarkably for more than the sample size 96 s of EGGs. These results indicate that the AE developed in this study can be used to classify the bio-state with the basis of the AI analysis for EGGs before and after caloric intake with an accuracy of F1-measure >0.9. This accuracy can be ensured by setting the sample size of the EGG to 96 s or more.

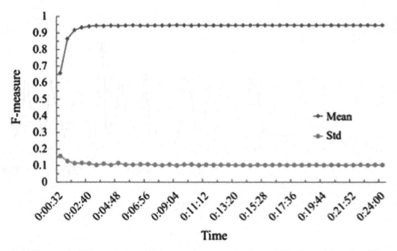

Fig. 6. Changes in F1-measure with increasing sample size of EGG used for classification.

5 Discussions

We classified 11 channels of EGGs recorded at 1Hz with the condition of before and after calorie intake. The following AI was used for the analysis of EGGs. Mathematical models of EGGs in the seated posture were also compared with those in the supine. Irregular components of the wavelength could be found in EGGs measured during the seated posture. It has been considered that the variations can not be described by the stochastic resonance as a mathematical model of normal EGGs in the supine.

In this study, we used AE, a kind of deep learning model, to classify them by clustering. 32-s time series of EGGs were input to the Encoder and embedded into two variables for each channel as latent variables. Since we wanted to embed the calorie intake condition included in the EGG into the metric plane as the principal component, we input the calorie intake condition into the Encoder at the same time as the time series and trained it. The classification accuracy of SVM was expressed as F1-measure, and the results showed that the classification accuracy was over 90% when using EGG of 96 s, suggesting the possibility of using AE for EGG classification before and after caloric intake.

Acknowledgments. This research has been supported in part by JSPS KAKENHI Grant Number JP06J07842, JP18K11417, JP20K11925, and JP20K12528.

Appendix

- Support vector machine (SVM) is an algorithm that finds a hyperplane in N-dimensional space consisting of N feature variables that classify data points.
- Precision is defined as the fraction of true positive examples among the examples that the classifier model classified as positive.
- Recall is defined as the fraction of examples classified as positive, among the total number of positive examples.
- F1-measure is defined as the value calculated as the harmonic mean between values of the precision and the recall.

References

1. Manning, G.W., Stewart, G.W.: Effect of body position on incidence of motion sickness. J. Appl. Physiol. **1**(9), 619–628 (1949)
2. Reason, J.T., Brand, J.J.: Motion Sickness, 3rd edn. Academic Press Inc., San Diego (1975)
3. Barmack, N.H.: Central vestibular system: vestibular nuclei and posterior cerebellum. Brain Res. Bull. **60**(5–6), 511–541 (2003)
4. Balaban, C.D., Porter, J.D.: Neuroanatomical substrates for vestibuloautonomic interactions. J. Vestib. Res. **8**, 7–16 (1998)
5. Takeda, N., et al.: Histaminergic mechanism of motion sickness neurochemical and neuropharmacological studies in rats. Acta Otolaryngol. **101**(5–6), 416–421 (1986)
6. Kennedy, R.S., Lane, N.E., Berbaum, K.S., Lilienthal, M.G.: Simulator sickness questionnaire: an enhanced method for quantifying simulator sickness. Int. J. Aviat. Psychol. **3**(3), 203–220 (1993)
7. Holmes, S.R., Griffin, M.J.: Correlation between heart rate and the severity of motion sickness caused by optokinetic stimulation. J. Psychophysiol. **15**, 35–42 (2001)
8. Himi, N., Koga, T., Nakamura, E., Kobashi, M., Yamane, M., Tsujioka, K.: Differences in autonomic responses between subjects with and without nausea while watching an irregularly oscillating video. Auton. Neurosci. **116**(1–2), 46–53 (2004)
9. Yokota, Y., Aoki, M., Mizuta, K., Ito, Y., Isu, N.: Motion sickness susceptibility associated with visually induced postural instability and cardiac autonomic responses in healthy subjects. Acta Otolaryngol. **125**(3), 280–285 (2005)
10. Alvarez, W.C.: The electrogastrogram and what is shows. J. Am. Med. Assoc. **78**, 1116–1119 (1922)
11. Couturier, D., Roze, C., Paolaggi, J., Debray, C.: Electrical activity of the normal human stomach: a comparative study of recordings obtained from the serosal and mucosal sides. Dig. Dis. Sci. **17**(11), 969–976 (1972)
12. Van Der Schee, E.J., Smout, A.J.P.M., Grashuis, J.L.: Application of running spectrum analysis to electrogastrographic signals recorded from dog and man. In: Motility of the Digestive Tract, pp. 241–250. Raven Press, New York (1982)
13. Chen, J.Z., McCallum, R.W.: Electrogastrography: Principles and Applications. Raven Press, New York (1994)
14. Nagai, M., Wada, M., Kobayashi, Y., Togawa, S.: Effects of lumbar skin warming on gastric motility and blood pressure in humans. Jpn. J. Physiol. **53**(1), 45–51 (2003)
15. Kawachi, N., Iwase, S., Takada, H., Michigami, D., Watanabe, Y., Mae, N.: Effect of wet hot packs applied to the epigastrium on electrogastrogram in constipated young women. Auton. Nerv. Syst. **39**(5), 433–437 (2002)

16. Matsuura, Y., Iwase, S., Takada, H., Watanabe, Y., Miyashita, E.: Effect of three days of consecutive hot wet pack application to the epigastrium on electrogastrography in constipated young women. Auton. Nerv. Syst. **40**(4), 406–411 (2003)
17. Cajal, S.R., Swanson, N., Swanson, L.W.: Histology of the nervous system of man and vertebrates. Oxford University Press, New York (1995)
18. Hinton, G.E., Salakhutdinov, R.R.: Reducing the dimensionality of data with neural networks. Science **313**(5786), 504–507 (2006)

Building an Ecologically Valid Facial Expression Database – Behind the Scenes

Francesca Nonis[1], Luca Ulrich[1]([✉]), Nicolò Dozio[2], Francesca Giada Antonaci[1], Enrico Vezzetti[1], Francesco Ferrise[2], and Federica Marcolin[1]

[1] Department of Management and Production Engineering, Politecnico di Torino, Torino, Italy
luca.ulrich@polito.it
[2] Department of Mechanical Engineering, Politecnico di Milano, Milano, Italy

Abstract. Artificial Intelligence (AI) algorithms, together with a general increased computational performance, allow nowadays exploring the use of Facial Expression Recognition (FER) as a method of recognizing human emotion through the use of neural networks. The interest in facial emotion and expression recognition in real-life situations is one of the current cutting-edge research challenges. In this context, the creation of an ecologically valid facial expression database is crucial. To this aim, a controlled experiment has been designed, in which thirty-five subjects aged 18–35 were asked to react spontaneously to a set of 48 validated images from two affective databases, IAPS and GAPED. According to the Self-Assessment Manikin, participants were asked to rate images on a 9-points visual scale on valence and arousal. Furthermore, they were asked to select one of the six Ekman's basic emotions. During the experiment, an RGB-D camera was also used to record spontaneous facial expressions aroused in participants storing both the color and the depth frames to feed a Convolutional Neural Network (CNN) to perform FER. In every case, the prevalent emotion pointed out in the questionnaires matched with the expected emotion. CNN obtained a recognition rate of 75.02%, computed comparing the neural network results with the evaluations given by a human observer. These preliminary results have confirmed that this experimental setting is an effective starting point for building an ecologically valid database.

Keywords: Facial expression recognition · Ecologically-valid data · 3D facial database · Basic emotions · Affective database · Human-robot interaction

1 Introduction

Automatic classifiers are spreading in a variety of fields and are strongly used even in facial expression recognition applications. The main problem in using supervised classifiers to perform facial expression recognition is to find valid data to train machine learning algorithms. Data that have to be inputted for the training phase must be labelled, and to do such an operation, a scientific approach to describe emotions is necessary.

The first study dealing with quantification of emotions was initiated by Wundt [1] and continued by Schlosberg [2], that introduced a three-dimensional model which dimensions were pleasant-unpleasant, tension-relaxation, and excitation-calm. Ekman

© Springer Nature Switzerland AG 2021
M. Antona and C. Stephanidis (Eds.): HCII 2021, LNCS 12768, pp. 599–616, 2021.
https://doi.org/10.1007/978-3-030-78092-0_42

[3] recommended to merge the two last dimensions because they resulted too similar each other, and Russell [4] developed the Circumplex Model of Affect, that has been taken as a reference in the present work and is shown in Fig. 1.

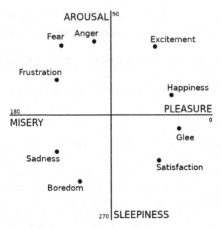

Fig. 1. Circumplex Model of Affect. On the left the eight affect concepts are arranged in a circular order, as well as the twenty-eight affect words that are displayed on the right.

Ecological validity refers to the possibility to generalize the data collected from observed behavior in the laboratory to the natural behavior in the real world [5]. In the current study, the facial expression of a subject must be due to a certain stimulus and not to boundary or artificial conditions. Within the context of an experiment, this means to find a trade-off between the experimental rigor, necessary to compare results obtained from different subjects, and the comfortability of the subjects themselves, who should express feelings by their nature only as a consequence to the stimulus received, not conditioned by constraints imposed by the experiment.

An experiment that aims to study facial expressions can be set up in different ways. First of all, participants can be asked to act or to express their spontaneous feelings as has been requested for the current work; then, the format of results must be established [6] and, consequently, the necessary equipment must be procured (a standard video camera, an RGB-D camera, sensors to obtain physiological data, a database to store answers to a questionnaire, etc.); moreover, stimuli to obtain spontaneous reactions must be defined.

Among the variety of stimuli raising emotions, such as audio-visual [7], movie clips [8], music tracks and game scenarios [9], for the present work images stored in IAPS and GAPED affective databases have been chosen.

The International Affective Picture System (IAPS) is the most known affective database. The version of the database used for this experiment is composed of 1182 images (the database has been subjected to updates through the years) subdivided into semantic categories to arouse different emotions. IAPS has been largely used in psychiatric applications. Taskiran et al. [10] have studied the responses to emotional stimuli in patients affected by attention-deficit hyperactivity disorder, Migliore et al. [11] have conducted a similar study in Relapsing-Remitting Multiple Sclerosis (RRMS) patients,

Moret-Tatay et al. [12] and Bekele et al. [13] have dealt with middle-aged adults and older men respectively affected by Schizophrenia, Peter et al. [14] have compared emotional responses in subjects with personality disorders, cluster-C personality disorders and non-patients. Furthermore, the ability of processing emotions after traumatic situations has been investigated, such as post-earthquake distress by Pistoia et al. [15] and violated women by Navarro Martinez [16], but also the dependence from alcohol can have implications in the way of processing emotions according to Dominguez-Centeno et al. [17]. The vast majority of the above-mentioned studies focused on evaluating subjects' emotions through the analysis of physiological signals: electroencephalography (EEG), electrocardiography (ECG) and magnetic resonance imaging (MRI).

The Geneva Affective Picture Database (GAPED) is composed of 730 images. The intent in building this new dataset was to overcome a problem that arouses in using IAPS extensively: the impact of those images seemed to drop in terms of efficacy both for positive and negative emotions. In particular, regarding the negative ones, GAPED designers subdivided images into four classes: two of them represents animals (snakes and spiders), one concerns the violation of the social norms (defined by legality), one concerns the violation of personal norms (determined by morality). According to Dan-Glauser and Scherer [18], estimation of low tolerability of the stimuli related to social norms becomes relevant in the elicitation of anger, but also in disgust, pity, guilt, shame, and contempt. There are predictable dissimilarities in valence marks among the positive, neutral, and negative categories, but also in arousal rates, indeed it is usually possible to find a correlation since valence scores are rarely independent from arousal levels.

To quantify an emotion is a critical task that has been largely discussed; what people refer to when using the term *feeling* is only the conscious experience of an emotion. Nonetheless, Mehrabian and Russell [19] have developed the Semantic Differential Scale to assess objects, events, and situations by using 18 opposite couples of adjectives related to three independent dimensions:

- Valence/pleasure: it describes the positivity or negativity of an emotion. In the work of Mehrabian and Russell, adjectives used to label valence were not only in the range happy-unhappy; the concept of positivity was also associated to pleasantness, satisfaction, content, hope and relaxation, while the concept of negativity was associated to annoyance, unsatisfaction, melancholy, despair, and boredom.
- Arousal: it describes the level of activation inducted by the received stimulus, in terms of psychophysical response. The continuum ranges from the lowest level associated with a status of boredom and sleepiness, to the highest level of frantic excitement. Adjectives used to label this dimension are aroused-unaroused, stimulated-relaxed, excited-calm, awake-sleepy, frenzied-sluggish, jittery-dull.
- Dominance: it describes how a subject feels with regards to the aroused emotion in terms of submission-dominance. It is the most critical dimension to define because of possible misinterpretations; for example, one subject may consider her/his sense of control in the situation presented, while another subject could consider whether the pictured object is perceived in control or not of that situation.

The Self-Assessment Manikin (SAM) [20] is a solution that maps the three dimensions into three non-verbal pictorial scales in order to directly assess the pleasure, arousal, and dominance associated in response to an object or event.

Valence ranges from pleasant to unpleasant; in the SAM implementation selected for this experiment, the lowest value is represented by a frowning figure, while the highest value is represented by a smiling figure.

Arousal ranges from calm to excited; in the SAM implementation selected for this experiment, the lowest value is represented by a sleepy figure, while the highest value is represented by a wide-eyed figure.

Dominance has not been used in this experiment not to move the focus of the participants forcing them to answer a too demanding questionnaire. Furthermore, in literature and in describing images in affective databases, it is the least used dimension.

SAM has been the selected scale representation in this study.

As reported in [21], participants responses have been collected on a 9-point rating scale for each dimension.

In the experimental setup for the current work, participants have seen images chosen from affective databases and have answered a short questionnaire to express their own feeling elicited by each image. They have been recorded using the RGB-D camera Intel RealSense SR300. The final aim of this project is to build an ecologically valid dataset within which RGB-D images are stored. These images should represent spontaneous facial expressions, indispensable to train deep learning neural networks, such as Convolutional Neural Network, or other supervised machine learning algorithms.

The result that has been obtained up to now is twofold: on one side, a comparison between elicited emotions and expected emotions has been drawn up; on the other side, a remarkable recognition rate of a CNN trained with the obtained images has been achieved.

2   Methods

In this Section, all the components involved in the experiment design and implementation phase are presented (Fig. 2).

2.1 Participants

Participants have been selected among students and PhD students of Politecnico di Torino, aged between 18 and 35, for a total number of thirty-five participants, fourteen female and twenty-one male subjects.

The experiment's nature has required to ensure that participants had at least a standard level of empathy and were not alexithymic; thus, every participant filled-in two tests before attending the experiment itself.

Empathy identifies the ability to identify and to understand others' points of view, thoughts, intentions, and beliefs and is fundamental to build interpersonal relationships [22]. Empathy has two main components: the affective one and the cognitive one. The first refers to the affective reaction to another person's emotional state, and the latter refers to the cognitive capacity to take the perspective of the other person [23]. The

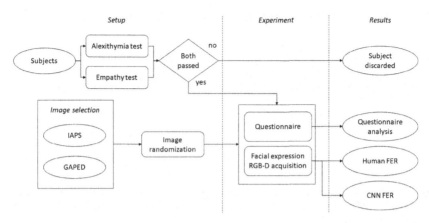

Fig. 2. Methodology steps.

Balanced Emotional Empathy Scale (BEES) proposed by Mehrabian and translated into Italian by Meneghini et al. [24] has been adopted to evaluate participants' empathy. This test is composed of thirty questions, and each answer requires a choice between strongly disagree and strongly agree on a seven-point scale. Results are subdivided into three ranges, namely below the average, standard and above the average.

Alexithymia identifies a reduced ability in recognizing, describing, and understanding one's own emotions [23]. It goes without saying that alexithymia and empathy are interlinked because if one has difficulties recognizing his own emotions, that person will have difficulties in recognizing others' emotions. The Toronto Structured Interview for Alexithymia (TAS-20) has been adopted to evaluate participants' alexithymia [25]; this test has a 3-factor structure: the first evaluates difficulty in recognizing feelings, the second evaluates the difficulty in describing feelings, the third one considers externally oriented thinking. There are twenty questions, and each answer requires a choice between strongly disagree and strongly agree on a five-point scale. Results are subdivided in three ranges, namely non-alexithymic, borderline and alexithymic.

Subjects' empathy and alexithymia results have been displayed in Fig. 3.

2.2 Images Selection

The choice of static visual stimuli, i.e., images, has been done to obtain an important advantage, which is to identify the exact moment during which the image is shown to the participants, namely the moment from which it is reasonable to search for a facial expression in the video acquired with the camera.

Databases from which to gather the pictures have been IAPS and GAPED. This choice has been made after the literature review and, also, a trial day dedicated to identifying weaknesses in the planned design of the experiment. The chosen pictures have been selected to arouse the widest range of stimuli possible and to represent a selection of a comprehensive sample of contents across the entire affective space.

Unfortunately, the literature lacks a unique validated system to relate the Russell model (Fig. 1), the six Ekman's expressions (happiness, sadness, anger, fear, disgust,

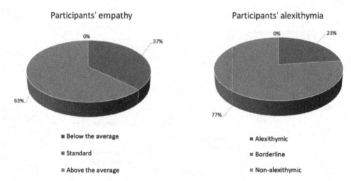

Fig. 3. On the left: participants' alexithymia according to the Toronto Structured Interview for Alexithymia (TAS-20). On the right: Participants' empathy according to the Balanced Emotional Empathy Scale (BEES).

and surprise), and the images stored in the IAPS database, that have been classified according to valence and arousal values. Nonetheless, an attempt to put in relation these dependent dimensions has been done, according to the theory of emotions elaborated by Plutchik [26]. This effort has been done to be able to select the IAPS proper images to arouse specific stimuli without having images organized by emotions (there is no emotion label on IAPS images), but only by valence and arousal values. Results of this mapping operation are shown in Fig. 4 and Fig. 5.

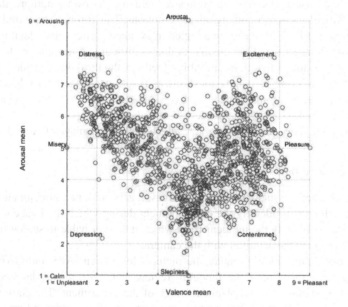

Fig. 4. Valence-arousal and Russel's model mapping (affective space).

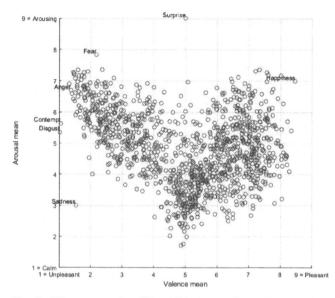

Fig. 5. Valence-arousal and Plutchik's theory of emotions mapping.

Images stored in the GAPED database had both a labelling system to describe which emotions should arouse and the scores of valence and arousal, even if ranging from 0 to 100, so a normalization has been performed. Despite this operation, a poor correlation between values of IAPS and GAPED associated with positive emotions has been obtained. Some examples of inconsistency are reported in Table 1.

Table 1. Valence and arousal comparisons for positive images in IAPS and GAPED databases.

Images subject	IAPS		GAPED	
	Valence	Arousal	Valence	Arousal
Puppies	8.34	5.41	8.68	3.3
Baby	7.86	5	8.37	3.2
Seal	8.19	4.61	8.61	1.68

These issues in making correspondences between the two datasets can be explained by the different characteristics of the images, IAPS ones look older, even if GAPED is only six years more recent the most used version of IAPS, but mostly because of cultural factors of people that evaluated the pictures; indeed, IAPS has been developed by the National Institute of Mental Health Center for Emotion and Attention at the University of Florida and images have been evaluated by one hundred people aged 18–24, while GAPED comes from Geneva, Switzerland, and images have been evaluated by sixty people aged 19–34.

To solve the issue, all the images have been carefully selected one-by-one.

GAPED images have been selected more easily since the database is arranged in folders (humans, animals, neutrals, spiders, snakes, and positive categories).

IAPS images have been selected assigning the correct labels of emotions to each picture considering in a first instance the work of Bradley & Lang [27, 28], and Bradley et al. [29]. The contents that generate the same emotion in the two genders has been considered, and the emotion with the major percentage has been taken as predominant (Table 2 has been reported from [28]).

Table 2. List of the most frequent specific emotion descriptors reported in [28, 29] and linked to the IAPS picture categories selected for our experiment. The table includes also the proportion of men and women selecting that specific emotion to describe their affective experience.

Picture category	Women		Men	
Families	Happy (.79)	Loving (.78)	Happy (.58)	Loving (.58)
Pollution	Disgust (.56)	Irritated (.43)	Disgust (.34)	Irritated (.26)
Loss	Sad (.79)	Pity (.56)	Sad (.61)	Pity (.59)
Illness	Pity (.67)	Sad (.69)	Pity (.58)	Sad (.51)
Contamination	Disgust (.88)	Irritated (.50)	Disgust (.78)	Irritated (.40)
Accidents	Sad (.63)	Pity (55)	Pity (.50)	Sad (.49)
Mutilation	Disgust (.81)	Sad (.47)	Disgust (.75)	Pity (.42)
Animal Threat	Afraid (.69)	Anxious (.31)	Afraid (.42)	Anxious (.23)
Human Threat	Afraid (.67)	Angry (.42)	Afraid (.37)	Angry (.35)

A final check with the affective space has been done before the following list of images was confirmed (24 IAPS images in Table 3, 24 GAPED images in Table 4). Images used in the training phase have not been reported.

The final list is also the result of an analysis conducted after the trial day; the number of 48 images was defined instead of the initial 60, a trade-off to use the greatest number of pictures preserving the participants' attention, and some images considered too dated (belonging to IAPS database) have been substituted. Images are uniformly distributed among the basic emotions: anger, disgust, fear, happiness, sadness, and neutrality. More-over, Fig. 6 identifies the images of the final dataset onto the Valence-Arousal plane. Surprise is not present among the labelled images.

Table 3. Selected IAPS images.

Description	Valence	Arousal	Emotion
Beaten woman	2.31	6.38	Anger
Soldiers	2.10	6.53	Anger
Soldier	1.51	7.07	Anger
Mutilation #1	1.79	7.26	Disgust
Mutilation #2	1.79	7.12	Disgust
Mutilation #3	1.80	6.77	Disgust
Mutilation #4	1.70	7.03	Disgust
Mutilation #5	1.48	7.22	Disgust
Mutilation #6	1.58	6.97	Disgust
Baby with tumor	1.46	7.21	Disgust
Injury	1.56	6.79	Disgust
Snake	3.79	6.93	Fear
Dog attack	3.09	6.51	Fear
Shark	3.85	6.47	Fear
Kiss	7.27	5.16	Happiness
Mushroom #1	5.42	3.00	Neutrality
Mushroom #2	5.15	3.69	Neutrality
Spoon	5.04	2.00	Neutrality
Bowl	4.88	2.33	Neutrality
Lamp	4.87	1.72	Neutrality
Toddler	1.79	5.25	Sadness
Sad child	1.78	5.49	Sadness
Injured child	1.80	5.21	Sadness
Car accident	2.34	6.63	Sadness

2.3 Experimental Setup

Participants were asked to fill-in the empathy and alexithymia tests before coming to the laboratory.

Regarding the part of the experiment held in presence, at the beginning participants have attended a presentation to become familiar with the context and to receive the main indications on what to do during the experiment, without influencing their emotionality in any way not to corrupt the results. They have been warned about the presence of images that could have potentially bothered their sensibility. The possibility of abandoning the experiment due to any kind of discomfort has been clarified.

The experiment has taken place in two phases: training and testing. The structure of both the phases has been the same: in a first instance one image provided by affective

Table 4. Selected GAPED images.

Description	Valence	Arousal	Emotion
Animal mistreatment #1	2.12	5.89	Anger
Animal mistreatment #2	2.08	6.46	Anger
Animal mistreatment #3	2.40	6.88	Anger
Animal mistreatment #4	1.15	7.23	Anger
Animal mistreatment #5	1.71	7.46	Anger
Snake #1	4.94	6.09	Fear
Snake #2	2.44	6.5	Fear
Spider #1	4.21	5.44	Fear
Spider #2	4.85	6.4	Fear
Spider #3	3.94	5.63	Fear
Baby #1	8.07	3.38	Happiness
Baby #2	8.03	2.86	Happiness
Baby #3	8.21	2.72	Happiness
Puppies #1	8.19	3.37	Happiness
Puppies #2	8.68	3.3	Happiness
Baby fox	7.83	3.11	Happiness
Kitten	7.77	3.10	Happiness
Antenna	5.4	2.97	Neutrality
Chairs	5.01	2.06	Neutrality
Lamp and sofa	5.84	2.10	Neutrality
Animal in captivity #1	3.20	6.43	Sadness
Animal in captivity #2	1.80	7.48	Sadness
Animal in captivity #3	2.11	6.38	Sadness
Animal in captivity #4	2.08	5.68	Sadness

databases was displayed in full-screen mode (Fig. 7), then the participants had to fill-in the questionnaire about valence, arousal and the prevalent felt emotion (Fig. 8). It has to be noticed that the label surprise has been inserted in the questionnaire, to let participants free of choosing the most proper basic emotion they felt, independently from the fact that images arousing surprise have not been inserted in the final dataset of 48 images.

The training phase has been useful mainly to get participants familiar with the questionnaire, because answers were forced to be given in no more than 15 s, to favor spontaneity. SAM icons are intuitive, but not so easy to interpret if never seen before.

The testing phase is composed of 48 images which are randomized for every participant and lasts about 20 min.

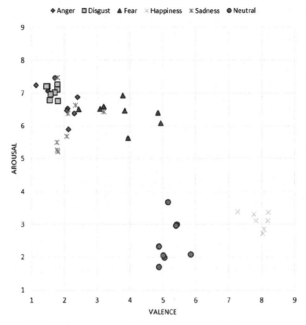

Fig. 6. IAPS and GAPED distribution in terms of valence and arousal.

Fig. 7. Example of image content selected to arouse happiness [30].

An ad-hoc software has been necessary to deal with both the management of images and questionnaire, maximizing the user experience not to distract the user from his task and the management of the RGB-D camera recording. Indeed, the Intel RealSense SR300 has been connected to the same application using a different thread and has been set up to record user's expression from the moment during which the affective image

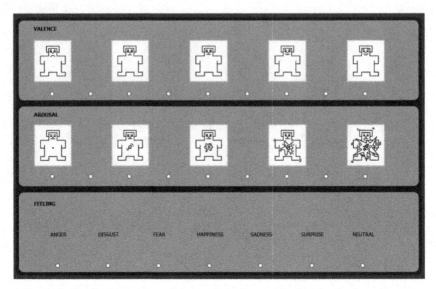

Fig. 8. Screenshot of the questionnaire used for the experiment.

appears on the screen to 2 s after it disappears, to be sure not to lose any expression. An idle interval of 2000 ms between the affective image and the questionnaire and between the questionnaire and the next affective image has been introduced. The affective image lasts 6000 ms on the screen; nonetheless, a smaller frame has been inserted next to the questionnaire as a reminder for the user.

In Fig. 9 the experimental setup is illustrated.

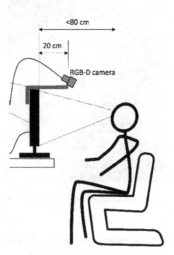

Fig. 9. Experimental setup.

2.4 Facial Expression Recognition via Deep Learning

The RGB-D camera was used to record spontaneous facial expressions aroused in participants, storing both the color and the depth frames, with the purpose of creating a facial depth map database to be adopted for testing novel face/facial expression recognition methodologies. Thus, it was necessary to preliminarily test the acquired data to verify that could be suitable for feeding a Convolutional Neural Network (CNN), the most used neural networks to identify objects and faces within frames. Deep learning methods provide some advantages, including the automatic features extraction and the possibility of retraining existing networks for other recognition activities, with cutting-edge recognition results [31].

Facial Expression Recognition has been performed starting by VGG-16, a convolutional neural network model proposed by Simonyan and Zisserman [32], trained on the Imagenet dataset [33], a database of images of generic objects. Then, the recognition task has been readapted to faces by training the CNN on the BU-3DFE database [34], a 3D facial expression database that presently contains 100 subjects (56% female, 44% male), ranging age from 18 years to 70 years old, with a variety of ethnic/racial ancestries. All the subjects involved in the database performed seven expressions in front of the 3D face scanner. Excluding the neutral expression, the other six basic emotions (i.e., anger, disgust, happiness, fear, sadness, and surprise) are represented with four levels of intensity resulting in a total of 2,500 3D facial expression models and the corresponding 2D texture images. The training phase is the most demanding step when dealing with deep learning because a huge amount of data is required [35].

Keras was used, an open-source neural-network library written in Python, running on top of TensorFlow, on Windows 10 Pro with NVIDIA GeForce RTX 2060.

Data obtained from the acquisitions, i.e., color and depth frames, must be processed before being used as input for the neural network. Three main steps can be identified: frame capture to manually extract the most significant frames (Maximum Criterion variation) to be analyzed through the neural network; Color to Depth alignment to both temporally and spatially synchronize the frames; Face Detection to identify the face only in its oval shape. The input layer of the network requires RGB images having a size of 224×224.

The testing phase results are discussed in the next Section, together with the other experimental results.

3 Results and Discussion

To evaluate the effectivity of the acquired data in order to create a facial database for emotion recognition, it was core to compare the emotions expected to be aroused and the emotions pointed out in the questionnaire by the participants. This comparison aims to verify if the images chosen from the affective database have been effective.

In Table 5 the six considered emotions are displayed in the first column. From the second column to the last one, the indication of the emotion pointed out by the 35 users has been reported.

It can be noticed that the prevalent emotion found in the questionnaires matches with the expected emotion in every case.

Table 5. Comparisons between expected emotions (first column) and questionnaire answers

	Emotions reported in the questionnaire						
	Happiness	Neutrality	Sadness	Disgust	Anger	Fear	Surprise
Happiness	79%	16%	1%	0%	0%	0%	4%
Neutrality	8%	75%	2%	1%	0%	1%	13%
Sadness	6%	7%	67%	1%	4%	7%	8%
Disgust	0%	3%	15%	67%	3%	5%	7%
Anger	0%	9%	23%	14%	44%	3%	7%
Fear	4%	26%	0%	26%	0%	27%	17%

To be coherent with the CNN training and the literature, surprise has been maintained as an available option to choose, even if not directly present among the affective images. In some cases, participants have chosen this emotion instead of neutrality because they did not know how to react. Anyways, 75% of matching between expected and aroused neutrality is remarkable, as well as the 79% of happiness.

Obtained results are perfectly coherent with Table 2. For instance, mutilations should arouse disgust both for men and women, then sadness in women and pity in men. Pity is not a basic emotion, the closest one is sadness, and in our study, the mutilations that have been chosen to arouse disgust, have aroused disgust in the 67% and sadness in 15% of the participants.

Anger images have been mostly evaluated as anger (44%) or sadness (23%) or disgust (14%) confirming the not so clear area of the affective space occupied by these three emotions.

Fear has been the emotion aroused with less success (27%). According to Edwards et al. [36], disgust can be part of the emotional reaction to certain phobic stimuli. This explains why it has been chosen from the 26% of the participants, as well as the neutrality, simple to explain that 26% of the participants have not felt these images frightful enough.

After that, emotions have been analyzed, a comparison between valence and arousal values expected from one side, valence and arousal pointed out in the questionnaires on the other side has been carried on.

The 48 images have been represented in the affective space (singularly in Fig. 10, compacted in Fig. 11), both with valence and arousal values reported in affective databases and with valence and arousal values given by participants' answers to the questionnaire. In this last case, valence and arousal have been averaged among the 35 participants for every image, and to choose the emotion that each valence-arousal couple represents, the most selected emotion by the participants has been used.

Surprise has not been reported in the graphs because, as expected, it has been chosen a few times by the users and not significant for this comparison.

Then, the CNN was run in order to have a preliminary classification of the emotions acquired by the RGB-D camera. An heterogeneous focus group was created to label users' emotions frame by frame. This allowed us to obtain a percentage accuracy.

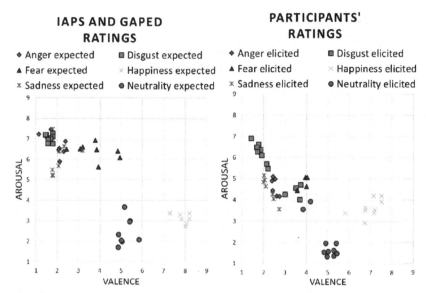

Fig. 10. Valence and arousal values comparisons in affective databases (on the left) and obtained during the experiment (on the right).

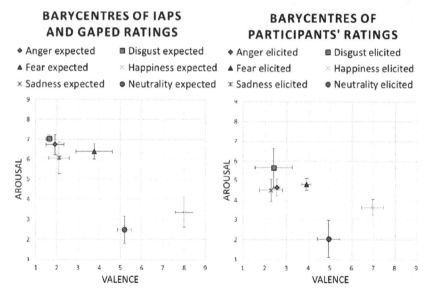

Fig. 11. Valence and arousal barycenter comparisons in affective databases and obtained during the experiments by participants' ratings. Lines represent the standard deviation.

The use of both the RGB and the 3D channels has returned three classifications for each image. The first one takes into account only the RGB data; the second one only the 3D data. Instead, the third classification results in an average between the two previous classifications. Results considering only depth images have not been satisfactory (55,20%), while RGB and depth's combined usage has led to a 72,65% of agreement. Best results have been obtained considering only RGB images, correctly recognized 3 times out of 4 (75,02%). Some considerations about these results must be made.

The participants' head orientation was not the most suitable one because the RGB-D camera has not been positioned in the center of the field of view of the participants; otherwise, the monitor would not have been visible. The need to keep the monitor size large enough was urgent, to guarantee the user the most immersive experience possible to ensure the spontaneity of facial expressions. Hence, to ensure the ecological validity of the experiment, a compromise with the data visualization has been requested. The result is that faces have been framed with a slight tilt angle relative to the camera; particularly, the CNN trained with depth images labeled many images as angry since areas highlighting anger have been pointed out this way (wrinkles between eyes). This consideration leads to the second one: the dataset for training is too limited, especially for negative emotions. The training set is uniformly split, nonetheless, negative emotions are really close to each other in the affective space. This means that the CNN, as well as most classifiers, needs more images to properly run, especially those images belonging to classes critical to be recognized. Finally, the participants in the experiment, the focus group, and the CNN were asked to evaluate the images assigning only one single emotion. Nonetheless, some images could have led to feeling more than an emotion.

The final recognition rate of 75,02% can be considered satisfactory for the purpose of testing the adoptability of our data for facial expression recognition purposes.

4   Conclusions

The present work has aimed to realize and test an ecologically valid facial expression database, realized by recording spontaneous facial expressions elicited during the designed experiment. Each person has been recorded by an RGB-D camera. Information about her/his emotions has been obtained through a questionnaire and a visual analysis provided by human observers, and an automatic recognition method based on CNN. The results reflect the distribution of the arousal and valence values in Russell and Plutchik's affective spaces taken as reference.

The next step will be the CNN training with an enlarged dataset both for RGB and Depth images. To improve the recognition rate of the basic emotions and increase the range of emotions, further images will be provided by different databases consisting of posed and spontaneous expressions. Nowadays, state-of-art results are obtained using a multimodal approach, a new promising research direction; the building of an ecologically valid RGB-D dataset that benefits from the accuracy of 2D and the flexibility of 3D data, aims to obtain cutting-edge results in the Facial Expression Recognition field.

Another improvement will be creating immersive virtual reality environments to arouse more pronounced and clear expressions, preserving the dataset's ecologically valid nature, chiefly for those emotions that occupy similar areas in the affective space. Furthermore, the usage of these environments will change the paradigm of the experiment, converting the user experience from passive to proactive.

References

1. Wundt, W.: Outlines of psychology. In: Rieber, R.W. (ed.) Wilhelm Wundt and the Making of a Scientific Psychology, pp. 179–195. Springer US, Boston, MA (1980)
2. Woodworth, R.S., Barber, B., Schlosberg, H.: Experimental psychology. Oxford and IBH Publishing, New Delhi (1954)
3. Ekman, P.: A methodological discussion of nonverbal behavior. J. Psychol. **43**, 141–149 (1957). https://doi.org/10.1080/00223980.1957.9713059
4. Russell, J.A.: A circumplex model of affect. J. Pers. Soc. Psychol. **39**, 1161 (1980)
5. Schmuckler, M.A.: What is ecological validity? A dimensional analysis. Infancy **2**, 419–436 (2001)
6. Zhang, Z., et al.: Multimodal spontaneous emotion corpus for human behavior analysis. In: Proceedings of the IEEE Conference on Computer Vision and Pattern Recognition, pp. 3438–3446 (2016)
7. Gross, J.J., Levenson, R.W.: Emotion elicitation using films. Cogn. Emot. **9**, 87–108 (1995)
8. Soleymani, M., Pantic, M., Pun, T.: Multimodal emotion recognition in response to videos. IEEE Trans. Affect. Comput. **3**, 211–223 (2011)
9. Chanel, G., Rebetez, C., Bétrancourt, M., Pun, T.: Emotion assessment from physiological signals for adaptation of game difficulty. IEEE Trans. Syst. Man Cybern. A: Syst. Hum. **41**, 1052–1063 (2011)
10. Taskiran, C., et al.: Clinical features and subjective/physiological responses to emotional stimuli in the presence of emotion dysregulation in attention-deficit hyperactivity disorder. J. Clin. Exp. Neuropsychol. **40**, 389–404 (2018)
11. Migliore, S., et al.: Emotional processing in RRMS patients: dissociation between behavioural and neurophysiological response. Multiple Scler. Relat. Disord. **27**, 344–349 (2019)
12. Moret-Tatay, C., Rueda, P.M., Bernabé-Valero, G., Gamermann, D.: Emotional recognition in schizophrenia: an analysis of response components in middle-aged adults. Psychiatr. Q. **90**, 543–552 (2019)
13. Bekele, E., Bian, D., Zheng, Z., Peterman, J., Park, S., Sarkar, N.: Responses during facial emotional expression recognition tasks using virtual reality and static iaps pictures for adults with schizophrenia. In: Shumaker, R., Lackey, S. (eds.) VAMR 2014. LNCS, vol. 8526, pp. 225–235. Springer, Cham (2014). https://doi.org/10.1007/978-3-319-07464-1_21
14. Peter, M., Arntz, A., Klimstra, T.A., Faulborn, M., Vingerhoets, A.: Subjective emotional responses to IAPS pictures in patients with borderline personality disorder, cluster-C personality disorders, and non-patients. Psychiatry Res. **273**, 712–718 (2019)
15. Pistoia, F., et al.: Post-earthquake distress and development of emotional expertise in young adults. Front. Behav. Neurosci. **12**, 91 (2018)
16. Martínez Navarro, A.M.: Medición de las Respuestas Emocionales en la Violencia contra las Mujeres: Una Revisión Sistemática (2019)
17. Dominguez-Centeno, I., et al.: Psychophysiological correlates of emotional-and alcohol-related cues processing in offspring of alcohol-dependent patients. Alcohol Alcohol. **55**(4), 374–381 (2020)
18. Dan-Glauser, E.S., Scherer, K.R.: The Geneva affective picture database (GAPED): a new 730-picture database focusing on valence and normative significance. Behav. Res. Methods **43**, 468 (2011)
19. Mehrabian, A., Russell, J.A.: An Approach to Environmental Psychology. The MIT Press, Cambridge (1974)
20. Bradley, M.M., Lang, P.J.: Measuring emotion: the self-assessment Manikin and the semantic differential. J. Behav. Therapy Exp. Psychiatry **25**, 49 (1994)

21. Lang, P.J., Bradley, M.M., Cuthbert, B.N., International Affective Picture System (IAPS): Technical Manual and Affective Ratings. NIMH Center for the Study of Emotion and Attention (1997).

22. Mul, C., Stagg, S.D., Herbelin, B., Aspell, J.E.: The feeling of me feeling for you: interoception, alexithymia and empathy in autism. J. Autism Dev. Disord. **48**, 2953–2967 (2018)

23. Moriguchi, Y., et al.: Empathy and judging other's pain: an fMRI study of alexithymia. Cereb. Cortex **17**, 2223–2234 (2007)

24. Meneghini, A.M., Sartori, R., Cunico, L.: Adattamento italiano della Balanced Emotional Emspathy Scale (BEES) di Albert Mehrabian [The Italian adaptation of the Balanced Emotional Empathy Scale (BEES) by Albert Mehrabian]. Giunti Organizzazioni Speciali, Florence, Italy (2012)

25. Michael Bagby, R., Parker, J., Taylor, G.: The twenty-item Toronto Alexithymia Scale—I. Item selection and cross-validation of the factor structure. J. Psychosom. Res. **38**, 23–32 (1994)

26. Plutchik, R.: A general psychoevolutionary theory of emotion. In: Theories of Emotion, pp. 3–33. Elsevier, Amsterdam (1980)

27. Coan, J.A., Allen, J.J.: Handbook of Emotion Elicitation and Assessment. Oxford University Press (2007)

28. Lang, P., Bradley, M.M.: The International Affective Picture System (IAPS) in the study of emotion and attention. Handb. Emot. Elicitation Assess. **29**, 70–73 (2007)

29. Bradley, M.M., Codispoti, M., Sabatinelli, D., Lang, P.J.: Emotion and motivation II: sex differences in picture processing. Emotion **1**, 300–319 (2001)

30. Kundu, S.: https://unsplash.com/@senjuti

31. Nonis, F., Dagnes, N., Marcolin, F., Vezzetti, E.: 3D approaches and challenges in facial expression recognition algorithms—a literature review. Appl. Sci. **9**, 3904 (2019)

32. Simonyan, K., Zisserman, A.: Very deep convolutional networks for large-scale image recognition. arXiv preprint arXiv:1409.1556. (2014)

33. Deng, J., Dong, W., Socher, R., Li, L.-J., Li, K., Fei-Fei, L.: Imagenet: a large-scale hierarchical image database. In: 2009 IEEE Conference on Computer Vision and Pattern Recognition, pp. 248–255. IEEE (2009).

34. Yin, L., Wei, X., Sun, Y., Wang, J., Rosato, M.J.: A 3D facial expression database for facial behavior research. In: 7th International Conference on Automatic Face and Gesture Recognition (FGR 2006), pp. 211–216. IEEE (2006).

35. Nonis, F., Barbiero, P., Cirrincione, G., Olivetti, E.C., Marcolin, F., Vezzetti, E.: Understanding abstraction in deep CNN: an application on facial emotion recognition. In: Esposito, A., Faundez-Zanuy, M., Morabito, F.C., Pasero, E. (eds.) Progresses in Artificial Intelligence and Neural Systems. SIST, vol. 184, pp. 281–290. Springer, Singapore (2021)

36. Edwards, S., Salkovskis, P.M.: An experimental demonstration that fear, but not disgust, is associated with return of fear in phobias. J. Anxiety Disord. **20**, 58–71 (2006)

Supervised Contrastive Learning for Game-Play Frustration Detection from Speech

Meishu Song[1][(✉)], Emilia Parada-Cabaleiro[2], Shuo Liu[1], Manuel Milling[1], Alice Baird[1], Zijiang Yang[1], and Björn W. Schuller[1,3]

[1] Chair of Embedded Intelligence for Health Care and Wellbeing, University of Augsburg, Augsburg, Germany
meishu.song@informatik.uni-augsburg.de
[2] Institute of Computational Perception, Johannes Kepler University Linz, Linz, Austria
[3] GLAM – Group on Language, Audio, & Music, Imperial College London, London, UK

Abstract. Frustration is a common response during game interactions, typically decreasing a user's engagement and leading to game failure. Artificially intelligent methods capable to automatically detect a user's level of frustration at an early stage are hence of great interest for game designers, since this would enable optimisation of a player's experience in real-time. Nevertheless, research in this context is still in its infancy, mainly relying on the use of pre-trained models and fine-tuning tailored to a specific dataset. Furthermore, this lack in research is due to the limited data available and to the ambiguous labelling of frustration, which leads to outcomes which are not generalisable in the real-world. Meanwhile, contrastive loss has been considered instead of the traditional cross-entropy loss in a variety of machine learning applications, showing to be more robust for system stability alternative in self-supervised learning. Following this trend, we hypothesise that using a supervised contrastive loss might overcome the limitations of the cross-entropy loss yielded by the labels' ambiguity. In fact, our experiments demonstrate that using the supervised contrastive method as a loss function, results improve for the automatic recognition (binary frustration vs no-frustration) of game-induced frustration from speech with an Unweighted Average Recall increase from 86.4 % to 89.9 %.

Keywords: Frustration recognition · Supervised contrastive learning · Speech recognition

1 Introduction

Automatically detecting frustration from users' audio-visual cues is becoming a more important part in ubiquitous sensing technology, used in a variety of applications, such as in-car-driver monitoring [44], or e-learning scenarios [13]. Although game-based applications—both entertainment and education

© Springer Nature Switzerland AG 2021
M. Antona and C. Stephanidis (Eds.): HCII 2021, LNCS 12768, pp. 617–629, 2021.
https://doi.org/10.1007/978-3-030-78092-0_43

oriented—would benefit from such a technology to achieve user evaluation and study feedback in real-time, the automatic analysis of frustration during game play is still an underdeveloped area of research. On the one side, the lack in research is due to the still limited amount of suitable data [37]. On the other side, due to the labels' ambiguity typical of emotional data, for which instead of an objective 'ground truth', a subjective 'gold standard' [33], i.e., an agreed-upon human annotation label, is typically available. Although methods for automatic recognition of frustration from audio-visual cues have been presented, most of these are based on end-to-end models applying cross-entropy loss [9], which despite their excellent convergence speed, present a sub-optimal performance when dealing with ambiguous labels [45]— note that frustration is usually annotated according to a gold standard. Furthermore, frustration can also be confused with other highly aroused emotional states, e.g., anger, or, irritation.

In recent years, the use of contrastive learning, able to compensate for the disadvantage of cross-entropy loss, i.e., the sub-optimal performance with ambiguous labels, has led to major advances in self-supervised learning, especially showing its potential on traditional visual classification tasks [5]. The main idea behind contrastive learning is to pull together an anchor, i.e., 'positive' sample of the class intended to be recognised, into an embedding space; then, push apart the 'negative' samples, by measuring their similarity w.r.t. the anchor [21]. Since in self-supervised tasks there is no label information, in order to adapt contrastive learning to a fully supervised setting, the Supervised Contrastive (SupCon) loss has been presented, which provides label information to the system by enabling multiple positives per anchor [23].

Inspired by this idea and by the successful performance shown by the use of contrastive learning and SupCon loss in previous works [23], we aim to overcome the shortcomings of using cross-entropy loss by applying supervised contrastive learning with Residual Convolutional Neural Networks (ResNet) to the detection of frustration from speech. By using this approach on the Multimodal Game Frustration Database (MGFD) [37], we aim to mitigate the influence of ambiguous labels—typical of emotional induced datasets [31]—in the frustration recognition task. The rest of the manuscript is laid out as follows: In Sect. 2, the related literature on frustration recognition and contrastive learning is described; in Sect. 3, the methodology is presented; in Sect. 4, the considered deep learning approaches are evaluated; in Sect. 5, the experimental results are discussed; finally, in Sect. 6, the conclusions and future work are given.

2   Related Work

2.1   Frustration Recognition

Frustration is a negative emotional state typically triggered by someone's inability to achieve the own goals [37]. In the realm of user experience research, traditional methods to measure frustration include the *Focus Group User Study* [28], the *User Questionnaire* [2], the *Expert Evaluation* [2], or the *Diary-Based*

Study [19]. Nowadays, with the advent of artificial intelligence, affective computing has opened new horizons in the automatic detection and measurement of frustration through machine learning [37]. In this regard, a variety of datasets aimed to develop frustration recognition systems has been presented in the literature. These include corpora containing spontaneous frustration in the context of driving, such as the UTDrive database [16], amongst others [26]. Similarly, educational scenarios have also been considered to record frustration, as shown by: the computer-mediated human tutoring corpus, which contains facial expression of frustration [11]; the ChIMP-Children's Interactive Multimedia Project database [3], collected during children-computer interactions, and containing verbal expressions of frustration; or the Microsoft Kinect sensors posture dataset, collected in a game-based learning environment for emergency medical training [18]. Another example is the AlloSat corpus [25], a speech-based dataset composed of real-life call centre conversations in French language recorded by Allo-Media. Finally, studies on frustration recognition from speech data have also been presented [10]. As every emotional reaction, frustration presents a variety of symptoms, which can be measured from different modalities, including physiological signals and audio-visual cues [34]. Furthermore, since frustration might arise in different situations, its recognition through such modalities has been applied in many contexts, mostly influenced by the existing corpora. For instance, driving in daily traffic scenarios has shown to be a prominent source of frustration, reason why this context has been considered to detect drivers' frustration from different modalities, such as finger temperature [44], or bimodal cues, i.e., heart rate and visual facial features [43]. Frustration is also a typical emotion that impairs a successful learning process [39].

Due to the importance of monitoring [36] and understanding students' emotions [30], systems such as ULearn, aimed to detect a student's level of frustration through computer vision techniques and natural language processing [13], as well as sensor-based methods which assess frustration through gesture and posture detection [18], have been presented. Indeed, the systems aimed to predict students' frustration and learning outcomes [12], by this enhancing student engagement [40], are always increasing. Another context very close to the educational, is the design of serious games, where motivational feedback is applied to counterbalance users' frustration, a method that can improve students' outcomes [7]. Nevertheless, despite the promising outcomes of applying automatic detection of frustration in serious games, the automatic recognition in game-interaction remains still underdeveloped [37].

2.2 Contrastive Learning

The origins of contrastive learning dates to the 90ies, and its development has spanned across many fields [24], such as, computer vision and natural language processing [22]. The core idea of this approach is learning by comparing between separate, although related, data points, without considering any supervised information like labels [1]. In 2005, Chopra et al. proposed a kernel able to map training data into a target area; thus, creating the foundation of the contrastive learning framework [6] [15]. The training stage minimises a discriminative loss function that drives the similarity metric for the samples of the same class [6]; by this, the contrastive pair loss learns a good representation of the data. This idea was tested on the Purdue face database, which includes a very high degree of variability [6]. Further improvements were subsequently presented, for instance, Oh Song et al. improved the efficiency of comparisons in an iteration by lifting the vector of pair-wise distances within the batch [29].

In 2010, Gutmann and Hyvärinen [14] introduced the Noise Contrastive Estimation (NCE), i.e., a simple conceptual strategy for estimating an unnormalised statistical model by contrasting the data w.r.t. an auxiliary noise. Nevertheless, how to select the auxiliary noise distribution remains still an open research question. To this end, a variety of solutions has been presented in the literature. Ceylan and Gutmann [4] proposed to formulate density estimation as a supervised learning problem that unlike NCE, leverages the observed data when generating noisy samples. Also based on NCE, Mnih and Teh [27] trained powerful natural language processing models to learn word embeddings on the Microsoft Research Sentence Completion Challenge dataset [46]. In 2018, Hjelm et al. [20] investigated data representations by maximising mutual information between an input and the output as well as minimising a contrastive loss.

Instead of learning from individual data samples one at a time, contrastive learning is based on the comparison amongst data pairs, i.e., it learns a representation by maximising the distance between samples organised into similar and dissimilar pairs [42]. As in other self-supervised learning tasks, such a similarity can be defined from the data itself, thus overcoming the limitation typical of supervised learning settings, where only a finite number of label pairs are available from the data. Furthermore, while some self-supervised methods need to modify the model architecture during learning, one of the main advantages of contrastive methods is that no modification to the model architecture is needed between training and fine-tuning [24]. Indeed, contrastive learning has recently achieved state of the art performance in the field of self-supervised representation learning [38].

3 Methodology

The experiments on frustration recognition were carried out on the Multimodal Game Frustration Database (MGFD) [37], an audio-visual dataset collected within the Wizard-of-Oz framework, aimed to investigate users' audio-visual expressions of frustration during game interaction on the CrazyTrophy game (cf. Fig. 1). MGFD contains 5 h of recordings from 67 healthy individuals (27 female, 40 male, with a mean age of 15 years old) experiencing different levels of spontaneous frustration elicited by a variety of (intentional) 'inconsistency'-based usability problems. Although MGFD is suitable to assess users' frustration from both audiovisual modalities [37], i.e., audio and video, it has been shown that the recognition of the emotion of frustration from speech shows a higher performance than from facial expressions [37]. This is mostly due to the fact

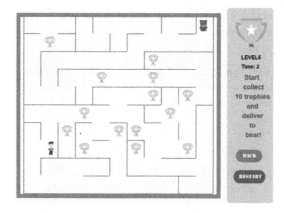

Fig. 1. Interface of the CrazyTrophy game on the sixth level. Through spoken direction words (left, right, up and down), the user controls the avatar movements in order to achieve the game's goal, i.e., to deliver the trophies to the bear (top-right of the interface). Due to a purposefully designed in-consistency usability problem, the user will receive 2 points for each collected trophy, which makes the game impossible to be won, by this intentionally eliciting frustration in the player.

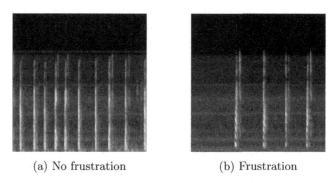

(a) No frustration   (b) Frustration

Fig. 2. Mel-spectrograms extracted from utterances of non-frustration and frustration (left and right, respectively). For non-frustration, the male user produces the words 'up, up, up, right, right, up, up, left, left'; for frustration, 'right, up, down, right'. Comparing the two Mel-spectrograms, we can observe that the user speaks considerably faster when not frustrated. The slower speaking during frustration might be due to the increased cognitive load: the player attempts to both win the game and to understand the usability problem [37].

that the participants of MGFD are Chinese, a culture in which it is particularly encouraged to conceal the own emotions [41]. In this regard, since facial expressions of emotion are generally accepted across cultures [8], we assume these are easier to control than speech; thus, frustration might be more difficult to hide in vocal than in visual cues. Due to this, in the present study, we will take only into account the audio signals for the prediction of users' frustration, since it is considered a more reliable modality in the MGFD corpus.

Table 1. Implemented distribution of speakers: m(ale), f(emale); and number (#) of instances: frustration, non frustration; for each set: Train(ing), Dev(elopment), and Test. Sums across sets (Σ) are also given.

#	Train	Dev	Test	Σ
Speakers	43	12	12	67
Gender (m:f)	28:15	6:6	6:6	40:27
Frustration	456	118	118	692
Non Frustration	3798	978	978	5754

Since in supervised learning, a model's performance might be influenced by the use of specific features, Mel-spectrograms (cf. Fig. 2), widely utilised in speech emotion recognition [35], were considered appropriate for the purposes of the present study. As a standard procedure in the field, the experiments were carried out in a speaker-independent manner, considering 43 speakers for training, 12 speakers for development (i.e., validation), and 12 speakers for test. In Table 1, descriptive statistics on the considered partitioning are given.

4   Deep Learning Approach

In this study, we utilise Residual Networks (ResNet) with two loss settings: Binary Cross-Entropy Loss (BCELoss) with Logits and Supervised Contrastive (SupCon) Loss. The machine learning models are implemented through the deep-learning framework `PyTorch` [32]. In the following, the proposed architectures for frustration recognition from speech are presented.

4.1   Binary Cross-Entropy with Logits Loss

Since we perform a binary classification task: *frustration* vs *non-frustration*, we take into account the common implementation of the BCELoss with Logits as a baseline in our experiments. The BCELoss with Logits for one sample is defined as

$$\mathcal{L}_{\text{BCE}} = -\sum_{i=1}^{2} y_i log(\hat{y}_i) = -y_1 log(\hat{y}_1) - (1 - y_1)log(1 - \hat{y}_1), \tag{1}$$

where the network assigns the probability $\hat{y}_i$ that the given sample belongs to class i. The target probability y_i of the sample belonging to class i is given by the label. Note that the right side of (1) results from the fact that only two classes are considered in binary cross-entropy, and that probabilities are normalised, which is ensured for the network's prediction by a softmax layer. As we consider a problem for which the target probabilities are either 0 or 1, only one term on the right side of (1) contributes to the loss. Nevertheless, changes to one of the two predictions $\hat{y}_i$ affects the other one via normalisation.

4.2 Supervised Contrastive Loss

The performance of a deep learning system is directly influenced by the choice and quality of the data representation [24]. For instance, labelled datasets, especially in affective computing, are often too small, something that might impair a learning system's performance. In such a scenario, focusing explicitly on learning representation, i.e., the process of learning a parametric mapping from the raw input data to a feature vector or tensor, might be beneficial [24]. Since contrastive loss can achieve a proper data representation for distinguishing different classes, it can be applied in this context. In constrastive learning, augmented samples are generated from samples of the anchor's class; then, the network extracts a strong inductive bias from both, the anchor and the augmented samples, by this attracting positive samples, i.e., those similar to the anchor, while repealing negative ones, i.e., those dissimilar. Unlike self-supervised contrastive learning [23], supervised contrastive learning draws positive samples not only from the augmentation of the sample, but also from the augmentation of other samples belonging to the same class as the anchor.

For each of N labelled samples in a given minibatch, we generate two augmentations, leading to $2N$ augmented samples in training. Our network computes the representations $\{z_l\}$ of the augmented samples in a 128-dimensional projection space. In this space, the supervised contrastive loss is defined as

$$\mathcal{L}_{\text{SC}} = \sum_{i=1}^{2N} \frac{-1}{|P(i)|} \sum_{p \in P(i)} \log \frac{\exp(z_i \cdot z_p/\tau)}{\sum\limits_{a \in A(i)} \exp(z_i \cdot z_a/\tau)}, \tag{2}$$

with the scalar product '·' and the temperature hyperparameter τ. For a given augmented sample i, considered the anchor of the loss, the set $A(i)$ contains all $2N$ indices except the ones for i and $P(i)$, i.e., the set of all positive samples. In other words, $P(i)$ contains the indices of $A(i)$ with the same label as i; where $|P(i)|$ is the cardinality of $P(i)$.

In order to train a classifier with the help of SupCon Loss, two subsequent steps are performed. First, the model learns the representations of the data, which are well separable utilising the SupCon Loss. In a second step, a classifier based on the BCELoss is trained on the learnt representations. Note that, during the training of the classifier backbone of the model is frozen, i. e., learning is disabled for any layer being involved in the calculation of the representations.

In Fig. 3, a visual representation of the procedure followed by the BCELoss and SupCon Loss for data representation is displayed. For the BCELoss training and optimisation, i.e., looking for a good data representation and for the optimal decision boundary, are performed simultaneously. Differently, when considering

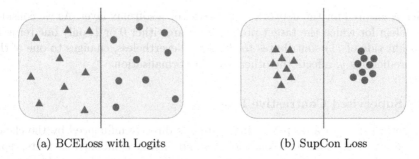

(a) BCELoss with Logits   (b) SupCon Loss

Fig. 3. Representation of the Binary Cross Entropy Loss (BCELoss) with Logits and the supervised Contrastive (SupCon) Loss, associated with a linear classifier.

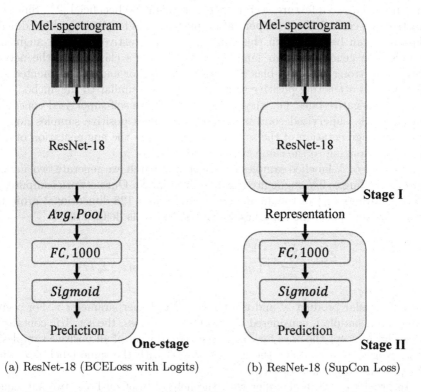

(a) ResNet-18 (BCELoss with Logits)   (b) ResNet-18 (SupCon Loss)

Fig. 4. ResNet-18 architectures: (a) with Binary Cross Entropy with Logits Loss (BCELoss); (b) with Supervised Contrastive Loss (SupCon Loss). For both architectures, in the last fully connected layer, a Sigmoid activation function is considered. For the model with SupCon Loss, we apply the ResNet model to extract a data representation; then, this is considered as input of a Multilayer Perceptron.

the supervised contrastive loss, finding a good representation and classification are two separate procedures, as at this moment, there is no sophisticated model for explicit training of a classifier using the supervised contrastive loss. It has previously been shown that this two step-training can facilitate the task of the linear classifier and therefore improve its performance [24].

4.3   ResNet Architectures

To assess the efficiency of the two evalauted losses, i.e., the BCELoss with logits and the SupCon Loss, we consider a ResNet architecture in our experiments. This was chosen since it has been shown that shallow networks with a Residual Block usually perform better than traditional convolutional neural networks [17]. Furthermore, this architecture does not need additional parameters, such as shortcuts, by this reducing computational complexity. The experiments were carried out on three types of RestNet: ResNet-18, ResNet-34, and ResNet-50; i.e., three convolutional networks with 18, 34, and 50 layers depth, respectively. The Residual Block enables the stacked layers to fit a residual mapping, i.e., the layers in a traditional network are learning the true output whereas the layers in a residual network are learning the residual. Specifically in our study, there are two steps utilising SupCon Loss. Firstly, we apply a ResNet and SupCon Loss to otain a data representation. Afterwards, we send these representation data into a classifier. In this study, we use a Multi-Layer Perceptrum (MLP) as classifier. The normalised activations of the final pooling layer are used as the representation vector. In Fig. 4, the ResNet-18 architecture with both BCELoss with logits and SupCon Loss is shown.

For the experiments with the SupCon Loss, the initial learning rate is 0.0001, the batch size is 64, training epochs are 1 000, and the SGD optimiser with momentum equalling 0.9 is considered. After getting all the data representations, these are considered as input for the MLP classifier with one hidden layer, for which, the BCELoss with logits is chosen as activation function. For the experiments with the BCELoss, we input the data directly into the different ResNet models. For comparability, the hyperparameters are setup as for the experiments with the SupCon Loss (described above).

5   Results

The models' performance is measured using Unweighted Average Recall (UAR), an evaluation metric suitable for class-imbalanced classification tasks [37]. In Table 2, the experimental results are given. For both ResNet-18 and ResNet-34, the experiments considering SupCon Loss outperform the ones given by BCELoss with logits: 79.3 % and 81.2 % vs 75.1 % and 78.5 % for Dev and Test in ResNet-18; 88.7 % and 89.9 % vs 84.2 % and 86.4 % for Dev and Test in ResNet-34; cf. SupCon Loss vs BCELoss, respectively, in Table 2.

Differently, for ResNet-50, the BCELoss with logits performs slightly better than the SupCon Loss: 84.1 % and 83.6 % vs 85.0 % and 84.8 % for Dev and Test; cf. ResNet-50 for SupCon Loss vs BCELoss, respectively, in Table 2. Yet, these differences are very small. The best UAR was achieved by ResNet-34 with SupCon Loss on the Test set (cf. 89.9 % in Table 2).

Table 2. Evaluation Results [%] of the ResNets models: ResNets-18, ResNets-34, and ResNets-50; with Supervised Contrastive Loss (SupCon loss) and Binary Cross Entropy Loss (BCELoss) with Logits. Results are presented both for the Dev(elopment) and Test sets. Unweighted Average Recall (UAR) is used as evaluation metric; the best results are highlighted in bold.

UAR [%]	Achitecture	Dev	Test
SupCon Loss	ResNets-18	79.3	81.2
	ResNets-34	88.7	**89.9**
	ResNets-50	84.1	83.6
BCELoss	ResNets-18	75.1	78.5
	ResNets-34	84.2	**86.4**
	ResNets-50	85.0	84.8

We interpret that the superiority of using the SupCon Loss is due to the fact that—through data augmentation—this architecture enables 2 views per sample; thus, its batch size is effectively double w.r.t. the BCELoss-based architecture. Furthermore, the model with BCELoss focuses on maximising the probability of recognising the correct class, but it does not take into account the samples distance to each other. Differently, the model with SupCon Loss aims to create a good representation where the samples of each class are close to each other and distant to the opposite class. Nevertheless, training an architecture with SupCon Loss is considerably more time-consuming than using BCELoss, a downside that should be taken into account.

6 Conclusion and Future Work

Our study confirmed that supervised contrastive learning is an appropriate method to recognise frustration from speech, showing to be robust in handling the inaccurate labels typical of emotional datasets. To the best of our knowledge, this is the first time that supervised contrastive learning has been applied in the detection of frustration from speech. Our experimental results demonstrate that the proposed method considerably outperforms the cross-entropy loss-based method, as shown by the comparison on the same model configuration. The promising outcomes show that supervised contrastive learning is a robust method to automatically detect users' frustration from speech, which suggest that the use of SupCon loss might also be a turning point in audio-visual applications for emotion recognition. In future work, one should further investigate how different percentages of noisy labels might alter the performance of a supervised contrastive learning framework in comparison to other loss functions.

Acknowlwdgement. The authors acknowledge funding from the German Research Foundation (DFG) under the Reinhart Koselleck Project grant AUDI0NOMOUS (No. 442218748). The responsibility lies with the authors.

References

1. Becker, S., Hinton, G.E.: Self-organizing neural network that discovers surfaces in random-dot stereograms. Nature **355**(6356), 161–163 (1992)
2. Bevan, N.: What is the difference between the purpose of usability and user experience evaluation methods. In: Proceedings of the Workshop UXEM, pp. 1–4. Uppsala, Sweden (2009)
3. Byrd, D., McLaughlin, M., Khurana, S., Landes, M., Ucar, T.: Chimp: Children interacting with machines project
4. Ceylan, C., Gutmann, M.U.: Conditional noise-contrastive estimation of unnormalised models. In: Proceedings of the International Conference on Machine Learning, pp. 726–734. Vienna, Austria (2018)
5. Chen, T., Kornblith, S., Norouzi, M., Hinton, G.: A simple framework for contrastive learning of visual representations. In: Proceedings of the International Conference on Machine Learning, pp. 1597–1607. Virtual (2020)
6. Chopra, S., Hadsell, R., LeCun, Y.: Learning a similarity metric discriminatively, with application to face verification. In: Proceedings of the Computer Society Conference on Computer Vision and Pattern Recognition. vol. 1, pp. 539–546. San Diego, USA (2005)
7. DeFalco, J.A., Rowe, J.P., Paquette, L., Georgoulas-Sherry, V., Brawner, K., Mott, B.W., Baker, R.S., Lester, J.C.: Detecting and addressing frustration in a serious game for military training. Int. J. Artif. Intell. Educ. **28**(2), 152–193 (2018)
8. Ekman, P., Keltner, D.: Universal facial expressions of emotion. In: Segerstrale U, P. Molnar, P., (eds.) Nonverbal communication: Where nature meets culture vol. 54 no. 2, pp. 27–46 (1997)
9. Franz, O., Drewitz, U., Ihme, K.: Facing driver frustration: towards real-time in-vehicle frustration estimation based on video streams of the face. In: Proceedings of the International Conference on Human-Computer Interaction, pp. 349–356. Virtual (2020)
10. Goetsu, S., Sakai, T.: Different types of voice user interface failures may cause different degrees of frustration. arXiv preprint arXiv:2002.03582 (2020)
11. Grafsgaard, J.F., Wiggins, J.B., Boyer, K.E., Wiebe, E.N., Lester, J.C.: Automatically recognizing facial indicators of frustration: a learning-centric analysis. In: Proceedings of the Humaine Association Conference on Affective Computing and Intelligent Interaction, pp. 159–165. Geneva, Switzerland (2013)
12. Grafsgaard, J.F., Wiggins, J.B., Vail, A.K., Boyer, K.E., Wiebe, E.N., Lester, J.C.: The additive value of multimodal features for predicting engagement, frustration, and learning during tutoring. In: Proc. International Conference on Multimodal Interaction, pp. 42–49. Istanbul, Turkey (2014)
13. Grewe, L., Hu, C.: Ulearn: understanding and reacting to student frustration using deep learning, mobile vision and nlp. In: Proceedings of the Signal Processing, Sensor/Information Fusion, and Target Recognition XXVIII. p. 110. Maryland, USA (2019)
14. Gutmann, M., Hyvärinen, A.: Noise-contrastive estimation: a new estimation principle for unnormalized statistical models. In: Proceedings of the International Conference on Artificial Intelligence and Statistics, pp. 297–304. Sardinia, Italy (2010)
15. Hadsell, R., Chopra, S., LeCun, Y.: Dimensionality reduction by learning an invariant mapping. In: Proceedings of the Computer Society Conference on Computer Vision and Pattern Recognition, pp. 1735–1742. New York, USA (2006)

16. Hansen, J.H., Busso, C., Zheng, Y., Sathyanarayana, A.: Driver modeling for detection and assessment of driver distraction: examples from the utdrive test bed. IEEE Signal Process. Mag. **34**(4), 130–142 (2017)
17. He, K., Zhang, X., Ren, S., Sun, J.: Deep residual learning for image recognition. In: Proceedings of the Computer Vision and Pattern Recognition, pp. 770–778. Las Vegas, USA (2016)
18. Henderson, N.L., Rowe, J.P., Mott, B.W., Brawner, K., Baker, R., Lester, J.C.: 4d affect detection: improving frustration detection in game-based learning with posture-based temporal data fusion. In: Proceedings of the Artificial Intelligence in Education, pp. 144–156. Beijing, China (2019)
19. Hertzum, M.: Frustration: a common user experience. DHRS2010 p. 11 (2010)
20. Hjelm, R.D., Fedorov, A., Lavoie-Marchildon, S., Grewal, K., Bachman, P., Trischler, A., Bengio, Y.: Learning deep representations by mutual information estimation and maximization. arXiv preprint arXiv:1808.06670 (2018)
21. Inoue, N., Goto, K.: Semi-supervised contrastive learning with generalized contrastive loss and its application to speaker recognition. In: Proceedings of the Asia-Pacific Signal and Information Processing Association Annual Summit and Conference, pp. 1641–1646. Virtual (2020)
22. Jaiswal, A., Babu, A.R., Zadeh, M.Z., Banerjee, D., Makedon, F.: A survey on contrastive self-supervised learning. Technologies **9**(1), 2 (2021)
23. Khosla, P., et al.: Supervised contrastive learning. arXiv preprint arXiv:2004.11362 (2020)
24. Le-Khac, P.H., Healy, G., Smeaton, A.F.: Contrastive representation learning: a framework and review. IEEE Access (2020)
25. Macary, M., Tahon, M., Estève, Y., Rousseau, A.: Allosat: a new call center French corpus for satisfaction and frustration analysis. In: Proceedings of the Language Resources and Evaluation Conference, pp. 1590–1597. Virtual (2020)
26. Malta, L., Miyajima, C., Kitaoka, N., Takeda, K.: Analysis of real-world driver's frustration. IEEE Trans. Intell. Transp. Syst. **12**(1), 109–118 (2010)
27. Mnih, A., Teh, Y.W.: A fast and simple algorithm for training neural probabilistic language models. arXiv preprint arXiv:1206.6426 (2012)
28. Oehl, M., Ihme, K., Drewitz, U., Pape, A.A., Cornelsen, S., Schramm, M.: Towards a frustration-aware assistant for increased in-vehicle UX: F-RELACS. In: Proceedings of the Automotive User Interfaces and Interactive Vehicular Applications, pp. 260–264. Utrecht, Netherlands (2019)
29. Oh Song, H., Xiang, Y., Jegelka, S., Savarese, S.: Deep metric learning via lifted structured feature embedding. In: Proceedings of the IEEE conference on computer vision and pattern recognition, pp. 4004–4012 (2016)
30. Parada-Cabaleiro, E., Batliner, A., Baird, A., Schuller, B.: The perception of emotional cues by children in artificial background noise. Int. J. Speech Technol. **23**(1), 169–182 (2020). https://doi.org/10.1007/s10772-020-09675-1
31. Parada-Cabaleiro, E., Costantini, G., Batliner, A., Schmitt, M., Schuller, B.W.: DEMoS: an Italian emotional speech corpus: elicitation methods, machine learning, and perception. Lang. Resour. Eval. **54**, 341–383 (2020)
32. Paszke, A., et al.: Automatic differentiation in PyTorch. In: NIPS-W (2017)
33. Schuller, B., Batliner, A.: Computational paralinguistics: emotion, affect and personality in speech and language processing. Wiley, Sussex, UK (2014)
34. Shoumy, N.J., Ang, L.M., Seng, K.P., Rahaman, D.M., Zia, T.: Multimodal big data affective analytics: a comprehensive survey using text, audio, visual and physiological signals. J. Netw. Comput. Appl. **149**, 102447 (2020)

35. Song, M., et al.: Frustration recognition from speech during game interaction using wide residual networks. Virtual Reality & Intelligent Hardware **10**, (2020)
36. Song, M., et al.: Predicting group work performance from physical handwriting features in a smart English classroom. In: Proceedings of the International Conference on Digital Signal Processing (ICDSP). Chengdu, China (2021)
37. Song, M., et al.: Audiovisual analysis for recognising frustration during gameplay: introducing the multimodal game frustration database. In: Proceedings of the Affective Computing and Intelligent Interaction, pp. 517–523. Cambridge, the UK (2019)
38. Tian, Y., Sun, C., Poole, B., Krishnan, D., Schmid, C., Isola, P.: What makes for good views for contrastive learning. arXiv preprint arXiv:2005.10243 (2020)
39. Tyng, C.M., Amin, H.U., Saad, M.N., Malik, A.S.: The influences of emotion on learning and memory. Front. Psychol. **8**, 1454 (2017)
40. Valdez, M.G., Hernández-Águila, A., Guervós, J.J.M., Soto, A.M.: Enhancing student engagement via reduction of frustration with programming assignments using machine learning. In: Proceedings of the International Joint Conference on Computational Intelligence, pp. 297–304. Funchal, Portugal (2017)
41. Wei, M., Su, J.C., Carrera, S., Lin, S.P., Yi, F.: Suppression and interpersonal harmony: a cross-cultural comparison between chinese and european americans. J. Couns. Psychol. **60**(4), 625 (2013)
42. Xiao, T., Wang, X., Efros, A.A., Darrell, T.: What should not be contrastive in contrastive learning. arXiv preprint arXiv:2008.05659 (2020)
43. Zepf, S., Stracke, T., Schmitt, A., van de Camp, F., Beyerer, J.: Towards real-time detection and mitigation of driver frustration using SVM. In: Proceedings of the Machine Learning and Applications, pp. 202–209. Florida, USA (2019)
44. Zhang, M., Ihme, K., Drewitz, U.: Discriminating drivers' fear and frustration through the dimension of power. In: Proceedings of the Humanist Conference, p. 98. Hague, Netherlands (2018)
45. Zhang, Z., Sabuncu, M.R.: Generalized cross entropy loss for training deep neural networks with noisy labels. arXiv preprint arXiv:1805.07836 (2018)
46. Zweig, G., Burges, C.J.: The microsoft research sentence completion challenge. Microsoft Research, Redmond, WA, USA, Technical report. MSR-TR-2011-129 (2011)

Parkinson's Disease Detection and Diagnosis from fMRI: A Literature Review

Guillermina Vivar-Estudillo[1], Nasim Hajari[2(✉)],
Mario-Alberta Ibarra-Manzano[1], and Irene Cheng[2]

[1] Electrical Engineering, Universidad de Guanajuato, Guanajuato, Mexico
{g.vivarestudillo,ibarram}@ugto.mx
[2] Department of Computing Science, University of Alberta, Edmonton, Canada
{hajari,locheng}@ualberta.ca

Abstract. Parkinson's disease (PD) is the second most common neurodegenerative and movement disorder affecting different groups of people, especially the aging community. According to research studies, a noticeable cause of PD is early and progressive deterioration of dopaminergic neurons in the Substantia Nigra Pars compacta (SNc). PD diagnosis from Magnetic Resonance Imaging (MRI) and functional MRI (fMRI) seems to offer promising results. However, comprehensive studies are needed to explore various brain atlases and their effects on accurate anomaly detection in substantia nigra basal ganglia. In this survey paper, we present the recent related works in automatic PD diagnosis using fMRI data. Our goal is to study and compare various automatic PD detection algorithms, bring up the current limitations and challenges in the literature and highlight the future possibilities to further improve this research area.

Keywords: Parkinson's disease detection · Neurodegenerative disorder · Neuroimaging techniques · MRI · fMRI

1 Introduction

Parkinson's disease (PD) is the second most common neurodegenerative disorder and movement disorder in the aging population [25]. PD is often associated with motor impairment including trembling, bradykinesia (slowness in movement), postural instability, gait difficulty and rigidity of the limbs. Furthermore, non-motor symptoms including olfactory dysfunction, cognitive impairment, psychiatric symptoms, sleep disorders, autonomic dysfunction, pain, and fatigue can be used in clinical diagnostics.

An important cause of PD is early and progressive deterioration of dopaminergic neurons in the Substantia Nigra pars compacta (SNc) [15,19,37]. Most of the physical symptoms of PD emerge after 50% or more of dopaminergic cells in the SNc have been lost [13,29]. The clinical symptoms and time span of

© Springer Nature Switzerland AG 2021
M. Antona and C. Stephanidis (Eds.): HCII 2021, LNCS 12768, pp. 630–638, 2021.
https://doi.org/10.1007/978-3-030-78092-0_44

PD progression is described in [15]. According to their experiment, non-motor symptoms of PD can develop up to 20 years before the development of motor symptoms.

Early diagnosis, before the onset of motor symptoms, can improve the patient's quality of life significantly by slowing down or stopping the progression of PD. However, the early non-motor symptoms of PD including constipation, depression and excessive daytime sleepiness (EDS) are quite common and can be caused by various conditions. Early PD diagnosis using neuroimaging technologies such as MRI, fMRI, CT and PET scan show promising results and researchers have been putting collective efforts in this domain in recent years.

In this review article, we present the recent works on PD diagnosis using resting fMRI data. The remaining of this paper is organized as follows: Section 2 describes the details about fMRI, its challenges and why it is a suitable neuroimaging technology for PD diagnosis. Section 3 shows the analytical methods that are used to study resting states functional connectivity. A comparison on some of the fMRI brain atlases are presented in Sect. 4. Finally Sect. 5 provides further discussion and concludes the paper.

2 Background on fMRI

Functional neuroimaging techniques are used widely in cognitive neuroscience to investigate aspects of functional specialization or segregation and functional integration in the human brain [34]. From a historical perspective, the distinction between functional segregation and functional integration relates to the dialectic between localizationism and connectionism [8]. Functional specialization suggests that different areas in the brain are specialized and functional integration refers to the interactions among specialized neuronal populations and how these interactions depend upon the sensorimotor or cognitive context [6] and is usually assessed by examining the correlation among activities in different brain areas. Moreover, functional integration is classified into functional connectivity and effective connectivity. Functional connectivity is the presence of statistical dependencies between two sets of neurophysiological data [33]. On the other hand, effective connectivity describes the causal influences that neural units exert over others [7]. The classification of the functional neuroimaging technologies is depicted in Fig. 1.

One of the existing functional neuro imaging approaches is functional Magnetic Resonance Imaging (fMRI). The fMRI has the capability to measure parameters related to several neuro-physiological functions including: changes in various metabolic byproducts, blood flow, blood volume and blood oxygenation. According to [14], fMRI provides an opportunity to observe the phenomenon called hemodynamic response (or increase in blood flow and oxygenation in the local vascular). This can be used to indirectly measure the neural activities of the brain. In other words, fMRI creates images based on the changes in the Blood Oxygenation Level-Dependent (BOLD). Thus, fMRI is a class of imaging methods developed in order to demonstrate regional, time-varying changes in brain

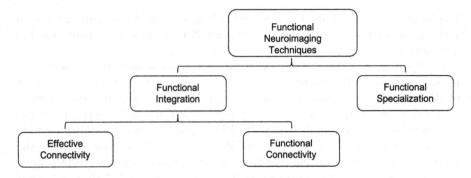

Fig. 1. Classification of functional neuroimaging techniques.

metabolism [10]. It is possible to estimate the brain activities by measuring these changes.

There are two types of fMRI for assessing the changes: task-based fMRI and resting-state fMRI. Task-based fMRI consists of assessing the BOLD signal intensity during the performance of a given behavioral task compared with the signal intensity during a control condition or rest. While in the resting-state fMRI, subjects do not need to perform any specific task. As discussed in [22], resting-state fMRI can be used in both healthy subjects and patients with various neurologic, neurosurgical, and psychiatric disorders. Also, fMRI has the ability to localize changes in brain activities with a high degree of spatial resolution [3]. This makes fMRI a good imaging technique for PD diagnosis.

Functional connectivity in PD patients can be assessed with resting-state fMRI (rs-fMRI), which measures the BOLD signal when patients are positioned in the scanner in an awake-state without performing any particular task.

There are three main challenges with PD detection and diagnosis from fMRI images:

- fMRI data has a dimensionality problem. The high dimensionality of the data (in the range of tens of millions of features) and the relatively few number of instances (in the range of hundereds of instances) can easily cause sparsity of the data in the feature space. This will cause problem for any algorithm that is based on statistical significance [28,38].
- Data preprocessing is an important step in medical applications. The main goals are to minimize the adverse influence of data artefacts, to validate statistical assumptions and to standardize the locations of brain regions across subjects in order to achieve increased validity and sensitivity in group analysis [21].
- Another common problem in medical applications is unbalanced data. Machine learning approaches usually assume that the training data is a good approximation of the real distribution of the data, which might not be the case with only a small set of instances in high dimensional space [42].

3   Analysis Methods for Resting-State Functional Connectivity

There are multiple ways to analyse rs-fMRI data, and each approach has implications in terms of what information can be extracted from the data [22, 29].

3.1   Functional Segregation Methods for Identifying Neural Networks

This model divides the brain into two regions according to their specific functions and is mainly used for brain mapping. The two main methods are Amplitude of Low Frequency Fluctuations (ALFF) and Regional Homogeneity Analysis (ReHo). ALFF is an index that describes the regional intensity of spontaneous fluctuations in resting state of the BOLD signals. ReHo is a voxel based measure that evaluates the similarity between the time series of a given voxel and the time series of its neighbouring voxels.

Singh et al. [32] used ALFF and ReHo to obtain the feature maps. They calculates the functional connectivity and correlation between the feature maps. They used PPMI IDA dataset with 10 Healthy Control (HC) (6 male, 4 female) and 10 PD patients (5 male, 5 female). The functional connectivity maps were generated with reference to cerebellum as the region of interest for PD group and control group. Paired t-test was performed on the resulting two functional connectivity map sets, and the regions of significant differences between them. The goal is to understand and explore the statistical analysis of various inherent features of neuroimages (fMRI) and compare the brain activation of the PD and normal subjects.

Tang et al. [36] used ALLF and fALFF (fractional ALFF) to measure the total power of the BOLD signals. They used a dataset with 50 PD and 50 age-and-sex matched healthy subjects. The accuracy of their method is 84.2% with 88.2% sensitivity and 80% specificity. The goal of this work is to determine whether the presence of PD could be predicted based on resting-state fluctuations in the BOLD signals.

3.2   Functional Integration Methods for Identifying Neural Networks

This model focuses on functional connectivity between different regions of the brain. It measures the degree of synchrony of BOLD time series. Researchers used methods such as Functional Connectivity Analysis (FCA), Independent Component Analysis (ICA) and Graph Theory Analysis (GTA).

Functional Connectivity Analysis (FCA). Abos et al. [1] proposed a method to discriminate PD patients according to cognitive status using machine learning. They used connection-wise patterns of functional connectivity to identify PD patients. The dataset had 38 healthy controls and 70 PD patients. They achieved a final accuracy of 80% for classifying the subjects into PD and healthy.

Independent Component Analysis (ICA). Rubbert et al. [31] used ICA to generate network definitions. They used Human Connectcome Project (HCP) and 1,000 BRAINS datasets. The evaluation was performed for each canonical network definition from HCP and 1,000 BRAINS. The average accuracy was 76.2%, average sensitivity was 81% and average specificity was 72.7%. The goal of this work was evaluation of a data-driven, model-based classification approach to classify (PD) patients from healthy controls (HC) subjects based on between-network connectivity in whole-brain rs-fMRI.

Szewczyk-Krolikowsi et al. [35] used ICA to enable isolation of resting-state brain networks. The goal is to investigate changes in the basal ganglia network (BGN) in PD patients and test whether it is possible to distinguish PD from healthy controls. Average BGN connectivity differentiated PD from controls with 100% sensitivity and 89.5% specificity. The connectivity threshold was tested on the validation cohort and achieved 85% accuracy.

Graph Theory Analysis (GTA). Kazeminejad et al. (2017) [16] used Graph Theory Analysis for quantifying neural relations, such as structural and functional differences between PD patient and healthy control (HC) groups to automatically diagnose PD. They used PPMI dataset with 18 HC (14 males, 4 female) and 19 PD (12 males, 7 female). They selected the 5 best features in the areas of cuneus (right hemisphere), precuneus (left), superior (right) and middle (both) frontal gyri. They achieved a classification accuracy of 94.6%.

Another graph based approach was proposed by Gellerup [9]. He used the graph brain as a simple model of functional connectivity patterns in the brain. He used a dataset with 45 subjects, 24 PD (17 males, 7 females) and 21 control individuals (9 males, 12 females). The final classification yields 80% accuracy, with 74% sensitivity and 93% specificity.

Table 1 summarizes the discussed approaches, datasets and their accuracy, specificity and sensitivity.

Table 1. Comparison of various fMRI-based PD detection methods in the literature.

Proposed method	Approach	Dataset characteristic	Accuracy	Specificity	Sensitivity
Tang et al. [36]	ALLF/fALLF	50 PD/50 HC	84.2%	80%	88.2%
Abos et al. [1]	FCA	70 PD/38 HC	80%	–	–
Rubbert et al. [31]	ICA	HCP/1000 BRAINS	76.2%	72.7%	81%
Szewczyk et al. [35]	ICA	–	85%	89.5%	100%
Kazeminejad et al. [16]	GTA	PPMI (19 PD/18 HC)	94.6%	–	–
Gellerup [9]	GTA	24 PD/21 HC	80%	93%	74%

4   Basal Ganglia Structure and Related Brain Atlas

As previous studies have shown, PD affects the nerve cells in basal ganglia and substantia nigra, which are deeply embedded parts of the brain [26,27]. The basal ganglia, or basal nuclei, are large masses of gray matter deep within the cerebrum, below its outer surface or cerebral cortex. The division of the structures known as basal ganglia has been confusing in the literature because various anatomists have categorized the structures differently [39]. A current literature indicates that most neuroanatomists include **caudate nucleus**, **putamen**, **globus pallidus**, **substantia nigra** and **subthalamic nucleus** in basal ganglia [30,39]. The mentioned structures sometimes group together and form other structures such as: **lentiform or lenticular nucleus** (putamen, globus pallidus), **striatum or dorsal striatum or neostriatum** (caudate, putamen) and **corpus striatum** (caudate, putamen, globus pallidus).

Over the years, researchers have proposed MRI or fMRI brain atlases that could segment basal ganglia and the corresponding structures. Lehéricy et al. [20], Melrose et al. [24] and Ferrandez et al. [5] mapped activation functions related to basal ganglia circuits into 3d brain atlases. Bardinet et al. [2] and Keuken et al. [17] proposed 3d probabilistic brain atlases that extract basal ganglia. Yaakub et al. [41] compared three different publicly available brain atlases to comprehensively analyze an adult brain from MRI images. The atlases used are Hammers-mith (HM) brain atlas [4,11,12,40], Desikan-Killiany-Tourville (DKT) classifier atlas [18] and OASIS atlas [23]. HM atlas can extract the substantia nigra region in basal ganglia, while the other two atlases do not provide this information directly. Based on various studies, substantia nigra is the brain region that is more affected by PD. However, as different researchers categorized and included slightly different brain structures into the basal ganglia region [39], identifying an appropriate and comprehensive atlas that can successfully extract the brain regions affected by PD, remains a challenging research task.

5   Discussion and Conclusion

Parkinson's disease (PD) is a neurodegenerative disorder, which is common among the elderly population. Automatic PD detection from brain medical imaging data, such as MRI, fMRI, CT and PET scan can be very beneficial to patients as it can help with the early diagnosis and treatment plan. Researches have shown that the main reason for PD development is progressive deterioration of dopaminergic neurons in the substantia nigra. This condition can occur long before the motor symptoms of the disease show up. Early intervention and treatment can improve patient's quality of life significantly.

Despite the great potential of automatic PD detection from brain medical imaging, it remains a challenging task and more researches and studies are needed. A major difficulty is the lack of unified public datasets that researchers use in their studies and extracting the brain regions that can be affected by PD conditions. Two main affected regions are substantia nigra and basal ganglia, which are the deeply embedded parts of the brain. Researchers define these regions slightly differently. Existing atlases provide very different numbers of segmented regions, from a few to over a hundred. Whether to analyse by grouping features in a larger region or a smaller neighborhood can deliver a better outcome, is still to be studied. Therefore, finding or developing a brain atlas that can identify and extract these regions is a challenging task. Another issue is analysing and comparing the performance of different automatic PD detection algorithms. These methods mostly work on local or private datasets, which are not accessible by other researchers.

In this survey paper, we presented the recent works in PD diagnostics using fMRI data. We classified the methods into two main categories including functional segregation methods and functional integration methods. The functional integration methods were further classified into functional connectivity analysis (FCA), independent component analysis (ICA) and graph theory analysis (GTA). This paper aims to shine light on some major issues in the research of automatic PD detection from fMRI data, and provide helpful information to support more in depth investigation in Parkinson's disease detection and diagnosis.

References

1. Abós, A., Baggio, H.C., Segura, B., García-Díaz, A.I., Compta, Y., Martí, M.J., Valldeoriola, F., Junqué, C.: Discriminating cognitive status in parkinson's disease through functional connectomics and machine learning. Sci. Rep. **7**, 45347 (2017)
2. Bardinet, E., et al.: A three-dimensional histological atlas of the human basal ganglia. ii. atlas deformation strategy and evaluation in deep brain stimulation for parkinson disease. J. Neurosurg. **110**(2), 208–219 (2009)
3. Brett, M., Johnsrude, I.S., Owen, A.M.: The problem of functional localization in the human brain. Nat. Rev. Neurosci. **3**(3), 243–249 (2002)
4. Faillenot, I., Heckemann, R.A., Frot, M., Hammers, A.: Macroanatomy and 3d probabilistic atlas of the human insula. Neuroimage **150**, 88–98 (2017)
5. Ferrandez, A.M., Hugueville, L., Lehéricy, S., Poline, J.B., Marsault, C., Pouthas, V.: Basal ganglia and supplementary motor area subtend duration perception: an fmri study. Neuroimage **19**(4), 1532–1544 (2003)
6. Friston, K.: Functional integration and inference in the brain. Prog. Neurobiol. **68**(2), 113–143 (2002)
7. Friston, K.J.: Functional and effective connectivity in neuroimaging: a synthesis. Hum. Brain Mapp. **2**(1–2), 56–78 (1994)
8. Friston, K.J.: Functional and effective connectivity: a review. Brain Connect. **1**(1), 13–36 (2011)
9. Gellerup, D.: Discriminating Parkinson's disease using functional connectivity and brain network analysis. Ph.D. thesis (2016)
10. Glover, G.H.: Overview of functional magnetic resonance imaging. Neurosurg. Clin. **22**(2), 133–139 (2011)
11. Gousias, I.S., Rueckert, D., Heckemann, R.A., Dyet, L.E., Boardman, J.P., Edwards, A.D., Hammers, A.: Automatic segmentation of brain mris of 2-year-olds into 83 regions of interest. Neuroimage **40**(2), 672–684 (2008)
12. Hammers, A., Allom, R., Koepp, M.J., Free, S.L., Myers, R., Lemieux, L., Mitchell, T.N., Brooks, D.J., Duncan, J.S.: Three-dimensional maximum probability atlas of the human brain, with particular reference to the temporal lobe. Hum. Brain Mapp. **19**(4), 224–247 (2003)

13. Hodaie, M., Neimat, J., Lozano, A.: The dopaminergic nigrostriatal system and parkinson's disease: Molecular events in development, disease, and cell death, and new therapeutic strategies. Neurosurgery 60, 17–28; discussion 28 (Feburary 2007)

14. Honorio, J.: Classification on brain functional magnetic resonance imaging: dimensionality, sample size, subject variability and noise. In: Frontiers of Medical Imaging, pp. 153–165. World Scientific (2015)

15. Kalia, L.V., Lang, A.E.: Parkinson's disease. The Lancet **386**(9996), 896–912 (2015)

16. Kazeminejad, A., Golbabaei, S., Soltanian-Zadeh, H.: Graph theoretical metrics and machine learning for diagnosis of parkinson's disease using rs-fmri. In: 2017 Artificial Intelligence and Signal Processing Conference (AISP), pp. 134–139. IEEE (2017)

17. Keuken, M.C., Forstmann, B.U.: A probabilistic atlas of the basal ganglia using 7 t mri. Data Brief **4**, 577–582 (2015)

18. Klein, A., Tourville, J.: 101 labeled brain images and a consistent human cortical labeling protocol. Front. Neurosci. **6**, 171 (2012)

19. Korczyn, A.D.: Parkinson's disease: one disease entity or many? In: Diagnosis and Treatment of Parkinson's Disease – State of the Art, pp. 107–111. Springer Vienna, Vienna (1999). https://doi.org/10.1007/978-3-7091-6360-3_5

20. Lehéricy, S., Bardinet, E., Tremblay, L., Van de Moortele, P.F., Pochon, J.B., Dormont, D., Kim, D.S., Yelnik, J., Ugurbil, K.: Motor control in basal ganglia circuits using fmri and brain atlas approaches. Cereb. Cortex **16**(2), 149–161 (2006)

21. Lindquist, M.A.: The statistical analysis of fmri data. Stat. Sci. **23**(4), 439–464 (2008)

22. Lv, H., Wang, Z., Tong, E., Williams, L.M., Zaharchuk, G., Zeineh, M., Goldstein-Piekarski, A.N., Ball, T.M., Liao, C., Wintermark, M.: Resting-state functional mri: everything that nonexperts have always wanted to know. Am. J. Neuroradiol. **39**(8), 1390–1399 (2018)

23. Marcus, D.S., Wang, T.H., Parker, J., Csernansky, J.G., Morris, J.C., Buckner, R.L.: Open access series of imaging studies (oasis): cross-sectional mri data in young, middle aged, nondemented, and demented older adults. J. Cogn. Neurosci. **19**(9), 1498–1507 (2007)

24. Melrose, R.J., Poulin, R.M., Stern, C.E.: An fmri investigation of the role of the basal ganglia in reasoning. Brain Res. **1142**, 146–158 (2007)

25. Mhyre, T.R., Boyd, J.T., Hamill, R.W., Maguire-Zeiss, K.A.: Parkinson's Disease, pp. 389–455. Springer, Netherlands, Dordrecht (2012)

26. Obeso, J.A., Marin, C., Rodriguez-Oroz, C., Blesa, J., Benitez-Temiño, B., Mena-Segovia, J., Rodríguez, M., Olanow, C.W.: The basal ganglia in parkinson's disease: current concepts and unexplained observations. Ann. Neurol. Off. J. Am. Neurol. Assoc. Child Neurol. Soc. **64**(S2), S30–S46 (2008)

27. Obeso, J.A., Rodriguez-Oroz, M.C., Rodriguez, M., Lanciego, J.L., Artieda, J., Gonzalo, N., Olanow, C.W.: Pathophysiology of the basal ganglia in parkinson's disease. Trends Neurosci. **23**, S8–S19 (2000)

28. Poldrack, R.A., Mumford, J.A., Nichols, T.E.: Handbook of Functional MRI Data Analysis. Cambridge University Press, Cambridge (2011)

29. Prodoehl, J., Burciu, R., Vaillancourt, D.: Resting state functional magnetic resonance imaging in parkinson's disease. Curr. Neurol. Neurosci. Rep. **14**(6), 448 (2014)

30. Rea, P.: Chapter 2 - essential anatomy and function of the brain. In: Essential Clinical Anatomy of the Nervous System, pp. 51–76. Academic Press, San Diego (2015)

31. Rubbert, C., Mathys, C., Jockwitz, C., Hartmann, C.J., Eickhoff, S.B., Hoffs-taedter, F., Caspers, S., Eickhoff, C.R., Sigl, B., Teichert, N.A., et al.: Machine-learning identifies parkinson's disease patients based on resting-state between-network functional connectivity. Br. J. Radiol. **92**(1101), 20180886 (2019)

32. Singh, A., Mehra, N., Singh, S., Akther, S., Jain, C., Khare, V.: Analysis and iden-tification of Parkinson disease based on FMRI. Int. J. Electron. Electr. Comput. Syst. IJEECS **6**(1), 201–205 (2017)

33. Stephan, K., Friston, K.: Functional connectivity. In: Encyclopedia of Neuroscience, pp. 391–397. Academic Press, Oxford (2009)

34. Stephan, K., Friston, K.: Analyzing effective connectivity with FMRI. Wiley Inter-disciplinary Reviews: Cognitive Science 1 (05 2010)

35. Szewczyk-Krolikowski, K., et al.: Functional connectivity in the basal ganglia net-work differentiates pd patients from controls. Neurology **83**(3), 208–214 (2014)

36. Tang, Y., et al.: Identifying the presence of parkinson's disease using low-frequency fluctuations in bold signals. Neurosci. Lett. **645**, 1–6 (2017)

37. Thomas, B., Beal, M.F.: Parkinson's disease. Hum. Mol. Genet. **16**(R2), R183–R194 (2007)

38. Vega Romero, R.I.: The challenge of applying machine learning techniques to diag-nose schizophrenia using multi-site FMRI data (2017)

39. Webb, W.G.: 2 - organization of the nervous system i. In: Neurology for the Speech-Language Pathologist (Sixth Edition), pp. 13–43. Mosby, sixth edition edn. (2017)

40. Wild, H.M., Heckemann, R.A., Studholme, C., Hammers, A.: Gyri of the human parietal lobe: Volumes, spatial extents, automatic labelling, and probabilistic atlases. PloS one **12**(8), e0180866 (2017)

41. Yaakub, S.N., Heckemann, R.A., Keller, S.S., McGinnity, C.J., Weber, B., Ham-mers, A.: On brain atlas choice and automatic segmentation methods: a comparison of maper & freesurfer using three atlas databases. Sci. Rep. **10**(1), 1–15 (2020)

42. Yu, L., Liu, H.: Feature selection for high-dimensional data: a fast correlation-based filter solution. In: Proceedings of the 20th international conference on machine learning (ICML-03), pp. 856–863 (2003)

State of the Art and Future Challenges of the Portrayal of Facial Nonmanual Signals by Signing Avatar

Rosalee Wolfe[1,2(✉)], John McDonald[1(✉)], Ronan Johnson[1], Robyn Moncrief[1],
Andrew Alexander[1], Ben Sturr[1], Sydney Klinghoffer[1], Fiona Conneely[1],
Maria Saenz[1], and Shatabdi Choudhry[1]

[1] DePaul University, Chicago, USA
{rwolfe,sjohn165,rkelley5,bsturr,sklingho,msaenz,
schoud12}@depaul.edu, jmcdonald@cs.depaul.edu
[2] Institute of Language and Speech Processing, Athens, Greece

Abstract. Researchers have been developing avatars to portray sign languages as a necessary component of automatic translation systems between signed and spoken languages. Although sign language avatar technology has improved significantly in recent years, there are still open questions as to how best portray the linguistic and paralinguistic information that occurs on a signer's face. Three interdisciplinary themes influence the current state of the art. The first, linguistic discovery, defines the facial activity that an avatar must carry out. The second, Computer Generated Imagery (CGI), supplies the tools and technology required to build avatars, and which determines the fidelity of an avatar's appearance. In contrast, the third theme, Sign Language Representation Systems, determines the fidelity of timing of facial co-occurrences. This paper discusses the current state of the art and demonstrates how these themes contribute to the overall goal of creating avatars that can produce legible signed utterances that are acceptable to viewers.

Keywords: Sign language · Nonmanual signals · Avatars

1 Introduction

For the past 20 years, researchers have been developing avatars to portray sign languages. The goal of these signing avatars is to display signed languages as 3D animation, in lieu of displaying video recordings of human signers. The appeal of signing avatars is in their flexibility and consistency. It is easier to change or add a sign to an utterance when using an avatar than it is to change or add a sign to a previously recorded video. Further, when a project requires repeated production sessions over a period of several weeks or months, it is easier to maintain presentation consistency in the lighting, camera angle, clothing, and hair length of an avatar than it is when recording human signers.

Signing avatars are also a necessary component of automatic translation systems. In situations where the interaction is highly predictable but an interpreter will never be

© Springer Nature Switzerland AG 2021
M. Antona and C. Stephanidis (Eds.): HCII 2021, LNCS 12768, pp. 639–655, 2021.
https://doi.org/10.1007/978-3-030-78092-0_45

available, a signing avatar can work in conjunction with an automatic translation system to provide rudimentary communication. Prototypes have translated weather reports [1, 2], facilitated interactions with a post office clerk [3] and airport security personnel [4], and created Deaf-accessible public address systems [5].

Although avatar technology has improved significantly in recent years, there are still open questions about how best to display the linguistic and pragmatic information that occurs on a signer's face. The focus of this paper is a discussion of the potential for linguistics and computer graphics to work together to portray facial nonmanual signals effectively through signing avatar technology.

2 Three Themes

An in-depth understanding of the state of the art requires examining several multidisciplinary themes. The first theme is the linguistic discovery of the purpose and properties of facial nonmanual signals, and the second is a visual recounting of the developments in computer generated imagery (CGI) that make the computer display of signing possible. The third theme is sign language representation systems which direct an avatar's face to produce nonmanual signals dictated by linguistics. Combining the best practices of these three areas will contribute to an improved clarity in avatar signing, which will lead to a greater acceptance of avatar portrayal of nonmanual signals as perceived by the target users.

These three themes provide a context for considering current challenges in portraying facial nonmanual signals, which currently lag the larger manual motions of signing in current avatars. These challenges include the ramifications of choosing a cartoon style versus human realism, improving avatar motion, acquiring finer detail in corpora for more in-depth study of facial detail, adapting an avatar to produce multiple sign languages and considering legibility on different display devices.

Although there are also nonmanuals that occur on the body, this paper will focus on the linguistic discoveries involving only the facial articulators. It omits nonmanual signals arising from the body (shifts, leans), the head (tilt, nod, shake, turn), and teeth.

2.1 Linguistic Discovery

Without the insights into the structure and meaning of signed languages, it would be impossible to create avatar technology with sufficient flexibility to produce animations that would be perceived as intelligible signed language. As a discipline, sign language linguistics has evolved rapidly. Less than twenty years after the pioneering efforts of Stokoe [6] which focused mainly on a signer's hands, Baker's [7] extensive study of American Sign Language (ASL) showed that a signer's face conveys more than emotion. She observed that although affect can alter the form of a syntactic signal, the signal is still readily perceivable.

In later work, Baker noted that syntactic constituents primarily occur on the upper half of the face, including topic marking, yes/no, wh-, and rhetorical questions [8]. Consistent with this finding, subsequent researchers found that signers use eye gaze to create synatic agreement by marking referents [9, 10] and they use eye blinks to mark prosodic as well as syntactic phrases [11].

In her 1983 work, Baker also noted that activity on the lower part of a signer's face tends to modify individual signs or phrases and to convey adjectival or adverbial information. An example is the use of pursed lips to convey that a surface is smooth [12]. Facial nonmanual signals can also operate on the phonemic level as seen in ASL when the presence of the nonmanual 'th' changes the lexical item LATE to NOT-YET [13].

Another facial activity occuring on the lower face is *mouthing*, which is derived from words in the circumambient spoken language. Linguists recognize mouthing as part of sign languages found in the Netherlands, the United Kingdom, Sweden, Germany, France, and the German-speaking regions of Switzerland [14–17].

This short survey of linguistic discoveries demonstrates that facial articulators can convey information at all linguistic levels, ranging from the prosodic down to the phonemic. In addition, pragmatic information can co-occur with linguistic informa-tion. Figure 1 is a diagram that summarizes the participation of facial articulators in producing linguistic and paralinguistic information.

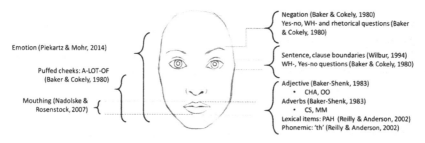

Fig. 1. Facial articulators

The segmentation of linguistic processes to particular areas of the face is a general characterization, but not a strict classification. Even though a linguistic phenomenon may be categorized as occurring on a particular facial feature, other features can participate in its production, but to a lesser degree. Figure 2 demonstrates how brow height and eye aperture can change when a signer produces the ASL adverbial modifier CS on the lower part of the face.

Another counterexample to the rule of thumb that "the upper face is used for syntactic and prosodic processes" is the role that the upper face plays in producing the ASL nonmanual VERY SMOOTH. Figure 3 demonstrates how a brow lowering and an eye squint can intensify the nonmanual adjective SMOOTH [18].

Further, facial nonmanual signals can co-occur and each can have an influence on a single facial feature. Consider a scenario where a signer poses a yes/no question about whether a surface is very smooth but does so in a concerned manner. In this case, affect, syntax and an adverbial modifier will have an influence on the brows. Lastly, these co-occurring facial nonmanual signals can have different spans and varying

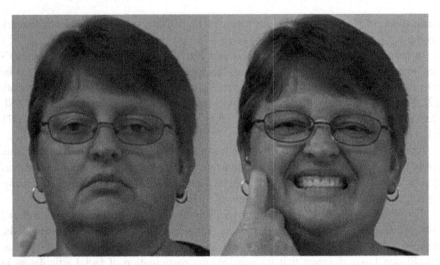

Fig. 2. Comparison of a neutral face and the nonmanual marker CS. Note that the upper face participates in the production of the adverbial modifier [19].

intensities. To accommodate this complexity Wilbur [20] proposes a layering of prosodic and phonological events.

Because linguistics forms the basis of the software specifications for an avatar, there are several takeaways to keep in mind when developing an avatar capable of facial nonmanual expressions:

- Facial articulators can convey information at all linguistic levels.
- A single facial articulator can be responsible for conveying multiple co-occurring nonmanual signals.
- Co-occurring facial nonmanual signals can have different onsets, durations, and intensity envelopes.

2.2 Advancements in Computer Generated Imagery (CGI)

The limitations of Computer Generated Imagery (CGI) pose challenges to creating facial nonmanual signals that are correct, believable and acceptable. One of the contributing barriers is the difficulty of portraying a human face that is convincing in appearance and which moves in a natural, lifelike manner.

Researchers are making excellent progress in creating an appealing and realistic rendering of human skin and cartilage [21], but the most efficient and effective representation of the underlying facial musculature is still an open question. Facial musculature varies greatly among individuals and some facial muscles are not present in all humans.

CGI depicting human figures began with primitive representations. The first recording of a computer-generated animation depicting human figures was *A Computer Generated Ballet* [22]. Figure 4 shows a frame from the movie. The dancers were simplistic stick figures drawn using white lines on a dark background.

Fig. 3. A lowered brow and squinted eyes intensity the nonmanual SMOOTH to convey VERY_SMOOTH.

It would be another twenty years twenty years before animators and developers would tackle the challenge of portraying emotions through facial expressions to support a storyline. *Tony de Peltrie* (Fig. 5) features an aging lounge pianist. His entire face reflects his thoughts and moods as he wistfully remembers the success of his youth [23].

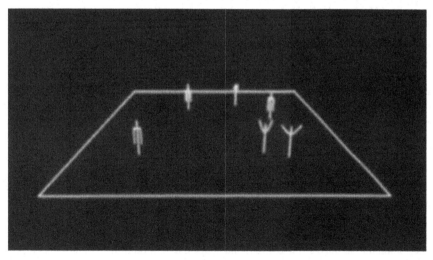

Fig. 4. *A Computer Generated Ballet* [22].

With this expressivity came greater complexity. Whereas the stick figures of Noll's *Ballet* used less than fifty line segments, *Tony* required thousands. It took three years to create the 7.5 min film.

Fig. 5. Tony de Peltrie [23].

Although *Tony* won numerous international prizes for innovations in computer animation and was hailed as groundbreaking, in recent years, younger viewers have often expressed an aversion to the Tony character. This is an example of the phenomenon known as the *uncanny valley* [24].

The robotics researcher Mori proposed that a person's reaction to a robot would change from empathy to aversion as its face approached, but failed to obtain, a lifelike appearance. He described this change as the uncanny valley, as seen in Fig. 6. This effect is intensified if the robot is in motion. If it appeared eerie in a still pose, it will appear even eerier in motion. Researchers have since found that this relationship also applies to computer generated human characters as well.

This is the reason that the first computer-generated movies deliberately portrayed eerie or alien humanoids. The pseudopod character in *The Abyss* (1989), capitalized on the uncanny valley. Another approach is to deliberately choose to give characters a cartoon-like look, as in as in *Toy Story* (1995) and *Avatar* (2009). Since their appearance is less human-like, they avoid the uncanny valley, and viewers are more accepting of their motion.

Although there was much enthusiasm in the early days of CGI, the reality is that creating animations takes a tremendous amount of manual labor, and the results aren't always that great to look at. Since the advent of CGI, two avenues of research have attempted to ameliorate the problem. One of them reduces the amount of manual labor required and the second attempts produce better visual effects. Several approaches to reducing manual labor include using blend shapes, a method of using static facial poses (the shapes) that are blended together to create motion moving from pose to pose [25], Improved 3D scanning techniques to record the shape of character faces and facial movement through *motion capture* now permit artists to combine the face of one virtual actor with the movements of another [26].

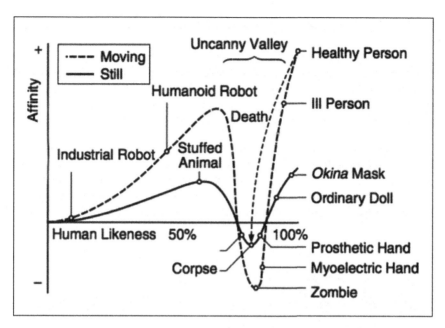

Fig. 6. The uncanny value is intensified by movement. After [24].

Other time-savers involve building libraries of frequently used gestures for repeated use in animation. One example is automatic lip sync. Manually animating lips to move when a character speaks is time consuming. First, artists create a library of *visemes*. A viseme is a shape that lips take when a speaker is producing a particular phoneme. See Fig. 7 for an example set of visemes for spoken English. Software deconstructs the character dialog into phonemes and chooses a corresponding viseme from the library for portrayal in the animation [27].

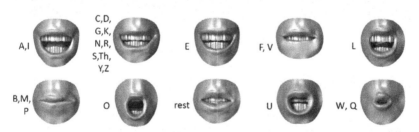

Fig. 7. Visemes and corresponding phonemes commonly used in automatic lip sync of spoken English. After Preston Blair [28].

As a result of the introduction of these time-saving techniques and the advent of ever-faster computers, movie effects have become increasingly realistic. Figure 8 shows the first extreme close-up of a CGI face, which appeared in the "Super Burly Brawl" scene in *The Matrix Revolutions* when the character Smith sustains a violent face punch [29].

A question naturally arises, "If movie effects are so realistic, why are avatars so unrealistic?" The answer lies in the time it takes to create the movies from the artist's work. Although many time-saving techniques have made it quicker for artists to animate, render times are still a bottleneck. Quoting Craig Good, a digital artist who worked at Pixar [30]:

There's something I call The Law of Constancy of Pain: Back in 1983 it took between half an hour and around 8 hours to render a frame… Today, computers are literally millions of times more powerful. And guess how long it takes Pixar to render a frame [today]? Yup. Between half an hour and around 8 hours, with a typical average of a couple or three hours. Rendering time has stayed essentially flat for three decades.

Fig. 8. "Super Burly Brawl" The Matrix Revolutions [29].

Such long rendering times are incompatible with interactive graphics applications, such as video games and signing avatar technology which must be rendered at a rate of at least 25 frames per second. Interactive graphics must respond instantly to user commands. Compare Fig. 9, a frame from the "Super Burly Brawl" scene of the video game *Matrix Online 2005* and Fig. 8, a frame from the movie. Figure 9 contains more primitive characters in a simpler environment. These reductions in realism result in greater interactivity.

Fig. 9. "Super Burly Brawl" *Matrix Online* video game released in 2005 [31].

The discussion of CGI has revealed the following insights into developing avatar technology:

– Avoid the uncanny valley,
– Avatars need the same level of responsiveness found in video games,
– Avatars also need the realism of CGI in movies,
– Creating animation is still an expensive process, even with automation.

2.3 Sign Language Representations

The third theme considers alternatives in representation which can direct an avatar's face to produce nonmanual signals. Multiple approaches to representing sign language have been explored in the past twenty years, varying degrees of success. Categories of these approaches include.

1. general-purpose representations adapted for sign languages
2. sign language notation and annotation systems
3. sign language representations supporting prosody.

A representation used in early analyses of facial nonmanual signals is the Facial Action Coding System (FACS), which records movements of individual muscles on a face from visually observing small instantaneous changes that occur [32]. Although used extensively in psychology and computer vision research, FACS could not encode the motivation for facial movements. For example, although FACS can effectively represent raised brows, it does not facilitate recording *why* the raise occurred. It may be due to syntactic or affective reasons or both [33].

Another general-purpose representation is MPEG-4 H-Anim, the Humanoid Animation International Standard [34]. It facilitates the display of 3D avatars in web browsers on any device, which means that applications using this representation will work on any computer or smart phone running an H-Anim enabled browser. H-Anim's Facial Animation Parameters dictate an avatar's facial movement. See Fig. 10 for a list of facial feature points in the representation.

Unfortunately, H-Anim is a coarse representation that does not capture important facial details. Figure 10 shows that each eye lid only has one control to open or close it. This suffices for animating an eye blink but is insufficient even to represent basic emotions. On the left side Fig. 11 is an eye of an angry face and on the right is the eye of a sad face. In each case, the upper lid forms a complex curve. A single lid control is not be able to define a curve.

The second category mentioned in the beginning of this section is sign language notation and annotation systems. Designed by researchers with in-depth knowledge of sign languages, these systems have the advantage recording linguistic intent. The earliest of these was Stokoe notation, the first phonemic notation for signed language [35]. Created for ASL, it provided for the notation of handshape (dez), location (tab), and movement (sig), but it did not provide for nonmanual signals.

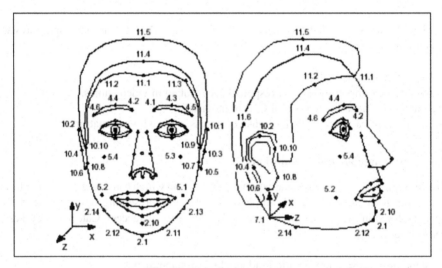

Fig. 10. H-Anim feature points

In contrast, HamNoSys (the Hamburg Notation System) can specify handshape, palm orientation, location, movement and nonmanual signals [36]. See Fig. 12 for an example. It is a phonetic system, so it is not limited to a particular sign language language. In fact, the Dicta-Sign project [37] used HamNoSys to create corpora in German, French, British and Greek sign languages.

One advantage of notation systems is that they are amenable to automatic analysis through statistical tools. However, these notation systems can express only sparse information about the timing of facial events within a sign or throughout a sentence. They do not effectively specify timing of co-occurrences.

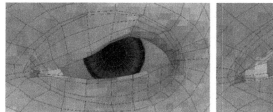

Fig. 11. Left: Angry eye. Right: Sad eye. Courtesy of Ronan Johnson

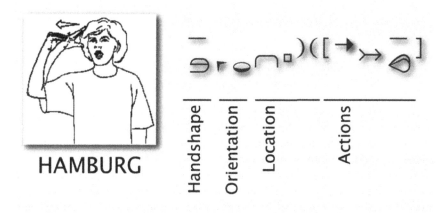

Fig. 12. Annotating the DGS sign HAMBURG: sign sketch and HamNoSys notation

Linguists have posited that are as many as fourteen channels of activity – on the head, hands and arms – where behaviors could co-occur [12]. Most of these occur on the face. Producing the onset, duration and intensity envelope, of each facial event is essential for clear communication via avatar.

Two useful annotation systems that can record co-occurrences are iLex [38] and ELAN [39]. Both systems support time-based annotations of video. They allow for the definition of tiers that correspond to the linguistic channels identified by researchers. Figure 13 is a partial screenshot from an ELAN file which contains multiple tiers representing nonmanual signals. There are many instances of co-occurrence in this short example.

The last category of representations support prosody. Knowledge of prosody enables avatars to produce natural, easy-to-read signed sentences. Without it, the animated signing "will be as unacceptable and potentially as difficult to understand as robotic speech lacking cues to phrasing, stress and intonation." [41].

Although Wilbur had previously identified several prosodic elements that are predictable enough for automation, many nonmanual signals are not as predictable and require additional information. To accomplish this, Adamo-Villani and Wilbur created

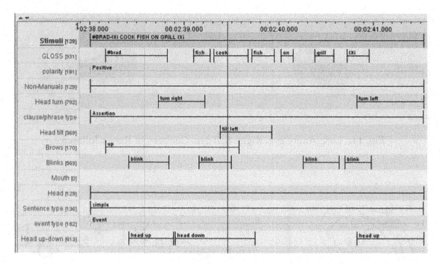

Fig. 13. An ELAN annotation with 14 tiers [40].

the representation ASL-Pro (ASL with prosody). The representation is time-based, similar to ELAN or iLex, but the annotations contain sufficient geometric information that an avatar can produce more lifelike motion.

A second representation supporting prosody is a hybrid approach [42] that relies on a mixture of traditional and procedural animation to build the basic elements for a discourse produced by avatar. A hierarchical description called AZee provides the coordination and timing of the animation data to create co-occurrences [43]. The goal is to build directly from linguistic descriptions rather than sequences of individual phonemes. Because it works with larger segments of the discourse, it achieves more natural animation.

Researchers have a wide variety of alternatives for representing sign languages for avatar display. When choosing, the following questions may prove useful:

- Generality of representation: Is it one that is project specific, or does it lend itself to data reuse for additional linguistic research?
- Availability of supporting software: Are there facilities to input, validate, store, retrieve, analyze, and display signed utterances?
- Level of detail of the representation: Does the representation facilitate linguistic abstraction or details of the timing and coordination of facial movements, or both?
- Acceptance within the research community: is the representation prevalent enough that there is a community to discuss challenges and future directions?

3 State of the Art

From the above description of the three themes – linguistic discovery, the limitations of CGI and the suitability of sign language representations – it is clear that substantial challenges remain. Recall that the goal is to create avatars that can portray facial nonmanual signals sufficiently clearly and correctly that the utterances they produce are acceptable to viewers.

All current avatars remain works-in-progress. Although there are avatars whose appearance is appealing and there are avatar systems that offer different characters, no avatar system to date can create convincing motion by drawing from a library of signs to synthesize the full range of new signed utterances. To be sure, there are many avatars that can display previously animated utterances but no one system can.

- retrieve lexical items from a database,
- modify their motion to add adverbial or adjectival modifiers,
- designate the characters in constructed dialog,
- respect the prosody,
- but still paying attention to the co-occurrence of facial articulators.

All of these are necessary for viewer comprehension and acceptance.

In the end, the avatar must be judged by the naturalness of its communication, the comprehensibility of the signing it generates and its acceptance by the Deaf community. To date, there has been little in the way of evaluations by end users of avatar comprehensibility [44]. The best published results from commercial efforts to date put comprehension rates at 52% [45]. This comprehension rate is not sufficient for effective communication.

The acceptability issue for current avatars is a tradeoff between the ability to generate new utterances and the naturalness of resulting motion. Motion capture systems, that supply some of the most natural human motion for pre-recorded signing, produce motion that is very difficult to edit and re-combine. Pre-recorded hand animation also produces very natural motion and is easier to edit but suffers from the high cost of animator time. On the other hand, synthesis driven directly from linguistic specification via mathematical procedural models, while very flexible, produces highly robotic motion. Hybrid systems that try to combine the naturalness of pre-recorded motion with the flexibility of procedural animation fall in between these two extremes.

4 Current Challenges and Future Directions

Several research directions will aid in creating an avatar that will produce credible facial nonmanual signals. The first direction is toward *integration*. Building on current work will achieve a new representation that will accommodate any sign language at any level of detail, ranging from the sublinguistic to the linguistic to the paralinguistic through the use of multiple channels. Researchers will still have the option of annotating the linguistic events that are pertinent to their study, but their data will be open to further modifications that add or refine annotations. Representing multiple channels is essential for specifying events that co-occur but do not coincide. All of the channels contribute to building message clarity for a viewer. Without this data, an avatar would be limited to producing motion based on developer's heuristics or an animator's best estimate.

The sublinguistic level must be part of the integration efforts because it is essential to legibility and acceptability of the signing produced by an avatar. Developers of a new sign language representation will need to work closely with avatar developers to ensure that the multiple methods for characterizing motion mentioned in Sect. 3 are specified, including motion capture, manual animation, procedural modeling, and constraint specification. Each of these has its strengths and will be beneficial to an avatar system.

A second research direction is toward *flexibility*. Any sign language representation needs to be sufficiently flexible to accommodate new discoveries in linguistics. Further, the avatar representation needs the flexibility to adapt its appearance to the needs of the audience. These can be surface changes such as modifications in the color of the hair, skin and clothing, or deeper changes such as accommodating diversity in ethnicity, age, and gender.

The last research direction is the development of evaluation techniques leading to standards. Most of the studies to date that have been shared with the research community involve such metrics as comprehensibility and appeal. These are common summative measures which are evaluated after a project has been completed. Since avatar technology is still a work-in-progress, developers need more *formative* feedback. Granted, much user feedback from a formative evaluation is qualitative which is more difficult to analyze.

Vital to creating a basis for formative evaluation is a way to generate the test stimuli (rendered animations) that an evaluation would require. Developing a set of *challenge data* for the avatar to perform would aid researchers carrying out formative evaluations. A set of challenge data could contain examples of facial nonmanual signals that have proved to be problematic in the past, such as lip coarticulation and eye aperture, as well as combining multiple channels of co-occurring linguistic events.

Developing challenge data and new methods for carrying out formative evaluation will aid in more rapid advancement in avatar technology. Such tools will save developers the work of creating test instruments "from scratch" and will provide a standard of comparison between systems.

5   Conclusion

Avatar technology is a new field, and the display of facial nonmanual signals is still an open question. The three themes that will support new innovations toward this goal are sign language linguistics, computer generated imagery and sign language representation. Possible directions of new research include the integration of current sign language representations to incorporate not only linguistic events, but sub-linguistic and paralinguistic events, and planning for sufficient flexibility to accommodate necessary changes based on linguistic discoveries and audience preference. Finally, developing challenge data and new evaluation techniques will help define the specification of new standards for avatar development.

References

1. Grieve-Smith, A.B.: English to American Sign Language machine translation of weather reports. In: Proceedings of the Second High Desert Student Conference in Linguistics (HDSL2), Albuquerque, NM (1999)

2. Verlinden, M., Zwitserlood, I., Frowein, H.: Multimedia with animated sign language for deaf learners. In: EdMedia+ Innovate Learning (2005)
3. Cox, S., et al.: The development and evaluation of a speech-to-sign translation system to assist transactions. Int. J. Hum.-Comput. Interact. **16**, 141–161 (2003)
4. Furst, J., Alkoby, K., Lancaster, G., McDonald, J., Wolfe, R.: Making airport security accessible to the deaf. In: Proceedings of the Fifth IASTED International Conference on Computer Graphics and Imaging, Kaua'i, HI (2002)
5. Ebling, S., Glauert, J.: Building a Swiss German Sign Language avatar with JASigning and evaluating it among the deaf community. Univ. Access Inf. Soc. **15**(4), 577–587 (2015)
6. Stokoe, W.C.: Sign Language Structure: An Outline of the Visual Communication Systems of the American Deaf (Studies in Linguistics, Occasional Papers 8). University of Buffalo, Buffalo, NY (1960)
7. Baker, C.: Focusing on the nonmanual components of American Sign Language. Understanding Language Through Sign Language Research (1978)
8. Baker-Shenk, C.: A Microanalysis of the Nonmanual Components of Questions in American Sign Language (1983)
9. Bellugi, U., Fischer, S.: A comparison of sign language and spoken language. Cognition **1**, 173–200 (1972)
10. Bahan, B.: Non-manual Realization of Agreement in American Sign Language (1997)
11. Wilbur, R.B.: Eyeblinks and ASL phrase structure. Sign Lang. Stud. **1084**(1), 221–240 (1994)
12. Wilbur, R.B.: Effects of varying rate of signing on ASL manual signs and nonmanual markers. Lang. Speech **52**, 245–285 (2009)
13. Reilly, I., Anderson, D.: FACES: the aquisition of non-manual morphology in ASL. Direct. Sign Lang. Acquisit. **2**, 159–182 (2002)
14. Crasborn, O.A., Van Der Kooij, E., Waters, D., Woll, B., Mesch, J.: Frequency distribution and spreading behavior of different types of mouth actions in three sign languages. Sign Lang. Linguist. **11**(1), 45–67 (2008)
15. Elliott, E.A., Jacobs, A.M.: Facial expressions, emotions, and sign languages. Front. Psychol. **4**, 115 (2013)
16. Sallandre, M.: Simultaneity in French sign language discourse. In: Amsterdam Studies in the Theory and History of Linguistic Science Series 4, vol. 281, p. 103 (2007)
17. Braem, P.B.: Functions of the mouthing component in the signing of deaf early and late learners of Swiss German Sign Language. In: Brentari, D. (ed.) Foreign Vocabulary in Sign Languages: A Cross-Linguistic Investigation of Word Formation, pp. 1–47. Erlbaum, Mahwah (2001)
18. Shumaker, C.: NMS Facial Expression, 2 Feb 2016. https://www.youtube.com/watch?v=NbbNwVwdfGg. [Accessed 15 Apr 2020]
19. Foster, H.: Non-Manual Markers in ASL/North Carolina Division of Services for the Deaf and Hard of Hearing, 12 Sept 2019. https://www.youtube.com/watch?v=8HIc0IRe-dE&feature=youtu.be
20. Wilbur, R.: Phonological and prosodic layering of nonmanuals in American Sign Language. In: Emmrey, K., Lane, H.L., Bellugi, U., Klima, E. (eds.) The Signs of Language Revisited: Festscrift for Ursula Bellugi and Edward Klima, pp. 213-241 (2000)
21. Nunes, A., Maciel, A., Meyer, G., John, N., Baranoski, G., Walter, M.: Appearance modelling of living human tissues. Comput. Graph. Forum **38**(6), 43–65 (2019)
22. Noll, A.M.: Computer-generated Three-dimensional Movies. Bell Telephone Laboratories (1965)
23. Bergeron, P., Lachapelle, P., Langlois, D., Robidoux, P. (Directors): Tony de Peltrie. [Film] (1985)
24. Mori, M.: The uncanny valley. Energy **7**(4), 33–35 (1970)

25. Marmor, D.: Facial Rigging Blend Shape, 22 Oct 2011. http://www.cgfeedback.com/cgfeed back/showthread.php?t=2119. Accessed 30 Mar 2020

26. Edwards, G. (Director): Rogue One: A Star Wars Story [Film]. Lucasefilm; Walt Disney Pictures; Allison Shearmur Productions, USA (2016)

27. Xu, Y., Feng, A.W., Marsella, S., Shapiro, A.: A practical and configurable lip sync method for games. In: Proceedings of Motion on Games, pp. 131–140 (2013)

28. Martin, G.C.: Preston Blair phoneme series, 4 May 2018 http://www.garycmartin.com/ mouth_shapes.html

29. Wachowski, L., Wachowski, L. (Directors): The Matrix Revolutions [Film]. Warner Bros, USA (2003)

30. Good, C.: When CGI artists say it takes "X" amount of time to render a frame, are they talking literally or figuratively? 11 Sep 2016. https://www.quora.com/When-CGI-artists-say-it-takes-X-amount-of-time-to-render-a-frame-are-they-talking-literally-or-figuratively

31. Royce, B: The Matrix is getting a fourth movie – so can we have The Matrix Online back now please?, 21 Aug 2019. https://massivelyop.com/2019/08/21/the-matrix-is-getting-a-fou rth-movie-so-can-we-have-the-matrix-online-back-now-please/. Accessed 16 Apr 2020

32. Ekman, R.: What the Face Reveals: Basic and Applied Studies of Spontaneous Expression Using the Facial Action Coding System (FACS). Oxford University Press, USA (1997)

33. Weast, T.P.: Questions in American Sign Language: A quantitative analysis of raised and lowered eyebrows. ProQuest, Ann Arbor, MI (2008)

34. Garchery, S., Boulic, R., Capin, T.: Standards for Virtual Human Animation: H-ANIM and MPEG4 (2004)

35. Stokoe, W.C., Casterline, D.C., Croneberg, C.G.: A Dictionary of American Sign Language on Linguistic Principles. Gallaudet College Press, Washington, DC (1965)

36. Hanke, T.: HamNoSys – Representing sign language data in language resources and language processing contexts. In: Fourth International Conference on Language Resources and Evaluation (LREC 2004). Representation and Processing of Sign Languages Workshop, Paris (2004)

37. Efthimiou, E., et al.: Dicta-sign–sign language recognition, generation and modelling: a research effort with applications in deaf communication. In: Proceedings of the 4th Workshop on the Representation and Processing of Sign Languages: Corpora and Sign Language Technologies (2010)

38. Hanke, T., Storz, J.: iLex – A database tool for integrating sign language corpus linguistics and sign language lexicography. In: Workshop on the Representation and Processing of Sign Language, at the Sixth International Conference on Language Resources and Evaluation (LREC 2008), Marrakech, Morocco (2008)

39. Brugman, H., Russel, A.: Annotating multi-media/multi-modal resources with ELAN. In: Proceedings of the 2nd Workshop on the Representation and Processing of Sign Languages: Lexicographic Matters and Didactic Scenarios, Paris (2004)

40. Fabian Benitez-Quiroz, C., Gökgöz, K., Wilbur, R., Martinez, A.: Discriminant features and temporal structure of nonmanuals in American Sign Language. PLoS ONE $9(2)$, e86268 (2014)

41. Adamo-Villani, N., Wilbur, R.B.: Asl-pro: American sign language animation with prosodic elements. In: International Conference on Universal Access in Human-Computer Interaction (2015)

42. Filhol, M., McDonald, J.: Extending the AZee-Paula shortcuts to enable natural proform synthesis. In: 8th Workshop on the Representation and Processing of Sign Languages, pp. 45–52 (2018)

43. Filhol, M., Hadjadj, M.N.: Juxtaposition as a form feature; syntax captured and explained rather than assumed and modelled. In: Language Resources and Evaluation Conference (LREC), Representation and Processing of Sign Languages, Portorož, Slovenia (2016)

44. Kipp, M., Nguyen, Q., Heloir, A., Matthes, S.: Assessing the deaf user perspective on sign language avatars. In: The Proceedings of the 13th International ACM SIGACCESS Conference on Computers and Accessibility. ACM (2011)
45. Pauser, S.: Prototypentest SiMAX im Rahmen des Innovationsschecks, 19 Mar 2019. https://www.equalizent.com/fileadmin/user_upload/News/2019_04_Avatar_Projektbericht.pdf

Author Index

Printed in the United States
by Baker & Taylor Publisher Services